EXPANDING THE PAST:
A READER IN SOCIAL HISTORY

EXPANDING THE PAST:

A READER IN SOCIAL HISTORY

Essays from the *Journal of Social History*

Peter N. Stearns, editor

NEW YORK UNIVERSITY PRESS
New York and London

Library of Congress Cataloging-in-Publication Data

Expanding the past.

  Bibliography: P.
  Includes index.
  1. Social history.   2. Sociology.   I. Stearns,
Peter N.   II. Journal of social history.
HN27.E96   1987   301   87-31365
ISBN 0-8147-7876-3
ISBN 0-8147-7877-1 (pbk.)

CONTENTS

PREFACE

This volume consists of essays previously published in the *Journal of Social History*, now nearing a quarter-century of rather lively existence. The *Journal of Social History* was launched early in the years of social history's research surge in the United States, its first issues appearing in 1967. Obviously the new journal did not create the social history surge. Older and excellent outlets abroad, such as *Annales: Economies, Sociétés, Civilisations* in France and *Past and Present* in England, played a more seminal role. Standard American historical journals have also promoted social history. Key early articles appeared in the *William and Mary Quarterly,* and other journals have opened their pages increasingly to social history over the years. Non-western social historians, indeed, routinely publish primarily in their area-specialist journals, at some cost to comparative and theoretical rigor. Finally, since the inception of the *Journal of Social History,* several other new historical journals in the United States have focused substantially on social history, though none with the centrality of interest that the *Journal of Social History* has maintained.

With all the modesty due the role of the *Journal of Social History,* however, it remains true that this journal has served as a central outlet for work in this genre in the United States, particularly in European and American history but with increasing outreach to Asian and Latin American subject areas. The *Journal of Social History* has led in the initial exploration of a host of new topics, such as the history of old age, that have since become staple items. It played a significant role in developing a genuinely sociohistorical approach to other topics that were initially started on more conventional, less illuminating bases; thus early articles explored women's history as social history as opposed to earlier approaches confined largely to a search for great women in the past or for formal ideas about gender. More recent pioneering efforts in social history's topical expansion are included in the present volume. The *Journal of Social History* has also contributed to periodic reviews of the state of the field, including problems of theory and method. It has worked to encourage provocative interpretations and syntheses, many of which are in turn widely cited in efforts to deal with historical phenomena over long time periods or comparatively, and to integrate social history with more conventional coverage. Indeed, the *Journal of Social History* has become one of the most extensively referenced historical journals in the United States during the past fifteen years.

This volume serves in a way to commemorate and highlight the achievements of the *Journal of Social History* in encouraging and shaping sociohistorical work. It is not a "best essays" collection. We deliberately omitted most articles that have been subsequently worked into book form and articles which, despite or because of their initial merits, have since publication been superseded by newer work. We chose articles around certain themes quite simply because not everything could be covered. Thus excellent pieces on black history or the social history of religion are not represented. Also for reasons of coherence, we did not try to represent premodern or non-Western essays, despite a current *Journal of Social History* campaign, beginning to bear fruit, to encourage more non-Western material in interests of interchange and comparison.

What the volume does attempt is the use of a few good articles (chosen from among many other qualified candidates) to illustrate key features and trends in social history, toward introducing students and a general public, still often ill-informed about this decisive historical field, to the social historian's world. The volume should serve also as a token of gratitude to the many authors and reviewers who have contributed and continue to contribute to the *Journal's* success.

The volume itself was produced on the advice of many of my fellow editors, several of whom suggested the idea of an anthology in the first place. To these editors, who have given such impetus to the *Journal of Social History* over the years—some, indeed, over the *Journal's* entire span to date—my sincere thanks.

PETER N. STEARNS
Carnegie Mellon University

CONTRIBUTORS

PETER BAILEY, an author on the history of leisure in Britain, is a member of the history department at the University of Manitoba.

MARY H. BLEWETT is a faculty member at the University of Lowell. Her further publications on women and work are appearing in book form.

JOHN BUSHNELL, author of a major study on the Revolution of 1905, teaches at Northwestern University.

GEORGE CHAUNCEY, Jr., is affiliated with Yale University.

CHRISTOPHER CLARK is in the history department of the University of York.

JAMES E. CRONIN, a member of the JSH editorial board and author of several books on British labor history, teaches at Boston College.

ALAN DAWLEY, of Trenton State College, and PAUL FALER, of the University of Massachusetts at Boston, have separately authored important studies in American working-class history.

ELIZABETH FOX-GENOVESE, of Emory University, and EUGENE D. GENOVESE, of the University of Rochester, have collaborated on several projects, in addition to their individual studies in European history and American social history respectively. Eugene D. Genovese has been a member of the JSH Board of Editors since its inception. The argument in the article published here was expanded in the book coauthored by Professors Fox-Genovese and Genovese, *Fruits of Merchant Capital.*

DAVID LEVINE, a leading demographic historian, is affiliated with the Ontario Institute for Studies in Education.

KENNETH A. LOCKRIDGE, one of the pioneering "new" social historians in American colonial history, teaches at the University of Michigan.

CONSTANCE M. MCGOVERN, an authority on the history of mental health in nineteenth-century America, teaches at the University of Vermont.

ARTHUR MITZMAN is a faculty member at the University of Amsterdam. He has published extensively in the history of social thought and in psychohistory.

ERIC H. MONKKONEN, widely known for studies in the history of urban crime and policing, teaches at the University of California, Los Angeles.

EWA MORAWSKA, a sociologist, teaches at the University of Pennsylvania. Her article in this volume deals with themes more fully explored in her recent book, *For Bread with Butter: Life-Worlds of East Central Europeans in Johnstown, Pa., 1890–1940.*

PATRICIA O'BRIEN has published on various aspects of French social history. She teaches at the University of California, Irvine.

CAROLE SHAMMAS has written many essays on trends in the early modern family and in women's roles, dealing both with Western Europe and North America. She is a member of the history department at the University of Wisconsin, Milwaukee.

EDWARD SHORTER, of the University of Toronto, has published widely in social history, on topics ranging from strike patterns to the social history of medicine.

PETER N. STEARNS, editor-in-chief of the JSH since its inception, has published on various topics in social history. He is Heinz Professor and Head, Department of History, Carnegie Mellon University.

I.
ON THEORY

1.

INTRODUCTION: SOCIAL HISTORY AND ITS EVOLUTION

Peter N. Stearns

During the past twenty-five years, social history has grown from noisy infancy to established adulthood, in the roster of approaches to the past and to the phenomenon of change over time. Social history has greatly widened the range of topics brought under serious historical scrutiny, using history in fact to provide perspective on most major facets of the human condition not strictly and immutably determined by biology. Social historians have also amended the way the past is approached, by focusing on changes in patterns and processes rather than a step-by-step narrative of events. These significant alterations in the definition of history and of the past have been confusing, productive of many untidy results, but they have also been exhilarating, truly expanding our grasp of how the human animal ticks. Despite challenges, despite some prosaic or inadequately conceptualized work, social historians have indeed provided some of the greatest empirical and theoretical gains in the social sciences over the past generation.

This volume explores what social history is about, by discussing some characteristic methods and sources, some of the new kinds of topics social historians deal with, and some of the syntheses they produce. There are of course lots of ways to introduce to social history, including a number of good definitional statements,[1] a host of compelling monographs, and many collections of articles in major topic areas such as family or social class. Oddly, however, there is no anthology designed to illustrate social history in general, toward an initial exploration, beyond abstract definition, of what the field is about. Following this essay, then, which seeks to define social history and its current status, while placing the subsequent articles in brief perspective, the book itself will illustrate some of social history's major approaches and concerns.

Without much question, the rise of social history has been the most dramatic development in American historical research over the past two decades. In a sense, most branches of historical writing have become "social," with political historians charting the link between social groupings and voting behavior, and intellectual historians studying such arcane fields as book publishing to discover how widely and by what means ideas spread. In history teaching, also, social historians have pushed strongly into college curriculum and are beginning to have impact in the schools.

This dramatic change in the way historians define what history is — for the rise in social history involves no less — can of course be assessed in narrowly academic terms. Written mainly for a scholarly audience, much of the new research seems highly specialized — partly because it is novel, but partly because many social historians have been trying to impress not only other historians but also a wider array of social scientists, and this can induce some very technical presentations indeed.

The field has significance beyond the confines of the academy, however. For one thing, the rise of social history runs partially counter to recurrent laments about the decline of history in the United States, standing as dramatic evidence that major sources of vitality remain. Furthermore, social history has remarkable implications for popular attention to history. Much of the flowering of adult historical interest in the United States, such as the concern with family and community roots, although not caused by academic social history, relates to it quite directly.

Simply put: social history can interest people — students and other regular people as well as academic types — in the past in new ways. Many social historians would argue that their specialty provides not only new insights into the past but also a new and dynamic sense of how the past has forged the present. This is not a unique claim. Any good history contributes to this kind of understanding, and social history most definitely is history. For some, however, social history gets closer to the stuff of life than other kinds of history do and thus contributes more directly to a grasp of the patterns of contemporary society as they continue or as they contrast with past trends, and sometimes to a sense of personal values.

Social history must be seen both as a set of topics and as an approach to history. The topical definition is simplest and carries us a good way into the field, but by itself it remains incomplete.

Social history involves two broad subject areas that conventional history has largely ignored. First, it deals with ordinary people, rather than the elite. The first excitement surrounding the surge of social history over the past two decades centered on the claim that the common folk — not just the movers and shakers of politics or intellectual life— have a vibrant past and contribute to larger historical processes. "History from the bottom up" was an early slogan that retains great validity. The people studied were relatively inarticulate, in that few of them spoke or wrote as a matter of public record, but social historians working imaginatively with new sources have found that few if any groups are really inarticulate. Records of protest, demographic data, diaries and anonymous writings, and artistic and artifactual evidence have filled in the gaps left by more conventional materials. The result has been rapid advance in historical knowledge of the working class, of blacks and ethnic groups, of women. The list of groupings steadily multiplies, with a concern for age categories as the most recent general addition. Children, youth, and the elderly all have solid histories. Increasingly, a given individual in the past, though perhaps never noted by name, is brought into a whole series of group analyses, by class, gender, ethnicity, or region.

While the development of categories for the historical study of ordinary people proceeds, a second topical approach moves to greater prominence: the history of ordinary activities, institutions, and modes of thought. Thus, age categories can be seen as groupings of people but also as stages of life that have histories of their own. The study of workers or the lower middle class edges into an examination of work and leisure as historical phenomena. Sexual behavior; social mobility; family roles and functions; attitudes and practices relating to death; popular health and medicine, including mental illness; crime and law enforcement — all these areas have rich and growing histories, in some cases with specialist journals attached. At their best, the histories deal both with behavior and with values and attitudes (what French social historians call mentalités). Thus we know the evolution of courtship behavior, but are also moving into some assessment of changes in the emotional experience and expectations that courtship entailed. In principle, there is no area of human behavior not purely and simply determined by biology, and thus unchanging, that cannot be illuminated by historical analysis. A few have not yet been tackled — we have no history of sleep habits, and only some hints about the history of boredom — but the goal is now clear. Social historians intend to bring into the historical record not only all kinds of people, but all aspects of behavior and value systems, as well.

The social historians' ability to generate a wide array of new historical topics explains much of the excitement in the field. The emphasis on ordinary people often related closely to political changes in American society. Concern for blacks, women, or youth derived important inspiration from contemporary developments, though the concern has now outstripped purely political impetus. The interest in ordinary aspects of life, though less obviously political, stems from growing concern about problems of crime or the stability of the family. It ties history to the ways we measure life, today, in our own society.

Many conventional historians, convinced that politics is the beginning and end of what is important in the past, were appalled at this effervescence of new historical topics, and some remain so. Social historians undeniably complicate our sense of what the past was, beyond the simple framework of constitutional changes and the ebb and flow of political parties. But social historians — nothing if not brash — do more than this, and that is why social history is not just a topical branch of history, such as political, economic, or intellectual history, but also a distinctive approach to the past. Obviously, social historians alter priorities in the historical record. They are saying, at least implicitly, that the great and famous cause less than we used to think, while ordinary people cause more. They are saying that political actions are not necessarily more important than changes in demographic behavior, that the history of great ideas must often yield to changes in the way people treat children.

As a result of their distinctive interest, social historians develop, as well, a particular approach to time. As historians, they are centrally concerned with change and therefore with making chronology intelligible; but they normally proceed in terms of relatively large sweeps, rarely by year-to-year analysis. Major change is identified in the framework of a decade or two, not a specific year. Relatedly, as social historians gain increasing command of their field, they develop alternative periodizations. Presidential administrations and even major wars may demarcate relatively little in social history, compared to the implications of changes in rates of illegitimate births or popular redefinitions of the possibility of social mobility, which often take shape rather gradually.

Compared to conventional historians, social historians are uncomfortable with events. They deal instead with processes, with distinctive trends within the periods they mark out. Single events like battles or individual cases of epidemic diseases rarely cause major or durable changes in the way ordinary people behave or in the ordinary activities of life — or, at least, so most social historians assume. When they do cause major changes — such as, for example, the impact of the Black Plague on the history of death or the role of World War II in altering women's work patterns — events must of course be included in discussions of periodization and causation. But social historians rarely explore events for their own sake. Their narrative focuses more on the unfolding of a process — such as the way Irish immigrants accommodated to the American mobility ethic — than on one event leading to another. Obviously also, social historians tend to treat individuals as illustrations of large groupings or trends.

Those characteristics make reading social history rather different from reading other kinds of history. They mean, as well, that historians cannot easily move back and forth between conventional and social history. The social historian's approach to names, dates, and events is more than just a reflection of the kinds of subjects he or she is interested in; it constitutes a distinctive way of viewing the past.

And some social historians go one step further; they claim that their approach will ideally yield a total history, in which poliltics, military developments, and seminal ideas merge with farmers' behavior, childrearing habits, and recreational patterns into an integrated picture of what society was like. Claims to total history have rarely been realized, at least as yet. In the United States, they have been most clearly approximated in a variety of exciting local studies, rather than in a larger regional or national frame. Even when incompletely realized, however, the claim is important. Social historians, in their most honest and imperialistic moods, mean to leave nothing out in their remaking of our map of the past.

Social history's surge in the United States, from the mid-1960s, had a number of roots, whose exploration can further define the field and move us toward an assessment of its trajectory in more recent years. There was of course the example of strong schools of social history abroad, particularly in France, where the new genre emerged between the wars. Indeed, as historians have been properly reminded, social history is not so much new as revived, for concerns with some features of popular life and with aspects of society beyond politics were commonplace in historical work before the later nineteenth century, when attention toward supporting the rise of nationalist states and using history for political socialization narrowed the approach toward the past.[2]

More specifically, American social historians built on three foundations. There was a strong ideological motive. Many born-again social historians in the 1960s sought to use history to dramatize the cause of various "inarticulate" groups, seeking to show the wrongs done them in past as well as present, and/or trying to show that political awareness and a sense of identity had strong precedent. This motive still runs strong in some social history fields, such as women's history or more recently gay history, but it has unquestionably declined as a wider variety of viewpoints have joined the social history parade. The loss of political thrust has confused or antagonized some social history supporters, yielding to calls for more rigorous, and politicized, theoretical underpinnings. This critique is echoed in the first essay in this volume, by Eugene D. Genovese and Elizabeth Fox-Genovese. Yet the political implications of social history were always somewhat ambiguous, even in the headier climate of the 1960s. Attention to the inarticulate can lead to empathy with their powerlessness, but it can also lead to admiration for their successful if incomplete adaptations. And while theoretically both points of view can be maintained simultaneously, in fact it has proved difficult to attend equally to exploitation and cultural creativity, particularly when outright protest is not the preeminent response. A political charge in social history remains, but it has unquestionably become more complicated over the course of time.

The second pillar for what was called the "new" social history rested on an attempt to blend historical with social science concerns. Many social historians chose topics and to some extent methodologies from sociology, seeking to apply to history what sociologists examined, often with scant historical sense and little patience for the subleties of empirical work on the past, in the present-day. Some practitioners hoped that social history would develop its own methodology, utilizing for example the growing resources of quantification, from its kinship with the social sciences. Some of these early hopes, too, have been dashed. Social historians continue to have some special methodological concerns, as they deal with the inarticulate and with an unusual array of evidence and gaps in evidence, but they do not have a distinctive single method. Quantification has declined in favor, perhaps because of insufficient zeal and training but in part because many leading issues cannot be addressed through numerical evidence alone. At the same time it long appeared that social scientists would as resolutely ignore social history as they did the other varieties of history. Despite the heroic efforts of some cross-disciplinary pollinators such as Charles Tilly, social history remained fairly strictly a historical province into the later 1970s.

More recently, however, some of the early expectations about interdisciplinary outreach have been given new support. Social historians continue to interact with other disciplines, turning recently to cultural anthropology, in an effort to find new ways to talk about popular beliefs or mentalities and to use evidence from ceremony or material artifacts, as well as to the various strands of sociology. At the same time, several of the social sciences — sociology, geography, as well as some branches of anthropology and political science — have developed a strong interest in historical perspectives. And specific topical fields, ranging from gerontology to alcohol studies, have discovered in the findings of social history a precious resource for dealing with trends and analogies from past to present. Social historians, as a result, publish increasingly widely in journals outside the historical discipline, and play an active role, beyond the provision of sterile background statements, in various social science agendas. Disciplinary boundaries have not crumbled yet, but there is growing interchange, and this continues to serve as exciting support for research and theory in social history.

The final pillar of social history, though closely related to the other two, involved a sense among many practitioners that some of the established fields of history had been sufficiently worked over that new approaches to the past were an essential research challenge. Too much of the human experience was being left out as historians picked over the carcasses of standard diplomatic and political archives; too many studies in conventional history seemed bent on filling small gaps, adding tiny details to a record that, however important, grew increasingly familiar. Add perhaps a bit of American suspicion that politics were a dirty business at best, a boring one at worst, and one has a final ingredient to the social history brew. The results of this motive were at best mixed. The determination of many social historians to "leave politics out," according to the hoary definition of social history offered by G. M. Trevelyan, needlessly antagonized many conventional historians and some of the radicals in the social history camp. It caused difficulties in reintegrating political and diplomatic concerns with the findings of social historians in fields such as crime, popular medicine, or even working-class culture. Yet it did give many social historians some breathing room in which they could pursue their newer topics unencumbered with the necessity of paying lipservice to conventional goals such as understanding the Civil War or providing a new perspective on the shufflings of British cabinets. To be sure, it is now a commonplace that the pieces of the past must be put back together, that politics is not a separate concern. But the period of indulgence, in which some social historians could pretend that the state scarcely played a role in their areas of inquiry, has allowed questions about social-political interactions to be raised in new ways, involving attention to the functions as well as the constitutional structures of government, to politics as process rather than a series of (often minor) events alone, to history as composed of a periodization not bounded (or at least not always bounded) by the more obvious political determinants.

The principal bases for the recrudescence of social history explains why the field has often seemed so exciting. They explain also why the social history effort has often been complex, fraught with internal disagreement. They explain, finally, why social historians continue to feel challenged: to relate their mission to diverse sympathies for the underprivileged of many sorts; to deal with an array of social scientific approaches that raise vital topics but sorely want historical data and perspective; and to provide a fresh start for inquiry into the past without, now, neglecting the central topics and findings of political, diplomatic, and intellectual historians.

Partly because of diverse origins and motivations, social historians often present confusing images to themselves as well as their various audiences. They develop hosts of topical subspecialties, in family, or mobility, or sports. Some can seem unconcerned about broader relationships, for example between family structures and changes in leisure outlets. Some seem unconcerned with change. In their enthusiasms over uncovering new topics and related new sources of information, many social historians have often been content with portraying conditions at one time period — the nature of skill in the 1850s — vaguely assuming that someday their findings would fit a larger pattern. More recently the excitement about anthropological approaches has generated "thick descriptions" of popular rituals in a single time period, predicated on a realization that the patterns uncovered differ from those that emerged later but without explicit attention to how change developed and how it was caused. Yet for all the confusions and inadequacies, some resulting quite understandably from pioneering efforts to plow new historical ground, most social historians remain roughly united in four respects. They are, as historians, concerned with the past, and ultimately with change and causation. They believe that a focus on groups outside the formal power structures reveals much about the past and about change, not only for the groups involved but for society at large. They believe that serious, analytical attention to the histories of activities not formally political, such as family life, serves the same function, in revealing important characteristics about society ultimately linked to other expressions such as politics. And they believe that history, in dealing with politics, or women, or eating habits, best captures the past by dealing with patterns and processes, rather than simply a series of discrete events.

As it has matured, social history has inevitably faced a number of new issues, though some of these relate to its initial motivations. It has not resolved its relationship to "conventional" history, as important bickering continues. It has not settled on a single mode of presentation. It has not met all the challenges, issued by social as well as conventional historians, to produce overarching theories and syntheses. Identifying each of these current areas of debate, mostly the products of social history's growing visibility and a certain maturity, can complete an evaluation of the field and turn us to the way the essays in this collection allow its exploration.

The Issue of Modes of Discourse. It is perhaps not accidental that, as social historians have turned away from a concentration on measurable incidence of protest or on family structures, toward exploration of value systems as manifested in meanings and in methods of expression, they have devoted more attention to how they present themselves. Even aside from the implications of inquiry into discourse, the passage of time has produced understandable questions about social history styles. If, as in the sociohistorical vision, events do not constitute the bedrock of the past, standard narrative modes that tell stories about events, and individuals' roles in them, do not always suit. In fact, some social historians (and many who use social history, as in museum presentations) are becoming increasingly imaginative about using individual vignettes and narrative data as illustrations of wider processes. It is also important to recognize that certain events can be more substantively explored in terms of what they reveal about social change, or what kinds of change they cause; and some periods of time allow more play to events, even from the social history vantagepoint, than others. Nevertheless, problems remain, and some thoughtful writers have urged that social historians develop renewed use of narrative forms, on grounds that these alone make change intelligible.[3] This approach may be too confining, unless the meaning of narrative is widened beyond normal recognition. It is true, however, the social historians must become more alert to clarity and grace. They must demarcate their periodization explicitly, so that their accounts have definite beginnings and ends, with causes for each, rather than serving as random interventions into slices of the past. The plea for new narratives, that take into account unfamiliar, ordinary events as well as conventional diplomatic or political occurrences, has some exciting potential. yet a vivid discussion of changes in patterns of mentality or behavior can offer its own drama and structure.

It remains unclear how uniform social history styles, and the conceptualization behind them, must be, or how severe any stylistic crisis is. The need to attend to presentation, particularly as social historians reach out to wide audiences, is quite real. The essays in this collection can and should be read, and possibly criticized, from the standpoint of their standards of presentation — very few, certainly, fall into a conventional narrative framework, though they lack neither sequence nor interest as a result. Many of the essays also present clearer statements of significance, clearer generalizations for comparison or analogy with other work, than many conventional accounts offer. Precisely because so many events are in fact miniscule in social history — the decisions of a single family about how many children to have — the need for delineation of basic patterns is unusually great, and with this the provision of conceptual building blocks toward larger historical arguments. It remains true, however, that discussions of methods of organizing and presenting history have loomed large as social history moves from novelty to centrality, and that the effectiveness of social historians in vividly presenting change provides a valid criterion for judging the progress of the field.

The Issue of Synthesis. Social history has generated so many new topics that it inevitably raises questions about putting the pieces together. Just as the field has produced no single methodology, so it has yielded no agreement on what the unifying forces are in causing change. There is as a result increasing clamor for more attention to synthesis and to formulations of general theory, and there is validity to the plea. Social history's lack of widely accepted, overarching frameworks is hardly unique in historical or social scientific study, but it is true that when attention turns from a single institution, such as the state, the lack of unity becomes at the least more obvious, at most more debilitating. Furthermore, the number of new topics that continue to enliven social history may be finite, and this too prompts attention to more sophisticated, general visions.

Here too, however, there is cause for rejoicing as well as concern. Many social historians have developed a number of topical inquiries, linking them to general developments such as industrialization; the centrifugal splintering of the field is hardly complete. Historians like Charles Tilly have plumped for several "big changes" that, in their view, provide basic coherence to developments in modern Western history, social and other; and while any specific list of big changes is open to debate — Tilly plumps for largely structural factors, in nation-state formation and the impact of capitalism, while others might include shifts in basic mentalities as well — the effort is already stimulating important efforts at integration.[4] Modernization theory, though long since cast aside in its simplest forms, has a related utility in focusing attention on how various social changes interrelate, and in more sophisticated statements, at least in Western history, the modernization model has real utility.[5] Comparative work, also, though still crying out for additional work beyond a few well-developed subspecialities such as patterns of slavery, has encouraged clearer statements about the relationships among social factors and social indices.[6] Finally, the plea for synthesis in social history is sometimes confused by an implicit belief that the resulting amalgam must somehow translate into generalizations about conventional political processes — a point to which we turn in the next section.

Social history is not, in sum, as wanting in integrative analyses as is sometimes claimed, which is not to say that more work will not be welcome, and not to deny that too many social historians remain content with narrow statements, small chunks of time, and reliance on limited segments of the possible source materials available. It is also true that important disagreements about whether material structures or cultures serve as the best basic units of analysis raise disputes — though often fruitful disputes — about what ties the past together. Yet growing ability to trace key phenomena over long stretches of time, or to translate social history into coherent general statements for student audiences, suggests that many social historians are working to meet the challenge increasingly obvious in the field. Many of the essays that follow offer various models of synthesis, in tracing patterns over several centuries or relating numerous social phenomena around a single set of factors. Certainly, the collection allows some assessment of how social historical pieces can fit into a coherent jigsaw, of how integration can be attempted, and of problems that remain.

The Issue of Political History. This category, in a sense the oldest of the problems faced in defining social history, remains perhaps the most bedeviling. The American historical profession continues to be divided between social and conventional historians, though there are many who serve both camps ably. It contrasts in this regard with countries like France, where social history is, for all intents and purposes, history at the postsecondary and research levels. The American division inevitably produces ongoing questions and confusions about how social history fits in. Some of the questions are silly; conventional historians have attacked social historians for their interest in private lives in the past (past violence is all right, in other words, because it fits into military history; but past sexuality is taboo) or for distracting from the themes of rationality and progress in history teaching (as though these themes were attainable only by examining the actions of elites, and as though history's purpose was described by uplift and moralizing obfuscation alone). Some of the questions, even from social historians themselves, reflect the tenacious durability of a conventional framework. Thus one eminent historian has lamented that social history has produced no new interpretations of the

Civil War, as if reexplaining familiar events is the ultimate litmus test. (In fact, social historians have contributed to a reevaluation of the context in which the Civil War occurred, so they might squeak through this test even though they should seek wider criteria.)

Without question, the continued rift between social and conventional history has encouraged too many social historians to shun political factors, and in this sense the plea for reintroducing the state is timely. But reintroducing the state and politics (never in fact totally absent in any event, as several of the following essays suggest) does not mean adhering to the conventional historical agenda. It does not mean forgetting the contributions of relatively inarticulate groups. Even diplomatic history, at least for the modern period, can benefit by analyzing contexts set by popular assumptions and interests, though policy details remain largely an elite province. Reintroducing the state does not mean a mindless return to a narrative mode, in which events monopolize center stage. Political consciousness, popular political action and state functions can be discussed in terms of patterns and processes, and thus rendered compatible with other social historical topics. A good bit of the "new" political history works in fact to this end, and thus erodes the dividing line between its concerns and those of social history. Finally, the reintegration of political patterns does not mean that all social history topics must be pulled into the conventional orbit, so that if they have no obviously political connections they become unworthy of serious attention. The ability of social history to enhance a grasp of phenomena such as death, or drinking, or emotion remains a vital contribution, and this topical array must not be artifically narrowed.

To be sure, social historians argue that politics itself must now be redefined, to include power relationships beyond those immediately connected to government. Thus gender relations, hierarchies at work, uses of leisure or emotion to promote social control all fit a redefined political history which becomes indistinguishable from social history. The point is that the eminently desirable, and increasingly feasible goal of putting the state back into serious history means preserving, not diluting, the social historian's vision of what the past consists of and how this past is best conveyed. This reintegration will include, of course, a recognition that some important political processes are politically caused, just as important developments in, say, popular health practices are *not* politically caused in the narrow sense.

It is thus possible to work toward a greater unification of history on the basis of a common concern for viewing the past in terms of changes in patterns of behavior and outlook, and a common concern also for seeking linkages among such changes on the basis of fundamental relationships such as the interaction between elites and their ideas and institutions, and commoners and theirs. Several essays in this volume, particularly in the final section, in fact sketch forms in which some of the reconnecting can take place. Whether the end result will be labeled social history or just history, that is in fact social, is really irrelevant. The point is that the new vision, of capturing the past in terms of whole societies and the full range of human endeavor, will be preserved.

The challenge that social history continues to pose for the larger discipline consists above all of the need to work out a new topical equilibrium through attention to the changing patterns of social and institutional life. Social history does not elevate a single process — such as voting habits, or economic forms — to unquestioned preeminence; it is not deterministic in this sense, and so contrasts with earlier subfields whose interest in process was overshadowed by claims that a particular kind of process, such as the evolution of great ideas or the actions of politicians, constituted the core historical inquiry. Thus social history continues to encourage an approach that contrasts with much conventional historical wisdom, even with the proliferation of "new" histories in various fields — a contrast which explains why social historians still often feel self-conscious and conventional historians often hostile to what remains to them an upstart method of envisaging the past.

For the concern with basic processes in society — including cultural processes or mentalities — is turning out to be social history's main contribution to broadening and refocusing history-in-general. In modern social history this refocusing adds up to an effort to determine, again in Charles Tilly's words, how people have lived through the "big changes," (but also, I would add, how they have helped shape these changes) which may of course be somewhat variously defined but on which there can now be considerable agreement. Social history has long suffered, and still draws skepticism, because of its lack of a coherent, continuous phenomenon as an object of study comparable to the state for political history. For a time social historians seemed to be offering the inarticulate as their alternative, but this is not provably a consistent rival to the state, in terms of coherence, and in any event now captures social history too narrowly, given advances in understanding elites as well as commoners. But if there is nothing exactly comparable to the state as social history's ultimate focus, the alternative, basic processes such as technological and demographic change or shifts in popular outlook or elite-mass cultural relationships, is genuine and workable. If such a focus lacks the simplicity of the state, which in fact is embraced in basic processes both as actor and as creature, it gains in comprehensiveness, in its enhanced ability to capture the complexity of social change. This challenging new focus, the essential product of social history's own maturation over earlier and narrow definitions, is the key device for relinking social history with history-in-general.

An agenda of reintegrating history substantially on social history's base is not without brashness. It has at least the merit of counterbalancing unrealistic attempts to simplify the discipline by pretending that, in crucial respects, social history has not happened or is about to stop. The bifurcation of history that has followed from social history's rise is not the result, primarily, of social historians' inattention to style or failures of synthesis; it also results from stubbornness on the part of some of the historians who charge themselves with particular responsibility for treating politics and diplomacy in the past. The bifurcation is not fundamentally fruitful; it differs from other kinds of tensions which lead to productive debate. It unduly complicates efforts, in teaching as well as research synthesis, to convey something of the wholeness of past periods — efforts which are doomed to imperfection even in the best of circumstances. Social history has, over the past quarter-century, provided not only considerable new knowledge about historical change. It has also provided an excitement that can usefully inform the whole historical discipline, and it is beginning to generate historically based contacts among the various specialties that examine the human condition that should involve the whole discipline as well. It is time to build on the growing sense that a period of confusion in the discipline needs to find resolution, and to do so on a basis that takes full advantage of the advances that social history has brought, though unevenly and incompletely, to the historical endeavor.

The essays in this volume were selected as interesting examples of social history and as an important contributions in various subfields. They are grouped, here, according to their ability to illustrate several key facets of social history, discussed in general in this introduction, though most of the essays in fact fit several categories.

After the critique of social history from a theoretical standpoint, in the contribution by Fox-Genovese and Genovese, a trio of essays illustrate the social historian's concern with the inarticulate, both in behavior and in mentalities. These contributions collectively reveal the diversity of sources, both quantitative and qualitative, that social historians have uncovered, and also the issues involved in using these sources to discuss basic motivations and values. David Levine uses demographic and literacy data to discuss the family motivations of key proletarian groups in Britain during the early industrial revolution. His essay shows the use of quantitative materials beyond a purely descriptive framework, while also revealing important complexity in the situations and motivations of people who might be lumped together as an undifferentiated proletariat. Relatedly, like most social historians he is at pains to demonstrate the rationality and purposefulness of ordinary people, in this case in their family behavior. Ewa Morawska, using qualitative evidence, similarly demonstrates important subtlety in the way poor Slavic immigrants reacted to their social and economic environment, showing an outlook that was neither peasantlike nor middle class. Finally, using printed sources and also behavioral evidence, Peter Bailey discusses the way British workers had learned to fit into their larger society by the later nineteenth century, while preserving an important subculture of their own.

Part Three focuses on how social historians have staked out new topics, or new dimensions of topics, in recent years, dealing with the evolution of concepts such as homosexuality and disease, adding a social base to discussions of military history, or expanding a well-developed field such as women's history into new aspects of the work experience. John Bushnell's essay deals with the interaction between peasant mentalities, the Russian social hierarchy, and military life, in ways that at once explain the behavior of ordinary soldiers and also illumine the meaning of military service to ordinary people. Military history as social history is just beginning to flower, and this essay demonstrates much of its potential. Patricia O'Brien shows how social history can explore patterns of crime and their social context, and how innovations in crime reveal larger social trends. The mixture of sources used in the article illustrates quite vividly how social historians work to develop a historical perspective where none previously existed, in this case for kleptomania, and also the meanings that must be squeezed from the sources to produce satisfactory patterns and explanations. Mary Blewett shows how work history and women's history intertwine in the early industrial period, moving women's history forward as a social history topic outside a purely familial context. In a somewhat similiar way Carole Shammas takes another social history staple, in this case the family, and explores a new dimension through the interpretation of prosaic budget and consumption documents intermixed with qualitative evidence. George Chauncey deals with an important aspect of the history of sexuality, showing clashing standards at a key point in the early twentieth century.

Constance McGovern uses a direct examination of patients' experiences in mental institutions to improve, though also to complicate, our judgment of the social history of mental disorder. Here is a topic that was once handled simply as an adjunct to the history of medicine and reform, utilizing the proclamations of leading practitioners as sole source; then the social control school of interpretation moved in, using much the same materials but evaluating motivations and impact in a much different light. In the social control approach, mental institutions were the product not of reform, but of a new desire to isolate and discipline. McGovern suggests that the actual social history of mental disease and its treatment must be more nuanced, with disease itself seen as a real entity as well as social construct, and with treatment serving both as amelioration and social control. Her work parallels social historians' findings in fields such as education and penology in suggesting that social control, though a useful model, has serious limitations in describing reality. Finally, Edward Shorter shows how social history illuminates the history of disease itself, serving as a crucial link between basic human biology and cultural forces in describing patterns of change in one of the most intimate aspects of human life. Shorter's essay, as befits social historians' work in essentially new topic areas previously felt to be the province of other disciplines, raises a number of questions yet to be answered, about how change in the incidence of mental disorders and the mental structures that underlay them can be explained, how they relate to larger processes of social change.

The final cluster of essays deals with efforts to synthesize findings in social history and in some cases relate them to concerns shared by conventional historians as well. The essays in this group derive from generalizations based on a wide range of social historical work, as well as specific research data. They demonstrate the positive strides social historians have made in creating coherent periodization over large stretches of time and in relating various facets of the social experience — though they do not of course suggest that the task of interpretation has ended.

The first essay in this group, by Kenneth Lockridge, suggests how a grasp of changing social context effects the interpretation of the American Revolution. The essay by Dawley and Faler links working-class structure and outlook to political trends a few decades later in American history. These two essays show how social history changes the face of political history in the revolutionary and early republican period without of course removing all familiar landmarks. Dealing with the same period but with less explicit political content, Christopher Clark treats the interaction of economic change and popular outlook under new market impulses. Social history has greatly amplified our grasp of the industrial revolution and of economic changes that preceded it, in part by translating larger economic processes into the terms of ordinary human lives and values. The overall interpretation of the industrial revolution and the rise of commercial capitalism — surely no small challenge to synthesis, but often avoided or narrowed before social history's advent — has been enriched and rendered more usable as a result.

In another social-political history link, James Cronin sketches the interaction between British Labour, class structure and working-class expectations, again enhancing both political coverage and a grasp of the twentieth-century working-class experience in the process.

Eric Monkkonen shows another important relationship, again over an extensive time period, in relating government functions — specifically, police functions — to social experience, showing among other things the interaction among police, crime and disorder patterns, and public perceptions, all variables open to significant change. Along with the pieces by Cronin and Dawley/Faler, the Monkkonen contribution shows two important facets involved in relinking social and political history: the social base of political parties and agitation, on the one hand, and the social impact of government activities and society's influence on defining these activities, on the other.

Finally, in a different kind of synthesis, Arthur Mitzman deals with a huge swath of time in terms of interactions among formal ideals (including religion and literature), government and elite institutions, and popular culture or mentality. He shows how the growing interest in mentalities lends itself to determination of overarching patterns that link "conventional" intellectual history to the world of ordinary people and ordinary activities such as leisure or protest. The suggestion that psychological change itself can be grasped through social history reminds us again of the field's topical range and its power to deal with fundamental elements of the human condition. Mitzman's approach rests heavily on cultural causation, in contrast to the emphases on material structure widely used in other social historical work, but he suggests some ways that even this gap might be bridged.

Social history remains enthralling. Research in new topic areas and sweeping interpretations continue to keep this field at the forefront. The tasks posed by maturation and critique, including the need for new integration, new dissemination in teaching and in historical presentations to the public, the extension of the full range of social history topics to world history[7] and careful attention to style, add to the excitement of social history's future. By showing new ways to deal with basic political change and new ways to capture human psychology as a changing entity, social history continues to enrich our grasp of the past and its uses. Almost two decades ago a British pioneer in social history, Eric Hobsbawm, wrote that the times were good for the social historian. Today, because of the validity of the initial new vision of the past but also because of the new tasks created by success, the days are still bright. The excitement persists.

NOTES

1. A series of definitions establishes what social history long has been and also how certain features and issues have changed. For a classic statement before the advent of the contemporary social history surge, see G. M. Trevelyan, *English Social History* (London, 1944), p. 1. More useful early efforts are Lucien Febvre, *A New Kind of History*, Peter Burke, ed. (New York, 1973) and Harold J. Perkin, "What Is Social History," *Bulletin of the John Rylands Library* 36 (1953): 56–74. See also Eric Hobsbawm, "From Social History to the History of Society," *Daedalus* C (1971); Samuel P. Hays, "A Systematic Social History," in G. Billias and G. Grob, eds., *American History: Retrospect and Prospect* (New York, 1971): 315–66; Peter N. Stearns, "Toward a Wider Vision: Trends in Social History," in Michael Kammen, ed., *The Past Before Us* (New York, 1980): 205–30; James Henretta, "Social History as Lived and Written," *American Historical Review* 84 (1979): 1293–1323; Charles Tilly, "The Old New Social History and the New Old Social History," *Review* 7 (1984): 363–406; Olivier Zunz, ed., *Reliving the Past: The Worlds of Social History* (Chapel Hill, 1985); *Theory and Society* 9 (1980), special issue on social history; James B. Gardner and G. R. Adams, eds., *Ordinary People and Everyday Life: Perspectives on the New Social History* (Nashville, 1983); Peter N. Stearns, "Social History and History: A Progress Report," *Journal of Social History* 19 (1985): 319–34.

2. J. C. Wilsher, "Power Follows Property — Social and Economic Interpretations in British Historical Writing in the 18th and Early 19th Centuries," *Journal of Social History* 16 (1983): 7–26.

3. Lawrence Stone, *Past and Present* (Boston, 1981); see also Tilly, "The Old New Social History" and Eric Hobsbawm, "The Revival of Narrative: Some Comments," *Past and Present* 86 (1980): 3–8.

4. Charles Tilly, "Retrieving European Lives," in Zunz, ed., *Reliving the Past*, pp. 11–52.

5. Raymond Grew, "Modernization and Its Discontents," *American Behavioral Scientist* 12 (1977); Peter N. Stearns, "Modernization and Social History: Some Suggestions, and a Muted Cheer," *Journal of Social History* 14 (1980): 189–210.

6. See for example the discussions in Rebecca Scott, "Comparing Emancipation," *Journal of Social History* 20 (1987): 565–84; and George Reid Andrews, "Comparing the Comparers: White Supremacy in the United States and South Africa," *Journal of Social History* 20 (1987): 585–600.

7. The situation of social-historical coverage of non-Western societies presents some intriguing anomalies and also key challenges for further work, including comparative study. On the one hand, social history is a standard approach in dealing with Russia, Asia, or Latin America. Conditions of peasants and other issues of social structure and protest are seen as fundamental, and a conventional/social history split is not pronounced. Relatedly, social historians dealing with non-Western societies have borrowed freely from sociologists, anthropologists and political scientists. On the other hand, the range of social history topics established for the West has not yet fully emerged. Family history and the history of mentalities, for example, are generally in a more rudimentary stage. Meeting the challenge and opportunity in applying social history approaches on a worldwide basis constitute an obvious, major next step in sociohistorical inquiry. For an assessment, though accentuating the positive, see Michael Adas, "Social History and the Revolution in African and Asian Historiography," *Journal of Social History* 19 (1985): 335–48.

2.

THE POLITICAL CRISIS OF SOCIAL HISTORY:
A MARXIAN PERSPECTIVE

Elizabeth Fox-Genovese and Eugene D. Genovese

Social history, recent fanfare and fashion notwithstanding, hardly qualifies as new: it dates from Herodotus. The novelty derives neither from its content nor from the increasing technical sophistication of its methods, but from its status. Chroniclers and historians have always described customs and behavior, albeit not always systematically. Since World War II, however, social history has gradually come to supplant political history as the dominant concern of the academy. Contemporary social history, in its prestigious, not to say pretentious, new forms can be roughly traced from the pioneering works of Lucien Febvre and Marc Bloch during the 1930s. They and their now numerous progeny attempted to renovate, rather than repudiate, extreme positivism by focusing away from the political narrative that had found quintessential expression in the great *Histoire de la France* directed by Ernest Lavisse. Febvre and Bloch directed their attention to the total *mentalité* or social and cultural texture of an age, and their method and sensibility, at peak performance, yielded such stunning works as Bloch's own classic *Feudal Society.* The trend they inaugurated, imprecisely identified with the *Annales,* still legitimates the general panoply of efforts covered by the umbrella of social history in its current and fashionable guise.[1]

Social history, particularly in its preestablishment days, had a prior ancestor: the collaborative work of Karl Marx and Friedrich Engels. The "social" of this social history carried an implicit socialist or at least anticapitalist political commitment. The "social" here also referred less to the totality of society than to the classes contending for state power and especially to the workers and other laboring peoples. In its early phases, in fact, this social history coincided almost completely with labor history, supplemented by some attention to the peasantry. After Marx's pathbreaking *Eighteenth Brumaire of Louis Bonaparte,* however, this tradition tended to converge with the reigning positivism of the late nineteenth and early twentieth centuries; and to the extent that labor history appeared as the history of organized labor or the history of the socialist movement, a work of "social" history could, by its manifestation of names, dates, and generously sprinkled initials, rival a history of monarchs or of bourgeois political parties. Socialist sensibility alone could not suffice to break through the methodological hegemony of accepted historical practice.

The early histories of the labor and socialist movements are hardly more widely read today than histories of the Capetian monarchs or the early liberal political parties, although the best in each category deserves a better fate. Those early histories breathed a commitment that transcended bourgeois positivism. Specifically, the early social historians remained preoccupied with the accession of the working class to power or with the degree of success in struggles to improve class interests. They reflected a commitment to the political process and to the decisive role of power in human relations. Whatever their limitations, they did not usually slip into a philistine disregard of the centrality of politics; on the contrary, they built on the assumption that the study of class relations in general and the life of the lower classes in particular would produce a deeper and broader understanding of political history.

Early Marxian social history made its major contributions in the documentation and chronicling of the conscious efforts of the working class in its political and economic struggles. By present standards it tended toward an "economist" Marxism in intellectual orientation, while espousing a politics appropriate to the Second International. Convinced of the realities of the class struggle as elaborated by Marx and Engels and sufficiently certain of pragmatic goals, it felt little need to move toward theoretical innovation. Like the classification that still obtains in the London Library, "capital and labor" defined its subject. However crude, unidimensional, and — let it be admitted — dull this history may appear today, it must be evaluated within the epistemological paradigm to which it belonged. These social historians, like their ideological opponents, thought in terms of the corridors of power. History "from the bottom up" incorporated a heavy and healthy dose of blood and iron.

In those halcyon days before the war — every real historian's Great War, of course — and in the grim and ideologically charged years following, historians of most persuasions remained reasonably certain that they could rely upon the reality of the fact. The epistemological uncertainty inaugurated in the closing years of the old century by the simultaneous publication of Planck's quantum theory and Freud's *Interpretation of Dreams,* as well as similarly disturbing works by Husserl, Russell, and others, had not yet permeated the collective consciousness of the academic intelligentsia. The uncertainty with respect to narrative or chronology could be explored in the literature of the period, but historians, well enough protected by their corporate organization and collective bias, enjoyed an institutional and emotional buffer against such disquieting intellectual currents. During the decades in which anthropology, sociology, and psychology developed as academic disciplines, historians by and large continued to "tell the story as it happened." Lenin, perceived as a politician, albeit a distressingly successful one, could safely be ignored. Antonio Gramsci, Lenin's most gifted western heir, who effected the major theoretical advance in the Marxian problematic, pursued his most important intellectual concerns in the inhospitable environment of Mussolini's prison and in the Italian language. The virulent anticommunism of the western academy during those happy days, when American liberals were cheering the local version of Show trials at which the leaders of the Communist Party were imprisoned by Harry Truman *et al.* on palpably trumped up charges, and the political atrocities of Stalinism in the Soviet Union did nothing to encourage public reconsideration of Marxian theory. And at least until the shock of the Hungarian counter-revolution and the painful exigencies of its suppression, and the official admission that the Father of the Peoples also qualified, to a disquieting extent, as their undertaker, western

Marxists enjoyed a luxury increasingly denied their liberal and radical-democratic colleagues: a combination of faith, hope, and purpose. Possessed of an ending to the story, they remained committed to its telling; they could discern the beginning, middle, and end of a historical process.

In the beginning, the social history deriving from the *Annales* school shared much of this perspective intellectually although little of it politically. A brief review of Bloch's work, in particular the centrality of the question of periodization to *Feudal Society,* reveals the extent to which the narrative preoccupations of his training had formed his historical sense. In effect, Bloch's work accomplished two things: It extended the range of historical vision to include a wide variety of subjects normally ignored; and it enveloped the relations of superordination and subordination (of authority) within a broad social canvass depicted as systemically interdependent. Feudal society figured as the subject of Bloch's narrative where in the hands of his predecessors the House of Capet or other worthies reigned unchecked. The collective subject, methodologically akin to historical forces, conveyed a density of texture and a sense of historical interconnectedness lacking in the more unilinear accounts of chanceries and palaces. In this respect, as in the contrapuntal relationship between rulers and ruled and the linking of relations of production to their juridical formulation, Bloch's work approached a Marxian standpoint. Marxian work of this period, however, had not, by and large, attained Bloch's measure of sophistication; and Bloch did not espouse an explicit class analysis. Moreover, the temporal distance of the medieval period partially mitigated the immediacy of political and moral passion and permitted a more dispassionate appraisal of total society.

The vigor of Bloch's work derived at once from his vision of integral relationships among all facets of human existence and from his analysis of historical dynamics — the changes in the internal relationships and in the social totality over time. It contained a number of threads, or lines of inquiry, that would subsequently develop into the characteristic preoccupations of the group of postwar historians loosely known as the *Annales* school. In particular, Bloch's use of areal photography and his preoccupation with the ecological base, technical practice, and human relations of agricultural production laid the groundwork for those rural historians whose magisterial *grandes thèses* have illuminated so many features of the French provinces during the feudal period and the *ancien regime.* In addition, his attention to ritual, to the symbolic aspect of political bonds, to the psychological and cultural density of social relations and their institutional codification reflected an anthropological and artistic sensitivity and indicated new avenues to the understanding of premodern and ultimately modern political practice and institutions. His emphasis on kinship ties and their fluctuating strength over time and in relation to political dynamics foreshadowed contemporary preoccupations with kinship and family patterns. The list could be extended indefinitely, for Bloch's work touched upon almost every facet of human experience. But, unlike the growing army of present-day epigones, he never allowed the synchronic or spatial to predominate over the diachronic or narrative; and he never allowed his theoretical and methodological sophistication to usurp center stage from the historical process itself.

Bloch's work constituted a privileged moment in historical practice, but it remained to his heirs to forge the legacy. It can be left to philosophers to debate the exact moment of tension at which the introduction of new questions or foci of attention accumulates sufficient momentum to shatter the older paradigm. Bloch's work appears to master the conflicting claims of spatial and temporal, substantive and theoretical, structural and dynamic. In the work of his successors that tension appears shattered. Post-Blochian, or rather post World War II, social history has both proliferated and fragmented at an accelerating rate. A mere catalogue of the books and journals devoted to topics in social history, or even in the range of inquiry claimed by social history, would occupy much more space than that allotted for this article.

The crisis within the historical profession, of which the current state of social history constitutes a telling illustration, pertains as much to intellectual and cultural currents within western consciousness as a whole as it does to the problems specific to the writing of history. The deep uncertainties with respect to duration, to objects of observation, and to communication are all transmitted, if in much diluted fashion, to historical work. In addition, the anxiety-ridden crisis of Eurocentrism, of faith in progress, of commitment to delayed gratification — in short, the loss of purpose — has forced a reexamination, and in many instances a deep repudiation, of the very notion of history. History as creative order or sense-conveying fiction has increasingly lost ground to static and conflict-denying myths. In the words of Frank Kermode, "Myth operates within diagrams of ritual, which presupposes total and adequate explanation of things as they are and were; it is a sequence of radically unchangeable gestures. Fictions are for finding things out, and they change as the needs of sense-making change. Myths are the agents of stability, fictions the agents of change."[2]

The influential structural enterprise that took shape in the hands of the anthropologist Claude Levi-Strauss favored the "cold" and unchanging in human experience at the expense of the "hot" or dynamic. Drawing upon the problematic developed by modern linguistics and adding an artist's sensitivity to the details of human activity, gesture, and record, Levi-Strauss elaborated an almost textual method of decoding human behavior. The impact of his work in disciplines from literary criticism through the several social sciences requires no review here. But the repercussions of that work upon the writing of history, especially social history, commands attention.

The introduction of a structuralist and anthropological — a spatial — sensibility into history can perhaps best be evaluated with respect to the work of the recognized dean of the *Annales,* its longtime director and head of the prestigious *sixième section,* Fernand Braudel. Undisputed heir to Bloch and Febvre, Braudel pushed their efforts beyond the balance of structure and dynamic to a decided emphasis upon structure. In his seminal book, *The Mediterranean,* he began with the topographical setting and moved up through the routine of material life with a loving and painstaking attention to detail that beautifully recaptured the texture of the material existence of a privileged corner of the world. His leisurely pages, for all their opacity of language, evoke that corner from the sea to the rocks and the dust rising from dry soil. The smell of lavender, the glistening of olives, the laborious motion of the oxen, the stooping, sowing, scything gestures of the men and women bound to that soil blend in his evocation of a total ecology. Regrettably, as J. H. Elliott has observed, the people who inhabit this earth do not fare so well in the story. Thus, the political narrative, the historical events of his focal period, occupies a few pages at the very end of the massive two volumes.[3]

In *Material Life and Capitalism* Braudel explicitly delineates his conception: material ife, the simple routine of reproduction of the race, constitutes the essential feature of most human life during most of recorded time. Over time an economy develops and intersects with material life at nodal points. Finally, and most recently, capitalism, which he defines or rather describes with suprising vagueness, emerges to appropriate and organize, within the limits of its powers, both the economy and the underlying material life. This is obviously not the place for a full critique of Braudel's great, and antiMarxist, work. Suffice it to note that his structural interpretation, with its anthropological, ecological, and archeological predilections, implicitly negates the historical process itself and distorts the temporal dimension. The traditional preoccupation of historians, that outmoded political narrative, figures in his work almost as accident or afterthought. This treatment not only minimizes the human or political dimension of change over time, it also — and more perniciously for social history — negates the centrality of relations of production, of authority and exploitation, within the given historial moment.[4]

Braudel's work, or at least his method and sensibility, has evoked enthusiasm and emulation, however paradoxically, especially for his minute examination of the details of the lives and material conditions of the most humble members of the human community. That attention per se can only be admired, but the context within which Braudel situates the social chronicle gravely weakens his contribution. For, the basic human community in his work figures more as part of nature — as an ecological feature — than as a collectivity acting upon nature. Yet as Marx, among so many, long ago indicated, the properly human, the properly historical, begins with the separation of human consciousness from the natural world. The earliest and most rudimentary form of agricultural production with its attendant primitive technology indicates that separation. And with the exploitation of nature by man is sown the seeds of the exploitation of man by man (and woman by man and even woman by woman).

Yet, at exactly the point at which bourgeois social history rejoins the earlier Marxist tradition of attempting to write the history of the lower classes in general and of the working class in particular, it undercuts the essentials of the Marxian theoretical model. Marx, concerned with political goals, never mistook socialist demands for justice and proletarian power for a celebration of previous working-class patterns of life. He could not afford to: as a great revolutionary committed to changing the world and raising the working class to power, one of his major projects had to be precisely a ruthless criticism of all popular movements and classes, especially the working class, in order to help steel it for battle. Hence, he had to view any attempt to cover the blemishes or to exaggerate the virtues not only as romantic nonsense but as counterrevolutionary politics.

The search for a revolutionary tradition for working and oppressed peoples has characterized much Marxian and, more generally, socialist social history and has distorted historical experience in three principal ways: (1) It has unduly emphasized the presence or absence of class consciousness in various oppressed classes and has sought class-consciousnessly revolutionary proletariats, in a virtually modern sense, where such were unlikely to have obtained. Discerning the political content of early modern peasant uprisings or of slave rebellions either in the ancient world or in the Western hemisphere, to take only two examples, remains a delicate historical and theoretical task. (2) Much of Marxian social history has suffered from a quasi-teological bias, derived from eighteenth-century ideas of progress and nineteenth-century ideas of determinism that seriously undermine a flexible and fruitful reading of the past. And (3) pre-occupation with the most active segments of the working and oppressed classes at any given moment has led to the slighting of women and children and to the neglect of important cultural forces, including religion, folk customs, and family life, not to mention the social and cultural fabric and contributions of the dominant classes.

In the 1960s these shortcomings began to be reversed throughout the historical profession, including its Marxian component. The *Annalistes* certainly made the decisive impact, although by no means the total one sometimes claimed. First sociological theory and then psychology, now succeeded by anthropology, were called upon to redress the mechanical naivete of an ossifying historical practice. The extensive application of quantitative methods permitted a vast expansion in the amount of data that could be processed, and the demographic methods, including family reconstitution, permitted the analysis of data that did not exist. To call the new quantitative political history, the population studies, and the so-called and disastrously short-lived cliometric revolution "social history" is, to say the least, debatable. But their methods and findings undoubtedly constitute an important dimension of the work of almost all social historians.

Indeed, the statistical method, their common denominator, has shaped the questions, and therefore the answers, favored by many historians. In extreme cases, as with François Furet, it even changes the nature of the historical fact. The popularity of this and other methods, together with their implicit social perspective, has corresponded to a larger epistemological and ideological climate. It has been no accident that so many of those historians who came to maturity or received their early training during the 1950s have been prepared to jettison any concern with purposeful political action and to view the world as a configuration of statistical patterns. The series of hard data has at least partially absolved the observer of the responsibility for conscious judgment, although as James Henretta has cogently argued against Stephan Thernstrom and his social mobility group, the ideological bias cannot so readily be exorcized.[5] Increasingly, that bias has emerged as a willful pretense at "value-free" analysis which drains out any notion of consciousness or intent. As Henretta has also argued with reference to the older consensus school, interpretation persists, but instead of being sought in the self-conscious political programs and actions of the elites, it is sought in the statistically ascertainable — and emasculated — behavioral patterns of masses of individuals. This viewpoint not only denies the centrality of political struggle but of social and, in the extreme cases, intrapsychic struggle as well. For, while it may claim to recognize conflict, it inherently denies irreconcilable conflict; moreover, its methodological bias, which immediately emerges as ideology, focuses on moments of conflict-resolution and generally collapses into a denial of any conflict worthy of the name. The observed phenomena, or better, the statistical norm of the observed phenomena, become the reality. Procedures to account for the perilous conjuncture at any given moment of observed time get lost. The abstracted empiricism, so harshly pilloried by C. Wright Mills, triumphs.

No one outside the ranks of dogmatic cranks denies the indispensability of empirical work or mindlessly castigates quantitative methods, which clearly have much to contribute when delicately handled. But we do insist that the new and higher forms of empiricism in social history have reflected back onto whatever theoretical apparatus directs the beginning of the work. On the face of it, the retrieval of behavior of large numbers of individuals who made no autograph impact upon the world of high politics and high culture makes accessible dimensions of human experience hitherto largely ignored. There should be no need to review *in extenso* the increasingly familiar arguments that much of the material available for quantification still depends upon the prior collection of information considered relevant or useful by those — generally the elite — keeping records at the time. Before the rather recent systematic recordkeeping by national states, beginning with census records, much serial information contained strong biases and was, in any case, shaped by the intentions of the observer, not the observed. Police records have, however sensitively analyzed, provided a particularly charged example, for they have been biased even with respect to political heroes and villains since detention has always been selective. Even where more general series can be obtained — and family reconstitution and related techniques have significantly advanced our understanding of a host of demographic problems — the program formulated by the historian shapes the answers yielded by the ostensibly neutral scientific materials. It is a truism of scientific research that hypothesis precedes experimentation — that the scientist proceeds with a reasonably good idea of what he is looking for, however willing he is to be disappointed. On the theoretical level, quantitative work differs little, except in amount of data, from those great Victorian novels so readily dismissed as biased literary accounts.

Like every method, the quantitative remains precisely that — a method. Quantification is a tool, which in skillful hands facilitates the work of a shaping intelligence — the human understanding. But the problems of extrapolation, weighting of variables, breathtaking margins of error, and assorted other inevitable atrocities should make historians wary of seeing in it a substitute for their own concerns, much less a recasting of their questions. And to extrapolate from the mean of observed behavior conclusions about attitudes, beliefs, and social processes is tantamount to ascribing to every resident of the Upper West Side of New York City the statistically observed mean of achievement orientation, work motivation, and social attitude.

Quantification has already established itself as part of the apparatus of many social historians across the interpretive spectrum, and we are now approaching the time when the same ideological divisions will be as discernible within the magic circle as without. The recent furor over *Time on the Cross* has demonstrated nothing so much as the inevitable recurrence of all the old arguments and interpretations, albeit in a new language.

One of the major themes to emerge from the debate over *Time on the Cross* has been the extraordinary attempt to extrapolate the culture of the slaves from economic and social statistics, which ended in the dismal portrayal of black culture in general and work ethic in particular as a reflection of the culture of the masters. (We must pass over the dubious portrayal of the masters themselves, not to mention the economic process, which has been the subject of harsh and generally effective criticism.) The problematic nature of the relationship between the masters and the slaves and between the experience of enslavement and the personality structure, social values, and possible political behavior of the enslaved touched upon questions that dominate the rest of the field of social history as well. Fogel and Engerman, in a caricature of the consensus interpretation that plagues so many of the social mobility studies, argued in effect that the consciousness of the slaves reflected the values of their masters.

The weaker of Fogel's and Engerman's liberal critics have argued the reverse: that the consciousness of the slaves developed in virtually complete independence of the values of the masters. This view, in emphasizing African origins, family life, and, in some measure, custom, abstracts the slave experience almost completely from its political conditions of incipient violence and from that work experience which consumed so many of the slaves' waking hours and constituted much of the *raison d'etre* of his or her enslavement It denies the decisive importance of the master — slave dialectic — i.e., of the specific and historically ubiquitous form of class struggle — and no amount of "radical" emphasis on black achievement and autonomy can disguise this retreat from class interpretation to a politically anesthetized idealism. Thus, in denying the power of the ruling class in the society in which the slaves were enmeshed, and in denying the minimally mediating experience of enslavement upon the intimate consciousness of the slaves, this liberal view — albeit without saying so and hiding behind discussions of the mass — focuses upon the private rather than public experience of the slaves.

This tendency to look to the private existence to redress the political impotence of the public characterizes much recent social history. The traditionally socialist concern with laboring people has emerged transformed as history from the bottom up and, safely shorn of its political content, engages the attention of scholars of all political persuasions. The paternalist ethos, transfigured as it may be, has never had such a field day — so many opportunities for sublimation, and a sublimation often clothed in radical rhetoric at that.

The most recent and by far most fashionable methods espoused by social historians include anthropology and ethnography. The plotting of kinship patterns, the detailed observation of custom, the analysis of festivals and charivari, and the meticulous examination of the apparently most irrelevant bits of information afford a picture of the lives of the lowest strata of society. These studies, the best of which have been splendid on their own chosen terrain, frequently direct attention to the features of life — to the space — not claimed by the ruling classes. Hence the relative privacy of village celebrations, communal practices, and the interstices of family life, including relations between the sexes and childrearing, take pride of place.

The picture that emerges from the best of these studies affords a healthy and much needed corrective to the narrower view that emphasized working people, as well as women and children, as mere objects of the attention of their betters. It fills the gaps to which those betters saw no need to direct attention. It restores subjective participation in their own existence to people much too long denied their just claims to dignity. It even contributes in important ways to a delineation of the contours of custom within which the ruling classes had to extract their dues.[6] And no small matter, the best of these studies make delightful reading — as great travelers' accounts always have. After all, the practices of the natives have afforded endless hours of spellbinding relaxation for the ruling classes for centuries, so why should they not now do as much for the liberal and radical intelligentsia? But, as the fascination with custom demonstrates, it also leads, particularly in the hands of left-liberals away from the political content of class relationships, for customs that favor the lower classes can hardly be attributed to God or anthropology. They emerge from the mechanisms of equilibrium within continuing class war, the analysis of which requires due attention to the rulers as well as the ruled and to the political antagonism between them.

The burgeoning interest in the history of marriage and the family owes much to the reigning preference for private satisfaction as against public purpose; to the perception of a corrupt and bureaucratic state upon which political processes, and even socialist revolutions, seem to make little impact; and, paradoxically, to the cries of anguish from within the Western family itself. These very concerns, however much disillusionment with public political life they may testify to, should alert self-conscious practitioners of the historical craft to the intimate and complex relationship between public and private life and between political power and the conditions of private satisfaction. The family, after all, has functioned in one way or another not merely as "a little commonwealth," but as, in Samuel von Pufendorf's phrase, the nursery of the state. Whatever the failings of Engels' *Origins of the Family, Private Property, and the State,* the very title and attendant subject matter splendidly posed the right questions and called attention to the decisive political terrain of historical process. The close attention to family life, characteristic of at least the last three centuries, owes much to an increase in the state's ambitions to absorb the private sphere in order, among other things, to insure an adequate population growth and a correct psychological disposition.

Adequate analysis and interpretation of the role of the family as mediator between the public and private spheres remain difficult, elusive, and necessarily controversial. The questions span a wide range, including not only relations between men and women; the induction of the young into the ranks of rulers, citizenry, or work force; the disposition of property; and the virtues and violence of intimate domestic life; but also the much thornier ones of the causal relationship between private preferences and public structures. Presumably, the family-polity relationship must ultimately be understood as a dialectical one that takes full account of changing modes and relations of production, as well as of changing ideological commitments. (And on this ground alone one would think that the fashionable disdain for intellectual history among social historians would be recognized as being as stupid as it in fact is. It is enough to note that a social history of slavery which ignores David Brion Davis's brilliant study of the ideological forces within the larger historical process is doomed to fail.)[7] Hence, Lawrence Stone has recently argued, with compelling force, for localizing the origins of the nuclear family — in the modern sense of psychological intensity, property formation, explicit position of women, and concern with the education of the young — in contradistinction to the conjugal unit, at roughly the late sixteenth-century period marked in England by increased market relations, consolidation of absolute (i.e., bourgeois) property, and the solidification of Protestantism. Other excellent recent work, including most notably that of J. H. Plumb and Leonore Davidoff among many, similarly point to probable relationships between political life and family practice in the broad sense that includes social relations, the role of women, and the education of children.[8]

Such work only begins to indicate the possible contours of the family-polity nexus. The dynamics of the relationship between the individual and society, mediated as it is by family relations and the exercise of political power, require extensive investigation. But such investigation cannot hope to elucidate the social texture of any group — rich or poor, black or white, male or female, young or old — if it contents itself with a rapt neo-Victorian fixation on the blessings of domesticity. The notion of family as sanctuary from the public world of power and labor — in the manner of an *image d'Epinal* — itself derived from the ideological hegemony of emerging and mature capitalism. Those who, like certain contributors to recent discussions of the black family in slavery, invoke "socialization" as if the family or, worse, the entire popular culture, can be understood as an autonomous structure, independent of class confrontation, cultural interpenetration, and political domination, end by treating with contempt those whose qualities they are supposedly celebrating. For, what this mythical autonomy reduces to is a denial of the class struggle, the mediation of which largely accounts for whatever degree of autonomy historically emerges and passes into political significance.[9]

To speak bluntly, in full awareness that our position will require subsequent elaboration and defense not only by ourselves but by the Marxist comrades with whom we are associated: as admirable as much of the recent social history has been and as valuable as much of the description of the life of the lower classes may eventually prove, the subject as a whole is steadily sinking into a neoantiquarian swamp presided over by liberal ideologues, the burden of whose political argument — notwithstanding the usual pretense of not having a political argument — rests on an evasion of class confrontation. It should therefore come as no surprise that so many leading lights are ex-Marxists, ex-new Leftists, and ex-Communists who have fallen silent on political matters as well as on the class content of historical process but who desperately cling to the subject matter of the lower classes to shore up eroding credentials. No amount of superficial enthusiasm for "popular culture" or the symbolic representation of lower-class dissent, much less for ostensibly new methods, can obscure the obfuscation of the continuing class struggle between contending social forces as manifested on politically decisive terrain. To become more than sentimental neoantiquarianism, however "leftwing," attention to the lower classes must address the question of political power and demonstrate the extent to which that culture, those symbols, provide safety valves or, alternatively, implicit challenges to the ruling class. And such putative implicit challenges demand attention to the primary question: Why did they not become explicit? In any event, it must address the process of class struggle and extract the political implications — which means a good deal more than demonstrating that the "people" have always resented being abused; it means subjecting their strengths and weaknesses to the most severe criticism.

By now, it ought to be obvious that we view the current fad of "anthropology" in social history as a bourgeois swindle. It should be no less obvious that we have no principled objection to anthropology as such or to the notion that every historian should become as good an anthropologist as his or her talent permits. But the notion that anthropology per se offers a way toward the reconciliation of historical viewpoints is as silly as the similar claims advanced for cliometrics, econometric history, and assorted other scientisms.[10] And let it be noted that some of the worst offenders claim to be opposing consensus history because they project a bizarre and ahistorical — and anti-Marxist — view of a lower class life autonomously divorced from the pervasive influence of, and therefore influence on, the ruling classes. They end with their consensus-school opponents in a denial of class confrontation as the dynamic of historical (read: political) process; by bypassing political history they wistfully attempt, notwithstanding all radical pretense, to bypass everything essential to the development of human society.

Anthropology, like economics, sociology, and every other social science, splits internally along the same ideological lines as history itself. The attempt to invoke anthropology as a way out of the dilemmas of historical interpretation quickly exposes itself as pointless, however much certain schools of anthropology and specific empirical anthropological work may illuminate historical problems. In the end, the same ideological schools reappear; and, in this case, much of the "radical" left-liberal fascination with lower-class life, once scratched, emerges as a good deal more liberal than left — as an attempt to put everything and anything ("race," "culture," "socialization," and ultimately Rabelais' *ergo Gluck* in place of class confrontation — of the fundamental problem of power and order — at the center of historical process.

In any historical society, the problems of power and order receive at least an approximate solution through the medium of political institutions and processes. The wielding of legitimate authority — the consolidation of hegemony — cannot, however, be reduced to the skin and bones of political life narrowly construed.

This very ossification of the political, best exemplified in its curtailement to series of electoral figures, accounts in no small measure for the disrepute into which it has fallen on itself prefigures the fate of much of the new social history. Authority deployed and accepted passes through a myriad of tributaries that saturate the social terrain. Culture in all its manifestations, particularly language, standards of education, rituals of deference, patterns of urban space, celebrations of human values, religious practice, social forms, all contribute to the plenitude of the authority enjoyed by the ruling class. As J.H. Plumb indicated, in a brilliant review of David Brion Davis's second volume, the exploration of these paths of influence and ideological preeminence constitutes the indispensable and as yet largely unaccompanied task of social history.[12]

Unfortunately, social history as a whole has had trouble in sustaining a dialectical balance and a properly historical — i.e. narrative and political — perspective on these matters. Too frequently the awareness of culture passes into studies of so-called political culture that sacrifice the ever-renewed tensions of domination to a new form of concensual harmony. Or, as frequently, the new sensitivity to the determined resistance of popular practice sacrifices the recognition of continuing struggle with and acceptance of ruling class assumptions. The process of mutual transmission between classes gets lost as does the necessary recognition that the control of elite institutions gives the ruling class a decisive edge in the struggle. The attempt to enforce a national language from the center during the French Revolution, as Michel de Certeau and Dominique Julia have argued, reflects a keen attention to the political value of cultural forms on the part of politically self-conscious revolutionaries. Culture, as Mary Douglass properly insists, should not be invoked as some disembodied deus-ex-machina: It can never be divorced from the individuals and social groups whose experience it simultaneously articulates and shapes.[13] In this context, our insistence upon the overriding importance of the political dimension of social history should be understood in the larger sense of "political," namely the formulation and implementation of class authority, with the full understanding that a true hegemony entails far more police power and defines itself within the customary limits established by the lower classes, but, nonetheless, cannot ultimately be severed from political processes in general and the use of force in particular — as the history of revolutions testifies.

The accelerating proliferation of methodological revolutions in historical studies had its grand takeoff after World War II, when social history came into its own. That conjuncture ought to have made everyone thoughtful; instead it seems merely to have encouraged premature celebrations of intellectual virtue. Historical credentials depend increasingly upon expertise in one or another alternate discipline and preferably several. Something called "interdisciplinary history" has swept all before it. (And this too is a political question: Was it an accident that our profession was overwhelmed with fads at the very moment at which the most vulgar instrumentalism was being peddled by the federal government and the great foundations within an increasingly prostituted academy? The moment at which history and the humanities were being reduced in the curricula and treated as playthings for effete snobs? Why, for example, has no one demanded that every anthropologist, economist, sociologist, and psychologist become a historian, if "interdisciplinary" studies are at issue? And why has our bourgeois academy somehow overlooked the harsh dictum of the great Marxist scientist and historian of science J. D. Bernal that social scientists talk about method when they have run out of things to say?) Of course, all good history must be interdisciplinary in the sense that it depends upon the maximum application of human sensitivity and intellectual rigor: It always has been, as anyone who has read, say, Gibbon will attest. The danger lies in allowing the methods to swallow the historical content to the point at which the qualifications of a historian rest upon his or her qualifications in another discipline of presumed relevance.

The various academic disciplines now being brought to the assistance of historical inquiry originated as poorly differentiated facets of a single science of society when that secular enterprise disengaged itself from the residual shackles of sacred history during the early modern period. Properly, the great early exponents of the new craft subordinated their diverse forms of inquiry to the larger project of understanding society as a whole. Accordingly, much of their investigation bore an explicit relationship to their search for political excellence within a just social order. One of the most important and influential of their programs for a comprehensive understanding has come down to posterity as the Scottish Historical School. In the work of the great eighteenth-century progenitors of modern social science, both the historical sensibility and the concern with social totality figured decisively.

Increased specialization and the more precise delineation of intellectual experience have eroded the mastery of the whole accessible to any single scholar. The preoccupation with interdisciplinary work has, at its best, attempted to address the exaggerated fragmentation. The epistemological shifts, and indeed anxieties, have restored the old concern for comprehensiveness under a new guise. The sense of historical process has, however, fallen victim to an understandable impatience with naive theology. The focus on change over time has lost much of its intellectual prestige because of its implicit equation in so many minds with unilinear progress. Ironically, social history, which like Hegel's owl of Minerva may be taking the last great flight of the historical sensibility, suffers most from this conjuncture, however great the temporary advantage. Social history, shorn of politics and of the struggles and tensions that bedevil the world, may easily pass into anthropology or behavioral psychology or functional sociology, for that politics and those struggles and tensions lie at the core of any society, based as it must be on force.

Political history will, needless to say, survive, and in a form marvellously convenient for the ruling classes: once liberated from a social history nicely reduced to cultural anthropology or its functional equivalent, political history may safely return to the chronicle of kings, palaces, republican intrigues, and coups, occasionally disturbed by the recorded necessity to shoot down those lower-class bastards who could not adjust to the required social equilibrium or who proved too undisciplined for the harem. We would exaggerate if we said that the outcome of this pseudoscientific ideological parlor game must be to write all history as if it resembled some caricatured versions of life under the Asiatic mode of production. We would exaggerate – but not much.

Social history may then tend toward the application of "method" so as to reduce its subject matter to case study; toward the interpretation of the social text; toward the deciphering of the underlying structural codes. Delicately handled, all of these procedures and the sensibilities informing them contribute to the elucidation of the historical past and help to mitigate the worst features of simplistic determinism and blind teleology. But their contribution to our mode of understanding the complex conditions within which and the tortuous paths through which classes confront and rule each other should not be taken as a substitute for the processes, conflicts, and struggles that characterize human social relations.

For the rest, we shall risk an apparent contradiction in our argument. Psychology, which also splits ideologically within itself, has, at this point, a good deal more to offer historians, not because it is more "scientific" than some other discipline, much less because it is, in its general aspect, closer to our Marxism. Rather, in its Freudian form – and yes, we take Freudian ground in general as we have in our own published work – it at least has the virtue of bringing us back to the irreconcilable antagonisms inherent in the human condition and, therefore, to that tragedy of historical process once addressed so eloquently by Christian theology. Thus, the assorted "modern" schools, from the Behavioralists to the Sullivanians to the Ericksonians, with their intrinsic bias toward conflict-resolution, represent various forms of the Grand Liberal Dream of a will-of-the-wisp human reconciliation – a Utopia.[14] It should surprise no one that the psychological presuppositions of so much contemporary social history, dominated as it is by liberal ideology, eschews Freudian psychology for one of the alternatives. No better illustration commends itself than the debate over *Time on the Cross*, which not only revealed Fogel and Engerman to stand on the same ground as Stanley Elkins, depsite a reversal of various conclusions, but revealed their liberal opponents, who shifted the conclusions once more, as standing there also.[15] The spokesman for the liberal schools of psychology, including not only the behavioralists but Sullivan and Erickson as well, stand in relation to Freud as Bernstein and those whom Lenin derided as the "Heroes of the Second International" stood in relation to Marx. And they end in a similar intellectual impasse and with a similar political impotence, not to say betrayal of values.

It matters not a whit that "psycho-history," as written today, is largely drivel. It matters a great deal that psychoanalysis encourages a sensibility capable of mastering a disordered world and a theory of cultural transmission that addresses the historical problem of mediating the contrary claims of order, authority, freedom, and rebellion. The elucidation of these matters will have to await another day.

For the moment, we would call attention to the words with which the distinguished conservative historian Eric Voeglin opened his challenging multi-volume work, *Order and History:* "The order of history emerges from the history of order." Or, in our decidedly less elegant Marxian language: History, when it transcends chronicle, romance, and ideology — including "leftwing" versions — is primarily the story of who rides whom and how. To the extent that social history illuminates this essentially political process, we should all aspire to be social historians. To the extent that it provides new and more sophisticated, or alternatively more populist, forms of evasion and obfuscation, we should recognize it for what it is: merely the latest version of liberal or even "radical" bourgeois cant.

FOOTNOTES

1. Marc Bloch, *La société féodale:* I. *La formation des liens de dependance;* II. *Les classes et le gouvernment des hommes,* 2 vols. (Paris, 1949). For an extended discussion of the *Annales* school, albeit from a somewhat different perspective than our own (and for more detailed bibliographical references), see, Traian Stoianovich, *French Historical Method. The Annales Paradigm* (Ithaca, N.Y. and London, 1976).

2. Frank Kermode, *The Sense of an Ending. Studies in the Theory of Fiction* (New York, 1967), 39.

3. Fernand Braudel, *The Mediterranean and the Mediterranean World in the Age of Philip II* (N.Y. 1972)

4. Fernand Braudel, *Civilisation matérielle et capitalisme* (Paris, 1967); English translation, 1973.

5. Henretta's critique, which he delivered in preliminary form at the University of Rochester in the fall of 1975, has appeared in *Labor History*.

6. The impact of E. P. Thompson's work in the United States deserves full-length treatment. For the moment let it be noted that his pathbreaking book, *The Making of the English Working Class* (1963), joined political and social history decisively, but that its attention to popular culture, phrased with exceptional literary grace, inadvertently opened the way to a distorted and depoliticized reading. This essentially "rightist" interpretation has notably marked the work of certain recent American historians of labor and the lower classes. From the beginning it has been a tendentious and unworthy reading of Thompson's rich thought, as should become obvious when his remarkable paper, "Eighteenth Century English Society: Structure, Field-of-Force, Dialectic," which we have been privileged to read and to hear delivered, is published. But also to the point are Thompson's own *Whigs and Hunters* (1975) and the studies which he edited with Doug Hay and Peter Linebaugh, *Albion's Fatal Tree* (1975).

7. David Brion Davis, *The Idea of Slavery in Western Culture* (Ithaca, N.Y. and London, 1966), and *The Problem of Slavery in the Age of Revolution, 1770-1823* (Ithaca, N.Y. and London, 1975). Davis breaks simultaneously with "the history of ideas" and with sociological reductionism. Thus, his great work on antislavery thought, the second volume of which takes basically Marxian ground, accounts for the ideological dynamics of the historical process as a whole; as such, it provides the indispensable link between the emergence of irreconcilable class forces and the self-consciousness of those forces without which their political implementation would remain a puzzle. The work of Eric Foner should also be noted here. In *Free Soil, Free Labor, Free Men. The Ideology of the Republican Party before the Civil War* (New York, 1970), he analyzed the emergent ideological reaction in the North to the developing social system of the South and thereby contributed much to an understanding of the special nature of the southern ruling class itself. Foner's sensitivity to the intersections of social and intellectual history appears again in his recent study of Tom Paine (New York, 1976). In a somewhat different vein, the remarkable work of Raymond Williams requires careful attention for its contribution to our understanding of the relationship between culture and social forces. See, among many, his *The Country and the City* (New York, 1973).

8. Lawrence Stone, "The Rise of the Nuclear Family in Early Modern England: The Patriarchal Stage," in Charles Rosenberg, ed., *The Family in History* (Philadelphia, 1975); J. H. Plumb, "The New World of Children in Eighteenth-Century England," *Past and Present* (1975); Leonore Davidoff, *The Best Circles* (Totowa, N.J., 1974). Our references to Stone and Plumb ought to make clear that we do not wish to be understood as advancing the absurd, not to say Stalinist, notion that only Marxists are writing good social history or are capable of linking social and political history or can address questions of class confrontation. To the contrary, the best liberal and conservative historians differ from us primarily in their denial of the centrality of class struggle to historical process, but since they share our concern with power and authority in society, and have alternative ways of viewing social conflict, they manage to live at ease with the classes themselves. We do say, however, that academic liberalism as a whole is in full flight from these matters and that, not accidentally, the Stones and Plumbs have themselves had to sound the alarm at the implicit betrayal of values — something they can do more easily since so much of the liberal retreat is being led by left-liberals and ostensible radicals. We also would argue, with St. Cyprian, that there is indeed no salvation outside the Church and that, in general, the further social history departs from a Marxian theory of social process, the weaker it becomes. From this admittedly self-serving standpoint we can only paraphrase Gibbon on Belissarius: the fault of Mssrs. Stone and Plumb are those of their residual bourgeois ideology; their virtues are entirely their own.

9. Historians have been as awed by sociology as by economics and anthropology. Hence, many have not noticed the deep ideological biases and even palpable absurdities in some of the theories they so uncritically grasp and apply. Christopher Lasch's forthcoming book on sociological theories of the family, with its excellent critique of assorted models of socialization, should help to arrest this trend.

10. We cannot afford to, if only because one of us has the honor to serve on the editorial board of *Dialectical Anthropology* and does not wish to antagonize his comrades. But that is the point: there is anthropology and anthropology, and in the end the same ideological issues recur. Thus, the work of Sidney Mintz or Eric Wolff, for example, may be seen to contribute toward a deeper understanding of politics and historical process, for they are, above all, historical anthropologists. See, e.g., E. D. Genovese, "Class, Culture, and Historical Process," *Dialectical Anthropology,* I (1975).

11. See Claude Meillassoux, *Femmes, greniers and capitaux* (Paris, 1975). And, for a non-Marxist, but extremely provocative attempt to find new ways of understanding the female role in social processes, see Shirley Ardner, ed., *Perceiving Women* (London, 1975).

12. *New York Times Book Review,* Jan., 1975. See also his, *In the Light of History* (London, 1972).

13. *Une politique du language* (Paris, 1975); *Times Literary Supplement* Aug., 1975.

14. See the superb critique of the American tradition of ego psychology by Bernard Apfelbaum, "Ego Psychology, Psychic Energy, and the Hazards of Quantitative Explanation in Psycho-Analytic Theory," *The International Journal of Psycho-Analysis,* 46, pt. 2 (1965).

15. See Elizabeth Fox-Genovese, "Poor Richard at Work in the Cotton Fields: A Critique of the Psychological and Ideological Presuppositions of *Time on the Cross,"* *The Review of Radical Political Economics,* 7 (1975).

II.
LISTENING TO THE INARTICULATE

3.

ILLITERACY AND FAMILY LIFE DURING THE FIRST INDUSTRIAL REVOLUTION

David Levine

In the centuries preceding the Industrial Revolution a gigantic effort was made by several generations of English reformers and divines to wean the common people from their traditional habits of time and work. This reformation of manners was intimately concerned with the persistence of popular mentalities which opposed both "rationality" and "modernization." The period of the first Industrial Revolution thus presents us with a heightened sense of paradox in that almost all aspects of the political economy were "modernized" while continuing to co-exist with the detritus of the popular mental world of the pre-industrial epoch.[1] This popular mental world, so ably described by Keith Thomas, does not appear to have declined in the eighteenth century but rather it became separated and isolated in a giant centrifuge of social distancing.[2] While their betters were attracted to a latitudinarian scepticism, the plebeians continued to be ruled by a potent brew of magic, mystery and authority that was occasionally supercharged with a heady admixture of evangelical piety. The development of "rationality" and "modernity" cannot therefore be neatly pigeon-holed in the chronology of English history.

In trying to chart the growth of "rationality," historians often use literacy as a yardstick with which to measure this aspect of social development. Lawrence Stone, in explaining what he calls "the growth of affective individualism," has argued that "Puritanism, introspection, literacy and privacy form a single affinity group of characteristics." Stone goes on to remark that "Literacy is probably a necessary pre-condition for the growth of introspection."[3] It is clear from the context of Stone's remarks that he is here equating literacy with what educationalists such as Jeanne S. Chall would define as "reading for learning the new" and that this skilled literacy is a quite different experience from functional literacy.[4] The treatment of literacy by historians, however, is fraught with difficulties. "Literacy" extends across a broad continuum of skill and experience so that the use of the concept is often ambivalent; it is not unusual for it to be employed in a variety of ways within a single argument. Stone's book again provides a very good example of this inconsistent usage. Thus, at one point we are told that "the growth of literacy and of printing, which created great divergences between high and low cultures, . . . [was a change] . . . of incalculable significance," while later on we are informed that "The removal during the day of the male child from the house between the ages of six and ten for education in basic literacy was a revolutionary innovation in the life of most families from the lower middle class upwards."[5] This kind of ambivalent definition of literacy provokes a series of questions regarding the implications of the spread of "rationality." Thus, if the possession of literacy was a civilizing influence then one might ask whether the reformation of manners accompanying this transition in the psychological characteristics of English society was reflected in forms of behavior that can be analyzed with quantitative measurements. Were the characteristics of individuation and privatization, that Stone considers to be the concomitants of skilled literacy, of similar influence among those who were functionally literate? Were those who were illiterate somehow different in their behavior from the functionally literate?

The demographic repercussions of illiteracy are thought to be simple and direct. There has been a belief that certain acts are evidence of a rational, calculating approach to family formation and child care and that such an approach to reproductive behavior is part of a larger rationality that pervades the lives of more "modern" groups in the population. The poor, the shiftless, the "traditional" residuum are not thought to have practiced such restraint. They are said to have possessed "low gradient personalities" and their family life, it is claimed, was bestial and brutal.[6] It is not my intention to discuss the overt manifestations of caring and sentimentality but, rather, I wish to examine some of the premises on which these arguments are erected, for the expected dichotomy of "modern"/"traditional" or literate/illiterate seems to be carried over into the realm of demographic behavior. Thus, "modern," literate families are held to be in the vanguard of social evolution and, correlatively, child-centered. Such people should, one expects, adopt a prudent approach to marriage, restrict fertility and, by valuing children as individuals, devote a good deal of attention to each child's care. "Traditional," illiterate parents should be expected to display comparatively uncaring, thoughtless behavior.

The connection between literacy and demographic behavior has usually been studied in an aggregate level. For instance, students of the "fertility transition" usually try to correlate age at marriage, marital fertility and mortality with a population's ability to read. It is often supposed that the more literate a community, the more sophisticated its intellectual atmosphere, the more likely it is to experience demographic modernization.[7] So far, however, historical demographers studying this problem have lumped together literate groups (e.g. merchants and gentlemen) and compared their attributes with those of illiterate groups (e.g. laborers, peasants and shepherds).[8] But it is possible to look at the problem in another way. The family reconstitution studies that are held by the S.S.R.C. Cambridge Group for the History of Population and Social Structure are so structured that we can use people's literacy as the critical variable in selecting our sample and by so doing determine if this skill distinguished behavioral patterns among the sub-populations (educationally-defined) of the community. In this essay I propose to report the findings of such an investigation for the Leicestershire village of Shepshed between 1754 and 1851.

In confronting the issue of mass literacy historians have adopted two approaches. The first method is essentially bibliographical in that it involves the tabulation of books in print and books in circulation and goes on to assume that there is some relationship between the volume of publications and size of the reading public. On a very general level such an assumption must, of course, be true. Unfortunately such a fit is most imprecise, to say the least. The second kind of analysis proceeds in a quite different manner because it tries to calculate what might be termed "functional literacy" by direct observation. That is, alas, only possible when it comes to measuring an event which has left documentary remains. Except for nineteenth century Sweden where annual invigilations of the population's educational and catechetical knowledge were scrupulously noted by the inquisitive Lutheran clerics, the only traces we possess are an individual's ability to sign his or her name. Roger Schofield has argued that the merit of this measurement is not so nugatory as may first appear to be the case.

Although at first sight this is not a particularly meaningful literacy skill, it has the advantage of giving a fairly "middle range" measure of literacy in this period. This is because, ever since the sixteenth century, school curricula had been so phased that reading was taught before writing, and the intermittent nature of school attendance thus ensured that large numbers of children left school having acquired some reading ability, but little or no ability to write. In this period, therefore, the proportion of the population able to sign was less than the proportion able to read and greater than the proportion able to write. Early nineteenth century evidence suggests that the proportion of the population claiming a basic level of reading ability may have been half as much again as the proportion able to sign, and that the proportion able to sign roughly corresponded with the proportion able to read fluently.[9]

Schofield has further argued that such a measure is direct and can be easily standardized by a researcher who carefully takes the time to prepare comparable samples. Before Lord Hardwicke's Marriage Act of 1753 historians have consulted a variety of sources — wills, depositions, parochial records, the 1642 pretestation oath, and marriage licenses — to probe the dimensions of literacy.[10] With the bureaucratization of marriage registration that was entailed in Lord Hardwicke's Act, the parochial register of marriages becomes a valuable source. It yields a measure which encompasses almost all of the population at a point in their lives when the ravages of time have not dimmed their mental powers nor impaired their physical capacities. In this paper information describing literacy was derived from the registers of marriages that were celebrated in the parish of Shepshed, Leicestershire, between 1754 and 1851.

Shepshed is located on the edge of Charnwood Forest, midway between Leicester and Nottingham, about 110 miles north of London. It was a major rural center of framework knitting, a domestic industry which had first appeared in the mid-seventeenth century and grew dramatically from the 1750s until the end of the Napoleonic Wars. After 1815 the industry entered a phase of severe depression, and wages fell by as much as forty per cent. Accurate census-type enumerations do not exist before 1801 when the village had some 2600 inhabitants. The 1676 Compton Census of communicants suggests that at that time when framework knitting first appeared in the village there were around 600 people living there. It would seem that down to the middle of the eighteenth century the village grew slowly — it may have had about 900 inhabitants in 1750 — and then demographic expansion took hold. By 1821 the village had increased four-fold — to 3700 — although after that date its population stabilized and in 1851 there were 3750 villagers.

Framework knitting in Shepshed was initially organized along the lines of the putting-out system but over the century after 1750 significant changes occurred partly in response to the mechanization of spinning and partly due to the need, especially after 1815, to provide more breadwinners for the family. Thus, women's role in the household process of production changes as their original contribution — spinning — was revolutionized by Arkwright's mills. Looking back from 1845 Thomas Briers noted that in his youth, in the 1790s, few women worked at the frame whereas it had later become a commonplace for married women to engage in production and so add valuable supplements to the family income.[11] Men's work also changed over this period as small frame-shops emerged in which a number of machines were concentrated under the same roof. While this development increased the supervisory control exercised by the masters it did nothing, by itself, to revolutionize production, which continued to be based on human energy. Mechanization and flow production were *not* part of the proto-industrial scene during our period.

The full-scale growth of proto-industry in Shepshed after 1750 had profound demographic reverberations — the age of marriage fell by about five years for both men and women, life expectation at birth dropped markedly after 1825 and while fertility rose after 1750 there were clear signs that family limitation was being practised after 1825.[12] Only after 1825 was it possible to disaggregate the population and to compare the demography of the framework knitters with the rest of the community. This differentiated analysis was instructive since the response to the deterioration in real wages seems to have been quite effective. The proto-industrialists' rate of replacement was about half that of the other villagers after 1825. They offset their somewhat earlier marriage by regulating their marital fertility after they had crossed over their "dependency hump" and reached what seems to have been a desired family size. Their straitened circumstances led to a sharp increase in their infants' mortality which was not experienced by the other villagers. The onset of declining real wages after 1815 was accompanied by substantial emigration. Lastly, in 1851 it was found that a substantial number of framework knitters were sharing their household with another family, apparently part of their strategy to increase the number of co-residing wage-earners. In more than fifty per cent of the stockingers' households in 1851 there were three or more wage-earners.

Shepshed entered the proto-industrial period with no formal educational establishments. As late as 1740 there was no endowment for education.[13] The major educational institutions in the village were the denominational Sunday Schools. The 1833 survey lists four Protestant Sunday Schools and a Roman Catholic one. The Anglicans had 383 students while the three non-conformist groups had a further 355. The enrollment in the Roman Catholic schools was estimated to be 150. Thus there were something like 900 children who were in attendance at these five Sabbath Schools which provided the first and last chance for many of the village children to receive instruction.[14] In a village population of about 3750 there were approximately 900 between the ages of five and fifteen, the prime years of youthful school attendance. After allowing for a drop-off among the teenagers it would appear that there was something approaching universal Sunday School attendance. All children in Shepshed, it seems, had the chance to be exposed to some instruction. It would appear, however, that for many children their attendance at Sunday School was perfunctory and did not leave a lasting impression. The parish registers reveal that in the period 1825-1844, 41.4% of men (N=589) and 68.6% of women were unable to sign their names when celebrating their marriage. In the previous seventy-year period, 1754-1824, the proportions of illiterates were almost exactly the same — men, 43.2% (N=1354) and women, 69.2%.

The central set of records used in my demographic study were the parish registers of baptisms, burials and marriages.[15] The information garnered from these records was reconstituted into family units which provided the basic group for analysis. As mentioned earlier, the marriage register provided for the bride's and groom's signature or mark. This evidence was used to supplement the family reconstitution study in ways that will become evident as I discuss the results of the calculations describing the interplay between literacy and family life. The family reconstitution study of Shepshed makes it possible to consider a few of the critical parameters of demography, those most basic of all social characteristics, and to determine whether real differences can be found in the behavioral regularities of our educationally-defined sub-groups. For the post-1825 cohort it will be possible to break down these sub-groups further by adding an occupational dimension to the analysis.

Table I
AGE AT FIRST MARRIAGE, BY LITERACY (SHEPSHED)

A) MEN

i) ABLE TO SIGN

	N	Mean	Standard Deviation	Median
1754-1824	245	24.8	5.4	23.5
1825-1851	194	24.3	5.0	23.7

ii) UNABLE TO SIGN

	N	Mean	Standard Deviation	Median
1754-1824	199	25.5	6.4	23.5
1825-1851	197	23.7	4.8	22.9

B) WOMEN

i) ABLE TO SIGN

	N	Mean	Standard Deviation	Median
1754-1824	198	24.0	4.7	22.5
1825-1851	111	24.5	5.4	23.0

ii) UNABLE TO SIGN

	N	Mean	Standard Deviation	Median
1754-1825	314	24.4	6.1	22.9
1825-1851	368	22.2	4.4	21.4

Table II
AGE AT FIRST MARRIAGE, BY LITERACY AND OCCUPATION, 1825-1851 (SHEPSHED)

A) Literate

i) MEN Framework

ii) WOMEN Framework

Knitters	Others		Knitters	Others
125	69	N	44	67
23.4	25.8	Mean	23.2	25.4
4.5	5.8	Standard Deviation	5.3	5.5
23.2	24.5	Median	22.1	23.6

B) Illiterate

i) MEN Framework

ii) WOMEN Framework

Knitters	Others		Knitters	Others
143	54	N	268	100
23.7	23.8	Mean	22.2	22.3
4.9	4.7	Standard Deviation	4.4	4.5
22.9	23.0	Median	21.2	22.0

For Western European populations, age at marriage has been the crucial variable in the demographic question. For pre-Malthusian populations it was the one area of demographic experience over which men and women exercised choice. Because of the importance of marriage it will be analyzed and described from a variety of viewpoints to try to determine whether significant correlations existed between literacy, marriage and (after 1825) occupation.

In Table I the basic distinction between literates and illiterates subdivides the population of each cohort. A striking change was evident after 1825. Illiterates, both men and women, married earlier than those who displayed "middle range" educational skill. For men who were literate there was no appreciable change over time. Literate women, in fact, married 0.5 years later after 1825. In contrast, male illiterates married 1.8 years earlier after 1825, while females who could not sign their name married 2.2 years earlier in the second quarter of the nineteenth century than before. If we look more closely at the results in Table I it will be seen that mean values drop more sharply than median scores. It would appear that a significant component of this reduction in the age of first marriage for post-1825 illiterates can be attributed to the decrease in the proportion of women much older than average who were marrying. The shape of the distribution was more peaked after 1825. The measurement of central tendency was subject to less variance and a smaller standard deviation.

If we turn to consider the occupational component in these shifts in the age at marriage after 1825 it should be pointed out that because of the small size of the various non-industrial occupations — farmer, carpenter, grocer, labourer, etc. — it was necessary to consider these sub-groups together. The agricultural labourers had a level of literacy that was more similar to that of the proto-industrialists — two-thirds of these men were illiterate — than to the farmers, artisans and tradespeople, of whom just eight per cent could not sign their name, and it may well be the case that the disaggregation in Table II has sorted out this effect. The illiterate, "other" villagers were similar to the framework knitters — literate or illiterate, men or women. It would seem that the lines of demarcation would oppose the literate, "other" villagers to all of their neighbours. The literate, "other" men married between 2.0 and 2.4 years later and the literate, "other" women were between 2.2 and 3.2 years older at the time of their first marriage.

Another way of getting at the changing configuration of marriage is through a comparison of what may be termed "literate endogamy" and "illiterate endogamy." We are contrasting couples in which both partners are literate with a group in which both partners are illiterate. In addition, those couples in which one partner could sign and the other could not have also been incorporated into Table III. Here, the most significant change between the two cohorts concerns the bifurcation in the experience of the literate endogamous, who married later after 1825, and the others who married earlier or, in the case of the literate women marrying illiterate men, at the same age.

When parental literacy is considered, and occupation is added onto the mix as well, the results become even more suggestive although the sample size diminished to much lower levels. There were twenty-five women marrying after 1825 who were literate, whose fathers were not framework knitters, whose parents were both literate, and whose husbands were also literate. They married at a (mean) average age of 26.4. In comparison, the thirty-six illiterate framework knitters' daughters whose parents and grooms were all illiterate married at 21.6, 4.8 years earlier. The men do not present such a stark opposition in behavior. The eight fully literate non-industrial men married at 24.5 while the twenty-six fully illiterate framework knitters whose closest relations were also illiterate had an average at first marriage of 22.0.

Table III
AGE AT FIRST MARRIAGE, BY COUPLE'S LITERACY (SHEPSHED)

1754-1824

A) MEN	N	Mean	Standard Deviation	Median
S/S	112	24.9	5.0	23.5
Mixed	165	25.0	5.8	23.5
X/X	168	25.5	6.5	23.5

B) WOMEN	N	Mean	Standard Deviation	Median
S/S	158	24.2	4.7	23.0
Mixed	190	24.6	8.1	22.5
X/X	164	23.9	5.3	23.0

1825-1851

A) MEN	N	Mean	Standard Deviation	Median
S/S	101	25.2	5.2	24.6
Mixed	137	23.6	4.7	22.6
X/X	153	23.6	4.8	23.2

B) WOMEN	N	Mean	Standard Deviation	Median
S/S	83	24.3	5.5	22.8
Mixed	188	22.3	4.4	21.8
X/X	208	22.5	4.6	22.3

S/S means both partners are literate
X/X means both partners are illiterate

NOTE: These figures were recalculated after I discovered some errors in the tabulations for the 1825-1851 cohort. For this reason the scores in this version are different from those in the earlier paper, "Immiseration, Illiteracy and Family Life During the First Industrial Revolution," which was presented to the History of Education Conference and the Social Science History Association Seminar on Proto-Industrialization.

These differences in age at marriage are substantial. They beg the question of the role of differentiation within the village community. An answer to this question requires that we first survey the other demographic variables — marital fertility and infant mortality. Only when we see the effect of marriage within the larger demographic equation can we properly interpret these differences in nuptiality. In presenting the data on marital fertility and infant mortality it was decided to join together the two sub-populations in which one partner was literate and the other was not. This decision was made because of the tiny number of cases for the group in which there was an illiterate man and a literate woman. Thus, we will be looking at three types of families: both partners literate; both partners illiterate; and mixed.

The age-specific fertility rates in Table IV seemingly contradict the impression yielded from our discussion of age at marriage. In both cohorts the literate couples had the highest levels of fertility while the illiterates had the lowest. This evidence questions the hypothesis that the higher age at marriage of literate women after 1825 was part of a prudent reproductive strategy. The literate woman seemingly

Table IV
AGE-SPECIFIC MARITAL FERTILITY, BY COUPLE'S LITERACY (SHEPSHED)

A) 1754-1824

S/S	Years at Risk	Children Born	Rate/000
U25	174	83	477
25-29	268	100	373
30-34	268	89	331
35-39	191	51	268
40-44	146	17	116
45-49	121	3	25

Mixed	Years at Risk	Children Born	Rate/000
U25	212	95	448
25-29	246	88	358
30-34	241	77	320
35-39	229	59	258
40-44	181	31	171
45-49	158	7	44

X/X	Years at Risk	Children Born	Rate/000
U25	151	62	411
25-29	211	61	289
30-34	223	64	286
35-39	155	36	232
40-44	120	12	100
45-49	91	0	0

B) 1825-1851

S/S	Years at Risk	Children Born	Rate/000
U25	165	68	412
25-29	220	89	404
30-34	199	68	342
35-39	128	33	258
40-44	94	13	138
45-49	91	0	0

Mixed	Years at Risk	Children Born	Rate/000
U25	502	226	450
25-29	473	167	353
30-34	349	107	307
35-39	200	45	225
40-44	90	13	144
45-49	33	—	0

X/X	Years at Risk	Children Born	Rate/000
U25	462	192	416
25-29	428	140	327
30-34	350	103	294
35-39	234	54	231
40-44	128	12	94
45-49	54	—	0

Table V
TOTAL FERTILITY, BY COUPLE'S LITERACY (SHEPSHED)

A) S/S

i) 1754-1824

	Years Married	Annual Fertility	Children Born
U25	0.8	.447	.38
25-29	5.0	.373	1.87
30-34	5.0	.331	1.66
35-39	5.0	.268	1.34
40-44	5.0	.116	.58
45-49	5.0	.025	.12
			5.95

ii) 1825-1851

	Years Married	Annual Fertility	Children Born
U25	0.7	.412	.29
25-29	5.0	.404	2.02
30-34	5.0	.342	1.71
35-39	5.0	.258	1.29
40-44	5.0	.138	.69
45-49	5.0	.061	.31
			6.31

B) Mixed

i) 1754-1824

	Years Married	Annual Fertility	Children Born
U25	0.4	.448	.18
25-29	5.0	.358	1.79
30-34	5.0	.320	1.60
35-39	5.0	.258	1.29
40-44	5.0	.171	.86
45-49	5.0	.044	.22
			5.94

ii) 1825-1851

	Years Married	Annual Fertility	Children Born
U25	2.7	.450	1.22
25-29	5.0	.353	1.77
30-34	5.0	.307	1.58
35-39	5.0	.225	1.13
40-44	5.0	.144	.72
45-49	5.0	–	–
			6.42

C) X/X

i) 1754-1824

	Years Married	Annual Fertility	Children Born
U25	1.1	.411	.45
25-29	5.0	.289	1.45
30-34	5.0	.286	1.43
35-39	5.0	.232	1.16
40-44	5.0	.100	.50
45-49	5.0	–	–
			4.59

ii) 1825-1851

	Years Married	Annual Fertility	Children Born
U25	2.5	.416	1.04
25-29	5.0	.327	1.64
30-34	5.0	.294	1.47
35-39	5.0	.231	1.16
40-44	5.0	.094	.47
45-49	5.0	–	–
			5.78

NOTE: The age at marriage is based on the mean measurement.

Table VI
INFANT MORTALITY, BY COUPLE'S LITERACY (SHEPSHED)

A) 1754-1824

	At Risk	Dying	Rate/000	Life Expectation	Surviving to Marriage
S/S	871	108	123	50.9	.763
Mixed	1223	215	176	41.6	.643
X/X	1200	213	177	41.6	.645

B) 1825-1851

	At Risk	Dying	Rate/000	Life Expectation	Surviving to Marriage
S/S	174	31	178	41.6	.640
Mixed	360	70	194	40.5	.646
X/X	298	72	242	35.3	.573

Table VII
SURVIVING CHILDREN, BY COUPLE'S LITERACY (SHEPSHED)

A) S/S   i) 1754-1824   ii) 1825-1851

24.2	age at marriage	24.3
5.95	total fertility	6.31
.763	proportion surviving to marriage	.640
4.54	children surviving to marriage	4.04

B) Mixed i) 1754-1824   ii) 1825-1851

24.6	age at marriage	22.3
5.94	total fertility	6.42
.643	proportion surviving to marriage	.646
3.82	children surviving to marriage	4.15

C) X/X   i) 1754-1824   ii) 1825-1851

23.9	age at marriage	22.5
4.59	total fertility	5.78
.645	proportion surviving to marriage	.573
2.96	children surviving to marriage	3.31

Table VIII
AGE AT FIRST MARRIAGE, BY COUPLE'S LITERACY AND OCCUPATION, 1825-1851 (SHEPSHED)

S/S   i) **MEN**   ii) **WOMEN**

Framework Knitters	Others		Framework Knitters	Others
47	54	N	33	50
24.0	26.3	Mean	22.4	25.6
4.5	5.9	Standard Deviation	5.3	5.7
23.7	25.3	Median	21.5	23.7

Mixed i) **MEN**   ii) **WOMEN**

Framework Knitters	Others		Framework Knitters	Others
108	29	N	145	43
23.4	24.2	Mean	22.1	22.8
4.5	5.4	Standard Deviation	4.6	4.1
22.6	22.7	Median	21.5	22.6

X/X   i) **MEN**   ii) **WOMEN**

Framework Knitters	Others		Framework Knitters	Others
113	40	N	134	74
23.7	23.5	Mean	22.5	22.5
4.9	4.7	Standard Deviation	4.4	5.0
23.0	23.7	Median	22.3	22.4

compensated for their later marriage with their higher marital fertility although at no point in time did the levels of marital fertility in Shepshed approach the "natural fertility" levels of the hutterites. Marital fertility in Shepshed was always below the physiological maximum and there was always room for considerable adjustments in its level. If we compare the interaction between age at marriage and age-specific marital fertility, in terms of completed family size, for a hypothetical, representative woman from each cohort who represents each literacy-defined sub-group, the results are very interesting. The simulation exercises depicted in Table V do not allow for ravages of adult mortality and so

Table IX
AGE-SPECIFIC MARITAL FERTILITY, BY COUPLES LITERACY AND OCCUPATION, 1825-1851 (SHEPSHED)

A)   Framework Knitters

i)

S/S	Years at Risk	Children Born	Rate/000
U25	70	24	343
25-29	69	26	377
30-34	70	16	229
35-39	44	7	159
40-44	39	5	128
45-49	14	2	142

ii)

Mixed	Years at Risk	Children Born	Rate/000
U25	267	126	472
25-29	270	97	359
30-34	201	56	279
35-39	126	31	246
40-44	55	9	164
45-49	14	—	0

iii)

X/X	Years at Risk	Children Born	Rate/000
U25	377	140	371
25-29	366	119	325
30-34	290	84	290
35-39	204	43	211
40-44	105	10	95
45-49	49	—	0

B)   Others

i)

S/S	Years at Risk	Children Born	Rate/000
U25	95	44	463
25-29	151	63	417
30-34	129	52	403
35-39	84	26	310
40-44	55	8	145
45-49	19	—	0

ii)

Mixed	Years at Risk	Children Born	Rate/000
U25	235	100	426
25-29	203	70	345
30-34	148	51	345
35-39	74	14	189
40-44	35	4	114
45-49	19	—	0

iii)

X/X	Years at Risk	Children Born	Rate/000
U25	85	52	612
25-29	62	21	339
30-34	60	19	317
35-39	30	9	300
40-44	23	2	87
45-49	5	—	0

they produce total fertility measures for women whose marriages have remained unbroken through the whole of their child-bearing peirod. The later marriage of the literate women was more than counteracted by their higher fertility within marriage (I possess no relevant information concerning pre-marital fertility). The comparatively low fertility of the pre-1825 cohort of illiterate women is noteworthy, and we shall return to this point later. The mixed literacy marriages were, in fact, the most prolific.

The full meaning of our figures describing nuptiality and fertility will only become apparent when the effects of infant mortality are added into the equation. In Table VI the reconstituted results describing this phenomenon are presented. The fourth column, "Life Expectations," denotes the average length of life of a group sharing that particular infant mortality rate.[16] The fifth column, "surviving to marriage," describes the rate of survival to the average age at marriage per 1,000 births sharing the specified life expectation and age at marriage. Using the information from our three variables I can now proceed to explicate the results of each sub-population's reproductive strategy. In Table VII I have shown how many of the children from each of our hypothetical families survived.

The figures in Table VII are meant to describe *relative* rates of replacement — by not taking adult mortality, and hence marital break-up, into account they cannot be construed as net rates of replacement. This caveat must be borne in mind since levels of infant mortality are not necessarily of the same order of magnitude as adult mortality rates. Even so, these results are very interesting. In particular, there is no evidence of a direct relationship between age at marriage and surviving children. Indeed, when we see the reproductive patterns of the educationally-defined groups in terms of their *total* strategy the earlier intimation of a connection between the late marriage of literate women and prudential reproduction withers. It was not the literates but, rather, the illiterates who had the smallest number of surviving children, in each cohort. A full explanation of these results will only be worthwhile after we have reanalyzed the post-1825 cohort's reproductive patterns by splitting each educationally-defined group along occupational lines. At that point we might be able to proffer an explanation which is less jeopardized by the influence of this most important intervening variable. Then, too, the question of culture and economic pressure can be properly addressed.

In many ways Table VIII echoes the earlier findings (see Tables II and III) in that the distinctly later marriages of the literate endogamous "others" are highlighted. The other five groups — regardless of occupation, husband's literacy, or wife's literacy — all shared a similar pattern of earlier marriages. Only 0.5 years separated the youngest-marrying from the oldest-marrying — men or women — among these five groups. These men married from 2.3 to 2.8 years earlier than the literate endogamous "others." These five sets of women were from 2.8 to 5.5 years younger when they first married than were the female partners in literate endogamous, non-industrial marriages.

The age-specific fertility of the various sub-groups after 1825 is presented in Table IX. The non-industrial couples in which both partners could sign had the highest levels of fertility. The literate proto-industrialists had the lowest fertility rates although this sample is very small. The next lowest rates were those of the illiterate framework knitters.

When we turn to the variations in infant mortality (Table X) we are once again bedevilled by small sample sizes which may, in some instances, yield the results liable to chance fluctuations. While there were no significant differences between

Table X
INFANT MORTALITY, BY COUPLE'S LITERACY AND OCCUPATION, 1825-1851
(SHEPSHED)

i)   Framework Knitters

	At Risk	Dying	Rate/000	Life Expectation	Surviving to Marriage
S/S	88	15	170	42.8	.656
Mixed	269	57	212	37.0	.588
X/X	249	63	253	30.6	.489

ii)   Others

	At Risk	Dying	Rate/000	Life Expectation	Surviving to Marriage
S/S	86	16	186	41.6	.635
Mixed	91	13	143	47.4	.721
X/X	49	9	183	41.6	.651

Table XI
SURVIVING CHILDREN, BY COUPLE'S LITERACY AND OCCUPATION, 1825-
1851 (SHEPSHED)

i) S/S	Framework Knitters		Others
	22.4	age at marriage	25.6
	5.99	total fertility	6.13
	.656	proportion surviving to marriage	.635
	3.93	children surviving to marriage	3.89

ii) Mixed	Framework Knitters		Others
	22.1	age at marriage	22.8
	6.61	total fertility	5.91
	.588	proportion surviving to marriage	.721
	3.89	children surviving to marriage	4.26

iii) X/X	Framework Knitters		Others
	22.5	age at marriage	22.5
	5.59	total fertility	6.75
	.489	proportion surviving to marriage	.6511
	2.73	children surviving to marriage	4.39

the infant mortality of literate parents' children — framework knitters and the rest of the population had almost identical scores — the unlettered proto-industrialists' children fared badly in comparison with the children of the other illiterate villagers. The framework knitters with mixed literacy saw their children die more frequently than the other parents with mixed literacy.

In Table XI the three demographic variables have been used in the kind of simulation exercise that has already been carried out for the undifferentiated results. It is extremely interesting that the illiterate proto-industrialists appear to have had substantially lower rates of replacement than all other groups. There is grist here for an argument which would see these double-exploited villagers as the members of a culture of poverty. But it was a group which was not reproducing itself with the energy of the other villagers. The broad similarity of these replacement rates among the other five sets of villagers seems again to militate against an argument that the later marriage of the literate-endogamous, non-industrial villagers was part of a prudent reproductive strategy. If anything, these results seem to illustrate the wide variety of ways in which people could arrive at a desired family size. Thus it would appear that, in families unbroken by parental death until the end of the wife's child-bearing years, something like six or seven children could be born, of whom about four would themselves survive to the age at marriage. Among the unlettered framework knitters, marriage was early but fertility was not high and so they had less children of whom not half survived to their mother's age at marriage, 22.5.

The results in Table XI appear to beg two questions and it is now time to address them. Specifically, what would account for the illiterate framework knitters' distinctively low levels of replacement? and, secondly, what, if anything, was the role of literacy in promoting population growth during the period of the first industrial revolution? I should like to address these questions in reverse order.

I had initially begun this research with the hypothesis that illiteracy was associated with population growth inasmuch as it distinguished early-marrying, high fertility, and high mortality groups whose numbers swelled as the demand for unskilled, industrial labour rose.[17] Being an unregenerate disciple of the "rising birth rate" school, it seemed to me that the higher mortality of the illiterates' children was probably of minor importance in comparison with the effective unleashing of the prudential check. Initially, I examined the undifferentiated results from the 1825-1851 cohort which suggested that my theorizing was likely to be accurate since the unlettered were marrying much earlier than the literate. The lower fertility of the illiterate after 1825 was, I thought, part of *their* prudential response to the depressed wage-levels in the framework knitting industry after 1825. Again, the higher infant mortality among the illiterates' children seemed to be explicable in terms of the deteriorating life expectation of the framework knitters who were themselves largely unlettered. Thus, I came to my further research with a set of hypotheses which seemed reasonable and, after some initial analysis, perhaps even correct. As the previous discussion has made abundantly clear, I could hardly have been more wrong. By extending the research backwards to embrace the 1754-1824 cohort I found that the expected association of illiteracy and earlier marriages, literacy and later marriage, was not provable; indeed it did not exist at all but was, if anything, the opposite of the post-1825 practice. Furthermore, the illiterates' marital fertility was also lower before 1825 while their children fared worse than the infants of literate parents. The illiterates did not make an extraordinary contribution to population growth in Shepshed after 1750. In fact, their replacement rate was less than that of the literate or mixed literacy parents. As if this exercise was not destructive enough, the process of disaggregating the post-1825 cohort, as we have just seen, definitively put paid to my inchoate hypothesizing. The evidence that has been presented in this paper has turned the problem of explanation upside down. What we need to understand is why the illiterate — and particularly the framework knitters after 1825 — had such low rates of replacement.

The problem of explaining the post-1825 illiterate framework knitters' low reproductive levels is trebly complicated: first, I do not know if the post-1825 occupational differences mirrored those from the earlier cohort; second, I do not know whether literacy was correlated with income and skill so that, for example, the illiterate framework knitters were also the worst paid; and, third, I have no knowledge if there were differences in the household structures of literates and illiterates. The lack of this evidence is unfortunate because an explanation of their reproductive behavior can only be rooted in the family economy of the unlettered framework knitters if we can make certain assumptions about the nature of that family economy.[18] The element of uncertainty is obvious. Thus, if the illiterate proto-industrialists were the worst paid, poorest members of the community, then an argument which would stress the rationality and prudence of their reproductive strategies could be made. And, if these illiterate framework knitters were also the most likely to have complex, co-residential households with several wage-earners, then the demographic response to the post-Napoleonic depression in wages could be understood within a larger argument which proposes that, in fact, literacy and "rationality" were not synonymous and that contemporary social reformers — and later historians of family life in England — were quite wrong in attributing this section of the working class with profligate and unthinking attitudes toward their domestic responsibilities. Such an argument would place the decision-making process firmly within the pullulations of the family's budget. The domestic economy would, therefore, have its own reason and calculation. Plebs — just as much as the bourgeoisie — would be recognized as being capable of understanding the nature of fiscal stringency for their family budgets as well as reacting against a careless, profligate reproductive strategy. But such hypothesizing must remain just that in the absence of firmer evidence.

The results of the Shepshed study provide evidence of substantial inter- and intra-group variations in demographic rates thereby making it difficult to argue for a homogeneous regime antedating the late nineteenth century decline in fertility and mortality. At no time, however, did marital fertility in Shepshed approach the physiological maximum so that there was considerable room for both upwards and downwards adjustments. Of primary importance is the extent to which it was possible for these villagers to adjust their rate of replacement in times of changing economic opportunity. This flexibility was most apparent in the behavior of the illiterate proto-industrialists who responded to difficult times by reducing their fertility at the same time as more of their infants were dying. Such a response on the part of the illiterate framework knitters is of particular interest in that it highlights the extent to which they acted to control their own destiny. This pattern of behavior is also noteworthy because in times of demographic equilibrium the birth rate and the death rate tend to fluctuate directly; but after 1825, in Shepshed, they fluctuated in an inverse manner.

Our conceptualization of demographic history is shifting its emphasis and the heterogeneity of reproductive systems antedating the demographic transition has come to the forefront. The static picture of high birth rates balancing high death rates has been undermined by empirical findings during the past two decades of research into parish register statistics. Perhaps the greatest casualty of this new work has been the theoretical framework which posits a dramatic dichotomy separating "pre-industrial" and "modern" demographic regimes.[19] The experience of Shepshed's illiterate proto-industrialists provides a striking illustration of the powers that a pre-Malthusian population could call upon to re-establish a balance between population and resources. Researchers are finding that variations between what David Gaunt has termed "eco-systems" created a substantial amount of variation within the overarching framework created by the laws of biology and the cultural demands of the European family system.[20] While mortality levels were high they seem to have fluctuated over time as well as varying quite substantially across space. Thus, in conditions of demographic equilibrium, it was possible for highly different levels of fertility to emerge.

Similarly, although there was a general assent to what John Hajnal has called the "European Marriage Pattern," there were substantial differences in its local interpretation.[21]

In stepping back from the grand theories of development and beginning to study ground-level activity, there has been an insistence on the primacy of local factors in the explanation of local social systems. Work at the grass-roots has revealed a welter of contradictory patterns. In an attempt to come to grips with these islands of sub-atomic activity it is as necessary for us to break with general theories as it was for Max Planck and Werner von Heisenberg. The fit between the world of the large and the world of the small is inexact and, hence, problematic. The explanation itself becomes a theoretical problem and we are required to devote intellectual energy to a consideration of the appropriate level of analysis. The upshot of this exercise has been a renewed emphasis upon discontinuity, unevenness and differentiation.[22] In such a world of pullulating forces individuals are assumed to make strategic decisions in order to optimize their circumstances.[23] Such strategic decisions are *not* overdetermined by the cultural milieu, as earlier theorists would have had it, but are themselves part of a continuously evolving definition of that milieu. Men and women are understood to interpret cultural norms in terms of their own experience. Thus when proto-industry undermined the prudential check marriage occurred earlier. A reduction of two, three or even four years may have still kept the marriage within the parameters of the "European Pattern" but it had an explosive effect on the rate of replacement. In the absence of any countervailing reduction in fertility or a rise in mortality, such a shift in the pattern of marriage resulted in demographic disequilibrium. And, to continue with the example of proto-industry, such developments were confined neither in time nor in space in the so-called pre-industrial world. Nor did they work solely to produce faster rates of growth since some proto-industrial areas were superceded and reverted to a later age at marriage and a more prudential replacement rate.[24] The point of this slight diversion has been to reiterate the heterogeneity of pre-transition demographic systems. It should also serve to introduce another factor into the discussion. To the extent that the argument which emphasizes unevenness, discontinuity and differentiation is based on an economic model stressing the integrity and independence of the family unit, the role of class cannot be left out. It is a factor of paramount importance but, alas, progress in this sphere has been halting. To no small extent the sources at our disposal are simply inadequate.[25] Parish registers are rarely specific in describing occupation and, by proxy, class positions. In the Shepshed study it was precisely at this point that the progress was most exciting and most frustrating. Thus, while it was possible to describe the pattern of earlier marriage on the part of the framework knitters after 1825 and to provide an explanation rooted in the deterioration of their living standards and the demo-economic demands of their household economy, it was not clear how the specific mechanisms operated to achieve an integration of the family's economic and demographic strategies.

So, the results of the demographic analysis remain inconclusive inasmuch as it is not possible to produce a solidly-based explanation of the illiterate framework knitters' motives and expectations when they experienced a significant decline in their rate of replacement after 1825. Furthermore, there is no conclusive evidence that the literacy-defined sub-populations were pursuing separate or distinct reproductive strategies before the second quarter of the nineteenth century when the living standards of the proto-industrial villagers deteriorated. Perhaps the most we can say is that illiteracy was not accompaied by mindless breeding nor was literacy associated with a prudential reproductive strategy in this first century of industrial revolution in Shepshed.

This paper has argued against the perspective of modernization theory which posits that the illiterate were somehow not fully rational in their family lives. I have suggested that functional literacy was not a significant indicator of differentiation among the popular classes in Shepshed. It might be objected that my heuristic framework has made an artificially stark dichotomy based on the possession of a simple, functional skill. In my defense I would agree that such an objection is precisely to the point. The possession of literacy seems to have been a relatively unimpressive signifier of special status.

FOOTNOTES

The author wishes to thank the members of the Davis Center Seminar in Princeton, as well as Harvey Graff, Michael Katz and Roger Schofield, for their advice and encouragement.

1. This sense of paradox has been neatly captured by E.A. Wrigley in his article "The Process of Modernization and the Industrial Revolution in England," *Journal of Interdisciplinary History 3* (1972), esp. 258.

2. *Religion and the Decline of Magic* (London 1971). Although the panoply of detail and the breadth of Thomas' reach (and grasp) are stunning, the book never quite explains (or even completely describes) the decline of magical practices and beliefs. James Obelkevich's research on popular religion in rural Lincolnshire suggests that the decline of magic was a class-specific phenomenon. (*Religion and Rural Society, South Lindsey 1825-1875* [Oxford, 1976].)

3. *The Family, Sex and Marriage in England 1500-1800* (New York, 1977), 224, 226.

4. "The Great Debate: Ten Years Later, with a Modest Proposal for Reading Stages," quoted in D.P. Resnick and L.B. Resnick, "The Nature of Literacy: An Historical Exploration," *Harvard Educational Review 47* (1977), 383.

5. Stone, *Family, Sex and Marriage*, 21, 132. In this paper, as will be discussed later, "literacy" refers to functional literacy and not "ce grand silence à la interieur duquel l'individu s'aménage une sphère privée et libre." (F. Furet and J. Ozouf, "Trois Siècles de Métissage Cultural," *Annales, E.S.C.* XXXIII [1977], 494.

6. Stone, *Family, Sex and Marriage*, 268-269. A number of reviewers have commented unfavorably on Stone's description of plebeian family life. See E.P. Thompson, "Happy Families," *New Society*, (8 September, 1977), 499-501; K. Thomas, "The Changing Family," *Times Literary Supplement*, (21 October, 1977), 1226-1227; Alan Macfarlane, "Review Essay," *History and Theory* XVIII (1979), 103-126; Christopher Hill, "Sex, Marriage and the Family in England," *Economic History Review* 2nd ser., XXXI (1978), 450-463.

7. See, for example, R.J. Lesthaeghe, *The Decline of Belgian Fertility 1800-1970* (Princeton, 1977), esp. 189-194.

8. A good example is provided by H. Charbonneau in his book *Tourouvre-au-Perche* (Paris, 1970), 42-46.

9. R.S. Schofield, "Dimensions of Illiteracy, 1770-1850," *Explorations in Economic History* 2nd ser., 10 (1973), 437-454.

10. A number of articles have been written on this subject. The most comprehensive is L. Stone, "Literacy and Education in England, 1640-1900," *Past and Present* 42 (1969), 69-139. The most recent is D. Cressy, "Levels of Illiteracy in England, 1530-1730" *The Historical Journal* 20 (1977), 1-23.

11. "Minutes of Evidence, Framework Knitters, Leicestershire," *Parliamentary Papers*, 1845, XV, Q. 5575.

12. A fuller discussion of the intricacies of Shepshed's demographic history can be found in Chapter 5 of my book, *Family Formation in an Age of Nascent Capitalism* (New York, 1977). Shepshed's social and economic development is the subject of Chapter 2.

13. B. Simon (ed.), *Education in Leicestershire, 1540-1940* (Leicester, 1968), 39, 78.

14. Simon (ed.), *Education in Leicestershire*, 234. The figures for the number of pupils in the Roman Catholic school are based on the estimate of its schoolmaster, Luigi Gentili. (C. Leetham, *Luigi Gentili* [London, 1965], 136).

15. The questions of the reliability of Shepshed's registration and the representativeness of the family reconstitution study are discussed in the "Appendix" to *Family Formation*.

16. The life expectation and survival rates were derived from the mortality projections based on infant mortality rates, provided by Sully Ledermann, *Nouvelles Table-Types de Mortalité* (Paris, 1969), 132-137.

17. An earlier version of this paper, "Immiseration, Illiteracy and Family Life during the First Industrial Revolution," was presented at the History of Education Society's conference in Toronto (October 14, 1977) and the Social Science History Association's Seminar on Proto-industrialization in Ann Arbor (October 23, 1977).

18. The lack of this kind of micro-level evidence makes it impossible to test the association between hardship and "famine amenorrhea." However, recent work by both physiologists and demographers seems to suggest that, short of catastrophic circumstances like the concentration camps or psychologically-induced trauma such as *anorexia nervosa*, there is no apparent association between maternal nutrition and fecundity. I am indebted to Susan Watkins for bringing some of the recent literature on this subject to my attention. The most useful works I read were: Sandra L. Huffman, A.K.M. Alauddin Chowdhury, J. Chakraborty and W. Henry Mosley, "Nutrition and Post-Partum Amenorrhea in Rural Bangladesh," *Population Studies* XXXII (1978), 251-260; J. Trussel, "Menarche and Fatness," *Science*, 200 (30 June, 1978), 1506-1509; R. Frisch, "Menarche and Fatness," *Science* 200 (30 June, 1978), 1509-1513. A related article of great value on this subject of maternal health and fecundity is: Fredric David Abramson, "High Fetal Mortality and Birth Intervals," *Population Studies* XXVII (1973), 235-242.

19. E.A. Wrigley, "Family Limitation in Pre-Industrial England," *Economic History Review* 2nd ser., XIX (1966), 82-109.

20. "Pre-Industrial Economy and Population Structure," *Scandanavian Journal of History* 2 (1977), 183-210.

21. "European Marriage Patterns in Perspective," in *Population in History*, D.V. Glass and D.E.C. Eversley, eds. (London, 1965), 101-143.

22. Perhaps the most concise and wide-ranging summary of this approach is by Charles Tilly, "The Historical Study of Vital Processes." In *Historical Studies in Changing Fertility*, edited by C. Tilly, 3-55. (Princeton, 1978).

23. A fine statement of the assumptions behind the economic study of fertility is provided by Stanley Engerman, "Economic Perspectives on the Life Course," in *Transitions: The Family and the Life Course Perspective*, T. Hareven, ed. (New York, 1979).

24. This point is the subject of my re-interpretation of E.A. Wrigley's essay on Colyton's demographic history. (*Family Formation*, 103-115; see, also, 9-15).

25. The skimpiness of class- and/or occupation-specific measures of demographic rates is well borne out by the difficulty researchers using English parish registers have discovered in trying to disaggregate family reconstitituion studies. (For a longer discussion of the problem see, Levine, *Family Formation*, 146-152). V. Skipp's admirable study of the ecological crisis of the early 17th century in the Forest of Arden provides a practical demonstration of this problem: *Crisis and Development.* (Cambridge, 1977), esp. 25-28.

4.

'FOR BREAD WITH BUTTER': LIFE-WORLDS OF PEASANT-IMMIGRANTS FROM EAST CENTRAL EUROPE, 1880-1914

Ewa Morawska

The image of late 19th century East Central European rural societies as in the process of "transformation" and "significant change" has, by now, replaced the old stereotype of the "stagnant villages" in the American historiography of immigration. Ethnic and labor historians today stress the complexity of world views of peasant-immigrants as they became industrial workers in America. However, there have been few analyses of the cultural and psychological implications and the actual *meaning* of these transformations for the actors themselves.[1].

The aim of this paper is to breathe a little more life into the static image of peasant-immigrants by showing how, under the impact of changing structural conditions in East Central Europe and of mass migrations, their situations became more diversified, options more open, and orientations more complex and multifaceted than has been usually assumed. The focus or leitmotif of this paper is to show that the sociocultural system of East Central Europeans, when analysed in its own terms, simultaneously contained a basic survival orientation — the "negative want," *and* the image of and desire toward accomplishment as measured by the standards of the peasant-immigrant society — the "positive wish." In the ongoing interaction with the surrounding environment, the actions of peasants who left their villages and settled in American cities were motivated by both these elements.

The cumulative effects of the enfranchisement of the East Central European peasants: the rapid fragmentation of land and the proletarianization of increasing segments of the rural society, coupled with explosive demographic growth and prolonged agricultural depression during the 1880's and 1890's, set thousands of people in motion.[2] The rapid increments in economic density in the rural parts of the region in the last decades of the 19th century and the unprecedented demographic "boom" which could not be absorbed locally, were the primary contributing factors to the huge and unceasing migratory movements of the peasantry whose paths criss-crossed in all directions — within provinces of East Central Europe, between them inside the region, and then reaching far outside to western Europe and further away across the Atlantic.

The colossal dimensions of these migrations sweeping throughout East Central Europe were evidenced in reports from virtually all quarters of the region, indicating that at the beginning of our century no less than 30 to 35 per cent of the adult agrarian population of the vast territory covering Hungary proper, Slovakia, all of Poland, the western part of the Ukraine, Subcarpathian Rus', Transylvania, Croatia-Slavonia, northern Serbia and Slovenia, lived or worked in places different from that of their birth.[3] The combined external migrations, both seasonal and permanent, from all of the Polish territories during the second half of the last century until 1914, affected about 9 million people. In the same period, in the Hungarian Monarchy, an estimated total of about 6 million people migrated from their permanent residences, either in seasonal movements to Western Europe or journeying across the ocean. In only six years from 1906 to 1911, nearly

3 million people migrated from Austria in seasonal movements across the continent and most of these migrants were peasants. Excluding a few pockets of the most isolated areas, it was the exception rather than the rule for an East Central European peasant at the turn of the century to have spent all his life solely in agriculture in his native village.

Migrant peasant-workers were the most active "diffusive agents" in the gradual modernization of the traditional sociocultural system, spreading new trends in village life through the whole region. Just as the old economic system was undergoing slow transformation from feudalism to modernity, the traditional cultural patterns of peasant societies in East Central Europe were in a state of flux with disjointed elements in the process of rearrangement toward a new pattern.

In traditional feudal society peasants paid most of their obligations in kind and labor, hardly exposed to a money economy. "In the world of serfdom," noted a Hungarian memoirist, grandson of a serf, "there was, truth to tell, no real need for money."[5] After the emancipation, however, peasants "needed money for the redemption payments, to carry them over a poor harvest, to improve their farms and to buy or rent more land or cattle. They needed money, too, for less material reasons such as to pay for a wedding or a funeral, events for which family pride demanded the greatest possible expenditure."[6] And so money, a new kind of value in peasant life, grew in importance as the modern economy gradually penetrated rural communities. Agrarian banks, co-operatives, credit agencies and loan associations which mushroomed in East Central Europe were created to assist the emancipated peasants in purchasing land and paying up mortgages, further enmeshing them in the cash nexus.[7] However, the most spectacular impact of money on the peasant's household economy, and with it on his behavior and attitudes, came with seasonal migrations. In 1900, the Warsaw Statistical Committee reported that the seasonal migrants from Congress Poland to Germany returned, in that year only, with a total sum nearing 8,000,000 *rubles* ($4,000,000). In 1901, the sum brought into the country by seasonal workers returning from Germany increased to 9,000,000 *rubles* ($4,500,000), and by 1904 it was already 11,425,174 *rubles* ($5,712,587).[8] A study conducted in 1899 in a Galician village revealed that in that one year alone returning male and female seasonal workers brought home more than 28,000 *kronen* ($5,600), which exceeded the total income from this village's local farming by 20 per cent. In 1911 the amount of money that came to that same village from Continental migrations more than tripled reaching 90,000 *kronen* ($18,000).[9]

In traditional peasant society work had been perceived as the attribute of human existence. It was a value in and of itself, its moral quality bearing little or no relation to its practical functions. The peasant did not work to obtain good results, he worked because "čovek mora da radi" — man must work — this Serbian saying had its exact counterpart in each and every corner of East Central Europe. Under the feudal system the peasant-serfs did not care whether their compulsory work for the seignor was efficient or not. Religion only strengthened the peasant's attitude toward labor as the obligatory task: "Man has to work" — stated one of the commandments most often repeated from the pulpits in the village churches — "it is a curse, but also his duty; the process of working is meritorious, laziness is bad, independent of any results."[10] There was certain mystical fatalism in the traditional peasant's acceptance of work. With all its monotony and hardship, he viewed work as part of the universal cosmic order of which he was an element.

After serfdom had been abolished and the quasi-isolation of the villages ultimately broken down, with thousands of peasants moving in and out, migrating through half of the Continent in search of work and pay, this attitude toward work was partially altered. Once the peasant discovered that work could bring money, that it brought practical, quantifiable results, it gradually began to assume a new and different meaning, entering his thinking alongside the old traditional orientation with which it was to coexist for a long time to come.

The forces of demographic pressure and economic necessity which prompted the peasants' movement out of the villages brought a new and important element into peasant thinking and attitudes: the concept of gain and the motivation to calculate in order to maximize the magnitude of possessions. The labor market became the first area in which this new approach was solidified.

The prospects for seasonal earnings differed quite substantially depending where and what one was doing. The average pay of the hired agricultural laborer in East Central Europe was 40-50% lower than that received by unskilled industrial workers in the same region. Moreover, the average earnings of industrial workers in East Central Europe were only about half of those paid in the western parts of the Continent.[11] For instance, a male peasant laborer would bring home approximately $20-25 or even occasionally $30 for a season's work on the native farms of Poland, Slovakia or Hungary. However, after having spent the summer laboring in the fields of a German *Bauer*, he could save as much as $50-55. Industrial work in Austria and Germany was even more rewarding if one found a good place. It allowed for savings of about $70 or more for the season. By way of contrast, after a long season's labor in one of the major local industries in Ostrava, Dabrowa, Diösgÿoor, Warszawa, Budapest or Lódź, a man could save no more than $40. In smaller industries, savings were even less impressive, approximating $30.[12] From the experience of their own and others' previous migrations and from German and Austrian agents combing the villages, peasant migrants learned what kind of earnings they could expect in what place, and within the social migratory patterns followed in the local area acted according to their particular needs.

Given the scarcity of economic resources of the East Central European peasants, the poverty in which most of them lived, and a threat of further decline of family status with the shrinking portions of land, it was unavoidable that their fundamental and ultimate need was for survival and for a minimal level of security. Alongside and above this basic "negative want," however, the increased monetization of rural household economy and the opening of external opportunities for additional income, also created a limited margin of "positive" options.[13] One important change that occurred as the result of the structural transformations taking place in the region, and which directly affected the *Weltanschauungen* of East Central European peasants, was increased exposure to forces outside of the peasant world. A peasant from Babica, a small Galician village, described this change poignantly, referring to the train which since 1893 passed every day by his native village: "This passing train [. . .] reminds us of our poverty here and tells us that somewhere else life is better, that the world is different, big, better, but not ours."[14] More than ever before, the villagers began to perceive the world around them as expandable and some increment in goods as feasible. Whether he stayed on the land, worked on nearby manor, or decided to move further, the East Central European peasant at the turn of the century was confronted with the *presence of choice*. Within the narrow limits of economic opportunity accessible to rural migrants, and within restricting bounds of the still very traditional peasant culture, there now appeared some space open for purposeful action, selected and executed according to the family needs, goals and preferences.

It was just at the time of such 'mobilization' of the East Central European peasantry in the late decades of the 19th century that there appeared the "American option" — the opportunity to extend the paths of seasonal or permanent labor migrations across the Atlantic into American cities and factories. I want to argue that for a large number of East Central European peasant immigrants, leaving for America was not solely a "negative" flight from misery and a declining status, but also and simultaneously a "positive" thrust toward an envisioned accomplishment. To argue that peasant emigrants were driven to America by the motive of accomplishment does not negate the determining role played in their decisions by external social and economic forces. The distinction between two kinds of motives proposed by Alfred Schutz in his essay *The Problems of Social Reality*, seems particularly useful here. He distinguishes, on the one hand, the "in-order-to" motive referring to the future, pre-fantasized state of affairs or the goal to be brought about by the action that is undertaken. The "in-order-to" motive may be interpreted as the mental readiness of an individual, as the *expectation* of the actor who thinks as it were in the future perfect tense. On the other hand, there exists another type of motive which Schutz proposes calling "because" motives, referring to the background conditions surrounding the individual which have influenced his actions.[15] It is the former type of motive that has received less attention in recent American ethnic historiography focusing for the most part on the "because" conditions of East Central European emigration. Therefore, while fully acknowledging the presence and impact of the "because" determinants — the push factors which forced peasants out of their villages — I will concentrate here on the interpretation of the "in-order-to" motives that brought them to America.

Of all places that were available to East Central European peasants, places where they could and did go, it was America that had its Great Legend and offered the greatest promise. It was, as the popular song went, the "incredible land" where within two weeks people made as much money as a peasant would earn working on a farm for the whole season from May through October. At the turn of the century, an industrial laborer in Hungary — in Budapest, Szeged or Kecskemet — made approximately $3.50 a week. Of this, he spent on the average $2.00, which left him with monthly savings of about $6.00.[16] In America, as peasants at home learned through letters and from returning friends, a man could save at least 150% more — about $15-17 a month, and a young woman over $10. The economic calculation was obvious: in Austrian *kronen* it meant an unheard of purchasing power enabling one to afford a full hectare of land for a single year's savings or four cows in six months or a large new brick farm building in nine. "For these minds" — noted a contemporary observer, himself of peasant origin — "accustomed to the poor local wages [and living conditions], it was like a fantasy, like a dream pay!"[17]

The principal creators of the opinions about America were the *Amerikanci* themselves — those who sent letters home, often exaggerating their good fortunes in order to appear more successful and, in particular, those who returned. With the results seen about the village in the households of the returnees, the "demonstration effect" — the tendency of people to raise their aspirations when they come into contact, particularly among their peers, with a standard of living higher than that to which they were accustomed — a phenomenon familiar to social scientists investigating modern societies, began working most forcefully.[18] However humble and insignificant an immigrant had been in America — a miserable uncivilized "Hunky" — if he acquired some means, he appeared to people in his own village the incarnation of success. A contemporary diarist described this phenomenon in his native Galician village: "When . . . after a few years in America returned Walenty Podlasek [and] with the dollars he brought with him purchased a dozen or so hectares and started to build one house in Wierzchoslawice and one in Tarnow, the people went wild from envy and desire."[19] Indeed, the enormous amounts of money that had accrued to East Central European peasant households as the result of American migrations, made plainly visible as they were turned into land, cattle, brickhouses, barns, etc., only augmented the hopes of those who had not yet gone themselves and fortified their belief that America was the peasant Eldorado. Thus during six years from 1900 to 1906, the total amount of money orders sent from America to Russia and Austria-Hungary alone was as high as $69,041,227 (not including sums put into letters, and those carried by the returnees which averaged from $500 *per capita* in Transylvania, to $850 in Galicia).[20]

Given, then, the presence of other "minor" options through seasonal migrations within the European Continent, we may conjecture with Thomas and Znaniecki that a peasant's decision to leave for America came as a result of his choice rather than a direct economic necessity, and that for a large number of them it contained an "in-order-to" motive to alter more seriously their ordinary course of life.[21]

What was the "inner vision" or a pre-fantasized state of future affairs behind, to use once more the Schutzian concept, the "voluntative fiat" — the decision *Let's Go!* of peasant-emigrants, which was to "transform the inner fancying into performance or action gearing into the outer world?"[22] The "better life" — the positive accomplishment prospective migrants saw in their dreams, was not some vague and imprecise notion, but, on the contrary, a concrete and practical one, defined according to the criteria of well-being, prestige and social status prevailing in the peasant culture. These were measured in terms of the amount of land owned and added by purchase, the number of cows in the field, by the size and the quality of farm buildings and the dowries given to daughters, by weddings and parties thrown for the village public, by the dress displayed on Sundays in church, and, finally, by the amount of money actually or purportedly possessed. In planning a future action to which they attach particular importance but whose outcome is uncertain, people usually have in mind some sort of a minimum-maximum *desiderata*, a vision of the least state of accomplishment, and, should things turn out well, at the other end of the continuum of wishes — the most achievement, timidly hidden in the depths of their consciousness. I think the peasant-emigrants' goals could be interpreted in the same way. Thus, at the minimum end of the continuum we would have the "negative want": to accumulate sufficient resources to make their precarious position relatively secure and safe from decline — the attitude ever-present in peasant thinking. At the "positive" end of the continuum, there was a vision of a more substantial status elevation relative to their present position in the village and measured by the multiplication of acres, cattle, buildings and money spent on material possessions. In between these extremes, there would be a range of middle-accomplishment goals. With such contingent visions of future accomplishments — monies to be earned in America and consumed back in the village, the peasants set off across the Atlantic. It was a decision with a calculated risk.

Soon after coming to this country, thousands of immigrants saw America for what it actually was: a promise perhaps, but one to be redeemed at the price of terribly hard work, dismal living conditions, recurrent insecurity and deteriorating health — a price much steeper than what they imagined in Europe. "Ameryka dla byka, Europa dla chlopa," America for the oxen, Europe for the men — went a popular saying of immigrants, implying that only those with unusual stamina and strength could meet the challenge of work demands in America, while men of average physique should stay in Europe. Their experience in this country was fundamentally ambivalent and their perception of it correspondingly equivocal — a complex attitude balancing the gains and losses in a "trade-off" of sorts. In 1895, a Polish newspaper published a poem about America in which each stanza ended with the same refrain: "Avoid excessive praise/Do not criticize too much/ Wherever flowers grow/You will also find thorns."[23]

On the one hand, the industrial environment in which the immigrants found themselves petrified some elements of the traditional peasant culture; on the other it simultaneously fostered, if incompletely and partially, further solidification of the new patterns that by the end of the 19th century were beginning to surface in peasant attitudes and behavior in Europe. The precariousness of the immigrants' economic existence in America fortified a blend of attitudes which were apparently inconsistent but experienced simultaneously by the actors: an underlying, deep anxiety for tomorrow, inextricably meshed with an intensified effort to maximize the desired goals. The former manifested itself in the wish to survive, not to "go under," deeply embedded in the minds of the immigrants. This was a "negative want," not unlike that experienced by peasants in Europe who strove to retain their subsistence. The other simultaneously experienced attitude was manifested in actions which had as their "in-order-to" motive the accomplishment of what had been *most achievable* under the circumstances. Faced with adversities, the immigrants "retreated" into their fatalism which made them accept repeated failures as a natural part of existence while also making them keep stubbornly, patiently at what they had set out to accomplish. Having experienced success, they expanded their goals just a little, setting their hopes somewhat further within the limited range of the accessible. The peasants' deep-rooted materialism and practicality found in America a particularly fertile soil as the immigrants' strivings for better existence — to be achieved back home upon return or in this country — were centered around *things* possessed, enjoyed and displayed in public as symbols of social standing.[24]

Steady work, the acknowledged desire of East Central Europeans, has been interpreted by ethnic historians as the mere instrument of the immigrants' survival-security orientation, and their "content[ment] simply with steady income" as an expressison of the "modest thrust of [their] aspirations."[25] In the remainder of this paper I suggest a more complex interpretation of the actions of East Central European peasant immigrants. As much as they strove for security, for a large number of immigrants steady work of a family collective was at the same time perceived as equivalent to steady income and thus as the means to accumulate some surplus capital, thereby improving somewhat the economic and social condition of the individual and the family. The majority of East Central European immigrants who came to America at the turn of the century had originally been sojourners, i.e., they had no intention of remaining in this country for good. As the years passed, amidst prolonged uncertainty and indecision, the plans for a great many of them to return to the native village gradually evaporated. For analytical purposes and for greater clarity of argument I will distinguish two general types of "achievement reaction" displayed by the peasant-immigrants during the first decades of their stay in this country. In one pattern, the "achievement reaction" was generated by the image of accomplishment to be enjoyed back home in Europe, with emigration perceived as the path toward the alteration of status in the native village. It was naturally conceived of according to the peasant criteria of well-being, prestige and social respect. In this pattern, the immediate goal of the immigrants was to work hard and incessantly in order to save as much money as possible and send it or take it home. The parallel "achievement reaction" of the East Central European immigrants often displayed simultaneously with the former, and gradually taking precedence among those who extended their stay and remained in this country, was to strive for and to enjoy the accomplishments measured in terms of achievements available through steady employment of the whole family, and consumed in the social context of the immigrant community in America: the optimal possible combination of wages and working conditions, food, dress, home furnishings, prestige among fellow-immigrants inside the foreign colony.

The following discussion of immigrants' behavior is based for the most part on the data I collected in my study of the adaptation of East Central Europeans in Johnstown, a steeltown of about 60,000 in Western Pennsylvania, whose social and economic development as dominated by the powerful Cambria Iron (later Bethlehem) Company.

In order to accomplish their goals the immigrants actively applied a battery of all available resources. In a steeltown, work opportunities for men were of primary consideration. Within the narrow scope of job opportunities available to East Central Europeans in Johnstown, there still remained some "horizontal space" open to choice and purposeful action on the part of the immigrants, depending upon their family situation, needs and individual preferences. Work that to an observer unacquainted with the lowest, unskilled level of labor seemed undifferentiated and monotonously identical, appeared to those who performed it as offering some real options. Among the jobs available to immigrants in the city there were indeed "better" and "worse" ones, which they evaluated according to at least two kinds of considerations: the basic wage and wage increase prospects, and the character of the work itself.

There were multiple reasons for very frequent immigrant moves inside Cambria, and within and out of town during the years following their arrival in Johnstown.[26] Without doubt, many of these movements were involuntary, caused by fluctuations in the local industry. Even when business conditions were good, the steel industry prior to World War I in Western Pennsylvania worked on the average only 290 days a year.[27] Involuntary movements, however, forced by irregular production, constituted only one type of the immigrants' spatial mobility. At the beginning of the century Cambria reported close to one hundred per cent labor turnover, which covered a substantial proportion of voluntary resignations by men whose family situations or individual needs and preferences prompted them to search actively for different employment.[28]

In the immigrants' voluntary shifting from job to job, money was of utmost consideration because there was so little of it and because getting it was their primary goal, the very purpose of coming to America and working so hard. So, for instance, at the beginning of the century East Central Europeans in Johnstown knew very well that a day-laborer without skills and the command of English could get, in prosperous times, from as little as $1.20 to as much as $1.60 for a ten-hour work day, and more than that for a 12-hour shift.[29] Besides the immediate financial considerations, there were additional reasons behind the maneuvers of immigrant job-shifters. First, there were jobs that were more or less independent — a high-rated value in the peasant society. "My uncle," recalls Anthony C., "he preferred working in the mine [Cambria also owned coal mines around the city] because he thought it was more independent. He was his own boss. In the mills one had to do what others told you."[30] Others preferred the mills, a "cleaner and less dangerous job," and because public opinion in the foreign colony considered mining as "lowly and dirty work, all day in darkness, in water up to your ankles." In the mills different jobs had varying work-time and shift schedules, a consideration important for many a young man who played and dated.[31] Further, there were jobs in the mills where conditions were better, cleaner, with more fresh air, and thus appreciated by peasant-immigrants accustomed to working outside in the fields.[32] On the other hand, a consideration important to those who tried to minimize the risk of irregular employment, different departments had different rates of work fluctuations. In the rolling mills and steel works departments they were usually more intense than in blast furnace production, where the reaction to seasonal slumps was generally delayed. It often happened that before the slump had reached these departments, work picked up again.[33]

Let us now re-examine the financial strategies immigrants used in pursuing their goals. For single male immigrants or those whose wives and children had stayed behind in Europe, work in the Cambria mills or coal mines was the sole source of income. The monthly average expenditures of single East Central European men in Johnstown in the beginning of the century oscillated between $17 and $19 (including room and board — approximately $12; a drinking bill which usually amounted to $2-3; insurance in an immigrant society — 50 cents; church dues and donations, if paid dutifully when asked — about $2; recreation and/or clothing purchased in the local immigrant "variety stores" — $1-1.50). With the average monthly wages of the unskilled mill laborer ranging between $30 and $40, a single man who Sundays attended church, dated and dressed a little, could put away (unless he spent most of his money on drinking), a minimum of $10-16 a month, after we have subtracted the average wage loss due to seasonal unemployment (if there was no voluntary or automatic transfer), or sickness not covered by his insurance benefits. A number of immigrants, determined to maximize their gains at the price of existence in the most unpleasant conditions and having no recreation, or those who held better jobs, saved even more, up to $25-30 a month.[34] During the year 1907 (before the depression set in), the Johnstown immigrants sent home to Europe the staggering sum of $400,000.[35]

While they strongly resented the pace and character of industrial labor, and cursed its lack of security, those who came "in-order-to" save the maximum amount of money to be transferred home, perceived their work as the instrument for the realization of goals cherished in the old country. Like Szabo Janoś, the immigrant from Baranya county in Hungary, they

> Kept on working and thinking . . . Every ten minutes he had made a nickel. What could he buy with that? Lots. Every twenty minutes — a dime . . . Every three hours and twenty minutes a dollar, and that was a landmark . . . And if you have been a farmhand in Baranya county, a dollar is not merely a piece of money, it is also power, prestige, and command over the universe . . .[36]

In his inner eyes, Szabo Janoś saw himself returning to his native village in a city suit and flashing a "golden" watch, in a high celluloid collar and a ribbon-trimmed "gentleman's" hat, with suitcases of gifts, and a round sum of dollars to be converted to *forints* and subsequently invested in a few acres of land or a pair of good cows, maybe an addition to the old house. The village would obviously notice and evaluate his acquisitions, and the appropriate status would be assigned to him. In the very least, he would be an *Amerikanac*, a wordly traveler with endless and exaggerated stories to tell while treating neighbors to drinks in a nearby tavern.

As the time passed and the prospects of going back to Europe became rather remote, the "in-order-to" actions of the immigrant families turned increasingly toward the accomplishments of the best possible life in America. These accomplishments were now measured in terms of dress and food consumed at home in the foreign colony, the optimal possible combination of pay and work conditions, some stable savings in the bank that would sustain the hope of purchasing a home one day, prestige among fellow-immigrants, a future for children materially more comfortable, better than that which would have awaited them had they stayed in Europe. While the local economic opportunities and their own foreign colony increasingly served as frames of reference in defining and delimiting their individual and family goals, the life in Europe had nevertheless remained a living memory, somewhat blurred with time and more distant, yet uneradicable in the immigrants' experience.

Before World War I it was possible for an East Central European family in Johnstown to subsist on a monthly income of $29-35: $6 for rent (the minimum rent for a two-room apartment in dilapidated "tenement rows" owned by Cambria); $12-15 for food; $2.50-3.00 for gas and fuel; $2 for the man's drinking bill; $2-4 for the church; $1 for the parochial school (50 cents for the first two children each, all others free); $1 for insurance (husband and wife); $3 for clothing and recreation.[37]

If the husband's earnings from the mill or coal mine were the only source of income in the family, and if his actual monthly wages did not exceed the average of $36, no savings were possible and life was a constant aggravating struggle with the unending debts, unpaid credits and shortages. A typical steel town, Johnstown provided only very limited opportunities for female employment and those almost exclusively for unmarried women. Keeping boarders was therefore the dominant secondary source of income for East Central European families — the financial contribution of women as household members. More than half of all East Central European households that were recorded by the 1900 census in Johnstown kept boarders and lodgers.[38] The typical income accrued to an immigrant family prior to World War I by the wife who kept boarders — five was the average — oscillated around $20-25 a month, i.e., between two-thirds and three-fourths of the standard earnings brought home by the husband. To support the minimum survival level of subsistence, it would have been sufficient for the majority of boarder-keeping families with the lowest income brought by the husband to keep seven or eight lodgers during no more than six months of the year. The accrued sum of $150-200 would have sufficed to shelter the immigrant family against "normal" unemployment and accidental sickness or injury. For the rest of the year, the desperately overworked immigrant women could rest a little, and limit their services to the members of their own household. They did not take this option however, not only because of the deep-seated distrust in the fate to come, an attitude which was a solid underlying element of the peasant culture in Europe and which the immigrants' industrial experience by no means eradicated. They kept on with the boarders also because they were stubborn and driven by the desire to make the best possbile life for themselves and their families, better than in the old country, and better than minimum survival in the "rotten row" at the edge of the foreign colony, with no money left over for coping with unpaid credits from the local stores, no meat on the table, no decent dress for the Sunday mass, no means to make a donation like everybody else for the church building, or to send a holiday check to the village.

Contributions of children constituted a third source of supplementary income for the immigrant families. Eighty per cent of the Slavic children in Johnstown before World War I dropped out of school after the sixth grade. By their fifteenth birthday, nearly all male youth held regular jobs. The average monthly contributions of adolescent boys who usually followed their fathers into the mills or coal mines oscillated between $10 and $25. Young females, if they were not needed at home to work in the household and for boarders, employed themselves as servants and maids, as laborers in the cigar factory, or in neighborhood stores. Their monthly earnings averaged $4-17.[39] Two young offspring gainfully employed meant an additional gain between about $10 and over $40, which equaled from one-third to more than a full extra subsistence income required for the survival of an East Central European household in Johnstown before World War I.

An important fourth element of the immigrant families' budgets in Johnstown was the fruit of their plots and gardens and other domestic productions consumed by the household as well as sold outside in the neighborhood. The major burden of this subsistence farming, practiced by virtually all East Central European families in the city, fell on the shoulders of women. Besides, these *omnibuses* of the immigrant households also made bread, butter, cheese and noodles, canned food for the winter, pickled and marinated, sewed and wove in order to minimize the costs of existence. I estimated the average reduction in the amount of money spent by the immigrant family made possible by these female activities at about $5-6 a month. These savings made it possible for East European households in Johnstown to limit their food expenditures to a minimum of about $12-15 a month, and the spending on clothing to about $25-odd annually.[40]

The Immigration Commission investigating working and living conditions in Johnstown in 1907 reported the average total income from all sources combined accruing to East Central European families as significantly larger than that brought home by the breadwinner alone. All in all, it amounted to a sum of $573 annually — an amount certainly very modest, yet about $200 higher than the average yearly wage of East Central European millworkers at Cambria. This increment, however, was unequally distributed. Approximately one half (54%) of East Central European households surveyed declared a total amount of annual income of less than $500 — this group we may call the actual *survivors*, the households which had existed on just about what was needed in Johnstwown, or at best a little more, for an immigrant family to carry on without "safety-belt" savings. The remaining 46% enjoyed an existence a little bit more relaxed by the prevailing immigrant standards: 27% lived on the total fund of $500-700, 16% on $700-1,000 and 3% on $1,000-1,500.[41]

The material objects which, in the second pattern of "achievement reaction," East Central European families in income groups higher than the subsistence level came to posses and consume: food, dress, furniture, recreation — usually interpreted by ethnic historians in the context of basic "survival orientation" — were inherently perceived and evaluated by immigrants in the old country frame of reference, which functioned alongside the comparative framework of the surrounding foreign colony. A Slovenian noted in his diary what one finds over and again in most immigrant letters and memoirs reflecting this double perspective that qualified their American experience: "Although my standard of living . . . was at its lowest compared with the American standards, it was splendid compared with that in the old country."[42] An old Polish immigrant who spent his whole life in Johnstown's foreign community recalls: "We had very little, but there was more of this bread here than there, and something on this bread, too."[43] Accustomed to the subsistence diet consisting of a monotonous rotation of cabbage, bread and noodles, East Central European peasants-immigrants measured and experienced their accomplishments in America by the amount and quality of food on their tables. A sad "program minimum" of the underprivileged — the American Dream for the poor, but these were the categories in which East Central European peasants immigrants genuinely experienced improvement in their life situations. Like sojourners, the immigrants who settled permanenetly in this country still calculated their earnings in two modes — in dollars and in the old country currency, thus evaluating their accomplishments against the opportunities in the home village as well as against the earnings of others in the immigrant community. "For a 48-hour week, after a week I received $12, and right away translated it into kronen, it was 60 kronen a week" — an immigrant wrote in his diary.[44]

Among the criteria used by the East Central Europeans to measure their accomplishments in America, the "gentility" of the new style of life was of particular importance, a carry-over from the old country social relations. A common reference made by the immigrants as they compared and evaluated their life in America was that of the "nobleman": pan or baron. "Don't worry about me, 'cause I live here like a pan," wrote an immigrant to his family in Galicia. Another says: "In America . . . a pound of the fattest meat costs 3 and 4 cents, the leaner the more expensive, a pound of sausage 3 cents. I am a pan here."[45]

As the immigrants quickly learned, however, family status, elevated a little above the bare survival level by the collective effort of all household members, could be easily lost. For the immigrants, America was not only unevenhanded, it was also fickle, which made things at once better and worse: bad in winter, better during the spring and summer, and maybe worse in the fall. But unlike the village, here there was some hope that the situation would improve again. It was a deceitful feeling, a hope often frustrated, but nevertheless present. By 1915, about one fourth of the East Central European immigrants recorded in Johnstown by the 1900 census who persisted in town, already owned their homes. By World War I, however, a total of almost one-third of one-time homeowners had lost their property. In 1915, eighty per cent of East Central European male immigrants—persisters in Johnstown since 1900, were still recorded as unskilled laborers. Yet during those fifteen years nearly one-third of the whole East Central European male population who had persisted in the city since the beginning of the century were recorded as holding an occupational position higher than that of an unskilled laborer at least once. Once attained, however, such better occupational positions were very often subsequently lost, then possibly regained, lost and regained.[46]

Even if only temporarily successful, the immigrants' climb after more money and cleaner and lighter jobs proved that such a move was áccomplishable, that is was possible — a new feeling for East Central European peasants. By 1915, owning a home had remained a very remote dream for the majority. But by that time one among four immigrants-persisters in Johnstown since 1900 already possessed it, and a sytematic increase in the number of homeowners was visible to all in the foreign colony. While many of the home-purchasers subsequently lost their property, they often regained it with time, and others joined in every year. In their European existence the peasants-immigrants were only too familiar with failure and bad luck, and certainly America had not spared them. Yet food, dress, the standard of living, small savings — however insignificant from the urban native American perspective — were genuinely experienced by East Central European peasants-immigrants as accomplishments, as something new and worth the striving of the whole family. While the "fluctuating reality" in America was deeply frustrating, at the same time it bred and sustained hope and mobilized the immigrants' repeated efforts to maximize the assets conducive to the fullfillment of culturally preferred goals. Once they settled in this country for good, they quickly abandoned the unrealistic dreams harbored in Europe about the "Eldorado." Their lives here were hard and insecure and their attitudes about America ambivalent. However, as compared with the alternative they had known in Europe, they perceived this country as a *lesser evil*: "America is not perfect, true, but elsewhere these failings are even more numerous and pronounced" — concluded an editorial in the Polish language newspaper *Zgoda* in 1910.[47] In their letters home, the immigrants repeatedly expressed this balanced, ambivalent judgment: "Nowhere there is heaven, everywhere misery, in America no good, but still better than the [old] country" — wrote an immigrant from Chicago to his mother in Europe.[48] The same attitude echoed in the words of Kracha, a Slovak hero of Thomas Bell's *Out of This Furnace*: " Braddock is no paradise, I admit, but have you forgotten how we had to live in the old country . . . ?"[49]

Research for this study has been made possible by a grant from the American Council of Learned Societies, grant #RS-20183-0487 from the National Endowment for the Humanities, and Andrew Mellon Fellowship.

FOOTNOTES

This paper is derived from a larger study that has appeared as a book under the same title.
1. By pointing to the need for more, and more refined analysis of the cultural and psychological *meaning* for peasant immigrants of the socioeconomic changes in East Central Europe at the turn of the century and of the mass rural migrations, I do not wish to imply that my effort here is wholly original or that there have been no successful attempts heretofore. Obviously, this would be inaccurate. Almost seventy years ago W. Thomas and Florian Znaniecki in their monumental work *The Polish Peasant in Europe and America* provided an exemplary sophisticated analysis of the transformations of the traditional peasant sociocultural system as it opened up ever-wider to the outside world. Among the present day analyses, Victor Greene's provides subtle insights into the psychocultural world of East Central European peasants-immigrants: *The Slavic Community on Strike: Immigrant Labor in Pennsylvania Anthracite* (Notre Dame, 1968); *For God and Country: The Rise of Polish and Lithuanian Ethnic Consciousness* (Madison, 1975). Also, informed and perceptive studies by Timothy Smith and his "school" have probed into some of the implications of the structural transformations occurring in East Central Europe at the turn of the century on the rural life styles and peasant *Weltanschauungen*: Timothy Smith, "Religion and Ethnicity in America," *American Historical Review*, No. 5, (1967); and by the same author "Immigrant Social Aspirations and American Education, 1880-1930," *American Quarterly*, (1969); Joseph Barton, *Peasants and Strangers: Italians, Rumanians and Slovaks in an American City*,

1890-1950 (Cambridge, Mass., 1975); Mark Stolarik, "Immigrant Education and the Social Mobility of Slovaks, 1870-1930," in Randall M. Miller and Thomas D. Marzik [eds.], *Immigrants and Religion in Urban America* (Philadelphia, 1977); Paula Benkart, "Religion, Family and Community Among Hungarians Migrating to American Cities, 1880-1930," Ph.D. dissertation, (Johns Hopkins University, 1975).

Inasmuch as these studies point to the increased complexity and "equivocality" of the life situations and world views of East Central European peasants-immigrants, this paper follows in a similar general direction, elaborating on some major themes.

2. On structural changes occurring in the economy of East Central Europe in the late nineteenth century see: Istvan Berend and Gÿorgi Ranki, *Underdevelopment and Economic Growth: Studies in Hungarian Social and Economic History* (Budapest, 1979); *Polish Encyclopedia*, Economic Life of Poland, vol. III (Geneva, 1922); Doreen Warriner, *Contrasts in Emerging Societies: Readings in the Social and Economic History of South-Eastern Europe in the Nineteenth Century* (Bloomington, Ind., 1961); C.A. Macartney, *The Habsburg Empire, 1870-1918* (London, 1968); Jerome Blum, *The End of the Old Order in Rural Europe* (Princeton, NJ., 1978).

3. Compiled from: Elzbieta Kaczynska, *Spoleczenstwo i Gospodarka Polnocno-Wschodnich Ziem Krolestwa Polskiego w Okresie Rozkwitu Kapitalizmu* (Warszawa, 1974); Jon Aluas, "Industrialization and Migration of the Transylvanian Peasantry at the End of the Nineteenth and the Beginning of the Twentieth Century," *East European Quarterly* 4 (1975); Ladislav Tajtak, "Slovak Emigration and Migration in the Years 1910-1914," *Studia Historica Slovaca* X (1978); Julianna Puskaś, "Emigration from Hungary to the United States Before 1914," *Studia Historica Academiae Scientiarum Hungariae,* (1975); Vladimir Dedijer et al., *History of Yugoslavia* (New York, 1974); Ireneusz Inhatowicz, et al., *Spoleczenstwo Polskie od X do XX Wieku* (Warszawa, 1979); Berend and Ranki, *Hungary: A Century of Economic Development* (New York, 1974).

4. Compiled from: Ihnatowicz et al., *Spoleczenstwo Polskie, op. cit.;* Benjamin Murdzek, *Emigration in Polish Social-Political Thought, 1870-1914* (New York, 1979); Caroline Golab, *Immigrant Destinations* (Philadelphia, 1977); Zanna Kormanowa (ed.), *Historia Polski* (Warszawa, 1978), vol. II; Part 1; Celina Bobinska and Andrzej Pilch (eds.), *Employment-Seeking Emigrations of the Poles World-Wide XIX and XX C.* (Krakow, 1975); Toussaint Hoćevar, *The Structure of the Slovenian Economy, 1848-1963,* (New York, 1965); Berend and Ranki, *Hungary: A Century of Economic Development,* op. cit, Macartney, *The Habsburg Empire, 1870-1918,* op. cit.; Richard Pfaunder, "Die Grundlagen der nationalen Bevölkerung gesentwicklung Steiermarks," *Statistische Monatschrift,* 1907; Wilhelm Hecke, "Binenwanderung und Umgangssprache in den östereischen Alpenändern und Südländern," *Statisticche Montaschrift, 1913;* and„ by the same author "Binnenwanderung und Umgangssprache in den nördlichen Ländern Östereichs," *Statistiche Monatschirift,* 1914; *Magyar Statisztikai Kózle menyek,* Budapest, vol. 64, 557-592.

5. Gyula Illyés, *Puszták nepe,* (Budapest, 1936), 55-56.

6. Blum, *The End of the Old Order in Rural Europe,* op. cit., 433.

7. On peasant banks, loan and credit agencies and cooperatives: J. Buckinger, *Der Bauer in der Kultur und Wirtschaftsgeschichte Osterreichs* (Vienna, 1952); Berend and Ranki, *Underdevelopment and Economic Growth,* op. cit.; D. Mitrany, *The Land and the Peasant in Rumania* (London, 1930); Bogdan Stojsavijevic, *Povijest Sela: Hrvatska-Slavonija-Dalmacija, 1848-1918* (Zagreb, 1973); Ivan Bryk and Mykhailo Kotsiuba, *The Ukrainian (Ruthenian) Co-operative Movement in Galicia* (1913); Hoćevar, *The Structure of the Slovenian Economy,* op. cit.; *Polish Encyclopedia,* Economic Life of Poland, vol. III. op. cit.; A.B. Petersen, "The Development of Cooperative Credit in Rural Russia, 1871-1914," Ph.D. dissertation (Cornell University, 1973).

8. Murdzek, *Emigration in Polish-Social-Political Thought*, op. cit., 152-153; Puskaś, "From Hungary to the United States," op. cit., 79.

9. Franciszek Bujak, *Maszkienice, Wies Powiatu Brzeskiego: Stosunki Gospodarcze i Spoleczne* (Krakow, 1901), 49-50; and by the same author *Maszkienice . . . Rozwoj od Roku 1900 do Roku 1911* (Krakow, 1914), 105.

10. W. Thomas and Florian Znaniecki, *The Polish Peasant in Europe and America*, (New York, 1958), vol. I, 173.

11. Compiled from: Berend and Ranki, *Hungary: A Century of Economic Development*, op. cit., 82-84; Murdzek, *Emigration in Polish Social-Political Thought*, op. cit., 145; Bujak,*Maszkienice . . . Stosunki Gospodarcze i Spoleczne*, op. cit., 43-55; and by the same author: *Maskienice . . . Rozwoj od R. 1900 do R. 1911, op. cit.*, 65-68, 94-95, 102-105; Jozef Okolowicz, *Wychodztwo i Osadnictwo Polskie Przed I Wojna Swiatowa* (Warszawa, 1920), 114-131; Maria Misinska, "Podhale dawne i wspolczesne," *Muzeum Archeologiczne i Etnograficzne w Lodzi*, 15, Seriaff3, 33-40; Jan Sveton, "Slovenske Vystahovalectvo w Obdobi Uhorskeho Kapitalizmu," *Ekonomicky Casopis*, ff2 (1956): 190; Emily Balch, *Our Fellow Slavic Citizens* (New York, 1969), 56; Irena Lechowa, "Tradycje Migracyjne w Klonowej," *Prace i Materialy Muzeum Archeologicznego i Etnograficznego w Lodzi*, Seria No. 3, 51; Wladyslaw Rusinski, "The Role of the Peasantry of Poznan (Wielkopolska) in the Formation of the Non-Agricultural Labor Market," *East European Quarterly*, No. 4 (1975): 521; *Polish Encyclopedia*, vol. III, op. cit., 217, Danuta Dobrowolska, *Gornicy Salinavni Wieliczki w Latach 1880-1939* (Wvoclaw, 1965), 110; Emil Lengyel, *Americans from Hungary* (Philadelphia, 1948), 114; Wojciech Saryusz-Zaleski, *Dzieje Przemyslie w Galicji 1804-1929* (Krakow, 1930), 194; Zanna Kormanowa (ed.), *Historia Polski*, vol. III, Part 1, op. cit., 225, 564-566, 643; Jerzy Fierich, *Broniszow Wies Powiatu Ropczyckiego* (Warszawa, 1933), 187; Franciszek Gusciora, *Trzy Kurzyny Wsie Powiatu Nieskiego*, (Warszawa, 1929), 68.

12. Caluclations based on the information in Bujak, *Maszkienice, Wies Powiatu Brzeskiego*, op. cit., 45-50, and *Maszkienice . . . Rozwoj od R. 1900 do R. 1911*, op. cit., 102-105, indicating that seasonal workers saved approximately 60-70% of their earnings. Also *Polish Encyclopedia*, vol. III, op. cit., 217, 220, 345, 539-540; Julius Mesaroś, *Dejiny Slovenska II. Od Roku 1848 do Roku 1900* (Bratislava, 1968), 345; 431-32; Macartney, *The Habsburg Empire*, op. cit., 717; Okolowicz, *Wychodztwo i Osadniċtwo Polskie*, op. cit., 279-80; Misinska, "Podhale dawne i wspolczesne," op. cit., 40; Lechowa, "Tradycje Emigracyjne w Klonowej," op. cit., 51.

13. The term "negative want" comes from an excellent study by Sol Tax, *Penny Capitalism: A Guatemalan Indian Economy* (Chicago, 1963), 204-206.

14. Krystyna Duda-Dziewierz, *Wies Malopolska a Emigracja Amerykanska*, (Warszawa, 1938) 30; also Maria Gliwicowna, *Drogi Emigracji* (Warszawa, 1937), 514-515.

15. Alfred Schutz, *Collected Papers* (The Hague, 1962), vol. I, 69-71.

16. Macartney, *The Habsburg Empire*, op. cit., 717; Lengyel, *Americans from Hungary*, op. cit., 113-115. These calculations, however, are based on the expenditures of a city dweller rather than a seasonal peasant worker. Routinely, peasant seasonal laborers boarded in large groups in rooms for which they paid 20-30 *kronen* ($4-6) a month; individually, it amounted to a contribution of approximately $.50 or less. Their meals consisted of coffee, bread and sausage or bacon during the day, and potatoes or gruel in the evening (meat was eaten only on Sundays). Their food expenditures ranged about 1-2 *kronen* a day (20-25 cents). Calculated from Bujak, *Maszkienice . . . Rozwoj od R. 1900 do R. 1911*, op. cit., 96-97.

17. Wladyslaw Orkan, *Listy ze Wsi* (Warszawa, 1925), op. cit., vol. I., 120.

18. First formulated by James S. Duesenberry, *Income, Saving and the Theory of Consumer Behavior.* (Cambridge, Mass., 1949). The notion of 'demonstration effect' has since become a common reference in the vocabulary of social sciences.

19. Wincenty Witos, *Moje Wspomnienia* (Paris, 1964), vol. I, 188.

20. Compiled from: Balch, *Our Slavic Fellow Citizens,* op. cit. 140-183, 471-73; Frank Sheridan, "Italian, Slavic and Hungarian Unskilled Immigrant Laborers in the United States," *Bulletin of the Bureau of Labor,* September 1907, No. 72, 480; Puskas, *From Hungary to the United States,* op. cit., 77; G. Maior, *Political agrara la romani* (Bucharest, 1906); M. Misinska, "Podhale dawne i wspolczesne," op. cit., 52; Bujak, *Maszkienice . . . Rozwoj od R. 1900 do R. 1911,* op. cit., 103-104.

21. Thomas and Znaniecki, *The Polish Peasant in Europe and America,* op. cit., vol. II, The same observation is also stated in the US Congress Reports of the Immigration Commission, *Emigration Conditions in Europe,* 61st Congress, 3rd Session, Sen. Doc. 748, p. 53.

22. Schutz, *The Phenomenology of the Social World* (Chicago, 1967), 87-89; also his *Collected Papers,* op. cit., vol. 1, 70.

23. *Przeglad Wszechpolski,* vol. I/IV, No. 6, February 15, 1895, 90.

24. In his otherwise very able essay "Immigration and Modernization: The Case of Slavic Peasants in Industrial America" (*Journal of Social History,* Fall 1976, 44-72), John Bodnar, having found in the East European foreign-language press at the beginning of the century repeated condemnations of the "Dollar God" and the material "excess and wantoness" prevailing in America, infers from it a "consistent anti-materialism [permeating] the Slavic-American culture." The peasant cultural tradition, transplanted to this country, contained — like many plebeian cultures in general — a strong materialistic current (see, for instance, the discussion of this and related topics in Thomas and Znaniecki, *The Polish Peasant in Europe and America,* Introduction, 156-205). The moralistic appeals of the Slavic-American press were in fact a confirmation of this tendency: there is no need to preach the ideal unless it is not being practiced. The Slavic-language newspapers in America at the beginning of the century very frequently lamented "bumptious materialism" among peasant-immigrants in the foreign colonies.

25. John Bodnar, Roger Simon and Michael Weber, *Lives of Their Own: Blacks, Italians and Poles in Pittsburgh, 1900-1960* (Urbana, Ill., 1982), 42, 102, 134, 143. Also Bodnar, "Immigration and Modernization . . . ," op. cit., 53-55; Caroline Golab, "The Impact of the Industrial Experience on the Immigrant Family: The Huddled Masses Reconsidered," in Richard L. Ehrlich (ed.), *Immigrants in Industrial America, 1850-1920* (Charlottesville, 1977), 8; Tamara K. Hareven and Randolph Langenbach, *Amoskeag. Life and Work in an American Factory City* (New York, 1978), 26-28.

26. With Cambria (Bethlehem) employment records destroyed, it was not possible to reconstruct the movements of East Central European workers inside the company. I calculated, however, persistence rates in the city of 2,399 male immigrants recorded in Johnstown by the 1900 census, checking their names in the city directories at five-year time intervals. Corrected for mortality, they appeared as follows: 1900/05—.57; 1900/10—.39; 1900/20—.31. (U.S. Census, Manuscript Population Schedule, 1900 — Johnstown, Pennsylvania — East Central European population subsequently traced in city directories; tabulations).

27. Compiled from: Commonwealth of Pennsylvania. Bureau of the Industrial Statistics. *Annual Report of the Secretary of Internal Affairs: 1904,* Part III, vol., XXXII, 82-92, and 1905, Part III, vol. XXXIII, 87-96; Commonwealth of Pennsylvania, *Second Annual Report of the*

Commissioner of Labor and Industry, 1914, Part I, Cambria County, 100-101; *Third Annual Report of the Commissioner of Labor and Industry*, 1915, Part I, 472-73; Commonwealth of Pennsylvania, Department of Labor and Industry, *Office of Information and Statistics*, 1914, 19; US Congress, Report on the Conditions of Employment in the Iron and Steel Industry in the United States, vol. III: *Working Conditions and the Relations of Employers and Employees*. 62nd Congress, 1st Session, Sen Doc. No. 110, 212-14.

28. *Johnstown Tribune*, 2/13/1907, 14; 2/18/1910, 12; 3/1/1910, 6.
   Surely, there was among the immigrants a good number who stuck to their jobs whatever they were, and did not move for years, determined to 'play it safe.' However, evidence from various sources: labor turnover data that indicate increased voluntary mobility in times of industrial prosperity, immigrant diaries and letters, written and taped biographies, foreign-language newspapers, does not support a generalization that for *"most immigrants [E.M.] once a job was secured, it was not easily abandoned,"* and that their goal was "simply to get a job, any job" to which they subsequently clung regardless of its nature (Bodnar, Simon and Weber, *Lives of Their Own*, op. cit., 42,134,143; same in Bodnar, "Immigration and Modernization . . . ," op. cit., 53.).
   The tabulations of my Johnstown data indicate that the more recent arrivals — most likely sojourners, and motivated predominantly by the first type of "achievement reaction," moved out of Johnstown in much greater proportions than the more settled immigrants burdened with families. However, the latter were also moving. Between 1900 and 1905, over 50 per cent of all East Central European males recorded as boarders by the 1900 census moved out of town, as compared with 25 per cent of the heads of the immigrant households.

29. Compiled from the data collected by the Immigration Commission investigating the employment and working conditions in Johnstown in 1907: US Congress, Reports of the Immigration Commission, *Immigrants in Industries*, Part 2, Iron and Steel Manufacturing, vol. I, "Community A," 61st Congress, 2nd Session, Sen. Doc. 633, 360-63, 441-46; also from David Brody, *Steelworkers in America. The NonUnion Era* (New York, 1960), 44, 107; John Fitch, "Wage-Earners of Pittsburgh," *Charities and the Commons*, March 6, 1909, 1061-63.

30. Interview No. 9, with Anthony C., (October 10, 1980).

31. Interview No. 8, with Frank S., (May 6, 1981).

32. "Laborer in a car or repair shop, or in the mechanical department, this was better jobs than blast furnace or open hearth where you suffocated from the heat" (Interview No. 9, with Anthony C., October 10, 1980; No. 4, with Nikola B., July 14, 1981).

33. US Congress, Report on the Conditions of Employment in the Iron and Steel Industry in the United States, vol. III, *Working Conditions and the Relations of Employers and Employees*, 210-14; Commonwealth of Pennsylvania *Annual Report of the Secretary of Internal Affairs*. Part III: Industrial Statistics, vol. XXXII, 1904, 82-92; vol. XXXIII, 1905, 87-96; vol. XL, 1912, 99-112, 329; *Second Annual Report of the Commissioner of Labor and Industry of the Commonwealth of Pennsylvania*, 1914, Part 1, 100-101.

34. The calculation compiled from: *Reports of the Immigration Commission*, "Community A," op. cit., 408, 468; Peter Roberts, "The New Pittsburghers," *Charity and the Commons*, January 2, 1909, 547; Isaac Hourwich, *Immigration and Labor*, (New York, 1922), 259, 269-271; Margaret Byington, *Homestead: The Households of a Mill Town* (Pittsburgh, 1975), 45, 68, 206-7. In particular, the average drink bill I calculated from *Slovenska Narodna Podporna Jednota*, Lodge No. 82 in Johnstown, Minute Book, vol. I, 1908-14, "pivo i wiski" (ekspens, dochotky); church dues — from St. Casimir's Polish Roman Catholic church, Minute Book, 1905-12; St. John the Baptist Ukrainian Catholic church, Minute Book (n/d); St. Rochus Croatian Catholic church, Minute Book, 1900-05; insurance — from the minute books of the immigrant societies: Slovak *Jednota*, Lodge No. 23 in Johnstown, 1890-1910, and the

Polish Roman Catholic Union, Lodge No. 503, 1900-12; food prices I calculated from *Johnstown Tribune* 4/10/1905, 1;5/2/1914,15.

The average annual loss of pay due to sickness and unemployment (assuming a worker was in fact idle and did not find substitute occupation), was calculated by the Congressional Commission at 13% (*Report on the Conditions of Employment in the Iron and Steel Industry in the United States*, Part III, op. cit., 214). But the immigrants who belonged to insurance societies were partially (50-60%) covered for sickness — for instance, for 30 days of sickness the Slovak immigrants-members of the *Jednota* received about $20 (Slovak *Jednota* Lodge No. 23 in Johnstown, Minute Book, 1907-08).

35. *Reports of the Immigration Commission*, "Community A," op. cit., 463, 478. The figure covers all foreign-born residents of Johnstown, i.e., including West European immigrants (in 1910 they numbered a total of about 5,000, as opposed to approximately 9,000 South and East Central Europeans).

36. Emil Lengyel, *Americans from Hungary*, op. cit., 143.

37. Calculated from Reports of the Immigration Commission, "Community A" op. cit., 405-407; Balch, *Our Fellow Slavic Citizens*, op. cit., 363-366; Byington, *Homestead. The Households of a Mill Town*, op. cit., 38-45, 50-57, 76-80; 138-143, 206-207 Interviews No. 36, with Henryk S., (March 12, 1981); No. 37a, with John O., (March 11, 1981), No. 41, with Paul M., (February 25, 1981), No. 62-62a, with Mrs. and Mr. Thomas B., (June 11, 1980); No. 75, with Frank G., (October 2, 1980), No. 25 with Mary K., (June 14, 1981).

38. Johnstown sample data.

39. St. Stephen's Slovak Catholic School — enrollment and attendance records, 1902-12. *Reports of the Immigration Commission*, "Community A," op. cit., 443-46; Harve-Mack Coal Company (Indiana, Pennsylvania) — payroll records (UMWA Health and Retirement Funds, Richland, Pennsylvania), 1905-14; Interviews No. 6 (UPJ), with Charles B., No. 47 (UPJ), with Gus M., No. 71a, with Mrs. Pete H., (December 18, 1980); No. 89, with Pauline H., (June 11, 1980) No. 25, with Mary K., (June 14, 1981). I wish to thank here Dr. Bruce Williams and Michael Yates from the University of Pittsburgh at Johnstown for letting me use their collection of taped interviews with the East Central European coalminers (noted here as *UPJ*).

40. Calculated by comparing the expenditures on food as listed in Slavic family budgets compiled by Byington in Homestead, (*Homestead*, op. cit., 45, 76-78, 139) with items listed by my Johnstown informants as grown or made at home.

41. *Reports of the Immigration Commission*, "Community A," op. cit., 369. As reported by the Commission, the distribution of income earned by the East Central European laborers from the mills was the following: 59% — less than $400, 28% — $400-600; and 13% — over $600 (ibid., 367).

42. Ivan Molek, "First Work with the Steam Boilers." in Mary Molek (ed.), *Slovene Immigrant History, 1900-1950* (Dover, Delaware, 1979), 28.

43. Interview No. 10, with Anthony C., (February 23, 1981).

44. Marian M. Drozdowski (ed.), *Pamietniki Emigrantow. Stany Zjednoczone* (Warszawa, 1977), vol. II, 259.

45. Witold Kula, Nina Assorodobraj-Kula and Marcin Kula (eds.), *Listy Emigrantow z Brazylii i Stanow Zjednoczonych* (Warszawa, 1973), 86-87, 90-91. Also Lengyel, *Americans from Hungary*, op. cit., 137.

46. Johnstown sample data.

47. *Zgoda* (Chicago), June 30, 1910.

48. Kula et al. (eds.), *Listy Emigrantow z Brazylii i Stanow Zjednoczonych*, op. cit., 254.

49. Thomas Bell, *Out of This Furnace* (Pittsburgh, 1976), 59.

5.

"WILL THE REAL BILL BANKS PLEASE STAND UP?" TOWARDS A ROLE ANALYSIS OF MID-VICTORIAN WORKING-CLASS RESPECTABILITY

Peter Bailey

Respectability is again respectable. Long employed as a convenient and unfocused shorthand for all that was taken to be typical of social correctness among the Victorian middle and lower middle class, the term has recently been invested with a new consequence and complexity. Historians now identify respectability as a highly specific value system of considerable normative power, whose most important consequence was to incorporate a minor but significant sector of the working class into the social consensus that assured mid-Victorian society in particular its overall cohesion and stability, and it is in the precise manner and degree of this incorporation that they discern a complexity unassociated with the previous simple portmanteau sense of the term. Published work on this phenomenon has already significantly expanded our understanding of cultural differentiation within the working class and raised important questions about the mechanisms of social control and cultural hegemony, but this paper will argue that present studies still underestimate the dynamic properties in working-class respectability and have yet properly to relate its operation to the human geography of the modern city and the behavior patterns of the modern city dweller. The case made here is largely speculative, but *prima facie* it suggests some further modification of the respectability thesis and offers a fresh perspective for new research.[1]

Let us first look more closely at the recent reassessments of respectability. Geoffrey Best, in his impressive text on the mid-Victorian period, claims that respectability exerted "a socially soothing tendency, by assimilating the most widely separated groups (separated socially or geographically) to a common cult." "Here," he maintains, "was the sharpest of all lines of social division, between those who were and those who were not respectable; a sharper line by far than that between rich and poor, employer and employee, or capitalist and proletarian."[2] This is brisk and conclusive in tone, and indeed Best claims to find nothing new or complicated about it, but in his discussion of respectability he does give some weight to its variations and ambiguities, particularly in working-class life, and it is these features of its operation rather than its unequivocal conformities that have impressed other students of the period. Whatever its net effect as a social emollient, it is plain from other work that respectability could be subtly, even abruptly differentiated in terms of class. Brian Harrison in his study of Victorian temperance interests shows how these coalesced into a pan-class movement which captured many working men for respectability, but argues that the movement's proletarian converts were far from deferential rubberstamps for its predominantly middle-class values —

rather they generated their own independent convictions that gave them confidence to criticise the existing social order on other issues.[3] The same phenomenon is more fully discovered in Trygve Tholfsen's suggestive examination of working-class radicalism in the period, which identifies a cadre of workingmen who subscribed to the new consensual ideology of "mid-Victorianism" with its seductively orchestrated rhetoric of progress and self-culture, yet at the same time sustained an independent radical critique of capital and its values.[4]

More particularised local studies of the labour aristocracy (the stratum long held to be most susceptible to some form of embourgeoisement) demonstrate how artisan elites evolved sub-cultures of respectability as class-specific responses to the social reality of their own world and the coercive structure of mid-Victorian capitalism.[5] Thus working people reformulated the official values of respectability and preserved a distinct and irreducible class identity in its practise. Clearly the integration of the skilled worker was a far from even or finite process, and the social peace of the period is increasingly represented as the product of continual negotiation between capital and labour in a muted, yet highly charged, sub-dialectic operating across the long and convoluted cultural frontier between the classes. Working-class respectability was, in a sense, a sublimation of the overt class hostility of the Chartist era, but it carried within it the tensions of unresolved social conflict.[6] The new studies are coloured by a variety of historiographical and ideological persuasions — liberal empirical or neo-Whig, idealist-functional, New Left Gramscian — but together they present us with a suggestive picture of the respectable working man (both individually and collectively) as a complex and autonomous social actor; however considerable the imprint of burgeois values, clearly not all working men so touched were its passive recipients.

So far this is convincing enough but it may well be that respectability was still more polyvalent than any or all of these interpretations allow; for notwithstanding their authors' sensitivity to the particular texture of working-class life, the respectable working man that they present us with is often too stolidly predictable and earnestly cerebral a social type to be readily believable. In the first instance, working-class respectability, whether primarily emulative or indigenous, is implicitly represented as a cultural absolute: once a respectable, always a respectable (with the corollary holding true for the non-respectables or roughs). Secondly, the working-class respectable is invariably cast as a ideologue; his respectability is primarily an intellectual consruct, a systematic body of values and beliefs thought through beyond the level of common sense or a merely ad hoc response to a particular social exigency. Thus have historians tended to reinforce the stereotype of a basic and exclusive duality in working-class culture while simultaneously fastening the working-class respectable into a characterologial strait-jacket. Such emphases seem to stem in large part from a situation of some piquancy, namely, that in response to their evidence, today's historians can still be governed by the most pristine of Victorian reflexes; for in this case, they appear to have unwittingly adopted 19th-century presumptions of behavioural consistency that ignore the changes wrought in patterns of personal conduct and social interaction by the new circumstances of modern city life. In consequence, they have scarcely taken into account the likelihood that respectability was practised in a more limited and situational sense than that of a lived ideal or permanent code of values, and thus have passed over the potentially fruitful proposition that respectability was assumed as a role (or cluster of roles) as much as it was espoused as an ideology.

I

There can, of course, be no doubt that respectability was a clearly recognised and much exalted contemporary ideal. Indeed it was considered a principal prerequisite for true citizenship. "To be respectable," declared the *Cornhill Magazine*, "is . . . to come up to that most real, though very indefinite standard of goodness, the attainment of which is exacted of everyone as a condition of being allowed to associate upon terms of ostensible equality with the rest of the human race."[7] Respectability primarily enjoined moral rectitude, but in addition, it also demanded economic continence and self-sufficiency. Though its possession was a badge of conformity, its attainment was a matter of independent individual achievement through an ongoing process of self-discipline and self-improvement. Essentially, a distillation of evangelical disciplines, it represented a secular version of election — minus the uncertainties — and in so far as it demanded an appropriate faith and conduct, it both incorporated an ideology and defined a life-style.

By the tests of respectability observers identified two discrete and exclusive constituencies in working-class life. Thus respectables and non-respectables clearly were distinguished in the reform strategy of Henry Solly — the middle-class founder of the working men's club movement — who appealed to "the more prudent, worthier members of the working class" to seek refuge in the clubs, away from "their reckless, drinking, cowardly, or dishonest neighbours."[8] This characterization of the dichotomy in more abrupt and emotively judgmental terms than those of respectable and non-respectable was common: other commentators also discriminated between respectables and 'roughs', 'thinkers and drinkers', or 'virtuous and vicious.' To the Victorian bourgeois there was no confusion as to the elect and non-elect in working-class life.

What evidence lent support to this formulation? For contemporaries there were several indicators of the firm establishment of respectability in working-class life. There were the heartening if anonymous statistics recording the accumulative deposits of small investors in the Post Office Savings Bank. On the evidence of the good behaviour on shilling days at the Great Exhibition, lower-class public manners had much improved — an impression reinforced locally by the view from the platform when middle-class visitors attended temperance soirées or other set pieces of rational recreation and charitable schemes of improvement. The behaviour of the Lancashire operatives during the cotton famine provided striking proof of a new self-control and moral forbearance among workers, and the industrial north in general seemed to

Victorian commentators to offer further convincing evidence of working-class progress on the approved model. The concentration of such improvement among an artisan elite was central to the reform case in the formulating of the Reform bill of 1867.[9] Certainly the establishment of such bridgeheads of respectability among the working classes was thrown into relief by the great wash of the non-respectable poor whose number and contumacy were both impressively offensive. In Belton, a correspondent wrote to the local paper complaining of "crowds of men and boys" loafing on the street corners, "for the most part all in their deshabille . . . applying the expression 'bloody' to almost every person and thing that came their way." The offence was compounded when working people made their mass break-out from the urban ghetto and thrust themselves in upon the privacy of their betters: after four weeks in Southend, the journalist Ewing Ritchie reported, "I began to tremble at the sight of an excursionist." Good manners were no defence against the boorishness of the non-elect, as seen in a Charles Keen cartoon of the period which records an exchange between a genteel tourist and a "powerful navvy" from whom he politely asks the way: "Can you kindly direct me to Slagley?" Powerfuly navvy: "Ah can poonch the head of thee." The tourist, we are told, retired hastily.[10]

Though less categorical in their classifications, modern historians have confirmed to their own satisfaction the dualist character of working-class culture. The roughs have had no difficulty in registering their presence, appearing in various guises from the simply pathetic to the alarmingly violent,[11] but it is the respectables who have received more precise attention. The line of economic differentiation between the aristocracy of labour and the rest have been represented as more or less coterminous with the social divide between respectables and non-respectables, and historians have achieved a sharper focus on the former where they have reconstructed something of the experience of distinct communities or sub-cultures of working-class respectability.[12] We can also know the more specific human face of respectability through modern biographical studies and the rescue from obscurity of personal working-class testimonies.[13] Here, where conduct and belief cohere in the continuum of an individual life-history, is convincing evidence of respectability as a monolinear and perennial commitment of a broadly ideological or ethical nature. Yet the evidence now taken to support the idea of stable and exclusive constituency of working-class respectables is often little different in kind from that which confirmed the formulations of Victorian observers, for it is still for the most part anonymous and disembodied, episodic and elliptical. The reconstructed world of working-class respectability, though now more sophisticatedly assembled and interpreted, is still an artificial composite, put together from limited instances of respectable behaviour and its rhetoric, rather than from a sustained collective biography of its constituents. In the present state of knowledge this is a necessary and legitimate technique for the historian, but what is inferred from such a construct is more dubious; for it suggests a continuity in casting where there may only have been a continuity in performance. This inference echoes that of contemporary commentators, and we may more readily appreciate the probability of a present day misreading of the evidence if we examine the presuppositions that governed the Victorians' conception of social reality and their ordering of experience in everyday life. A simple ecological model of the urban process, derived from the writings of the Chicago School, defines the context.

II

In the 19th-century, the expansion of the urban population and the development of a society ordered by the priorities of industrial growth fragmented social interaction, and the coherent and readily comprehensive pattern of social life shared within the small-scale traditional community was increasingly exchanged for a pattern of life notable for its discontinuities of experience in terms of time, space, and personnel. In the city, segregation and the introduction of new work routine compartmentalised social classes and the basic activities of work, leisure, and home life to such a degree that man the social actor was obliged to play out his encounters in an ever greater number of discrete situational settings.[14] According to Gerth and Mills, in the more intimate social milieu of the pre-industrial village or small town, "the various situations in which men play roles are not so widely different from one another and are transparent to all . . .The variety of roles which any given person plays is not very wide, and each is translatable into the others."[15] In such a world, men's conduct and intentions answer to an homogeneous "vocabulary of motives." In an industrial city, however, conduct is segmentalised and justified according to various and more private vocabularies of motive; the diversification of social context allows for a greater variability in personal behaviour as role activites become insulated from the continuous observation of actual and potential role others.[16]

Insulation was most pronounced in inter-class relationships; here physical discontinuities were compounded by the bourgeois concern to maintain social distance. But although there was frequent acknowledgment among middle-class commentators of how little they were acquainted with working men and their world — it was, in a much used phrase, 'terra incognita' — they had a rudimentary interpretative scheme of the territory, peopled with stereotypes that represented imaginary projections of the role-specific behaviour met with in the intermittent social exchanges of real life. Only rarely were they confronted with evidence which revealed their mistake in presuming upon a consistency in role progression that followed from the expectations of conventional behaviour in their own lives. The Birmingham manufacturer, William Sargant, realised as much when he discovered, by accident, that one of his steadiest and, as he had thought, most temperate workmen was a heavy drinker.

> Most of us (recorded Sargant) know very little about what goes on among workmen in the evening. We see them in their places during the day, we find them always ready to labour when they are called upon, and we set them down as men of temperate habits; inferring from their regularity that they are not guilty of excesses in their leisure hours. It is sometimes startling to find that we are entirely mistaken.[17]

Sargant's surprise suggests how little cognisant of role discontinuities his contemporaries could be.

That the co-existence of seemingly contradictory modes of behaviour within a single life-style was not an aberration can be evidenced from other sources, particularly those relating to leisure-time activities, which provided a striking new area of free choice for all classes by the mid-Victorian period — "a sort of neutral ground which we may fairly call our own," as one observer noted.[18] The leisure choice of one contemporary working man is recorded in "Bill Banks's Day Out", a suggestive piece of documentary fiction by Thomas Wright, the 'Journeyman Engineer,' published in 1868.[19] Bill is a London railwayman who goes 'St. Mondaying' with his wife and friends in Hampton Court. They meet outside a local pub, admire each other in their best dress, and start the excursion with a morning pint. They travel out to Hampton Court by hired van, complete with cornet player to enliven the journey. On arrival they tuck into a dinner provided by the van-owner at 2s/6d a head — "a first-rater; beef and mutton and ham, and any quantity of rolls, and lots of fruit-tarts, in the way of eating, and bottled ale and small cask of porter to wash 'em down." The harmony of the occasion is disturbed when Bill, somewhat flushed with drink, takes exception to the superior airs of a young shopman in the company; after a scuffle, peace is restored and the party continues, finishing up in late evening back in town, at the Alhambra, the famous Leicester Square music hall. Bill and his wife together with two friends share the cost of a cab home, enjoying the prospect of scandalising the neighbours by arriving in such style.

Retailed in the first person, the piece has an internal consistency which suggests how a working man at play could move through several different roles, all cohering into a single life-world, but each in turn likely to be interpreted by an outsider as the behaviour peculiar to a distinct, separate, and exclusive type within the working classes. On the evidence of his home life Banks would pass as the self-improving artisan: he is a considerable and intelligent reader who borrows books from the local Institute to supplement his own small library. In taking an excursion Bill appears at first to be a further credit to his class. His expenditure can be reckoned at between ten and fifteen shillings for him and his wife, yet the day out is not the reflex action of a poor family gobbling up a sudden windfall, but the happy product of careful budgeting which, so we gather, owes something to Mrs. Banks' good management. Hampton Court, an historic house on which Bill is well read, represents a 'rational' choice for a visit, and in their concern with their appearance the party displays that "pardonable vanity" that reformers recommended as a tonic both for trade and self-respect.[20] Thereafter, however, Bill Banks' respectable image disintegrates, as he regresses into the time-honoured role of the English workman on a spree. To a middle-class observer he then would appear drunk, gluttonous, and unruly. Detected among the music hall crowd he would serve as an example of the feckless new breed of workingman who surrendered himself to the temptations of the 'fast' life. Thus might random snapshorts of working men at play confirm the bourgeois categorisation of working-class life, whereas the synoptic documentary of Wright's account suggests a congruency that questions its reliability.

The easy association of rationality and traditional play patterns — respectability and non-respectability — represented above appears in institutional form in the case of the friendly societies — which retained much of the older style of conviviality while mostly commending themselves to middle-class observers as improving agencies in working-class life. At the national meeting of the Friendly Society of Ironfounders held in Bolton in 1866, the chairman opened proceedings by declaring that they were met for two principal objects: "enjoyment and pleasure, and to show the country that the ironfounders were not behind other bodies of workpeople in this age of improvement." Improvement here was measured on a different scale from that used by politicians and reformers — it came by the bellyful. Accordingly, the ironfounders demolished a mountain of food and indulged an impressive thirst. To cater to the delegates "the whole length of the west side of the pavilion had been appropriated to a refreshment department, in which were to be seen a multitudinous array of glasses, jugs and beer barrels." Afterwards the ironfounders and members of local allied trades disported themselves till daybreak. The local press made but few disapproving noises on reporting such occasions: "After all their drawbacks," concluded the *Bolton Chronicle* in a review of the Lancashire societies in the late seventies, "they . . . provide an education in the duties of citizenship through the practice of self-government."[21] The consolidation of friendly societies into regional or national organizations of increasing financial probity encouraged observers in the belief that orthodox values of improvement were well on their way to superseding the obsolescent survivals of an older and intemperate way of life, the hangovers from a semi-barbarous folk culture which would soon be extinguished.

Yet working-class culture in its adaptation to an urban industrial setting was more additive than substitutive. What outsiders chose to see as anomalies were its normalities: to members of the friendly societies and other major insittutions in common life the concurrent pursuit of 'thinking and drinking', 'virtue and vice' represented not so much a conflict of value systems as a reconciliation. Thus did the working men's clubs of the '80s combine sociability with instruction, though their unabashed informality (the constant traffic, the cries of the pie-boy and the pot-boy, the smoking and bantering) — produced a bad press among visiting middle-class lecturers. For Frederick Rogers, an unbendingly respectable working-class autodidact, disenchantment came in the middle of his Sunday morning talk on Shakespeare, when the club chairman called a break to let the man come round with the beer.[22] The trappings of respectability were on occasions readily assumed in working-class life, but they did not mean the displacement of older conformities. Climbing into the sober garb of the Sunday suit, for example, was no prophylactic against the customary resort to the pub, and best clothes could be openly surrendered to the pawnbroker on Monday morning without loss of face.[23]

Where the working-class neighbourhoods of big cities later took on the closed and parochial character of "urban villlages", the possession of Sunday best clearly became an important ongoing test of status and identity,[24] but respectability could also function in a more limited and situational sense as a tactic for dealing with the external world beyond one's most immediate class and community reference group. It could, for example, be assumed as a defensive device. Mouthing a few passwords about respectability might secure immunity from the 'badgering' of middle-class charity workers or district visitors.[25] In the sensitive matter of dress, the accessories of respectability might offer some protection against arbitary arrest or conviction for implication in one of the 'nuisances' which provoked recurrent purges of street life by the police — in cases of prosecution of the players and spectators of the street games in Bolton, police witnesses thought it material to inform the courts whether or not the defendants were apprehended with or without a jacket or collar on.[26]

Acknowledging respectability as a choice of role rather than a universal normative mode can make us more alert to its instrumental or calculative deployment in working-class relationships with outsiders. Signing the pledge or otherwise subscribing to tests of membership for middle-class sponsored associations for improvement would have passed as professions of or aspirations to respectability, yet may well have represented only a limited attachment to its norms. Lay workers in Bolton noted that occasional booms in Sunday School attendance could be attributed to the announcement of some treat or excursion and were never sustained beyond that point, and there were other reports in the same vein.[27] Among the early football teams formed by working men in the '70s and '80s a good number were connected with religious bodies, yet the short-lived nature of these connexions and the ease with which they were severed suggests that, in the practical and eclectic fashion of their culture, working men used such institutions as a convenient and socially neutral locus for realising their own initiatives, taking calculated advantage of the various amenities at their mentors' disposal.[28] Thus, by meeting the role demands of their class superiors, working people could extract practical benefits often unobtainable from the resources of their own culture.

In arguing for a calculative function in working-class respectability the assumption is that working people were capable of playing *at* roles as much as role playing.[29] The recovery of intention is a difficult exercise but the application of Goffman's concept of role distance gives us some leverage on the problem.[30] Goffman points out how, in the interests of social expediency, the social actor can perform a role with sufficient conviction to meet the expectations of the role-other, while injecting some expression into the performance which conveys his psychic resistance to any fundamental attachment to the obligations of that role. The signs of detachment are often miniscule, and displayed in any number of possible deviations from the conventional grammar of social encounter. Goffman finds considerable evidence of this in relationships between social actors in situations governed by a clearly ascribed authority structure:

> At such times, we often find that although the subordinate is careful not to threaten those who are, in a sense, in charge of the situation, he may be just as careful to inject some expression to show, for any who care to see, that he is not capitulating completely to the (work) arrangement in which he finds himself. Sullenness, muttering, irony, joking, and sarcasm may allow one to show that something of oneself lies outside the constraints of the moment and outside the role within whose jurisdiction the moment occurs.[31]

Can anything like these innuendos of disaffection be detected in the interplay of the classes in mid-Victorian England? Perhaps. G.M. Young offered sound advice to the apprentice historian by stressing the need to read, read, and read in the sources of the period until one could almost hear the characters talk. What we must be careful to do here, is to adjust our hearing to catch the tone of speech as much as its content. One of Canon Barnett's eager young settlement workers recorded the welcome he received from East End working men: "We are," said one of the latter, "always pleased to see a gentleman."[32] How gratifying to be so readily awarded the title and status of gentleman! How likely that the term was delivered with the slightest inflexion of mock respect? Expressions of disassociation are there, says Goffman, "for any who care to see," to which we might add, for any who are *capable* of seeing, or otherwise comprehending. What was recorded as quaint or curious in working-class life may well have had more significant social undertones than middle-class observers could perceive. Workers in the Black Country, reported one witness in the 1860s, had so little social intercourse with their betters that they were almost totally ignorant of the correct forms of address; thus when confronted with a bishop or senior officer of the church they addressed him as 'Madam'.[33] An example of backward manners or a jest inwardly savoured by an outwardly respectful working-class audience? Certainly the middle-class reader of this extract was unlikely to know that the misidentification of a bishop as a lady in an advanced state of pregnancy was a staple of the comic routines on the music halls.

If, at this point, it be objected that the sources will not bear the strain of such a reading, it can at least be countered that certain forms of source material advanced as evidence of respectable or compliant behaviour among the working classes have been awarded too much significance and most likely have also been misinterpreted. We have recently been warned in convincing manner how inadequate and misleading was the representation of contemporary city life in Victorian magazine illustration; a combination of artistic convention and technical constraints served to distance the polite reader from social reality and protect him from exposure to anything startling or threatening.[34] Similar caveats ought to be attached to the general run of magazine and newspaper reporting in the period. Reporters relied on the stock phrases of a narrowly stylised vocabulary, pairing noun and modifier in standard fashion, in the interests of balance rather than accuracy. When local worthies or philanthropists addressed gatherings of working men, the clichés of Victorian journalism assured them of 'hearty thanks' and 'vociferous applause' though the actual response may have been a good deal less encouraging.[35] Social reformers who promoted institutions or occasions for rational recreation several times found working-class behaviour less than auspicious and the sanctions of respectability imperilled. One reformer commented on the difficulty of maintaining a happy medium between "weak tea and a rollicking free and easy" and the bourgeois promoter of the Manchester Lyceums, Benjamin Heywood, wrote to his son bemoaning the collapse of propriety in these 'improving' institutions:

The character of the thing is changed. I am glad you were there, however, for old time's sake, but it is somewhat humiliating that the sober speakers should be the stopgaps between the acts.[36]

When Emma Cons opened an extension of Tom Hughes' Cat and Comfort coffee house in Drury Lane for working girls, the latter "marked their appreciation of efforts made for their comfort by smashing the lights, breaking the windows, and tearing the inside out of the piano."[37] Incidents like the above may have been exceptional, but they do suggest the persistence of a considerable social tension in reportedly fraternal exercises in respectability. The official reports of the Working Men's Club and Institute Union (initially officered by the middle-class) repeatedly emphasised the well-mannered behaviour of club audiences at lectures and the respect accorded visiting middle-class speakers, which suggests a need for reassurance that all was truly what it seemed.[38] The unease of a bourgeois patron in the presence of working men can be attributed to several factors, but one of them may well have been apprehension at the tenuous hold of the normative sanctions of respectability, particularly in the new open-ended social territory of modern leisure. To reverse another cliché, a good time was not had by all.

Middle-class discomfiture on these occasions was compounded by a more general fear for the security of their status in an operationally protean social order. "The social sorrow of our times," observed the Rev. J. Baldwin Brown, in charting the "social revolution" of the mid-century, is that men do not know their places . . .

no man knows surely either his neighbour's, or his own. There is no sort of fixity in any of the institutions of society, no sort of continence in any of its orders. No order keeps to itself; they all interlock and interpenetrate. All things are in constant flux; and above all things the habits, pursuits, callings and social status of men. We do not know where to find men, and large classes do not know where to find themselves. There are no broad platforms on which men stand together with those of the same rank and calling . . .Now every man, every class tries to make a law for itself. There is a complete break-up and mixture of social orders."[39]

On close investigation, mid-Victorian England appears remarkable not only for its volatile social order but for the plasticity of its human geography. Thus there were as yet no adequate physical *cordons sanitaires* to protect the assumptions and apparatus of class superiority. Residential segregation provided some protection for the middle class, but the suburbs did not yet offer services and job opportunities sufficient to relieve the necessity of business and social commuting to the city, where social hauteurs could be badly bruised in the heavy human traffic of the streets (carriage trade alone excepted). Letters to the Bolton press frequently complained at the inadequate policing of the town's thoroughfares and the prevalence of 'nuisances' — bad language (as noted above), the road-running nuisance, the snowballing nuisance, etc. On vacation, as we have seen above, the middle-class family could not be certain of territorial security, for the excursion train made all classes mobile, and custom and price differentials had not yet confirmed the class rating of specific resorts.[40] Where strong economic sanctions obtained, as at work, in the market place or — more commonly significant for the conditioning of social responses

— in relationships with domestic servants in the home, interclass contacts conformed more closely to class protocol (though even here the master class was apprehensive of the subversive alter ego that lay behind the face of conformity).[41] Elsewhere in the social landscape encounters were much less personal, formalised, or predictable, and took place along a shifting and discontinuous situational frontier peopled by anonymous strangers.

To be abroad in this territory was not not often physically dangerous, but it constituted something of a normative void whose uncertainties threatened the fundamental structure of social control, and it was a signal virtue of the respectable/non-respectable formulation that it imposed some conceptual order and stability on the bewildering and elliptical experience of city life.[42] By its criteria a man could assess the likely extent to which other members of a volatile and congested public milieu shared common expectations in face to face encounters. A good deal of the business of an urban industrial society could no longer wait on any meticulous examination of individual credentials, and the pattern of social encounter had in any case changed to the extent where the empirical confirmation of another's character was mostly beyond the reach of personal witness, but the inventory of respectable behaviour and appearance provided a mental checklist by which to read both status and intention, thereby expediting social transaction and reducing vulnerability to rebuff, exploitation, or worse. Contemporaries were far from unaware that men might take advantage of the discontinuities of big city life to default upon their respectability. In the 1850s Ewing Ritchie inveighed against the suburban businessmen who drank heavily in Town but passed as models of virtue in their home neighbourhoods, and Samuel Smiles' commandment "Be what you seem" was a warning against the inherent duplicities of modern living.[43] But despite such misgivings the middle classes proceeded on the conviction that respectability was a social imperative whose internalised values commanded the conformity of an individual's actions beyond the public knowledge of his reference group. Encouraged by this model, the middle class felt able to extrapolate from the various instances of respectable behaviour in working-class life and presume upon a constituency of working-class respectables whose putative presence sustantially extended the safety zone of social contact in their cognitive map of the city.

III

The opacity of working-class life and the need to believe obscured the deficiencies of such a thesis. There were undoubtedly working men and their families for whom respectability was a stable and regular way of life, but in this period they were most likely rarer birds than contemporaries or today's historians have allowed. Many men registered as respectables in the mental dossiers of middle-class observers were known as such on the evidence of a single role-performance, a performance perhaps regularly repeated, but in many cases, isolated and anonymous or both. Much of this behaviour answered to the established constraints and expectations of inter-class encounter, but

formed part of an independent working-class culture with its own patterns of
behavioural consistency and homogeneity, a culture with a tangential rather
than an emulative relationship to that of the middle class. To the middle-class
mind, role enactments of respectability were like so many beads which they
restrung along axes of their own wishful construction; that the beads led in
other directions or conformed to different patterns was something that the
middle-class outsider could not easily have known. Mostly, one suspects, he did
not want to know, for the concept of a regiment of working-class respectables
recruited from the unlikely denizens of the 'terra incognita' of Victorian
England was a necessary prop to the self-esteem of his own class, proof of the
middle-class capacity to remake society in their own image, and a preservative
too of the flattering fiction of an open society in which working men could
advance to "ostensible equality" with their betters. The myth of substantial
working-class respectability served, moreover, as a source of reassurance in a
period whose conventional appellation as an age of equipoise obscures the
extent to which the bourgeoisie were still mindful of the social and political
combustibility of the urban masses.[44] Identifying the respectable working man
was more of a prescriptive than a descriptive exercise.

This need to believe reduced bourgeois sensitivity to calculative or
instrumental adoptions of respectability by working people. Given this
predisposition on the part of the role-other and the episodic or otherwise
limited nature of most class exchanges, respectability was an undemanding role
to play for working men wko possessed the basic equipment in dress, speech,
and demeanour which conformed to its standardized public image. In his social
classification of The Nether World, George Gissing offered that the broad
distinction lay between two great sections of working men — "those who do,
and those who do not, wear collars."[45] However circumstantial, there is
evidence that respectability was assumed or discarded as easily as the collar
which was its symbolic accessory.

Before concluding, I must revert briefly to the defensive. The case made here
depends upon the interlocking and retrospective application of behavioural
models generated by 20th-century American society, a unique culture, it may
be argued, whose more loosely-textured social structure and higher rate and
range of social and geographical mobility has produced more abrupt
discontinuities and normative confusion than can wisely be allowed for mid-
Victorian England. Perhaps then my argument only makes sense as a personal
attempt to resolve the cultural schizophrenia that afflicts an expatriate Britisher
teaching Victorian studies in Canada. Yet the transposition is admissible on
more than ad hominem grounds. Clearly the work of the Chicago School of the
1920s and '30s is of that city and that era,[46] but the ideal type that it presented
was influenced by the evidence of late 19th-century London — the locus
classicus of Victorian behaviour — and its scheme of distinct patterns of urban
segregation has recently been revalidated, not only for late- for for mid-
Victorian England.[47] Historians have left the sociological concept of role largely
unused,[48] and its application does not seem to have recommended itself to
literary scholars. No Victorian formulated a role theory of behaviour, but the

characteristic anxieties of contemporary literary consciousness do reveal an increasing sensitivity to the opacity of modern city life. By the '80s, novelists like Gissing plainly recognised that they could no longer assume the continuity between private consciousness and public reality that had typified an earlier society, and Stevenson's Jekyll and Hyde can be seen as a striking metaphor for the divided self in a new urban world, a moral fable that was quoted from a thousand pulpits.[49] Recently disclosed case histories of double lives are also significant, for their revelations provide more than a simple addition to our gallery of Other Victorians; they are the rattle of skeletons in a closet that may yet be found to contain innumerable other examples from an extensive seam of more or less "moral" deviancy (Robert Park's coinage) that stretched through the life of the period, and was practised by all sorts and conditions of men and women. After all, Arthur Munby's inamorata, the maid of all work, Hannah Cullwick, proved just as capable of a double consciousness as her bohemian and eccentric master.[50]

But the test of this hypothesis on working-class respectability, particularly where it is represented as a manipulative mode, must depend upon its correlation with a broader range of concrete historical evidence. Given the nature of the case made here this will be no easy matter, but I hope enough has been said to encourage a greater sensitivity to the situational contexts of behaviour, particularly in inter-class relationships. What exactly were the short-run social and geographical mobilities of city living and how did they determine role progression? What were the sites and occasions of class encounter, whether by design or accident, in the individual trajectories of daily life? What was the vocabulary of class encounter, and when and how did it chime with the semi-official rhetoric of respectability? What were the cues in its non-verbal exchanges, in the paralanguage of tone, and the silent language of gesture and appearance? We may find clues in music hall parody, in the graphic satire of popular periodicals, or in the behaviour of the marginal or economically unincorporated worker — the "sort of working-class Bohemian" who Raphael Samuel discovered among the free spirits of Headington Quarry.[51] Certainly for the later period new questions could be asked in oral history interviews, for it is from studies of the individual that we may best discern the pattern of movement in and out of respectability and thus illuminate the broad territory that lies between its two idealised poles.

It can be admitted that however disjunctive or calculative the practice of respectability among the working class, taken in toto it denotes a measure of compliance with bourgeois norms that largely justifies its interpretation as a "socially-soothing tendency." But the recent analyses of respectability still underestimate the ambiguity of its operation in working-class life, and the extent to which it cloaked a form of deviancy or new style of counter-theatre.[52] Where its practice served to extract material and social benefits from class superiors it functioned as a kind of exploitation in reverse; where its returns offered more psychic satsifactions, it served as a kind of private saturnalia in a society that had all but extinguished carnival. Despite the tightening constraints of social organisation that mark the development of modern industrial society its expansion provides a diversity of situational contexts whose lack of correspondence enables the individual to manipulate the social order in such a way as to preserve what Burns identifies as "a kind of second-order self-realisation and autonomy."[53] The preservation of a satisfying inner life in a self-contained working-class culture may have had more to do with the maintenance of social stability in mid-Victorian England than the blandishments of embourgeoisement or a collective modification of its norms. In the manner of their resistance to middle-class tutelage the working class may thus appear both less than doggedly heroic and more than boorishly bloody-minded — in truth, perhaps rather a shifty lot — but this interpretation may be more consistent with the changing patterns of consciousness and behaviour in a modern society than those we have yet been offered.

FOOTNOTES

1. An earlier draft of this paper was read to the Canadian Historical Association of Edmonton, June 1975. For various forms of encouragement I have to thank my colleague John Finlay, Leonore Davidoff of the University of Essex, E.P. Pickering and my social history seminar for 1976-77, my wife Bonnie, and the small research grant fund of the University of Manitoba.

2. G. Best, *Mid-Victorian Britain, 1851-1875* (London, 1971), 256-263.

3. B.Harrison, *Drink and the Victorians: The Temperance Question in England, 1815-1872* (London, 1971), 24-25, 195, 366-367, 394-395. See also, T.W. Laqueur, *Religion and Respectability: Sunday Schools and Working-Class Culture, 1780-1850* (New Haven, 1976).

4. T.R. Tholfsen, *Working-Class Radicalism in Mid-Victorian England* (London, 1976), 17-18, 216-221. See also his article, "The Intellectual Origins of Mid-Victorian Stability," *Political Science Quarterly* 86 (1971), 57-91. Tholfsen defines respectability in a limited and almost pathological sense as the narrowly emulative sub-bourgeois mentality that followed from an uncritical subordination to middle-class values, but his radical workingman epitomises the contrary element in working class social consciousness that is commonly admitted within the term in other reinterpretative scholarhip. His usage echoes that of Engels, for whom respectability connoted submission and pusillanimity. It was, wrote the latter, "the most repulsive thing" and "bred into the bones of the workers." Engels to Sorge, 7 December, 1889, in *Marx-Engels on Britain* (Moscow, 1953), 522-523.

5. G. Crossick, "The Labour Aristocracy and its Values: A Study of Mid-Victorian Kentish London," *Victorian Studies* 19 (March, 1976): 301-328 and "An Artisan Elite," *New Society*, 23/30 (December, 1976); C. Reid, "Middle-Class Values and Working-Class Culture in Nineteenth Century Sheffield: The Pursuit of Respectability," in S. Pollard and C. Holmes, eds., *Essays in the Economic and Social History of South Yorkshire* (Sheffield, 1976), 275-295. For a somewhat later period, see R.Q. Gray, "Styles of Life, the 'Labour Aristrocracy' and Class Relations in Later Nineteenth Century Edinburgh," *International Review of Social History* 18 (1973), 428-452. See also his "The Labour Aristocracy in the Victorian Class Structure," in F. Parkin, ed., *The Social Analysis of Class Structure* (London, 1974), 19-38 and *The Labour Aristocracy in Victorian Edinburgh* (Oxford, 1976), ch. 7. For a valuable discussion of the historiography of the concept of a labour aristocracy see H.F. Moorhouse, "The Marxist Theory of the Labour Aristocracy," *Social History* 3 (January, 1978), 61-82.

6. Tholfsen's characterisation of the mid-Victorian city as "a stable culture in a state of inner tension" is apt; see his *Working-Class Radicalism*, 11. For such tension at its most explosive, see R. Price, "The Other Face of Respectability," *Past and Present*, No. 66 (February, 1975), 110-132.

7. (Fitzjames Stephen), "Anti-Respectability," *Cornhill Magazine* 8 (September, 1863), 282-293. G.M. Young, *Portrait of an Age* (Oxford, 1936) 25, catches the right tone: "Respectability was at once a select status and a universal motive. Like Roman citizenship, it could be indefinitely extended, and every extension fortified the state."

8. From an address to the T.U.C. in 1871, recorded in *Occasional Papers of the Working Men's Club and Institute Union*, No. 20 (January, 1872).

9. Such were the staple observations of the 'then and now' genre in social commentary, e.g. J.M. Ludlow and L. Jones, *Progress of the Working Class, 1832-1867* (London, 1867), and J. Kay-Shuttleworth, "The Laws of Social Progress, as Illustrated in the History of the Manual Labour Class in England," in *Thoughts and Suggestions on Certain Social Problems* (London, 1873), 3-39. See also, G. Stedman Jones, *Outcast London: A Study in the Relationship Between Classes in Victorian Society* (Oxford, 1971), 8-11; R. Harrison, *Before the Socialists: Studies in Labour and Politics, 1861-1881* (London, 1965), 33.

10. Bolton Chronicle, 18 March, 1871. See also evidence from Liverpool in "Street Ruffianism," *Porcupine*, 11 November, 1865. J.E. Ritchie, *Days and Nights in London* (London, 1880), 49-50. C. Keene, *Our People* (London, 1881), 155.

11. Most historians of mid-Victorian England have their favorite horror stories of the roughs on the rampage, e.g., Best, *op cit*, 203; G. Kitson Clark, *The Making of Victorian England* (London, 1962), 62.

12. See above, n.5, though note also that Reid, *op cit*, 278 does adumbrate a more flexible typology by identifying a significant middle ground between respectables and non-respectables. For other relevant studies see L.L. Shiman, "The Band of Hope Movement: Respectable Recreation for Working-Class Children," *Victorian Studies* 18 (September, 1973), 49-74, and "The Birstall Temperance Society," *Yorkshire Archaeological Journal* 46 (1974), 128-139. See also, R.J. Morris, "The History of Self-Help," *New Society*, 3 December, 1979, on the Woodhouse temperance community in Leeds, and R. Moore, *Pit Men, Preachers and Politics: The Effects of Methodism in a Durham Mining Community* (Cambridge, 1974), 140-155. Among the late Victorian and Edwardian working class social and cultural distinctions weakened somewhat, and the line between respectables and non-respectables conformed less exactly to the craft and income differentials between the skilled artisans and the rest. See Gray, *Labour Aristocracy*, 120, and cf. S. Meacham, *A Life Apart: The English Working Class, 1890-1914* (London, 1977), 26-29.

13. E.G., F.M. Leventhal, *Respectable Radical: George Howell and Victorian Working-Class Politics* (Cambridge, Mass., 1971); B. Harrison and P. Hollis, "Chartism, Liberalism and the Life of Robert Lowery," *English Historical Review* 82 (July, 1967), 503-535.

14. Robert Park, "The City: Suggestions for the Investigation of Human Behaviour in the Urban Environment," and Louis Wirth, "Urbanism as a Way of Life," reprinted in Richard Sennett, ed., *Classic Essays on the Culture of Cities* (New York, 1969), 91-130, 143-164. For the urbanisation of consciousness as part of the more general process of modernisation, see P.L. Berger, B. Berger, and H. Kellner, *The Homeless Mind: Modernisation and Consciousness* (Harmondsworth, 1974), 62-77.

15. H. Gerth and C. Wright Mills, *Character and Social Structure* (New York, 1964), 120. In general I have adopted the concept of role employed by these authors: "technically, the concept 'role' refers to (1) units of conduct which by their recurrence stand out as regularities and (2) which are oriented in the conduct of other actors." *Ibid.*, 10-11. See also, M. Banton, *Roles: An Introduction to the Study of Social Relations* (London, 1965).

16. On observability, see the important article by R.K. Merton, "The Role-Set: Problems in Sociological Theory," *British Journal of Sociology* 8 (1957), 112-20. See also, Gerth and Mills, *op cit*, 122-124; R. Frankenberg, *Communities in Britain: Social Life in Town and Country* (Harmondsworth, 1966), 240-242.

17. W.L. Sargant, *Economy of the Labouring Classes* (London, 1857), 353.

18. W.C. Lake in J.E. Kempe, ed., *The Use and Abuse of the World* (London, 1873-1875), I, 39-56. On the new saliency of leisure, see Peter Bailey, *Leisure and Class in Victorian England: Rational Recreation and the Contest for Control, 1830-1885* (London, 1978). On the greater independence of leisure roles, see Banton, *op cit*, 33-34 and A. Southall, "An Operational Theory of Role," *Human Relations* 7 (February, 1959), 17-34.

19. Thomas Wright in A. Halliday, ed., *The Savage Club Papers* (London, 1868), 214-230.

20. The phrase was used by an early champion of rational recreation, R.A. Slaney, MP, in evidence to the Select Committee of the House of Commons on Public Walks, *Parliamentary Papers*, 1833, XV, 9, and the theme found common expression among reformers, e.g. S.W. Jevons, "Methods of Social Reform: Amusements of the People," *Contemporary Review* 33 (1878), 499-513.

21. *Bolton Chronicle*, 14 July, 1866, 26 May, 1877. See also P.H.J.H. Gosden, *The Friendly Societies in England, 1815-1875* (Manchester, 1961).

22. See the comments of Shaw and William Morris on lecturing engagements at clubs, quoted in J. Taylor, *From Self-Help to Glamour: The Working Man's Club, 1860-1972* (Oxford, 1972), 59, and F. Rogers, *Labour Life and Literature: Some Movements of Sixty Years* (London, 1913), 96-97.

23. Jones, "Working-Class Culture and Working-Class Politics in London, 1870-1900; Notes on the Remaking of a Working Class," *Journal of Social History* 7 (1974), 476-476.

24. R. Roberts, *The Classic Slum: Salford Life in the First Quarter of the Century* (Harmondsworth, 1973), 22-24.

25. Jones, "Working-Class Culture," 471-472.

26. Bailey, *op cit*, 83-84.

27. Report of a Wesleyan Sunday School Convention, *Bolton Chronicle*, 8 April, 1876.

28. Members of the Christ Church football club in Bolton deserted their patron, Rev. J.F. Wright, four years after he had formed the club; they walked out of a meeting in the church school rooms, crossed the road to the Gladstone Hotel and reconstituted themselves the Bolton Wanderers. P.M. Young, *Bolton Wanderers* (London, 1961), 19. Gray, "Styles of Life," 449-450, finds evidence of a calculative relationship with the churches.

29. This capability would seem to be part of the general expressive repertoire of modern urban man, though a case has been made that the dramaturgical resources of today's working class are severely limited by early socialization patterns, see J. Ford *et al*, "Functional Autonomy, Role Distance and Social Class," *British Journal of Sociology* 18 (December, 1967), 370-381.

30. E. Goffman, "Role Distance," in *Encounters: Two Studies in the Sociology of Interaction* (Harmondsworth, 1972), 75-134.

31. *Ibid.*, 101.

32. So well have I taken Young's advice to heart that this phrase has been resonating in my skull

for years; unfortunately the vibrations have shaken it loose from the anchorage of an exact reference. May I offer, with apologies, that it is recorded somewhere in J.M. Knapp, ed., *The Universities and the Social Problem* (London, 1895).

33. "Our Working People and How They Live," *Good Words* 2 (1870), 246-255.

34. M. Wolff and C. Fox, "Pictures from the Magazines," in H.J. Dyos and M. Wolff, eds., *The Victorian City*, 2 vols. (London, 1973), II, 559-582.

35. See the illustrations 7 & 9 in Best, *op cit*, following 142.

36. J. Keningale Cook, "The Labourer's Leisure," *Dublin University Magazine* 90 (1877), 174-192; T. Heywood, *A Memoir of Sir Benjamin Heywood* (Manchester, 1863), 201.

37. L. Bayliss, *The Old Vic* (London, 1926), 267-268.

38. *Club and Institute Journal*, July 1875 - Feb. 1878.

39. J.B. Brown, *First Principles of Ecclesiastical Truth* (London, 1871), 278.

40. See also, J.K. Walton, "Residential Amenity, Respectable Morality, and the Rise of the Entertainment Industry: the Case of Blackpool, 1860-1914," *Literature and History* 1 (March, 1975), 62-78; Bailey, "'A Mingled Mass of Perfectly Legitimate Pleasures': The Victorian Middle Class and the Problem of Leisure," *Victorian Studies* 21 (Autumn, 1977), 7-28.

41. Recent studies reveal how servants practised a wide range of disruptive tactics behind the increasingly ill-fitting mask of occupational deference, to the considerable disquiet of their employers. See L. Davidoff, "Mastered for Life: Servant and Wife in Victorian and Edwardian England," *Journal of Social History* 7 (1974), 406-428; P. Branca, *Silent Sisterhood: Middle-Class Women in the Victorian Home* (London, 1975), 30-34, 56, 57; T. McBride, *The Domestic Revolution: The Modernisation of Household Service in England and France, 1820-1920* (London, 1976), 25, 109, 120. Similar forms of worker resistance and unpredictability in other fields of employment deserve attention.

42. L. James, *Print and the People, 1819-1851* (London, 1976), 80, points out that the use of reductionist dichotomies — town and country, moral and immoral — had already become a basic literary technique by the 1840s and a central mental structure for organising experience in the modern city.

43. Ritchie, *The Night Side of London* (London, 1857), 132-138. For the tension created by the claims of two incompatible ideals of urban living: individual privacy and public accountability, see D. Olsen, "Victorian London: Specialisation, Segregation, and Privacy," *Victorian Studies* 17 (March, 1974), 265-78.

44. For the nature and extent of middle-class fears on this count, see Jones, *Outcast London.* Working-class respectability may have been to the new self-regarding middle class patriciate what plebeian deference had once been to the squirearchy. For a suggestive study of deference as a form of social interaction, see Howard Newby, "The Deferential Dialectic," *Comparative Studies in Society and History* 7 (1975), 139-64.

45. G. Gissing, *The Nether World* (London, 1903), 69.

46. Herbert J. Gans, "Urbanism and Suburbanism as Ways of Life: A Re-evaluation of Definitions," in A.M. Rose, ed., *Human Behaviour and Social Processes* (London, 1962), 625-648.

47. David Cannadine, "Victorian Cities: How Different?," *Social History* 2, (January, 1977), 457-482. See also, Olsen, *op cit.* For historians who have used the Chicago School's work to define the

urban context in Victorian England, see Jones, *Outcast London,* and H.E. Meller, *Leisure and the Changing City, 1870-1914* (London, 1976).

48. E.J. Hobsbawm suggests that the term may be useful to historians but does not offer possible applications, "From Social History to the History of Society," in M.W. Flinn & T.C. Smout, eds., *Essays in Social History* (Oxford, 1974), 7. Some suggestions on the applicability of role theory are made by T.C. Cochran, "The Historian's Use of Social Role," in L. Gottschalk, *Generalisations in the Writing of History* (Chicago, 1963), 103-110.

49. See A. Poole, *Gissing in Context* (London, 1975), 31-59; I.S. Saposnik, *Robert Louis Stevenson* (London, 1974), 88-101. On Stevenson, see also, *Dictionary of National Biography.*

50. *See Derek Hudson, Munby, Man of Two Worlds: The Life and Diaries of Arthur J. Munby, 1828-1910* (London, 1972). See also, J.R. Ackerley, *My Father and Myself* (New York, 1975) for an Edwardian double life.

51. Rafael Samuel, "'Quarry Roughs': Life in Headington Quarry, 1860-1920: An Essay in Oral History," in Samuel, ed., *Village Life and Labour* (London, 1975), 242.

52. Cf. E.P. Thompson, "Patrician Society, Plebeian Culture," *Journal of Social History* 7 (Summer, 1974), 382-405, for the dramaturgy of class encounter in the previous century.

53. T. Burns, "Leisure in Industrial Society," in M.A. Smith, S. Parker, and C. Smith, *Leisure and Society in Britain* (London, 1973), 50-53. See also, D. Wrong, "The Oversocialised Conception of Man," *American Sociological Review* 26 (April, 1961), 183-193, and Goffman on "inner autonomy" in "The Nature of Deference and Demeanour," in *Interaction Ritual* (Harmondsworth, 1972), 58. Michel Crozier, *The World of the Office Worker* (Chicago, 1971), 212-213 is also suggestive on this point: "The multiplicity of alienations possible, and the incoherence which naturally emerges as a result, tend to liberate the individual. The more the choices offered allow him a diversity of combinations, the more easily he can escape the determinism of his group, of his condition, and even of his society." For a wider examination of the various tactics employed by modern man to counter or subvert the oppressive reality of daily life, see S. Cohen and L. Taylor, *Escape Attempts: The Theory and Practice of Resistance to Everyday Life* (Harmondsworth, 1978).

III.
EXPANDING HISTORY'S RANGE:
SOCIAL HISTORY AS NEW TOPICS

6.

PEASANTS IN UNIFORM:
THE TSARIST ARMY AS A PEASANT SOCIETY

John Bushnell

A colonel in the Tsarist army by the name of A. Rittikh wrote in 1893 that service in the army turned ignorant peasants into civilized human beings. The peasant conscript's military career began "with a bath and a haircut," then proceded to "cleanliness and neatness in dress." At the same time, conscripts were "taught to speak, look, turn and move with military precision." They learned new words and concepts. In sum, "the wholly rough-hewn and rude [peasant conscript] receives, in the broad sense of the word, a human finish."[1] This has a familiar ring. What Col. Rittikh thought of as the civilizing process we have lately called modernization, and it has been argued that service in the armed forces is one of the routes through which peasants in underdeveloped countries are modernized. To take just one example, Lerner and Robinson have observed that the Turkish army performed a modernizing function in the 1950's because for the army to absorb large quantities of sophisticated weaponry Turkish soldiers had to be educated in its use and maintenance. An important byproduct of this military schooling was that Turkish soldiers "acquired new habits of dress, of cleanliness, of teamwork. In the most profound sense, they acquired a new personality." The army became "a major agency of social change precisely because it spread . . . a new sense of identity — and new skills and concepts as well as new machines. Young Turks from isolated villages now suddenly felt themselves to be part of the larger society."[2]

It might be conceived that the Tsarist army played a similar modernizing role in the late 19th and early 20th centuries. Following its defeat in the Crimean War, the Russian army under the leadership of Minister of War Dmitrii Miliutin embarked on an ambitious program of reforms. One of Miliutin's many goals was to upgrade the army's weaponry, but because the change in weapons technology was undramatic by mid-20th century standards, the starting point for a modernization process cannot be located here. On the other hand, we might look for a similar ripple effect from the implementation of Miliutin's principal goal, the capstone of his reforms: the conversion of the Tsarist army from long-term (25 years) to short-term service (6 years as of 1874, reduced to 3 by 1906). One immediate consequence of reducing the conscript's term of service was that military training had to be greatly compressed: the leisurely development of military skills possible in the pre-reform army had to give way to more intensive instruction. To this end, Miliutin introduced compulsory schooling in the 3 R's for all conscripts, and for a time the Tsarist army became the single most important source of literacy for Russian peasants (25-30 percent of all males of draft age went into the army in the last quarter of the 19th century).[3]

Since the intended effect of all of the many military reforms introduced by Miliutin was to make the Tsarist army a more modern and more professionally competent institution, it is reasonable to ask how these reforms affected peasant conscripts. Was the Tsarist army a modernizing institution, did it instill the habits of discipline and regularity, a sense of abstract order, an openness to change, an orientation toward the future, and all those other traits we associate with modernity? Was service in the army at the least a qualitatively new experience for peasants, bringing them — even if against their will — into contact with a world beyond their villages?

It must be noted at the outset that after Miliutin's retirement in 1881 the army high command lost interest in educating soldiers, and many officers shared the feeling of their new chief, Vannovskii, that education was positively harmful. Junior officers who continued to think of themselves as educators were suspect and were occasionally ordered to cease teaching the rudiments of literacy to conscripts. While some peasants who came into the army with a semblance of literacy — reading newspapers rather than smoking them, as the saying went — did receive further instruction if they were chosen to be NCO's, the mass of peasant soldiers left the army no more literate than they had entered it.[4]

However, the lack of a program of formal education need not mean that the army failed to impart modern attitudes. The civilizing experience described by Col. Rittikh could proceed whether or not soldiers could read and write, and many officers shared Col. Rittikh's perception that military service in and of itself was an educational experience.[5] At any rate, service in the army, with its formal hierarchy, its abstract rules and complex patterns of behavior, seems at first glance a world away from life in the village and might be presumed to have undermined the traditional mentality of peasant soldiers. Furthermore, in the late 19th century Dragomirov's precepts on training were gospel: soldiers were not simply to be drilled, they were to be made to internalize military discipline, to think about and understand the rationale behind the military system.[6] We might add that it was precisely in this period — from the 1880's on — that the army became a predominantly urban institution. While before, many regiments had been scattered about the countryside and soldiers quartered in peasant huts, units were now concentrated in the cities and housed in proper barracks.[7] Military society thus became more self-contained, while what extra-military experience soldiers had was now urban rather than rural.

The case for modernization by way of military service can be taken one step farther: the conscript's initial experience in the army was utterly unlike anything he had ever known. During the first four months of service the conscript was immersed in an intensive process of military socialization. It was during this period that the soldier was taught, none too gently, to "speak, look, turn and move with military precision," that he memorized the intricate grammar of the military hierarchy, and that he was catechized on the duties of a soldier and the military virtues. It was in this period, too, that soldiers were introduced to the complete spectrum of the Tsarist army's vices — beatings, extortion by non-coms, outright theft, and so on. Naturally enough, this was for the conscript a time of extreme disorientation, depression and homesickness; he frequently wasted away bodily, and occasionally maimed himself for the sake of a discharge.[8] The severity of the psychological stress was proportionate to the abruptness of the transition from village to barracks. The conscript was well on the way to being modernized, or at least uprooted.

At that point, however, the modernizing process — if that is what it was — ended; of his initial military experience only the vices carried over in any major way to the remainder of the soldier's term of service. The case for socio-psychological modernization breaks down as soon as it becomes clear just how unmilitary life in the Tsarist army was. The soldier's duties, his *byt*, were functions of the economic rather than the properly military life of his unit. In fact, the Russian regiment's economic functions left little room for martial matters. Not only did the regiment cook its own food and bake its own bread; where possible it grew its own fruit and vegetables and even kept some cattle. The regiment produced its own uniforms and boots. (As of 1907, 150,000 soldiers — 12 percent of all enlisted personnel — spent their duty hours tailoring.) All regiments produced or otherwise provided for themselves — at no cost to the government — blankets, coats, *valenki*, utensils and other military accoutrement. Every regiment maintained a production complex — *masterskie* — staffed by soldiers permanently detailed to provide for its economic needs. However, soldiers from line companies as well did duty as tailors, cobblers, carpenters, carters, cooks, and gardeners. They also served as stable hands, singers, musicians, church attendants, batmen and lackeys in the officers' club. (If this incomplete list calls to mind the organization of a large estate before the emancipation, it should.) During the 8 or 9 months a regiment spent in its barracks, 40 or more of the 100-odd men in a company were performing these unsoldierly duties. Since most other soldiers were on guard duty or serving as duty orderlies, the total number of men free for the training that was called for in the regulations was low. One estimate put it at 1 or 2, rarely as many as 10. This figure is surely too low, but just as surely, after the first four months of intensive training, roughly half the strength of the company on any given day were on details that were in no way military, while most of the rest were simply standing guard. What military training a soldier received was episodic, and it is not difficult to believe a report that a Russian soldier's military skills deteriorated the longer he was in the army.[9]

The unsoldierly life of the Tsarist soldier was due above all to the fact that, once provided with some working capital by the commissariat, regiments were expected to be economically self-sufficient. However, the commissariat was stingy, and the regiment's capital was insufficient to provide for its needs. The only resource the regiment had in excess was labor, so in order to make good the deficit in material soldiers were dispatched to earn money in the civilian economy, a practice known as "*vol'nye raboty*." General Dragomirov observed that

> In July enlisted personnel fan out in hay-mowing, in forests, along railway lines, in town for building; they spoil their clothing; they acquire an external aspect entirely unsuitable [for military service], they become unaccustomed to discipline and lose their military bearing.[10]

The soldiers' migratory labor was so obviously detrimental to the army's military mission that there was frequent discussion of ending the practice. Yet as one officer noted, his men needed blankets, the blankets had to be paid for, and the only recourse was to collect the money soldiers earned at their civilian work.[11] *Vol'nye raboty* were built into the military economy.

If the money earned through migratory labor balanced the regimental budget, it did not entirely balance the individual soldier's budget. Prior to 1906, soldiers were required to provide their own soap, spoons, boot brushes and polish, oil and rags for cleaning rifles, bed linen, shirts, in many instances blankets, and on and on. Equipment that *was* issued to the soldiers was so inadequate that considerable expense was involved in keeping it up to specifications. Army-issue boots, for instance, were of such poor quality that they lasted no more than three months. Soldiers had either to purchase their own or pay for repairs — and repairs, even if performed by the company cobbler, could easily cost the soldier as much as four rubles a year — yet before 1906 soldiers were paid only 2r. 70k. a year. The soldier's minimum monthly budget ranged anywhere from 90k. to 1r. 74k. a year. However calculated, it far exceeded his monthly pay of 22½k. (raised to 50k. per month as of January 1906).[12] Soldiers were allowed to keep for themselves some of the money from their *vol'nye raboty*, roughly half the soldiers received money from home; and in addition soldiers sold part of their daily bread ration to civilians, this providing up to 30 extra kopeks per month.[13] In any event, in addition to the regiment's involvement in the civilian economy, soldiers as individuals were also peripheral participants in the market.

It should be evident by now that as an economic entity the Tsarist regiment functioned in a way quite familiar to the peasant soldier. Like the peasant household and village, the Tsarist regiment aspired to self-sufficiency, but was bound up in a larger market system. Individual soldiers sold what surplus they had in order to cover the expense of maintaining their military household. But since the regiment's marketable surplus was meager, soldiers joined the migratory labor force and sent their earnings "home."

The similarity between the peasant and military economy extended to the seasonality of the military-economic cycle. Units set off for their summer encampments in early May. Field exercises — the most exhausting part of the yearly cycle — were over by the end of July or early August. At that point, soldiers who had completed their term were discharged from service, others were given home leave, and most of the rest went off in search of civilian work. The regiment withered from 1800 to roughly 300 men, with no more than 20 present in a company. Military duties were supposed to resume in mid-October, but with soldiers off doing one thing or another no start could be made until mid-November — at which point end-of-the-year holidays intervened. What training there was during the winter was confined to the four months between the new year and the onset of field exercises — but as we have seen, training was hardly regular even then.[14] Not only was military life as cyclical as peasant life, the modulations of the two cycles were virtually identical.

Relations between officers and men, too, were congruent with the peasant experience. It was not just that officers thought of their men as the rude peasants they had been prior to service, though this was an important element of the overall pattern. Denikin remarked in 1903 that officers just could not conceive of their soldiers as fellow men.[15] This attitude came through most clearly in the distinction officers drew between ordinary conscripts and the educated volunteers: striking a simple soldier was a matter of course, but it was unthinkable to strike a volunteer, who came from a social world much like the officer's own and might actually file charges. The simple soldier was quite aware of his inferior standing, which was entirely independent of his subordinate position in the military hierarchy. That he could be beaten was as natural to him as it was to his officer. Soldiers drew the line only at officers from other companies — their own officers could strike them, but the *barin* from another company who did so was violating the social proprieties.[16]

These attitudes were of course reminiscent of the master-serf relationship, but they were rooted more in the socio-economic reality of the unit than in tradition. The structure of which such attitudes were a part was most exposed to view in the *vol'nye raboty*. General Dragomirov commented that so-called "civilian work" is in essence *forced labor*, with overtones of serfdom. Formerly the *pomeshchik* hired out his own peasants, now the military commander does the same . . . Such an application of authority sometimes leads to an individual who does not want to do civilian work being courtmartialed.[17]

Another officer added that not only did *vol'nye raboty* "accustom the commander to view his men as serfs; from this it is not far to the use of soldiers as free labor."[18] And indeed, officers employed their men not only to sustain the unit, but also for personal labor and other services. The attitude of officers toward the regimental shops was frankly proprietary: outfitting an apartment with new table, desk and curtains was as simple as issuing an order. Setting soldiers to constructing comfortable summer cottages at the regimental camp was just as easy. In Saratov in the early 20th century, one enterprising regimental commander ran a funeral procession business, employing in this enterprise the men and horses of his unit. Less imaginative officers merely used their men as household labor.[19]

Like peasants, soldiers were at the mercy of the strong of the world, and the world was one in which formal regulations against striking soldiers or exploiting them for economic gain — formal regulations of any kind — were irrelevant. Custom alone counted, and Tsarist military custom was weighted heavily against the soldier. Yet the soldier's peasant *persona* was more deeply rooted in military society than that. Even where regimental custom conformed to military regulations, the ordinary functioning of the unit recalled for the soldier the familiar peasant world. The officer was not just the soldier's military superior, he was simultaneously master of the unit's economy. If nothing else, this was a situation ripe for abuse. There was ample opportunity — indeed, necessity — for officers to divert money intended for provisioning soldiers to other needs of the unit, or to their own pockets. (To the soldier, of course, it made no difference whether money meant to purchase their food was gambled away by the company commander or was spent repairing barracks.) Furthermore, whether or not officers were in fact "stealing" from their men, they could be doing so, and it was impossible for soldiers to complain — because the officers' economic functions were vested in their authority as military superiors. This may seem a minor point. But if officers had had primarily military functions, if they had not controlled the finances for feeding and clothing their men, if they had not allocated their men to production duties, they would not automatically have been perceived to be living at the expense of the soldiers. (As one contemporary observer put it delicately, the fact that the officer's military and economic functions were indivisible undermined his moral authority.) As things stood, there was nothing more natural than for soldiers to view their officers as economic drones, or at least as competitors for scarce goods.[20] Certainly, officers alone were not responsible for this situation — the military economy was in fact one of scarcity. Yet the socio-economic pattern that derived from the army's scarcity economy could only reinforce the prototypically peasant "image of limited good." Given the economic reality of peasant (and military) life, one man's gain was indeed another's loss. While this image was obviously congruent with the distribution of material goods, it also held — in the peasant's view — for the distribution of psychic goods.[21] Since the image of limited good was fundamental to the peasant way of looking at the world and was reinforced by life in the army, it is scarcely credible that military service could have done much to reshape the peasant mentality.

Officers, then, employed their peasant soldiers to maintain the regimental estate and to benefit themselves, and if they did not, no matter — soldiers suspected them of doing so. To complete the picture of the army as a peasant society, it remains only to consider the officer's role as outsider, a role that was, again, built into the daily routine of military life. The fact is that officers, junior officers included, spent very little time with their men. Much of their time was given over either to management and related paperwork, or to verification of the management of other officers. Officers sat on countless commissions that checked the books of the various economic subunits, revolving funds and permanent capital that made up the regimental economy. Officers were rated more for their proficiency as economic managers than for their ability to train and lead men — which, given the predominance of the regiment's economic functions, was logical enough. Little wonder, then, that the road to success lay through the company and regimental offices. It was there that junior officers came to the attention of their superiors, it was there that they could perform services genuinely useful to the regiment and its commander and could hope to reap a suitable reward. Whether or not their formal duties called for them to be in the offices, that was where they congregated at every opportunity. It was anyhow boring to spend time with soldiers, much more interesting to be involved in the social life centered on the offices. Little wonder, again, that a company commander's contact with his men was ordinarily limited to a cursory look-through (and that not every day), or that lieutenants — when forced into the barracks against their will — idled on the sidelines, smoking, gossiping and telling jokes.[22] Lack of contact between officers and men was certainly detrimental to training, but then a regiment's economic functions had priority. Since the economic life of the unit was routine, only routine dispositions had to be made.

If officers were distant, periodically intrusive figures, who was in day-to-day charge of the men? Obviously, the NCO's. However, after the Miliutin reforms the Tsarist army had proportionately fewer long-term NCO's than any other European army, because few soldiers reenlisted after completing their appointed term. From the 1880's on, there were at most the company Sgt. Major and perhaps one or two long-term senior sergeants — but only perhaps. All the other non-com slots were filled by literate conscripts given some extra training, but only on the company roster could these be distinguished from privates. The Sgt. Major was certainly the most important authority with whom soldiers regularly came into contact, but he was the *only* authority with whom they were in regular contact. The Sgt. Major kept no closer track of the men under him than was necessary to satisfy the company commander, or alternatively grossly abused his authority because the company commander had so little knowledge of what went on in the unit.[23]

Mostly, in fact, soldiers were left to themselves, the Sgt. Major merely maintaining a patina of proper military order and discipline. Since soldiers were more or less free to organize themselves, it is not at all surprising that they fell back on the type of social organization that Russian peasants away from their villages had employed for centuries, the *artel'*. (The recrudescence of familiar civilian patterns was made all the easier by the fact that most soldiers in a unit were, due to the recruiting system, *zemliaki — Landsleute —* often from the same or neighboring villages.) The company chose an *artel'shchik* who was responsible for purchasing food and sundry other of the soldiers' necessities with funds provided by the company commander, and it was the self-constituted soldier *artel'* that concluded contracts for *vol'nye raboty*.[24] It seemed so natural to the soldiers that they should manage their own affairs — because that was their experience as peasants, and because that was the norm in the army — that invariably the most detested officers were those who actually attempted to supervise their men. It was the very principle of officer intrusion in the barracks that soldiers resented, not the results. It made no difference that units in which officers played an active supervisory role were the best clothed, the best shod and the best fed. Soldiers preferred — and performed best for — the officer who let his unit run itself, even if they suffered some privation in consequence.[25] In the soldiers' view, the officer's proper role was that of an outsider — the improving officer was as much resented as the improving landlord.

Yet the Tsarist officer was not simply an outsider, he was a mediating outsider, a necessary part of the soldier's world. Only he could provide the link between the relatively autonomous, unit-level soldier community and the larger military world. And like mediating outsiders in peasant society, the Tsarist officer combined in his person the roles of socio-political middle man, economic intermediary, intercessor, and patron.[26] In anthropological terms, the relationship between officer and soldier was multiplex rather than single-interest (i.e., specialized) — a distinction in modes of authority that has been called the watershed between traditional and modern society.[27]

Other analogies can be found between peasant and military societies, but surely enough has been said to demonstrate that the Tsarist army was not a modernizing institution. In defiance of formal tables of organization and the prescriptions of training manuals, the soldier's socio-economic experience replicated that of peasant society, the similarity extending even to types of contact with the non-peasant (or non-military) world. Though the army had on paper a hierarchy of command and discipline that had no analogue in peasant society, in practice the pattern of officer-soldier relations was familiar — even if by the late 19th century it was somewhat archaic by civilian standards. The peasant remained a peasant even while in uniform.

This is not to say that service in the army had no impact on individual Russian peasants. The peasant soldier was, after all, stationed far from home and in an urban environment. Still, this sort of contact with the modern urban world was itself part of the Russian peasant's ordinary experience. Millions of peasants in the late 19th and early 20th centuries were engaged in migratory seasonal labor (and had been for generations), and other millions were engaged in non-seasonal, but temporary, labor in the cities. Yet the urban setting had a muted impact on peasant migrants, because urban peasants had traditional social institutions that set them apart from the city proper.[28] If the urban peasant was in but not of the city, how much truer must this have been of the peasant soldier, whose urban experience was mediated by the peasant structure of his military unit? Whatever new experience came to the peasant soldier while in the army was being more efficiently acquired by other peasants in the civilian world. As all contemporaries reported, it was the returned peasant migrant who brought change to the village, not the ex-soldier.

In the final analysis, then, answering the question posed at the outset — was the Tsarist army a modernizing institution — does not contribute very much to our understanding of socio-cultural change in the Russian peasantry. It has, however, been a useful way to get at what a soldier's life in the Tsarist army was really like. This in turn throws some light on other aspects of Tsarist military experience, and suggests new approaches to some old issues. These can only be briefly adumbrated here.

We are in a better position, first, to understand the behavior of the Tsarist army during periods of civil turmoil. For instance, the mutinies of 1905 and 1906 exhibited similarities at a number of levels to contemporaneous peasant disturbances. Allowing for differences in the organizational framework within which they occurred, mutinies and peasant disturbances had a very similar internal dynamic — the way they started, and the way they worked themselves out. They coincided, too, in their timing (responding to the same external stimuli) and in their frequency curves (they peaked at roughly the same time both in 1905 and 1906). Finally, the ultimate objects of mutiny and peasant riot were similar. Given what we know of soldier society, it would be strange if it had been otherwise — yet the mutinies have ordinarily been treated as political demonstrations, or as responses to military conditions narrowly construed.[29]

We may also be in a better position to understand the Russian soldier's performance in battle. Russian soldiers were renowned for their endurance and bravery — for their stolidity — but were also renowned for their lack of initiative and their tendency to deteriorate into a helpless herd as soon as their officers were put out of action.[30] The virtues of the Russian soldier were characteristic of peasant society. His defects, too, were rooted in peasant social organization, which was entirely inappropriate on the battlefield. A Tsarist military unit was cohesive so long as its officers were present — but a unit without officers had lost not just its appointed leaders, it had lost as well its intermediary to the world beyond the unit. On the battlefield, Russian soldiers without officers were not so much militarily as socially isolated. They had no sense of being part of an integrated military machine, nor could they have, since this was not their peacetime experience. Soldiers without officers had no more notion of how to comport themselves than would a Russian village suddenly materialized in the midst of a battle.

Finally, what has been said of soldier society suggests a number of ways to approach the Tsarist officer corps. In the final analysis, soldier society was what it was because officers permitted it to be so. Officer society was functionally complementary to soldier society, and not just in the way I suggested earlier; a more detailed analysis of this aspect of the officer corps would be well worth the while. It has, for instance, recently been suggested that many of the ills of the Tsarist army on the eve of World War I can be attributed to uncontrolled rivalry among cliques of generals (the generals' inability to coordinate their activities also made itself felt prior to and during the Russo-Japanese War), which negated otherwise beneficial military reforms.[32] Clearly, rivalry between high-ranking cliques was only one of several end products of the functioning of the Tsarist military system. Furthermore, the reforms hastily enacted after the Russo-Japanese War failed not because of accidental personal rivalry, but because they were incompatible with the reality of the Tsarist army — they were obliterated by self-perpetuating (officer-perpetuated) military routine. And just as there was a connection between the soldiers' peacetime experience and battlefield performance, there must certainly have been such a connection for the officer corps. Indeed, a few military commentators after the Russo-Japanese War placed the blame for defeat squarely on habits acquired by officers in the course of their economic chores.[33] In any event, to appreciate properly the service habits of Tsarist officers in peace and war, we need a structural — if you will, an anthropological — analysis of the officer corps much like that offered here for enlisted personnel.

FOOTNOTES

1. A Rittikh, *Russkii voennyi byt v deistvitel'nosti i v mechtakh* (Spb., 1893), p. 20. Rittikh makes similar observations on pp. 38 and 263.

2. Daniel Lerner and Richard D. Robinson, "Swords and Ploughshares: The Turkish Army as a Modernizing Force," *World Politics* 13, (Oct. 1960), p. 32. Others who make much the same point are Lucian W. Pye, "Armies in the Process of Political Modernization," in John J. Johnson, ed., *The Role of the Military in Underdeveloped Countries* (Princeton, 1962), pp. 80-84; James S. Coleman and Belmont Brice, Jr., "The Role of the Military in Sub-Saharan Africa," *ibid.*, pp. 396-98; Morris Janowitz, *Military Institutions and Coercion in the Developing Nations* (Chicago, 1977), pp. 156-8; W. Raymond Duncan, "Development Roles of the Military in Cuba: Modal Personality and Nation Building," in Sheldon W. Simon, ed., *The Military and Security in the Third World: Domestic and International Impacts* (Boulder, Col., 1978), pp. 77-121.

3. On the Tsarist army at the time of the Crimean War: John Shelton Curtiss, *The Army of Nicholas I, 1825-1855* (Durham, N.C., 1965). On Miliutin's reforms: P.A. Zaionchkovskii, *Voennye reformy 1860-1870 godov v Rossii* (M., 1952), and Forrest A. Miller, *Dmitrii Miliutin and the Reform Era in Russia,* (Nashville, 1968). P.A. Zaionchkovskii, *Samoderzhavie i russkaia armiia na rubezhe XIX-XX stoletii, 1881-1903* (M., 1973), pp. 116-17, provides figures on draftees.

4. Required instruction was dropped in the mid-1880's then restored, for the infantry alone, in 1902. Even when literacy instruction was required, however, it frequently — perhaps ordinarily — remained a dead letter. The officer in charge filled out and presented the proper forms during brigade inspection, and no one asked whether instruction had actually been provided. Ziaonchkovskii, *Samoderzhavie i russkaia armiia*, pp. 276-9; A. Gerua, *Posle voiny. O nashei armii* (Spb., 1907), pp. 54-5; *V tsartsve shtykov* (N. Novgorod, 1908), pp. 21-2; A.A. Ignatyev, *A Subaltern in Old Russia* (New York, 1944), p. 150; M. Grulev, *Zapiski generala-evreia* (Paris, 1930), pp. 112-13, 130-31; M. Grulev, *Zloby dnia v zhizni armii* ([Brest-Litovsk], 1911), pp. 76, 78, reports a lack of enthusiasm for educating soldiers even after the Russo-Japanese War. A.I. Denikin, *Put' russkogo ofitsera* (New York, 1953), p. 123, claims that at least after 1902 hundreds of thousands of Russian soldiers did become literate while in the army, but the weight of the evidence is against him.

On the instruction provided in the *uchebnye roty* for future non-coms: A. Rittikh, *Russkii voennyi byt*, pp. 55-6; Col. Mamontov, "Sovremennoe polozhenie 'untr-ofitserskogo voprosa' v Rossii i za granitseiu," *Obshchestvo revnitelei voennykh znanii*, kn. 4 (1906), p. 82.

5. W. Barnes Steveni, *The Russian Army from Within* (New York, 1914), pp. 35, 44, 47, reports this as the common sentiment among Russian officers. Other officers felt not so much that the Russian army was carrying out a civilizing mission as that it should be doing so: Captain Veselovskii, *K voprosu o vospitanii soldata* (Spb., 1900), p. 164; Mstislav Levitskii, *Vospitanie soldata* (Spb., 1911), p. 4 and passim, M. Galkin, *Novyi put' sovremennogo ofitsera* (M., 1906), pp. 19, 53-5.

6. Dragomirov's ideas on this subject are laid out in, *inter alia, Opyt rukovodstva dlia podgotovka k boiu* (many editions), especially Part I, and *Podgotovka voisk v mirnoe vremia* (Kiev, 1906). Both are reprinted in M.I. Dragomirov, *Izbrannye trudy. Voprosy vospitaniia i obucheniia* (M., 1956). Dragomirov's influence is remarked by German Miuller, "Moral'noe vospitanie voisk v Germanii, Rossii i Iaponii. Sravnitel'nyi etiud na osnovanii Russko-Iaponskoi voiny," *Voina i mir* (1907), no. 3, passim; A. Gerua, *Posle voiny*, pp. 73-4, 100-1; and by most other contemporary commentators.

7. In 1882, only 53.6 percent of the army was housed in regular barracks; by 1903, all field troops were quartered either in barracks or in private apartments under barrack conditions. Zaionchkovskii, *Samoderzhavie i russkaia armiia*, pp. 270-1; Rittikh, *Russkii voennyi byt*, pp. 138-141.

8. Actually, the introduction of conscripts to the vices began before they arrived in their regiments, as they were subject to blatant extortion by non-coms who conveyed them from the induction centers (Gerua, *Posle voiny*, pp. 105-7). On the experience of the conscripts during their first four months of service, see *V tsarstve shtykov*, pp. 2-4, 7, 14; M. Zenchenko, *Obuchenie i vospitanie soldata* (Spb., 1902), pp. 71-85; Rittikh, *Russkii voennyi byt*, pp. 38-9, 42; B.v. Rechenberg-Linten, *Russische Soldaten und Offiziere aus der Zarenzeit. Nach Selbsterlebnissen in einer russischen Garnison* (Bern-Leipzig, 1924), pp. 8-9, 14-18; N.D. Butovskii, *Sbornik poslednykh statei* (Spb., 1910), pp. 128, 131.

On the high rate of sickness during the first four months, see N. Butovskii, *Nashi soldaty. (Tipy mirnogo i voennogo vremeni)* (Spb., 1893), pp. 10-11, 79, 145. M. Grulev, *Zloby dnia*, pp. 241-3, points out that much of the sickness was due to the fact that many draftees went into the army "under protest" — the list of medical exemptions did not cover them, but they were not really fit for service. Grulev estimates that as many as 10-15 percent of all draftees were discharged on medical grounds, often after hospitalization, soon after arriving in their units. N.N. Golovin, *The Russian Army in the World War* (New Haven, 1931), p. 22, also refers to the high proportion of draftees who arrived at their units "under protest."

The references to beatings, theft and extortion are innumerable, the only question being how prevalent they were in fact. Whatever the true incidence, it is clear that newly-arrived conscripts were the most vulnerable, but that all soldiers considered these phenomena a normal feature of military life.

9. Rittikh, *Russkii voennyi byt*, pp. 86-8; A. Gerua, *Posle voiny*, pp. 51-2, 65-6, 103, 107-8, 111; A.P. Voznesenskii, "O voennom khoziaistve," *Obshchestvo revnitelei voennykh znanii*, kn. 1 (1906), pp. 109-11, 118; A.A. Ignatyev, *A Subaltern*, p. 75; Grulev, *Zloby dnia*, pp. 154, 229; A.M. Volgin, *Ob armii* (Spb., 1908) pp. 114-16. A.I. Denikin, *Staraia armiia* v. 1 (Paris, 1929), p. 93, explicitly compares the running of a regiment at the turn of the century — especially in the interior — to running a *pomest'e*.

10. Zaionchkovskii, *Samoderzhavie i russkaia armiia*, pp. 272-3.

11. *Razvedchik*, no. 539, 13 Feb. 1901. The sources on this curious practice are numerous, for it was widely discussed in the military press at the turn of the century. See John Bushnell, "Mutineers and Revolutionaries. Military Revolution in Russia, 1905-1907," Ph.D. dissertation, Indiana University, 1977, pp. 18-20 and notes. In addition: Rittikh, *Russkii voennyi byt*, p. 52; M. Grulev, *Zapiski*, p. 93. *Vol'nye raboty* were finally suppressed in 1906: *Razvedchik*, no. 796, 29 Jan. 1906.

12. The two budgets (others were offered as well) are in R. Maksheev, "Zhalovan'e i pensii nizhnym chinam," *Intendantskii zhurnal*, 1903, no. 5, pp, 44-7; *Razvedchik*, no. 565, 14 Aug. 1901. On the items soldiers had to provide for themselves, and the cost involved in maintaining uniforms and, especially, boots in required order, see Bushnell, "Mutineers," pp. 16-18. In addition, see Voznesenskii, "O voennom khoziastve," pp. 105, 107. On the increase in pay and the December 1905 increase in equipment issued to soldiers: "Ulushenie byta nizhnikh chinov," *Russkii invalid*, no. 255, 6 Dec. 1905.

13. Bushnell, "Mutineers," p. 18; Ignatyev, *A Subaltern*, pp. 146-7; Steveni, *Russian Army*, pp. 65-6; Grulev, *Zapiski*, p. 94; Denikin, *Put'*, p. 120; Rechenberg-Linten, *Russische Soldaten*, p. 16.

14. The seasonal cycle is laid out in the most detail by Rittikh, *Russkii voennyi byt*, pp. 44-7, 54, 100, 143, 146, 153. No other source offers contrary evidence. Grulev, *Zloby dnia*, comes up with a figure of 25-30 in a company after summer camp even after the *vol'nye raboty* had been abolished — the rest were detailed to other duties temporarily.

15. A. Denikin, "Soldatskii byt," *Razvedchik*, no. 661, 24 June 1903. On the inferior social status of Tsarist soldiers in general, see Bushnell, "Mutineers," pp. 21-3.

16. *Golos iz russkoi armii. Rzaoblacheniia* (Berlin, 1902), pp. 44, 62, provides direct soldier testimony on this point. The known behavior pattern in the army — frequent striking of soldiers and the soldiers' acceptance of same — is at least circumstantial evidence.

17. *Russkii invalid*, no. 235, 28 Oct. 1900.

18. "Eshche o vol'nykh rabotakh," *Varshavskii voennyi zhurnal*, 1902, no. 1.

19. N.D. Butovskii, *Stat'i na sovremennye voprosy* (Spb., 1907), pp. 62, 64; Grulev, *Zloby dnia*, pp. 228-9, 237-8; Denikin, *Staraia armiia*, v. 1, p. 93.

20. Voznesenskii, "O voennom khoziastve," pp. 111-12, 122.

21. George Foster, "Peasant Society and the Image of Limited Good," *American Anthropologist* 67 (1965), no. 2, pp. 293-315.

22. Veselovskii, *K voprosu*, p. 12; Gerua, *Posle voiny*, pp. 47-51, 54, 118; Voznesenskii, "O voennom khoziaistve," pp. 97, 112-18; Zenchenko, *Obuchenie*, pp. 59-63; Rittikh, *Russkii voennyi byt*, p. 75; Galkin, *Novy put'*, pp. 49-52; Rechenberg-Linten, *Russishche Soldaten*, pp. 13-22; Butovskii, *Sbornik*, pp. 63-70, 120-22; Grulev, *Zloby dnia*, 54, 57-8, 155-7. There was little contact between officers and men even during guard duty, because the officers and men on guard detail came from different units: Levitskii, *Vospitanie*, p. 10. Peter Kenez, "A Profile of the Prerevolutionary Officer Corps," *California Slavic Studies* 7, (1973), pp. 129, 133-34, notes that a disproportionate number of Tsarist officers were assigned to staff work, while the ratio between officers (including staff officers) and men was the lowest of any major European army.

23. Ignatyev, *A Subaltern*, p. 85; *V tsarstve shtykov*, p. 8; Grulev, *Zapiski*, pp. 92, 94, 98, 133; Zenchenko, *Obuchenie*, p. 59; *Golos iz russkoi armii*, pp. 4-5; Rittikh, *Russkii voennyi byt*, pp. 48-9; Mamontov, "Sovremennoe polozhenie 'untr-ofitserskogo voprosa'," pp. 97, 101; K.V., "Sravnenie nashikh uslovii obuchenii soldata s zagranichnymi," *Russkii invalid*, no. 154, 20 July 1905; P. Sagat-skii, "K unter-ofitserskomu voprosu," *Razvedchik*, no. 821, 18 July 1906; Zaionchkovskii, *Samoderzhavie i russkaia armiia*, pp. 120-23; Butovskii, *Stat'i*, p. 25; Golovin, *Russian Army*, p. 29.

24. *V tsarstve shtykov*, p. 13; Voznesenskii, "O voennom khoziastve," p. 110; Rittikh, *Russkii voennyi byt*, pp. 51-2; Gerua, *Posle voiny*, pp. 86, 88; Bushnell, "Mutineers," pp. 20-21.

25. *V tsarstve shtykov*, pp. 23-4. There is some indication that the "improving officer" was more common after 1905 than before, and that the soldiers' perception of the proper role of their officers may gradually have been changing. But the change could only have been gradual, because the bulk of the Tsarist officers were still immersed in office paperwork.

26. On the officer's role as patron (in providing special treats out of his own pocket, helping out soldiers in time of need, and so on), see Ignatyev, *A Subaltern*, pp. 86-7, 89, 144; B.V. Gerua, *Vospominaniia o moei zhizni*, 1 (Paris, 1969), p. 58. The patron role was filled most often in the Guards, where officers were independently wealthy. It may well be that where soldiers felt that the patron role was being adequately filled they were more likely to be loyal to their officers; this may have been one of the reasons why some units did not mutiny during the epidemic of mutinies in late 1905. See Bushnell, "Mutineers," pp. 95-7 (the evidence is therein presented, but the point is not stated in the same terms).

27. E.G. Bailey, "The Peasant View of the Bad Life," *The Advancement of Science*, 23 (Dec. 1966), p. 401.

28. There is a nice discussion of the peasant's place in the city in Joseph Crane Bradley, Jr., "*Muzhik* and Muscovite: Peasants in Late Nineteenth-Century Urban Russia," Ph.D. dissertation, Harvard University, 1977, pp. 98-117, 170-73, and passim.

29. Bushnell, "Mutineers," pp. 68-97, 145-52, 295-343, discusses the mutinies of 1905 and 1906, though not quite in the same terms (the peasant analogy is suggested, but not developed).

30. Representative comments from the late 19th and early 20th centuries: "Report of Captain Carl Reichman," in U.S. War Department, General Staff G-2, *Reports of Military Observers attached to the Armies in Manchuria*, Part I, 1906, p. 244; F.V. Greene, *Sketches of Army Life in Russia* (New York, 1880), pp. 24-5, 124-5; Steveni, *Russian Army*, p. 50; Grulev, *Zloby dnia*, pp. 55, 85.

31. Veselovskii, *K voprosu o vospitanii*, pp. 7-10, does an intelligent job in deriving the Russian soldier's martial virtues from his peasant background.

32. Norman Stone, *The Eastern Front 1914-1917* (New York, 1975), pp. 17-35; W. Thomas Wilfong, "Rebuilding the Russian Army, 1905-1914: The Question of a Comprehensive Plan for National Defense," Ph.D. dissertation, Indiana University, 1977, pp. 170, 174-5.

33. Gerua, *Posle voiny*, 50, 57, 61, 332; Voznesenskii, "O voennom khoziastve," p. 97.

7.

THE KLEPTOMANIA DIAGNOSIS: BOURGEOIS WOMEN AND THEFT IN LATE NINETEENTH-CENTURY FRANCE

Patricia O'Brien

"Then there were the women with a mania for stealing, a perversion of desire, a new kind of neurosis that was classified by a mental specialist who had observed the acute result of the temptation exercised on them by the department stores."

Emile Zola, *Au Bonheur des dames*[1] (1883)

In the second half of the nineteenth century, an unusual body of case studies appeared in the annals of French forensic medicine. These were individual histories of kleptomaniacs —women, for the most part, diagnosed as stealing out of compulsion. The case studies are unusual for their growing and unprecedented numbers, especially after 1880, and for the uniform behavior patterns they reveal. This article proposes to examine these individual case studies and the psychiatric literature surrounding them with the intention of discovering something about the domain of forensic medicine and the assumptions that were made by it regarding woman's nature, and, more broadly, something about social attitudes towards women as deviants in late nineteenth-century France. There is a further social dimension to kleptomania. The diagnosis became popular in a society marked by new consumer behavior in the marketplace. The forensic literature itself suggests a relationship between the diagnosis and changing social patterns and a social critique of bourgeois values in the France of the early Third Republic.[2]

I propose to examine the nineteenth-century diagnosis of kleptomania on three levels:

1) the case studies themselves, the assumptions made, and the procedures followed by the examining specialists;

2) the concept of kleptomania, how it developed in nineteenth-century forensic medicine (the introduction of medical knowledge into the process of justice), especially in relation to theories of legal irresponsibility;

and 3) the social meaning of kleptomania, and the context in which the diagnosis took root and flourished. The hypothesis is that the diagnosis of kleptomania allows us to glimpse professional interpretations of female behavior and, less reliably, the behavior itself. It serves as a window on social and professional assumptions about woman's nature.

The Case Studies. Before turning to the individuals examined, two related circumstances should be briefly considered: the emergence of forensic medicine as a specialization; and the increase in the incidence of shoplifting.

The existence of these case studies is, in part, explained by the establishment of forensic medicine as a discipline with its own methods and procedures and its battle for the legitimacy and acceptance of medical testimony in the courts. The publication of case studies was intended as a teaching device in the training of forensic specialists and as a weapon against magistrates who doubted medicine's place in determining guilt or innocence. In the case of kleptomania, *médecins légistes* were waging a winning battle at the turn of the century to demonstrate the utility of psychiatry as expert testimony in the law courts. Their collective concern was further enhanced by the passage of a law on 30 November 1892 that was intended to regulate the exercise of medicine, in general, and that addressed itself, in particular, to the mode of operation, fees, and certification of forensic experts. Many of the published case studies were the consequence of court requests for medical examinations of defendants and reflected increased judicial reliance on the medical specialist in the process of judgment.

A second factor influenced the context of the kleptomania diagnosis. Shoplifting, or more specifically, department-store theft, was on the rise. Psychiatrists and forensic specialists joined department store owners and lawyers in focusing a growing attention on what was widely considered an "epidemic" of stealing after 1880. Shoplifting had become, as the leading alienist Alexandre Laccasagne declared, a "social phenomenon."[3] The case studies take their place, therefore, in a broader literature on the subject of department store theft.

Unfortunately not much can be said about the statistical relationship between the number of kleptomaniacs and the general incidence of shoplifting. Furthermore, the data on "real" crimes — those actually committed versus those detected — lack substance and reliability. Even our picture of detected crimes remains murky for several reasons. Official statistics on theft were undifferentiated: shoplifting was lumped together with all other types of theft, with the exception of domestic theft, which was recorded separately. Second, department stores actively suppressed information on thefts out of fear that publicity would adversely affect sales. A third reason for our inability to determine the extent of the shoplifting epidemic is that the vast majority of thefts committed resulted in neither arrest nor conviction. This is only partially explained by the notorious ineffectiveness of detection in department stores, a problem that owners were seeking to correct.[4] More significantly, the stores, the courts, and the legal and medical professions sought to protect from public scrutiny many of the individuals arrested, especially if they were otherwise respectable bourgeois women. With kleptomania, protection was even more certain because of concern for the patient and her family's honor.

In spite of the variety and extent of the limitations on the data, we do know that at the height of the reported epidemic, two department stores alone (the Bon Marché and the Louvre) were responsible for bringing over 1,000 individuals to court in a single year.[5] Even this, we are assured, was only the tip of the iceberg. Vicomte d'Avenel, a philosopher of sorts of modern consumption, estimated that each of the major department stores in Paris lost 100,000 francs a year in unreported thefts: this meant that, with the average theft amounting to no more than 50 francs, there were twice as many thefts that went unreported as those that reached the courts.[6] We can take this to be a reasonable — and unsubstantiated — guess. Observers like Avenel employed a variety of ways to estimate actual thefts — none with outstanding success. On the basis of these estimates, we are only safe in concluding that there was general agreement on two points: that shoplifting after 1880 was dramatically different in type and extent from retail theft before that period; and that between 1880 and 1920 shoplifting was indisputably on the rise.

One additional aspect of the shoplifting phenomenon that fascinated criminologists and that should be mentioned here is that it was a crime committed almost exclusively by women. The only other crime with a similar profile was prostitution. It was, therefore, understandably the source of curiosity and concern among contemporaries studying the phenomenon.

In was in this atmosphere, then, that the psychiatric case studies made their appearance. The histories are scattered throughout a variety of similar sources:

works specifically analyzing kleptomania as a psychic disorder, broader studies of legal irresponsibility, textbooks on forensic medicine and the practice of medical jurisprudence, studies of department store thefts, clinical reports on mental illness, journals of psychiatry, psychology, and forensic medicine, and psychiatric manuals. Most of the studies were published between 1880 and 1905. "Classic" cases were frequently repeated from one work to another. Both the criteria used and symptoms discovered reveal common concerns and highly similar findings.

After 1880, kleptomania was recognized almost universally as "a morbid impulse to steal perfectly useless objects or those that could be easily paid for."[7] Both monomaniacal and hysterical manifestations figured heavily in the determination of the diagnosis. These were "catchall" categories,[8] which encompassed a broad variety of behavior under a general rubric that emphasized loss of reason. The diagnosis was based on the assumption that it was irrational to steal things one did not need. The forensic specialist concluded that people who did so were not legally responsible for their acts. A confluence of psychiatric literature supported the principle of legal irresponsibility of the kleptomaniac in the commission of a crime and had a determining impact on the judicial treatment of bourgeois women caught shoplifting: nearly all the individuals in the case studies were acquitted by the courts.

In addition to the fact that most of these individuals were acquitted for their acts, nearly all of them were women accused of theft. They were also apparently and predominantly bourgeois. Dubuisson, the forensic specialist for the Tribunal of the Seine, was typical in his emphasis on wealth as a critical factor in determining the diagnosis: he found most of the women he examined to be "well-to-do" and even "rich."[9] Dr. Dupouy likewise found it relevant to his diagnosis that one of his patients accused of stealing an umbrella worth 3 francs 95 centimes had 70,000 francs in her purse at the time of the theft.[10] This led to another generalization about the individuals examined: if they were women who had money and who still stole, one could conclude that they were suffering from a *débilité mentale.* [11] By this means, shoplifting came to be associated with low intelligence and weakness of spirit in bourgeois women.[12]

Over 200 case studies are included in the published material. Information is not consistently recorded in all cases but what is there allows us to conclude that most of the diagnosed kleptomaniacs were not guilty merely of isolated acts but appear to have stolen over long periods of time without having considered the possibility of detection. When these individuals were confronted in the act of stealing, they often expressed their relief at being caught. Many confessed to numerous past crimes that had gone undetected. Most of the individuals in the case studies described themselves as in some way "driven" or "compelled" to steal. Common explanations included: "It was stronger than I"; "I didn't know what I was doing"; "I lost my head." Most kleptomaniacs also appear to have acted as packrats, amassing quantities of goods, often of little value, and hiding them, some still retaining their store ticket and "serving no purpose."

The case studies also reveal that the examining specialist was more than just a filter through whom the patient's testimony passed. One is struck by the degree to which he created the diagnosis by reconstructing the past life of the patient. Personal history came to determine the meaning of the present behavior of the accused individual. The theft itself was nearly lost sight of in the psychiatrist's concern with pathology — those diseased events that preceded, resulted in, and survived the act of theft and were woven together to form the fabric of a pathological condition.

Two components in particular were carefully investigated — heredity and sexuality. The main concern in both cases was the reconstruction of the past in terms of the recent, allegedly criminal event. Mental disturbances in either parent, for example, or in a close relative assumed central importance. Sexual problems explained nervousness and tension in accused patients and were sought out as the key to maniacal behavior. The medical specialists looked for "sexual physiological accidents" or *situations critiques,* like menstration, pregnancy, and menopause, that led to what they called the "auto-toxic" condition.[13] These alone could serve as justification for certification of irresponsibility. Many of the women examined, not surprisingly, exhibited some "symptoms." In one study of 104 department store thieves examined, 35 were women between the ages of 15 and 24 undergoing menstruation; 10 were menopausal; and 5 were pregnant.[14] This meant that about half the women accused were immediately considered in a weakened and monomaniacally susceptible state.

In a similar group study of "60 to 80 medico-legal reports" — psychiatrists in general were often imprecise regarding the statistical aspects of their work — "many" of the women were discovered to be menopausal, widowed, suffering from irregular menses, or the loss of a mate. All were considered to have *prédispositions héréditaires.*[15]

Deviant behavior, therefore, could be traced to physiological origins — women were *diseased* by their sexuality. As a result, all women, even the most honest, were, at various periods in their lives — "genital stages" — susceptible to criminal behavior.[16] The most dangerous stage of all was menopause.[17] Pregnant women also suffered from their own special madness —*folie puerpérale* — that was extended in certain studies to include the period beginning with pregnancy until about forty days after delivery and encompassed menstruation as well.[18] Even when social factors were recognized as influencing deviant behavior in women, this was never completely to the exclusion of biological determinants.[19] Pyromania, dipsomania, homicidal and suicidal monomania were all labeled "menstrual psychoses." By including kleptomania on this list, correlations were established between women's menstrual cycles and shoplifting, the onset of menopause and shoplifting.[20] Women stole or committed other crimes because they were having problems of a pathological nature with their reproductive organs. The argument at its most extreme at the turn of the century was that all menstruating, lactating, ovulating, newly delivered, newly sexually initiated, and menopausal women were prone to crime.[21] Significantly, these categories were more slowly applied to working-class women.

In addition to the physiological approach, there was also the less widely held opinion that women sought sexual gratification through theft. Fetishism, the extreme obsession or mania for an object, could be physiologically based but certain specialists focused primarily on the perverted sexual pleasure women were said to experience in shoplifting. Orgasmic reactions were frequently recorded in the clinical case studies. "The sexually perverted fetishist draws her sensual pleasure, for example, from crumpling a certain fabric — generally silk. . . ."[22] As one women frankly explained it, she got more pleasure from her thefts than from "the father of her children."[23] Another woman under examination explained that she entered the Bon Marché in "a genuine state of joy," feeling much the same as if she were going to meet a lover.[24] Yet even in the cases of diagnosed sexual depravity and fetishism, perversions were often traced to physiological and not only psychological origins.

A case that exemplifies many of the identifying characteristics is Madame M., widow of an estate agent. When caught in the act of shoplifting, she claimed that she didn't know what she was doing, that she was unable to stop herself. Nervous by temperament, she was found to have "marked hereditary antecedents." It was considered significant that her mother was an alcoholic, her aunt mentally ill, and that her mother's brother had committed suicide. Madame M. herself had had convulsions in early childhood and had experienced tremendous difficulty at the beginning of her menstrual history. She reportedly suffered monthly from headaches and bodyaches and had frequent attacks of nerves. Her crime was that she had stolen a remnant of alpaca wool valued at 43 francs. The medical assessment concluded that "the idea of possessing it had dominated her to the point of subjugating her will and her reason." She was acquitted of the crime of theft by virtue of irresponsibility.[25]

Another typical case involved Madame C., a 52-year-old woman who was declared to have a pathological family history. Her father was an alcoholic and her mother a paralytic. Having stolen a chicken from a display case, she claimed that she had been robbed of her wallet and could not pay for it. In reconstructing her past, the examining specialist discovered that Madame C. had been caught stealing twice before, once in 1857 and again in 1871, both times during pregnancies. Widowed in 1890, she had remarried an older man who, the testimony tells us, was unable to control her. She, too, was acquitted.[26]

Family problems and sexual disturbances — either physical or emotional — were areas of inquiry general enough to have been self-fulfilling in most cases. Psychiatrists appear to have found what they were looking for with great frequency. Women with regular or difficult pregnancies, bad marriages, dead husbands, irregular cycles, menopause, nervous conditions, bad health, and suicidal inclinations were all considered prime candidates for the designation of kleptomania.

Men, too, could be designated kleptomaniacs but here the exception proved the rule. One 40-year-old doctor stole books, which, as Dr. Paul Granier observed, he did not need. It was discovered that in his childhood he had displayed neurasthenic and hysterical tendencies and that later he engaged frequently in masturbation. In his adult life problems of sexual performance and premature ejaculation were followed by frenzies of maniacal theft.[27] Another male kleptomaniac displayed a nervous temperament and marked hereditary antecedents. His mother was an alcoholic who went mad; his mother's sister had been mad from the age of 20. An uncle, also on the mother's side of the family, had committed suicide. This man, like so many women with similar case histories, was judged to be a kleptomaniac.[28] A 56-year-old man whose thefts were discovered only after his death and who had filled three apartments with contraband pictures, medallions, umbrellas, place settings, and the like, was judged to be kleptomaniacal simply because the objects he stole were considered to be useless and because the man made no profit from his thefts.[29] The particular issue of utility, especially striking in the cases of these two men, is one that we shall return to shortly.

With regard to physical pathology, the exception also proved the rule. Even in cases where no sickness was evident, the examining specialist was capable of locating a problem. One young woman in excellent health with a "robust constitution" and "regular menses" was, nevertheless, certified as a kleptomaniac by the examining specialist. She had been caught stealing silk cloth, a camisole, two pillowcases, and two shawls in Au Printemps. The magistrate listed large quantities of other materials found hidden in her home: twenty-two wool and silk remnants, twenty-four handkerchiefs, fifty-six pairs of black stockings, and thirty-three pairs of wool socks. The dilemma was further complicated by the absence of a hereditary pathology. But it was considered critical that she, as the wife of a wine merchant, was rich enough to buy whatever she had stolen. The psychiatrist concluded that she was suffering from "a weakness of spirit," demonstrated in visions and loss of hearing she had experienced years before following her marriage. This otherwise forgotten moment in her history became crucial in the diagnosis of maniacal behavior.[30]

On the whole, then, what were called women's sicknesses, hysteria, and hereditary weaknesses became the essential elements in the etiology of kleptomania. The examining specialist clearly sought these out when he encountered a woman of the bourgeoisie charged with theft. The significance of the diagnosis, however, goes beyond menstrual psychoses and neurotic mothers. But before turning to its social meaning, a few words should be said about the intellectual history of the diagnosis in the nineteenth century.

Theories of Kleptomania. Kleptomania was "discovered" by André Matthey, a Swiss doctor whose work appeared in France in 1816.[31] The diagnosis of stealing as a form of madness existed before that time but he was important in formulating a theory of certain behavior, *klopémanie* as he called it, that was monomaniacal because of the impulsive nature of the thefts.

Monomania stood as an amorphous medical term intended to describe delirium or obsession with an object — for Matthey it was the object stolen, which was often insignificant and of little value. Although women who stole had been released by the courts before 1816 for mental imbalance,[32] they did not have the benefit of a systematic judicial defense before Matthey's work laid the groundwork for it.

The concept of kleptomania as a legal designation for an extenuating circumstance in the commission of a crime received fuller development in 1840 by Dr. Marc, a leading forensic specialist and physician to Louis-Philippe. In acknowledging that certain individuals were driven to steal by an abnormal, persistent impulse that was not characterized by need, Marc built upon the work of Matthey, Pinel and Esquirol. The first to use the word *kleptomanie,* he defined it rather loosely as "a distinctive, irresistible tendency to steal."[33] Marc was concerned above all with the social position and background of the accused.

In his discussion of the significance of heredity, Marc pointed the way for later works. And he foreran the heavy emphasis placed on biological determinants in the late nineteenth century, when he spoke of the influence of "certain secretions and excretions," like milk and menstrual flow, and the *perturbations nerveuses* caused by pregnancy.[34] Other factors that he considered worthy of the special attention of the forensic specialist were: the value of the object stolen, and the social class and educational level of the culprit. It is safe to assert that if the patient was both bourgeois and female, certification as a kleptomaniac was a virtual certainty. In the case of a man, bourgeois origins and the theft of an apparently useless object resulted in the same diagnosis.

The case studies of Matthey and Marc were the models for later observations and were cited regularly in subsequent works. Their investigations and the diagnoses they produced differed substantially from later studies only in locale of the crime: unlike Matthey and Marc, who wrote before the creation of the Bon Marché or Au Printemps, most works after mid-century identified kleptomania exclusively with the newly created department stores. In addition, men were more frequently mentioned in earlier works, although they remained a distinct minority both before and after mid-century. In other criteria, however, there was a predictable similarity. In the treatises kleptomaniacs were above all from bourgeois families stealing objects they apparently did not need and should have been able to pay for. The cases proliferated.

Twenty years later Morel extended the concern with family history even further with his notion of *dégénérescence*.[35] What for Marc had been an unhealthy tendency in an otherwise healthy person now emerged in Morel's work as a symptom, a syndrome indicating abnormality.[36] Morel influenced the further acceptance of kleptomania as a defense plea for acquittal. In the 1880s and 1890s Magnan and his disciples augmented Morel's work and publicized it with a more developed concept of *dégénérescence mentale héréditaire*.[37] Magnan's contribution to the theory of kleptomania in forensic medicine came at the height of the "epidemic" of department store thefts and at the moment when the forensic specialist was being more formally integrated into judicial investigation procedures.

At about the same time, kleptomania was also being diagnosed more explicitly as another form of hysterical behavior — *impulsion au vol du forme hystérique* — by Janet and Raymond in their influential clinical study, *Névroses et idées fixes*.[38] These alienists insisted on the relationship between the *idée fixe* and hysteria in "weak spirits," that is, kleptomaniacs. The work of Raymond and Janet joined a body of psychiatric studies in general agreement about the causes and symptoms of kleptomania, in spite of a variety of umbrella terms for the phenomenon: *vol morbide, propension instinctive, monomanie instinctive, folie impulsive, folie lucide*.[39] Accompanying the diversity of associations was a general agreement that victims of kleptomania stole because of a loss of reason, either temporary or hereditary, and were motivated by physiological malfunction, sexual frustration, or both.

The kleptomania case studies embodied themes that were representative of a larger body of literature on women and women's illnesses that appeared in France in the 1880s and 1890s. For the later decade alone, Susanna Barrows has estimated that 372 books were published about women including 149 "devoted to their 'illnesses and hygiene'."[40] In her study, *Distorting Mirrors*, Barrows explains, "On at least one issue, most French scientists could agree. Women, they argued, were rightly described as the 'weaker sex.' When compared to men, females were less intelligent, more emotional, and more susceptible to violent outbursts and mental illness."[41] The kleptomania case studies were another proof of female inferiority.

We can see in this brief survey of the theoretical development of the designation, as well as in the case studies themselves, that the kleptomania diagnosis incorporated assumptions from a growing body of literature about women's sicknesses and, in turn, used these assumptions to absolve what formerly had been considered criminal behavior. Furthermore, through the kleptomania diagnosis, we will now consider a new professional awareness of patterns of consumption, the causes of crime, and women as criminals. Kleptomania itself stands as a description of a mutation in bourgeois behavior. As with mutations in nature, it has something to tell us about the species in which it occurred — in this case, bourgeois society of late nineteenth-century France.

The Social Context. In the first place, the kleptomania diagnosis contributed to a critique of consumption and the consumer revolution at the end of the nineteenth century. As we have seen, kleptomania was necessarily embedded in new patterns of consumption associated with the rise of the department store and mass retailing after mid-century. Several recent studies have, from different perspectives, signalled the transformation in consumption and its implications for bourgeois culture in this period.[42] The rise of the "irresistible cult of consumption"[43] involved moral and ethical issues in a growing literature of social criticism with kleptomania constituting only a more deviant form of the need to consume.

Suprisingly, certain medical experts were, in spite of the dominance of biologically grounded analysis in the profession, among the first to view kleptomania as a means of evaluating the changing habits of the bourgeoisie, as an indicator of an important social change. This shift toward the social meaning of the phenomenon and its utility as a social critique constituted a rejection of exclusively biological and hereditary determinants. By 1900 some medical experts were taking a different tack closer to a consumerist analysis of the behavior than to the monomaniacal designation by placing the blame for the epidemic on the department stores. Open display cases and easily accessible goods were temptations "better than Satan himself could devise,"[44] placed in the path of weak and impressionable creatures. The reorientation reflected a new emphasis on environmental factors. Large retailers created artificial needs for goods by "seducing" their clients with clever advertising and marketing. It was reported that some women were "driven" to go to stores, "visiting the Bon Marché, the Louvre, Au Printemps every day in the same way that they paid weekly visits to Church."[45]

Shopping patterns and expectations were changing. The department store created new opportunities for handling goods not possible in the smaller boutiques and provided greater freedom to customers to pocket these goods in its more anonymous atmosphere. Acquisition became a form of fulfillment in itself, regardless of the utility of the object. After all, weren't the department stores trying to sell these women what they did not need?

This consumerist point of view also permitted a reconsideration of a critical element in the kleptomania diagnosis: hoarding of goods no longer demonstrated a loss of will or reason. We can look at the case of a 35-year-old man who stole daily for a six-month period, amassing the goods in his home. He, like most female kleptomaniacs, was symptomatically nervous, headachy, pale, and slept little. But while he was stealing, as he later lucidly testified, "I was happy. . . . I felt pleasure at possessing, at knowing that these things were mine."[46] Similar claims for happiness and fulfillment through theft were made by female kleptomaniacs.[47] Dubuisson and Vigouroux argued that the need to acquire and possess was normal: the kleptomaniac only extended that need beyond acceptable limits.[48]

This consumerist concept of utility and need permitted, therefore, a different interpretation of the acts of women who stole. The identifying characteristic in the new consumerist culture was not the purchase or even the use of goods — it was the possession of them. Nor, contrary to the findings of forensic specialists, did all women steal goods that were useless in a more traditional sense. One woman certified for maniacal behavior was proud that she had never spent any money on her dresses or those of her daughters, although they were always carefully and stylishly groomed.[49] Utility was in certain cases deliberately and systematically considered. And if it was true that kleptomaniacs were stealing apparently useless goods, did that not also mean that many honest women were buying them?

An additional qualification to the diagnosis put forward by Antheaume, a psychiatrist concerned with debunking the kleptomania "fiction," was that, although the women who stole were often the wives of wealthy men, they did not always have control over the purse strings. One woman questioned by him confessed to stealing silk stockings to please her lover and to avoid the suspicions of her frugal husband.[50] A new consumer mentality also played a central role in the justification of one of Dr. Dubuisson's patients. Having spent 60 francs during a visit to a department store, she stole a change purse worth 15 sous as a present for her cook: "I stole it because, having made a number of purchases with cash, I felt that this little addition was my due."[51] In so explaining her act, this woman combined a peculiar sense of justice with an adversarial concept of herself in relation to the department store to produce a mental outlook both thoroughly modern and criminal — "it was my due."

Laccasagne's condemnation of consumerism fostered by department stores was especially strong. They were for him "dangerous places"[52]: "These display-case provocations are one of the factors of theft. They exist in order to arouse desire. They are the preparation of an illusion. They fascinate the client, dazzle her with their disturbing exhibition. [Department stores] stir up the social order and can be called the 'apértifs' of crime."[53]

From this point of view, Laccasagne developed several categories of kleptomania that constituted a general critique of consumption. Laccasagne's kleptomaniacs were women overwhelmed by the presence of goods, standing in the middle of the vast halls of the new department stores, disoriented, "basking in the dazzling brightness of the chains of electric lamps."[54] In spite of his emphasis on female susceptibility of the *collectionneuse* and *deséquilibrée*, Lacassagne's analysis is one more closely linked to a theory of consumerism than to one based on psycho-sexual disturbances.

If Lacassagne was concerned with the satanic workings of the department store, it was Emile Zola who described its devilish ruler. In the person of M. Mouret, a mass retailing genius, we are given the fictitious representation of a department-store owner, the "conqueror of women," someone who trapped women and held them captive in his "temple." "He racked his brains day and night in search of bright, new ideas" to intoxicate, flatter, exploit, and ensnare female customers. The secret behind his fabulous success, Zola tells us, was the knowledge that women who thought they were getting a bargain would buy things they didn't need. For some of Zola's female shoppers, theft was the ultimate bargain, shoplifting no more than another means of consumption.[55]

On one level, then, there is an evolution apparent in the case studies (and matched in Zola's fictional representations) away from a pathological vision of femaleness and toward a more socially reflexive analysis. Woman was still, of course, a "weak spirit," governed by her senses and with low moral strength in the latter version as in the former. The difference was that there was now a social base to her reprehensible acts. The shift was a mild but perceptible one — not a stampede — in the forensic literature of late nineteenth-century France.

A second area in which the kleptomania diagnosis incorporated, if not always mirrored, aspects of changing social meanings was criminology, the study of crime and its causes. Shoplifting by bourgeois women was a perplexing problem for criminological specialists because it seemingly contradicted traditional notions of both bourgeois and criminal behavior. Conventional wisdom explained theft primarily in terms of need and deprivation, or moral failures associated with these factors. As we have seen in the work of Marc and later forensic specialists, the absence of need had become the chief identifying characteristic of shoplifting by bourgeois women. A new formulation was required: if working-class men and women stole because they were needy or even greedy, bouregois women stole because they were sick. The extenuating circumstance moved with a new legitimacy to center stage of the judicial process.

Kleptomania also seemed to defy the emphasis placed in sociological theory on the environment. Bad homes, bad upbringing, bad friends, criminologists reassured, caused crime. But these shoplifters were otherwise respectable and honest women who were *bien élevées* and who came from and lived in solid family environments. As Zola's department-store owner Mouret pointed out, "Very well-bred women do it. Last week we had a pharmacist's sister and a court counsellor's wife."[56] Kleptomania is one of the best examples of the tension between class and crime and of the debate surrounding environment and crime within criminology. Beginning from a class-based issue — thefts committed by bourgeois women — there emerged a new emphasis on personality and family history as explanatory factors in the commission of a crime. The kleptomania diagnosis indicated a general shift in criminological theory at the end of the century away from issues associated with class and toward factors surrounding personality formation as explanations for crime. Even though this particular process involving bourgeois women resulted temporarily in the decriminalization of behavior, it contributed to and drew upon a general orientation toward the mediation of the specialists, forensic doctors and psychiatrists, who interposed themselves between the accused and the courts.

Finally, in terms of criminality and behavior, the glimpses provided by the diagnosis into the lives of bourgeois families is startling. The frequency of madness, depression, drunkenness, suicide, and sexual disturbances among these women, their mates, and close relatives reveals a darker side of bourgeois culture worthy of further exploration. These seething and troubled family backgrounds exposed in the case studies require a broader study of bourgeois values and virtues. What can be affirmed here is that the case studies of bourgeois women who stole suggest some of the tensions and strains in the private world of the bourgeoisie. The intention has been to show that an episode in forensic history — the moment at which the kleptomania diagnosis was at its peak — reflected a series of assumptions about woman's nature, about consumption, and about crime, that were in the process of change in late nineteenth-century France.

FOOTNOTES

1. *Au Bonheur des dames* (Paris, 1971), p. 277.

2. For a different but complementary approach to the relationship between a diagnosis, hysteria, and politics in the same period, see Jan Goldstein, "The Hysteria Diagnosis and the Politics of Anti-Clericalism," *Journal of Modern History* (June, 1982), 54: 209-239.

3. Alexandre Lacassagne, "Les Vols à l'étalage et dans les grands magasins," *Revue de l'Hypnotisme et de la Psychologie Physiologique* (September, 1896), II: 77.

4. By the 1890s department-store owners recognized the necessity of special policing forces to patrol both the customers and the salesclerks. Only a handful of inspectors — usually six men and six women — policed the larger department stores. They were vastly outnumbered, it was felt, in their losing battle against customer crime. Roger Didier, *Les Vols des grands magasins* (Paris, 1929), pp. 110-11.

5. Vicomte d'Avenel, *Le Mécanisme de la vie moderne* (Paris, 1896), p. 71.

6. Ibid., pp. 75-76. Didier further estimated that the number of arrests made constituted about one-third of the actual thefts committed. *Les Vols des grands magasins*, p. 109.

7. J. Rogues de Fursac, *Manuel de psychiatrie* (Paris, 1903), p. 280.

8. Michael Miller astutely observes the open-endedness of these designations in *The Bon Marché: Bourgeois Culture and the Department Store* (Princeton, 1981), pp. 198-99.

9. Paul Dubuisson, *Les Voleuses de grands magasins* (Paris, n.d.), p. 2.

10. Roger Dupouy, "De la Kleptomanie," *Journal de Psychologie normale et Pathologique* (September-October, 1905), II: 412.

11. Camille Granier, *La Femme criminelle* (Paris, 1906), p. 248. Dr. Trélat claimed that kleptomania was common among imbeciles, *La Folie lucide, étudiee et considerée au point de vue de la famille at de la société* (Paris, 1861), p. 261.

12. Dubuisson was explicit in his discussion of arrested development, "hereditary" and "constitutional" causes of low intelligence, and their links with kleptomania, *Les Voleuses*, pp. 67-71.

13. "The psychoses of auto-toxication are more than an hypothesis subject to doubt thanks to the interesting work of E. Régis ["Les Psychoses d'intoxication," *Archives de Neurologie* (1899)] and the applications of it to pregnancy that have been made by Saint-Blaise [G. Bouffe de Saint-Blaise, *Les Auto-intoxications de la grossesse* (Paris, 1899)]," cited in G. Morache, *La Responsabilité. Etude de socio-biologie et de médecine-légale* (Paris, 1906), p. 208.

14. A. Pitres and E. Régis, *Les Obsessions et les impulsions* (Paris, 1902), recapitulates this study conducted at the Depôt de la Préfecture de police between 1868 and 1881 by Dr. Legrand du Saulle, p. 320. Dr. Legrand du Saulle developed his observations in more detail in *Les Hysteriques. Etat physique et état mental. Actes insolites, délictueux et criminels* (Paris, 1883).

15. Dr. Charles Lunier, "Des Vols aux étalages," in *Annales Médico-Psychologiques* (September 1880), pp. 213-214.

16. Morache, *La Responsabilité*, pp. 203-204.

17. Ibid., pp. 207-208.

18. L.V. Marcé, *Traité de la folie des femmes enceintes, des nouvelles accouchées et des nourrices et consideration médico-légales qui se rattachent à ce sujet* (Paris, 1858), pp. 1-2.

19. Louis Proal, *La Criminalité feminine* (Paris, 1890).

20. Séverin Icard, *La Femme pendant la période menstruelle, étude de psychologie morbide et de médecine légale* (Paris, 1890).

21. A work that recognized physiological determinants as well as economic and class correlates is: Camille Granier, *La Femme criminelle*.

22. Dupouy, "De la Kleptomanie," pp. 412-413.

23. Ibid., p. 413.

24. A. Miaret, *La Responsabilité. Etude psycho-physiologique* (Montpellier, 1907), pp. 90-91.

25. H. Dagonet, *Traité des maladies mentales* (Paris, 1894), pp. 464-465.

26. Dubuisson, *Les Voleuses*, pp. 67-70.

27. Paul Granier, *La Folie à Paris. Etude statistique, clinique et médico-légale* (Paris, 1890).

28. Dr. Girard, *Annales Médico-Psychologiques* (1845) cited in Dr. Dagonet, *Traité de maladies mentales,* p. 464.

29. Trélat, *La Folie lucide,* pp. 263-64.

30. Dubuisson, *Les Voleuses,* pp. 70-72.

31. André Matthey, *Nouvelles recherches sur les maladies de l'esprit, precédees de considérations sur les difficultés de l'art de guérir* (Paris, 1816).

32. The earliest nineteenth-century case is cited in C.C.H. Marc, *De la Folie considérée dans ses rapports avec les questions médico-judiciaires* (Paris, 1840), II: 464-465.

33. Ibid.

34. Ibid., II: 260-261.

35. B.A. Morel, *Traité des maladies mentales* (Paris, 1860).

36. Dubuisson, *Les voleuses,* pp. 11-12.

37. V. Magnan, *Leçons cliniques sur les maladies mentales. Le délire chronique* (Paris, 1890); *Recherches sur les centres nerveux. Pathologie et physiologie pathologique* (Paris, 1876). François Boissier and Georges Lachaux, "Contribution à l'étude clinique de la kleptomanie," *Annales Médico-Psychologiques* (January 1894), 19:42-54. Boissier and Lachaux recognized Magnan as "our master" (p. 43).

38. P. Janet and F. Raymond, *Névroses et idées fixes,* volume 2: *Fragments des leçons cliniques du mardi sur les névroses, les maladies produites par les émotions, les idées obsédantes et leur traitement* (Paris, 1898).

39. Pitres and Régis, *Les Obsessions,* pp. 316-323, provides a good overview of the use of these terms in relation to kleptomania.

40. Susanna Barrows, *Distorting Mirrors: Visions of the Crowd in Late Nineteenth-Century France* (New Haven, 1981), p. 46.

41. Ibid., p. 57.

42. Michael Miller's *The Bon Marché* provides a first-rate treatment of these developments. The work is more than the study of an individual store. It convincingly analyzes "bourgeois culture" in the period 1869 to 1920 and offers important insights to its consumerist component. Rosalind H. Williams, *Dream Worlds: Mass Consumption in Late Nineteenth-Century France* (Berkeley, 1982) analyzes the development of "consumer lifestyles" and the late nineteenth-century critique of the phenomenon. From a different perspective, Bonnie G. Smith, *Ladies of the Leisure Class: The Bourgeoises of Northern France in the Nineteenth Century* (Princeton, 1981) considers the role played by consumption in the domestic world of the bourgeoisie of northern France. New needs appeared that gave definition and order to the world of women.

43. Miller, *The Bon Marché,* p. 178.

44. Dubuisson, *Les Voleuses,* p. 43.

45. *Ibid.,* pp. 42-43.

46. Ibid., pp. 78-83.

47. Magnan, *Recherches,* p. 343.

48. P. Dubuisson and A. Vigoroux, *Responsabilité pénale et folie. Etude médico-legale* (Paris, 1911).

49. Trélat, *La Folie lucide,* pp. 264-265.

50. A. Antheaume, *Le Roman d'une épidémie parisienne. La kleptomanie?* (Paris, n.d.), pp. 30-31.

51. Dubuisson cited in Lacassagne, "Les Vols à l'étalage," p. 81.

52. Lacassagne, "Les Vols à l'étalage," p. 82.

53. Ibid., pp. 77-78.

54. Didier, *Les Vols,* pp. 23-26.

55. Zola, *Au Bonheur,* chapter 9.

56. Ibid., p. 277.

8.

WORK, GENDER AND THE ARTISAN TRADITION
IN NEW ENGLAND SHOEMAKING, 1780-1860

Mary H. Blewett

In the 1970s American labor history was transformed into a new labor history by the influential work of British historians, especially Edward P. Thompson. Following Thompson's model of examining the cultural expressions of working-class experience, American scholars looked at artisan life in the pre-industrial cities and towns of the Eastern seaboard and located a major source of resistance to early capitalism in artisan culture. Seventies historiography was also challenged by the development of women's history as a distinct field in social history, but many labor historians who were swift to study worker culture concentrated on the cultural, religious and political activities of male artisans, generally assuming that the experience of other family members was subsumed under male experience or was indistinguishable from it.[1] These historians need to borrow the analysis of gender relations in the family and at work from women's history to fully realize the meaning of worker culture and, in the case of pre-industrial artisan life, understand the limitations which the gender perceptions of artisan ideology placed on labor protest. The work of Thomas Dublin on the Lowell mill operatives best combined the new labor history with women's history to analyze the work experience and culture of women in early industrial capitalism.[2] Dublin's work, however, located the ideological source of labor protest among the textile operatives, not in artisan culture, but in the ideology of the Yankee freehold farmer.

This essay examines the relationship between gender and work in the shoe industry in Essex County, Massachusetts before the Civil War. Large numbers of men and women were employed in the putting-out system of domestic production as the boot and shoe industry of New England expanded prior to 1860. Pre-industrial methods of shoemaking involved an initially close relationship between work and family, production and the home, in which the interrelationships of gender and work can be observed. Men and women shared the work and traditions of artisan life in the family, but each gender experienced work, culture and consciousness in different ways. What were the attitudes of male artisans toward women who worked in shoe production and how did these attitudes shape artisan ideology? Did the cultural traditions and ideology of artisan life reflect or serve the interests of pre-industrial women workers who were drawn into production in the early nineteenth century? How did the differences in gender and work affect the ability of artisans to protest the rise of industrialization?

The pre-industrial phase of New England shoe production was a golden age of artisan life, and shoemakers were central to the rise of worker protest against early industrial capitalism. The group experience of training and work in the apprentice system and its traditions of mutual obligation defined artisan culture. Its locus was the shoe shop where the craft was learned and practiced. Decentralized production allowed groups of male artisans significant control over the process of work and fostered a strong tradition of militant resistance to the reorganization of production by employers. Its mechanics' ideology, analyzed by Paul Faler for the shoemakers of Lynn, Massachusetts, rested on the labor theory of value and republicanism as a political heritage from the American Revolution. Alan Dawley has seen this "equal rights" ideology as central to the activities of protesting shoemakers throughout most of the nineteenth century.[3] The ideology of artisan culture also included perceptions of gender relationships in the family and at work which defined and separated the roles of men and women and based collective action on the craftsman and householder.

For women workers, the pre-industrial period was a time of submersion in the family and in the family wage economy. The sexual division of labor placed them outside of the vitality of life, politics and work which centered in the artisan shop.[4] While male artisans defended their craft and its traditions before 1860, women workers experienced the cutting edge of change in the reorganization of work after 1780: a sexual division of labor which denied them craft status, the disassociation of their work from the family labor system, the increasingly direct contact of the individual worker with the employer, the isolation and vulnerability of the outworker and the mechanization and centralization of work in the factory. These changes in women's work affected artisan shoemakers. They faced a loss of control over the coordination of production and a loss of wages for the family economy. In the 1850s mechanization and centralization of women's work altered the size and composition of the male work force, a factor which helped precipitate in 1860 the largest pre-Civil War demonstration of labor protest. However, for many women workers in factory production, the artisan tradition of collective resistance represented neither their work nor their cultural experience. This new generation of female factory workers came into conflict with the striking shoemakers of Lynn over the objectives and strategy of the regional strike in 1860. This division of interests weakened labor protest in 1860 and pointed to the conflict between ideology and reality in the gender perceptions of New England artisans. Women shared the work in shoe production with men, but after 1860 they would need to create an ideology to justify labor protest based on their distinct experience. To understand this experience before 1860 will enrich the meaning of worker culture in early industrialization. The submersion of women's work experience within artisan culture has obscured the penetration of home-life and the work process by early capitalism and has sustained the illusion of the early nineteenth family as a refuge from the market place. The failure of artisans to perceive and accommodate the interests of women as workers weakened their ability to challenge the reorganization of work by early industrial capitalism.

How did women come to share the work of artisans? There is no evidence in primary or secondary sources of any female participation in colonial shoemaking. Men's work was either itinerant or custom work. In the 1750s higher standards for the production of women's shoes based on the European artisan model were introduced in Lynn by John Dagyr, and the master-journeyman-apprentice system was expanded to teach and practice a more refined craft. This system spread throughout Essex County, Massachusetts and was also common in New York, Pennsylvania and New Jersey.[5] Before the expansion of the artisan system, shoemakers had worked alone in the kitchens of their houses (or other people's houses), in an el or an attached shed. This was a domestic setting for work where shared family labor might have evolved as in hosiery making or spinning and weaving in England. However, with the expansion of the artisan system and an increase in production, shoemaking required its own work space to accomodate several men and boys on various levels of the craft. A small out-building called a "ten footer" began to appear in Essex County by the 1780s as a self-contained work area for men.[6] Many wives must have been pleased to rid their kitchens of the clutter, dirt and smell of the shoemaker's paraphernalia.

In the 1780s with the rise of tariff protection, the decline of English imports and the development of a potentially large domestic market, merchant capitalists began to expand production of shoes for a ready-to-wear market. John R. Commons analyzed the evolution of production in the industry and saw the crucial factors as new markets and the influence of competitive forces acting to stimulate the investment of capital and labor in shoemaking. Paul Faler also emphasized the expansion of markets in the transformation of production. Dawley focused on the primary role of the merchant capitalist who supplied the artisan shoemaker with leather, paid him wages and sought out new markets for shoes. Commons, Faler and Dawley ignored the implications of the introduction of the sexual division of labor into shoemaking as a craft. They do, however, point to the rough division of labor in the shoe shop in the 1780s: the separation of the major steps of shoemaking into cutting, sewing and making.[7] The shoemaker continued to be trained as an apprentice to make the entire shoe. When the division of men's work did not fill the demands of production, a solution was found within the shoemaking family.

The motive for the recruitment of women in shoemaking families to new work appears to have been made in the context of a shift in the control of profits as production expanded between 1780 and 1810. Production was expanded by merchant capitalists who bought leather and provided it to shoemakers. The merchant capitalist owned the shoes and marketed them. This control over raw materials meant control of profits as all cordwainers knew, and master shoemakers borrowed capital if they could to purchase leather.[8] Those shoemakers who owned no leather and who accepted work from capitalists had only their labor from which to profit. They divided up the work among the men in their shops and augmented their wage income from labor by recruiting additional family members for work: their women. The male head of the shoemaking family disciplined and controlled women's work in the home. The merchant capitalist, who had no control over the assignment of work in the artisan shop or family, welcomed the new potential for production. As entrepreneurs, they paid no wages directly to women workers and did not need to supervise their work. By adapting to the new work, women added their traditional household labor to their family's income in ways which continued to permit them to combine family and work roles.[9]

Why didn't the apprentices do the sewing of uppers to meet the needs of expanded production? They had learned the skill as part of their apprenticeship, and some did sew uppers whenever bottlenecks in production occurred. Specialization in sewing uppers, however, would have disrupted the apprenticeship system as an orientation to the male world of the artisan and to its work, rituals and hierarchy of subordination and dominance, as well as limiting the various services apprentices provided for the master and journeymen. To use apprentices would not have solved the labor shortage in an expanding market, for in a few years apprentices would become journeymen, no longer available to sew seams. Some more dependable source of new labor was needed, one which the capitalist would accept in the interests of expanded production, yet would not have to pay wages or supervise. The utilization of women in shoemaking families was a solution that would avoid changes in the apprentice system, meet the needs of both capitalist and artisan and threaten no alteration in the traditional patterns of gender formation. The origins of the sexual division of labor in the shoemaking craft was a conscious decision made by artisans and accepted by merchant capitalists to expand production.

Historians of the New England shoe industry have regarded the recruitment of female labor in the late eighteenth century as the natural evolution or inevitable outgrowth of women's involvement in household work or as the fitting of an excess female population in Essex County into a work process which drew on their abilities as needleworkers.[10] The recruitment of women in shoemaking families was instead a carefully controlled assignment of work designed to fit the role of women and to maintain gender relationships in the family, while preserving the artisan training system in its social as well as its craft aspect. Women were recruited to only a small part of the work, the sewing of the upper part of the shoe, and not to the craft itself. They were barred from apprenticeships and group work and isolated from the center of artisan life: the shoe shop. The artisan shop has come to be seen by historians as the center of pre-industrial political and cultural life for New England shoemakers and the source of the ideology and consciousness which many regard as representing the origins of the American working class. It was a world of men and boys.

The introduction of the sexual division of labor into an artisan craft represented a major change in the mode of production. Work was redefined and relocated, new words were coined and new procedures devised for supervision. The work assigned to women took on social meanings appropriate to their gender. Female family members adapted their traditional needle skills to hand sew the leather uppers of shoes in their kitchens without disrupting their domestic duties or their child care tasks. Needle work on leather uppers, a relatively clean part of the job, was accompanied by a new tool designed exclusively for women's work: the shoe clamp. The woman shoeworker would not have to straddle a shoemaker's bench, but would use a long, flexible wooden clamp which rested on the floor and which she held between her knees, holding the pieces of shoe upper together and freeing her hands to ply her needle. Her work was given a new name: shoebinding, which became a major category of women's work in the early nineteenth century.[11]

Binders in shoemaking families earned no wages between the 1780s and the 1810s, but they did contribute their labor to family production and to the wage it commanded. The emergence of shoebinding testified to the adaptibility and persistence of women's labor in household production. At this time, women in Essex County had few alternatives to hard, seasonal agricultural work or barter to add income to their families. The introduction of the sexual division of labor into an artisan craft was carefully controlled, guaranteeing the subordinate role of women by separating the work of shoebinding from any knowledge of the other various skills of the craft and by maintaining separate work places for men and women.[12] These patterns survived the transformation of the industry into the factory system and, therefore, constituted a fundamental social dimension of work.

Although shoebinders worked in their kitchens where domestic tasks and child care continued, the artisan shop and its demands for work intruded. No work in the shop could proceed without a few pairs of sewn uppers. The binder's work in her kitchen was essential to the timing and pace of production in the shop, and she had to keep ahead of the requirements of the shop workers with a ready supply of sewn uppers.[13] Her kitchen was transformed into a workplace where external demands from the ten footer shaped her time and tasks. The collective nature of men's work in the shoe shop, the locus of artisan culture, supported a militant tradition of resistance to the reorganization of production. This tradition did not mirror the experience of women workers who had no craft status and did not share in the political and religious discussions in the shop. The relationship of binders to this tradition was limited by their isolation from group production and mediated through their role in the family.

There were, however, limits to the capacity of female members of shoemaking families to fulfill the needs of the shoe shop for sewn uppers. Increasing numbers of shoes per lot strained the family labor system. Around 1800, ten to fourteen pairs of shoes made up a unit of production. By 1820 fifty, sixty and seventy pairs per lot were common, as most capitalists had organized cutting operations into central shops. Because shoebinding was typically combined with domestic work, the capacity of the binder who was both wife and mother to complete work on large lots had limits. In a pinch for more labor, shoemakers recruited the wives and daughters of neighbors, but this required some kind of a payment.[14] Gradually after 1810, shoebinding, while still performed in the home, shifted to work paid first in goods (often factory-made textiles) and later in wages, provided to the worker by the shoe boss, and increasingly disassociated from the family labor system.[15]

The surviving account books of storekeepers and shoe bosses in Essex and neighboring Middlesex Counties between 1810 and 1830 illustrate the slow development of what would become a widespread practice of giving out work to shoebinders who then returned it to the central shop before it was given out to the makers.[16] By the 1820s homework for women in textiles had shifted decisively into the factory, and those women who wished to contribute income to their families but who also needed or wanted to remain at home had few alternatives: outwork in straw and palm leaf hat making, sewing coats and shirts and, increasingly in Essex County, binding shoes.[17] According to calculations based on the untitled stock book of one Lynn manufacturer (1830-1831), less than 20% of the work put-out by this shoe boss was given to shoemakers and their wives or daughters to make and bind as a family work unit. The rest of the work was given out in separate lots to individual shoemakers and shoebinders whose work was coordinated by the boss in the central shop.[18]

By the 1830s shoe manufacturers had assumed much of the responsibility for hiring binders for wages and replaced husbands and fathers as employers. Even if her husband made shoes, a binder might work on uppers for ladies' boots while her spouse made coarse work shoes for Southern slaves. This disassociation of women's work from the family labor system affected the ability of the shoemaker to coordinate the work process. The shoe boss assumed responsibility not only for hiring female workers, often from non-shoemaking families, but also directed and coordinated the work process from his central shop. The shoemaker had to wait, sometimes for hours, for the shoe boss to provide him with bound uppers.[19] The shift in the coordination of the work of binding and making to the central shop represented a decline in the power of artisans to exert control over the work process.

The disassociation of shoebinding and shoemaking, the direct payment of wages to the binder and the increasing control of women's work by the shoe boss made it essential for binders to organize themselves in order to protest against their employers.[20] Two outbreaks of early labor protest occurred in Eastern Massachusetts shoe towns in the early 1830s over persistent low wages for shoebinding despite a rising market for shoes. Although these women sought and received the support of organized shoemakers especially in Lynn, the shoebinders created separate societies to represent their interests and acted independently. They did not challenge the sexual division of labor, but saw themselves as women workers unjustly treated by their employers and organized to demand a response to their grievances. They also attempted to utilize the mechanics' ideology in new ways to justify their protest and argue for new rights for women.

The shoebinders of Reading and the surrounding towns in Essex and Middlesex Counties formed a society of two to three hundred members in the summer of 1831 to protest low wages and to obtain a uniform wage scale for binding various kinds of work. The objective of the society was to encourage binders to cooperate in resisting individual wage bargains with their shoe bosses, so that inexperienced women would not "work for nothing and find themselves [furnish their labor free]."

Five shoe bosses in the Reading area rejected the demands of the binders' society for increases in wages which they claimed had been customary for ten years. The shoe manufacturers maintained that ". . . we are unacquainted with this new mode of doing business, and firmly protest against it, but are willing to employ them [the binders of the Reading society] on fair and honorable terms as heretofore."[21] Although nothing more was published about the activities of the Reading society, these shoebinders in 1831 were conscious of the vulnerability of the individual woman worker outside of the family labor system. Drawing on their cultural identification with the dignity and independence of artisan life, they expressed expectations of fairness and good treatment from the shoe bosses and were critical of the unwillingness of employers to share the profits of a rising shoe market. Perhaps the most impressive aspect of this early case of collective resistance by shoebinders was the ability of women workers living in different towns to establish a network of protest.

Two years later shoebinders in Lynn organized more resistance. By 1833 there were about 1,500 women in Lynn who earned wages as shoebinders. A wage cut prompted over half of them to organize the "Female Society of Lynn and vicinity for the protection and promotion of Female Industry." In their public statements, the shoebinders voiced the mechanics' ideology, blending it with expressions of their grievances as wage earners and using it as a defense of the worth of their labor as female members of artisan families. Most important, however, was their claim to new rights: the right to public action as women and the right to support themselves respectably and independently on their wages, independently in the sense of making a significant contribution to the family wage economy.[22]

The Lynn binders who organized the Female Society met at the Friends' Meetinghouse on December 30, 1833 where, as the *Lynn Record* noted, women as well as men could speak freely in public. They were joined a few days later by 125 binders who met at the Methodist church in neighboring Saugus and adopted the same objectives, ideology and constitution.[23] In the preamble to the society's constitution, the Lynn binders pointed to ". . . a manifest error, a want of justice, and reasonable compensation to the females; which calls imperiously for redress. While the prices of their labour have been reduced, the business of their *employers* has appeared to be improving, and prosperous, enabling them to increase their wealth. *These things ought not so to be!*" Their demand for higher wages was based on the labor theory of value. As workers, they believed they were not earning a just compensation; their independence and respectability were threatened. Furthermore, this economic injustice enriched the shoe boss. This was a violation of the dignity of their labor and a "moral outrage."

To redress their grievances, the shoebinders of Lynn demanded an extension of the equal rights doctrine of the artisan tradition to women. "Equal rights should be extended to all — to the weaker sex as well as the stronger." Many of the women who attended the society's first meeting on December 30, 1833, the preamble claimed, either supported themselves or their families on their earnings as binders and had become dependent on their wage labor. The disadvantages that women experienced "by nature and custom" should not be aggravated by "unnecessary and unjust" treatment as workers. The preamble expressed the belief that ". . . women as well as men, have certain inalienable rights, among which is the right at all times of 'peaceably assembling to consult upon the common good.'" In this, the Lynn binders were responding to criticism that they were forming a combination against the manufacturers which endangered the town's prosperity. They replied that the shoe bosses combined together themselves to hold down wages and to pay the binders in store orders for goods. The women in the Lynn society equated their interests as workers with the interests of the community, regarding the welfare of the town as consisting, ". . . not in the aggrandizement of a few individuals, but in the general prosperity and welfare of the industrious and laboring classes."

The preamble went on to criticize the recent reduction in wages for shoebinding which prevented them from obtaining "a comfortable support." This concept represented the shoebinders' claim to a just wage, a feminine version of the "competency" sought by artisans, an income sufficient to support their families and permit a little savings for old age.[24] However, in computing the wage which would earn them their comfortable support, the shoebinders used as a measure — not their work in production — but their duties and responsibilities as female members of artisan families. The shoebinders used their gender roles as the wives, daughters and widows of New England mechanics to insist upon a wage level that would confer dignity and independence on them. They calculated the price of the household services that a wife performed as a seamstress, washwoman, nurse and maid and demanded a wage high enough to cover these expenses. By extending the analogy of wage work into their domestic sphere, the wives of mechanics who bound shoes were bridging over the gap between work and domesticity. For a daughter, wages should be high enough to cover room, board and personal upkeep so as not to constitute a drain upon her father's income nor induce her to leave home for factory work. As for a mechanic's widow with dependents, her wage level should ensure a livelihood without the necessity of applying to the town for poor relief.[25]

To be effective the Lynn shoebinders' society had to organize all working women in the local industry, whatever their attachment to the mechanic's family or dependence on their earnings. However, the ideology which the society's members borrowed from the artisan tradition and which they reshaped to their experiences of gender hierarchy within the family betrayed a contradiction between their demands for equal rights for men and women workers and the calculations of a just wage for women. Equal rights for women as workers suggested the primacy of work; wages computed on the expenses of household services indicated that, in family terms, domestic duties were primary for women. For the Lynn shoebinders, their gender role in the family and in artisan ideology transformed the labor theory of value into a measure of their domestic work.

The artisan shoemakers of Lynn promptly offered their support to the Female Society in early 1834, voting as a group to refuse to take work from any manufacturer not agreeing to the wages demanded by the binders. When the Lynn shoemakers had organized a Society of Journeymen Cordwainers in 1830 to defend the wages and privileges of the craft, they regarded the low wages paid to the shoebinders as an injury to themselves as male heads of families. "Look and see how they [the shoe bosses] have depressed the price of female labor, and reduced it down to almost nothing! This has an effect on us as husbands, as fathers, and as brothers."[26] They perceived the grievances of the binders strictly in family terms.

The mechanics and the wives, daughters and widows of mechanics found cooperation easy enough based on the sharing of cultural and work traditions in the family, but the public demand of the binders for a wage sufficient to make a reasonable contribution to family income and their use of the mechanics' ideology as their justification involved an explicit claim to new rights for women. The leadership of the society demanded a new moral role for women which involved public activity on behalf of new rights, and some of the leaders of the binders' society would continue this activity on behalf of public morality in the Lynn Female Anti-Slavery Society in 1836.[27] The shift of women's work out of the family labor system had carried with it implications for change in gender relationships. In the typology of traditionalist, loyalist and rebel developed by Paul Faler and Alan Dawley, the shoebinders of Lynn and Saugus in 1834 were early rebels. They saw their interests as workers opposed to those of their employers and regarded collective action as the only means to secure accustomed living standards and independence.[28] They added, importantly, the dimention of gender to the expression of their consciousness as workers.

By the summer of 1834 the Lynn shoebinders' society was in trouble; three-fourths of its members were working for wages below the society's scale or had not paid their dues. One of the society's leaders, probably the President Mary A. Russell, used the *Lynn Record* of June 18 to urge the lagging membership to become "a band of sisters, each considering the welfare of the society as her own peculiar interest." She referred to the example of ". . . that liberty which other females have, that of setting their own prices upon their work." In what appeared to have been a reference to the March 1834 turnouts of the Lowell textile operatives, the writer urged a similar firmness and determination from the binders to become "equally free from oppression." Plans to divide work, share wages during dull times, start a manufacturing cooperative and exhortations to "think seriously, make exertions, be not discouraged" produced little response.[29] The society fell apart as the Reading society had in 1831.

In her study of middle-class New England women from 1780 to 1835, Nancy Cott analyzed the emergence of women's sphere as a vocation based on gender after production and male workers had left the home. A cult of domesticity defined this sphere and encouraged the development of a group consciousness with a positive social role expressed as sisterhood. Cott argued that this sense of sisterhood was a pre-condition to nineteenth century feminism.[30] Working women in New England shoe production also experienced a sense of consciousness as a gender, defined not only by domesticity but also by their work for wages. Shoebinders did not face a shift of production out of the home, but an assignment of new work for women in the home and its intensification in the outwork system. The sexual division of labor in shoe production reinforced the idea of a separate sphere for women and provided a class basis for the cult of domesticity among working women. By the 1830's, however, the family labor system had given way to the employment of women directly by the shoe boss in the outwork system. Sharing the bonds of womanhood both in work and in their domestic sphere, shoebinders in 1834 tried to organize themselves in terms of a female community of workers committed to self improvement and the improvement of society. Mary Russell actively sought to extend the idea of sisterhood as an organizing principle, but the shoebinders of Lynn could only respond hesitantly. The conditions under which many shoebinders labored — isolated from each other, employed by the shoe boss outside a group labor system and combining wage work with domestic responsibilities — discouraged collective activity. The tensions between their relationship to the artisan system and its equal rights ideology and their subordinate role as females in the family were exposed by their arguments for a just wage for women. Neither the social relations of the artisan family nor the realities of working as a woman for a shoe boss encouraged the shoebinder of Lynn to identify with her working sister in the Lowell mills or conceive of herself as a worker capable of supporting herself who could unite with her peers to protest mistreatment.

The efforts of the Lynn Female Society had limited success in 1834. Payments in store orders were temporarily suspended, but wages for binding shoes never even approached the wages offered to women workers in textile factories. Instead of raising wages to local shoebinders, shoe bosses in Eastern Massachusetts built networks of rural outworkers throughout the region extending into New Hampshire and Maine. By 1837, more women (15,366) were involved in shoe production in Massachusetts than female workers (14,759) in cotton textile factories.[31] The decline in the importance of the shoemaking family as a work unit left wives increasingly dependent on their shoemaker husbands for economic support. As the shoe bosses became more important to the coordination of production and the recruitment of binders, the relationship between the shoemaker and his employer changed. The shoemaker was regarded less and less as a middle-man in the recruitment of outwork for the boss, who now ran the central shop and directed the work of both binder and maker. This change in the relationship between shoeworker and shoe boss plus the pressure on the family wage economy may be underlying reasons for the outbursts of collective activity among Essex County shoemakers in the 1840s.

The decade of the 1840s represented a high point of activism among shoemakers in Eastern Massachusetts, who organized on a regional basis and held conventions with other working men and women. The Cordwainers' Mutual Benefit Society of Lynn began to publish a labor paper, *The Awl*, in 1844 and tried to summon support for the society among women including shoebinders.[32] In the first issue of the *Awl* on July 17, 1844, the editors developed a constituency and a set of objectives which limited and subordinated women's relationship to their organization. Oblivious to the implications for women of the disassociation of shoebinding from the family labor system and into a vulnerable isolation from group work and artisan ideology, the shoemakers' society in the 1840s perceived women as persons whose lives were defined primarily by family and morality. The origins of these attitudes may lie in the adjustment of shoemakers to the new industrial morality developing in Lynn as described by Paul Faler or in the claim of Lynn women to the right to act publicly on behalf of moral causes such as the binders' society in 1834 and the anti-slavery society in 1936-38.[33] Women's activities in local temperance groups in Essex County and especially in Lynn in 1841-43 indicated a fervent dedication by female members of shoemaking families to the total abstinence cause of the Washingtonian societies of Lynn. The Washingtonians of Lynn were close to the cordwainer's society and emphasized the special moral role of females and their dedication to family interests.[34] The editors of the *Awl* vigorously sought the support of women, but the circumscribed position for women in the society offered most shoebinders no ideological or strategic foothold with which to associate themselves as workers with the society.

In the first issue, the clearest statement of the aims of the society was contained in a draft circular to "all brothers of the craft" throughout New England.[35] The organization was seeking uniform wages for shoemaking in all New England shoe towns in order to restore the economic and social status of shoemakers in a society which they perceived as rapidly developing invidious class distinctions. The denial of a competency or reasonable income which would support an artisan's family comfortably and supply for old age threatened the equality and rights which freemen had won in the American Revolution. The society of cordwainers was especially sensitive to the declining status of those whose only wealth lay in the useful pursuit of a trade. The *Awl* championed the fundamental values of manly labor and linked its interests with all mechanics and artisans, as well as with the female operatives in the textile mills of New England, and with all working people, male or female, free or slave, who could not live decently and respectably in the economy of the 1840s.

At a meeting of the society on June 29, 1844, the members agreed to urge "the ladies" to lend their support and influence to the men's organization. Membership in the society was, however, defined by craft. The sexual division of labor prevented women from becoming members by learning the craft, although the society did accept as members three women trained as cordwainers: Mrs. Eliza Tuttle and two female apprentices.[36] The appeal for the presence of the ladies at the society's meetings became a persistent theme in the *Awl* during its year and a half of publication. The presence of these ladies, like the membership of Mrs. Tuttle, was to be used for its exemplary and, more importantly, for its moral influence. These requests for women to attend the society's meetings every Saturday night at the Town Hall were predicated not on their status as wage-earners or their work as shoebinders, but on their abilities as wives, mothers and sweethearts to persuade other shoemakers in Lynn to join.[37] The economic interests of most women in the objectives of the society were assumed to be familial: by bettering the wages of men — be they husbands, fathers or sons — women's own interests would be served.

In the December 21 issue of the *Awl*, the editors published under the title, "Woman," a special appeal for female support which illustrated how they viewed the nature of women and the limits this view placed on women's involvement in the activities of the society. Women were perceived as moral beings and were called upon to "hallow and enoble" the objectives of the society. The appeal to them was based on their capacity for self-sacrifice. The editors sought to enlist their energies to serve the interests of others; "the poor and down-trodden" and "her lovely sisters toiling . . . to gain a scanty subsistence."[38] Earlier, the *Awl* had reassured women that it was as moral for them to meet with the cordwainers every Saturday night as to attend church on Sunday. Indeed, their presence at these meetings would guarantee their propriety.[39] The *Awl* regarded women's power as moral, unselfish and spiritual, not as material, self-interested or political. These attitudes seemed to blind the cordwainers' society to the vulnerability and isolation of shoebinders.

The appeal of the *Awl* for female participation was deeply ambivalent. If women were seen as essentially moral and spiritual, characteristics that suggested gentility and the pious, private virtues that historians have identified as the cult of true womanhood, the ideology of the cordwainers' society pointedly rejected the values of the genteel, non-working classes who by their unearned wealth and leisured lives threatened the basic values of artisan culture. This side of their attitudes toward women revealed a fear of genteel or middle-class social behavior in females within their own families which would unfit them for the useful life of a mechanic's wife. These attitudes are best illustrated in several moral tales published in the *Awl* which explore this issue.

One story, reprinted from *The Family Visitor*, entitled "Old Fudge of an Uncle," demonstrated the triumph of a shoebinder over the "demon" of gentility.[40] Mary Burchstead was the niece of Mr. Goodrich, a shoemaker who had rescued her from childhood poverty by teaching her to make her own living binding shoes. Since her marriage to a sea captain, Mrs. Burchstead had fallen victim to gentility, altering at great expense the house which her husband had bought her, acquiring fine, new furniture and placing her husband deeply in debt. At the beginning of the story, Mary Burchstead puzzles over why her uncle has sent her — a lady — shoes to bind, but feels ashamed over her ingratitude and her neglect of relatives:

"But," she argued, "If a captain's wife bound shoes, what would people think?"

As she glances into her mirror, she finds that her displeasure had marred the beauty which the serenity found in binding shoes had once placed on her face:

"Mercy!" cried Mrs. Burchstead, "I look like a fright! . . . I must dress and call on uncle Goodrich, and expostulate, or, he will send a bundle of *cowhide brogans* next. I do wish the old man could know a little of gentility, or what belongs to it."

Stung by the incivility of her relatives, Mary visits her uncle and aunt. She is told that her husband has mortgaged their house to pay for the alterations and new furnishings and that, because of a general business depression, the voyage he is on may bankrupt him. Mary blames herself and sets to work, spurns the visitors who look down their noses at her occupation, rents the house and sells the furniture. Her husband returns, overjoyed at his wife's change of heart and her decisions which have cleared him of debt. In admiration of Mary's determination, his employer says to him:

Now you may congratulate yourself, not only for being in good circumstances, but for having a wife who has dared to sacrifice herself, as I may say, for she has defied gentility by binding shoes.

This story was chosen by the editors of the *Awl* for its criticism of the false social values which Mary Burchstead had chosen over the virtues of hard work and plain living. Her gentility as demonstrated by her rejection of shoebinding as unfitting for a captain's wife was symptomatic of the growing class divisions in American life and a betrayal of the equal rights ideology of Lynn mechanics.

In the February 22, 1845 issue, the editors made their views more explicit by publishing an original story, "Charles-Do-Well," written by one of the *Awl's* frequent contributors, "Noggs." "Charles-Do-Well" is a moral tale set in Lynn about the contest between the social virtues of the mechanic and the false values of the merchant class. The story begins as a young woman tries to decide whom she should marry:

It is no use talking mother said the pert though somewhat handsome Eliza D_____, as I am determined I will never no *never* marry a *mechanic*.

Eliza's father was a merchant, and she believes that it is up to a daughter to "keep up the dignity of [her] father's house," by marrying in the same class. Her inclination to marry a merchant is encouraged not by her kindly, sensible mother, but by the vapid Sarah Amelia Sudora Norton who objects to her friend Eliza's visits with shoebinders and rejects Charles Do-Well, the shoemaker, because "he smells of wax so." On the other hand, Eliza thinks, as she ponders her decision, Charles is handsome, well-informed and very interesting, even ". . . if he does make shoes." Her other suitor is Mr. Cheatem, a merchant who is received in all the best houses, but who has a reputation among working people as a liar and a "tricky trader." She wonders:

> But some how or other it seems strange to me that a man because he sells tape and buckram, small beer and ginger bread should be any more respectable than he who makes shoes . . . !

Charles has opened Eliza's eyes to the changing prospects of the mechanics of Lynn. He has told her that the:

> . . . times were fast altering, that things were beginning to be called by their right names; he says the common people are better informed than they used to be, now, and that it is beginning to be considered no disgrace to get a living honestly.

Thrillingly, this vision of change seems to include Eliza:

> Women too, he says, are beginning to be acknowledged as responsible creatures, as beings who have souls as well as hearts, who were born equal with the man, and who by every right, human and divine, are entitled to a voice in our councils, and are deserving of an equal recompense for their labors.

In contrast, Eliza reflects on Cheatem's philosophy:

> . . . that some people were born to be drawers of water, and hewers of wood, for his part he didn't see what the reformers wanted to make such a d____d fuss about the "niggers" and the poor folkes for.

Eliza observes:

> Oh how ugly he did look, as he with his sneering laugh uttered the above. I could not help contrasting him with the Charles Do-Well, who always takes sides with the oppressed. . . .

She is awakened from her reveries by her mother, and Eliza announces that she is done with girlish dreaming and that she is:

> . . . determined, henceforth, to be a woman, and see if I can't do something for a living. I will go immediately and join the "shoe binders' society of mutual improvement," and what is more I mean to bind shoes myself, for I have come to the conclusion that if we would be good members of society we must be useful.

Sarah Amelia is horrified to find Eliza binding shoes and drops her socially, saying she never did "keep company with the working class," but Charles Do-Well is enchanted to find Eliza binding shoes and dares to hope that his influence on her has produced her reformation. He has always thought that under her surface vanity and frivolity was "strong good sense." Some day, he believes, "she would dare be herself, a sensible, intelligent, *useful* woman." Eliza married Charles and Sarah Amelia married Cheatem. Six months later, Sarah Amelia is a deserted wife with a child left in poverty by her unscrupulous husband. She is wretched when Eliza calls on her, but otherwise much improved by her disastrous fate:

> She [Sarah Amelia] was not now ashamed herself, to bind shoes, aye was thankful, that there was so respectable and easy way for a poor stricken widow [?] to support herself and her child.

Eliza's story was a vehicle for the social criticism implicit in the mechanics' ideology, but when Charles explains to her the new conception of woman as an equal partner in the moral struggle against the merchant class, it becomes clear that the new fields opening to females are designed to permit them only to be sensible, intelligent and, most of all, useful family members: the paradigm of a mechanic's wife.[41] "Noggs" portrayed shoebinding as essential for the useful woman. Ignoring the objective conditions of the shoebinders whose work, if respectable, was never easy, the writer regarded binding shoes as appropriate, necessary and even chastening work for idle women. The useful woman is a much more flattering vision than the images of the shallow, materialistic women of the genteel class, but it is neither self-interested nor does it spring from the aspirations or dilemmas of working women themselves. In contrast to the energetic appeals in the *Awl* for female participation were the constant laments in its pages over the lack of response to these appeals. However, the explanation for this lack of response may lie less in the *Awl's* ambivalence over woman's nature or its fear of genteel values lurking within female members and more in the failure of the cordwainers' society to offer a solution for the vulnerable position of the female outworker in the structure of shoe manufacturing.

The cordwainers' society claimed benefit to shoebinders who associated with the organization, but the advice offered by the society suggests that the cordwainers refused to confront the implications of the isolated situation of most shoebinders in comparison with the collective nature of their own work. The folklore of artisan life in the 1840s and 1850s reflected the growing tensions between the shoemakers and the shoe boss over the quality of work turned into the central shop. Some shoe bosses treated their artisans with careful courtesy, while others did not. Shoemakers expressed resentment against hard bosses like Christopher Robinson of Lynn who tried in the late 1840s to alter the standards of work. Attempts to limit supplies or inspect work still in the shop were stoutly resisted.[42] The cordwainers of Essex County were better able than the individual shoebinder to resist attempts by the shoe boss to control and discipline the work process.

In an early appeal for female participation in the September 11, 1844 issue, the shoebinders were exhorted by the editors of the *Awl* to come to the society's meetings and identify any shoe boss in Lynn who had cheated women by the order system. The order system was an arrangement by which wages were paid in goods rather than in cash, a profitable convenience for merchants and shoes bosses and, according to the *Awl*, one of the greatest evils of the system of production. Widows with dependents were urged to point out the manufacturers who discounted their wages by 10% if they insisted on cash. Name the boss, the appeal went on, so that the world will know him. The strategy of publicly humiliating shoe bosses by focusing the moral power of indignant women on their oppressors did not persuade any shoebinders to come forward.

In addition to this advice, one of the editors, E.C. Darlin, championed a Lynn binder whose wage accounts he had examined and who, he charged, had been cheated by shoe manufacturer, Nathan D. Chase.[43] The case of Mrs. Jane Atherton illustrates the futility of the *Awl's* strategy for helping the shoebinders confront their employers. Darlin charged that Mrs. Atherton had been defrauded by Chase when he did not make it clear to her, when she began binding shoes for his firm in 1840, that the wages were paid 4 cents in cash or 5 cents in store orders. Although she played no direct role in the controversy, Mrs. Atherton had felt surprised and disappointed at the differential between cash and goods, and later thought the arrangements were rather hard, but worked for Chase for the next three years. During the controversy, Chase insisted that Mrs. Atherton had never said she had been defrauded. Darlin pointed out the injustices of the differential between goods and cash, whether Mrs. Atherton had agreed to it or not. He noted that Mrs. Atherton had not known the wage terms until after she had begun to work and referred to her "weakness" in relation to the shoe boss, but failed to analyze how her vulnerability influenced her behavior during the controversy. Mrs. Atherton, whose husband was away from Lynn during early 1845, was probably horrified that the *Awl* had chosen her wage record as the issue with which to attack the practices of the shoe bosses. Her chances for work as a binder were contingent on the good will of the shoe manufacturers whom she placated with reticence and meekness during the interviews which she had with them. Interestingly, as the controversy over the treatment of Mrs. Atherton developed between January 4 and February 22, shoebinders at last began to contribute letters and poetry to the *Awl*, but none of them even alluded to the Atherton case.[44] On the whole, the cordwainers' society of Lynn received little support from shoebinders. Its ideology implied a limited and subordinated role for most women. Its strategy to threaten the shoe bosses with public shame made the individual shoebinder even less likely to make an issue of mistreatment, fearing a stratagem which would focus the combined anger of Lynn shoe manufacturers on her and deprive her of work.

In the 1840s and 1850s the number of women working as shoebinders in Massachusetts grew rapidly, and by 1855, 32,826 women were recorded as employed in the boot and shoe industry in comparison with 22,850 employed in cotton textiles.[45] The number of women employed by Essex County shoe bosses grew from 7,027 in 1837 to 12,395 in 1855, an increase of 76%. By 1855 shoe manufacturing in Essex County had developed four major centers of outwork: Danvers and South Danvers, Haverhill (located near the New Hampshire boarder), Lynn and its neighbor Marblehead. These four centers of production accounted for 51% of all females in Massachusetts who worked in shoe production, and Lynn manufacturers who listed 11,021 women workers in 1855 had developed an extensive outwork system which reached beyond Eastern Massachusetts into Southern New Hampshire and Maine.

Low wages, irregular employment and low productivity plagued both the shoebinder and the shoe boss in the outwork system. Binding shoes was often characterized by intensive periods of effort over several weeks' duration followed by long periods of no shoebinding at all. The account books of John and Charles P. Preston of Danvers (1824-1845) and of James P. Hutchinson also of Danvers (1846-1860) indicate that the shoe bosses came to rely on a relatively small group of steady binders for most production, while employing a widespread and numerous group of casual binders whose work was conducted at irregular intervals. Account books from the 1840s also illustrate a further division of labor within the tasks which the binders performed which limited their earnings. A woman might be assigned only part of the work on uppers, for example, only the most poorly paid work of "closing" or sewing up side seams rather than "fitting" or seaming cloth linings into the upper which earned better pay. The debit side of the account books revealed the continuation of the custom of "furnishing" by which the binder assumed the costs of thread, needles and lining material, thereby further reducing her wages.[46] Much of women's work on shoes continued to be conducted separate from the family labor system by the wives and daughters of non-shoemaking families: farmers, other artisans, mariners and laborers.[47] Work had not yet left the home, but the home setting of women's work was less and less likely to revere the traditions and values of the shoemakers' craft.

With the invention of the sewing machine for leather in 1852 and the subsequent introduction of the factory system, the wages and the work available to shoebinders began to decline. But the adaptation of the sewing machine for cloth to stitch leather uppers did not immediately separate home and work for shoebinders. Neither did mechanization of women's work create a large scale factory system. Over the decade between 1855 and 1865, the process of shoe production slowly evolved toward the steam-powered factory, but the work process retained many features of pre-industrial production, including the sexual division of labor. John B. Nichols, who had succeeded in converting the I.M.

Singer sewing machine to stitch light leather, went to Lynn in 1852 in the employ of Singer who had sold exclusive rights to lease his new machines in Essex County to three Lynn manufacturers. Nichols organized stitching rooms for them and instructed young women in the use of the leather sewing machine. By 1855 several other sewing machine companies: Grover & Baker, Wheeler & Wilson and Nichols & Bliss, were producing and selling machines for work on leather uppers.[48] Shoebinding as women's needle work in the home seemed to face oblivion.

In the shoe centers of Lynn and Haverhill, the shoebinders organized to resist the introduction of the machines. A.S. Moore, one of Singer's agents in Essex County and the employer of machine operatives in Lynn, faced a committee of angry binders in 1852 who tried to pressure Moore and the women operatives to abandon the machines. In Haverhill shoebinders and shoemakers expressed bitterness at Isaac Harding who had brought the first stitching machines into town in 1853. Some of the women shook their fists in the face of Daniel Goodrich, Harding's partner. The binders were convinced that the machine would destroy their work. Many must have realized that centralized machine operations would force them to choose between their domestic duties and their ability to earn wages. Contributing to their distress was their unfamiliarity with the sewing machine for cloth. The marketing strategy of the early sewing machine companies concentrated on the use of the machines for the manufacture of clothing and shoes, ignoring the potential they would later realize in the domestic market for family sewing. Several experienced Haverhill binders who worked for the firm of Sawyer & Wheeler tried the new machines without success and gave up in despair.[49]

Although the binders were correct to fear mechanization, the system of household production accommodated itself to the introduction of the leather stitching machine. Not all work on uppers was mechanized. Suspicions regarding customer acceptance of machine stitched shoes somewhat retarded mechanization. But if hand work was still available in the home, the wages for shoebinding fell rapidly as the productivity of machine work rose and labor costs declined. In 1860 the piece rate for machine sewing was estimated at one quarter the price of hand work, while the operative earned nearly three times as much as the binder.[50] The shoebinder faced an uncertain future, working more intensively if she could obtain the work and at a severe wage reduction. Some binders rented or purchased leather stitching machines with hand cranks or foot treadles for use at home. Estimates differ on the extent of home use of stitching machines. They were expensive; in the mid-1850s the price ranged between $75 to $125. The most widespread use of home operated machines was apparently in Lynn, Salem and Marblehead where manufacturers rented machines to be used at home. Home use of a machine allowed women workers to continue to combine domestic duties with wage work and escape the discipline and long hours of centralized production.[51] Until the introduction of steam power and the invention of a pegging machine to mechanize the work of shoemakers, followed in 1862 by the McKay stitcher, home operations based on foot power provided work for many women.

Some of the shoe manufacturers centralized stitching operations by adding a story to central shops where the leather was cut out or had two story buildings constructed to contain the activities of the central shop on the ground floor and the stitching room on the second floor. Stitching was also sub-contracted by the central shop owners to shops like that of John B. Nichols of Lynn which specialized in stitching uppers.[52] The pre-industrial isolation of the female shoeworker from other operations in production was thereby maintained despite centralization. The work force in these little shops of thirty to fifty workers were "girls," that is, young, unmarried women who left their homes to work all day at stitching machines. *The Lynn News* estimated in 1855 that there were 1,500 to 1,800 sewing machines in operation and that most of them were run in shops by young women who earned an average weekly wage of about $6.00.[53] Many of these young women were members of local families, but by 1860 a sizeable portion of them had left their homes in the towns of Eastern Massachusetts, New Hampshire, Maine and the Maritime Provinces of Canada to board with families in Lynn and Haverhill and work for the attractive wages in the shoe shops. In the 1850s native-born, young New England women were abandoning work in the textile mills in the Merrimack Valley for employment in the shoe shops of Essex County.[54]

The depression years of the late 1850s created a crisis in the rapidly changing New England shoe industry. The crisis involved a collapse in the pre-industrial wage patterns of the family economy as shoe manufacturing moved toward mechanization, centralization and the factory system. In the early 1850s an expanding market for boots and shoes in the developing West had drawn additional male workers into the process of bottoming: the attachment by hand of machine or hand-sewn uppers to soles. Heeling and finishing operations were reorganized and performed separately along with cutting operations in the central shops. Groups of workmen in the surrounding towns of Essex County served by a network of teamsters bottomed shoes for Lynn and Haverhill shoe bosses, but an even more extensive rural outwork system, reaching into Central New Hampshire and Southern Maine and served by railroad, supplied additional male workers for bottoming.[55]

Machine productivity by female factory operatives increased the demand for bottomers, and Irish and German immigrants as well as migrants from New England came to the shoe towns of Massachusetts, crowding the local labor market. While the numbers of men who worked as bottomers increased, stimulated by machine productivity, the sex ratio of male to female shoeworker sharply reversed. The numbers of women employed in Massachusetts shoe production dropped off steadily in the 1850s. In Lynn the number of females employed on shoes shrank sharply by 41% between 1850 and 1860. The mechanization of women's work intensified the hard conditions of labor for both men and women involved in outwork in Essex County. The productivity of the new machine stitchers had stimulated the demand for bottomers, while cutting the demand for shoebinders. By contemporary estimates, one factory girl at her stitching machine could supply enough work for twenty bottomers, while replacing eleven binders. The woman who operated a sewing machine at home still faced the custom of "furnishing," that is, providing thread, needles and lining materials. A considerable gap developed after 1855 between the wages of factory operatives and the wages of women working at home whether by hand or by machine.[56]

Downward pressure on wages during the hard times after 1857 cut sharply into the shoemaker's family wage and helped precipitate the largest American demonstration of labor protest prior to the Civil War. A regional strike, beginning in February 1860 and spearheaded by activities in Natick and Lynn, disrupted production.[57] The values and patterns of the pre-industrial family economy confronted the emerging factory system. This confrontation divided not only the workers and their employers, but also divided the strikers into groups promoting the family wage economy through the artisan tradition and groups of female factory operatives whose place in centralized production and whose status as temporary residents of the shoe city created a different set of interests in the 1860 strike.

The strikers in Lynn, led by the bottomers, hoped to organize the country shoemakers to refuse outwork, while they simultaneously halted production in the Lynn shops. Important to this strategy was the interruption of teamster activities which carried sewn uppers and cut soles to country workshops. Significantly, the first serious conflict in Lynn involved express teams which carried shoe uppers machine-sewn by female factory workers to Marblehead bottomers for the John Wooldredge Company.[58] Wooldredge had pioneered both the adoption of the Singer sewing machine in 1852 and the introduction of steam power in 1858 for heeling and stitching operations. His firm symbolized the emerging factory system.

The strike leadership in Lynn had been considering the organization of the 3,000 shoebinders and stitchers as an auxiliary force to encourage community support and boycott uncooperative shoe bosses. Their decision to organize women workers was made after a violent incident on February 23 between strikers and expressmen which provoked widespread regional criticism in the press, precipitated the arrival of outside police forces and threatened to undermine the crucial support of shoemakers in the neighboring towns of Essex County for the strike.[59] In 1860 the Lynn strike committee attempted to utilize the moral stature of women for the same family and community purposes as had the Lynn cordwainers' society in the 1840s. Women's participation would restore morality to the strike, help generate community support in Lynn and throughout Essex County and mitigate criticism. The involvement of local women would erase the images of violence and disorder and emphasize the nature of the strike as a defense of the New England family.

The strike committee in Lynn was not, however, prepared to acknowledge or represent the interests of the female factory operatives whose leaders quickly seized control of the women's meetings. The interests of these women workers, who were nearly 40% of the female work force in Lynn by 1860, conflicted with artisan conception of the family wage economy.[60] The factory operatives disagreed with the advancement of the wages of male shoeworkers as the only objective in the strike and convinced the women workers of Lynn to strike for higher wages as binders and stitchers. They also began to organize women workers in the neighboring towns of Danvers, Newburyport and Marblehead.[61] Realizing the importance of their strategic position to stop work in centralized production, the factory girls in Lynn proposed a coalition with female homeworkers to raise wages in both categories of work: homework for wives and mothers and factory work for single girls. This alliance of gender represented a bridge between the pre-industrial patterns of women's work and the developing factory system. Unity as a gender would protect the wages of the married and the unmarried, the homeworkers and the shop girls, by linking the cause of working women to the new sources of wages and power in factory work. Mechanization and centralization of women's work had meant higher wages for factory workers, but reduced the numbers of women employed, relegated wives and mothers to homework and depressed the wages of outworkers. For homeworkers, an alliance with the young factory girls represented a real chance in 1860 for women working at home to make a valuable connection with the new industrial workers. In return, factory girls could anticipate marriage and a chance to work at home for decent wages. The family wage economy would be protected by a coalition of women workers acting together on behalf of their own interests.

The factory girls, led by twenty-one year old Clara Brown, a native of Massachusetts, who boarded in Lynn with a shoemaker's family, won several crucial votes on raising women's wages in the strike meetings held by Lynn women. They challenged the male strike committee for leadership of the women workers and to articulation of their interests. The factory girls identified with other women in the industry as workers and as a gender, not unlike the brothers of the craft. The ideology of artisan life did not figure in their vision of an alliance of women workers at home and in the shops, nor did they identify with the bottomers on familial or on ideological grounds. Conscious of the power of factory stitchers in this alliance whose productivity could shut down production in the industry and halt outwork, Clara Brown declared: "Girls of Lynn, . . . strike at once . . . Don't work your machines; let them lie still until we get all we ask." At a later meeting she challenged: ". . . we've got the bosses where we can do as we please with 'em. If we don't take the work, what can the bosses do?"[62]

The male strike committee quickly moved to oppose this unwelcome development. The committee members failed, however, to persuade the women at a meeting on February 28 to reconsider the list of wage demands which had been adopted the night before, a wage list which in the eyes of the striking shoemakers overvalued factory stitching and jeopardized homework. They feared that if the women's wages were raised, all stitching of uppers would be centralized in factories and homework eliminated. For the bottomers, the best protection for the family wage lay in obtaining higher wages for men's work and maintaining homework for women. In a bold move, the strike committee and its supporters among the women homeworkers ignored the high wage list adopted by votes taken at several of the women's meetings and substituted a lower list of wages which they circulated as the official wage list for the women workers of Lynn to sign.[63] On March 2 the supporters of the men's strike committee and the factory girls confronted each other at a tumultuous meeting. James Dillon, representing the bottomers, pleaded for the support of the women as wives and mothers of shoemakers and appealed to them not to alienate the bosses of the stitching shops by demanding an "unfair" increase in wages.[64] Other speakers dismissed the shop girls as interested only in money and in "the right to switch a long-tailed skirt [extravagant dress]."[65] Wage decisions, it was argued at the March 2 meeting, should be made by "sober, and discreet women" and not by "laughing" and "thoughtless girls."[66] Clara Brown countered by insisting that the machine girls of Lynn had the power to protect homeworkers, but that the factory girls would only strike for "something worth having." She pointed out that the low wage list prepared by the homeworkers actually cut wages on factory work. Despite her warnings, representatives of the bottomers' committee persuaded the majority of the women at the meeting to reject the high wage list and the factory girls, accept their recommendations on behalf of the family and community in Lynn and join the striking men in great show of community support for the strike.[67]

The legendary parade of striking women on a snowy March day through the streets of Lynn represented a great victory for the defenders of decentralized production and for the artisan tradition in Lynn. The images of the women's procession printed in the pages of *Frank Leslie's Illustrated Newspaper* have come to epitomize the involvement of women in the 1860 strike, but these sketches obscured the battle which took place over the relationship of women workers to the strike. The political stance of the majority of the women workers who rejected the strategy of the factory girls and supported the bottomers was reflected in the familial values on one of their banners:

> Weak in physical strength but strong in moral courage, we dare to battle for the right, shoulder to shoulder with our fathers, husbands and brothers.[68]

The decision of the homeworkers to support the men's strike committee was taken at the risk of ignoring the implications of mechanization, the factory system and the potential of the shop girls who, as workers in centralized production, represented the reorganization of industrial life in Lynn. Many Lynn women continued to support the bottomers until the strike slowly fell apart in late March, while the factory girls who boarded in Lynn returned to work or to their homes.[69]

The bottomers of Lynn had fought in 1860 to maintain the traditions and ideology of decentralized production, including women's work in the home. The artisan ideology had operated successfully to unite the heterogeneous work force of male workers — rural migrants, Irish, Germans and shoemakers in country shops and shoe towns — in the 1850s, but cut off the new female factory workers from contributing to labor protest. The leaders of the Lynn strike failed to perceive or respond to the strategic potential of female machine operators in centralized production and had ignored and opposed their articulated interests. The perceptions which shoemaking artisans had developed of work and gender made it difficult for them to regard women as fellow-workers outside of family relationships, to include them in the ideology and politics built on artisan life or see in the experience of working women what awaited all workers as capitalism in the New England shoe industry moved toward the factory system.

Historiography in the 1970s on women's work was dominated by a lively debate on the impact of economic change on women and their relationship to the family. Two major interpretations emerged. Joan Scott, Louise Tilly, Jane Humphries and Leslie Tentler emphasized the limitations of changes in women's lives as a result of industrialization, and they regarded the family as primary in defining the work and social roles of women employed at home or in the factory. Edward Shorter, Patricia Branca, Thomas Dublin and Heidi Hartmann have argued for a variety of levels of change in women's lives as a result of new work. All acknowledge the sexual division of labor as a fundamental condition of women's work in the nineteenth century.

This overview of changes in women's work in New England shoe production and the relationship of women shoeworkers to the artisan tradition suggests that tension between women workers and the family values of artisan culture remained constant and unresolved as work reorganized during the shift toward industrialization from 1780 to 1860. Contradictions between perceptions of the proper gender role for women in the family and their consciousness as workers in production prolonged these tensions for women workers into the early factory system and the 1860 strike. This struggle, most visible during moments of labor protest, had been initiated by the recruitment of women into production in the artisan system and maintained by the differences in the location of work and the exposure of the individual worker to the increasing control of the work process by the employer. For the most part, women shoeworkers negotiated those tensions between family and work within the value system of artisan ideology, but in doing so they built limits into their consciousness as workers and into their ability to act together as women to defend their interests or claim new rights. The gender perceptions of artisan ideology as articulated by male shoeworkers in ante bellum New England defined the role of women primarily as family members and as moral agents in society. Gender-based ideology and work experience cut women off from the most vital tradition of collective resistance in the early nineteenth century.

FOOTNOTES

I would like to thank Helena Wright, Tom Dublin, Milton Cantor, Carole Turbin, Paul Faler and Bruce Laurie for their useful suggestions, helpful criticism and support as this essay developed. The research and writing were aided by grants from the Andrew W. Mellon Foundation and the National Endowment for the Humanities. An earlier and shorter version of this paper was read at the Social Science History Association Conference, November 1982.

1. Edward P. Thompson, *The Making of the English Working Class* (New York, 1966); David Brody, "The Old Labor History and The New: In Search of an American Working Class," *Labor History* 20 (1979): 111-126; Herbert Gutman, *Work, Culture and Society in Industrializing America* (New York, 1976); David Montgomery, "The Working Classes of the Pre-Industrial American City, 1780-1830," *Labor History* 9 (1968): 3-22; Paul G. Faler, *Mechanics and Manufacturers in the Early Industrial Revolution: Lynn, Massachusetts, 1780-1860* (Albany, 1981); Alan Dawley, *Class and Community: The Industrial Revolution in Lynn* (Cambridge, 1976); Bruce Laurie, *The Working People of Philadelphia, 1800-1850* (Philadelphia, 1980); Susan E. Hirsch, *Roots of the American Working Class: The Industrialization of Newark, 1800-1860* (Philadelphia, 1978) and Howard B. Rock, *Artisans of the New Republic: The Tradesmen of New York City in the Age of Jefferson* (New York, 1979). For overviews, see Sean Wilentz, "Artisan Origins of the American Working Class," *International Labor and Working Class History.* 19 (1981): 1-22 and Jim Green, "Culture, Politics and Workers' Response to Industrialization in the U.S." *Radical America* 16 (Jan.-April, 1982): 101-128. Bruce Laurie provided a succinct definition of the new conception of class consciousness: ". . . culture and consciousness are made and remade by the interplay of living and working conditions and by what individuals bring to communities and workshops from prior experience," p. 27. Laurie, however, refrained from examining the experience of women's involvement in worker culture in pre-industrial Philadelphia despite the evidence he located on their participation in work, temperance groups and religious activities, pp. 12-13, 30-34, 43, 49-51. Hirsch explored women's involvement in pre-industrial work in Newark and its connections with family life, but she viewed the male artisan as the typical worker and the industrialization of male crafts as the touch-stone of economic change from 1800-1860. Her definition of status included ethnicity but not gender. In their review articles, Wilentz and Green call for more work on early industrialization from the perspective of rearrangements in gender relations as well as the relations of production. My research on women's relationship to the pre-industrial artisan tradition has been influenced by a workshop on "Family History: A Critique," at the Women and Power Conference, University of Maryland, 1977, later published as Rayna Rapp, Ellen Ross and Renate Bridenthal, "Examining Family History," *Feminist Studies* 5 (Spring, 1979): 174-200; by the work of Thomas Dublin on the Lowell textile operatives and by the work of Heidi Hartmann, especially "The Family as the Locus of Gender, Class, and Political Struggle," *Signs* 6 (Spring, 1981): 366-394.

2. Thomas Dublin, *Women At Work: The Transformation of Work and Community in Lowell, Massachusetts, 1826-1860* (New York, 1979).

3. Faler, *Mechanics*, chapter 3, 9 and Dawley, *Class and Community, passim.* For a critique of Faler and Dawley, see Friedrich Lenger, "Class, Culture and Class Consciousness in Ante Bellum Lynn: A Critique of Alan Dawley and Paul Faler," *Social History* 6 (1981): 317-332.

4. Mary Blewett, "Shared But Different: The Experience of Women Workers in the Nineteenth Century Work Force of the New England Shoe Industry," in *Essays from the Lowell Conference on Industrial History, 1980 and 1981* (Lowell, 1981): 77-85.

5. Faler, *Mechanics*, pp. 11-12. For the patterns of pre-industrial shoemaking in Eastern Massachusetts, Blanche Hazard, *The Organization of the Boot and Shoe Industry in Massachusetts Before 1875* (Cambridge, 1921); David Newhall Johnson, *Sketches of Lynn or the Changes of Fifty Years* (Lynn, 1880) and John Philip Hall, "The Gentle Craft: A Narrative of Yankee Shoemakers," (Ph.D. diss., Columbia University, 1953).

6. Alonzo Lewis and James R. Newhall, *History of Lynn* (Boston, 1865): 50-65.

7. John R. Commons, "American Shoemaking, 1648-1895: A Sketch of Industrial Evolution," *Quarterly Journal of Economics* 24 (1909): 39-83. Commons pointedly dismissed Marxian analysis of changes in the mode of production and ignored the introduction of the sexual division of labor. Dawley, *Class and Community* chapter 1 and Faler, *Mechanics*, chapter 2.

8. Dawley, *Class and Community*, pp. 16-25.

9. Johnson, *Sketches of Lynn*, pp. 336-340; Hazard, *Boot and Shoe Industry*, pp. 4-53; Dawley, *Class and Community* pp. 16-25; Philip C. Swett, "History of Shoemaking in Haverhill," unpublished reminiscences; William Stone, "Lynn and Its Old-Time Shoemakers' Shops," *Lynn Historical Society Register*, (1900): 49-100; Hall, "The Gentle Craft," pp. 49-145; Helen L. Sumner, *History of Women in Industry in the United States*, vol. 9 of *Report on Condition of Woman and Child Wage-Earners in the United States* (Washington, D.C., 1910): 167-170; Edith Abbott, "Women In Industry: The Manufacture of Boots and Shoes," *American Journal of Sociology* 15 (1909): 335-360. In his discussion of Philadelphia shoemaking, Laurie argued that the division of labor did not uniformly reduce craft work to semi-skilled jobs, but created a new hierarchy of occupations at the bottom of which was shoebinding, p. 22.

10. Dawley noted, but does not explain the origins of the involvement of women in shoe production, pp. 17-18. Faler discussed the importance of the assignment of work to women in shoemaking, pp. 19-27, but he moved too fast in his argument to speculate on the social dynamics of this decision within the shoemaking family. In attempting to account for the origins of the sexual division of labor (a term which he does not employ), Faler used a circular argument, stating that although women did not participate in shoemaking before the 1780s, the basis of their involvement in production ". . . was an outgrowth of the domestic system of manufacture in which the entire family of a cordwainer, working in the home participated in the productive process," p. 24. He cited the "muted growth" of powerful craft customs in Lynn in comparison with Philadelphia to explain the recruitment of women, but did not explain why women were recruited only to binding and were not admitted into the shoe shop, p. 24. Faler cited evidence on the surplus of females in Essex County, 1790 to 1810, as a labor pool for the ladies' shoe industry, but noted that these women probably resided in non-shoemaking families of seafarers and fishermen, p. 25. This surplus of females in Essex County would indeed be tapped by shoe bosses, but not until *after* the shoemaking family ceased to be the locus of combined production. Faler saw no implications for the mechanics' ideology or the artisan community in the physical and social separation of the workplaces of shoebinders and shoemakers, although he did identify the beginnings of class division in a similar separation between the workplaces of the journeymen in the ten footer and the master, later the shoe boss, in the central shop, pp. 23, 27, 167. On the whole, although he acknowledged the importance of the division of labor, Faler assumed that there were no important changes in women's work until mechanization in 1852. Anna Davin

discussed the neglect of the sexual division of labor as both an object of study and as a tool of analysis in "Feminism and Labour History," *People's History and Socialist Theory*, Raphael Samuel, editor (London, 1981): 178. For two discussions of the involvement of the sexual division of labor in the female experience of work and labor protest, see Louise Tilly, "Paths of Proletarianization: Organization of Production, Sexual Division of Labor and Women's Collective Action," *Signs* 7 (Winter, 1981): 400-417 and Temma Kaplan, "Female Consciousness and Collective Action: The Case of Barcelona, 1910-1918," *Signs* 7 (1982): 545-566.

11. On mechanization, the sexual division of labor and the social uses of technology, see Judith A. McGraw, "Women and the History of American Technology," *Signs* 7 (1982): 798-828. For a general interpretation of the sexual division of labor and capitalist development, Julie A. Matthaei, *An Economic History of Women in America* (New York, 1982).

12. In her study of French women and the artisan system of production in sixteenth century Lyon, Natalie Zemon Davis argued that the work identity of female workers was subordinated to their gender roles in the family, "Women in the Crafts in Sixteenth-Century Lyon," *Feminist Studies* 8 (1982): 45-80. For the separation of men and women in the artisan experience of London, Gareth Stedman-Jones, "Working-Class Culture and Working-Class Politics in London, 1870-1900; Notes on the Remaking of a Working Class," *Journal of Social History* 7 (1974): 485, and Sally Alexander, "Women's Work in Nineteenth Century London: A Study of the Years 1820-1850," in Juliet Mitchell and Ann Oakley, *The Rights and Wrongs of Women*, (New York, 1976): 59-111.

13. For a compelling image of the family labor system, see Johnson, *Sketches of Lynn*, pp. 337-338. In a critique of E.P. Thompson's concept of task and time labor, Lise Vogel pointed to the necessity of combining both task and time labor in a pre-industrial but capitalist productive system. The shoebinders' work, even as a contribution of unwaged labor performed in their kitchens, began to assume a timed and, therefore, industrial character, "Rummaging Through the Primitive Past: A Note on Family, Industrialization, and Capitalism," *The Newberry Papers in Family and Community History* (Nov. 1976): 19-26.

14. For example, see the correspondence between William Richardson, a shoe boss of Stoneham, Massachusetts, with shoemakers, Jesse Reed of New Ipswich, New Hampshire and William Cooke of Bedford, Massachusetts, Richardson Papers, Baker Library, Harvard University.

15. The accounts of Israel Buffum (1806-1847) and Aaron Breed (1805-1817) Lynn Historical Society. John Goodwin Accounts (1810-1834) of Reading, Massachusetts, Mrs. C. Nelson Bishop, Reading.

16. Among the account books which illustrate the shift of binders' work out of the family labor system are Jonathan Boyce (1793-1813) Lynn Historical Society; John Burrell (1819-1820) Lynn Historical Society; Samuel Bacheller Papers (1795-1845) Vol. 2, Sturbridge Village Archives; Untitled Ledger, Lynn (1790-1820) Lynn Historical Society; James Coburn, Boxford (1804-1821); Robert Brown, West Newburyport (1813-1828); Caleb Eames, Wilmington (1819-1825) Sturbridge Village Archives.

17. Percy Bidwell, "The Agricultural Revolution in New England," *American Historical Review* 25 (1921): 685-702. For statistics on the putting-out system in Essex County, Secretary of the Treasury, *Documents Relative to the Manufacturers in the United States, 1832* (Reprint, New York, 1969), Vol. 2, pp. 590-610 and Commonwealth of Massachusetts, *Statistical Information Relating to Certain Branches of Industry in Massachusetts, for the year 1837* (Boston, 1837). For a quantitative analysis of the early Massachusetts censuses, Claudia Goldin and Kenneth Sokoloff, "Women, Children, and Industrialization in the Early Republic: Evidence from the Manufacturing Censuses," *Journal of Economic History* 42 (1982): 741-774.

18. Unidentified Shoe Manufacturer's Stock Book, Lynn (1830-1831) Lynn Historical Society. Based on the figures of cut stock given out to workers in March 1830 and in March 1831, the annual production of this shoe manufacturer was about 30,000 pairs in 1830 and 70,000 pairs in 1831. According to the 1832 report of the Treasury or the McLane Report, only the eleven largest shoe manufacturers in Lynn had this capacity for production. *Documents Relating to Manufacturers, 1832*, Vol. 1, pp. 224-235.

19. See the Journal of Joseph P. Lye, Jr. of Lynn (1819-1830) Lynn Historical Society and the Diaries of Isaac W. Merrill of Haverhill (1828-1878) Haverhill Public Library. For worker control as crucial to class struggle in nineteenth century America, David Montgomery, *Workers' Control in America* (Cambridge, 1976).

20. In the early 1830s there was evidence of widespread collective resistance by shoebinders in Essex and Middlesex Counties in Massachusetts as well as in Philadelphia, New York City and Newark. John B. Andrews and W.D.P. Bliss, *History of Women in Trade Unions* (Reprint, New York, 1974): 41-45 and Augusta Emile Galster, *The Labor Movement in the Shoe Industry: With Special Reference to Philadelphia* (New York, 1924): 22-28. Hirsch in *Roots of the American Working Class* noted shoebinders' activity in Newark in 1836 and observed that "[t]he existence of a separate union for women . . . suggests that the days of domestic manufacture were long gone in shoemaking. The women binders and fitters hired out as individuals and were not wives and daughters helping craftsmen who worked within households," pp. 28-29. See also, Keith Melder, "Women in the Shoe Industry: The Evidence From Lynn," *Essex Institute Historical Collections* 115 (1979): 272-273.

21. The issues of *The New England Christian Herald* (printed briefly in Boston under this name, later *Zion's Herald*) are lost for 1831, but Hall quoted from them at length in his dissertation, pp. 152-154. In the August 12 issue of the *Christian Herald*, the binders' society challenged the figures of the shoe bosses, criticized payment in goods and insisted it represented 227 shoebinders. See also the *Lynn Mirror*, Aug. 6, 1831.

22. "Preamble to the Constitution of the Female Society of Lynn and vicinity for the protection and promotion of Female Industry," *Lynn Record*, January 1, 1834 and "Address of the Shoebinders of Lynn" by Chairman Mary Russell, *Lynn Record*, Jan. 8, 1834. All quotes are from the *Lynn Record*. Andrews and Bliss, *Women in Trade Unions*, quoted the Constitution of the Female Society, but not the preamble, pp. 42-43.

23. Based on the 1837 statistics of manufacturing in Massachusetts, the women of Saugus who met to affiliate with the Lynn Society represented almost the entire work force of binders in town.

24. Faler, *Mechanics*, pp. 172-173.

25. "Address," *Lynn Record*, Jan. 8, 1834. The association of fear and shame with the poorhouse was one of the products of a new industrial morality skillfully described by Faler, *Mechanics*, pp. 110-116.

26. Faler mistakenly dated the Female Society as organized in 1830, p. 198. Although the cordwainers listed the low wages of shoebinders in the 1830 grievances as a society, the Female Society did not appear until 1833 under its own leadership, *Lynn Mirror*, Aug. 14, Sept. 4, 1830. Although the leadership of the Lynn societies did not represent an association of family or kin, the two groups worked together closely in 1834.

27. Lynn Female Anti-Slavery Society, Minutes, 1836-1838, Lynn Historical Society.

28. In this typology developed by Dawley and Faler in "Working Class Culture and Politics in the Industrial Revolution: Sources of Loyalism and Rebellion," *Journal of Social History* 9 (1976): 466-471, gender was not explored. Lenger, "Class, Culture and Class Consciousness," is critical of Dawley and Faler's typology, but not on gender analysis, pp. 325-329.

29. *Lynn Record*, June 18, 1834. Mary Russell greatly exaggerated the results of the 1834 Lowell turnouts which failed to prevent a wage cut or even create an organization such as the binders' society in Lynn, Dublin, *Women At Work*, pp. 89-98.

30. Nancy F. Cott, *The Bonds of Womanhood: "Women's Sphere" in New England, 1780-1835* (New Haven, 1977).

31. Massachusetts, *Statistics of Manufacturing, 1837.*

32. Faler regarded the *Awl* as the most influential labor paper published by shoemakers, its circulation in Lynn probably reaching most of them, *Mechanics*, p. 200.

33. In his fascinating discussion of the impact of a new industrial morality on the social customs and attitudes of Lynn society, Faler analyzed attempts by moral reformers after 1826 to undermine the relaxed morality of the eighteenth century by imposing discipline on sexual practices, such as bundling, on public social occasions, on school yard behavior and on sexual conduct in general, *Mechanics*, pp. 109-138. Whether this new social morality also produced new working-class attitudes on the nature of women as purified, moral beings is a tantalizing question. Faler and Dawley have argued elsewhere that the "rebels" who identified with *Awl* utilized the new industrial morality for purposes of working-class resistance, see "Working Class Culture and Politics." The same argument may apply to the *Awl*'s attempt to utilize women as moral agents in support of working-class objectives in the 1840s and later in the strike of 1860. The concept of women as moral agents in society is crucial to women's history in the early nineteenth century and underlies the public activities of organized middle-class women, see for example, Carroll Smith-Rosenberg, "Beauty, the Beast, and the Militant Woman: A Case Study in Sex Roles and Social Stress in Jacksonian America," *American Quarterly* 23 (1971): 562-584.

34. *Essex County Washingtonian*, Dec. 29, 1842, Jan. 5, 26, 1843 calls attention to the temperance activities of women in the Woodend section of Lynn, the home of a large portion of Lynn's journeymen. On Woodend and temperance activities in Lynn, see Faler, *Mechanics*, pp. 197, 104, 130-136, 206-210. The activity of these women may also indicate their economic dependence on their families as a result of low wages for shoebinding.

35. *The Awl*, July 17, 1844.

36. The training of women as shoemakers in Essex County was not entirely unknown, but reflected the tradition of a widow or daughter carrying on the trade of a husband or father. On Mrs. Tuttle, *The Awl*, Aug. 28, 1844.

37. For appeals for female participation, *The Awl*, Sept. 11, 18, Dec. 7, 1844. For laments over lack of response, Dec. 14, 17, 21, 1844.

38. *The Awl*, Dec. 21, 1844.

39. "Letter to the Editor from Centre Street," *The Awl*, Sept. 18, 1844.

40. *The Awl*, Sept. 11, 1844.

41. "Mechanics' Wives," *The Awl*, June 18, 1845. See also "Frank Russell or the Village Blacksmith," an original story published in the September 4, 1844 issue which argued that the natural and acquired virtues of a mechanic's life could overcome and harmonize class divisions.

42. Stone, "Lynn," pp. 87-93. Faler argued that Robinson was a "good boss" during the 1840s as compared to the "grinders" who were regarded as highly exploitative by the journeymen, *Mechanics*, pp. 177-178. Robinson, however, introduced higher standards of

quality for work, issued printed directives to both makers and binders about how the work should be performed and inspected the work personally. He also apparently paid good wages in return for tighter discipline over work. For Danvers, William L. Hyde, "Reminiscences of Danvers in the Forties and Fifties," *Historical Collections of the Danvers Historical Society* 5 (1917): 1-20 and Edwin Mudge, "The Shoe Trade of Danvers," in Charles B. Rice, *Proceedings at the celebration of two hundredth anniversary of the first parish at Salem Village, now Danvers* (Boston, 1874): 235-243.

43. In 1845 the *Awl* announced an advanced position on women's rights and supported equal compensation for women workers and an absolute equality of rights, including the right to subscribe to a free press. *The Awl*, Jan. 4, 1845. Nathan D. Chase was regarded as a "grinder" by Lynn shoemakers, Faler, *Mechanics*, p. 178.

44. For the manufacturers' side, *The Awl*, Jan. 25, Feb. 22, 1845; for Darlin's side, Feb. 22, 1845. For the shoebinders' contributions, *The Awl*, Feb. 1, 22, 1845. For a complaint by one woman about being subordinated while participating in the activities of the cordwainers' society, see Constance, "On the Art of Shoemaking," *The Awl*, Feb. 22, 1845. The *Awl* supported labor activist Sarah Bagley and *The Voice of Industry*, defended the factory girls of Lowell and the seamstresses of Boston, but did not perceive shoebinders in terms of their vulnerability and isolation.

45. Commonwealth of Massachusetts, *Statistical Information Relating to Certain Branches of Industry in Massachusetts, for the year, 1855* (Boston, 1856).

46. Surviving accounts from the 1830s, the 1840s and 1850s on the outwork system in Essex County are rare. See the accounts of Jeremiah Chapman (1839-1849) Danvers and James P. Hutchinson (1836-1860) Danvers, Essex Institute, Salem, Massachusetts, the accounts of Bartlett Gage (1829-1834) Haverhill and John Tappan (1827-1843) Bradford, Haverhill Public Library and the personal accounts of Edward Poor (1828-1869) Georgetown, Essex Institute.

47. Mary H. Blewett, "'I Am Doom to Disapointment': The Diaries of a Beverly, Massachusetts, Shoebinder, Sarah E. Trask, 1849-1851," *Essex Institute Historical Collections* 117 (1981): 192-212. Trask and her fellow binders had fathers who were laborers, carpenters, mariners and shoemakers. These young women formed female networks with little connection to shoemaking artisans. The Preston accounts of Danvers, Essex Institute, revealed the employment of eleven shoebinders who formed the core of productive workers between 1836 and 1845 of which four were the wives or daughters of farmers. William Mulligan saw the shoemaking family as a harmonious work unit in operation from 1780 to 1850 and analyzed the impact of the close connections between work and family on the fertility of shoemaking families in the Lynn census of 1850. He found that shoemaking families had a fertility rate lower than other skilled workers and produced children in a more concentrated period of their lives. Mulligan contended that the role of women in shoemaking families as workers in family labor units was economically valuable and this valued economic role explains the fertility patterns of the shoemaking family in 1850. See William Mulligan, "The Family as Factory: Shoemaking in the North Shore District of Massachusetts, 1750-1850," paper presented to the American Historical Association, December, 1980. However, the census of population of 1850 does not give information on the occupations of women. The evidence in this essay on the disassociation of women workers from the family work unit suggests that the 1850 fertility patterns of the shoemaking families might better be explained by the penetration of the family by the putting-out system which divided women's work from a family labor context. Lower fertility, possibly evidence of domestic feminism, might reflect the breakdown rather than the continuity of families as work units. The family was still an economic unit, a family wage economy, but no longer a family labor economy. This useful distinction is explored in Joan Scott and Louise Tilly, *Women, Work, and Family* (New York, 1978).

48. Ross David Thomson, "The Origins of Modern Industry in the United States: The Mechanization of Shoe and Sewing Machine Production," (Ph.D. diss., Yale University, Economics, 1976): 245-250; *The Lynn Item*, (Reminiscences of John B. Nichols and Obituary) Nov. 10, 1903, Aug. 30 and Sept. 8, 1913.

49. Swett, "Haverhill," pp. 16-17; (Reminiscences of Charles Buffum) *The Lynn Item*, Oct. 5, 1901; *Lynn Weekly Reporter*, Feb. 28, 1863; "First Introduction of the Sewing Machine into the Shoe Business," *Shoe and Leather Reporter*, Dec. 12, 1867 and Thomson, "Origins of Modern Industry," pp. 247-261.

50. Thomas P. Kettel, "Manufacturers," in *Eighty Years' Progress of the United States* (New York, 1864): 428. See also the wages of Maria Poor in the account book of Edward Poor of Georgetown. Her wages rose in the 1850s just before mechanization and fell in the early 1860s to levels reminiscent of the 1830s as a result of the introduction of the factory system.

51. An examination of the Lynn Tax Assessments in 1860 and the schedules of the United States Census of Manufacture revealed no information on sewing machines owned by manufacturers or individuals. For impressions of the extent of their use in the home, see Johnson, *Sketches of Lynn*, p. 340; Hazard, *Boot and Shoe Industry*, pp. 95-96; *Eighty Years*, p. 428 and Thomson, "Origins of Modern Industry," pp. 69-70.

52. *Lynn Item*, Jan. 1, 1897 and Thomson, "Origins of Modern Industry," pp. 69-71, 138.

53. *Lynn News*, July 20, 1855. The Massachusetts state census of population for 1855 does not list the occupations of women.

54. On the decline of Yankee women as textile workers, Dublin, *Women at Work*, pp. 201-207. Calculations based on the federal manuscript census of population in Lynn for 1860 indicate that 52% of the total number of the 371 female machine operatives (stitchers) boarded in Lynn with private families or in small boarding houses. Of the boarding stitchers, 31% were natives of other states, principally New Hampshire and Maine and 19% were foreign-born, principally in Nova Scotia (7% were Irish natives). The remaining 48% of the boarding stitchers were natives of towns and cities of Massachusetts, assuming that Lynn natives were living with their families or kin.

55. Local observers noted a drop of one third in shoemakers' wages between 1857 and 1860. *Lynn Weekly Reporter*, Mar. 31, Apr. 16, 1860 and the *Salem Observer*, Mar. 3, 1860. Sumner, *Women in Industry*, p. 172, commented on the high productivity of the machine girls in relation to the bottomers after the introduction of the sewing machine. Also see, *Lynn Reporter*, Mar. 31, Apr. 21, 1860; *Marblehead Ledger*, Feb. 29, 1860.

56. See the comments of James Haines, a Boston shoemaker in the *New York Herald*, Mar. 22, 1860 on the relationship of machine stitchers to bottomers in terms of productivity in 1860. Also see letters deploring the development of two wage scales for women, *Tri-Weekly Publisher* (Haverhill), Mar. 3, 10, 1860. For the custom of furnishing by homeworkers, see the testimony of women at the Lynn strike meetings, *Boston Journal*, Feb. 28, 1860.

57. The regional shoe strike of 1860 was the largest demonstration of labor protest before the Civil War and as such has had some attention from historians, but little systematic analysis. The most detailed examination appeared in Philip S. Foner, *Women and the American Labor Movement: From Colonial Times to the Eve of World War I* (New York, 1979): 90-97. Foner emphasized the heroic and exemplary aspects of the strike, especially women's militancy and the unity between working-class men and women, but he dismissed the dissension over strike objectives as "some discussion," pp. 92-93. See also Norman Ware, *The Industrial Worker, 1840-1860* (New York, 1964): 47 and Andrews and Bliss, *Women in Trade Unions*, p. 108. Dawley analyzed the strike, *Class and Community*, pp. 79-90, as a product of mechanization and declining wages, but doesn't pick up the conflict between

women workers and the strike committee. He did, however, note the subordination of women in the ideology and rhetoric of the shoemakers' resistance. Faler saw the strike as marking the end of a community of interest in Lynn and as the beginning of class conflict, but he emphasized the role of the mechanics and overlooked the conflict within the women's organization, see *Mechanics*, chapter 11. Overreliance by Dawley and Faler on local newspaper reporting, especially in the pro-strike (Lynn) *Bay State* whose editor, Lewis Josselyn, acted as an advisor to the bottomers' strike committee and smoothed over evidence of conflicts within the strike, gave them an overly harmonious view of strike events. The preponderance of evidence from the out-of-town press, which sent reporters to Lynn to cover events in detail as eye-witnesses reveals the conflict between the homeworkers and factory girls, especially in the coverage of the women's strike meetings. See the lengthy, eye-witness accounts in the *Boston Herald*, the *New York Times*, the *New York Herald*, the *Boston Post*, the *Boston Journal*, and the *Boston Advertiser*. The *Bay State* and the other Lynn newspapers covered the women's meetings only briefly. Patricia Branca has suggested that women's experience with work has differed significantly from men's experience in ways which must be taken into account in assessing the motivations and behavior of women at work, in strike situations and in unions, *Women in Europe Since 1750* (New York, 1978): 45-46.

58. The *Bay State*, Feb. 23, Mar. 1, 1860.

59. The timing of the involvement of the women in the strike after the outbreak of violence on February 23 is crucial to understanding the motives of the strike committee. Alonzo Draper of the committee issued a call for the first meeting of women on the night of February 23 by urging crowds of striking men to send their wives and sweethearts to a public meeting. Later in a dispute among strike committee members in April 1860 reported in the *Lynn Reporter*, Apr. 14, 1860, a member of the Executive Board of the strike committee, John R. Parrott said: ". . . there was not a word said about the running of machines, or of the women striking, for some time after we struck."

60. Comparisons between data on women workers in Lynn in the United States Census of Manufacture for 1860 and newspaper estimates of women participating in the strike as homeworkers suggest that about 60% of the approximately 3,000 female shoeworkers in Lynn supported the strike committee. The remaining 40% represented the boarding shop girls, a minority of the total work force in Lynn, seasonally employed, but who, as full-time machine operatives in centralized production, were capable of crippling the industry.

61. See the Feb. 28, 29, 1860 issues of the *Boston Journal*, the *Boston Post*, the *Boston Herald*, and the *New York Herald*. For organizational work by the women, the *Boston Herald*, Mar. 6, 12, 1860 and the *Boston Traveler*, Mar. 2, 1860.

62. The *New York Times*, Feb. 29, Mar. 6, 1860.

63. The *New York Times*, Mar. 6, 1860.

64. The *New York Times*, Mar. 6, 1860; the *New York Herald*, Mar. 5, 1860 and the *Boston Journal*, Mar. 3, 1860.

65. The *New York Times*, Mar. 6, 1860.

66. The *Boston Herald*, Mar. 3, 1860.

67. The *New York Times*, Mar. 6, 1860; the *Boston Herald*, Mar. 3, 1860 and the *Boston Journal*, Mar. 3, 1860. Marxist-feminists have recently debated whether the family wage served the interests of patriarchy or served the ability of working-class families to resist exploitation by employers. See Heidi Hartmann, "The Unhappy Marriage of Marxism and Feminism: Towards a More Progressive Union," *Capital and Class* (Summer, 1979): 1-43

and Jane Humphries, "Class Struggle and the Persistence of the Working-Class Family," *Cambridge Journal of Economics* I (1979): 241-258. Both the Hartmann and the Humphries model appear to have operated in the Lynn strike in 1860. The family wage as a strike objective meant that homeworkers defended an increase in men's wages and wanted work in the home to be preserved in the interests of family income. They accepted the male strike committee's strategy. The factory girls led by Clara Brown seemed unconsciously to challenge patriarchal control in the family and in the strike by offering an alliance with the homeworkers based on gender and the sexual division of labor. They were defeated in the Lynn strike by the actions and rhetoric of the male strike committee and outnumbered by those who responded to the ideology of the bottomers' family wage argument. In mid-March, however, the bottomers demonstrated their willingness to jeopardize even homework to win their increases. The *New York Herald* Mar. 19, 1860; the *Boston Journal,* Mar. 20, 1860.

68. The *Bay State*, Mar. 8, 1860.

69. The *Lynn Reporter* denied that by the end of March the women's strike was having any effect at all on the manufacturers, March 21, 1860. To test whether the boarding stitchers who came from other communities to work in Lynn formed attachments to local men and, therefore, might identify with the bottomers' interests in the strike, the 192 boarding stitchers were linked to the Massachusetts marriage records between 1860 and 1870. Forty-five or 23% of the boarding stitchers did marry in Lynn, but only 29 or 15% married between 1860 and 1865 and might be said to have had sweethearts during the 1860 strike. Another sixteen of the 45 boarding stitchers who married in Lynn did so between 1865 and 1870. Three-fourths of the boarding stitchers did not marry in Lynn. Maris Vinovskis warned, however, that migration can affect and distort the evidence of marriage registers. Marriages may be performed in the town where the bride lived, yet the new couple may reside in the community where the groom lived and worked, *Fertility in Massachusetts from the Revolution to the Civil War* (New York, 1981): 49-50.

9.

THE DOMESTIC ENVIRONMENT IN EARLY MODERN ENGLAND AND AMERICA

Carole Shammas

Currently in the United States we are emerging from a long period of intensive investment in domesticity. By domesticity, I mean making home the center for most non-market social interaction. The creation of this environment, where family members relax together and entertain select members of the outside world, has invariably fallen to the woman, the "homemaker." The widespread re-entry of married females into the labor force, the drop in fertility, the rising number of divorces, and other demographic phenomena are now resulting, however, in a decline in the quantity and quality of goods and labor devoted to the home.[1] Vinyl upholstery, double-knits, and fast food restaurants all herald the dawn of the new age.

The change in attitude toward domesticity in the last few years has also been pronounced. From *Diary of a Mad Housewife* to *Interiors*, the message clearly reads that too refined a sensibility in regard to such things as turkey dressing or furniture placement can lead to familial strife and mental instability. In her recent novel, *Happy All the Time*, Laurie Colwin has valiantly attempted to rehabilitate the image of the household aesthete by making her heroine, Holly, a strong character who cogently argues the case for the "domestic sensualist." How persuasive such arguments can be, though, when the real life exponents of the ideal have become dress manufacturers and book editors, is doubtful. In fact, it should be noted that those who express themselves most vehemently on the importance of domesticity, the Total Woman crowd, concentrate on new ways to serve up sex, not tuna.

The passing or at least alteration of an institution always sparks interest in its origins, because people want some reassurance that what they are abandoning is not one of life's constants without which civilization will collapse. It is not surprising, therefore, that there is a growing literature on the rise of domesticity in Western society. Although domesticity is usually associated with the Victorian middle class during industrialization, historians of the family have detected signs of it developing as far back as the sixteenth century. At that time, according to one interpretation, the aristocratic households of Western Europe began a retreat into privacy. While the medieval nobility had eaten, slept, and lived "publicly" with a large number of retainers, kin, and servants in constant attendance, by the early modern period the concept of hospitality and display had declined and the desire to withdraw into the nuclear family manifested itself. A century or so later, the bourgeoisie began constructing their cozy nests.[2]

In the latest, detailed examination of domestic relations in pre-industrial England, Lawrence Stone labels the transformation that occurred in the sixteenth and seventeenth centuries as one from an open lineage to a patriarchal nuclear family.[3] The decline of kinship and clientage as well as the break with the Catholic

Church transferred considerable power to the household. Unlike some historians of the Puritan family, Stone does not see more equality and warm feelings between spouses or parents and children as the immediate product of intense Protestantism: "Although it cannot be proved that the power of the husband and father was more authoritarian and patriarchal than had been in the late middle ages," he writes, "there are certain theoretical reasons why this should have been so."[4] The father, as head of the household, was the prime beneficiary of the family's new authority. In Stone's opinion, the emotional bonds we assume to exist within nuclear families only began to surface in the late seventeenth century among urban, upper-middle-class households and did not take hold among the landed classes until the eighteenth century. This second shift, resulting in what he calls the domesticated nuclear family, featured more companionship between husband and wife and freedom of choice for children in their marriages and careers. It was not yet the contemporary marriage, he cautions, whose shaky structure is built on the "twin" bases of "sex and romantic love," but unions predicated upon affection and suitability. Earlier research has described similar behavioral alterations occurring from the mid-eighteenth century on in colonial America.[5]

While this interpretation offers a careful description of the changes that occurred in the emotional lives of family members in elite households, it is a far from complete picture of the way domesticity developed in early modern society and leaves several major questions unanswered. First, it covers only a portion of domestic behavior because it largely ignores the labor and commodities involved in the promotion of a house into a home.[6] Heightened household sociability implied a shift in the work patterns of housewives and servants. Although much ink has been spent on the female's loss of the so-called "productive" role, we do not know what replaced it and when.

Second, there is the question of how widespread the changes that Stone and others believe occurred within the family actually were. Almost all of the evidence produced (diaries, letterbooks, and autobiographies) relates to the landed elite, the top echelon of the business community, and clergymen. Did these changes also occur among the remaining 90 percent of families? In the research of Europe and America that has attempted to get at the affective relations of these people, only that on colonial New England explicitly aruges for a pre-industrial shift in feelings similar to Stone's schema.[7] However else they differ, other studies seem to conclude that as long as people lived in agricultural villages few alterations occurred in household relations or the home environment, and because most people lived in such surroundings until the late nineteenth century, domesticity was not of relevance to them until then.[8]

Finally, one wonders about the role of women in these developments. Family historians of the early modern period tend to explain the household's closing of the door on the outside world and domestic impulses as the result of individualism nurtured by affluence. But money can be spent in many different ways, and, as we know from current experience, a heightened sense of self does not necessarily mean flowers in the entry hall or clean kitchen floors. One of the sexes has exhibited a special concern with such matters in the past, and it would be unwise to assume, a priori, that the interest of men and women coincided when it came to expenditures of time and money on homemaking. The literature of Victorian sex roles has suggested men and women waged a silent power struggle in the home and historians have portrayed domesticity alternately as a tool used by a male-dominated society to control females and a means whereby women could exert influence over society.[9] It is an issue that has to be confronted in regard to earlier periods too.

One way to gain a sense of the work behind domesticity, include a broader spectrum of households, and evaluate the interests of the sexes in the development of homemaking during the early modern period is to examine the contents of probate inventories. Routine recording of personal estates began in England during the early sixteenth century and petered out around the second quarter of the eighteenth. In America detailed enumeration of goods continued longer, in some places through the 1800s. These documents contain information on ordinary householders, reveal the physical surroundings in which they lived, and indicate whether money was being channelled into the tools of domesticity or not. In the absence of time allocation studies for past societies, artifacts can help uncover work patterns. If the household had family dinners, morning tea, and home entertainment the evidence should be there in the form of more elaborate eating utensils, teapots, comfortable furniture, musical instruments, and so forth. In this paper, I will rely primarily upon three samples of probate inventories each from a different century and different locations: Oxfordshire, England 1550-1591; central and southern Worcestershire, England 1669-70; and Massachusetts 1774.[10] While each of these areas has its unique characteristics, all could be described as provincial, settled, and predominantly agricultural. As inventories list people's belongings at death, the average age of the sample is older than that of the population. We may assume, therefore, the records reflect the consumption habits of people a decade or so earlier than the dates listed.

Let us begin with the sixteenth century household. It was common for books giving advice on husbandry during the Tudor period to include a section toward the end, after plowing, harvesting, and animal diseases had been thoroughly discussed, that related to the obligations of the "huswife." One of the earliest of the genre was Fitzherbert's *The Book of Husbandry*, published in 1534. The list of housewifely duties he reeled off is rather awe inspiring and has been quoted many times, but what he left out or gave short shrift is also significant. Fitzherbert counselled the wife,

> First in a morning when thou art waked, and proposeth to rise, lift up thy hand, and bless thee, and make a sign of the holy cross . . . in the name of the father, the son and the holy ghost. And if thou say a Pater noster, an Ave, and a Creed, and remember thy maker, thou shalt speed much the better. And when thou art up and ready, then first sweep thy house, dress up thy dishboard, and set all things in good order within thy house: milk the cows, suckle thy calves, sye up thy milk, take up thy children and array them, and provide for thy husbands breakfast, dinner, supper and for thy childrens and servants, and take thy part with them.[11]

That was all he had to say about family dining, childcare, housecleaning, and decoration. The rest of the schedule concerned food, drink, and cloth production for the household: taking grain to the mill, checking the miller did not cheat you, baking, brewing, processing butter and cheese, feeding the pigs, caring for the poultry, planting the herb and vegetable garden, sowing flax and hemp, and making linen and wool cloth. If the farm had no sheep then Fitzherbert directed the housewife to "take wool to spin of clothmakers and by that means . . . have a convenient living." In time of need she should help her mate "fill the dung cart, drive the plough, load hay, corn, and such other." She might also go to the local market to buy and sell commodities. Here Fitzherbert cautioned both her and her husband to be honest with one another and not try to cheat by lying to their spouse about the prices paid and received.

What about after supper when all the tasks had been accomplished? The author quite clearly instructed the head of the household to go to bed unless some work activity was going on.

> One thing I will advise thee to remember, and specially in wintertime, when thou
> sittest by the fire, and hast supped, to consider in thy mind, whether the works that
> thou, thy wife, & thy servants shall do, be more advantage to thee than the fire, and
> candlelight, meat and drink that they shall spend, if it be more advantage, then sit
> still: and if not, then go to thy bed and sleep.[12]

Now obviously few housewives performed all the tasks Fitzherbert outlined, and
not every peasant couple promptly retired after supper in order to rise early the
next morning and repeat the whole regimen over again. What is amazing,
however, was Fitzherbert's assumptions about the proper conduct of the peasant
family, particularly the low value he attached to sociability and human interaction
within the household. His peasant home resembled a workplace. It was unclear if
the husband and the rest of the family ate together, whether the mother's
childcare duties involved more than dressing and feeding her offspring, and how
families relaxed with each other at home. Not only did husbands and wives have
to be on their guard constantly to prevent people from cheating them, but they
could not even trust one another. This is the kind of document that has prompted
historians of the family to conclude that the emotional ambiance in the
preindustrial home differed markedly from that found in *Little Women*.[13]
Fitzherbert's people exhibited their respect and concern for one another by
getting their work done rather than by attending to each other's personal
development.

What did the houses of Fitzherbert's husbandmen and "huswives" look like?
What investments, if any, did they make in domesticity? Most of the inventories
in the earliest sample, the one from Oxfordshire, are post 1570, and, even
allowing for the fact that those being probated are older than the rest of the
population and thus best reflect the living habits of a slightly earlier time, they
would seem to be at least a generation removed from Fitzherbert's day.
Contemporaries and modern historians of Tudor England have claimed that
within this generation substantial improvements had been made in the dwellings
of the populace. William Harrison, writing in the late 1580s, remarked that the old
men in the village where he lived "noted three things to be marvelously altered in
England within their sound remembrance." The first was the increased number of
chimneys:

> in their young days there were not above two and three, if so many, in most uplandish
> towns of the realm (the religious houses and manor places of their lords always
> excepted, and peradventure some great personages), but each one made his fire
> against a reredos [back of an open hearth] in the hall, where he dined and dressed his
> meat.

The second was the replacement of mats by beds:

> for (said they) our fathers, yea, and we ourselves also, have lien full oft upon straw
> pallets, on rough mats covered only with a sheet, under coverlets, made of dagswain
> of hapharlots [I use their own terms], and a good round log under their heads instead
> of a bolster or pillow.

The pillow was thought only appropriate for women in "childbed." After many
years of marriage, Harrison asserted, the head of household considered himself
well off if he could purchase a flock mattress. Lords might not have feather beds,
and servants lacked even a sheet to protect them from the straw irritating their
skin. Finally, the old men remarked upon the substitution of pewter for wooden
eating equipment: "for so common were all sorts of treen stuff in old time that a
man should hardly find four pieces of pewter (of which one was peradventure a

salt) in good farmer's house."[14] Richard Carew, writing in 1602, reported like improvements in West Country standards of living even in the remote area of Cornwall and claimed the "Cornish husbandman conformeth himselfe . . . to the Easterne patterns."[15]

Modern social historians have identified the late sixteenth and early seventeenth century as the time of the "great rebuilding of rural England."[16] What began earlier with churches and houses of the aristocracy by the Elizabethan period had filtered down to the dwellings of yeomen and husbandmen. According to this view, householders started constructing more brick buildings and fireplaces, just as Harrison mentioned, partitioning rooms, and installing glass windows, steps that provided warmer, lighter interiors, and more privacy.

The evidence from the Oxfordshire inventories substantiates several of these suppositions about Tudor-Stuart domestic existence. By the sixteenth century many people no longer lived in just a hall, where cooking, eating, working, sleeping, and general activities took place, and a loft. Poor and average Oxfordshire households* had a mean of 3.6 rooms indicating that some modest differentiation of living quarters was fairly widespread.[17] In Worcestershire about a hundred years later, the same wealth groups had 4.6 rooms. It became less and less necessary to go outside the home to obtain a limited kind of separation from other family members.

Gradually, even in urban laboring class households, people chose to partition rooms although the resulting space amounted to little more than a cubicle. One study of East London in the late seventeenth century describes the average home as a "small two-storied dwelling with an area of about 200 square feet on the ground floor. A house of this size might have as many as eight rooms, two on each floor and two each in cellar and attic . . ."[18] Most households, the author adds, did not have as many as eight, but people routinely divided up the limited space on a floor into smaller areas. As it also appears that the occupation of houses by several families at this time was the exception rather than the rule, these divisions cannot be simply explained as renovations to accommodate additional households.

Although the inventories give difficult to decipher information about the use of brick or stone in buildings and the presence of fireplaces, one may assume that because the government by the 1660s used chimneys as the basis for a national tax, increases had occurred on all levels of society. Glass windows probably had a somewhat slower diffusion pattern. In sixteenth century Oxfordshire, the only sample to list the then novel luxury, no more than 3.8 percent of poor and average wealth decedents had them and among those richer a mere 9.3 percent did. The custom, however, must have spread quickly thereafter. While the state did not levy a window tax until the 1690s, contemporaries proclaimed the near universality of glass usage by the Restoration.[19]

In regard to furnishings, the inventories definitely support contemporary comments about bedding and pewter investments. Between a fourth and a fifth of the total investment in consumer goods went into bedding in all three periods.

*In this paper four personal wealth categories will be used: poor denotes 1-20 pound sterling group; 21-100 pounds is labelled average; 101-300 pounds above average; and over 300 pounds affluent. The evaluations come from the probate inventories, and wealth in real estate, buildings, and slaves/indentured servants is not included. As I explain in more detail in note 17, all the figures have been adjusted for inflation by making them correspond to 1660-1674 prices.

Probated decedents, as a group, had more invested in bedding than they had in their own apparel, household linen, brass and pewter, plate and jewelry or any other single category of goods. The percentage of investment reached a peak in the seventeenth century Worcestershire sample and then declined about five points in eighteenth century Massachusetts. Pewter/brass had its heyday in terms of the proportion of consumer wealth dedicated to it in the sixteenth century (10.8%) and then slowly dropped in the following samples as plate investment increased and pottery came into vogue.[20]

At this point one must ask what is the significance of this miscellany of household changes? I would contend that the changes encouraged household member to spend more time at home. If you were warm, could separate yourself from others occasionally, and had a comfortable bed to retreat to when tired or ill, the desire to escape from so many people living in a small, dingy place must have been diminished.

What about new domestic rituals? This was, of course, the era of the Puritan movement with its emphasis on family and family devotionals. Bibles and pious works that could be used by the household head in leading group prayer sessions did increase between the sixteenth and seventeenth centuries. In Tudor Oxfordshire almost no one had books (1%), but by the Restoration in Worcestershire more than one in six probated decedents possessed a volume or more. To some extent then post-Reformation trends and alterations in the domestic environment reinforced one another.

Having said all this, I believe it would be going too far to suggest that the average household in the sixteenth or even seventeenth century showed many of the signs of the affective or sociable side of domesticity. Stone's patriarchal nuclear family may have had sufficient tools for its needs, but a closed domesticated nuclear family would have had trouble getting along. The furniture needed for comfortable talks, the utensils necessary for true dining, the instruments and games for entertainment cannot be found. Even with the improvements that have just been discussed, the ordinary home still looked as if the occupants expected a flash flood to sweep away their belongings at any moment. Special expenditures were largely confined to bedding, linens, and pewter/brass goods. The wooden part of the bed generally cost less than the textile portions, the flock or feather mattress, coverlets, curtains. Expenditure on other furniture was negligible and consisted of small outlays for tables, benches, and chests. In effect, all the valuables in the house could be quickly grabbed and stuffed into those chests without fear of breakage or of great expense in moving.[21] Households may in fact have kept their linens in them most of the time. Hangings appear to have been the principal kind of decoration, and they also could be packed up easily.

Table I shows the frequency with which commodities turned up as the most heavily invested in consumer item for various wealth groups in sixteenth century Oxfordshire, seventeenth century Worcestershire, and eighteenth century Massachusetts. As mentioned above, bedding dominated the field, both over time and among wealth groups, although the group whose members most frequently made sleeping gear their biggest investment changed from the sixteenth to the eighteenth century. In Elizabethan times, the poorest group had fewer decedents with bedding as their most expensive good (44.6%), presumably because they could not afford the feather mattress and the lush coverings that more substantial families owned or they boarded with someone and had no furnishings. Instead the crude planks joined together that passed for furniture and simple wearing apparel

Table I
PERCENTAGE OF DECEDENTS HAVING A
PARTICULAR GOOD AS MOST EXPENSIVE CONSUMER ITEM

Place and Wealth Group	N	Bedding	Linen	Brass & Pewter	Plate & Jewlery	Furniture	Wearing Apparel	Other
1550-1591 Oxfordshire								
Poor	83	44.6%	12.0	10.8	0.0	16.9	15.7	0.0
Average	113	50.4	15.9	14.2	0.0	4.4	12.4	2.7
Above Average and Affluent	42	64.3	14.3	9.5	9.5	0.0	2.4	0.0
1669-1670 Worcestershire								
Poor	64	76.6	0.0	9.4	0.0	0.0	10.9	31.
Average	128	83.6	0.8	4.7	0.8	0.0	9.4	0.8
Above Average and Affluent	75	66.7	5.3	4.0	9.3	0.0	12.0	2.7
1774 Massachusetts								
Poor	66	60.6	0.0	3.0	1.5	16.7	16.7	1.5
Average	137	59.1	.7	1.5	5.1	7.3	26.3	0.0
Above Average and Affluent	91	48.4	1.1	0.0	20.9	9.9	18.7	1.1

NOTE: For Pound sterling equivalents to wealth descriptions see the note at the bottom of page 7.

SOURCE: See note 10.

registered as "most expensive." None of those with above average wealth or in the affluent group in Tudor Oxfordshire had furniture as their most expensive item. In seventeenth century Worcestershire none of the wealth categories listed furniture, but in pre-Revolutionary Massachusetts furniture made a reappearance, surfacing among the richer groups as well as the poorer. The trend was for bedding initially to be the most expensive good with all those who could afford it and had their own household. As time went one, the same groups became the ones, with bedding needs satiated, who invested in other things — plate, wearing apparel, furniture, and carriages. The poorest wealth group became the one which had the most decedents with beds as the most expensive commodity. Increased investment in consumer goods, as opposed to producer, declining prices in some manufactured goods, and inheritance made these changes possible.

Another observable trend in Table 1 is the declining popularity of linen and brass/pewter as most favored commodities after the sixteenth century. Initially, a quarter of the decedents with wealth in the top category invested most heavily in one or the other. By the seventeenth century the percentage had fallen to under 10 percent, and a hundred years later only 1 percent had either as most expensive. The proportion of consumer goods investments in linen and brass/pewter mimicked the pattern discernible in Table I. Whereas in Tudor Oxfordshire they took up 25 percent of all consumer goods investment, their share dropped to 17.6 percent in Restoration Worcestershire, and then to 11.5 percent in Massachusetts. Declining real prices cannot account for a fall of this magnitude.[22]

The Tudor practice of devoting over one half of consumer goods investment to bedding, linen, and brass/pewter followed a medieval pattern that had been established by the richer elements in the society and had filtered down to the plebs by the sixteenth century.[23] The soft, warm, decorated bed was an isle of refuge in a household sea of discomfort. Neither linen stored in chests nor pewter bowls contributed greatly to relieving the spareness or unsociability of the total environment. Women worked on linens and accumulated stocks as part of their dowries. If their husbands died, they could pack up the linens and move on. Pewter, like linen, made the table look nicer, but it did not denote any major change in dining behavior. It, too, had unequivocal investment value.

Homes were to work, sleep, and, increasingly, to pray in, but not great centers for relaxation and recreation. The average meal, for example, was usually a hurried affair that was not intended to be an occasion for family togetherness. While, according to a contemporary, the Tudor upper class spent much more time eating than ever before, "the poorest sort generally dine and sup when they may so that to talk of their order of repast it were but a needless matter." Domestic economy experts railed against servants being talkative at the table and lingering over food: at dinners, portions should be eaten and then work resumed promptly; at suppers portions should be eaten and then to bed directly.[24]

There is an amusing scene in the late seventeenth century diary of the English apprentice, Roger Lowe, confirming the suspicion that the meals of the "common sort" proceeded at a lively pace. Lowe told of going on an errand to a nearby village and being asked to dinner by the local minister. He sat down next to the servants, received a bowl of porridge, and waited to be given a spoon. The others, having horn spoons in their pockets, quickly polished off their portions and then moved on to the tastier but less plentiful communal dishes. Lowe, noting "their nimbleness in the exercise of their hands from dish to their mouth," realized that the "Hungry Amalakites" would devour all the goodies before he could figure out a way to eat his porridge. Deciding finally to gulp the troublesome mixture down all at once, he merely succeeded in badly burning his mouth.[25] Meals in this period must have often taken on the characteristics of an athletic contest as diners vied with one another to be the first to scrape clean the trenchers.

Of course many working people, even those who had their own cottages, did not regularly dine at home but received victuals at the table of their employer or in the alehouse. Unlike the Victorian establishment who considered the working class pub an unmitigated evil, the Tudor-Stuart authorities actually granted alehouses some legitimacy. The statutes passed condemning the drunkenness and illegal activities that sometimes occurred in these places also recognized the need for each parish to have one "for such supply of the wants of those people who are not able by greater quantities to make their provision of victuals."[26] The alehouse might be little more than a widow's shack, but it provided a place where poor people and laborers, lacking the time or means to prepare meals at home, could resort. They also became the spots where neighbors congregated to drink, hear the news, and play games. By going to an alehouse rather than relaxing at home, one saved the expense of firewood and candles.[27] The government, however, did not approve of *this* use of alehouses and tried to limit the amount of time that could be spent in them and restrict the clientele on Sunday to travelers.

The primary times set aside for leisurely enjoyment of food, drink, and one's fellow human beings came on feast days. Rather than sociability being mixed in with everyday life in the home, people of this period seemed to go more for orgies of it on special occasions. This mentality comes out in the housewifery literature where the woman is told not to "keep companie" with her neighbors "except when she may doe them good, or helpe them," *or* "when she maketh some marriage or assemblies of great companie."[28] Major feasts in England included harvest dinner, the churchales, and Wake or Saint's day, and the celebration of most of them occurred elsewhere than inside the average home. They took place in the hall of the local great man, the church house, a mill, a large barn or in the village square. Lasting often all day and into the night, many feasts involved such an array of dishes that the requisite supplies, labor, and space exceeded the resources of the individual husbandman and his wife, so the community pooled its provisions and dishes for the special day. Most of the recipe books of this period seem primarily directed towards these feasts and banquets. After going through menus for such elaborate events, one early seventeenth century writer then turned to what he called a "humble feast" of two courses with sixteen dishes each day that *any* housewife could prepare herself with little or no help. Needless to say, even the "humble feast" was not the kind of meal you served to a few friends who happened to drop by for dinner.[29]

By the eighteenth century, the investment patterns found in the inventories imply some further changes in the household environment had occurred. Bedding, linen, and brass/pewter assets only took up a third of consumer goods investment in pre-Revolutionary Massachusetts as opposed to one half in sixteenth century Oxfordshire, and a whole group of commodities that promoted domesticity began to surface in ordinary households.

Some hints of this change can be gleaned from Table II which gives the percentage of decedents in various places and times (beyond just the three main samples) that had selected domestic goods. The usefulness of such a table is limited because it does not control for wealth and thus samples that contain more rich decedents than others must show greater ownership of luxuries even though the population as a whole might have less. In this instance, however, that bias matters little because not until the eighteenth century did most of the goods show up at all in the probate records.

Table II
PERCENTAGE OF DECEDENTS WITH SELECTED CONSUMER GOODS

Consumer Goods	Oxford. 1550-91	Worcs. 1669-70	E. London 1661-64	Virg. 1660-75	Worcs. 1720-21	E. London 1720-24	Virg. 1720s	Va. & Md. 1774	Mass. 1774
	N = 253	N = 272	N = 123	N = 133	N = 235	N = 168	N = 298	N = 141	N = 294
Eating & Drinking Equip.									
1. knives and forks	00.0%	00.7	00.0	00.0	2.6	18.5	15.8	70.7	52.7
2. glassware	00.0	1.1	1.6	00.0	3.0	16.7	7.1	45.4	55.9
3. china	00.0	00.0	0.8	00.0	1.7	38.7	1.3	35.5	35.0
4. tea equipment	00.0	00.0	00.0	00.0	1.7	31.6	2.7	48.9	55.4
5. coffee equipment	00.0	00.0	00.0	00.0	2.1	23.2	1.3	19.1	23.5
Furnishings									
1. mahogany furniture	00.0	00.0	00.0	00.0	00.0	00.0	00.0	2.8	15.3
Home Entertainment									
1. musical instruments	.8	0.4	3.2	0.0	0.3	.6	7.1	9.2	0.0

SOURCE: All samples collected by author except Oxfordshire from Michael Ashley Havinden, ed., *Household and Farm Inventories in Oxfordshire* (London, 1965) and the Virginia-Maryland 1774 and Massachusetts 1774 which are in Alice Hanson Jones, *American Colonial Wealth* 3 vols. (New York, 1977).

I decided to examine the extent of ownership of three categories of goods. First, Table II lists items that are associated with eating and drinking in the home: knives and forks, glassware, china (including all queensware and English-made delft), tea and coffee equipment. The presence of these items and others like them indicates that meals in the home had become more elaborate and leisurely events. Eating with knives and forks, I imagine, resulted in slower paced meals, ones that allowed for conversation between bites. Glassware and china decorated a table and were cleaner. The hot drinks, tea, coffee, and chocolate, taken at home, provided more opportunities for domestic get-togethers during the day.

The second category to be looked at is furnishings. I chose mahogany furniture as the indicator of increased commitment to the house beautiful and sociability, the possession of even one piece suggesting aspirations in that direction.

Finally, musical instruments were chosen as an indicator of home entertainment. In the nineteenth century the piano became the great mark of domestic conviviality among a wide range of households. One survey of Massachusetts working-class families in 1876 showed most of them had one.[30] While in the period being studied here, pianos would not be found, other types of instruments might be.

Table III
MASSACHUSETTS 1774 SELECTED CONSUMER ITEMS
OWNED BY EACH WEALTH GROUP

	Poor[a]	Average	Above Average	Affluent
Consumer Goods	N = 66	N = 137	N = 62	N = 29
Eating and Drinking eq.				
1. knives and forks	30.3%	50.4	67.7	82.8
2. glassware	40.9	56.2	58.7	82.8
3. china	18.2	29.2	41.9	86.2
4. tea equipment	42.4	50.4	64.5	89.7
5. coffee equipment	15.2	20.4	21.0	62.1
Furnishings				
1. mahogany furniture	9.1	11.7	11.3	55.2
Home Entertainment				
1. musical instruments	0.0	0.0	0.0	0.0

SOURCE: See Table II
[a]For the pound sterling equivalents of the wealth categories, see note at the bottom of p 7.

Apart from tea, coffee, and mahogany, which came into vogue after the Restoration, and certains kinds of musical instruments, all of the commodities had been in circulation among the European elite since the sixteenth century.[31] Table II indicates, however, that they all remained restricted to this group until the eigthteenth. In the first decades of the 1700s, eating and drinking equipment started showing up much more frequently in the inventories of East Londoners. While this section of London possessed more than its fair share of poor inhabitants, it also had some very rich ones who frequently found their way into the probate records. The metropolis effect probably did mean Londoners bought innovative items earlier than provincial consumers, but this unadjusted table overstates the difference. What cannot be dismissed, however, was the widespread presence of certain of these goods in America by the time of the Revolution.

Before the mid-eighteenth century, then, it is not necessary to break down ownership of these domestic items by wealth group because it is quite apparent that ownership was largely confined to the rich. Afterwards, though, such an analysis becomes worthwhile. Table III gives the breakdown for Massachusetts, and it shows the impact of wealth was quite uniform. Without exception the richer the group the higher the percentage of decedents who possessed the commodity. The table also suggests that decorative furnishings had a way to go yet, as only in the top wealth group did a majority possess a piece of mahogany (55.2%). Musical instruments had made no impact on family life. The 7 and 9 percentage figures for the Chesapeake in Table II reflect the fiddles possessed by a few poorer households. These people probably played at community events, perhaps for money, not for home entertainment.

What really marked the mid-eighteenth century off from previous periods, then, was the diffusion of eating and drinking goods into the ordinary household. As one student of eighteenth century domesticity has suggested, dinner was probably the most popular form of entertainment.[32] Knives and forks, glassware, and tea equipment appeared in a majority of inventories of decedents in the average wealth category. Small craftsmen, husbandmen, and even some laborers fall into this classification, and not only did the majority of them have these goods but nearly a third owned some pieces of china and a fifth possessed coffee equipment. Research on Maryland and on France indicates an increase in tableware around the same time or even a few decades earlier.[33]

Table III proves the importance of wealth in deciding the presence of the tools of domesticity, but what about other factors in determining their dispersion — occupational status, sex, education, urban location, age, and so forth? The influence of these elements on eating and drinking equipment is of particular interest because these goods even show up with regularity among those in the low wealth categories, so obviously other elements come into play.

Perhaps the eighteenth century artifacts that reveal the most about changes in the domestic environment are those associated with tea drinking. Early in the century, the use of this beverage was the preserve of the upper classes. When the *Spectator*, the gossipy London journal, first began publication in 1711, one of the editors recommended the paper "to all well regulated families, that set apart an Hour in every Morning for Tea and Bread and Butter." Make it "a Part of the Tea Equipage," he joked.[34] As has been shown in Table III, however, the practice of drinking tea spread beyond the *Spectator* readership and those with mahogany tea tables and silver spoons. Tea became the drink of the people probably because, in adulterated form, it could be drunk at home without the expense of preparation entailed with beer or even cider, and eighteenth century households did seem to show a preference for goods that could be consumed *en famille*. The breakfast at home with tea replaced the morning draft gulped down at the alehouse or at the abode of an employer.

When tea drinking reached the "common sort" it touched off a long debate in respectable society. Critics of the poor chastised them for squandering their money on tea and sugar and their time on gossip while consuming it. An alleged American "farmer" in one journal complained that breakfast used to take ten minutes when milk and porridge had been served but now took an hour with tea. Women were identified as the heaviest users. On the other hand, defenders of the drink, while admitting that tea might be an "unfortunate shrine of female devotion," argued that there had to be "some relaxation from labour" and tea drunk at home was preferable to liquor imbibed in the alehouse.[35]

Table IV
MASSACHUSETTS 1774, THE EFFECTS OF OCCUPATIONAL
STATUS AND BOOKOWNERSHIP ON THE PROBABILITY
OF DRINKING TEA

N = 276

The probability of tea drinking at home by a decedent with 100 pounds personal wealth (1660-1674 prices), over the age of forty-five, residing in a rural area, and owning no slaves or indentured servants who is a

	Bookowner	Not a Bookowner
1. Gentleman, professional, or merchant	66.6%	44.3%
2. Craftsman, tradesman, or of dual occupation	66.6	44.8
3. Yeoman	44.3	24.2
4. Husbandman or farmer	35.6	17.6
5. Laborer or mariner	77.6	57.9
6. Woman	85.5	68.8

SOURCE: See Table II
For maximum likelihood estimates and their significance levels see Appendix I.

Thus tea became one of those consumer goods that people connected with a change of lifestyle. They linked it with a mass consumer market in non-essentials, with leisure-time sociability in the home, and with women. Was tea especially attractive to the laboring classes? To women? Did proximity to a major marketing center make a difference? The multivariate technique most suitable for investigating these questions is probit analysis.[36] The presence of tea equipment presumably denotes tea drinking, and the probability of tea drinking is what we want to predict for the Massachusetts 1774 sample. *Wealth, Occupational Status, Urban Location, Bookownership* (a proxy for education), *Age, Slave/Indentured Servant Ownership,* are the variables culled from the probate inventories that will do the predicting. Although we already know from Table III that *Wealth* has a strong positive effect on the likelihood of tea drinking, it has to be included in the probit analysis for control purposes. *Occupational Status* allows us to consider the impact of laborers, agricultural types such as yeomen and husbandmen, and women. Because the inventories give no occupational information about females, it is necessary to include them as a category of *Occupational Status* and omit sex as a variable. *Urban Location* measures the commercial influence exerted on consumers by the provincial center of Boston and prominent towns such as Salem as opposed to rural villages. *Bookownership* as a proxy calculates the role of education or literacy in acquiring new tastes. *Age* and the *Ownership of Slaves/ Indentured Servants* were also thrown in because most consumer goods have a life-cycle appeal and the presence of servants accompanies the acquisition of some market commodities. As it happened, *Wealth, Age, Occupational Status* and *Bookownership* all turned out to be significant (see Appendix I), but because we already know about the effects of *Wealth* and because *Age* simply showed the usual affinity of household goods for the prime family building time, the years between 26 and 45, I have concentrated in Table IV on the impact *Occupational Status* and *Bookownership* had on *Tea Drinking.* The reader should be warned that by holding variables constant a rather unreal situation is set up. For example, in Table IV both gentlemen and laborers are assumed to possess 100 pounds of personal wealth while we know gentlemen seldom had so little or laborers so much. Such distortion is necessary, however, to allow the other variables to perform.

Table IV shows that, all other things being equal, laborers were more likely to drink tea than other male occupational groups. If they less often had such equipment in their inventories, therefore, it was due to the fact that they were poorer or less educated, or younger than other males. What is most interesting though, is the sharply lower probabilities of the farm owners, yeomen and husbandmen. This result agrees with other findings I have showing that the farming population had lower total investment in consumer goods and below average holdings in most of the commodities used to indicate domesticity. The role of occupation rather than accessibility to the market seems to have been the problem in the case of tea because living in the provincial center of Boston or the larger towns did not raise the probability to a statistically significant level. It is, of course, difficult to separate out the effects of *Occupational Status* and *Urban Location* due to the obvious relationship between the two. Because husbandmen tended to live in rural areas, craftsmen in towns, and so forth, the two variables explain some of the same variance.

Why the difference between farmers and others? I suspect it was related to the organization of agricultural labor. Farm households found it more difficult to adopt the new meal patterns because too many times a year large amounts of food had to be prepared for farm hands, harvesters, and other workers. Tea and bread would not suffice for field labor in the morning, and a reasonably large farm might find brewing essential. The family could not easily nor economically withdraw themselves from meals with their laborers, so they crept more slowly from the eating schedule described at the beginning of this essay.

But creep away they did, eventually. Writing in the 1820s the Tory essayist, William Cobbett, bemoaned the passing of the good old days when

> Squire Charington used to sit at the head of the oak table with his men, say grace to them, and cut up the meat and the pudding. He might take a cup of strong beer to himself, when they had none; but that was pretty nearly all the difference in their manner of living. So that all lived well.[37]

The present squire, Cobbett reported, had wine decanters, wine glasses, a dinner set, and a breakfast set that "must of necessity have greatly robbed the long oak table if it had remained tenanted." "The Labourers retreated to hovels, called cottages; and instead of board and lodging, they got money," he added ruefully. The farmhouses still had the space for agricultural servants, but the family's lifestyle precluded their presence.

Table IV also shows that women, holding other variables constant, had a higher probability of being tea drinkers (68.8% among those not owning books and 85.5% among those who did) than any male occupational group, lending credence to the contemporary assertion that females had a special attachment to the beverage and its accompanying rituals. It also supports the argument that domesticity was largely a female cause. One, of course, has to be careful in interpreting the findings about women from inventories because it is impossible to control for *Occupational Status*, and only unmarried women (primarily widows) could leave inventories. Consequently the high probability registered for women may be partially attributed to other variables, and the practice of husbands leaving tea equipment to their widows regardless of their preference. I must say the latter proposition does seem highly unlikely, though.

Bookownership did improve the probability of tea drinking although the exact meaning of the finding is not clear. It may mean that literacy encouraged more sophisticated use of the market, or perhaps there was some third variable encouraging both the use of books and tea in the home. This thought occurs because of what we know about the importance of religious works in family devotionals.

What the tea equipment, the knives and forks, crockery, glassware and such seem to indicate is that, during the course of the eighteenth century, the family meal began to take shape along with more entertainment of small groups of outsiders in the home. Besides the shift in breakfast that I just discussed, the evidence from domestic economy books reinforces the impression given by the artifacts found in the inventories that other everyday meals, dinner and supper, became more sociable occasions. For one thing, cookery books dealt more with problems encountered in daily food preparation — giving advice on marketing, recipes for Lenten meals, menus for farm servants and sick people — while feasts received less and less emphasis. In 1708, the *Ladies' Diary*, an almanac popular in England and the colonies, contained in its calendar the fixed and moveable feast days, biblical passages to be read on those days, the times during the year marriages were allowed, and fillers at the bottom of the page giving further information on holiday activities. By 1771, all that material, except for the name of the saints days, had been excluded. The passing of the housewife as server also was an important benchmark. By mid-century she less often stood and served throughout the meal, carving and attending to the needs of those at the table, but more frequently sat down with the rest and ate with them.[38]

In addition, literary evidence indicates some increased attention to washing and cleaning although I do not have sufficient quantitative materials to show when this evolved and who was affected.[39]

The change in relations between household members identified by historians of the early modern family was accompanied by alterations of a material nature that implied a change in the allocation of household labor and involved the purchase of consumer goods. Domesticity cannot be described solely in terms of feelings, for the conversion of homes into centers of sociability required a shift in female work patterns. The change might be described as one of specialization: women's labor in behalf of home consumption gradually ceased being spread thinly over primary, intermediary, and final processes and became concentrated on the last stage. This alteration eventually took place not only in the production of food but clothing, furnishings and even children. Cooking, sewing, decorating, cleaning, and childrearing are final processes, and the special attention devoted to these activities is what domesticity was all about. While female participation in primary and intermediary processes hardly disappeared, more and more it occurred within the context of market production.

The inventories reveal that more than just the elite experienced a change in living habits, for laboring class households readily purchased the more expensive tools of domesticity, teapots, knives and forks, cheap crockery, and so forth. The concept of two stages between the sixteenth century and 1800 seems a sound one. The changes in the domestic environment that began occurring during the sixteenth century made the house a more comfortable place to live for many people as improvements once enjoyed by only the privileged members of society started cropping up in the inventories of husbandmen. The evidence does not suggest, however, the acquisition of new commodities or additional expenditures of female time to promote sociability in the home. Only the increased presence of

Bibles indicates a new domestic function and it was a religious one supervised by the male household head. So what one finds in the first period is a type of patriarchal domesticity.

By the mid-eighteenth century, though, all levels of society showed some traces of new, secular, domestic activities, particularly in relation to eating and drinking. Yeomen and husbandmen households moved slowest into the domestic revolution, but they did move. My samples, of course, are limited in area, and what happened in Germany or France or other areas of the West I cannot tell. Still, it would be a mistake, I think, to assume New England or London were completely different from all other communities and that no changes in domesticity among average households occurred elsewhere until industrialization. Wherever researchers investigate the subject of early modern material culture, whether in the Dutch countryside, on Maryland plantations, or French villages many of the same patterns discussed here can be found.[40]

Increased affluence was undoubtedly necessary for these changes. Bedding, tableware, and furnishings cost money. Plus no one would have wanted to invest in these things and retreat into the home unless the house itself had not grown sturdier, warmer, and lighter — improvements that also require investment. Something else, though, happened. Over the three century period, the same wealth groups progressively invested a higher proportion of their wealth in consumer goods.[41] This trend, I suspect, resulted from the substitution of market for home produced commodities. If you did not manufacture certain goods at home you did not have to invest in the goods needed to produce them. In the long run, it probably raised the family's standard of living because household production of a wide variety of items was inefficient and beyond the economic reach of the laboring class. Non-farm households, both rich and poor, most quickly made this transformation as can be seen in the tea equipment probabilities. These households of course were also growing in number among the general population over time.

It was probably no coincidence that increased investment in domesticity occurred at a time when according to some sources, new "opportunities" for female employment opened up.[42] The availability of wage labor for women and children during the eighteenth century allowed families to purchase more on the market and more of what they bought reflected feminine interests.

In many ways women had the most to gain, considering the constraints placed on their conduct, by added investments in homemaking. They, traditionally, had been in charge "within doors," the house and surrounding yard comprised their workspace. The nature of their work and their childbearing-childcare responsibilities meant they were more tied to the house than men and probably could take less advantage of community gathering places. The evolution of the house into a home made social interaction more accessible to women and put it more under their control. And, then, much of the work connected with the home production of cloth and food could only be described as physically gruelling. Women might have to engage in such activities for wages, but release from some of these tasks — such as bleaching linen or making malt — must have been a welcome relief. Moreover, the improvements they promoted in the domestic environment are those that modern society identifies with a higher standard of living.

Certainly in the historical record one finds much less ambivalence about domesticity among women than men. Males complained about housecleaning upsetting their routine, about the expense of substituting crockery for trenchers and adding parlors, about more elaborate cookery, and so forth.[43] The pub evolved into an anti-domesticity hangout for men, something, for all its rowdiness, the alehouse had never been because there was no need for it. It is difficult not to see a contest of wills in all this. The oppressive interiors and constricting social conventions that stifled the middle-class Victorian female and the technologically complex home whose labor-saving devices drove the twentieth century housewife up the wall may in their origins have been a source of power and influence for the physically vulnerable and legally unequal woman of the early modern period.

Appendix I
CONDITIONAL PROBABILITIES OF TEA DRINKING

Variable	Maximum Likelihood Estimate	Standard Error	Significance Level
Constant	-2.012	.398	.000
Wealth (ln)	.284	.083	.001
Occupational Status[a]			
Gentlemen, mercs., prof.	.566	.291	.050
Husbandmen, farmers	- .233	.316	.470
Craftsmen, trades, dual occup.	.571	.229	.013
Laborers, mariners	.900	.313	.005
Women	1.194	.379	.002
Urban Location[a]			
Provincial center-Boston	.321	.255	.206
Large towns	.373	.341	.275
Book Ownership[a]	.565	.191	.004
Age[a]			
25 and under	- .922	.528	.078
26-45	.502	.184	.007
Slave/Ind. Servt. Ownership[a]	.106	.364	.291

[a]Dummy variables. Reference categories for dummies: occupational status — yeomen; urban location — rural; bookownership — no books; age over 45; slaves/ind. servants ownership — none owned.

-2 times the log likelihood ratio: 65,448, chi square with 12 df significance level = .001
% predicted correctly 71.4

Table of Actual vs. Predicted on Tea Drinking

		Predicted	
		Yes	No
	Yes	79	43
Actual			
	No	36	118

FOOTNOTES

Earlier versions of this paper were presented at the Philadelphia Center for Early American Studies and the OAH-Newberry Library Conference on Women's History and Quantification. I would like to thank those who participated in those sessions for their comments and criticisms. Lloyd Velicer, my research assistant, helped with the coding and computer runs.

1. Scott Burns, *The Household Economy* (Boston, 1977) has argued that the household economy is expanding, but what he is referring to really is an increase in consumer goods and services not the tools and labors of domesticity.

2. Philippe Aries, *Centuries of Childhood* (New York, 1962); Lawrence Stone, *Crisis of the Aristocracy* (Oxford, 1965); and Edward Shorter, *The Making of the Modern Family* (New York, 1976).

3. Lawrence Stone, *The Family, Sex, and Marriage in England 1500-1800* (New York, 1977).

4. Stone, *Family*, p. 216. Stone differs here from Edmund Morgan, *The Puritan Family* (Boston, 1944) and John Demos, *A Little Commonwealth* (New York, 1970), who present the post-Reformation marriage as more companionate. Philip Greven, in *The Protestant Temperament* (New York, 1977) joins Stone in emphasizing the authoritarian element in the intensely religious Protestant family. Also see Ruth H. Bloch, "Untangling the Roots of Modern Sex Roles: A Survey of Four Centuries of Change," *Signs* 4 (1978): 238.

5. Herman R. Lantz, Eloise C. Snyder, Margaret Britton, and Raymond Schmitt, "Pre-Industrial Patterns in the Colonial Family in America: A Content Analysis of Colonial Magazines," *American Sociological Review* 33 (1968): 413-27; and Daniel Scott Smith, "Parental Power and Marriage Patterns: An Analysis of Historical Trends in Hingham Massachusetts," *Journal of Marriage and the Family* 35 (1975): 419-28.

6. On the value of studying the personal services involved in the creation of a domestic environment see Patricia Branca, "Image and Reality: The Myth of the Idle Victorian Woman," in *Clio's Consciousness Raised*, eds. Mary S. Hartman and Lois W. Banner (New York, 1974), 179-89; and W. Elliott Brownlee, "Household Values, Women's Work and Economic Growth 1800-1930," *Journal of Economic History* XXXIX (1979): 199-210. On the relationship of social life and furnishings see Kenneth L. Ames, "Meaning in Artifacts: Hall Furnishings in Victorian American," *Journal of Interdisciplinary History* IX (1978): 19-46.

7. Smith, "Parental Power," and Nancy F. Cott, "Eighteenth-Century Family and Social Life Revealed in Massachusetts Divorce Records," *Journal of Social History* 10 (1976): 20-43.

8. See Shorter, *Modern Family*, pp. 229-43; Hans Medick, "The Proto-Industrial Family Economy: The Structural Function of Household and Family during the Transition from Peasant Society to Industrial Capitalism," *Social History* 3 (1976), especially 303; Olwen Hufton, "Women and the Family Economy in Eighteenth Century France," *French Historical Studies* IX (1975): 11; and Louise A. Tilly and Joan W. Scott, *Women, Work, and Family* (New York, 1978), 208.

9. See Nancy F. Cott's discussion of this literature in her conclusion to *The Bonds of Womanhood: 'Women's Sphere' in New England 1780-1835* (New Haven, 1977), and also Ann Douglas' interesting *The Feminization of American Culture* (New York, 1977).

10. The Oxfordshire inventories are printed in Michael Ashley Havinden, ed. *Household and Farm Inventories in Oxfordshire 1550-1590* (London, 1965); and the Massachusetts inventories are in Alice Hanson Jones, *American Colonial Wealth* II (New York, 1977). I collected the 1669-70 inventories for central and southern Worcestershire. The area and

sample is described in Carole Shammas, "The Determinants of Personal Wealth in Seventeenth Century England and America," *Journal of Economic History* XXXVII (1977): 677-78.

11. Master Fitzherbert, *The Book of Husbandry* (1534) edited by Walter W. Skeat (London, 1832), p. 95. I have modernized the spelling of the words.

12. Ibid., pp. 95-97, 101. Dorothy Davis, *A History of Shopping* (London, 1966), p. 39, comments on Fitzherbert's lack of appreciation for domestic sociability.

13. This conclusion has raised some controversy. For example, see Alan Macfarlane's review of Stone's book in *History and Theory* XVIII (1979), pp. 103-26. While Stone's characterization of the coldness in personal relations may be overdrawn, his argument seems more compelling than Macfarlane's assertion "that the English now have roughly the same family system as they had in about 1250" (*The Origins of English Individualism* [New York, 1979], p. 198).

14. William Harrison, *The Description of England* edited by George Edelen (Ithaca, 1968), pp. 200-01. James Deetz (*In Small Things Forgotten: The Archeology of Early American Life* [New York, 1977]) notes p. 52 that the wooden trenchers were communal tableware.

15. Richard Carew, *Survey of Cornwall* (London, 1602), p. 66.

16. W.G. Hoskins, *Provincial England: Essays in Social and Economic History* (London, 1963), pp. 131-48.

17. The figures in all three samples are in pounds sterling including the Massachusetts numbers. To correct for inflation, I used the Phelps-Brown and Hopkins index ("Seven Centuries of the Prices of Consumables, compared with Builders' Wage-Rates," in *Essays in Economic History*, vol. 2 edited by E.H. Carus-Wilson [New York, 1962], pp. 179-96) to inflate sixteenth century Oxfordshire amounts to 1660-1674 price levels and deflate Massachusetts to that same level, leaving the Worcestershire sample as it is. To reconvert to the original numbers, one can simply multiply the Tudor figures by .558 and the ones for Massachusetts by 1.177. In other words, the Oxfordshire decedent with 100 pounds wealth in my tables actually was listed in the inventory as having 55.8 pounds. the .558 conversion rate was obtained by averaging the prices from 1573-1590 (very few inventories fell into the 1550-1572 period) and comparing that sum with the average from the years 1660-1674. For Massachusetts the years 1760-1774 were used.

18. M.J. Power, "East London Housing in the Seventeenth Century," *Crisis and Order in English Towns 1500-1700* edited by Peter Clark and Paul Slack (London, 1972), pp. 237-62. Alan Everitt and his chapter on farm laborers in the *Agrarian History of England and Wales 1500-1640* edited by Joan Thirsk (Cambridge, 1967), pp. 443-44 reports that a quarter of the Tudor-Stuart inventories of this low status group specified rooms and out of those in the 1560-1600 period 56 percent had three or more rooms and by 1630-40 79 percent did. The rooms most frequently mentioned in descending order were hall, chamber, parlor, buttery, kitchen, dairy (cheese room or milkhouse).

19. Edward Chamberlayne, *Angliae Notitia or the Present State of England* second edition (London, 1669), pp. 29-30 states that "the windows everywhere [were] glazed, not made of Paper or wood, as is usually in Italy or Spain." Carew remarked that at the beginning of the century that Cornish husbandmen commonly had them, , *Survey*, p. 66.

20. The percentages of investment in a specific category of total consumer investment are listed below. I obtained the percentages by dividing the *mean* of the specific good by the *mean* of consumer investment.

	N	Mean Consumer Investment* pounds sterling	Bedding	Pewter/ Brass	Linen	Plate & Jewelry	Apparel	Other
Oxfordshire 1550-91	195	9.8	24.6%	10.8	14.9	4.2	11.8	33.7
Worcestershire 1669-70	198	21.7	26.7	9.5	8.1	4.3	11.1	40.2
Massachusetts 1774	270	32.0	21.9	4.9	6.6	13.2	17.4	36.0

*1660-73 prices

21. Demos, *Little Commonwealth* suggests linens were kept as assets in chests, p. 37.

22. See note 20 for percentages for each item. Accounting for inflation by reducing all prices to those of 1660-74, one finds that in Tudor Oxfordshire the valuations for most linen per sheet and brass per pound actually were below those in eighteenth century Massachusetts and that pewter was only 14 percent cheaper per pound.

23. John Burnett, *A History of the Cost of Living* (Baltimore, 1969), pp. 35-36. Jan deVries, "Peasant Demand Patterns and Economic Development: Friesland 1550-1750," in *European Peasants and Their Markets*, William N. Parker and Eric L. Jones, eds. (Princeton, 1975), pp. 205-68 also finds a decline in linen during the seventeenth century. He attributes it to a fall in household size, but that explanation seems inadequate for the English-American data.

24. Harrison, *Description*, p. 144; and Thomas Tusser, *Five Hundred Points of Good Husbandry*, William Navor, ed. (London, 1812 [collation of 1573, 1580, and 1585 editions]), 249ff. Also see R.N.K. Rees and Charles Fenby, "Meals and Meal-Times," *Englishmen at Rest and Play*, Reginald Lennard, ed. (Oxford, 1931), pp. 208-9.

25. *The Diary of Roger Lowe, 1663-1674* edited by William L. Sachse (New Haven, 1938), pp. 39-40.

26. *A Collection of English Statutes Now in Force* (London, 1611), 6ᵛ, the preamble to 1 James 1 c. 9.

27. On the traditional use of alehouses see Harrison, *Description*, p. 201; *The Diary of Roger Lowe* passim; Sir Frederic Eden, *The State of the Poor* (London, 1797), I, 253; *The Journal of Nicholas Assheton* edited by F.R. Raines *Chetham Society* 14 (1898), 1; and R.F. Bretherton, "Country Inns and Alehouses," in *Englishmen at Rest and Play*. Gathering places on the continent may have been different. See: Lucienne Roubin, "Male Space and Female Space within the Provincial Community," in *Rural Society in France*, eds. Robert Forster and Orest Ranum, trans. Elborg Forster and Patricia Ranum (Baltimore, 1977), 152-80, and Shorter, *Modern Family*, 124-7.

28. Charles Stevens [Estienne] and Jean Liebault, *Maison Rustique or the Country Farms* (London, 1616), Richard Surflet, trans., augmented by Gervase Markham, p. 38.

29. G[ervase] M[arkham], *Countrey Contentments, or the English Huswife* (London, 1623), p. 128. In 1660, the Samuel Pepys' gave a "humble" feast prepared by Mrs. Pepys and her maid, but they held it in the lodgings of his patron, Lord Montagu, presumably because they had not the room in their London house, *The Diary of Samuel Pepys*, Robert Latham and William Matthews, eds. (Berkeley, 1970), I, p. 29. On feasts see Harrison, *Descriptions*; E.B. Robinson, ed. *Rural Economy in Yorkshire, 1641, Being the Farming and Account Books of Henry Best, Surtees Society* 33 (1857), 93; and "Extracts from the Journal of Timothy Burrell . . . 1683-1714," *Sussex Archaelogical Collections* III (1850): 168-69. By Burrell's time, the harvest or Christmas dinner the gentry gave for the locals apparently had become just about what we think of as a dinner. Christina Hole, *The English Housewife in the*

Seventeenth Century (London, 1953), p. 169ff. Discusses the English feasts as does W.P. Baker, "The Observance of Sunday," in *Englishmen at Play*, pp. 79-144. Shorter, *Modern Family*, 129ff, analyzes the phenomenon in Europe.

30. Jeffrey G. Williamson, "Consumer Behavior in the Nineteenth Century: Carroll D. Wright's Massachusetts Workers in 1875," *Explorations in Entrepreneurial* [now *Economic*] *History*, 4, 2nd ser., (1967): 108. On the adoption of the piano by households at the end of the eighteenth and early nineteenth centuries consult the *Oxford English Dictionary* under piano and pianoforte.

31. On the timing of the introduction and diffusion of consumer items in England and America see Burnett, *Cost of Living*, Francis W. Steer, ed., *Farm and Cottage Inventories of Mid-Essex 1635-1749* (Chelmsford, 1950); Ivor Noel-Hume, *A Guide to Artifacts of Colonial America* (New York, 1970); and Marion Day Iverson, *The American Chair* (New York, 1957). Fernand Braudel, *Capitalism and Material Life*, Miriam Kochan, trans. (New York, 1973), gives the big picture.

32. Rosamond Bayne-Powell, *Housekeeping in the Eighteenth Century* (London, 1956), p. 103.

33. Lois Green Carr and Lorena S. Walsh, "Changing Life Styles in Colonial St. Mary's County," *Working Papers from the Regional Economic Research Center, Eleutherian Mills-Hagley Foundation* 1, No. 3 (1978): 85-86, 96-99; and Micheline Baulant, "Niveaux de Vie Paysans Autour de Meaux en 1700 et 1750," *Annales: Economies, Sociétés, Civilisations*, 30 (1975): 513-14.

34. David F. Bond, eds., *The Spectator* (Oxford, 1965), I, 44-45, March 12, 1711 issue. On America see Rodus Roth, "Tea Drinking in Eighteenth Century America," *Contributions from the Museum of History and Technology*, bulletin 225 (1961): 61-91.

35. *American Museum* I, January 1787, 12; John Scott, *Observations on the Present State of the Parochial and Vagrant Poor* (London, 1773), 56. Also see C. Deering's comments in 1739 quoted in J.D. Chambers, "The Vale of Trent, 1670-1800," *Economic History Review Supplement* 3 (1959), 24; John Holt, *General View of Agriculture in Lancaster* (London, 1794), 24-25 quoted in Elizabeth Gilboy, *Wages in Eighteenth Century England* (Cambridge, 1934), 199-200; and David Davies, *The Case of Labourers in Husbandry* (London, 1795), 50ff.

36. Probit analysis is used here because the dependent variable, ownership of tea equipment, is dichotomous. On the technique see Robert S. Pindyck and Daniel L. Rubinfeld, *Econometric Models and Economic Forecasts* (New York, 1976), pp. 247-49. Appendix I contains the maximum likelihood estimates and significance levels for the conditional probabilities listed in Table IV.

37. William Cobbett, *Rural Rides* (New York, n.d.), p. 266-67.

38. E. Smith, *The Modern Husbandman* (Williamsburg, 1742); William Ellis, *The Modern Husbandmen* (London, 1744); William Ellis, *The Country Housewife's Family Campanion* (London, 1750); [Hannah Glasse], *The Art of Cookery* (London, 1758); Susannah Carter, *The Frugal Housewife or Complete Woman Cook* (London and Boston, 1772); and Julia Cherry Spruill, *Women's Life and Work in the Southern Colonies* (Chapel Hill, 1938), p. 70.

39. We do know that soap, blue, and starch were basic items in the budgets of the poor by the 1790s, Eden, *State of Poor*, II and III.

40. Jan deVries, "Peasant Demand Patterns and Economic Development: Friesland, 1550-1750," in *European Peasants and Their Markets*, Willian N. Parker and Eric L. Jones, eds., pp. 205-68; Carr and Walsh, "Life Styles," and Baulant, "Niveaux de Vie Paysans."

41. See my unpublished paper "Consumer Demand in Early Modern Society." Joan Thirsk, *Economic Policy and Projects: The Development of a Consumer Society in Early Modern England* (Oxford, 1978), discusses the new kinds of consumer goods manufactured in England from the mid-sixteenth century on.

42. Neil McKendrick, "Home Demand and Economic Growth: A New View of the Role of Women and Children in the Industrial Revolution," in *Historical Perspectives: Studies in English Thought and Society*, McKendrick, ed. (London, 1974), pp. 152-210.

43. Linda K. Kerber, "The Politicks of Housework," *Signs* 4 (1978): 402-06; *History of the Connecticut Valley in Massachusetts*, I (Philadelphia, 1879), p. 388 — a reference I owe to John Brooke; Margaret Blundell, ed. *Blundell's Diary and Letter Book 1702-1728* (Liverpool, 1952), p. 53; Alice E. Messing, "American Foodways: The First Hundred Years of Domestic Cookery," (unpublished paper, Department of American Civilization, University of Pennsylvania).

10.

CHRISTIAN BROTHERHOOD OR SEXUAL PERVERSION? HOMOSEXUAL IDENTITIES AND THE CONSTRUCTION OF SEXUAL BOUNDARIES IN THE WORLD WAR ONE ERA[1]

George Chauncey, Jr.

In the spring of 1919, officers at the Newport (Rhode Island) Naval Training Station dispatched a squad of young enlisted men into the community to investigate the "immoral conditions" obtaining there. The decoys sought out and associated with suspected "sexual perverts," had sex with them, and learned all they could about homosexual activity in Newport. On the basis of the evidence they gathered, naval and municipal authorities arrested more than 20 sailors in April and 16 civilians in July, and the decoys testified against them at a naval court of inquiry and several civilian trials. The entire investigation received little attention before the navy accused a prominent Episcopal clergyman who worked at the Y.M.C.A. of soliciting homosexual contacts there. But when civilian and then naval officials took the minister to trial on charges of being a "lewd and wanton person," a major controversy developed. Protests by the Newport Ministerial Union and the Episcopal Bishop of Rhode Island and a vigorous editorial campaign by the *Providence Journal* forced the navy to conduct a second inquiry in 1920 into the methods used in the first investigation. When that inquiry criticized the methods but essentially exonerated the senior naval officials who had instituted them, the ministers asked the Republican-controlled Senate Naval Affairs Committee to conduct its own investigation. The Committee agreed and issued a report in 1921 that vindicated the ministers' original charges and condemned the conduct of the highest naval officials involved, including Franklin D. Roosevelt, President Wilson's Assistant Secretary of the Navy and the 1920 Democratic vice-presidential candidate.[2]

The legacy of this controversy is a rich collection of evidence about the organization and phenomenology of homosexual relations among white working class and middle class men and about the changing nature of sexual discourse in the World War I era. The two naval courts of inquiry and the minister's second civilian trial produced some 3,500 pages of testimony from the decoys, suspected "perverts," ministers, and town and naval officials about their relations with men, their often conflicting understandings of sexuality, and their reactions to the investigation itself.[3] On the basis of this evidence it is possible to reconstruct the organization of a homosexual subculture during this period, how its participants understood their behavior, and how they were viewed by the larger community, thus providing a benchmark for generalizations about the historical development of homosexual identities and communities. The evidence also enables us to reassess current hypotheses concerning the relative significance of medical discourse, religious doctrine, and folk tradition in the shaping of popular understandings of sexual behavior and character. Most importantly, analysis of the testimony of the government's witnesses and the accused churchmen and sailors offers new insights into the relationship between homosexual behavior and identity in the cultural construction of sexuality. Even when witnesses agreed that two men had engaged in homosexual relations with each other, they disagreed about whether both men or only the one playing the "woman's part" should be labelled as "queer." More profoundly, they disagreed about how to distinguish between a "sexual" and a "nonsexual" relationship; the navy defined certain relationships as homosexual and perverted which the ministers claimed were merely brotherly and Christian. Because disagreement over the boundary between homosexuality and homosociality lay at the heart of the Newport controversy, its records allow us to explore the cultural construction of sexual categories in unusual depth.

The Social Organization of Homosexual Relations

The investigation found evidence of a highly-developed and varied gay subculture in this small seaport community, and a strong sense of collective identity on the part of many of its participants. Cruising areas, where gay men and "straight" sailors[4] alike knew that sexual encounters were to be had, included the beach during the summer and the fashionable Bellevue Avenue close to it, the area along Cliff Walk, a cemetery, and a bridge. Many men's homosexual experiences consisted entirely (and irregularly) of visits to such areas for anonymous sexual encounters, but some men organized a group life with others who shared their inclinations. The navy's witnesses alluded to groups of servants who worked in the exclusive "cottages" on Bellevue Avenue and of civilians who met at places such as Jim's Restaurant on Long Wharf[5]. But they focused on a tightly-knit group of sailors who referred to themselves as "the gang,"[6] and it is this group whose social organization the first section of this paper will analyze.

The best known rendezvous of gang members and of other gay sailors was neither dark nor secret: "The Army and Navy Y.M.C.A. was the headquarters of all cocksuckers [in] the early part of the evening," commented one investigator, and, added another, "everybody who sat around there in the evening. . . knew it."[7] The Y.M.C.A. was one of the central institutions of gay male life; some gay sailors lived there, others occasionally rented its rooms for the evening so that they would have a place to entertain men, and the Black elevator operators were said to direct interested sailors to the gay men's rooms.[8] Moreover, the Y.M.C.A. was a social center, where gay men often had dinner together before moving to the lobby to continue conversation and meet the sailors visiting the Y.M.C.A. in the evening.[9] The ties which they maintained through such daily interactions were reinforced by a dizzying array of parties; within the space of three weeks, investigators were invited to four "fagott part[ies]" and heard of others[10]

Moreover, the men who had developed a collective life in Newport recognized themselves as part of a subculture extending beyond a single town; they knew of places in New York and other cities "where the 'queens' hung out," made frequent visits to New York, Providence, and Fall River, and were visited by gay men from those cities. An apprentice machinist working in Providence, for instance, spent "week-ends in Newport for the purpose of associating with his 'dear friends,' the 'girls,' " and a third of the civilians arrested during the raids conducted in the summer were New York City residents working as servants in the grand houses of Newport. Only two of the arrested civilians were local residents.[11]

Within and sustained by this community, a complex system of personal identities and structured relationships took shape, in which homosexual behavior per se did not play a determining part. Relatively few of the men who engaged in homosexual activity, whether as casual participants in anonymous encounters or as partners in ongoing relationships, identified themselves or were labelled by others as sexually different from other men on that basis alone. Most observers recognized that many "straight" sailors (their term) had sex with members of the gang, but, as I will explain below, few believed that this alone meant such sailors were homosexual. The determining criterion in labelling a man as "straight" or "queer" was not the extent of his homosexual activity, but the gender role he assumed. The only men who sharply differentiated themselves from other men, labelling themselves as "queer," were those who assumed the sexual and other cultural roles ascribed to women; they might have been termed "inverts" in the early twentieth-century medical literature, because they not only expressed homosexual desire but "inverted" (or reversed) their gender role. [12]

The most prominent queers in Newport were effeminate men who sometimes donned women's clothes — when not in uniform — including some who became locally famous female impersonators. Sometimes referred to as "queens," these men dominated the social activities of the gang and frequently organized parties at their off-base apartments to which gay and "straight" sailors alike were invited. At these "drags" gang members could relax, be openly gay, and entertain straight sailors from the base with their theatrics and their sexual favors. One gay man described a party held in honor of some men from the USS Baltimore in the following terms:

> I went in and they were singing and playing. Some were coked up that wasn't drunk. And there was two of the fellows, 'Beckie' Goldstein and Richard that was in drags, they call it, in costume. They had on some kind of ball gowns, dancing costumes. They had on some ladies' underwear and ladies' drawers and everything and wigs. . . . I saw them playing and singing and dancing and somebody was playing the piano. . . . Every once in a while 'Beckie' (Goldstein) would go out of the room with a fellow and . . . some would come back buttoning up their pants. [13]

Female impersonation was an unexceptional part of navy culture during the World War I years, sufficiently legitimate — if curious — for the *Providence Journal* and the navy's own magazine, *Newport Recruit*, to run lengthy stories and photo essays about the many theatrical productions at the navy base in which men took the female roles. [14] The ubiquity of such drag shows and the fact that numerous "straight"-identified men took part in them sometimes served to protect gay female impersonators from suspicion. The landlord of one of the gay men arrested by the navy cited the sailor's stage roles in order to explain why he hadn't regarded the man's wearing women's clothes as "peculiar," and presumably the wife of the training station's commandant, who loaned the man "corsets, stockings, shirt waists, [and] women's pumps" for his use in *H.M.S. Pinafore*, did not realize that he also wore them at private parties. [15]

But if in some circles the men's stage roles served to legitimate their wearing drag, for most sailors such roles only confirmed the impersonators' identities as queer. Many sailors, after all, had seen or heard of the queens' appearing in drag at parties where its homosexual significance was inescapable. According to the navy's investigators, for instance, numerous sailors in uniform and "three prize fighters in civilian clothes" attended one "fagott party" given in honor of a female impersonator visiting Newport to perform at the Opera House. Not only were some of the men at the party — and presumably the guest of honor — in drag, but two men made out on a bed in full view of the others, who "remarked about their affection for each other." [16] Moreover, while sailors commonly gave each other nicknames indicating ethnic origin (e.g., "Wop" Bianchia and "Frenchman" La Favor) or other personal characteristics (e.g., "Lucky" and "Pick-axe"), many of them knew the most prominent queers *only* by their "ladies' names," camp nicknames they had adopted from the opera such as "Salome," "Theda Bara," and "Galli Curci." [17]

Female impersonation was only the most extreme form of the effeminacy that queers and straights alike considered to be the basis for labelling a man as an invert. Several of the navy's witnesses described other signs of effeminacy one might look for in a queer. A straight investigator explained that "it was common knowledge that if a man was walking along the street in an effeminate manner, with his lips rouged, his face powdered and his eye-brows pencilled, that in the majority of cases you could form a pretty good opinion of what kind of a man he was, . . . a 'fairy.' " [18]

One gay man, when pressed by the court to explain how he identified someone as "queer," pointed to more subtle indicators: "He acted sort of peculiar; walking around with his hands on his hips. . . . [H]is manner was not masculine. . . . The expression with the eyes and the gestures. . . . If a man was walking around and did not act real masculine, I would think he was a cocksucker."[19] A sailor, who later agreed to be a decoy, recalled that upon noticing "a number of fellows. . . of effeminate characters" shortly after his arrival at Newport, he decided to look "into the crowd to see what kind of fellows they were and found they were perverts."[20] Effeminacy had been the first sign of a deeper perversion.

Although a man's effeminacy was regarded as the outward sign of his being queer, his distinctively *sexual* tastes were equally important in the construction of his social role and identity. The inverts grouped themselves together as "queers" on the basis of their effeminate gender behavior,[21] and they all played roles culturally defined as feminine in sexual contacts. But they distinguished among themselves on the basis of the "feminine" sexual behavior they preferred, categorizing themselves as "fairies" (also called "cocksuckers"), "pogues" (men who liked to be "browned," or anally penetrated), and "two-way artists" (who enjoyed both). The ubiquity of these distinctions and their importance to personal self-identification cannot be overemphasized. Witnesses at the naval inquiries explicitly drew the distinctions as a matter of course and incorporated them into their descriptions of the gay subculture. One "pogue" who cooperated with the investigation, for instance, used such categories to label his friends in the gang with no prompting from the court: "Hughes said he was a pogue; Richard said he was a cocksucker; Fred Hoage said he was a two-way artist. . ." While there were some men about whom he "had to draw my own conclusions; they never said directly what they was or wasn't," his remarks made it clear he was sure they fit into one category or another.[22]

A second group of sailors who engaged in homosexual relations and participated in the group life of the gang nonetheless occupied a more ambiguous sexual category because they, unlike the queers, conformed to masculine gender norms. Some of them were heterosexually married. None of them behaved effeminately or took the "woman's part" in sexual relations, they took no feminine nicknames, and they did not label themselves — nor were they labelled by others — as queer. Instead, gang members, who reproduced the highly genderized sexual relations of their culture, described the second group of men as playing the "husbands" to the "ladies" of the "inverted set." Some husbands entered into steady, loving relationships with individual men known as queer; witnesses spoke of couples who took trips together and maintained monogomous relationships.[23] It was on the basis of the husbands' sexual — and sometimes explicitly romantic — interest in men that the queers distinguished them from other men: one gay man explained to the court that he believed the rumor about one man being the husband of another must have "some truth in it because [the first man] seems to be very fond of him, more so than the average man would be for a boy."[24] But the ambiguity of the sexual category such men occupied was reflected in the difficulty observers found in labelling them. The navy, which sometimes grouped such men with the queers as "perverts," found it could only satisfactorily identify them by describing what they *did*, rather than naming what they *were*. One investigator, for instance, provided the navy with a list of suspects in which he carefully labelled some men as "pogues" and others as "fairies," but he could only identify one man by noting that he "went out with all the above named men at various times and had himself sucked off or screwed them through the rectum."[25] Even the queers' terms for such men — "friends" and "husbands" — identified the men only *in relation to* the queers, rather than according them an autonomous sexual identity. Despite the uncertain definition of their sexual identity, however, most observers recognized these men as regular — if relatively marginal — members of the gang.

The social organization of the gang was deeply embedded in that of the larger culture;

as we have seen, its members reproduced many of the social forms of genderized heterosexuality, with some men playing "the woman's part" in relationships with conventionally masculine "husbands." But the gang also helped men depart from the social roles ascribed to them as biological males by that larger culture. Many of the "queers" interrogated by the navy recalled having felt effeminate or otherwise "different" most of their lives. But it was the existence of sexual subcultures — of which the gang was one — that provided them a means of structuring their vague feelings of sexual and gender difference into distinctive personal identities. Such groups facilitated people's exploration and organization of their homosexuality by offering them support in the face of social opprobrium and providing them with guidelines for how to organize their feelings of difference into a particular social form of homosexuality, a coherent identity and way of life. The gang offered men a means of assuming social roles which they perceived to be more congruent with their inner natures than those prescribed by the dominant culture, and sometimes gave them remarkable strength to publicly defy social convention.

At the same time, the weight of social disapprobation led people within the gang to insist on a form of solidarity which required conformity to its own standards even as it offered release from the behavioral imperatives of the dominant culture. To be accepted by the gang, for instance, one had to assume the role of pogue, fairy, two-way artist, or husband, and present oneself publicly in a manner consistent with that labelling. But while men chose to assume one or another role on the basis of which most closely approximated their sexual preferences, they appear to have maintained a critical perspective on the significance of the role for their personal identities. Even while assuming one role for the purpose of interaction in the gang, at least some continued to explore their sexual interests when the full range of those interests was not expressed in the norms for that role. Frederick Hoage, for instance, was known as a "brilliant woman" and a "French artist" (or "fairy"), but he was also reported surreptitiously to have tried to "brown" another member of the gang — behavior inappropriate to a "queer" as defined by the gang.[26]

Gang members, who believed they could identify men as pogues or fairies even if the men themselves had not yet recognized their true natures, sometimes intervened to accelerate the process of self-discovery. The gang scrutinized newly arrived recruits at the Y.M.C.A. for likely sexual partners and "queers," and at least one case is recorded of their approaching an effeminate but "straight"-identified man named Rogers in order to bring him out as a pogue. While he recalled always having been somewhat effeminate, after he joined the gang Rogers began using make-up "because the others did," assumed the name "Kitty Gordon," and developed a steady relationship with another man (his "husband").[27] What is striking to the contemporary reader is not only that gang members were so confident of their ability to detect Rogers' homosexual interests that they were willing to intervene in the normal pattern of his life, but that they believed they could identify him so precisely as a "latent" (not their word) pogue.

Many witnesses indicated they had at least heard of "fairies" before joining the service, but military mobilization, by removing men like Rogers from family and neighborhood supervision and placing them in a single-sex environment, increased the chances that they would encounter gay-identified men and be able to explore new sexual possibilities. Both the opportunities offered by military mobilization and the constraints of hometown family supervision were poignantly reflected in Rogers' plea to the court of inquiry after his arrest. After claiming that he had met gay men and had homosexual experiences only after joining the navy, he added:

I got in their company. I don't know why; but I used to go out with them. I would like to say here that these people were doing this all their lives. I never met one until I came in the Navy. . . . I would like to add that I would not care for my folks to learn anything about this; that I would suffer everything, because I want them to know me as they think I am. This is something that I never did until I came in the Navy.[28]

Straight witnesses at the naval inquiry demonstrated remarkable familiarity with homosexual activity in Newport; like gay men, they believed that "queers" constituted a distinct group of people, "a certain class of people called 'fairies.' "[29] Furthermore, almost all of them agreed that one could identify certain men as queer by their mannerisms and carriage. At the second court of inquiry, a naval official ridiculed the Bishop of Rhode Island's assertions that it was impossible to recognize "fairies" and that he had never even heard of the term as if claiming such naïveté were preposterous:

Then you don't know whether or not it is common to hear in any hotel lobby the remark, when a certain man will go by, and somebody will say, 'There goes a fairy.' You have *never* heard that expression used in that way?[30]

Not only did most people recognize the existence of individual "fairies," but they knew that such men had organized a collective life, even if they were unfamiliar with its details. As we have seen, many sailors at the naval training station knew that the Y.M.C.A. was a "headquarters" for such people, and Newport's mayor recalled that "it was information that was common. . . in times gone by, summer after summer," that men called "floaters" who appeared in town "had followed the fleet up from Norfolk."[31] In a comment which reveals more about straight perceptions than gay realities, a navy officer described gay men to the Newport Chief of Police as "a gang who were stronger than the Masons. . . [and who] had signals and a lot of other stuff. . . [T]hey were perverts and well organized."[32]

"Straight" people's familiarity with the homosexual subculture resulted from the openness with which some gay men rejected the cultural norms of heterosexuality. Several servicemen, for instance, mentioned having encountered openly homosexual men at the naval hospital, where they saw patients and staff wear make-up and publicly discuss their romances and homosexual experiences.[33] The story of two gang members assigned to the Melville coaling station near Newport indicates the extent to which individual "queers," with the support of the gang, were willing to make their presence known by defying social convention, even at the cost of hostile reactions. "From the time that they arrived at the station they were both the topic of conversation because of their effeminate habits," testified several sailors stationed at Melville. Because the men refused to conform to masculine norms they suffered constant harassment; many sailors refused to associate with them or abused them physically and verbally, while their officers assigned them especially heavy work loads and ordered their subordinates to "try to get [one of them] with the goods."[34] Straight sailors reacted with such vigor because the gay men flaunted their difference rather than trying to conceal it, addressing each other with "feminine names," witnesses complained, and "publish[ing] the fact that they were prostitutes and such stuff as that."[35] At times they were deliberately provocative; one astounded sailor reported that he had "seen Richard lying in his bunk take one leg and, putting it up in the air, ask everyone within range of his voice and within range of this place how they would like to take it in this position."[36]

Even before the naval inquiry began, Newport's servicemen and civilians alike were well aware of the queers in their midst. They tolerated them in many settings and brutalized them in others, but they thought they knew what they were dealing with: perverts were men who behaved like women. But as the inquiry progressed, it inadvertently brought the neat boundaries separating queers from the rest of men into question.

Disputing the Boundaries of the "Sexual"

The testimony generated by the navy investigation provided unusually detailed information about the social organization of men who identified themselves as "queer." But it also revealed that many more men than the queers were regularly engaging in some form of homosexual activity. Initially the navy expressed little concern about such men's behavior, for it did not believe that straight sailors' occasional liaisons with queers raised any questions about their sexual character. But the authorities' decision to prosecute men not normally labelled as queer ignited a controversy which ultimately forced the navy and its opponents to define more precisely what they believed constituted a homosexual act and to defend the basis upon which they categorized people participating in such acts. Because the controversy brought so many groups of people — working- and middle-class gay and straight-identified enlisted men, middle-class naval officers, ministers, and town officials — into conflict, it revealed how differently those groups interpreted sexuality. A multiplicity of sexual discourses co-existed at a single moment in the civilian and naval seaport communities.

The gang itself loosely described the male population beyond the borders of its inner circle of "queers" and "husbands" as "straight," but its members further divided the straight population into two different groups: those who would reject their sexual advances, and those who would accept them. A man was "trade," according to one fairy, if he "would stand to have 'queer' persons fool around [with] him in any way, shape or manner."[37] Even among "trade," gay men realized that some men would participate more actively than others in sexual encounters. Once they had confirmed a straight sailor's sexual availability, gay men who were so inclined felt free to indicate their own interests, even though the sailor clearly set the limits. Most gay men were said to prefer men who were strictly "straight and [would] not reciprocate in any way," but at least one fairy, as a decoy recorded, "wanted to kiss me and love me [and]...insisted and begged for it."[38] The etymology of the term, which was widely used by gay men in the United States from the turn of the century until the 1960s, is unclear, but "trade" accurately described a common pattern of interaction between gay men and their straight sexual partners. In Newport, a gay man might take a sailor to a show or to dinner, offer him small gifts, or provide him with a place to stay when he was on overnight leave; in exchange, the sailor allowed his host to have sex with him that night, within whatever limits the sailor cared to set. The exchange was not always so elaborate: the navy's detectives reported several instances of gay men meeting and sexually servicing numerous sailors at the Y.M.C.A. in a single evening. Men who were "trade" normally did not expect or demand direct payment for their services, although gay men did sometimes lend their partners small amounts of money without expecting it to be returned, and they used "trade" to refer to some civilians who, in contrast to the sailors, paid *them* for sexual services. "Trade" normally referred to straight-identified men who played the "masculine" role in sexual encounters solicited by "queers."[39]

The boundary separating trade from the rest of men was easy to cross. As we have seen, there were locations in Newport, such as the Y.M.C.A., a bridge, and sections of Bellevue Avenue, where straight men knew they could present themselves in order to be solicited. One decoy testified that to infiltrate the gang he merely sat with its members in the Y.M.C.A. lobby one evening. As the decoy had already been in Newport for some time, presumably without expressing any interest in the gang, a gang member named Kreisberg said

> he was surprised to see me in such company. I finally told him that I belonged to the gang and very soon after that Kreisberg...said 'So we can consider you trade?' I replied

that he could. Very soon Kreisberg requested that I remove my gloves as he, Kreisberg, wanted to hold my hands. Kreisberg acknowledged that he was abnormal and wanted to spend the night with me.[40]

Almost all straight sailors agreed that the effeminate members of the gang should be labelled "queer," but they disagreed about the sexual character of a straight man who accepted the sexual advances of a queer. Many straight men accepted it as a matter of course that young recruits would accept the sexual solicitations of the perverts. "It was a shame to let these kids come in and run in to that kind of stuff," remarked one decoy; but his remarks indicate he did not think a boy was "queer" just because he let a queer have sex with him.[41] The nonchalance with which many sailors regarded such sexual encounters was strikingly revealed by the ways in which they defined "queers" to the court of inquiry. Most pogues defined themselves as "men who like to be browned," but straight men casually defined pogues as "[people] *that you can brown*'" and as men who "offered themselves in the same manner which women do."[42] Both remarks imply that "normal" men could take advantage of the pogues' availability without questioning their own identities as "straight;" the fact that the sailors made such potentially incriminating statements before the naval court indicates that this was an assumption they fully expected the board to share (as in fact it did). That lonesome men could unreservedly take advantage of a fairy's availability is perhaps also the implication, no matter how veiled in humor, of the remark made by a sailor stationed at the Melville coaling station near Newport: "it was common talk around that the Navy Department was getting good. They were sending a couple of 'fairies' up there for the 'sailors in Siberia.' As we used to call ourselves...meaning that we were all alone."[43] The strongest evidence of the social acceptability of trade was that the enlisted men who served as decoys volunteered to take on the role of trade for the purpose of infiltrating the gang, but were never even asked to consider assuming the role of queer. Becoming trade, unlike becoming a queer, posed no threat to the decoys' self-image or social status.

While many straight men took the sexual advances of gay men in stride, most engaged in certain ritual behavior designed to reinforce the distinction between themselves and the "queers." Most importantly, they played only the "masculine" sex role in their encounters with gay men — or at least claimed that they did — and observed the norms of masculinity in their own demeanor. They also ridiculed gay men and sometimes beat them up after sexual encounters in order to distance themselves from them. Other men, who feared it brought their manhood into question simply to be approached by a "pervert," were even more likely to attack gay men. Gang members recognized that they had to be careful about whom they approached: some men might respond violently to the mere suggestion of a sexual encounter, and others to the fact of its consummation. They all knew friends who had received severe beatings upon approaching the wrong man.[44] The more militant of the queers even played on straight men's fears in order to taunt them. One of the queers at the Melville coaling station "made a remark that 'half the world is queer and the other half trade,'" recalled a straight sailor, who then described the harassment the queer suffered in retribution.[45]

It is now impossible to determine how many straight sailors had such sexual experiences with the queers, although Alfred Kinsey's research suggests the number might have been large. Kinsey found that 37% of the men he interviewed in the 1930s and 1940s had engaged in some homosexual activity, and that a quarter of them had had "more than incidental homosexual experience or reactions" for at least three years between the ages 16 and 55, even though only 4% were exclusively homosexual throughout their lives.[46] Whatever the precise figures at Newport, naval officials and queers alike believed that very many men were involved. Members of the court of inquiry never challenged the veracity of the numerous reports given them of straight sailors having sex with the queers; their chief investigator informed them on the first day of testimony that one suspected pervert had fellated "something like fifteen or twenty young recruits from the Naval Training Station" in a single night. As the investigation progressed, however, even the court of inquiry became concerned about the extent of homosexual activity uncovered. The chief investigator later claimed that the chairman of the first court had ordered him to curtail the investigation because " 'If your men [the decoys] do not knock off, they will hang the whole state of Rhode Island.' "[47]

While straight sailors disagreed about the boundaries between "friends," "trade," and "straights," naval officials sought to distinguish the actively "perverted" from the merely complicit in their own way. As we have seen, they were aware of the number of sailors whom engaged in occasional homosexual activity at Newport. But they never considered prosecuting the many sailors who they fully realized were being serviced by the fairies each year, because they did not believe that the sailors' willingness to allow such acts "to be performed upon them" in any way implicated their sexual character as homosexual.

Instead, the navy chose to prosecute only those men who were intimately involved in the gang, or otherwise demonstrated (as the navy tried to prove in court) that homosexual desire was a persistent, constituent element of their personalities, whether or not it manifested itself in effeminate behavior. The fact that naval and civilian authorities could prosecute men only for the commission of specific acts of sodomy should not be construed to mean that they viewed homosexuality simply as an act rather than as a condition characteristic of certain individuals; the whole organization of their investigation suggests otherwise. At the January 1920 trial of Rev. Kent the prosecution contended that

> we may offer evidence of other occurences similar to the ones the indictment is based on for the purpose of proving the disposition on the part of this man. I submit that it is a well known principle of evidence that in a crime of this nature where disposition, inclination, is an element, that we are not confined to the specific conduct which we have complained of in the indictment, that the other incidents are gone into for their corroborative value as to intent, as to disposition, inclination.[48]

As the investigation and trials proceeded, however, the men prosecuted by the navy made it increasingly difficult for the navy to maintain standards which categorized certain men as "straight" even though they had engaged in homosexual acts with the defendants. This was doubtless particularly troubling to the navy because, while its opponents focused their questions on the character of the decoys in particular, by doing so they implicitly questioned the character of *any* man who had sex with a "pervert." The decoys testified that they had submitted to the queers' sexual advances only in order to rid the navy of their presence, and the navy, initially at least, guaranteed their legal immunity. But the defendants readily charged that the decoys themselves were tainted by homosexual interest and had taken abnormal pleasure in their work. Rev. Kent's lawyers were particularly forceful in questioning the character of any man who would volunteer to work as a decoy. As one decoy after another helplessly answered each question with a quiescent "Yes, sir," the lawyers pressed them:

Q. You volunteered for this work?
A. Yes, sir.
Q. You knew what kind of work it was before you volunteered, didn't you?
A. Yes, sir.
Q. You knew it involved sucking and that sort of thing, didn't you?
A. I knew that we had to deal with that, yes, sir.

Q. You knew it included sodomy and that sort of thing, didn't you?
A. Yes, sir.
Q. And you were quite willing to get into that sort of work?
A. I was willing to do it, yes, sir.
Q. And so willing that you volunteered for it, is that right?
A. Yes, sir. I volunteered for it, yes, sir.
Q. You knew it included buggering fellows, didn't you?[49]

Such questions about the decoys' character were reinforced when members of the gang claimed that the decoys had sometimes taken the initiative in sexual encounters.

The defendants raised questions about the character not only of men who volunteered to be decoys but of any man capable of responding to the advances of a pervert. Such questions forced the navy to reexamine its standards for distinguishing "straight" from "perverted" sexuality. At the second naval court of inquiry, even the navy's judge advocate asked the men about how much sexual pleasure they had experienced during their contacts with the suspects. As the boundaries distinguishing acceptable from perverted sexual response began to crumble, the decoys recognized their vulnerability and tried to protect themselves. Some simply refused to answer any further questions about the sexual encounters they had described in graphic detail to the first court. One decoy protested that he had never responded to a pervert's advances: "I am a man...The thing was so horrible in my sight that naturally I could not become passionate and there was no erection," but was immediately asked, "Weren't [the other decoys] men, too?" Another, less fortunate decoy had to plead:

Of course, a great deal of that was involuntary inasmuch as a man placing his hand on my penis would cause an erection and subsequent emission. That was uncontrollable on my part...
Probably I would have had it [the emission] when I got back in bed anyway...It is a physiological fact.[50]

But if a decoy could be suspected of perversion simply because he had a certain physiological response to a pervert's sexual advances, then the character of countless other sailors came under question. Many more men than the inner circle of queers and husbands would have to be investigated. In 1920, the navy was unprepared to take that step. The decision of the Dunn Inquiry to condemn the original investigation and the navy's decision to offer clemency to some of the men imprisoned as a result of it may be interpreted, in part, as a quiet retreat from that prospect.

Christian Brotherhood under Suspicion

The navy investigation revealed that even when two men engaged in what was generally regarded as a "sexual" relationship, whether both or only one of them should be labelled a sexual pervert was still disputed. But the investigation raised even more fundamental questions — concerning the definition of a "sexual relationship" itself — when it reached beyond the largely working-class milieu of the military to label a prominent local Episcopal clergyman, Samuel Kent, and a Y.M.C.A. volunteer and churchman, Arthur Leslie Green, as homosexual. When Kent fled the city, the navy tracked him down and brought him to trial on sodomy charges. Two courts acquitted him despite the fact that five decoys claimed to have had sex with him, because the denials of the respected minister and of the numerous clergymen and educators who defended him seemed more credible. Soon after Kent's second acquittal in early 1920, the Bishop of Rhode Island and the Newport Ministerial Union went on the offensive against the navy. The clergymen charged that the navy had used immoral methods in its investigation, by instructing young enlisted men "in the details of a nameless vice" and sending them into the community to entrap innocent citizens. They wrote letters of protest to the Secretary of the Navy and the President, condemned the investigation in the press, and forced the navy to convene a second court of inquiry into the methods used in the first inquiry. When it exculpated senior naval officials and failed to endorse all of the ministers' criticisms, the ministers persuaded the Republican-controlled Senate Naval Affairs Committee to undertake its own investigation, which eventually endorsed all of the ministers' charges.[51]

The simple fact that one of their own had been attacked did not provoke the fervor of the ministers' response to the navy investigation, nor did they oppose the investigation simply because of its "immoral" methods. Close examination of the navy's allegations and of the ministers' countercharges suggests that the ministers feared that the navy's charges against the two churchmen threatened to implicate them all. Both Green and Kent were highly regarded local churchmen; Kent had been asked to preach weekly during Lent, had received praise for his work at the Naval Hospital during the influenza epidemic, and at the time of the investigation was expected to be named Superintendant of a planned Seaman's Church Institute.[52] Their behavior had not differed markedly from that of the many other men who ministered to the needs of the thousands of boys brought to Newport by the war. When the Navy charged that Kent's and Green's behavior and motives were perverted, many ministers feared that they could also be accused of perversion, and, more broadly, that the inquiry had questioned the ideology of nonsexual Christian brotherhood that had heretofore explained their devotion to other men. The confrontation between the two groups represented fundamentally a dispute over the norms for masculine gender behavior and over the boundaries between homosociality and homosexuality in the relations of men.

The investigation threatened Newport's ministers precisely because it repudiated those conventions that had justified and institutionalized a mode of behavior for men of the cloth or of the upper class that would have been perceived as effeminate in other men. The ministers' perception of this threat is reflected in their repeated criticism of the navy operatives' claim that they could detect perverts by their "looks and actions."[53] Almost all sailors and townspeople, as we have seen, endorsed this claim, but it put the ministers as a group in an extremely awkward position, for the major sign of a man's perversion according to most sailors was his being effeminate. As the ministers' consternation indicated, there was no single norm for masculine behavior at Newport; many forms of behavior considered effeminate on the part of working-class men were regarded as appropriate to the status of upper-class men or to the ministerial duties of the clergy. Perhaps if the navy had accused only working-class sailors, among whom "effeminacy" was more clearly deviant from group norms, of perversion, the ministers might have been content to let this claim stand. But when the naval inquiry also identified churchmen associated with such an upper-class institution as the Episcopal Church of Newport as perverted because of their perceived effeminacy, it challenged the norms which had heretofore shielded men of their background from such suspicions.

One witness tried to defend Kent's "peculiar" behavior on the basis of the conventional norms when he contended that "I don't know whether you would call it abnormal. He was a minister."[54] But the navy refused to accept this as a defense, and witnesses repeatedly described Kent and Green to the court as "peculiar," "sissyfied," and "effeminate." During his daily visits to patients at the hospital, according to a witness named Brunelle, Green held the patients' hands and "didn't talk like a man — he talk[ed] like a woman to me."[55] Since there is no evidence that Green had a high-pitched or otherwise "effeminate" *voice*, Brunelle probably meant Green addressed men with greater affection than he expected of a man. But all ministers visited with patients and spoke quiet, healing words to them; their position as ministers had permitted them to engage in such conventionally "feminine" behavior. When the navy and ordinary sailors labelled this behavior "effeminate" in the case of Green and Kent, and further claimed that such effeminacy was a sign of sexual perversion, they challenged the legitimacy of many Christian social workers' behavior.

Even more disturbing to the ministers was the navy's charge that perverted sexual interest had motivated Kent's and Green's ministry to young enlisted men. During the war, Newport's clergymen had done all they could to minister to the needs of the thousands of boys brought to the Naval Training Station. They believed they had acted in the spirit of Christian brotherhood, but the naval inquiry seemed to suggest that less lofty motives were at work. Ministers had loaned sailors money, but during the inquiry they heard Green accused of buying sex. They had visited boys in the hospital and now heard witnesses insinuate that this was abnormal: "I don't know what [Kent's] duties were, but he was always talking to some boys. It seems though he would have special boys to talk to. He would go to certain fellows [patients] and probably spend the afternoon with them."[56] They had given boys drives and taken them out to dinner and to the theater, and now heard Kent accused of lavishing such favors on young men in order to further his salacious purposes. They had opened their homes to the young enlisted men but now heard Kent accused of inviting boys home in order to seduce them.[57] When one witness at the first court of inquiry tried to argue that Green's work at the Y.M.C.A. was inspired by purely "charitable" motives, the court repudiated his interpretation and questioned the motives of *any* man who engaged in such work:

> Do you think a normal active man would peddle stamps and paper around a Hospital and at the Y.M.C.A.?...
> Do you think that a man who had no interest in young boys would voluntarily offer his services and work in the Y.M.C.A. where he is constantly associated with young boys?[58]

To question the motives of Green in this manner was to raise questions about the motives of all the men who had worked with him during the war, and this posed personal and professional dangers of the greatest magnitude. Rev. Deming of the Ministerial Union reported that numerous ministers shared the fear of one man who was "frantic after all he had done for the Navy:"

> When this thing [the investigation] occurred, it threw some of my personal friends into a panic. For they knew that in the course of their work they had had relations with boys in various ways; they had been alone with them in some cases. As one boy [a friend] said, frequently boys had slept in the room with him. But he had never thought of the impropriety of sleeping alone with a navy boy. He thought probably he would be accused.[59]

The ministers sought to defend Kent — and themselves — from the navy's insinuations by reaffirming the cultural interpretation of ministerial behavior as Christian and praiseworthy. While they denied the navy's charge that Kent had had genital contact with sailors, they did not deny his devotion to young men, for to have done so would have implicitly conceded the navy's interpretation of such behavior as salacious — and thus have left all ministers who had demonstrated similar devotion open to suspicion. Rather than deny the government's claim that Kent had sought intimate relationships with sailors and devoted unusual attention to them, therefore, Kent and his supporters depicted such behavior as an honorable part of the man's ministry. Indeed, demonstrating just how much attention Kent had lavished on boys became as central to the strategy of the ministers as it was to that of the government, but the ministers offered a radically different interpretation of it. Their preoccupation with validating ministerial behavior turned Kent's trial and the second naval inquiry into an implicit public debate over the cultural definition of the boundaries between homosociality and homosexuality in the relations of men. The navy had defined Kent's behavior as sexual and perverted; the ministers sought to reaffirm that it was brotherly and Christian.

Kent himself interpreted his relations with sailors as "[t]rying to be friends with them, urging them to come to my quarters and see me if they wanted to, telling them – I think, perhaps, I can best express it by saying 'Big Brotherhood.' " He quoted a letter from another minister commending his "brotherly assistance" during the influenza epidemic, and he pointed out that the Episcopal War Commission provided him with funds with which to take servicemen to the theater "at least once a week" and to maintain his automobile in order to give boys drives "and get acquainted with them."[60] He described in detail his efforts to minister to the men who had testified against him, explaining that he had offered them counsel, a place to sleep, and other services just as he had to hundreds of other enlisted men. But he denied that any genital contact had taken place, and in some cases claimed he had broken off the relationships when he realized that the *decoys* wanted sexual contact.

Kent's lawyers produced a succession of defense witnesses – respected clergymen, educators, and businesspeople who had known Kent at every stage of his career – to testify to his obvious affection for boys, even though by emphasizing this aspect of his character they risked substantiating the navy's case. The main point of their testimony was that Kent was devoted to boys and young men and had demonstrated such talent in working with them that they had encouraged him to focus his ministry on them. Kent's lawyers prompted a former employer from Kent's hometown of Lynn, Massachusetts, to recall that Kent, a "friend of [his] family, and especially [his] sons and sons' associates," had "[taken] charge of twelve or fourteen boys [from Lynn] and [taken] them down to Sebago Lake," where they camped for several weeks "under his charge."[61] The Bishop of Pennsylvania recalled that, as Kent's teacher at the Episcopal Theological School in Cambridge in 1908, he had asked Kent to help him develop a ministry to Harvard men, "because [Kent] seemed peculiarly fitted for it in temperment and in experience, and in general knowledge of how to approach young men and influence them for good."[62] The rector of the Holy Church of the Communion in New York, where Kent had served as assistant minister from 1913-1915, testified that he had also assigned Kent to youth work because of his obvious talents and called Kent "a perfectly splendid manly man among men and boys."[63] The sentiments of Kent's character witnesses were perhaps best summarized by a judge who sat on the Episcopal War Commission which employed Kent. The judge assured the court that Kent's reputation was "excellent; I think he was looked upon as an earnest Christian man [who] was much interested in young men."[64]

The extent to which Kent's supporters were willing to interpret his intimacy with young men as brotherly rather than sexual is perhaps best illustrated by the effort of Kent's defense lawyer to show how Kent's inviting a decoy named Charles Zipf to sleep with him was only another aspect of his ministering to the boy's needs. Hadn't the decoy told Kent he was "lonesome" and had no place to sleep that night, the defense attorney pressed Zipf in cross-examination, before Kent invited him to spend the night in his parish house? And after Kent had set up a cot for Zipf in the living room, hadn't Zipf told Kent that he was "cold" before Kent pulled back the covers and invited him to join him in his bed?[65] The attorney counted on the presumption of Christian brotherhood to protect the minister's behavior from the suspicion of homosexual perversion, even though the same evidence would have seemed irrefutably incriminating in the case of another man.

Kent's defense strategy worked. Arguments based on assumptions about ministerial conduct persuaded the jury to acquit Kent of the government's charges. But Newport's ministers launched their campaign against the navy probe as soon as Kent was acquitted because they recognized that it had succeeded in putting their devotion to men under suspicion. It had raised questions about the cultural boundaries distinguishing homosexuality from homosociality that the ministers were determined to lay to rest.

But while it is evident that Newport's ministers feared the consequences of the investigation for their public reputations, two of their charges against the navy suggest that they may also have feared that its allegations contained some element of truth. The charges reflect the difference between the ministers' and the navy's understanding of sexuality and human sinfulness, but the very difference may have made the navy's accusations seem plausible in a way that the navy could not have forseen. First, the ministers condemned the navy for having instructed young enlisted men — the decoys — "in the details of a nameless vice," and having ordered them to use that knowledge. The naval authorities had been willing to let their agents engage in sexual acts with the "queers" because they were primarily concerned about people manifesting a homosexual disposition rather than those engaging occasionally in homosexual acts. The navy asserted that the decoys' investigative purpose rendered them immune from criminal prosecution even though they had committed illegal sexual acts. But the ministers viewed the decoys' culpability as "a moral question...not a technical question at all;" when the decoys had sex with other men, they had "scars placed on their souls," because, inescapably, "having immoral relations with men is an immoral act."[66] The sin was in the act, not the motive or the disposition. In addition, the ministers charged that the navy had directed the decoys to entrap designated individuals and that no one, no matter how innocent, could avoid entrapment by a skillful decoy. According to Bishop Perry, the decoys operated by putting men "into compromising positions, where they might be suspected of guilt, [even though they were] guiltless persons." Anyone could be entrapped because an "innocent advance might be made by the person operated upon and he might be ensnared against his will."[67] Implicitly, any clergyman could have done what Kent was accused of doing. Anyone's defenses could fall.

The ministers' preoccupation with the moral significance of genital sexual activity and their fear that anyone could be entrapped may reflect the continued saliency for them of the Christian precept that *all* people, including the clergy, were sinners subject to a variety of sexual temptations, including those of homosexual desire.[68] According to this tradition, Christians had to resist homosexual temptations, as they resisted others, but simply to desire a homosexual liaison was neither a singular failing nor an indication of perverted character. The fact that the ministers never clearly elucidated this perspective and were forced increasingly to use the navy's own terms while contesting the navy's conclusions may reflect both the ministers' uncertainty about it and their recognition that such a perspective was no longer shared by the public whose opinion they wished to influence.

In any case, making the commission of specified physical acts the distinguishing characteristic of a moral pervert made it definitionally impossible to interpret the ministers' relationships with sailors — no matter how intimate and emotionally moving — as having a "sexual" element, so long as they involved no such acts. Defining the sexual element in men's relationships in this narrow manner enabled the ministers to develop a bipartate defense of Kent which simultaneously denied he had had sexual relationships with other men and yet celebrated his profound emotional devotion to them. It legitimized (nonphysical) intimacy between men by precluding the possibility that such intimacy could be defined as sexual. Reaffirming the boundaries between Christian brotherhood and perverted sexuality in this manner was a central objective of the ministers' very public debate with the navy. But it may also have been of private significance to churchmen forced by the navy investigation to reflect on the nature of their brotherhood with other men.

Conclusion

The richly textured evidence provided by the Newport controversy makes it possible to reexamine certain tenets of recent work in the history of sexuality, especially the history of homosexuality. Much of that work, drawing on sociological models of symbolic interactionism and the labelling theory of deviance, has argued that the end of the nineteenth century witnessed a major reconceptualization of homosexuality. Before the last century, according to this thesis, North American and European cultures had no concept of the homosexual-as-person; they regarded homosexuality as simply another form of sinful behavior in which anyone might choose to engage. The turn of the century witnessed the "invention of the homosexual," that is, the new determination that homosexual desire was limited to certain identifiable individuals for whom it was an involuntary sexual orientation of some biological or psychological origin. The most prominent advocates of this thesis have argued that the medical discourse on homosexuality that emerged in the late nineteenth century played the determinative role in this process, by creating and popularizing this new model of homosexual behavior (which, in order to emphasize the centrality of medical discourse in its development, they have termed the "medical model" of homosexuality). It was on the basis of the new medical models, they argue, that homosexually-active individuals came to be labelled in popular culture — and to assume an identity — as sexual deviants different in nature from other people, rather than as sinners whose sinful nature was the common lot of humanity.[69]

The Newport evidence indicates that the role of medical discourse has been exaggerated in this thesis, and it also suggests how we might begin to refine our analysis of the relationship between homosexual behavior and identity. First, and most clearly, the Newport evidence indicates that medical discourse still played little or no role in the shaping of working-class homosexual identities and categories by World War I, more than thirty years after the discourse had begun. There would be no logical reason to expect that discussions carried on in elite journals whose distribution was limited to members of the medical and legal professions would have had any immediate effect on the larger culture, particularly the working class. In the Newport evidence, only one fairy even mentioned the favored medical term "invert," using it as a synonym for the already existing and widely-recognized popular term "queer." Moreover, while "invert" was commonly used in the medical literature there is no reason to assume that it originated there, and the Newport witness specified that he had first heard it in theater circles and not through reading any "literature." The culture of the sexual underground, always in a complex relationship with the dominant culture, played a more important role in the shaping and sustaining of sexual identities.

More remarkably, medical discourse appears to have had as little influence on the military hierarchy as on the people of Newport.[70] Throughout the two years of navy investigations related to Newport, which involved the highest naval officials, not a single medical expert was invited to present the medical perspective on the issues at stake. The only member of the original board of inquiry who even alluded to the published literature (and this on only one occasion during the Foster hearings, and once more at the second inquiry) was Dr. E.M. Hudson, the welfare officer at the naval hospital and one of the decoys' supervisors. Hudson played a prominent role in the original investigation not because of his medical expertise, but because it was the flagrantly displayed (and normally tolerated) effeminacy and homosexuality of hospital staff and patients that first made naval officials consider undertaking an investigation. As the decoys' supervisor, Hudson drew on his training in fingerprinting and detective work considerably more than his medical background. Only after he became concerned that the decoys might be held legally culpable for their homosexual activity did he "read several medical books on the subject and read everything that

I could find out as to what legal decisions there were on these cases."[71] But he never became very familiar with the medical discourse on sexual nonconformity; after his reading he still thought that the term "invert," which had first appeared in U.S. medical journals almost 40 years earlier, was "practically a new term," less than two years old.[72]

Moreover, Hudson only accepted those aspects of the medical analysis of homosexuality that confirmed the common beliefs about "queers" he already shared with other, non-medical naval officials. Thus he accepted as authoritative the distinction that medical writers drew between "congenital perverts" (called "queers" in common parlance) and "normal people submitting to acts of perversion, as a great many normal people do, [who] do not become perverts themselves," such as men isolated from women at a military base. He accepted this "scientific" distinction because it only confirmed what he and other naval officials already believed: that many sailors had sex with the queers without being "queer" themselves. But when the medical literature differed from the assumptions he shared with most navy men, he ignored it. Rather than adopting the medical viewpoint that homosexuals were biological anomalies who should be treated medically rather than willful criminals who should be deterred from homosexuality by severe legal penalties, for instance, he agreed with his colleagues that "these conditions existed and should be eradicated and the men guilty of offenses should be rounded up and punished."[73] In the course of 109 days of hearings, Dr. Hudson referred to medical authorities only twice, and then only when they confirmed the assumptions of popular culture.

It thus appears more plausible to describe the medical discourse as a "reverse discourse," to use Michel Foucault's term, rather than as the central force in the creation of new sexual categories around which individuals shaped their personal identities. Rather than creating such categories as "the invert" and "the homosexual," the turn-of-the-century medical investigators whom Hudson read were trying to describe, classify, and explain a preexisting sexual underground whose outlines they only vaguely perceived. Their scientific categories largely reproduced those of popular culture, with "queers" becoming "inverts" in medical parlance but retaining the characteristic cross-gender behavior already attributed to them in popular culture. Doctors developed generalizations about homosexuals based on their idiosyncratic observations of particular individuals and admitted from the beginning that they were responding to the existence of communities of such people whose mysterious behavior and social organization they wished to explore. As one of the first American medical commentators observed in 1889, in explaining the need to study sexual perversion, "[t]here is in every community of any size a colony of male sexual perverts; they are usually known to each other, and are likely to congregate together."[74] By the time of the Newport investigation, medical researchers had developed an elaborate system of sexual classification and numerous explanations for individual cases of homosexuality, but they still had little comprehension of the complex social and cultural structure of gay life. One of the country's most prominent and best-informed medical investigators asserted in 1916 that

> Chicago has not developed a euphemism yet for these male perverts. In New York they
> are known as 'fairies' and wear a red necktie (inverts are generally said to prefer green).
> In Philadelphia they are known as 'Brownies.'[75]

That gay men in a single city might use the terms "fairy" and "Brownie" (or "pogue") to refer to two different kinds of "inverts" had not even occurred to him.

The Newport evidence helps put the significance of the medical discourse in perspective; it also offers new insights into the relationship between homosexual behavior and identity. Recent studies which have established the need to distinguish between homosexual behavior (presumably a transhistorically evident phenomenon) and the historically specific concept of homosexual identity have tended to focus on the evolution of people whose *primary* personal and political "ethnic" identification is as gay, and who have organized a multidimensional way of life on the basis of their homosexuality. The high visibility of such people in contemporary Western societies and their growing political significance make analysis of the historical development of their community of particular scholarly interest and importance.[76] But the Newport evidence indicates that we need to begin paying more attention to *other* social forms of homosexuality — other ways in which homosexual relations have been organized and understood, differentiated, named, and left deliberately unnamed. We need to specify the *particularity* of various modes of homosexual behavior and the relationships between those modes and particular configurations of sexual identity.

For even when we find evidence that a culture has labelled people who were homosexually active as sexually deviant, we should not assume *a priori* that their homosexual activity was the determinative criterion in the labelling process. As in Newport, where many men engaged in certain kinds of homosexual behavior yet continued to be regarded as "normal," the assumption of particular sexual roles and deviance from gender norms may have been more important than the coincidence of male or female sexual partners in the classification of sexual character. "Fairies," "pogues," "husbands," and "trade" might all be labelled "homosexuals" in our own time, but they were labelled — and understood themselves — as fundamentally different kinds of people in WWI-era Newport. They all engaged in what we would define as homosexual behavior, but they and the people who observed them were more careful than we to draw distinctions between different modes of such behavior. To classify their behavior and character using the simple polarities of "homosexual" and "heterosexual" would be to misunderstand the complexity of their sexual system. Indeed, the very terms "homosexual behavior" and "identity," because of their tendency to conflate phenomena that other cultures may have regarded as quite distinct, appear to be insufficiently precise to denote the variety of social forms of sexuality we wish to analyze.[77]

The problems that arise when different forms of homosexual activity and identity are conflated are evidenced in the current debate over the consequences of the development of a medical model of homosexuality. Recent studies, especially in lesbian history, have argued that the creation and stigmatization of the public image of the homosexual at the turn of the century served to restrict the possibilities for intimacy between all women and all men, by making it possible to associate such intimacy with the despised social category of the homosexual. This thesis rightly observes that the definition of deviance serves to establish behavioral norms for everyone, not just for the deviant. But it overlooks the corollary of this observation, that the definition of deviance serves to legitimize some social relations even as it stigmatizes others; and it assumes that the turn-of-the-century definition of "sexual inversion" codified the same configuration of sexual and gender phenomena which "homosexuality" does today. But many early twentieth-century romantic friendships between women, for instance, appear to have been unaffected by the development of a public lesbian persona, in part because that image characterized the lesbian primarily as a "mannish woman," which had the effect of excluding from its stigmatizing purview all conventionally feminine women, no matter how intimate their friendships.[78]

Similarly, even though Newport residents were familiar with a particular image of "queers," they did not classify ministers who were intimate as Christian brothers with other men or sailors who had sex with effeminate men as "queer," because the character of neither group fully corresponded to the public's image of what a queer should be like. Moreover, both the sailors and clergymen defined sexual behavior and perversion in ways which excluded their own behavior from being labelled as either, no matter how suspect their behavior might seem from another perspective. The sailors legitimized their physical sexual contact with the queers by restricting the form of that contact and by proscribing effeminate behavior and emotional intimacy with their partners. The ministers interpreted the boundaries between acceptable and unacceptable male relations in precisely the opposite manner: for they defended their apparent effeminacy and emotional intimacy with men by defining sexuality as physical contact, which their moral code proscribed.

At the heart of the controversy provoked and revealed by the Newport investigation was a confrontation between several such definitional systems, a series of disputes over the boundaries between homosociality and homosexuality in the relations of men and over the standards by which their masculinity would be judged. The investigation became controversial when it verged on suggesting that the homosocial world of the navy and the relationships between sailors and their Christian brothers in the Newport ministry were permeated by homosexual desire. Newport's ministers and leading citizens, the Senate Naval Affairs Committee, and to some extent even the navy itself repudiated the Newport inquiry because they found such a suggestion intolerable. Although numerous cultural interpretations of sexuality were allowed to confront each other at the inquiry, ultimately certain cultural boundaries had to be reaffirmed in order to protect certain relations as "nonsexual," even as the sexual nature of others was declared and condemned. The Newport evidence reveals much about the social organization and self-understanding of men who identified themselves as "queer." But it also provides a remarkable illustration of the social nature of the boundaries established between the "sexual" and the "nonsexual" in human relations and reminds us that cultural struggles over the demarcation of those boundaries are a central aspect of the history of sexuality.

FOOTNOTES

1. This is a revised version of a paper originally presented at the conference, "Among Men, Among Women: Sociological and Historical Recognition of Homosocial Arrangements," held at the University of Amsterdam, June 22-26, 1983. I am grateful to Allan Bérubé, John Boswell, Nancy Cott, Steven Dubin, James Schultz, Anthony Stellato, James Taylor, and my colleagues at the Amsterdam conference for their comments on earlier versions.

2. The Newport investigation was brought to the attention of historians by Frank Freidel, *Franklin D. Roosevelt: The Ordeal* (Boston, 1954), 41, 46-47, 96-97, and Jonathan Katz, *Gay American History: A Documentary* (New York, 1976), 579n. Katz reprinted the Senate report in *Government Versus Homosexuals* (New York, 1975), a volume in the Arno Press series on homosexuality he edited. A useful narrative account of the naval investigation is provided by Lawrence R. Murphy, "Cleaning Up Newport: The U.S. Navy's Prosecution of Homosexuals After World War I," *Journal of American Culture* 7 (Fall, 1984): 57-64.

3. Murphy J. Foster presided over the first Court of Inquiry, which began its work in Newport on March 13, 1919 and heard 406 pages of testimony in the course of 23 days (its records are hereafter cited as *Foster Testimony*). The second court of inquiry, convened in 1920 "to inquire into the methods employed . . . in the investigation of moral and other conditions existing in the Naval Service; [and] to ascertain and inquire into the scope of and authority for said investigation,"

was presided over by Rear Admiral Herbert O. Dunn and heard 2500 pages of testimony in the course of 86 days (hereinafter cited as *Dunn Testimony*). The second trial of Rev. Kent, *U.S. v. Samuel Neal Kent*, heard in Rhode Island District Court in Providence beginning January 20, 1920, heard 532 pages of evidence (hereinafter cited as *Kent Trial*). The records are held at the National Archives, Modern Military Field Branch, Suitland, Maryland, R.G. 125.

4. I have used "gay" in this essay to refer to men who identified themselves as sexually different from other men — and who labelled themselves and were labelled by others as "queer" — because of their assumption of "feminine" sexual and other social roles. As I explain below, not all men who were homosexually active labelled themselves in this manner, including men, known as "husbands," who were involved in long-term homosexual relationships but nonetheless maintained a masculine identity.

5. *Foster Testimony*, Ervin Arnold, 5; F.T. Brittain, 12, Thomas Brunelle, 21; *Dunn Testimony*, Albert Viehl, 307; Dudley Marriott, 1737.

6. Frederick Hoage, using a somewhat different construction than most, referred to them as "the inverted gang" (*Foster Testimony*, 255).

7. *Foster Testimony*, Arnold, 5; *Dunn Testimony*, Clyde Rudy, 1783. For a few of the many other comments by "straight" sailors on the presence of gay men at the Y.M.C.A., see *Dunn Testimony*, Claude McQuillin, 1759, and Preston Paul, 1836.

8. A man named Temple, for instance, had a room at the Y where he frequently took pick-ups (*Foster Testimony*, Brunelle, 207-8); on the role of the elevator operators, see William McCoy, 20, and Samuel Rogers, 61.

9. *Foster Testimony*, Arnold, 27; Frederick Hoage, 271; Harrison Rideout, 292.

10. Ibid., Hoage, 267; Rogers, 50; Brunelle, 185.

11. Ibid., Gregory A. Cunningham, 30; Arnold, 6; *Dunn Testimony*, John S. Tobin, 720-21.

12. For an elaboration of the conceptual distinction between "inversion" and "homosexuality" in the contemporary medical literature, see my article, "From Sexual Inversion to Homosexuality: Medicine and the Changing Conceptualization of Female Deviance," *Salmagundi* 58-59 (Fall 1982-Winter 1983): 114-46.

13. *Foster Testimony*, Rogers, 50-51.

14. E.g., an article which included the following caption beneath a photography of Hughes dressed in women's clothes: "This is Billy Hughes, Yeo. 2c. It's a shame to break the news like that, but enough of the men who saw 'Pinafore' fell in love with Bill, without adding to their number. 'Little Highesy,' as he is affectionately known, dances like a Ziegfeld chorus girl . . ." ("We Sail the Ocean Blue': 'H.M.S. Pinafore' as Produced by the Navy," *Newport Recruit*, 6 [August 1918]: 9). See also, e.g., "Mayor Will Greet Navy Show Troupe: Official Welcome Arranged for 'Jack and Beanstalk' Boys," which quoted an admiral saying, " 'It is a corker. I have never in my life seen a prettier "girl" [a man] than "Princess Mary." She is the daintiest little thing I ever laid eyes on' " (*Providence Journal* [26 May 1919]: 9). I am grateful to Lawrence Murphy for supplying me with copies of these articles.

15. *Dunn Testimony*, John S. Tobin, 716; *Foster Testimony*, Charles Zipf, 377; confirmed by Hoage, 289, and Arnold (*Dunn Testimony*, 1405). The man who received the women's clothes was the Billy Hughes mentioned in the newspaper article cited in the previous note. I am grateful to Allan Bérubé for informing me of the regularity with which female impersonators appeared in navy shows during and immediately following World War I.

16. Ibid., Hoage called it a "faggot party" and "a general congregation of inverts" (267); Brunelle, who claimed to have attended the party for only 15 minutes, noted the presence of the sailors and fighters; he also said only one person was in drag, but mentioned at least two (194, 206); John E. McCormick observed the lovers (332).

17. For the straight sailors' nicknames, see *Foster Testimony*, William Nelson Gorham, 349. On the ubiquity of nicknames and the origins of some of them, see Hoage, 253, 271; Whitney Delmore Rosenszweig, 397.

18. *Dunn Testimony*, Hudson, 1663.

19. *Foster Testimony*, Rideout, 76-77.

20. Ibid., Cunningham, 29. For other examples, see Wade Stuart Harvey, 366; and *Dunn Testimony*, Tobin, 715.

21. *Foster Testimony*, George Richard, 143; Hoage, 298.

22. Ibid., Rideout, 69; see also Rogers, 63; Viehl, 175; Arnold, 3; and *passim*.

23. An investigator told the navy that one gay man had declined to make a date with him because "he did not like to 'play with fire'. . .[and] was afraid Chief Brugs would beat him up" (*Foster Testimony*, Arnold, 36); the same gay man told the court he had travelled to Providence with Brugs two weekends in a row and gone to shows with him (Rogers, 53-54). Speaking of another couple, Hoage admitted he had heard "that Hughes has travelled with Brunelle separately for two months or so" and that "they were lovers." He added that "of course that does not indicate anything but friendship," but that "naturally I would suspect that something else was taking place" (Hoage, 268).

24. Ibid., Hoage, 313.

25. Ibid., Arnold, 5.

26. Ibid., Viehl, 175; Brunelle, 235; Rideout, 93. Hoage, when cross-examined by Rosenszweig, denied another witness's charge that he, Hoage, had *boasted* of browning Rosenszweig, but he did not deny the act itself — nor did Rosenszweig ask him to do so (p. 396).

27. Ibid., Hoage, 271; Rogers, 131-36.

28. Ibid., Rogers, 39-40; other evidence tends to confirm Rogers' contention that he had not known openly gay men or women before joining the navy. For other examples of the role of the war in introducing men to gays, see Brunelle, 211; and in the *Dunn Testimony*, Rudy, 1764. For extended discussions of the similar impact of military mobilization on many people's lives during World War II, see Allan Bérubé, "Marching to a Different Drummer," in Ann Snitow, Christine Stansell, and Sharon Thompson, eds., *Powers of Desire: The Politics of Sexuality* (New York, 1983), 88-99; and John D'Emilio, *Sexual Politics, Sexual Communities: The Making of a Homosexual Minority in the United States, 1940-1970* (Chicago, 1983), 23-39.

29. *Foster Testimony*, Rideout, 78.

30. *Dunn Testimony*, E.M. Hudson questioning Bishop James De Wolf Perry, 609 (my emphasis).

31. Ibid., Jeremiah Mahoney, 698.

32. Ibid., Tobin, 717.

33. Witnesses who encountered gay men at the hospital or commented on the presence of homosexuals there included Gregory Cunningham, *Foster Testimony*, 29; Brunelle, 210; John McCormick, *Dunn Testimony*, 1780; and Paul, 1841. Paul also described some of the open homosexual joking engaged in by patients, *Foster Testimony*, 393-94.

34. *Foster Testimony*, Hervey, 366; Johnson, 153, 155, 165, 167; Smith, 221.

35. Ibid., Johnson, 153; Smith, 169.

36. Ibid., Smith, 171.

37. *Ibid.*, Hoage, 272. Hoage added that "[t]rade is a word that is only used among people tempermental [i.e., gay]," although this does not appear to have been entirely the case.

38. Ibid., Hoage, 269, 314; Rudy, 14. The decoy further noted that, despite the fairy's pleas, "I insisted that he do his work below my chest."

39. Frederick Hoage provided an example of this pattern when he described how a gay civilian had taken him to a show and dinner, let him stay in his room, and then "attempted to do what they call 'browning.'" But he devoted much of his testimony to *denying* that *his* "tak[ing] boys to dinner and to a show," offering to share his bed with sailors who had nowhere else to stay, and giving them small gifts and loans had the sexual implications that the court obviously suspected (*Foster Testimony*, Hoage, 261, 256, 262, 281-82). For other examples of solicitation patterns, see Maurice Kreisberg, 12; Arnold, 26; *Dunn Testimony*, Paul, 1843. Edward Stevenson described the "trade" involved in military prostitution in *The Intersexes: A History of Semisexualism* (privately printed, 1908), 214. For an early sociological description of "trade," see Albert Reiss, Jr., "The Social Integration of Queers and Peers," *Social Problems* 9 (1961): 102-20. It is possible that "trade" originally took on sexual connotations because of the frequency with which boys and young men who were engaged in "street trades" such as newspaper hawking earned extra money by having sex with older men (see Helen Kitchen Branson, " 'Street Trades' and Their Sex Knowledge," *Sexology* (April 1949): 568-71).

40. *Foster Testimony*, Rudy, 13.

41. *Dunn Testimony*, Paul, 1836; see also, e.g., Mayor Mahoney's comments, 703.

42. *Foster Testimony*, James Daniel Chase, 119 (my emphasis); Zipf, 375.

43. Ibid., Walter F. Smith, 169.

44. See, e.g., the accounts of Hoage, *Foster Testimony*, 271-72, and Rideout, 87.

45. *Foster Testimony*, Smith, 169.

46. Alfred Kinsey, Wardell Pomeroy, and Clyde Martin, *Sexual Behavior in the Human Male* (Philadelphia, 1948), 650-51.

47. *Foster Testimony*, Arnold, 6; *Dunn Testimony*, Arnold, 1495.

48. *Kent Trial*, 21.

49. Ibid., defense attorney's interrogation of Charles McKinney, 66-67. See also, e.g., the examination of Zipf, esp. pp. 27-28.

50. Ibid., Zipf, 2113, 2131 (the court repeatedly turned to the subject). The "manly" decoy was Clyde Rudy, 1793.

51. The ministers' efforts are reviewed and their charges affirmed in the Senate report, 67th Congress, 1st session, Committee on Naval Affairs, *Alleged Immoral Conditions of Newport (R.I.) Naval Training Station* (Washington, D.C., 1921), and in the testimony of Bishop Perry and Reverend Hughes before the Dunn Inquiry.

52. *Dunn Testimony*, Rev. Deming, 30; Rev. Forster, 303.

53. Hudson quoted in the Senate report, *Alleged Immoral Conditions*, 8; see also *Dunn Testimony*, Tobin, 723, cf. Arnold, 1712. For the ministers' criticism, see, e.g., Bishop Perry, 529, 607.

54. *Foster Testimony*, Hoage, 319.

55. Ibid., Brunelle, 216. He says the same of Kent on p. 217.

56. *Kent Trial*, cross-examination of Howard Rider, 296.

57. Ibid., Malcolm C. Crawford, 220-23; Dostalik, 57-71.

58. *Foster Testimony*, interrogation of Hoage, 315, 318.

59. *Dunn Testimony*, Deming, 43.

60. *Kent Trial*, Kent, 396, 419, 403.

61. Ibid., Herbert Walker, 318-20.

62. Ibid., Bishop Philip Rhinelander, 261-62.

63. Ibid., Rev. Henry Motett, 145-49, 151.

64. Ibid., Judge Darius Baker, 277.

65. Ibid., interrogation of C.B. Zipf, 37-38.

66. *Dunn Testimony*, Rev. Deming, 42; Bishop Perry, 507.

67. Ibid., Perry, 678.

68. Jonathan Katz argues that such a perspective was central to Puritan concepts of homosexuality, "The Age of Sodomitical Sin, 1607-1740," in his *Gay/Lesbian Almanac* (New York, 1983), 23-65. But see also John Boswell, "Revolutions, Universals and Sexual Categories," *Salmagundi* 58-59 (Fall 1982-Winter 1983): 89-113.

69. This argument was first introduced by Mary McIntosh, "The Homosexual Role," *Social Problems* 16 (1968): 182-92, and has been developed and modified by Jeffrey Weeks, *Coming Out: Homosexual Politics in Britian from the Nineteenth Century to the Present* (London, 1977); Michel Foucault, *The History of Sexuality: An Introduction*, transl. by Robert Hurley (New York, 1978); Lillian Faderman, *Surpassing the Love of Men: Romantic Friendships and Love Between Women From the Renaissance to the Present*(New York, 1981); Kenneth Plummer, ed., *The Making of the Modern Homosexual* (London, 1981); and Jonathan Katz, *Gay/Lesbian Almanac: A New Documentary* (New York, 1983). Although these historians and sociologists subscribe to the same general model, they disagree over the timing and details of the emergence of a homosexual role, and McIntosh's original essay did not attribute a key role in that process to medical discourse.

70. The situation had changed considerably by World War II, when psychiatrists occupied a more influential position in the military, which used them to help select and manage the more than 15 million men and women it mobilized for the war. See, for instance, the role of psychiatrists

in the records of courts-martial conducted from 1941-43 held at the National Archives (Army A.G. 250.1) and the 1944 investigation of lesbianism at the Third WAC Training Center, Fort Oglethorpe, Georgia (National Archives, Modern Military Field Branch, Suitland, Maryland, R.G. 159, Entry 26F). Allan Bérubé's important forthcoming study, *Coming Out Under Fire*, will discuss at length the role of psychiatrists in the development and implementation of WWII-era military policies.

71. *Dunn Testimony*, Hudson, 1630.

72. *Foster Testimony*, 300. The transcript does not identify the speaker, but the context strongly suggests it was Hudson.

73. *Dunn Testimony*, 1628, 1514.

74. George Frank Lydston, "Sexual Perversion, Satyriasis, and Nymphomania," *Medical and Surgical Reporter* 61 (1889): 254. See also Chauncey, "From Sexual Inversion to Homosexuality," 142-43.

75. James Kiernan, "Classification of Homosexuality," *Urologic and Cutaneous Review* 20 (1916): 350.

76. John D'Emilio has provided the most sophisticated analysis of this process in *Sexual Politics, Sexual Communities: The Making of a Homosexual Minority in the United States, 1940-1970* (Chicago, 1983). See also Toby Moratta, *The Politics of Homosexuality* (Boston, 1981), and the pioneering studies by Jeffrey Weeks and Lillian Faderman cited above.

77. One would also hesitate to assert that a single definition of homosexuality obtains in our own culture. Jonathan Katz has made a similar argument about the need to specify the meaning of homosexual behavior and identity in his *Gay/Lesbian Almanac*, although our analyses differ in a number of respects (see my review in *The Body Politic*, no. 97 (1983): 33-34).

78. Lillian Faderman, in "The Mordification of Love Between Women by 19th-Century Sexologists," *Journal of Homosexuality* 4 (1978): 73-90, and *Surpassing the Love of Men*, is the major proponent of the argument that the medical discourse stigmatized romantic friendships. Alternative analyses of the role of the medical literature and of the timing and nature of the process of stigmatization having been proposed by Martha Vicinus, "Distance and Desire: English Boarding-School Friendships," *Signs: Journal of Women in Culture and Society* 9 (1984): 600-22, Carroll Smith-Rosenberg, "The New Woman as Androgyne: Social Disorder and Gender Crisis, 1870-1936," in *Disorderly Conduct: Visions of Gender in Victorian America* (New York, 1985), 245-96, and Chauncey, "From Sexual Inversion to Homosexuality." On the apparent ubiquity of the early twentieth-century public image of the lesbian as a "mannish woman," see Esther Newton, "The Mythic Mannish Lesbian: Radclyffe Hall and the New Woman," *Signs* 9 (1984): 557-575. Nineteenth-century medical articles and newspaper accounts of lesbian couples stigmatized only the partner who played "the man's part" by dressing like a man and seeking male employment, but found the "womanly" partner unremarkable, as if it did not matter that her "husband" was another female so along as she played the conventionally wifely role (see Chauncey, 125ff). The medical reconceptualization of female deviance as homosexual object choice rather than gender role inversion was underway by the 1920s, but it is difficult to date any such transition in popular images, in part because they remained so inconsistent.

11.

THE MYTHS OF SOCIAL CONTROL AND CUSTODIAL OPPRESSION: PATTERNS OF PSYCHIATRIC MEDICINE IN LATE NINETEENTH-CENTURY INSTITUTIONS

Constance M. McGovern

On April 14th, 1882, Henry Smith brought his brother Caleb to a state hospital for the mentally ill.[1] Caleb was a thirty-three year old iron worker, single, and had been "dissipated" for four years. For the first eighteen months of his hospitalization, the doctors kept no record of Caleb Smith. In late 1883 he began working around the hospital. Only then was his chart marked; the doctors entered an "a" for each day he worked. On February 12th, 1884, Caleb Smith died at the asylum.[2]

On August 17th, 1883, the Directors of the Poor ordered Ophelia Brown's husband to bring her to a state hospital. The doctors learned that Ophelia had married a teamster nine years earlier at the age of seventeen; she had borne four children and had not been "entirely well" physically since the birth of her first child. During the previous three weeks she had suffered from a bout of malarial fever, threatened suicide, destroyed much of her clothing and furniture, and insisted that she had "power to heal the sick and bring the world to an end." The doctors diagnosed her illness as acute mania, and in their preliminary examination discovered that she suffered from lacerations of the uterus and inflammation of the cervix. In their monthly reports, they noted her mental state (she persisted in her belief about her supernatural powers), observed her behavior (she was "very talkative and obstinate" and "at times very noisy indeed"), and prescribed bromides and tonics. Later they observed that Ophelia experienced a relapse after she had visitors, remarked that she was "more quiet and less unreasonable," and attached to her casebook record a letter she wrote in which she expressed her religious ramblings and suggested that her mental illness had been caused by having "to[o] many little ones in to[o] short a time." Within seven months, Ophelia Brown left the hospital bodily and mentally improved.[3]

If critics and historians of nineteenth-century institutions for the insane are correct, Caleb Smith's sparse record indicating neglect on the part of the doctors was far more typical than the attention paid to Ophelia Brown. As early as the 1880s, both self-interested critics like the neurologists and thoughtful lay and medical reformers concerned about abuse or neglect attacked the asylums as repressive, unscientific establishments. They characterized the institutions as "places of last resource" and as "despotisms" run by superintendents who neglected patients, indulged in "mystery" and "secrecy" within their asylum walls, and practiced "professional metaphysics." And medical superintendents, by the sheer quantity and pessimism of their self-defense in the face of these critics, created the image that their efforts were fruitless in holding back the tide of custodialism.[4]

Some modern commentators have argued that the idea of an asylum was repressive in its conception and naturally resulted in institutions which dehumanized patients and "confused the health of the patient with the health of the institution." They have ample fodder in the case of Caleb Smith and thousands of others like him. The asylum did function on the principles of a highly segmentized day and routinized activities. Smith did not appear as part of that routine until he participated by working on a regular schedule; for the record, he was non-existent as long as he merely occupied a bed or strolled aimlessly about the wards. Others, exploring the more halcyon days of asylum building, moral treatment, and the high curability claims of the 1830s and 1840s, explain that custodialism emerged from changing concepts of social control or from the changing nature of the patient body. When asylums no longer stood as models for reestablishing social order or when middle-class doctors, alienated from their growing numbers of lower class, foreign-born patients retreated to their administrative offices, therapy became a function of class and ethnicity and asylums served a custodial function. These historians can point to Ophelia Brown's letter attached to her casebook record by her doctor. Middle-class doctors had little appreciation of working-class values or lifestyles and translated them into predisposing causes of insanity. It is clear that the doctor, in this case, saw Brown's acknowledgment of too frequent child-bearing as acceptance of middle-class attitudes and, therefore, as evidence of her recuperation.[5]

Unrelieved custodialism was not the hallmark of nineteenth-century asylums, however. My examination of patient records, a hitherto untapped source, offers new evidence and alters the conceptualizations of asylums as custodial institutions or as totally repressive, dehumanizing places. Combining an analysis of institutional policy, the career patterns of medical personnel, and these patient records makes it clear that many variables, ranging from patient demographics to the individual doctor's dedication, influenced the role of psychiatric institutions in this period. This complex interaction of the internal histories of the hospitals, political struggles within them, competing models of psychiatric care, differences among doctors, and reactions of the patients and their families illustrates the variety of ways in which late nineteenth-century asylums actually worked.

The casebook records kept on the patients offer a surprisingly full and frank picture of the asylum.[6] Both state law and the Association of Medical Superintendents' policy contributed to the nature and consistency of the type of information recorded. There are, of course, limits to the use of these records. The medical and behavioral history of the patient, for instance, was supplied by the person who brought the patient to the hospital. Thus behavioral manifestations or causality and the link made between them were put forth by a husband, wife, father, friend, neighbor, or town authority. The doctors made little attempt to verify the information. There is, also, no way to know what really went on in these hospitals on a daily basis, but some data such as those on the length of stay for a patient, and his or her age, marital status or birthplace are without doubt accurate. And, with the exception of one hospital, the doctors practiced a remarkable degree of forthrightness about their reactions to patients and about keeping track of prescriptions and the use of restraining devices.

The determination of the regularity with which doctors saw individual patients is more problematic. Hospital rules required that the head physician see or be informed of the status of every patient on a daily basis and that one of the assistant physicians actually visit each patient every day. State lunacy commissions demanded monthly entries for recent and curable cases and quarterly notes for chronic patients. The records reveal that the doctors followed the lunacy commissions' rules and we can only speculate about the hospital's rules since they did not call for written records of those daily visits. Yet a doctor's obligatory monthly or quarterly remark that a patient "*continues* to resist all attempts to engage her in conversation" implies a greater degree of daily attention than is explicit in the written record. And the observations of doctors who perceived that a patient who otherwise behaved quite rationally still had a "lurking idea that certain persons" stalked her implies a similar regularity of contact. The criteria used to determine "recovery" or an "improved" mental condition, moreover, were sometimes as puzzling for the nineteenth-century doctors as they are for historians. All the institutionalized patients were not necessarily ill in modern terms and, of course, in some cases "recovery" meant changing one's behavior patterns or attitudes to fit the doctor's or community's expectations. Discharge did not necessarily mean cure in a current medical sense (although less than fifteen percent were rehospitalized). The standard apparent from the records was that if patients demonstrated an ability to carry out the ordinary tasks of life (in the hospital this usually meant speaking rationally and being willing to participate in work or social activities) and returned to the community for an extended period of time they were considered "recovered" or "improved." This consistency and candidness of record keeping, even in the relatively bare form ordered by the lunacy commissions, allow for considerable comparative analysis of the patient populations.

These patient records and the political and social structure of four hospitals, therefore, offer a gamut of possibilities to explore patterns of psychiatric medicine in late nineteenth-century institutions. Two of the institutions, the Norristown Hospital and the Harrisburg Hospital in Pennsylvania, were state hospitals. They were obligated to take all applicants from their districts, they were at the mercy of the vagaries of state funding, their patients were largely lower class, their hospitals understaffed, and the sheer size of their patient bodies (especially Norristown with well over 2000 patients by 1900) made a kind of anonymous herding difficult to avoid. The Vermont Asylum for the Insane in Brattleboro served as both a state-supported and privately-endowed hospital from 1845 to 1891. During this period it contracted to take indigent state patients, yet tried to maintain a policy of accepting a number of paying patients. The Institute of the Pennsylvania Hospital in Philadelphia was a private asylum. It was small (363 patients in 1885; only 436 by 1901) and five to seven doctors served its patients. One-third of these patients were from the families of professionals and businessmen; nearly another ten percent were farmers. Few were either foreign-born or unskilled laborers.[7] The Institute took pride in its long-standing reputation for offering specialized therapeutic care.

If middle-class status and American birth brought preferential treatment and more optimistic prognoses, the Institute of the Pennsylvania Hospital is a likely yardstick. From its founding in 1841 as a separate Department for the Insane of the Pennsylvania Hospital, the Board of Managers and Thomas Kirkbride, the medical superintendent for the insane, pursued a policy of selective admissions. Although publicizing the asylum as one whose "advantages have been denied to no class of society," in practice they carefully limited the numbers of indigent and chronic cases so that their program of therapeutic care for the more promising patients was not endangered. In the early 1840s Kirkbride retained as much as twenty percent of his patient body as "free" patients; by 1882, that proportion dwindled to just above ten percent. His successor, John Chapin, cut the "free" patients even more and boasted that the "Department [for the Insane] has been nearly self-sustaining from receipts for board of patients."[8]

Additionally, the active pursuit of private donations, substantial legacies, and tax exemptions that characterized the policy of the general hospital over the decades was imitated by the managers and superintendents of the Department for the Insane. Kirkbride's administration was marked by successful fund-raising; Chapin followed in his footsteps. Chapin delighted in reporting that in the first decade of his superintendency the fiscal concerns of the Department had been so well managed that "no impairment of its capital ha[d] occurred."[9]

Selective admissions and sound fiscal planning protected the Institute from a pile-up of chronically ill patients and from the constrictions of limited financial resources. The Institute maintained a middle-class clientele, close doctor-patient relationships, and commodious accommodations. As a result, the patterns of treatment and therapeutic results changed little over the course of the century. In the 1880s and 1890s, doctors in this small, middle-class hospital visited two-thirds of their patients more frequently than required by regulations. Sixty percent of the patients spent less than a year in the hospital and the same proportion left the hospital discharged as "recovered" or as in an "improved" state.[10] The Institute's mortality rate was under eight percent. It was a record worthy of the earlier, more optimistic decades and offers testimony for the historians who explain that cultural homogeneity, rather than inherent flaws in institutionalization, determined the quality of care.

For a time, for some patients, and in some hospitals, however, doctors under quite different institutional circumstances achieved similar results. These doctors worked at the large, understaffed state hospitals, yet saw their patients as frequently and released their charges as "improved" or "recovered" in as short a period of treatment as the doctors at the more selective Institute of the Pennsylvania Hospital.[11] This suggests that neither class and ethnicity nor doctor-patient ratios alone determined the quality of treatment. Rather, factors external to the institutions, the inner history of the asylums, and the personal sagas of the doctors all interacted to make hospitalization more of a therapeutic than a custodial experience for many patients.

The experience of the patients under the care of one male doctor at Harrisburg during the 1880s illustrates this multiplicity of factors which contributed to the fate of the patient who entered the asylum in late nineteenth-century America. To a large extent, the treatment of the male patients at Harrisburg is the story of the developmental history of the institution and the personalities of its administrators.

Pennsylvania opened its first state hospital for the care of the insane at Harrisburg in 1851. The trustees selected as medical superintendent a man trained by Thomas Kirkbride at the Institute of the Pennsylvania Hospital, John Curwin. Over the course of the next thirty years, Curwen governed his institution in the tradition established by the first moral therapists, supervised numerous building projects, and rose to prominence in the Association of Medical Superintendents of American Institutions for the Insane. Throughout the 1870s, however, John Curwen was involved in a number of controversial issues which distracted him from hospital duties and eventually altered the structure of the institution and the quality of life for the male patients at Harrisburg. Curwen opposed the centralization of asylums under the State Board of Charities and campaigned against the appointment of women doctors in public institutions which housed women. Particularly troublesome to Curwen had been the rising political power of one of his own trustees, Hiram Corson. Corson had led a struggle for the recognition of women doctors and spearheaded a plan to appoint women doctors to the staffs of state asylums. Additionally, Corson was an especially acerbic critic of the asylum superintendents.[12]

In the last decade of Curwen's reign at the Harrisburg hospital, his political battles consumed more energy than his patients commanded as Corson and the other trustees maneuvered Curwen out of the superintendency. Early in 1881 they voted a fifteen percent reduction in his salary; ignored letters from Thomas Kirkbride, Isaac Ray, and other equally well-known superintendents who wrote "certifying to the competence" of Curwen; closed the private road to his property and "accepted" his resignation. They then reorganized the hospital, appointing Margaret Cleaves as "Female Physician" in charge of the women patients and Jerome Z. Gerhard as superintendent for the male patients.[13]

Gerhard had been the assistant physician at the hospital during the chaotic seventies. In almost every respect he was unlike Curwen. He attended the annual meeting of the Association of Medical Superintendents for the first time in 1881 and found that "there was not as much of professional interest, as one could have desired." Moreover he was nonplussed by the Association's refusal to accept his colleague, Margaret Cleaves, as a member. He seldom attended after that. Gerhard had little reason to push the expansion of the hospital since Pennsylvania had embarked on the building of a number of other regional asylums, and so he settled down to the care of his patients. He reported to the trustees in minute detail about them and worked together with Cleaves with "hearty cooperation," offering her "much valuable aid, and many acts of kindness."[14]

The decade-long travails of John Curwen had created this golden opportunity for Gerhard. Disgruntled with the work and politics of Curwen, the trustees had given Gerhard a vote of confidence by promoting him to the superintendency. Gerhard welcomed the chance. For eleven years as assistant physician he had chafed under the administration of Curwen. Immediately, Gerhard reorganized the occupational and recreational therapy programs and in his first annual report recommended "prudence and economy" in refurbishing the buildings. He boasted that *he* would have no trouble in covincing the legislature "to appropriate the funds necessary to rebuild" and noted that the hospital "should be a model," although "it never has been." He promised that he would bring a new "epoch" of "moral force and power" to the institution.[15] And he did.

Because the Harrisburg trustees had hired a woman doctor for the female patients, Gerhard and his assistant dealt with a comparatively small number of patients. In 1881 the doctor-patient ratio in the male wards at Harrisburg was 1:77 and only rose to 1:105 by 1891. In essence, Gerhard had the atmosphere of a small, intimate asylum and the opportunity to offer specialized care: both elements believed crucial to the creation of a therapeutic environment. With a patient population that was less than ten percent middle class, from 1881 until 1891 Gerhard matched the record of the prestigious Institute of the Pennsylvania Hospital.

Gerhard visited his patients as frequently as did Chapin at the Institute and his success at improving their health was the same; both doctors released approximately one-quarter of their patients as mentally restored and one-third in an improved condition. The only difference between the record of Gerhard and Chapin was that Gerhard needed an additional year to achieve restorative results with some of his patients because they had been mentally ill for a longer period before they reached the hospital.[16]

Gerhard, however, could not touch Pennsylvania's mortality rate. Nearly one-quarter of Gerhard's patients died in the asylum. But a state hospital could neither choose to treat only active cases, refuse the chronically ill, nor send home persons on the brink of death and thus remove them from the hospital's death rolls. And whatever the effects of the internal and external history of the asylum and Gerhard's own drive for success, he exercised little control over the attitudes of the patients and their families about the asylum. Perhaps because his tenure was relatively short, Gerhard's reputation for success with a substantial proportion of his patients did not inspire families to bring men to the hospital at the first signs of mental disturbance. More likely, it was simply less acceptable for men to be sick. Doctors were often reluctant to place the stigma of certified insanity on men who needed to support families and families endured men's eccentric behavior longer out of economic necessity or legal hurdles. Gerhard was not alone in this experience; in general men entered the hospitals with longer-running illnesses than women. The result was that men stayed longer in the asylums and a smaller proportion of them recovered.[17] Nevertheless, Gerhard managed to discharge far more patients in an improved condition than Curwen had.

A change in state policy, in the purposes of the asylum, and in the nature of the patient body yielded yet another set of therapeutic circumstances and helps to fill in the picture of the complexity of psychiatric treatment in the late nineteenth century. At the Vermont Asylum for the Insane in Brattleboro, Joseph Draper was superintendent from 1873 to 1892. Draper's administration was marked by lengthy sparring with the state's Commissioners of the Insane. He complained about overcrowding and state niggardliness and they grumbled about everything from their inability to control the management of the asylum to the temperature of the patients' rooms. Particularly contentious for both parties was the question of out-of-state, private patients. Although the asylum had opened as a private hospital in 1836, from 1845 on it had an uneasy agreement with the state to take its transient and criminal insane and with the towns to take their indigent insane at a reduced cost. The situation was only exacerbated by the 1886 Poland

Pauper Law which made the state responsible for the support of all indigent insane. With the state footing the bill, town selectmen were far more willing to send their insane to the asylum at Brattleboro. By 1891, three-quarters of the patients at Brattleboro were supported by the state.[18]

As a result, Draper was hampered in his ability to provide high quality, individualized care. He made virtually no remarks about the behavior of patients, and when he did, the notes were largely negative in nature. One of the few comments about an old man, for instance, was simply that "for pure inborn cussedness he takes the prize" and, about a younger man, that "a couple of days in seclusion in his room has a very beautiful effect changing the very 'nature' of the animal." Draper regularly used drugs with the patients but kept no records of them, as he admitted to an 1878 legislative investigating committee.[19]

In 1891, Vermont finally opened a state hospital in Waterbury. Draper died within the year and Shailor Lawton, the new superintendent at Brattleboro, no longer had to deal with large numbers of state patients, especially the indigent and criminally insane. Like Gerhard at Harrisburg, Lawton had served as an assistant physician for eleven years and was eager to try his hand at administration. Although he claimed he could pay no "better reverence" to Draper "than to take up the work where [Draper] left it" and "continue the course marked out by him," the transference of most state patients to Waterbury allowed Lawton a brighter prospect than Draper.[20]

By 1896 Lawton had changed the name of the asylum to the Brattleboro Retreat and was working with a small clientele of just 162 patients (there had been 570 in 1891). But the Retreat borrowed funds that year just to keep its doors open. Despite the overcrowded conditions and the therapeutic pessimism engendered by large numbers of chronically ill, state-supported patients, the withdrawal of those patients had left the asylum's coffers depleted. Facing financial collapse, Lawton and the trustees launched a publicity campaign promoting Brattleboro's "pure air," and "homelike appearance" of the Retreat's wards, its "commodious and well-equipped gymnasium," and the management's desire "to receive private patients, at moderate cost."[21]

More crucial, however, they announced their intention to make the Brattleboro Retreat not only "second to none as a *hospital* for acute and curable cases," but also a "pleasant *home* for chronic mental invalids." In the following years, they extended their efforts by issuing more elaborate promotional booklets, by advertising the "merits of the Retreat" in medical journals, and by reserving one building for "summer guests requiring more or less medical attention." By 1900, they had salvaged the financial status of the asylum.[22]

Despite the distractions of this decade of reorganization and economic jeopardy, Lawton outdid Draper in his attention to patients. He saw four times as many patients on a weekly basis as Draper had and discharged as restored to full mental health twice as many. Even with his small number of patients and his desire to shape a therapeutic environment for the curable cases, he did not manage to create the same climate as the Institute of the Pennsylvania Hospital. While he saw one-third of his patients weekly, the doctors at the Institute visited two-thirds of theirs. The Institute doctors released sixty percent of their patients in at least an improved condition, but Lawton managed this progress for only forty-five percent of his. Lawton's greatest distinctiveness, however, compared to the Institute and the other hospitals considered, was that over fifty percent of his male patients died at the Retreat.

The explanation lies in the Retreat's responses to its financial experiences. Never certain that the appeal for private patients would guarantee solvency, in 1900 the trustees contracted once again with state officials; they would share the state patients with Waterbury. More importantly, their campaign to promote the Retreat as a home for invalids attracted patients who were not necessarily mentally ill and who were likely to die at the institution. Of the patients admitted between 1892 and 1910, one-third were over the age of fifty-five; Lawton spent considerable effort in his annual reports explaining his high mortality rates and bemoaning the havoc wreaked by advanced age and senile exhaustion. Additionally, Lawton cared for three times as many alcoholics and drug addicts as Draper had, and more than any other hospital. Each year, from one-quarter to one-third of Lawton's new male patients were brought to the hospital because they were intemperate. The care of the indigent insane, the elderly, and the male alcoholics interfered with Lawton's ability to return the hospital to the halcyon purposes of its founding in the 1830s.[23]

In this case, a hospital reorganization, stemming partially from outside the control of the institution itself, had a different result. The withdrawal of state patients offered the opportunity for creating the intimate climate of the antebellum moral therapists. And Lawton was as eager to implement his ideas about how to run the Retreat as Gerhard had been to create a new "epoch" for Harrisburg or as Chapin had been to maintain the tradition of therapeutic care at the Institute of the Pennsylvania Hospital. But Lawton's willingness to accept the hardest cases for the income they provided encouraged him to keep these people at the asylum; the Brattleboro Retreat became a home for alcoholics and the elderly as well as a hospital for the treatment of the insane. And because in the reporting of statistics Lawton did not distinguish between the patients he was treating and those he simply cared for, the Retreat's public record suggested a policy of across-the-board custodialism.

Despite the implications of this public record, the hindrances of state policies and cultural assumptions about men's illnesses, and the abdication of family responsibility for alcoholics or the elderly, both Lawton and Gerhard had far more success with their patients than their predecessors had managed. There were patients, of course, they could not reach, especially those suffering from somatically-based diseases like senile dementia or general paresis (the tertiary stage of syphilis). But for patients who temporarily had overtaxed their adaptive capacities or suffered from chronic emotional strain, the doctors' enthusiasm arising from their new career opportunities exerted considerable influence. Their renewed efforts and their determination that they could help their patients, plus the smaller number of patients, decreased staff apathy as well, allowing a greater degree of attention for the patients. Moreover, the doctors' faith in their own regime and expectations about recovery carried the "ability to evoke the patient's expectancy of help," an element far more conducive to healing than a pessimistic prognosis.[24]

Neither the vagaries of state policies nor the personal aspirations of doctors, however, cover fully the variety of circumstances which affected the types of treatment that patients received. The casebook records reveal that demographic factors and cultural assumptions often played a role in a hospitalized patient's fate. For instance, in many cases, women received substantially different treatment from that offered to men. This gender difference was intimately connected with the way in which doctors determined the causes of mental illness and formulated prognoses.

The "supposed cause" of the illness was one of the first bits of information the doctors asked for when a patient was brought to the hospital. For nearly one-quarter of all patients, male and female, the family suggested or the doctors assigned ill health as the culprit.[25] Sometimes this characterization took the specific form of injury, exposure, sunstroke, apoplexy, or lead poisoning, but mostly, ill health simply designated general physical debilitation. Indeed, so accustomed had the doctors become to seeing their new charges in a run-down condition that they prescribed tonics on admission as a matter of course.

Half of their patients, however, suffered from other difficulties and it was in the determination of causality in these cases that a gender-related pattern emerged. Doctors (or others) attributed women's problems to aberrations related to their reproductive functions (menstruation, child birth, or menopause), uncontrolled emotions, or the inability to cope with family relationships. They blamed men's instability on alcohol or drug abuse, overwork, heredity, or sexual excesses. These causality categories are not necessarily useful for hindsight guesses about etiology, but the descriptions employed did make a difference in the way doctors perceived patients and, ultimately, in the doctors' attitudes about treatment and the chances for recovery.

Doctors perceived men's illnesses as largely physical in nature. While taking refuge in alcohol may have been a way of dealing with emotional frustrations for many men, most doctors did not acknowledge these emotional sources and focused their therapeutic efforts on plans to "dry out" the alcoholic or enforce a "cold turkey" withdrawal on drug addicts. They seemed even more pessimistic about the men whose illness they attributed to sexual excesses (usually masturbation) and implicitly connected the use of tobacco or alcohol with masturbation. This attitude arose from their own socialization and training that engendered discomfort about sexual matters and predicted dire consequences for the masturbator.[26] Doctors used restraint with these patients more than with others, employed therapeutic drugs less, and generally despaired of being able to convince patients to change their behavior. Even Jerome Gerhard at Harrisburg, with all his initial optimism, slipped into stereotyping drinkers as masturbators and characterizing them as "dull and rather low" types who "always" remained "the same." And once in the asylum, these gender and diagnostic stereotypes yielded few advantages for men patients. Men had more difficulty playing the invalid role and adjusting to the asylum environment which called for passive behavior and unquestioning submission to authority.[27] These circumstances, plus the doctors' propensity to use heredity as a catchall category for determining the cause of men's mental illness, both contributed to the growing pessimism about the benefits of therapy and added to the momentum of the eugenics movement.[28] For at least one-third of their patients, doctors who were treating mentally ill men generally agreed there was little they could do.

It was a different story for some women patients because of the doctors' ideas about the emotionally-rooted causes of their ailments. While these women patients were hardly indicative of the ways in which most nineteenth-century women coped with their family situations, by simply entering the hospital, some women incapable of dealing with personal relationships or emotional trauma were removed from the stressful environment that had supposedly caused their illness. They no longer had to face those daily frustrations nor did they, temporarily, have to take responsibility for the disruption in their homes. Certainly the woman whose stepchildren verbally abused her and the women whose husbands beat them welcomed, however unconsciously, the escape the hospital offered. Hospitalization played a similar alleviating role for the women who struggled under the burdens of grief, worry, or disappointed affections. One woman's first signs of mental illness appeared at the time of the birth of her eighth child; her seven other children had all died in infancy. Presumably, risking institutionalization if she threatened to poison her husband was of smaller consequence to her than facing the daily reminders of her grief and the possibility of confronting yet another deep loss.[29]

But the doctors recorded the cause of nearly twenty percent of all women's illnesses (thirty percent of married women's) as gynecological in origin. For the women at the Harrisburg and Norristown hospitals diagnosed as suffering from gynecological disorders, the intersection of the history of the institutions, the commitment of particular doctors, and the medical theory that assumed a physiological connection between the female generative organs and the nervous system created a therapeutic environment for many patients. In 1881, Alice Bennett became the "Female Physician" at the Norristown Hospital; Margaret Cleaves held a similar post at Harrisburg. Both Bennett and Cleaves, like Gerhard at Harrisburg and Lawton at Brattleboro, took advantage of their new positions to implement some of their ideas about therapeutic practices. They embarked immediately upon a plan of gynecological examinations and treatment. Year after year, they increased the proportion of patients treated. Bennett, for one, delighted that her program had become a "large and laborious part of the medical work of the department."[30]

Women's gynecological problems were real. Doctors found pathological conditions ranging from fairly common inflammations to rampant infections and from retroverted and prolapsed uteri to severely malformed and dysfunctional organs. All patients, men or women, were treated for obvious physical ailments, but one of the crucial differences for the female patients at the Norristown and Harrisburg hospitals was that these doctors looked for gynecological disorders and took steps to alleviate the difficulties. They treated infections with iodine and glycerine, prescribed pessaries, and generally did everything they could to increase the physical comfort of their patients.[31]

More important, however, these gynecological ministrations also meant that doctors saw these women patients on a more regular basis. Frequent contact with doctors and even the increased attention from the attendants on the wards (checking drains and packings, for instance) could make the hospital a less frightening and anonymous place. And the acknowledgment of a real physical problem, plus active medical intervention, relieved some patients of the fear that they were simply out of control of themselves and their lives. In one case, for example, the doctors treated a woman suffering from an ovarian tumor, a vaginal blockage, and a cervical infection. For weeks they used every medical means to relieve the excruciating pain of the patient. After five months, they discharged her in an improved physical and mental condition. Yet on admission this patient's friends had explained her mental illness in terms of her husband's desertion three years earlier. They obviously thought she imagined the headaches, backaches, and general discomfort and pain she complained about and that these were merely symptoms of a now chronic depression.[32]

Given the taxing chores of wife and mother in a working-class world and the socialization of women to their self-sacrificing roles, it is apparent that at least some of these hospitalized women appreciated being the focus of this kind of attention. One patient had developed abscessed breasts while nursing her last child. She had been brought to the hospital by her husband and "several men" who had dragged her up the hospital steps "kicking and struggling wildly;" three nurses were needed to take her to the ward. Upon examination the doctors immediately ordered a warm bath, warm milk, a body rub and medicated poultices for her breasts. "She submitted to the bath and other attentions quietly," the doctors noted and as they visited her daily she thanked them for their "attentions" and asked for more baths and continued bed rest. This woman had five children under the age of nine at home and even in the pain created by her abscessed breasts her husband reported her as merely irritable and scolding. Indeed, the only time this patient appeared irritable during the month she spent in the asylum was when she received a letter from her husband.[33]

Women patients also received attention when the doctors prescribed drugs for them. Twice as many women as men received sedatives during their hospital stays and both male and female doctors prescribed drugs more frequently for women than for men patients. In a society that deemed women the weaker sex and in need of protection, doctors probably perceived the use of drugs with women as a less heinous procedure than mechanical restraint and as an acceptable substitute for physical force. Of all the female patients whose behavior was described as violent, only 6% of them were mechanically restrained, while 20% of the men were. On the other hand, nearly 40% of these violent women were drugged, but only 8% of the men.

Bennett, Cleaves, and other doctors frequently used drugs for therapeutic purposes, however. Closely following the course of the drugs' effects increased the level of attention women patients received from their doctors. At the least, they were on the doctors' minds because all prescriptions had to be entered both in the casebooks and in the hospital's prescription books. Usually these doctors were more than mere record keepers; they were conscientious about following up on their patient's conditions. For instance, at Harrisburg, Cleaves finally gave a hypodermic injection of hyoscyamine to a woman who had been "exceedingly noisy, destructive, and violent" during the first two weeks of her commitment. It had a "slight restraining influence, but not so much as desired," the doctors noted as they watched her closely and worried that "her constitution" had been "greatly enfeebled by the excitement under which she labored." The patient continued to be "filthy," throw food around her room, tear her clothing, assault other people, and exhaust herself. After a few days of hyoscyamine, the doctors tried bromides, but noticed they had little effect on her actions and, furthermore, constipated her. Only then did they resort to morphine to bring the patient to a calmer state.[34]

The stages of drugs used in this case are illustrative of both the history of drug usage in the nineteenth century and of the therapeutic plan of Cleaves and other doctors. Hyoscyamine was a relatively mild narcotic which acted both as a sleep inducer and pain killer with fewer side effects and a lesser addictive quality than the opium which had been used widely in the earlier part of the century. When the hyoscyamine was ineffective, Cleaves moved to older drugs – bromides and chloral hydrate – which also were less addictive than opium or its derivative, morphine. Only as a last resort did she turn to morphine. Moreover, she had waited through two weeks of destructive behavior before she even considered administering drugs. Another indicator that not all doctors used drugs out of merely punitive or coercive motives is the fact that a higher proportion of middle-class patients and those committed by their families received drug treatment than did working-class patients and those committed by the courts. And because doctors were twice as likely to see patients on drug programs either on a daily or weekly basis as patients who did not receive drugs, these patients received virtually the same kind of "individualized nursing care" as the women under gynecological treatment.[35]

This additional contact with the doctors, and the careful handling of their medical problems that women received at the Norristown and Harrisburg hospitals, affected their chances for recovery. Fifty-seven percent of the women who underwent gynecological treatment left the hospital restored to mental health, while only twenty-five percent of those without the specialized attention recovered; half of the women who received drugs recovered, and only thirty-five percent of the others did. The same factors explain why married women did slightly better than single, for they were the women who had the edge in the competition for the doctors' attention; they were far more likely to receive gynecological treatment and slightly more likely to undergo drug therapy.[36]

Because doctors believed that the mental illness of many women arose from environmental stresses or gynecological sources, the therapeutic techniques they used adventitiously contributed to the higher recovery rate of many of their working-class female patients. Modern researchers suggest, for instance, that the drugs used in nineteenth-century asylums acted essentially as placebos and that a placebo "gains its potency through being a tangible symbol of the physician's role as a healer." Doctors used drugs more with women patients and anticipated therapeutic results. Thus the doctors' expectations, and their transference of those expectations to the patients, coalesced. Additionally, for those women who were reacting to stressful personal or family relationships, their gender socialization to dependent, compliant, and emotionally reactive behavior increased the potential for them to respond positively to the drugs, as well as to the increased attention they received. For the women suffering from gynecological disorders, the amount of contact they experienced with doctors and staff may have exercised a similar influence. Their increased physical comfort, however, remained a major factor that undoubtedly affected the mental condition of many of them. Again, contemporary studies have illustrated that the scientific model of mental illness often "fails to acknowledge that psychological and bodily processes can profoundly affect each other" and that the "relief of symptoms by whatever means" can help patients "to make better use of the parts" of their personalities to function "more effectively in general."[37]

While these factors help to explain differences in the experiences of the institutionalized women patients, there is no disputing the fact that the recency of a patient's illness upon entering the hospital affected the likelihood of his or her recovery. Married women especially were brought to the institution at an earlier stage in their illness. Nearly seventy percent of these women had two or more children at home and had been committed within six months of the first appearance of their symptoms. In industrial environments, these working-class families lived in close quarters. Men worked away from home, leaving the daily routine of the household and child care to their wives. The irresponsible or eccentric behavior of these wives and mothers disrupted the family's ability to function. In rural families, child care could be shared more easily by the father; in middle-class families, hiring help to care for the sick person or the children was not such a financial burden.[38]

It is clear that this confluence of gynecological and drug therapy, the doctors' expectations, and the needs of working-class families changed lay attitudes toward the hospital, especially at Norristown. While state hospitals (including the male wards at Norristown) regularly admitted twenty-five percent of their new patients with an illness that had run its course for six months or less, by 1883 the doctors on the women's wards at Norristown were admitting one-third of their patients with recent illnesses. By 1896, fifty-five percent of the women who entered Norristown had been ill for only this short period of time. This reputation for restoring mental health (and offering much needed gynecological services probably otherwise unavailable) created an increasing faith in the hospital. Families, hoping that the doctors' appeals about treating mental illness early would enhance chances for a speedy recovery, and trusting in the medical success illustrated by the doctors, turned to the hospital for help for their wives, mothers, daughters, and sisters. The responses of these families affected the lives of the thousands of women patients who used the Norristown Hospital and, for many, altered the purposes of the asylum. At least at Norristown, the community perceived the hospital as an institution that offered medical and social services in addition to its psychiatric and custodial functions.[39]

It is not so much that custodialism did not exist in late nineteenth-century asylums. In each asylum there occurred a pile-up of chronically ill patients; about one-third of the patients who entered the hospitals left only in a coffin. Many of these patients suffered from maladies that the doctors could do little about; others were so far advanced in their illness that the doctors held out little hope for them or they were wards of the state who were not really mentally ill. As their numbers increased, many doctors became overwhelmed with the difficulties of offering care for these people while still trying to manage treatment for their more promising patients.

But to imply that this very real element of custodialism was an attempt on the part of middle-class doctors to exercise social control over the lives of their working-class patients is simply too easy and, indeed, misleading. As Richard Fox has warned, it is dangerous to posit "an abstract conflict between a group of controllers and their victims." [40] A case in point is Margaret Cleaves, the female physician at the Harrisburg Hospital. To suggest that she was interested only in restructuring the lives of her patients like Ophelia Brown to rid her middle-class society of the problems of working-class deviant behavior is to overlook the complexity of Cleaves's world. Although she said she hoped to ameliorate the sufferings of her female patients, diminish the incidence of mental illness among women, and change the prevailing attitudes toward women's mental health problems, she had equally strong self-interested goals in mind. She was a woman professional breaking ground in a male-dominated profession and when it became clear that remaining on the staff at Harrisburg would not advance her career, she moved to New York, opened a private practice, and spent the rest of her professional life treating middle class neurasthenic women.[41] Additionally, Shailor Lawton's policies at Brattleboro had little to do with his desire to control lower class patients; he had been glad to be rid of them until he realized the necessity of their contribution to the economic well-being of the asylum.

Equally a problem with social control explanations is the assumption that the patients and their families were passive victims of state policies and institutional programs. One of many examples of a patient manipulating the hospital staff, however unconsciously, occurred at the Harrisburg Hospital. This patient had been in the hospital for two months and the doctors had performed minor genito-urinary tract surgery on her. Upon receiving a letter from her husband "saying he was anxious to get her home" and that he would do so in a few days, she told her doctors "she was not fit to go home" and then suffered "hysterical convulsions" that kept her in the hospital for another two months. Moreover, both the increased use of the hospital by the families of Norristown's female patients and the greater reluctance of men's families to commit them to an asylum illustrate the exercise of considerable choice on the part of the so-called victims. It is time to shed social control interpretations that not only have been "applied carelessly" but have "become trite through excessive use" as well.[42]

It is also time to ask new questions.[43] Patient records are a rich and relatively unmined source which allow us to get inside the asylum walls to discover the inadvertent deceptions that superintendents like Shailor Lawton practiced upon us. Had Lawton distinguished between the patients he was actively treating and the residents of the Brattleboro Retreat who were simply using the asylum to live out their old age or invalidism, he would not have had to excuse his low recovery or high mortality rates. Lawton, like other superintendents, reported results in formulaic tables which changed little from the 1830s through the 1920s and which ultimately obscured both nuances of attitudinal differences and changes in psychiatric theory and practice over the course of the century.

Historians also must explore the inner history of asylums to discover the multiple functions that asylums played in the lives of nineteenth-century Americans. Immediately apparent is the existence of two kinds of service: one custodial, one therapeutic. They were not always separate, nor always predictable.

Some doctors, invigorated by new career opportunities or inspired by the chance to implement fresh psychiatric theories, changed the institutional experiences, and even the lives, of their patients. And even purely medical care such as routinized gynecological exams and treatment altered the hospital experience of thousands of women in some institutions and in some cases changed the purposes of the asylum, at least as viewed through the eyes of the patients and their families. Additionally, gender stereotypes made a difference in both the rate of usage of the hospital and the type of treatment men and women received.

If we add to these circumstances the individual doctors' ideologies (and self-interest), the intricacies of financing state hospitals and even private asylums like Brattleboro, and conflicts between the state and the institution, a generalization about custodialism encourages us to ignore the wide variety of psychiatric medicine in the late nineteenth century and to overlook the elements of the asylum that worked and hold lessons for current social policy and psychiatric practice. For instance, there was a bias practiced on the part of doctors, but that bias was not always one of class and ethnicity; it was often one of preferential treatment for those patients about whom the doctors were most hopeful. Institutional working conditions, the doctors' career aspirations and commitment, and patients' expectations about receiving help shaped that optimism as much as medical practice.

The data from the patient records of these four hospitals also suggest that social and cultural factors such as gender, marital status, and age affected definitions of mental illness and determined assumptions about diagnoses and prognoses which could hasten a return to the family, or sometimes condemn a patient to extended hospitalization. If we are to understand the social values that still affect the ideology of mental illness and the practice of psychiatry, historians must continue to examine this complex vortex of institutional politics, medical theory and practice, career exigencies, doctor-patient interactions, and the perceptions of the public.

FOOTNOTES

Research for this paper was funded in part by a National Endowment for the Humanities Summer Stipend and by a Summer Research Fellowship from the University of Vermont.

1. The names of these two patients are fictitious to protect the confidentiality of the records.

2. The only further information on Caleb Smith from his brother was that he was naturally good-hearted and had recently threatened suicide. The doctors thought Caleb seemed "exalted" and exhibited a "poor memory." On admission, they noted also that he was in a fair state of health, had a good appetite, regular bowels, but "wakeful sleep." An uncle on his father's side had suffered from paralysis and there was consumption on his mother's side of the family. Other than this formulaic information collected on all patients, there is no record of Caleb Smith's nearly two-year stay at the hospital.

3. The admission and casebook records on Ophelia Brown were much fuller than Caleb Smith's. Besides the information cited in the text, the doctors noted her natural disposition as "amiable and even-tempered," although she was sometimes "self-willed." They remarked that this was her first experience with mental aberration and suggested that her acute mania was brought on by ill health and uterine disease, complicated by heredity. Her paternal grandmother had been insane for a short time and a maternal uncle died in that condition. Ophelia, at admission, suffered from poor eating habits, irregular menstruation, constipated bowels, and some insomnia. Ophelia did not receive gynecological treatment because she had seemed disturbed by the examination, but she regularly took tonics and medicine when she was ill with a cold.

4. S. Weir Mitchell, "Address before the Fiftieth Annual Meeting of the American Medico-Psychological Association," *American Journal of Nervous and Mental Disease* 21 (July, 1894): 413-437 and Dorman B. Eaton, "Despotism in Lunatic Asylums," *North American Review* 132 (March, 1881): 263-275. Mitchell and Eaton are only the most cited critics of the asylum superintendents; their remarks reflect the dissatisfactions of dozens of others. For the responses of the superintendents and their concerns about the changing nature of their asylums, see Gerald N. Grob, *Mental Institutions in America* (New York, 1973) and *Mental Illness and American Society, 1875-1940* (Princeton, 1983); Charles E. Rosenberg, *The Trial of the Assassin Guiteau* (Chicago, 1968); and Constance M. McGovern, *Masters of Madness* (Hanover, NH, 1985).

5. Christopher Lasch, employing Erving Goffman's concept of the "total institution," asserts that confinement was inherent in the very nature of asylums. Michel Foucault came to a similar conclusion based on an emerging capitalist society's inability to tolerate the deviant's incapacity for productive work. David Rothman finds external pressures from demographic changes and shifting state policies produced new ways of dealing with social dislocation and Gerald Grob explains that the interaction of admission policies, state boards of charity, legislative expectations, and the appearance of increasing numbers of lower class patients created an unbridgeable gap between doctor-administrators and their charges. See Christopher Lasch, "Origins of the Asylum" in *The World of Nations* (New York, 1973); Erving Goffman, *Asylums* (New York, 1961); Michel Foucault, *Madness and Civilization* (New York, 1965) and *Discipline and Punish* (New York, 1979); David J. Rothman, *The Discovery of the Asylum* (Boston, 1971) and *Conscience and Convenience* (Boston, 1980); and Gerald N. Grob, "Class, Ethnicity, and Race in American Mental Hospitals, 1830-1875," *Journal of the History of Medicine and the Allied Sciences* (July, 1973): 207-229; "The Social History of Medicine and Disease in America," *Journal of Social History* 10 (June, 1977): 391-409; "Rediscovering Asylums" in Morris J. Vogel and Charles E. Rosenberg, eds., *The Therapeutic Revolution* (Philadelphia, 1979); *Mental Institutions*; and *Mental Illness and American Society*.

6. The data are based on a random selection of 1140 patients from four hospitals. In general, the extant records yield information about age, marital status, number of children (for some), occupation, place of birth and residence, the nature of the admitting agency and source of support, admission and discharge dates, condition at time of discharge, and causes and forms of illness. Most contain accounts of contacts between patient and doctor, as well as remarks about behavior before admission and during commitment, assessments of temperament and hereditary factors, and notes on the uses of treatment techniques ranging from drugs and restraint to work and persuasion. It is apparent that the doctors were candid in their notes in the casebooks. Many expressed rather negative biases and freely reported the use of muffs or cribs to restrain patients and solitary cells to isolate the violent ones. And it is not unusual to find reports of attendants who abused patients or the occasional assistant physician who became addicted to opium.

7. Of the 229 patients from the Institute of the Pennsylvania Hospital sample, 6.4% were farmers; 22% unskilled laborers; 19.3% skilled laborers; 34.5% were of the managerial or professional classes; and 17.9% had no identifiable occupation. This last category largely reflects women for whom there were no occupations listed and none designated for their fathers or husbands. The Harrisburg patient population (N=413) included 15% farmers; 31.5% unskilled laborers; 24% skilled laborers; 9.7% professionals or managers; and 19.9% unidentified. The

Norristown Hospital figures (N =175) were 4.7% farmers; 42.1% unskilled workers; 28.7% skilled; 12.9% professionals and managers; and 11.7% unidentified. Comparable figures for Brattleboro (N =249) were 10.8% farmers; 34.9% unskilled; 14.5% skilled; 7.2% professionals and managers; and 32.5% with unidentified occupations.

8. For the history of this policy, see Nancy Tomes, *A Generous Confidence: Thomas Story Kirkbride and the Art of Asylum Keeping* (Cambridge, Eng., 1984) and Thomas G. Morton, *The History of the Pennsylvania Hospital* (Philadelphia, 1895).

9. Morton, *History of the Pennsylvania Hospital*, p. 194.

10. These patterns of the admission and discharge of patients are evident from the tables in Morton, *History of the Pennsylvania Hospital*, p. 243.

11. *Doctor-patient contacts, hospitalization length, discharge condition, and mortality rates for four hospitals, 1880-1910:*

	Pennsylvania (N =299)	Harrisburg (Gerhard,men) (N =109)	Norristown Harrisburg (women) (N =396)	Brattleboro (Lawton) (N =150)
Frequent doctor-patient contact	68.2%	69.7%	62.6%	34.7%
Hospitalization (1 year or less)	59.2%	45.9%	55.6%	59.3%
Discharged (recovered or improved)	58.2%	59.4%	55.8%	44.0%
Mortality	7.7%	28.3%	28.3%	47.3%

The records for male patients at Norristown before 1895 were so sparsely kept that they are useless for statistical analysis and the available records on women at Norristown did not include those patients who died at the hospital. The statistics which include the Norristown women are adjusted by the addition of a "worst possible case" based on the mortality rates as reported in the annual reports of the hospital. In other words, fifty cases were added, none of whom received frequent doctor visits (defined as more often than quarterly) and all of whom were hospitalized for more than a year and died at the hospital.

12. For the institutional history of the Harrisburg Hospital, see Henry M. Hurd, ed., *The Institutional Care of the Insane in the United States and Canada* (Baltimore, 1916), vol. 3; for the professional career of Curwen, see McGovern, *Masters of Madness*; for the centralization of asylums under state boards, see Grob, *Mental Institutions* and *Mental Illness and American Society*; for the reforming efforts of Corson, see Hiram Corson, *A Brief History of Proceedings in the Medical Society of Pennsylvania to procure the Recognition of Women Physicians by the Medical Profession of the State* (Norristown, Pa., 1894); for the discussion of the issue of women doctors on institutional staffs, see John Curwen to Thomas Kirkbride, 12 May 1881, Kirkbride MSS, Pennsylvania Hospital, Philadelphia, and Constance M. McGovern, "Doctors or Ladies?," *Bulletin of the History of Medicine* 55 (Fall, 1981): 88-107.

13. For the specific actions of the trustees against Curwen, see Harrisburg State Hospital (HSH) Trustees' Minutes, 13 January, 17 February, and 14 April, 1881. For the reorganization of the hospital, see these Minutes, 10 July 1879 through 30 December 1880.

14. See HSH Trustees' Minutes, 14 July 1881, for Gerhard's reaction to the meeting of the Association of Medical Superintendents. The dispute over seating Cleaves is chronicled in "Proceedings of the Thirty-Seventh Annual Meeting of the Association of Medical Superintendents of American Institutions for the Insane," *American Journal of Insanity* 38

(October, 1881): 174-177. Cleaves also had reported to the trustees in July that her credentials had been "laid upon the table" at the Association and that she had found that the meeting "afforded very little of professional interest." Cleaves did appreciate the professional collegiality of Gerhard, however; in the *Thirty-First Annual Report of the State Lunatic Hospital at Harrisburg* (Harrisburg, Pa., 1881) and in her reports to the trustees, Cleaves praised Gerhard's "cooperation" and "kindness." See especially HSH Trustees' Minutes, 13 January and 14 April, 1881.

15. See the *Thirty-First Annual Report---Harrisburg*, pp. 9-12.

16. At the Pennsylvania Hospital, for instance, as early as 1807 the managers had accepted the poor on trial. If these patients showed no signs of improvement within six months, however, families had to make other arrangements. Thomas Kirkbride and his successors in the Department for the Insane pursued the same policy – as did other private hospitals. See "Rules and Regulations of the Pennsylvania Hospital" as reprinted in Morton, *History of the Pennsylvania Hospital*, pp. 561-562.

17. In her study of nineteenth-century British ideas about female insanity, Elaine Showalter suggests that many doctors may have been chary of placing the stigma of certified insanity of men who needed to support families and that "families seem to have been more resistant to incarcerating mildly disturbed or potentially curable male members." Elaine Showalter, "Victorian Women and Insanity," *Victorian Studies* 23 (1980): 163.

18. The essence of the relationship between the Vermont Asylum and the state of Vermont can be followed in Hurd, *Institutional Care*, vol. 3, pp. 672-700; the *Annual and Biennial Report of the Officers of the Vermont Asylum for the Insane* (variable publishers), 1836-1910; the Minutes of the Trustees' Meetings housed at the Brattleboro Retreat (BR); [Joseph Draper], *The Vermont Asylum for the Insane: Its Annals for Fifty Years* (Brattleboro, VT, 1887); and Constance M. McGovern, "The Insane, the Asylum, and the State in Nineteenth-Century Vermont," *Vermont History* 52 (Fall, 1984): 205-224.

19. See BR Casebooks, patients #4903 and 4948 for the remarks. For Draper's comments on drug usage, see *Report of the Special Commissioners Appointed Under the Provisions of Joint Resolution No. 137 entitled "Joint Resolution in Relation to the Insane of the State and Statutes in Relation to their Confinement and Treatment." Approved Nov. 28, 1876. Presented by* M. Goldsmith, O.F. Fassett, W.H. Walker, *Commissioners* (Rutland, VT, 1878).

20. Both the removal of the bulk of state patients and Lawton's tribute to Draper appear in the *Biennial Report---Vermont Asylum for the Insane* (Rutland, VT, 1892).

21. For 1891-1892, the Vermont Asylum received nearly $123,000 from the state; receipts from private patients (and "other sources") amounted to another $58,000. In the following year with the withdrawal of 185 or more state patients, Vermont paid only $52,000 to the asylum and the amount from private patients dipped to $28,000. For the financial status of the asylum, see BR Minutes of the Trustees' Meetings for July 1892 and July 1893; for the discussion about the name change, see these Minutes, 27 May and 12 July 1892 and 27 May 1893. See also the pamphlet entitled "Brattleboro Retreat" (n.p.: 1896?) filed with the records of the Retreat and the Trustees' Minutes for 3 November 1896 for evidence of the newly launched publicity campaign to attract paying patients.

22. The emphasis on the double purpose of the Retreat was announced in "Brattleboro Retreat." The continuing efforts to attract patients are evident in the BR Trustees' Minutes, 8 June 1897, 5 April 1898, and 11 January 1899. An 1898 pamphlet subtly shifted the earlier pamphlet's wording about a "pleasant home for chronic mental invalids" to the Retreat as "an institution for the care and relief of nervous and mental invalids" and advertised "attractive apartments for special cases." See "A Hospital Home" (n.p.: 1898?) and the reference to this in the Trustees' Minutes, 8 June 1897. On 5 April 1898, the trustees voted to open Linden Lodge for these "summer guests."

23. Starting in 1900, the state agreed to send at least 200 patients to the Brattleboro Retreat (another 500 to Waterbury) and by 1910 the state treasury once again was contributing large sums annually to the institution in Brattleboro ($93,000 in 1910). By that time it was clear that the publicity campaign had worked; private patients contributed over $135,000 in revenue that year. For evidence of the increased numbers and proportions of male patients who suffered from alcohol or drug abuse and for the growing numbers of the elderly of both sexes, see Lawton's *Biennial Reports*, 1892-1910. For turn-of-the-century evidence of this relationship between geriatric-related mental illness and pessimism about discharge, see Grob, *Mental Illness and American Society*, and for early twentieth-century studies of this pattern, see Morton Kramer, Hyman Goldstein, Robert Israel, and Nelson Johnson, *A Historical Study of the Disposition of First Admissions to a State Hospital: Experience of the Warren State Hospital During the Period 1916-1950*, U.S. Department of Health, Education, and Welfare, Public Health Service Monograph No. 32 (Washington, 1955).

24. For a penetrating analysis of these factors, see Jerome D. Frank, *Persuasion and Healing: A Comparative Study of Psychotherapy*, rev. ed. (Baltimore, 1973). I am grateful to Gerald N. Grob for bringing this study to my attention.

25. *Causality of mental illness by gender in four hospitals, 1880-1910:*

Women			Men		
Illness	131	23.0%	Illness	134	23.5%
Ob/Gyn	104	18.2%	Habits	76	13.3%
Emotions	58	10.2%	Work	50	8.8%
Domestic trouble	44	7.7%	Heredity	39	6.8%
			Sexual	36	6.3%
Other (7)	94	16.4%	Other (5)	78	13.7%
Unknown	139	24.4%	Unknown	157	27.6%
	570			570	

Besides the eight categories listed above, doctors determined causality in a few cases of both genders as related to financial concerns, religious excitement, or old age.

26. For the pervasiveness of the link between masturbation and insanity and doctors' generally pessimistic attitudes, see Peter McCandless, "Liberty and Lunacy," *Journal of Social History* 11 (1978): 366-386; E.H. Hare, "Masturbation and Insanity," *Journal of Mental Science* 108 (1962): 1-25; H. Tristram Englehart, "The Disease of Masturbation: Values and the Concept of Disease," *Bulletin of the History of Medicine* 48 (1974): 239-248; and R.P. Neuman, "Masturbation, Madness, and the Modern Concepts of Childhood and Adolescence," *Journal of Social History* 8 (1975): 1-27. At the Institute of the Pennsylvania Hospital in the 1880s and 1890s, for instance, masturbation was one of the few behavioral actions for which patients were kept in restraints, especially at night. Otherwise doctors restrained only suicidal or homicidal patients – and these for much shorter periods of time. See Medical Journals, volumes 1-6, of the Department for the Insane of the Pennsylvania Hospital, Pennsylvania Hospital, Philadelphia.

27. Gerhard, for instance, disputed the claims of some that at least three-quarters of recent cases "recovered, under proper treatment." Noting that the statistics for the men in his hospital "do not warrant this assumption," he continued, "nor do I believe that those of any other Hospital would if the real facts were given." For Gerhard, it was "the very nature of the disorder" in the cases of masturbation that precluded recovery. For the remarks of the doctors at Harrisburg about some of these patients, see HSH Casebooks, patients E.E., admitted May 1882; A.L.S., admitted November 1882; W.S., admitted November 1896; M.D., admitted January 1906; and L.M. and H.R., admitted May 1906. Gerhard and his successors also regularly recorded heredity as a complication in descriptions of their male patients.

28. For the emergence of the eugenics movement in the United States, see especially Charles E. Rosenberg, *No Other Gods* (Baltimore, 1976), chapters 1, 4, and 12.

29. For this and other particularly poignant examples of frequent child-bearing and infant deaths, see HSH Casebooks, patients #394, 516, 518, 523, and 524 and for samples of women suffering physical and emotional abuse, see patients #433 and 512.

30. For the history of the appointment of women doctors to the staffs of psychiatric institutions, see McGovern, "Doctors or Ladies?" and for analysis of women in the general medical profession, see Regina Markell Morantz, "The 'Connecting Link' " in Judith Walzer Leavitt and Ronald L. Numbers, eds., *Sickness & Health in America* (Madison, WI, 1978); "The Lady and Her Physician" in Mary Hartman and Lois Banner, eds., *Clio's Consciousness Raised* (New York, 1974); and Regina Markell Morantz and Sue Zschoche, "Professionalism, Feminism, and Gender Roles," *Journal of American History* 67 (1980): 568-588.

31. Edward Shorter, in his controversial work on women's illnesses, has demonstrated, nonetheless, that most nineteenth-century women suffered from multitudinous physical ailments connected especially with child-bearing. Edward Shorter, "Women's Diseases before 1900" in Mel Albin and Dominick Cavallo, eds., *Family Life in America* (St. James, N.Y., 1981). And although the particular doctors' commitments to surgery contributed to their eagerness to use ovariotomies as a means to gain mental recovery for their patients, Wendy Mitchinson illustrates that many institutionalized women suffered from gynecological disorders. Wendy Mitchinson, "Gynecological Operations on Insane Women: London, Ontario, 1895-1901," *Journal of Social History* 15 (1982): 467-484. The plan of treatment that the women doctors at Harrisburg and Norristown devised emerges from Margaret Cleaves's reports to the Harrisburg trustees, HSH Trustees' Minutes, 1880-1883, and *Thirty-First* through *Thirty-Third Annual Report--- Harrisburg* (1881-1883) and from Alice Bennett's reports to her trustees, Norristown State Hospital Executive Committee (of the Board of Trustees) Minutes, 1885-1899, and *First* through *Sixteenth Annual Report of the State Hospital for the Insane of the South-Eastern District of Pennsylvania at Norristown* (Norristown, PA, 1881-1896).

32. See HSH Casebooks, patient #455. Showalter, in "Victorian Women and Insanity," suggests that doctors expected women to be "quiet, virtuous, and immobile" and especially long-suffering; these men objected to women "chattering about their grievances" (p. 169). The fact that this patient's friends attributed her physical "grievances" to an emotional source suggests that middle-class doctors' attitudes about women's illnesses had penetrated the working class. Barbara Sicherman has found that many working-class patients at the Massachusetts General Hospital suffered from similar "misdiagnosis" as the patient described here, but nevertheless benefited from (and even seemed to enjoy) the "psychological as well as physical care that they could obtain in no other way." Barbara Sicherman, "The Uses of a Diagnosis" in Leavitt and Numbers, *Sickness & Health in America*, pp. 34 and 38.

33. See HSH Casebooks, patient #518.

34. The doctors at all three Pennsylvania hospitals were meticulous about recording the administration of drugs. At Harrisburg, for instance, the entries made in the casebook records and the drug prescription record were strikingly consistent. See HSH Casebooks, 1880-1883, and HSH Prescription Book, 1880-1882. For the example, see HSH Casebooks, patient #533, as well as patients #409, 432, and 540 for other illustrations.

35. For the history of the changing use of therapeutic drugs, see Eric T. Carlson, "Cannabis Indica in 19th-Century Psychiatry," *American Journal of Psychiatry* 131 (1974): 1004-1007 and Eric T. Carlson and Meribeth M. Simpson, "Opium as a Tranquilizer," *American Journal of Psychiatry* 120 (1963): 112-117. For nineteenth-century treatises on the dosages and purposes of drugs, see Frank T. Foster, ed., *Appleton's Medical Dictionary* (New York, 1904); George M. Gould, *The Student's Medical Dictionary* (Philadelphia, 1900); T. Gaillard Thomas, *Practical Treatise on the Diseases of Women* (Philadelphia, 1868); John Charles Bucknill and Daniel H. Tuke, *A Manual of Psychological Medicine* (Philadelphia, 1858); Charles K. Mills, *The Nervous System and Its Diseases* (Philadelphia, 1898); and various articles, such as John P. Gray, "Hyoscyamia in Insanity," *American Journal of Insanity* (1880): 394-403 and Henry M. Hurd, "A Plea for

Systematic Therapeutic, Clinical, and Statistical Study," *American Journal of Insanity* (1881): 16-31. For the intellectual and cultural climate, see Charles E. Rosenberg's, "The Therapeutic Revolution" in Vogel and Rosenberg, *The Therapeutic Revolution*. "Individualized nursing care" is Mitchinson phrase in "Gynecological Operations."

36. The differences between women and men, moreover, were dramatic. In the figures on recovery alone, 33.3% of the women were discharged as fully recovered, while only 20.5% of the men were.

37. See Frank, *Persuasion and Healing*, especially ch. 6; for the citations, pp. 46, 138, and 156. Hypnotics, sedatives, and narcotics, of course, had the indirect medical effect of calming the patient and anodynes served medical purposes as well.

38. The argument about the connection between the recency of illness and chances of recovery dates back at least to the initial building of therapeutic asylums in the 1820s. Statistics cited throughout the nineteenth century, as well as more contemporary studies, illustrate the link. For twentieth-century studies dealing with this factor, see Richard C. Erikson, "Outcome Studies in Mental Hospitals: A Review," *Psychological Bulletin* 82 (1975): 519-540; H. Warren Dunham and Bernard N. Meltzer, "Predicting Length of Hospitalization of Mental Patients," *American Journal of Sociology* 52 (1946): 123-131; and Philip Hilmar Person, Jr., *The Relationship between Selected Social and Demographic Characteristics of Hospitalized Mental Patients and the Outcome of Hospitalization*, U.S. Department of Health, Education, and Welfare, Public Health Service Monograph (Washington, 1964). Current studies illustrate the more prevalent use of psychiatric hospitals by married women than by other women or any men. See Walter R. Gove, "The Relationship between Sex Roles, Marital Status, and Mental Illness," *Social Forces* 51 (1972): 33-44; Earl S. Pollack, Richard W. Redick, and Carl A. Taube, "The Application of Census Socio-economic and Familial Data to the Study of Morbidity from Mental Disorders," *American Journal of Public Health* 58 (1968): 83-89; and Person, *The Relationship between Selected Social and Demographic Characteristics*. Once in the asylum, an analysis of the records of a Canadian asylum reveals that for women the chances of discharge were higher if they were housewives rather than if they were working women. See Barry Willer and Gary Miller, "Classification, Cause and Symptoms of Mental Illness, 1890-1900, in Ontario," *Canadian Psychiatric Association Journal* 22 (1977): 231-238.

39. Mitchinson, in "Gynecological Operations," also found that the claims of success by the doctors at the London (Ontario) asylum resulted in an increased use of the hospital "service" of gynecological surgery. For suggestions about the effects of public attitudes toward the mental hospital in the first half of the twentieth century, see Kramer, Goldstein, Israel, and Johnson, *A Historical Study of the Dispositions of First Admissions to a State Hospital*.

40. Richard Fox, *So Far Disordered in Mind* (Berkeley, 1978), p. 14.

41. For the details of Margaret Cleaves's career, see McGovern, "Doctors or Ladies?"

42. HSH Casebooks, patient #454, and Richard Fox's review of Allan Horlick's *Country Boys and Merchant Princes*, "Beyond 'Social Control:' Institutions and Disorder in Bourgeois Society," *History of Education Quarterly* 16 (1976): 203-207.

43. More recently historians of other types of institutions have raised some of these "new" questions, but even they accept the pervasiveness of custodialism. See especially, Jamil S. Zainaldin and Peter L. Tyor, "Asylum and Society: An Approach to Industrial Change," *Journal of Social History* 13 (1979): 23-48; Steven Ruggles, "Fallen Women: The Inmates of the Magdalen Society Asylum of Philadelphia, 1836-1908," *Journal of Social History* 16 (1983): 65-82; and Grob, *Mental Illness and American Society*.

12.

PARALYSIS: THE RISE AND FALL OF
A "HYSTERICAL" SYMPTOM

Edward Shorter

After doing research on hysteria for a certain time, I should like to attempt a *mise au point*. The following represents some preliminary findings, circulated now in an effort to encourage wider discussion. I offer a few speculations, fewer still fixed conclusions, and wish to hear other views about the difficult subject treated on the following pages.

What is "Hysteria"?

There have been several histories of "hysteria." Inevitably, they discuss medical ideas on the subject rather than the reality of the disease itself.[1] What has remained unexplored is the history of hysteria as a genuine psychiatric disorder, just as schizophrenia and depression, also real disorders, have as yet unwritten histories of their own.

"Hysteria" may be taken to mean simply physical symptoms of psychological origin. But a major difficulty for the historian is separating symptoms that truly arise in the mind ("psychogenic") from those arising in organic disease ("somatogenic"). "Fits," for example, could be psychogenic or arise from organic epilepsy, or both. Thus for many symptoms it is difficult to distinguish retrospectively those caused by organic processes from those arising in the mind. An exception to this, however, is symptoms affecting the legs. I propose in this paper to use disorders of walking as an "index" of the frequency of hysteria in past times. In these disorders especially, the underlying cause is more readily apparent from the patients' history than is generally the case. For example, a sudden paraplegia in a young woman of 17 that is "healed" in two weeks with electrotherapy is unlikely to have resulted from an organic disease. On the other hand, seizures, disorders of vision, and lumps in the throat − to take examples of other symptoms often deemed "hysterical" − may well have been caused by some organic process not apparent to the physician or from the patient's history.

Developing an index of the occurrence of hysteria in past times is of particular interest to the social historian because, unlike many other psychiatric diseases, the presentation of "hysterical" symptoms tends to be molded by the surrounding culture. The particular form in which schizophrenia or dementia present is probably not much influenced by the patient's surroundings. But with hysteria we enter a gray zone in which the underlying incidence of the disorder may well be constant across the ages but its form changeable, in accordance with such cultural influences as what is deemed to be "feminine" behavior, how much autonomy the individual is expected to demonstrate vis-a-vis community pressures, and so forth.

We might think of the culture as possessing a "symptom repertoire," a range of physical symptoms available to the unconscious mind for the physical expression of psychological conflict. In some epochs convulsions, the sudden inability to speak or terrible leg pain may loom prominently in the repertoire. In other epochs patients may draw chiefly upon such symptoms as abdominal pain, false estimates of body weight and enervating weakness as metaphors for conveying psychic stress. A whole range of symptoms is thus available in the repertoire, and what interests the cultural historian is *why* certain symptoms are selected in certain epochs.[2]

In the following pages I shall argue that psychogenic paraplegias and gait disturbances were relatively uncommon before the end of the eighteenth century. Then in the nineteenth century they begin to increase in frequency, culminating towards the *belle époque* in a veritable plague of "invalidism," young ladies unable to walk, or at best capable of tottering along with crutches until leg or hip pain pulled them down. After the First World War these motor disturbances vanish as swiftly and mysteriously as they arose. We thus have a classic kind of "rise-and-fall" problem, similar to the story of "chlorosis" or of "neurasthenia": the rapid coming into vogue of a pattern of symptoms, its drum-beat rise to a climax, and its sudden falling out of fashion. Those stricken with a psychogenic hemiplegia (one side of the body paralyzed) or an ataxic (unsteady) gait do not, of course, believe themselves to be following the dictates of fashion, but rather that they are the tragic victims of an inexplicable nervous disease which leaves them, against every conscious effort, hopelessly paralyzed until the healing medical hand appears brandishing a "faradic brush," or a jarful of leeches, or whatever medical treatment provides relief through suggestion.

I am not arguing that motor disorders constituted the only form of hysteria before the First World War. To keep the blizzard of symptoms once labeled "hysterical" in order, it might be useful to define hysteria generally as any psychogenic disorder of the "sensorimotor" part of the nervous system which the patient believes to be physical in origin.[3] Thus to qualify as "hysterical" the symptom must:

1. Be psychological in origin, and not the result of some organic disease process, not in other words the result of an anatomical, physiological or biochemical "lesion."

2. Be situated in the voluntary muscles of the body or in the patient's subjective perception of sensory impulses, and not in the motor functions of the autonomic nervous system. Thus visceral *pain* may be hysterical, but I would like to exclude such conditions as irritable bowel syndrome and hypertension.

3. Be perceived by the patient as beyond the control of his conscious mind, even though the symptom may very well be abolished through the operation of the unconscious mind, via suggestion or psychotherapy. For patients, in other words, "hysterical" symptoms are real.

4. By this standard, therefore, hysteria over the past three centuries may encompass a considerable spectrum of symptoms, ranging from classic "fits" to muscle contractures and paralyses in the motor system, to patches of skin "anaesthesia," sudden attacks of "blindness" and persistent unchanging deep abdominal "pain" on the sensory side. In focusing upon paresis of the lower limbs and on problems in walking I am by no means denying the frequency of these other deficits. I am, however, arguing that a whole range of other disorders, which both historians and the doctors of the time have tended to consider "hysterical," be removed from the definition:

– Disorders of mood and of states of consciousness: modern psychiatry is sufficiently advanced to give us more precise descriptions of what were once deemed "hysterical" psychoses, fugue states, and dissociation. It simply confuses things to continue labeling "split" states of consciousness or attacks of amnesia as "hysterical." The same is true of "hypochondria": as long as the victim does not perceive an actual physical symptom, the disorder is not hysterical.

– Disorders of personality, especially the so-called "hysterical personality" with its supposed animated, emotionally labile presentation and its imputed dark substructure of frigidity and pathological self-absorption. The entire construct corresponds to a set of psychoanalytic assumptions about sexual repression in mental disorder which have not been scientifically established. Empirically, there is little overlap between the hysterical personality and the occurrence of the physical symptoms that interest us here (in the Freudian tradition called "conversion symptoms"). And many scholars are inclined anyway to see this personality "disorder" more as an artifact of male-female relations, and quite particularly of relations between male doctors and female patients, so there is doubt whether it may be considered a true disorder of the personality at all.[4]

Thus outfitted with a definition of exactly what it is we wish to study, we may turn to the social history of a certain kind of hysterical symptom.

Separating Hysteria from Organic Disease: Some Issues

Studying the occurrence of hysteria in the past has been plagued by two problems. One is the overinclusiveness of the term, so that every organic disease imaginable — including tuberculosis, congestive heart failure, and neurosyphilis — has at one time or another been classified as hysteria. A second is the overinclusiveness of many organic diagnoses, so that somatically-oriented physicians have often ascribed to "polyneuritis" or "spinal tuberculosis" symptoms that were basically psychological in origin. This latter problem will concern us throughout the paper. The first occupies us here, because without guidelines for retrospectively ruling out from the flood of "hysteria" reports the many real organic affections, there can be no hope of studying the pure article.

Even for neurologists today, separating hysteria from organic disease is not easy. Eliot Slater traced the records of 85 patients who had been given the diagnosis "hysteria" at the National Hospital in London in selected years during the 1950s. Of these predominantly young and middle-aged individuals, it turned out nine years later that 12 had died, the vascular diseases, neoplasms and so forth that ultimately killed them not being diagnosed at the time; a number of epileptics were missed; drug intoxication, dementia and other disorders of the central nervous system all had been deemed "hysteria," and this at Britain's foremost neurological hospital in the 1950s. "In such cases," wrote Slater, "one wonders what the clinician had in mind which led him to speak of 'hysteria.' "[5]

The historian should take heart, nonetheless, for several reasons. One, the wrongly-diagnosed "hysterias" at the National Hospital were largely difficult referrals. The straightforward cases — a clear majority, never reached these consultants.

Secondly, most psychiatric and neurological cases today are, despite the existence of sophisticated machines for investigation, nonetheless diagnosed on the basis of "history," the patient's account of his illness plus his subsequent course. With the exception of multiple sclerosis, much neurological disease that might be confused with hysteria has an irreversible, downhill course. Despite remissions, the patient never really recovers, and sooner or later the organic nature of the problem is revealed in stark wasting of muscles, disorders of eye movement, or unmistakable dementia. The temporal course of disease of the mind is often different from that of organic nervous disease. And even though placebo therapy may relieve organic symptoms for a while, it never "cures" them, whereas it often cures psychological disease.

Acute paralysis is a particular problem. It may either be psychogenic or somatogenic. A young man goes to bed at night and wakes up unable to walk the next morning. What's wrong with him? If he displays a hemiplegia (paralysis on one side), the most probable diagnoses are a stroke, some other sudden brain event, or hysteria. The following case shows the possibilities that rush to mind:

On 21 April 1890 a German-Jewish industrialist, a somewhat "nervous" man, fainted in a restaurant. He was 42 and had suffered since age 18 from heart palpitations whenever he became excited. Upon awakening 24 hours later in a hospital, he noted that his left leg was paralyzed and his left hand stiff and painful. Sensation had also departed from the left leg ("anaesthesia"). He had a headache on both sides and disturbances of vision.

So far this sounds like a stroke. But the doctors discovered his left leg to be completely stiff and immobile. He could move his toes slightly and the deep tendon reflexes ("knee jerk") were abolished, but maybe because he was holding his leg so stiffly. This now sounds less like an organic disease, given all this muscular contraction, and when we discover that the man was cured after two sessions of "electrotherapy," we are inclined to think his problem may have been psychogenic.[6] Or perhaps he did suffer a mild stroke, spontaneous recovery from which happened to coincide with the "faradizations" and "galvanizations" of the day whose therapeutic benefit was entirely psychological. The point is that even before the advent of scientific biochemical and radiologic investigations, the historian often has enough information to permit serious analysis.

More challenging are the acute paralyses of both lower limbs ("paraplegias") because they occurred almost epidemically in young women in the nineteenth century. Here the "differential" diagnosis (assuming the victim has not been in an accident) is not stroke but acute inflammation in the nervous system, either infectious or autoimmune in nature. The young woman stricken so tragically might well indeed have a disease of the spinal cord (a myelitis, for example) or an affection of the peripheral nerves to the legs, such as the Landry-Guillain-Barré disease, or as it is now called acute immune-mediated polyneuritis ("AIMP"). This disease is not uncommon and was described in part by the doctors in Jean-Martin Charcot's Salpêtrière Hospital in Paris, just as important developments were occurring in the intellectual history of hysteria. Indeed, perhaps she does. But the account will usually tell us if she has lost the ability to urinate, for example. If she can still pass water, she probably does not have a myelitis. Or the history might reveal an instantaneous recovery as the result of receiving a massive purgative, which would rule out organic disease generally.

The above treats the acute paralyses. But of interest in the history of women particularly are the chronic paralyses and gait disorders, whose onset consists of scattered little deficits, separated in time and anatomical place, and whose course may lead to years of indisposition, culminating in invalidism. Consider, for example, "H.J.," a 17-year-old female servant who in 1881 was being treated by a chemist "for a wart on her knee." "The leg became stiff one night, and the next morning the patient could not use it." The leg remained "weak and useless" for five months until a session of electrotherapy at St. Thomas's Hospital in London seemed to cure it. But 18 months later, back home in her native Birmingham, the problem recurred, this time virtually immobilizing both lower limbs. On examination in June, 1884, at the Queen's Hospital in Birmingham, her body shook and the toes dragged when she attempted to walk. Her eyelids drooped. Everything else was in order, at least until somewhat later she developed "incontinence of urine and feces for a day or two, but after a stern admonition recovered control." By late July of 1884, after sessions of electrotherapy, she could "walk without assistance, although not well." We lose her from view at this point.[7]

What is one to make of such a case? Dr. Cornelius Suckling, who reported it, thought that she had hysteria. The insidious advance of the symptoms, the absence of sensory findings, the diffuse spread of the motor deficits (eyelids, legs) suggest that she might have had one of the ominous "motor neuron diseases" such as poliomyelitis or amyotrophic lateral sclerosis (ALS, also called Lou Gehrig's disease), or perhaps a neuromuscular disease called "myasthenia gravis."

Or maybe she had multiple sclerosis, which is the major competitor to hysteria in these chronic cases. "MS," a disease involving demyelination in the central nervous system (loss of the covering of the nerve fibers), is difficult to disentangle from hysteria because its course is often marked by remission (thus suggesting a "cure" has occurred);

the patchy motor and sensory deficits of MS correspond closely to those the mind may produce on its own accord. Unquestionably some of the disease classed as "hysteria" by past doctors was in fact MS. and "H.J." above, preoccupied with her failing legs, might not even have noticed sensory losses until she disappeared from Dr. Suckling's sight.

A neurologist in the 1980s would immediately think "MS" upon being told of double vision or "numbness in the sole of my foot." What therefore is the historian to make of the following 27-year-old single woman who had to abandon her profession as actress in Germany because of illness? "From then on she lives with her mother, who spoils her." Her present symptoms began to develop after her fiancé had been killed two years earlier by his former girlfriend: a burning sensation in the toes, inability to stand or walk much. At the end of March, 1911 she had a urinary tract infection, followed by "great weakness." She could now scarcely speak, and her gait was unbalanced. She had fainting spells, headaches, insomnia, and saw images in the dark. Her sense of the position of her feet was decreased, her "knee jerks" increased. There were no other "hard neurological findings." The author deemed it hysteria; Adolph Strümpell, a distinguished neurologist in the audience at this medical "rounds," considered the case MS.[8] Decades later, is the historian supposed to know better?

Of course no judgment is possible in this case. But in numerous similar cases one might, perhaps, attempt a judgment if the *outcome* is known. Dr. Byrom Bramwell presented to the medical students at the Edinburgh Royal Infirmary a patient much like the above, displaying the customary scattered deficits associated with MS. But this young woman was "told, in the most definite and emphatic way, that she would [shortly] get quite well." They gave her a variation of the Weir Mitchell "Rest Cure," with its social isolation and milk feeding. After faradization, water injections and other placebo treatments to produce a "profound psychological effect," she did in fact get better. After five days she was able to run "up and down the ward in 20 seconds." Three months later she was still "quite well."[9] Dr. Bramwell considered the case "functional paraplegia" (hysteria) rather than MS. And for the historian to insist on more rigorous evidence in making the diagnosis would effectively rule out writing the history of psychiatric disease: no case reports would ever be considered complete enough. But we must be mindful that early MS does wax and wane, that some of its victims — just as hysteria victims — may recover perfectly, and that, also as hysteria, it strikes electively the population of young women. My feeling is that the medical record often suffices to let us differentiate hysteria from the common organic diseases. But it is useful to remind ourselves what some instances of "hysteria" might otherwise be.

The Relative Absence of Paralysis in "Traditional" Motor Hysteria

This section makes two points. One, that "hysteria," however defined, was quite common among smalltown and village women before 1800. Two, to the extent that we find motor (affecting motion) symptoms among the variety of premodern "hysterical" complaints, they tend to be epileptiform seizures rather than paralyses and gait disorders.

Hysteria was often seen in the little communities of precapitalist Europe. In 1786 the doctor in the Alsatian village of Guebwiller noted that "the women are subject to many nervous illnesses, to hysterical affections. These diseases are passed on from mothers to daughters; one sees entire families in which girls at the blossom of youth have been struck. The abuse of coffee. . . sometimes coquetry, perhaps even the wine are the various causes."[10] In 1821 François-Emmanuel Foderé was surprised to see in the "cold valleys" of the Alpes-Maritimes department "many hysterical women; what at first surprised me even more was that these women lead a very active life, and at the same time a very sober one. I have had occasion to observe this in Provence as well, and to convince myself that it is not always the luxury of the cities and the reading of novels that gives rise to hysteric affections."[11] The doctor in the little town of Parckstein found hysteria "a customary disease" among women, especially during their period.[12] In the Württemberg town of Gmünd around the same time hysteria was thought the result of the "very frequent" leukorrhea.[13]

Nor are these generalized references to hysteria limited to *Spiessbüger* and subsistence peasants. The complaint is commonly mentioned among the fast-growing population of cottage workers. In 1793 Doctor Georg Wilhelm Consbruch associated "hypochondriacal, hysterical women and atrabiliary men" with the stinking, suffocating huts of rural linen weavers.[14] And Dr. J.G. Stemler noted hysteria, among other conditions, to be "very frequent" in the cottage-industrial district of Zeulenroda.[15]

Although these physicians do not always explain what they mean by "hysteria," seizure disorders figure prominently in their endless lists of symptoms. In 1784 the recent Viennese medical graduate Bartholomäus von Battisti offered a list of the incidents (*Zufälle*) that he regarded as hysterical: "Headaches that occur at a given site, a sudden strickening of the senses, timidity, fright at a bagatelle, sweating, hot flashes, a sudden dizziness. . . ." This list continues for a number of lines, including many symptoms to which the autonomic nervous system is heir. But then Battisti concludes the enumeration: "Sometimes they get a momentary kind of hysterical attack [*Schlagfluss*], a sudden twitching of the lips, swiftly passing paralysis of the tongue, of the arms and so forth, all these accidents coming in separate attacks."[16] Although Dr. Battisti evidently included a number of organic diseases under "hysteria," of interest is the importance he attaches to seizure-like symptoms. He said nothing about paralyses of the legs or problems in walking.

As a folklorist described the neurological beliefs of the Metz region "a hundred years ago," people of the day referred to "mild hysteria" as "la marice" (from "matrice," or uterus?). What symptoms were assigned to *la marice*? "Sensation of ballooning, of a ball, especially in the umbilical region, climbing towards the stomach along the intestines and provoking more or less violent rigors, a sense of suffocation, nausea and vomiting. Sometimes the patient falls into syncope and complains of visual and hearing troubles, suffers convulsive contractions of the limbs, muscular jerks of the abdomen, palpitations, and emits cries, having irregular and unfounded laughing attacks. Formerly this *mal de mère* was considered as a uterine crisis."[17] So again, seizures dominate the picture.

When local doctors spell out what they mean by "hysteria," epileptiform symptoms, though scarcely exclusive, come to the fore. Dr. F. Wilhelm Lippich described the "medical topography" of Ljubljana in the 1830s: "Hysteria, convulsions and epilepsy are frequently seen among young servant women from the countryside who take up an overly strenuous way of life in order to protect their virtue or to atone for misdeeds."[18] In the little Austrian town of St. Pölten in 1813, "nervous weakness, convulsions and agonizing uterine conditions provoke moans and lamentations daily from the pretty sex." The author commented that many "fits" ended fatally and that better diagnoses of these cases was required.[19] The center of gravity in these accounts is clearly upon motor twitches. It does not matter that many "hysterical" convulsions may in fact have been epilepsy; for the doctors of the time, the motor symptoms associated with hysteria were fits rather than paralysis.

To be sure, cases of psychogenic paralysis were reported before 1800, but more as medical curiosities than as run-of-the-mill symptomatology. Just as there are no new symptoms under the sun, there have always been young women stricken with fleeting pains and paralyses that made walking impossible. Mrs. Martha Greswold, 23, "a comely gentlewoman" from Solyhill in Warwickshire, was brought to Bath in May, 1663, "so weak as not able to use hand nor foot nor so much as to lift her hand to her head, but was carried from place to place and lifted into and out of her bed." She also had some cognitive disturbance, and remembered nothing of what was said to her. After seven weeks of hydrotherapy under Dr. Robert Peirce, she rode home and was well for the next ten years. Mrs. Budghill of Exeter, 25, "a comely young gentlewoman," was brought to Bath in June, 1682, "all parts enfeebled and benumbed, but especialy the lower parts, so that she could neither stand nor go, and the sense of feeling was depraved in all parts." Dr. Peirce's usual treatment ensured her a perfect recovery.[20]

Watering places have always attracted these psychological cases. But we have occasional reports from "society" doctors as well, whose upper-class practices since time out of mind have included non-organic paralyses. Thus Dr. Pierre Pomme of Paris and Montpellier, "médecin consultant du roi," described in his treatise on the "Vapors" Mlle. Autheman, 19, who in 1774 complained of horrible pains in her big toe, an 11-day right hemiplegia, and fits if one touched her or poured even a drop of water on her. Her case had dragged on for eight years, punctuated by poetry recitations during periodic trances. Dr. Pomme started her on a massive program of bathing and she was cured.[21] For Madame de Cligny of Lyon, a "continual trembling in the legs which had obliged her to take to her bed" for 25 years had commenced in the first year of her marriage. A course of cold bathing, "eau de poulet" and hot foot baths permitted her at 50 to walk again.[22] The application of electrotherapy in the second half of the eighteenth century cured a whole flock of paralytic patients.[23] So in all likelihood a few psychological paralyses had always been lurking upon the sofas and sedan chairs, waiting for a "bath doctor" or "magnetizer" to inspire in them a cure by suggestion.

Yet for the great masses of society before 1800 these psychological paralyses were quite uncommon. They are not mentioned by authors who otherwise discuss hysteria, "spleen" and "vapors." Jane Sharp's 1671 midwifery textbook, which discourses upon numerous mental disturbances thought to be the result of womb disease, such as headache, epilepsy, fainting and coma, says nothing about paralysis.[24] Richard Blackmore wrote in 1725 about a hysterical form of "spleen" common to women. He found convulsions, "globus" (a lump in the throat), a sense of oppression, and so forth, but does not mention motor symptoms in the lower limbs.[25] I am, in short, aware of no pre-1800 physician outside of spa or society practice who considered common the afflictions which concern us in this paper.

Perhaps pre-1800 doctors simply took these paralyses at face value and never questioned that they were organic? Is an improved medical appreciation of "psychogenesis" responsible for increased reporting of "hysteria"? Let me for a moment forecast the argument of the next section. To be sure, it is possible for new medical concepts to suggest a whole population into disease, and we shall see this in the case of "spinal irritation." But these new medical theories do not draw upon the mind: until perhaps the middle of the nineteenth century doctors believed they were dealing with organic disease.

Another disturbing possibility: Did peasants with these afflictions seek treatment at shrines before 1800, rather than from doctors? In other words, is the post-1800 "increase" mainly the result of a shift from shrines to physicians? I am unable to rule this out. Even before the rise of mass-healing at such shrines as Lourdes, we find references to crutches being thrown away after praying at the tomb of one divine or another.[26]

Rather than refuting dogmatically this alternative explanation, let me offer two tentative objections to it. One, these paralyses were completely disabling, spectacularly visible when they crushed the lives of young women (as opposed to elderly stroke patients), and they often mobilized the entire community to help the victims find relief.[27] Had these incidents been frequent in the eighteenth century, they would surely have prompted notice in administrative correspondence, among the clergy, or in other sources that paid routine attention to the mobilization efforts of popular life. In my previous work, I have not seen such mentions. Other historians may be able to show me wrong. Secondly, the "pilgrimages" explanation will not account for the almost epidemic spread of paralysis among nineteenth-century urbanites, a group that previously had relied upon shrine-going and miracle-healing less than did the peasantry. Thus overall, even if some of the increase turns out to be an artifactual consequence of "medicalization," some of it was doubtlessly genuine.

The Rise of Hysterical Paralyses in the Nineteenth Century

At the end of the eighteenth century cases of lower-limb paralysis without apparent organic cause become much more frequent. Hector Landouzy, who had a private practice in Reims, tells us of Madam X who, having lost her husband and one of her children "in the great frights caused by the political conspiracies of the Restoration," began to feel pain in the joints of her lower limbs. "Then one morning upon awakening she found herself completely immobile. The slightest movements of her limbs were completely impossible, and she had to be fed." Thus far a piteous quadriplegic. "That was during the day," Dr. Landouzy continues. "Each night, towards 11 o'clock, a delirium would come over her; without light she would rise and walk or run about the different parts of the house. When day returned, this kind of somnambulism would cease, and movement would once again become impossible, her sensibility obtunded, just as during the previous day."[28] Madame X had been under terrible strain, but of interest to us is that the somatic language she chose for responding to it was the language of paralysis.

These cases start to emerge in the medical literature all over Europe. John Wilson described a series he had treated in London's Middlesex Hospital in the early 1830s:

— Winnifred Dowty, 24, was admitted 28 April 1832 with headaches and abdominal pain. Several days later she developed a pain in the right groin which extended down to the knee. She was unable to move the leg or bear weight on it, but was restored four months later following a therapy of sticking needles into the leg plus putting a "moxa" (burning a tuft of thread) on her lumbar spine. Perhaps she had an organic problem, such as a psoas abscess. Yet there were so many similar patients.

— Rebecca Webster, 24, "a month ago was seized with a pain in the left side and back, with inability to walk which have continued ever since." Now she had so much pain in her left groin and hip that she was "scarcely able to bear the slightest touch." A therapy of massive purgation finally permitted her to throw away her crutches, and six weeks later she was discharged cured.

— Cordelia Smith, 20, was assailed by a vitual blizzard of symptoms, among which was that her right knee doubled up so that she could not walk. Meanwhile she was tormented by powerful fits in which "six women and the house surgeon all pressed upon her to restrain the convulsions." Cold douches to the knee every morning soon brought relief, and four months later she was "walking well and is only lame towards the evenings." Finally discharged, "free from lameness [she took] a situation behind the counter in a pastry-cook's shop."[29]

The penny takes rather long to drop in the medical profession that these deficits are hysterical. Among the first to describe "hysteria complicated with paraplegia" was Dr. Henry J.H. Bond of Addenbrooke's Hospital in Cambridge. Mary Dockley, 19, a history of seizures behind her, took a large dose of calomel and developed a paraplegia. "On admission into the hospital her state was as follows: A total inability of moving the feet, which were extended by gravitation as she lay in bed, nearly in the same line with the legs. She could with difficulty produce a semiflexion of the knees. Total insensibility of the left leg, and to a considerable extent above the knee; the right leg nearly as insensible; both extremities chilly and damp, while the rest of the body was warm, and covered with perspiration." A tumor in the spinal cord perhaps? They give her many laxatives.

A month later she had had a considerable change in mood; "from being morose and intractable, she became cheerful and patient." Strychnine pills were added to her regimen, and she "menstruated for the first time since she became paralytic." An aggressive policy of blistering her lower limbs effected a final return of sensibility, and slowly motive power came back as well. "In December last she again presented herself at the hospital nearly free from any paralysis. . . . She had continued the occasional use of small blisters to the extremities to the time of her recovery."[30] Thus blistering had suggested her back to health.

In 1844 Maurice Macario noted in his account of "hysterical paralysis" how little attention doctors had paid to the disorder. "Each day we discover new forms, some times so obvious that one is entitled to be astonished that they failed to discover it earlier."[31] Perhaps his medical colleagues were entirely imperceptive, but a more likely explanation is that paralytic symptoms were increasing in frequency. Other fragmentary evidence also suggests a rise in the incidence of the disorder, quite apart from the increase in the number of reported cases, which might simply be interpreted as due to the general growth of medical literature. Here is Dr. George Lefevre, back in London in the early 1840s after 14 years in St. Petersburg. "Dr. [Matthew] Baillie said, in his day, that palsy was on the increase. I have been much surprised, since my return to England, at the number of people whom I meet in the streets dragging a leg along."[32]

We have thus far skirted the margin of most of these early nineteenth-century paralyses, which the doctors of the time explained not at all as "hysteria," but as the results of "spinal irritation." The kinds of symptoms patients bring in stands in some relationship to the dominant medical ideas of an epoch: if new breakthroughs in neurophysiology were to discover that standing on one's head was a sign of grave pathology, there would soon be scads of patients on their heads. What happened medically early in the nineteenth century was the extension of Broussais's concept of "irritation" to the spine, and thus a new willingness to explain many symptoms in the limbs and belly as a consequence of that disorder. The spinal irritationists did not believe that gross, structural changes in the spine were involved – such as might be found in spinal tuberculosis or in neoplasms – but rather that tiny, invisible (though nonetheless physical) lesions in the cord were causing both viscera and voluntary muscle to act up. Spinal irritation acted with particular fury upon the lower limbs.

Already in 1809 the surgeon John Abernethy was seizing upon the spine. "A young lady, whose stomach and bowels were disordered . . . became gradually affected with weakness of the lower extremities, and pain in the loins. . . . This lady could scarcely walk, and gave a description of the state of her limbs so exactly resembling that which is sometimes consequent to diseases of the vertebrae, that I thought it right to examine the spine." Indeed he discovered the lumbar vertebrae were very painful. "Under these circumstances I placed a blister on each side of the spine, and kept up a discharge from the surface. . . . These means, with rest, relieved her sufferings."[33]

Abernethy, it is true, does not use the term "irritation." But when in 1824 Edward Sutleffe looked back over 38 years of medical and surgical practice, he recalled many cases of spinal "inflammation" and nervous "irritation." "A Lady, aetatis 24, stepping out of a coach, fell with such violence that she was unable to rise. The lower limbs became instantly paralytic and insensible." Assiduous cupping, leeching and vesication soon restored her, but so treacherous is the spine that the inflammation soon ascended to the "cerebellum" (sic). "Nymphomania, with all its attendant horrible circumstances, became conspicuously manifest, both by word and actions." Dr. Sutleffe, however, directed the "moveable artillery of local depletion" to the cervical spine. And after a few weeks the young lady returned to "her accustomed activity with unimpeached chastity." On another occasion the "anxious parents" of Miss Sarah P. of Brixton brought her to Dr. Sutleffe, unable to walk. "Instantly recognizing the law of sympathy, I replied that the disease was in the spine." "From this time she was kept in a recumbent posture, leeches were applied to the spine, and subsequently vesications were persisted in, till she could jump and hop about the room."[34] Thus spinal affections became the rage.

In 1828 the Glasgow physician Thomas Brown drew observations about "irritation of the spinal nerves" together into a doctrine: diseased spinal nerves could irritate the periphery, and disease on the periphery could cause irritation of the spine. Thus a diseased uterus could, via its impact on the spine, cause a paraplegia, or groin pain, or any symptom imaginable.[35] The way had now been laid for:

1. Encouraging physicians to select as an "acceptable" disease whatever transient, subjective sensations of lower-limb weakness their patients might perceive, acceptable because "paralysis from spinal irritation" had now become a treatable disorder. It was treatable with local therapy to the back plus "rest."

2. Encouraging patients to spend long hours recumbent on a sofa in the treatment of their "irritated" spines. Whatever the original symptoms of the spinal irritation had been, the longer these patients stayed in bed, the more they would suggest themselves into paresis and paralysis of the lower limbs.

These two circumstances conspired to produce an epidemic of "spinal" cases in England in the first half of the nineteenth century: young women whose medical attendants would find a painful vertebra, diagnose spinal irritation, and send the patient to rest upon the couch. Many of these prolonged rests produced paraplegias of psychological origin, referred to as "sofa disease." Dr. Thomas Watson, in his *Practice of Physic*, described a lady who "had been lying I know not how long on her back, the position having been prescribed to her by some medical man for a presumed disease of the spine. She lost all power of using her legs." Sir Benjamn Brodie, we learn, was sent to see her. "Now Sir Benjamin, to use a vulgar phrase, is *up* to these cases, and he wished to see her *try* to walk; but she declared that the attempt to do so would kill her. He was resolute, however, and had her got out of bed; and in a few days' time she was walking about quite well...."[36]

In 1866 Frederic Skey mocked before the students of St. Bartholomew's Hospital in London these "spinal" diagnoses. "You are consulted by a lady in reference to a daughter 18 or 20 years of age, who has exhibited failing health for some time, and now complains of her inability to walk in consequence of a pain in her back. You examine her, and discover that she suffers extremely on pressure" over the vertebrae. "You make a report to the mother that her daughter has 'spinal disease.' The result of your opinion is two or more years' confinement to her couch...." The spine, Skey noted, was in these cases perfectly normal.[37]

Skey, who in the early 1820s had apprenticed to the spinal specialist John Abernethy, well remembered the epidemic of sofa patients. "Thirty or 40 years [ago]," he wrote in 1867, "these cases were... far more common than at present. At that date, and for how many years anterior I know not, all the sea-side towns were crowded with young ladies between 17 and 25 years of age and beyond it, who were confined to this horizontal posture, and were wheeled about on the shore in Bath chairs, on the supposition that they were the subjects of spinal disease.... The large majority carried a pair of handsome issues [pus discharging from sites where some foreign matter, called an "issue-pea," had been surgically implanted] in the back. Brighton, Worthing, Hastings, and other places on the South Coast were largely tenanted by these unfortunate females."[38]

Early in the nineteenth century, not just in England but all across the Continent, the spas were peopled with these spinal "paraplegics." At the Bohemian spa of Franzensbad, Augustus Bozzi Granville was "shown a young lady who had arrived... with her legs and feet completely paralyzed, and who, after six immersions in the mud-bath, could walk without any assistance."[39] The waters of Baden-Baden were no less potent, for there Granville encountered a Dutch family. "The whole party were in high spirits at the recovery of their [mother's] health. The good lady had arrived at Baden a perfect cripple. Her limbs were lifeless – her power of feeling annihilated – all her internal functions damaged. Three months' bathing in the Ursprung (source), and *no medicine* (Oh! how she rejoiced at that!) enabled her to join her family at this festive board."[40]

By the middle of the century spinal irritation had largely fallen away as the explanation of these phantom paralyses. In retrospect this whole bogus pathophysiology was important mainly in medically legitimizing the symptom to both doctor and patient. Once launched, however, these psychogenic paralyses would increase in frequency until the end of the century.

The Range of Symptoms

But these psychological symptoms were not limited to paraplegias. A wide range of deficits would result in the inability to walk, or work properly, and all flourished alongside acute paralysis in the nineteenth century. We class them in terms of how much immobility they produced (Figure 1).

Least disabling were the monoplegias, meaning a paralysis of just one limb. Outside of fits, they probably were the commonest of all motor hysterical symptoms, although some differences evidently prevailed from country to country.[41] Of the 100 cases of hysteria of all kinds that Jean-Albert Pitres selected in the 1880s from the Saint-André Hospital in Bordeaux, 17 were "paralysis," and of these 10 were monoplegias, four hemiplegias, and the others a mix.[42]

Typical of the monoplegias was a 51-year-old female cook, admitted to the Birmingham Workhouse Infirmary on 22 September 1888, "suffering from cramp and paralysis of the right leg." She had worked in a large factory kitchen, "and had been accustomed to standing for many hours a day, the usual hours being from 6 A.M. to 9 P.M." It does not surprise us to learn that she "had always left her work completely tired out. Latterly she had noticed that her right leg felt tired towards the end of the day." After a particularly exhausting siege of overtime her right leg became "completely paralyzed," and the numbness afflicting the leg extended as well up the right side of the body to the breast. They gave her massage therapy and in ten days she was ready to return to work.[43]

Hemiplegias were widespread as well, if only because psychologically-caused paralyses often model themselves upon organic illnesses, and paralytic strokes of an entire side of the body offered a frequent enough model. But even though the arm would be involved in these hysterical hemiplegias, the paralysis in the leg would be worse. According to Paul Richer, "The two limbs are rarely affected to the same degree; the lower limb is always much more paralyzed."[44]

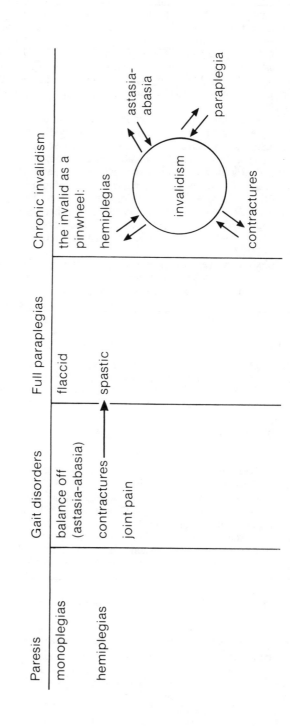

Figure 1 Types of "paralysis"
———▶ Degree of immobility

Even though Dr. Margaret Cleaves, a self-diagnosed "neurasthene," had suffered from many symptoms over the years, she saw their dramatic culmination in a weakening and "paralysis" of one side of her body which occurred in the course of a trip to Europe, whither she had fled to restore "the integrity of my intellectual centers." Even before docking in Hamburg she noted, "My right leg and arm had no reserve of strength, and a few moments' effort was enough to bring about a condition of motor inability." By the time she reached the château at Fontainebleau, however, her right leg had quite given out on her. "The increasing helplessness of my right leg was so great that I turned to the door and fled incontinently to the grounds of the château. Never shall I forget how wearily I crept down the massive and beautiful Escalier du Fer-à-Cheval and how heartbroken I felt." On the voyage back: "So profound was the exhaustion of my left motor centers [the motor nerves from the left brain cross to the right body] that the loss of strength and the feeling of being paralyzed, extended throughout the entire right side of my body...."[45] Thus we are maneuvering in a kind of shadowland between subjective sensations of "weakness" in a limb and the patient's belief that the limb is actually paralyzed and cannot be moved through any act of will.

The next step up the scale of disability were the gait disorders, in which it was impossible for the patient to stand upright or walk without losing his balance, even though the leg muscles themselves seemed perfectly in order. Although these had been known throughout the century, and doubtless even before, only in 1883 did Jean-Martin Charcot and Paul Richer identify them as "abasia" (the inability to walk).[46] Then in 1888 another Charcot student, Paul Blocq, called them collectively "astasia-abasia," astasia meaning the inability to stand.[47] Yet unlike many of the "hysterical" disorders identified by Charcot, which were rarely seen outside of his own hospital, astasia-abasia was found all over Europe and North America.

In November of 1893 a 31-year-old woman was admitted to Dr. William Osler's wards of the Johns Hopkins Hospital, "complaining of inability to walk or stand." The patient's history showed nothing remarkable, save a 30-pound weight gain in the last three years. "Was always a great pet at home and has a very kind husband." Four years ago, just after the birth of her last child, she had an attack of jerking in her arms and legs, "and the next morning, on trying to get out of bed, would have fallen had she not caught hold of a chair."

Since then a number of other attacks had occurred. "Sometimes she is unable to stand or walk for some days, then is perfectly well for two days, and suddenly relapses into her former condition.... When she has the attacks she is unable to move a limb except in bed."

Now the Hopkins resident reporting the case introduced another dimension: "A physician who has known the patient all her life says the relapses have on more than one occasion followed coitus." (The husband denied this.) In hospital she continued to have attacks and might, for example, walk down the corridor and then find herself "unable to get back [to her room] without assistance." The Hopkins diagnosis: hysteria.[48]

Perhaps the best-known case of astasia-abasia was Freud's 24-year-old patient "Elisabeth von R." This middle- or upper-class Viennese woman was first seized with leg pains and locomotor weakness at a spa "after she had had a warm bath in the bath establishment.... A few days earlier she had been for a long walk." As Freud plunged further into Elisabeth's past, it became apparent to him that various traumatic events in her life were associated with each different ache and pain. "Every fresh psychical determinant of painful sensations had become attached to some fresh spot in the painful areas of her legs." And the long walk, for example, was linked to her repressed love for her brother-in-law. Thus her abasia was the sum of these individual painful sensations. She concluded in her own mind (Freud thought) "that there was a legitimate connection between her pains and standing up."[49]

A second gait disorder, which too fell short of full paralysis, was "contracture" of the hip, knee or ankle joints, in which the muscles would go into a single, massive contraction and stay "seized up" for weeks and months on end. The patient might end up with a psychogenic form of "clubfoot," in which the ankle would be turned up or in, or see the knee rigidly extended, or perhaps the thigh flexed right up on the abdomen. Some of these patients could hobble about on crutches, others would be bedridden until whatever psychological mechanism causing the contracture had finally released. Even sleep might not bring relief, and only deep anaesthesia would permit the surgeons to unbend the contracted joint — and satisfy themselves that the problem was psychological.[50] These contractures were not like muscle cramps in that it required little energy to maintain them. Nor were they necessarily painful; feeling might be lost altogether from the limb. Thus the mind might maintain a muscle contracture for years on end.

So common were these contractures that lay people referred to them as "drawing spells," and might stand around anxiously to see if their or their children's limbs were about to "draw up."[51] In 1864 a 16-year-old girl was brought to see Frederic Skey. "For eight months prior to her visit to me she had been suffering from inversion of the left foot, which was so twisted as to bring the point of the foot... at nearly a right angle with the foot of the opposite side." Previous orthopedic attempts to correct the contracture with splints and such had failed, so Skey sent her to the country, "to rely on the kindly offices of Nature." While there "she accompanied her family to a ball, her foot, as she entered the ball-room, being not yet restored to its normal position. She was invited to dance, and under this novel excitement she stood up, and, to the astonishment of her family, she danced the whole evening, having almost suddenly recovered the healthy muscular actions of the limb!"[52] Thus eight months a cripple, not an uncommon event.

Or the contracture might last only briefly, "cured" in a moment of distraction. A 24-year-old Dutchman with a history of seizures, of drinking, and of a somewhat unstable personality, developed a contraction of the gluteal muscles at his right hip so that he was only able to lurch along bizarrely with a cane. The cure supervened nine days later when he dropped his stick somewhat drunkenly and sprang down to get it. He felt something "go" in his hip and was well.[53]

From contracture one could slide into a full-scale paralysis, just as one might also drift from astasia-abasia, from fits, or from "chronic invalidism" into paraplegia. The Tübingen neurologist Armand Hückel considered paraplegias the commonest kind of hysterical paralysis following that of the vocal cords.[54] A typical example was Berthe G. of Bordeaux, who at 23 had already a long history of "neuropathic accidents" behind her, and had been plagued with various contractures of the right upper limb and both lower limbs. "Two weeks ago, following a convulsive attack... Berthe G. remained paraplegic, both lower limbs immobilized in forced flexion, her heels almost touching her ischial tuberosities [buttocks]." This was a full-scale "spastic" (muscles contracted) paraplegia: "it is impossible to extend [the legs] forcibly, and the patient is incapable of moving them voluntarily."[55]

Most paraplegias were, however, "flaccid" rather than spastic, in that the muscles were limp and apparently without power. Many of the cases we saw above were of this variety, and only two points need be made here.

One, the "paraplegia" might result more from painful joints than from flaccid, "powerless" muscles. In 1837 Benjamin Brodie first called attention to the frequency of hysterical joint pain in young women. "I do not hesitate to declare that, among the higher classes of society, at least four-fifths of the female patients, who are commonly supposed to labor under diseases of the joints, labor under hysteria, and nothing else." The patient, generally "not much above the age of puberty," might be bedridden for months, or years, screaming when the joint was touched.[56]

Nor was the patients' sickbed behavior mere play acting, for, as in all hysteria, victims perceived the subjective symptoms as real. The surgeon Benjamin Travers noted that "Such cases go on for years and the patients are cured by perseverance in bandaging or a residence at the sea coast, or. . . by a sacrifice of the limb at their own earnest request."[57] Thus these young women were willing to endure a hip or knee amputation, in the days before anaesthesia, to rid themselves of the pain. Indeed Frederick Skey first became aware of "hysteric disease" in attending "a young lady of 19." He and a colleague thought at first the joint was inflamed. "I remember that we discussed with some anxiety the probable issue in abscess, destruction of ligaments, absorption of cartilage, and ultimate amputation of this limb!"

Then the young woman informed Skey that she was going to attend her sister's wedding at any cost. After remonstrating with her about the terrible potential consequences, Skey strapped up the joint with adhesive plaster. "On the following day I visited her. She told me she had stood throughout the whole ceremony, had joined the party at the breakfast, and had returned home without pain or discomfort in the joint."[58] This kind of immobilizing pain produced numerous of the nineteenth century's "paralysis" cases.

Second, full-scale paraplegias often formed a way station in a larger procession of symptoms. Just as astasia and contracture might drift into paraplegia, the paraplegia itself might be terminated by fits, or pass to a contracture, or be replaced by abdominal pain and headaches. In all these psychogenic motor deficits, one notes the lability of the unconscious mind, deciding one day upon a "paraplegia," the next upon some other symptom in order to communicate some deeper message. Because these apparently interchangeable symptoms flow in and out of larger patterns of deficits in locomotion, it is unwise to analyze in isolation any given one.

All these deficits, singly or together, conspired to produce the "nineteenth-century invalid." "Hysterical motor ataxia," wrote S. Weir Mitchell in 1881, "adds many recruits to that large class which someone has called 'bed cases,' and which are above all things distinguished by their desire to remain at rest."[59] The German neurologist Oswald Bumke associated contractures in particular with "the familiar figure of the 'suffering' lady, who from bed, wheelchair or sofa tortures and tyrannizes over her parents, her husband, her children and her doctor; she lies in a half-darkened room with cool compresses on her head, surrounded by an entire arsenal of devices for the care of the sick plus the latest novels; although she is not busy, she keeps the servants in an uproar, knows all the gossip, and spends her time in intrigue."[60]

Unlike older women bedridden with genuine internal disease, chronic invalidism started young. An irritated spine or an ankle contracture would send her to bed, where the idea would slowly instill itself that she was incapable of ever again rising. Many of these patients would thus spend decades recumbent, visited by "the burnings, the flutterings, the quiverings, the throbbings, the tensions, the relaxations" that were the lot of what the Boston psychiatrist Robert Edes called "the New England invalid."[61] Frau A., a mother of three, was struck at age 25 by a paraplegia which sent her to bed for the next two and a half years. Her concerned husband instructed Dr. Rudolph Burkart to meet with a stretcher the railway ambulance-car in which his wife would be arriving in Boppard am Rhein, a spa where Dr. Burkart had a "hydrotherapy institute." His wife, the husband explained, "is so sensitive to being shaken around that even a slight bump against her bed can cause the greatest exacerbation of her already terrible back pains." But despite the attentiveness of the railway personnel and the relatives, Frau A. went into a deep fainting spell as she was being transferred onto the stretcher, and was able to say goodbye to her concerned family only six hours later.

The next day Dr. Burkart began his examination. "When the patient is recumbent, her feet and legs lie slackly upon the bed. . . . Normal muscle tone seems absent from both lower extremities. The position of the legs corresponds fully to that of a complete paraplegia, and in fact the patient is not at all capable of voluntarily moving the muscles of the upper and lower thigh." (Her tendon reflexes, however, were very lively.) A finger's touch on certain zones in the soles of her feet would send her in to "more or less deep syncope." This helpless paraplegic was placed upon the Weir Mitchell "Rest Cure," and two months later she was taking long walks, indeed climbing in the hills nearby.[62]

The chronic invalid thus represented a kind of pinwheel from which the different psychogenic disorders of locomotion spun off. Some, like Frau A., complained of flaccid paraplegias, others contractures, still others astasia-abasia or unremitting hip pain. In Weir Mitchell's rather cruel portrait, "They lie in bed, or on sofas, hopeless and helpless, and exhibit every conceivable variety of hysteria."[63] Rather than being an extreme form of locomotion disorder, invalidism was its very distilled essence, and no historian will be able to account for "hysteria" who is unable to explain why these women took to their beds and stayed there.

Peak and Decline

In the late nineteenth or early twentieth century, hysterical paralyses reached their peak, thereafter to decline to unimportance. It is difficult to quantify matters. An index of frequency escapes us because we have no reliable way to "sample" hysteria in a population at risk. But neurologists themselves felt these psychological paralyses to be run-of-the-mill in office practice. Apropos "bed cases" alone, Weir Mitchell wrote in 1881, "There must be in every country thousands of these unhappy people."[64] Charles F. Taylor, the New York neurologist who treated Alice James among other society women, wrote about the same time, "I may here remark that loss of power, especially in the lower extremities, is a common effect of excessive erotic feeling. I have seen many cases of the kind. It sometimes happens that girls approaching womanhood are so affected. In the latter case, it generally is but partial, and they regain the use of their powers of locomotion soon after menstruation is established."[65] In 1907 the Hamburg neurologist Max Nonne found astasia-abasia "quite common in private practice, especially among children."[66]

It is difficult to take specialists' reports as evidence of frequency, because so many of their cases come as referrals rather than as walk-ins (to go simply by the accumulation of reports, one might imagine such neurological rarities as "Wilson's disease" or "Creutzfeldt-Jakob disease" to be frequent). But general practitioners encountered towards the turn of the century much obviously psychological paralysis as well. It is often remarked on, for example, in the memoirs of American country doctors. William A. Pusey wrote of his medical father, Robert B. Pusey, "I have known him to trick hysterical women in walking and talking when they thought they could not."[67] Arthur Hertzler, a country doctor in Kansas, describes encountering "paralyzed" patients as though it were not a medical curiosity. He recalled "a maiden lady 46 years of age. She had not walked a step for 18 years." He cured her by performing a hysterectomy.[68]

By the late nineteenth century, paralysis had become a widespread metaphor in western culture for the expression of distress. In Theodore Fontane's novel *Effi Briest*, Effi fakes a "neuralgia" and "rheumatism" that leave her unable to travel back home to see her husband. The husband believes her, these symptoms seeming perfectly credible to the Germans of the 1890s in a healthy young woman of 20.[69] Augustus

Hoppin's 1883 novel *A Fashionable Sufferer, or Chapters from Life's Comedy,* has as its heroine a bed case.[70] In short, western culture had in many ways incorporated by 1900 into its "symptom repertoire" paralysis and inability to walk.

During the next 50 years this metaphor would virtually vanish. The medical literature on hysterical paralysis starts to thin out dramatically after the First World War. In the "Surgeon General's Catalogue," the standard medical bibliographic source for these years, the entry on "Hysteria (Manifestations of) by Disorders of Motion" published in 1902 contained references that extend for 51 column inches. The comparable "hysteria" entry in the next series, published in 1926, had dropped to 22 column inches, and the entry in the final series of this catalogue, published in 1942, was only 12 column inches.[71]

Alternative explanations for this decreasing medical attention to the subject might be that (a) doctors were losing interest in the disease, while it continued at unchanging levels, and (b) improvements in diagnosis were now assigning to organic categories such as "vasculitis" or "scleroderma" afflictions that formerly had been misdiagnosed as "hysteria."

I find it unlikely that medical interest waned. Indeed, as the number of "ambulant" patients increased in private-practice psychiatry and neurology, doctors were avid for as much practical advice from colleagues as they could lay hands on. Neurologists even today have remained fascinated with "pseudo-neurological" symptoms, which is to say psychogenic symptoms, and when they encounter them, report eagerly to colleagues.

As for improved diagnosis, better knowledge undoubtedly shifted some of the anaesthesias and tremors from the category of "hysteria" to that of "multiple sclerosis" or "basal ganglia disease," where they properly belong. Part of the apparent decline is therefore owing to the ability to discriminate the psychogenic from the somatogenic. But I think only a small part, because the cases that mainly interest us in this paper − acute paralyses in young women which vanish of themselves or are "cured" by suggestive therapy − have a distinctive course and are difficult to confuse with organic diseases of the nervous system. Much of what was defined as "hysteria" in people over 40 was probably not. But I am convinced that the apparent decline in "paralysis" among the young was real, and not an artifact of changes in reporting.

Psychiatrists and neurologists in our own century have equally been convinced of a decline. Freud's work launched the term "conversion disorder" for what I have been calling psychogenic motor disorders. And in Freud's own experiences, most "conversion disorders" were the kind of leg paralysis and astasia-abasia we we have been examining. But for second-generation Freudians, hysteria would start to mean "hysterical personality," a concept quite different from classical sensorimotor hysteria. Psychiatrists saw fewer and fewer "conversion disorders." Paul Chodoff commented in 1954 on "the present widely held opinion that conversion hysteria is disappearing."[72] Two years later the psychiatrist Henry Laughlin wrote of the dramatic "conversions" such as paralysis and blindness, "In my personal experience, these major cases are less frequent." He argued that they "are today rather rarely seen in the civilian practice of psychiatry," and that even during World War Two "the gross types of somatic conversion as described in World War One were relatively rare."[73] In 1979 Harold Merskey, a leading specialist, said, "Conversion hysteria involving paralyses or anaesthesias is not a common disorder in routine psychiatric work. In times of peace general psychiatrists . . . usually see only a few such cases in a year."[74]

It might be argued that psychiatrists were seeing fewer "major conversions," because these patients, in the belief that their problems were not "all in their head," were seeking out family doctors and neurologists. Yet these doctors too were encountering less paralysis in the 1920s and after. The Columbia neurologist Israel Wechsler wrote in 1929, "Hysteric paralysis has become a comparatively infrequent phenomenon in civil practice, but it does occur sufficiently to confuse the unwary."[75] Dr. Patria Asher, a physician in the Royal Army Medical Corps, commented in 1946 apropos a young female soldier with a psychogenic paralysis of her right arm, "Frank conversion hysteria is. . . rare."[76]

In the half year that I spent in the mid-1980s as an observer in the Neurology Department of a large general hospital, I was surprised at how little paralysis of a psychogenic nature was seen. The odd case that came in — for example, an unwed mother struck with paraplegia until her family agreed that she did not have to give her baby up for adoption — excited the curiosity of the entire Neurology and Neurosurgery departments. One contrasts the exceptionality of motor hysteria today with its complete banality in the wards of any large English hospital late in the nineteenth century.

Statistics confirm these impressions that motor hysteria has become infrequent. Among 31 cases of "hysterical neurosis" seen at Toronto's Clarke Institute of Psychiatry in 1969-76 (itself not a large number for a big referral center over a seven-year period), only nine were "paralysis," and of those only three involved the legs. The non-paralytic "hysteria" was a grab-bag of fits, aphonia, blindness, and of some mental and cognitive changes outside the sensorimotor system.[77] A survey of conversion disorders seen by psychiatrists in Monroe County, New York (Rochester), found only 28 cases per 100,000 population in 1960-64, scarcely a high incidence. Of the 37 patients with "conversion disorder" seen at a university general hospital in Monroe County in 1960-69, the majority complained of pain; substantial numbers had difficulty in breathing and "anaesthesia or paresthesia" (a tingling sensation), and only 10 had "paralysis or weakness."[78] A house-to-house survey of psychiatric illness in the early 1980s in the United States found high levels of some disorders. "Major depression," for example, existed in as many as 3.5 people per 100. But "somatization," the current psychiatric term for hysteria involving physical symptoms, was found only in one of every thousand people surveyed.[79] In sum, hysteria of any kind is not frequent today, and paralytic disorders of the lower limbs have become curiosities.

Males and Females

The rest of this paper is devoted to making sense of this puzzling rise and fall of a striking disability. Presenting a comprehensive explanation of the increase of psychogenic paralysis in the nineteenth century, and its sudden diminution in the mid-twentieth, would be a tidy intellectual accomplishment. Unfortunately, at this stage of the research I feel like the blind men who each described a different part of the elephant, and I am not yet able to put all the pieces together into a bigger picture. Yet some themes do emerge.

One concerns the gender balance. It is not just that "hysteria" was diagnosed overwhelmingly in females, and had been so since the Ancient Greeks identified the disease with the uterus. Motor disorders in particular before the First World War happened mainly to women. The spas and hydrotherapy institutes specializing in "paralysis," the private nervous hospitals, the electrotherapists, "Rest Cure" specialists and "society nerve doctors" who treated these affections — all saw mainly females. I shall not support this statement quantitatively, yet it is apparent to anyone who has done research in the world of sofa-prone nineteenth-century "nervousness." A gynecologist — not a urologist — was on the staff of any important nerve clinic.

Yet men were not exempt. Herr A.T. of Berlin, 28 and single, had completed the written exams for his legal clerkship in the winter of 1883-84 and now began preparing for the orals. "He studied very strenuously and unremittingly for days on end. After he had worked in this way for perhaps 6-8 months he began. . . to get twitches in all of his muscles, especially in the arms and legs. In writing, his pen started running unintentionally off the page. Early in August, 1884, disorders of motility began to affect his legs. In midstride his left knee might suddenly and painlessly collapse." Soon both knees were collapsing, and as he fell he took to giving several involuntary hops. Soon he acquired a bizarre kind of hopping gait. "Treatment" over the next two months brought him back to normal.[80]

Herr A.T. was, however not entirely typical of male hysteria. Male cases tended to cluster at two particular foci: men in dangerous occupations, and the "traumatic neuroses." The military, a dangerous occupation par excellence, supplied a steady trickle of "paralysis." One young man, 19, had no sooner stepped off the boat in Capetown to fight in the Boer War than he developed "weakness of limbs, exaggerated knee-reflexes, some incoordination, and great difficulty in walking." He was invalided back to England and supplied with a hand-propelled "bicycle-wheeled chair." When Dr. Frederick Smith, major in the Royal Army Medical Corps, examined him, he evidenced an "absolute motor paralysis." Smith noted contemptuously, "He was allowed as much food and drink as he liked. . . being, so to speak, one of the war heroes." Dr. Smith discovered telltale signs of hysteria and ordered the wheeled chair to be taken away. "He was given a walking machine, and told that he *had* to walk. A week later he was walking fairly well. . . ."[81]

In the First World War "male hysteria" rushed into full medical view with the great number of "shell shock" cases, young men whose paralysis, blindness, or aphonia owed its origin to combat. While it is not true, as some writers have claimed, that "male hysteria" was discovered only in the Great War, the psychogenic paralyses among soldiers nonetheless occasioned much medical writing. No attempt is made here to review this literature.[82]

A second setting for male paralyses was work accidents. Typically the victim would be involved in a fall, burn, or scrape and then develop several days later a locomotion disorder in no particular anatomical relationship to the original lesion. A healthy young Londoner of 20, for example, received an "accidental kick just above the left public spine" in August of 1893. "The place was marked by a superficial scar. He had formed the notion that the left hip joint had been dislocated by the kick and was still out of joint," so he limped about holding his left leg rigid at the hip. Walter G. Spencer, a surgeon at Westminster Hospital, "diverted the patient's attention for a moment," then began to flex the knee and forced it up to the abdomen. "After this free movement [the man] seemed convinced that there was nothing wrong with the joint," and walked away normally.[83] Mr. S., a 25-year-old Russian who had lived in Cleveland about six months, "became entangled in coils of red-hot wire, in an iron-works in which he was employed, fell to the ground and sustained several burns. . . on the forearm and around one lower extremity, midway between the knee and the ankle." When he had finally recovered, he discovered that "he was unable to stand." In a sitting position all his leg muscles worked fine, but once erect, "all the coordinative power is lost." He was treated with strychnine and "absolute rest." "Patient made a good recovery in about three months."[84]

These cases became known as "traumatic neuroses," psychologically-caused deficits following physical trauma. A rich body of writing exists on them, which I shall not rehearse,[85] because the point is that, while female "paralyses" declined greatly in the first half of the twentieth century, these male paralyses seem scarcely to have changed in frequency. They were never terribly common, but they do not appear to have declined much either.

A considerable amount of male paralysis continued to be reported in the 1930s and after. In 1948 the Scottish physician and public-health officer James Halliday wrote, "In civilian practice my observations made in the 1930s on insured persons showed that hysteria was most frequently seen in males engaged in dangerous occupations – notably workers at depths (such as underground miners), workers at heights (such as steeplejacks...), and workers with explosives." In females, he found hysteria commonest among domestic servants and nurses.[86] In the Veterans Neuropsychiatric Hospital in Salem, Virginia, 25 to 30 percent of all patients showed "manifestations of conversion hysteria at some time during hospitalization." The men tended to be local people who had drifted into such laborious occupations as coalminer once back in Appalachia. Of the 16 patients selected for detailed study, 12 had some kind of motor or sensory problem in a limb, and the number of hemiparesis cases suggests that the lower limbs were often involved. Violence ran throughout the men's lives, and they used violent language to describe their "dead" limbs. Nobody could be further removed from the delicate "couch cases" of the nineteenth century, yet here was a thoroughly "hysterical" group of men.[87]

The unemployed miners of Eastern Kentucky, described by Hart Ransdell and Tressa Roche, evidenced a variety of "psychosomatic" and "conversion" symptoms, numerous of which affected the lower limbs. Mr. W., for example, an illiterate miner of 31, married with two children, had to be carried into the clinic in May of 1964 by his father because he "said he could not walk." "His recent reapplication for public assistance had just been denied the week before."[88] These authors are often imprecise about which limbs exactly are affected (since psychiatrists now assign no particular significance to upper or lower). But Charles Watson and Cheryl Buranen, who studied 40 male patients with the diagnosis of "hysteria" at the Minneapolis Veterans Administration Hospital between 1963 and 1966, found that 42 percent of them had "paresis" (weakness in a limb), and that 15 percent demonstrated ataxic gaits.[89]

Dr. Norval Watson noted a virtual epidemic of hysterical paraplegia among young men seen in a Sheffield hospital during the winter of 1977-78. Among them was a deep-sea diver, 21, who "12 hours after his last dive while drinking ashore... felt tingling in his legs." It turned into a complete paraplegia, with anaesthesia below the knees. His wife was pregnant, and on the day the baby was born he started moving his legs. After being told his diagnosis was "hysteria," he got better at once, and "discharged himself from hospital the same day, not only walking normally but carrying all his diving equipment to the bus stop."[90] In colorfulness these anecdotes rival those of the nineteenth-century schoolgirls who become paraplegic after seeing a frog in the road. But in the late twentieth century they happen as much if not more to males.

This persistence of motor hysteria among males is important because it suggests that the great decline occurred mainly among females, and that the factors accounting for that decline will have to address in some way the lives of women. It would be tempting to explain the experience of women with hysteria in terms of being "trapped at home" or "stifled by Victorian sex roles." In view of information still to be presented about social class, however, I shall refrain from doing so.

An Attack of Paraplegia: Aspects of Its Course

Of special interest in the typical attack of paraplegia are the precipitating events and the patient's other symptoms. In both areas dim patterns begin to emerge.

In women, the onset was most often associated with emotional trauma, a fright perhaps or receiving bad news. Thus Virginie Joannot, a 17-year-old linen maid who had been living in Paris for a year, was startled when a young man dressed in a shroud appeared in the middle of a field. Thinking she had seen a ghost, she spent the next 48 hours convulsing and crying, "Il est auprès de moi, il veut me saisir." A hemiparesis on the left side then appeared, and was cured by blistering her neck and by baths.[91] A 25-year-old Württemberg woman was seated at the window during a storm. She saw lightning strike a neighbor's house and immediately lost her voice, acquired a drooping right eyelid (ptosis) and a paralysis and contracture in her right arm and leg. These symptoms vanished after the Tübingen doctors applied "faradization" (alternating electrical current), only to recur four years later, and again a year after that. Her little daughter also developed a hysterical paraplegia. All were successsfully treated at the Tübingen clinic.[92]

A 16-year-old girl from Pomerania who had been in service in Berlin for a year was startled late one December evening at the noise of an attempted break-in. She tripped on the stairs, tumbled forward, then walked trembling to her room. The next day she was all right. Then on New Year's Eve she drank a glass of punch, got a colossal frontal headache, and when she awoke New Year's morning her limbs were so weak that she could not even get dressed. On the 2nd of January she was admitted to the Charité Hospital with a flaccid paralysis and sensory loss in all four limbs. Thus when Dr. Ernst von Leyden presented her at rounds 11 days later she was a total quadriplegic except for her head, neck and backside. A tragic case, but fortunately after faradization she could, three weeks later, be presented at rounds fully healed.[93]

In another scenario, conflicts over love and sex ignite the symptoms. Mrs. S. had been imprisoned in an unhappy marriage. "One morning, however, after a dispute with her husband of more than usual heat and acrimony, she suddenly felt a severe pain in the dorsal region of the spine and was seized with a fit of nausea and vomiting." For several months she was "unable to walk and almost entirely confined to her bed. There was no paralysis, but the muscular effort of standing or even getting up was certain to cause an increase of the local pain in the spine. . . ."[94] On the face of it, therefore, marital unhappiness had made her a bed case.

A young Philadelphia woman "of good position and in comfortable circumstances" had recently broken up with her fiancé. One night "she was roused from sleep at midnight by a ring at the bell. She hurried into her wrapper and slippers and opened the door to receive an indifferent telegram from a member of the family in another city." The next day she was unable to get out of bed. "With the assistance of her maid, she could cross the room, but unsupported sank to the floor." "My leg," she said, "feels as though it were made of cotton." With faradization, her leg symptoms went away, to be replaced by "vomiting, intermittent tremor of the hands, vertigo, sensation of throbbing in the abdomen, emotional manifestations, weeping, and excitement without apparent cause."[95]

A woman, 22, of St. Gallen, Switzerland, had just given birth to an illegitimate child. Just before she was to testify in the paternity suit, she found that both her hands and feet were paralyzed, and that she could not talk clearly. Pressure on her ovaries produced an epileptoid fit. Dr. H. Sutter was obliged to issue a certificate excusing her from appearing in court.[96]

Whether these cases are as straightforward as they seem is another question entirely. Maybe the flashes of lightning, young men in shrouds, unhappy romances and such did not "cause" the paralysis. How about all the young women with unhappy romances who failed to become paralyzed? Perhaps these emotional shocks merely precipitated a latent tendency to "somatize" as a way of dealing with conflict. Generations of scholars have argued whether patients were "predisposed" to these symptoms by oedipal events in early childhood, by genetic inheritance and "constitution," or whether the painful events of adult life account for these events sufficiently without a lot of murky speculation about "poisoned heredity" and the like. The question for us is a wisp.

The onset in males is another wisp. Unlike women, symptoms in men were often precipitated by some association with physical bodily harm. During the French Second Empire, for example, the 24-year-old Monsieur X. unwittingly accepted an invitation to the recruitment dinner of a secret conspiratorial society. At dinner a quarrel ensued in which "threats" were exchanged, and he strode out. But already on the way home he realized he was walking with difficulty. He had vertigo, his ears rang, and he saw double. As he struggled to fall asleep, he noted that his lower limbs seemed paralyzed. Et cetera.[97] Was it merely "stress," or the prospect of being injured in a brawl that unbalanced him?

An insult to an intimate body cavity evidently precipitated the symptoms of a "Dr. Douglas" of Sydney, Australia. As he was recovering in February, 1864, from an attack of dysentery, he noticed that he had hemorrhoids ("piles"). He had one of the hemorrhoids ligated, or tied off. In his own words, "I experienced intolerable pain, with indescribable sensation in the nates and rectum while sitting." As the pile dropped away a week later, he noticed the left side of his body was numb. By mid-July he was unable to move either hands or feet, and would recover only a year later. He ascribed his own symptoms to "reflex paralysis"[98]; it is possible (as we do not know his age) that he had had a stroke; but as the onset of his symptoms was associated with diarrhea and anal trauma, on balance it sounds more likely that he suffered from a problem in his mind rather than his brain. Numerous other instances of physical insult touching off paralysis in men are described in the literature. There may be genuine differences between the two sexes.

An Attack of Paralysis: Other Symptoms

The actual incidence of paralysis was like a boxcar hooked together in a larger train of symptoms. Other symptoms might appear during an episode, or before or after. There are two contrasting patterns. In one the disturbances are confined mainly to the sensorimotor system, in the second a mixture prevails of motor, sensory and autonomic symptoms.

Illustrating the first pattern is Jeanne L., 29, of Bordeaux, who had been a garment maker before she fell ill. She was a "small brunette, alert and intelligent," who after her menarche at 13 started to develop a "violent, quick-tempered personality, and she cried without the least excuse." At 19, she had a seizure after a fire broke out in her home, remaining somewhat "nervous" thereafter. Married at 20, she had three children in a row and, in the fall of 1884, was pregnant for the fourth time. "Three months later she started to feel painful pricklings in her knees," followed then by lasting contractures in both lower limbs.

Now a variety of symptoms began racing about her head and limbs. She took fright when a balloon landed nearby, had a fit, and when she awoke she was completely blind with her right leg contracted. She took to her bed at that point. Two weeks later the blindness vanished, but her valetudinarian state, not even modified by her delivery in October, 1885, would last until her admission to Jean-Albert Pitres' clinic in Bordeaux two years later.

On examination she had a complete hemianaesthesia on the right, her right eye was blind and the visual field on the left was contracted. All of her other special senses (hearing, smell, etc.) had deficits too. "Moreover we found on different points of her body spasmogenic zones, that is to say, points at which pressure could provoke convulsive attacks; we also found spasmo-frenic zones, where pressure could stop the convulsions." At the moment, however, her chief complaint was her painful right knee, which was keeping her in bed. "Whenever Jeanne L. tried to move her right leg or we tried to induce passive movement in the right knee, she experienced intense suffering of an extreme violence." She felt, she said, "as though her knee was being torn apart inside by thousands of tiny needles inside the joint." Et cetera. We shall not further follow her various symptoms, and note merely that over a period of three years many parts of her voluntary motor and sensory system had been implicated in her illness.[99]

In a contrasting pattern, the boxcars in the train of symptoms alternate between "voluntary" symptoms of the sensorimotor system and "involuntary," or "autonomic," symptoms of the viscera and blood vessels. Autonomic symptoms have always been judged "psychosomatic" (as opposed to "hysterical"), and yet they are often found in hysteria. The point is important because unlike hysterical symptoms − which may be abolished by hypnosis or by other "suggestive" psychotherapy − the unconscious mind cannot instantly abolish visceral symptoms (although it seems to be able to produce them easily enough).

In 1885 Henriette W., a young French woman of 20, began to be plagued by stomach cramps, which she would have daily over the next 14 months, along with abdominal swelling, nausea, and vomiting bile. They would start about four in the afternoon and be followed by a headache which lasted all night. Shortly· after the appearance of the cramps, Henriette W. also suffered a complete paralysis of her right arm and leg, with loss of feeling in the leg. The hemiplegia ceded after six months of electrotherapy at the Rothschild Hospital in Paris, but for three months after this she lost the power of speech, the ability to swallow, and found that her tongue was paralyzed.

At the hospital they rinsed out her stomach regularly, "douched" her daily, and fed her via a tube for five or six months. She vomited after every feeding. By the time she reached Dr. Hippolyte Bernheim's clinic in Nancy, she was drinking only milk and bouillon, and vomiting after every meal. "The vomiting is accompanied with pain in thorax and dyspnea [shortness of breath]. Cramps every evening."

Midst all these internal problems she also had a limp: "a continuous and intense sensation of constriction in the right leg and foot."

Once in the clinic almost every imaginable symptom began to appear: fits, fainting, her back arched rigidly in bed ("opisthotonos"), headache, palpitation, "pain upon pressure of lower part of right arm-pit," loss of hearing which changed from the left side to the right side. She was blind on the right side, and had diminished vision on the left. More fits, more vomiting. Her sensorimotor symptoms were cured by hypnosis, the diarrhea, anorexia, and "chronic stomach catarrh" persisted longer.[100]

Thus Jeanne L. and Henriette W. evidenced differently composed "trains" of symptoms. Both patterns, however, show that the mind was not content to ensnare just one muscle group, but reached across the body, tugging with what seems in retrospect random arbitrariness at different organs and limbs. Why Henriette's appetite and digestive tube would have been tugged during her paralysis and Jeanne's not is unclear, yet surely the process was not random.

Whether the viscera, responsible for many "autonomic" symptoms, were involved or not, two other ancillary symptoms often appeared in these lower limb paralyses: aphonia (loss of voice) and anorexia nervosa. In many of the cases above, the victim loses her voice or finds her vocal cords "paralyzed." She cannot communicate. Or, like a young German woman whose case was otherwise quite similar to those of Jeanne L. and Henriette W., she is only able to scream out words like "Rabe" and "Vetsera."[101] (The first means raven in German, the second has no meaning at all.) Another hemiplegic young French woman put the letter "T" in front of every word she said, making it difficult to understand her.[102] Whatever message intended by the paralysis itself, therefore, it was often modulated by the patient's loss of voice.

Another recurrent symptom in paralysis was loss of appetite, or disorders centering somehow about food. One gets a sense of how common anorexia nervosa was in the past from the regularity with which the "Rest Cure" insisted upon "overfeeding." With a diet heavy in milk fats and rich food, Weir Mitchell and his followers attempted to restore the weight of wasted women to normal, which often entailed gains of 30 or 40 pounds.[103] The young German woman mentioned in the paragraph above suffered from anorexia, in addition to her crippled left leg and contracted foot, "so that for weeks she had to be nourished through enemas." Suddenly thereupon she would show a strong appetite, "and now consume unbelievable quantities of food, for example, in a single day, 16 eggs, 25 apples and so forth."[104] Freud's patient Emmy von N. complained of loss of appetite alongside of her paralysis. Freud wrote, "I can adduce Frau von N.'s anorexia as proving that this mechanism [uncathected affect] is the operative one in certain abulias [loss of will], and paralysis."[105] Whether Freud was right about the mechanism of anorexia and paralysis remains to be seen. Yet it is perhaps important that just at the historical moment when paraplegias and the like decline in frequency, anorexia nervosa takes off.

Social Class and Development

The view has somehow established itself that these paralyses were in the nineteenth century a monopoly of "middle-class" women. Thus Barbara Ehrenreich and Deirdre English say that "a curious epidemic seemed to be sweeping through the middle- and upper-class female population both in the United States and England... hundreds of women slipping into hopeless invalidism."[106] This view was derived from such sources as the diaries and letters of well-to-do women and the writings of such "society nerve doctors" as S. Weir Mitchell. But in sources that give lower-class people a chance to appear, such as in case reports from hospitals or doctors with socially diverse practices, it becomes apparent that the great majority of all women stricken with these phantom paralyses belonged to the working classes, if only because these classes are most numerous. Of course the young ladies of Mayfair and Kensington were not exempt; we have seen many above; but they were not especially affected. Thomas Dixon Savill, a prominent London physician, wrote in 1909, "When I first went to the Paddington Infirmary I expected to be deprived of the field which the better classes of hospital practice afforded, but it was not so. I found that hysteria was as rife among the poor and destitute as among the wage-earners and the affluent." He calculated that the rate of hysteria among those "in easy circumstances, not obliged to work," was about 67 per 1000 patients; among "those who work for their living," 53 per 1000; and among "those who are destitute" 60 per 1000.[107] Thus according to Savill there was no important difference in the incidence of "hysteria" as a whole among the social classes.

It is instructive to contrast the experience of two young New England women who were "bed cases," each from a very different social class. The nervous problems of Alice James, sister of William and Henry James, began at the age of 19 as the family occupied their new home in Cambridge, Mass. Although the nature of her symptoms at this point was somewhat vague, she nonetheless went in November of 1866 to New York for treatment by Charles F. Taylor. Because Taylor's main interest was orthopedic surgery, especially the variety of disability resulting from "spinal irritation," we may assume that she had some problem related to locomotion. In June, 1867 she had a further "nervous attack," and refers to "my bed of sickness." She was brought home from Brookline, Mass., where she had been visiting, in a carriage.

What had happened? Her later account is maddeningly indirect, but there are references to a fight between "my body and my will," in which the body triumphed. Further she recalled of 1867-68: "Owing to some physical weakness, excess of nervous susceptibility, the moral power *pauses*, as it were for a moment, and refuses to maintain muscular sanity. . . ." This sounds like an account of paresis. In the spring of 1868 we find that Alice "lies upon the bed or sofa pretty much all day" and that her mother is already using the term "invalid."

Only ten years later, however, did Alice take "spectacularly to her bed," just as it became apparent, in April, 1878, that her brother William was about to become engaged to another Alice. Her illness lasted into the fall. She wrote a friend a year later that "I am growing stronger all the time, although I cannot do much or walk much yet."

This 1878 episode was the beginning of a long series of periodic collapses, with intermittent admissions to private nervous clinics such as the Adams Nervine Asylum in Boston, or consultations with specialists in "galvanotherapy" such as the New York society doctor William Neftel.

She travels to England in November, 1884, lonely for her friend Katharine Loring — for whose benefit many of these "collapses" seem to have been performed — and her brother Henry. She is carried off the ship by two stewards. Specialists prescribe salt-water sponges of the spine. "Now her legs would not move at all," writes her biographer. There are "weeks of steady pain in her legs, head or stomach." Et cetera. Years pass in which because of her "delicate and critical" spinal condition, she cannot move.[108] Alice James thus seems a classic "New England invalid," the victim of a major psychiatric illness plus the inability to walk.

But an 18-year-old Rhode Island woman who worked in a woolen mill was also a "New England invalid." In a fainting spell at work in July, 1892, she injured her head and right hip a bit as she fell to the ground. After resting at home for two days she was well again until, about a month later, her hip "began to be painful and tender, and to keep her awake at night." The doctors blistered her hip.

By December she had to be carried to the Out-Patient Department of the Rhode Island Hospital. "Patient could walk a little, but would fall after a few steps had been taken." She became bedridden. "The parents now gave up all hope of ever seeing her walk again."

When Dr. Frank Peckham saw her in May, 1893, she was "thin and anemic, and apparently of a very nervous disposition. On manipulating the leg she would groan continuously," and arrived in a wheel chair for Dr. Peckham's sessions of hypnosis. On the seventh session, "she opened her eyes and started across the floor." Four months later she was completely well again.[109] Who knows why this factory worker was cured of her invalidism and Alice James was not. But in the nineteenth century, these afflictions struck without discrimination of class, sparing only the peasantry early in the century.

Both Alice James and the young Rhode Islander were caught up, in disparate ways, in "early industrialization": the one the beneficiary of a family's mercantile fortune, the other an operative in a factory. We do not find young shepherdesses stricken with paraplegia: it is only when they rush into the city as servants, or industrial cooks, or otherwise entangle themselves in the tar baby of social change, that locomotive disaster strikes. Thus one of the few "medical topographies" written about an industrial population is the only one, in my knowledge, to mention these symptoms. In 1898 Dr. Jean-Auguste Crouzet noted that among the population of the French factory town of Lodève, "Hysteria strikes preferentially the girls and women under 30 and is sometimes complicated with hemiplegia and paraplegia."[110] Such snippets of evidence at least justify one to speculate that something about the logic of capitalism may have been acting in historically unprecedented ways to produce these paralyses.

Finally, then, early industrialization is left behind. In mature industrial society the drenching of popular culture in the mass media begins, and people become more sophisticated about which body symptoms are "legitimate" and which mean "it's all in your mind." Motor hysteria then vanishes from mainstream life. Only at that point do paralyses and the like seem to become confined to those groups in the population that are relatively less advanced, rather than disseminated among all classes as in the nineteenth century.

When today we encounter motor hysteria, it is among these "backward" populations. Of the 40 cases of sensorimotor hysteria studied at Government Hospital in Ness Ziona, Israel, in 1966-71, two-thirds occurred among Sephardic Jews from Asia and Africa (almost all men, moreover), rather than the more urbane Ashkenazic Jews from Europe.[111] Among the 61 patients with the diagnosis of conversion disorder attending the psychiatric clinic in Khartoum General Hospital (Sudan) in 1975-77, 13 had "motor disturbances." Almost all were cured by "suggestion under faradic stimulation" and by an "electro-sleeping machine."[112]

Those pockets of motor hysteria which by the twentieth century had remained in Europe tended to occur in the countryside, where a hundred years previously little had been found. Oswald Bumke wrote in his 1919 psychiatry textbook, "The most elemental psychogenic phenomena such as severe contractures and fits are seen most often among young girls of the villages."[113] He considered them due to a lack of the "self-control" which urbanites had presumably learned. An Austrian psychiatrist who had studied the psychoneuroses both in a small provincial town and in Vienna wrote in 1969, "It is... striking that the most diffuse autonomic phenomena strongly predominate in the symptom picture of the big city, while in the small town motor symptoms and especially symptoms of the respiratory tract prevail."[114]

What is it about paralyses and the like that makes "backward" working-class and rural patients in the twentieth-century choose them, rather than sophisticated middle-class patients? The current view is that lower-class patients are verbally less adroit, and for that reason decide to "express psychological distress in physiological terms," as two authors put it.[115] By contrast, in the nineteenth century nobody knew much about anatomy or physiology, and paralyses might have seemed a reasonable metaphor to all social classes. That, at least, is one possibility.

But why did traditional peasants not choose this metaphor? Why did these nineteenth-century servants and merchants' daughters choose the metaphor of disorders of locomotion, rather than "paralyzed" eye muscles or "paralyzed" fingers? If fashion dictates the symptom repertoire, why, after Europe's main industrialization had passed, does motor hysteria become identified with those who lagged behind?

Let me sum up the findings to now. "Hysteria," it appears, is a real psychiatric disease, in addition to being an epithet with which men have stigmatized women across the ages. Even after we have stripped away the cultural layers of male hostility and medical uneasiness in the face of female sexuality which the diagnosis has often conveyed, we still confront a group of predominantly female patients who are unable to walk, or get out of bed, or relax their contracted ankle muscles. That these deficits occurred particularly in the nineteenth century intrigues us: a whole new set of gestures suddenly drifts into the repertoire of symptoms that are available for expressing psychic conflict, and then drifts out again. Of the reasons behind this we know practically nothing, save that it happens to women from all walks of life, which argues against explanations that focus upon the middle classes.

Yet the great social and cultural changes of the nineteenth century hover like a low cloud. We know that industrialization is shaking popular life with bone-rattling force.

We know that in the twentieth century psychological disease becomes "legitimated," so that it becomes unnecessary to evidence solely somatic symptoms if one requires a sympathetic hearing. Some historians might point to improved motorized transport, which diminishes perhaps the symbolic significance of "paralysis." Students of medical history will highlight improvements in knowledge, such as Joseph Babinski's famous "toe" sign, that made it possible to differentiate some somatogenic and psychogenic disorders of the nervous system. Cultural historians will smile at the sheer incongruity of flappers with short skirts and cigarettes being couch-ridden. The potential explanations are sufficient to enliven the discussion in any senior common room. What we need now is information.

FOOTNOTES

For their comments on an earlier version, I would like to thank Lorie Cappe, M.D., Peter Carlen, M.D., Kenneth Mark Colby, M.D., Marcel Gauchet, Edward Hare, M.D., Erna Lesky, M.D., David Levine, William McIlroy, M.D., Harold Merskey, M.D., Roy Porter, Gladys Swain, M.D., Carol Stearns, M.D., and Peter Stearns.

1. Ilza Veith, *Hysteria: The History of a Disease* (Chicago, 1965); Henri Cesbron, *Histoire critique de l'hystérie* (Paris, 1909), which contains many references.

2. Laurence Kirmayer refers to the sufferer as a "poet in search of metaphors adequate to express his predicament." "Culture, Affect and Somatization, Pt. II," *Transcultural Psychiatric Research Review*, 21 (1984), 249.

3. For a discussion of these definitional issues see Edward Shorter, "Les désordres psychosomatiques: sont-ils 'hystériques'? Notes pour une recherche historique," *Cahiers internationaux de sociologie* 76 (1984): 201-224.

4. Harold Merskey defends the concept of hysterical personality in *The Analysis of Hysteria* (London, 1979), p. 198. For an attck, see Eliot Slater, "What is Hysteria?," in Alec Roy, ed., *Hysteria* (New York, 1982); Slater sees the diagnosis as expressing the male physician's condemnation of the sexually responsive female patient (pp. 39-40).

5. Eliot Slater, "Diagnosis of 'Hysteria,' " *British Medical Journal* (29 May 1965): quote from p. 1398.

6. Hermann Determann, "Hysterische Monoplegie," *Neurologisches Zentralblatt* 9 (1890): 425-430.

7. Cornelius Suckling, "Hysterical Paraplegia," *British Medical Journal* (31 January 1885): 228-229.

8. Dr. Nissl-Mayendorf, "Über eine Form von hysterischer Gangstörung," *Berliner klinische Wochenschrift* (6 May 1912): 916-917.

9. Byrom Bramwell, "Functional Paraplegia," *Clinical Studies* N.S., 1 (1902-03), 332-344.

10. Académie de médecine, Paris, file S.R.M. 175 ms. "Topographie médicale à Guebwiller... par M. Méglin."

11. François-Emmanuel Foderé, *Voyage aux Alpes Maritimes*, 2 vols. (Paris, 1821), II, 246-247.

12. Joseph Steiner, *Versuch einer medizinischen Topographie vom . . . Parckstein* (Sulzbach, 1808), p. 130.

13. F.J. Werfer, *Versuch einer medizinischen Topographie der Stadt Gmünd* (Gmünd, 1812), pp. 138-139.

14. Georg Wilhelm Consbruch, *Medicinische Ephemeriden nebst einer medicinischen Topographie der Grafschaft Ravensberg* (Chemnitz, 1793), p. 56.

15. J.G. Stemler, *Entwurf einer physisch-medizinischen Topographie von Zeulenroda*, 2nd ed. (Neustadt an der Orla, 1820), p. 67.

16. Bartholomäus von Battisti a S. Georgio, *Abhandlung von den Krankheiten des schöenen Geschlechts* (Vienna, 1784), pp. 58-59.

17. R. de Westphalen, *Petit dictionnaire des traditions populaires messines* (Metz, 1934), p. 458. "Hystérie" as such is described as a "maladie très rare" (p. 346).

18. Fr. Wilhelm Lippich, *Topographie. . . Laibach* (Laibach [Ljubljana], 1834), p. 155.

19. Franz Strohmayr, *Versuch einer physisch-medicinischen Topographie von . . . St. Pölten* (Vienna, 1813), p. 246. In another publication Strohmayr related "Krampfhafte Beschwerden" and "Convulsionen" in a hysteria case from 1807. *Medicinisch-praktische Darstellung gesammelter Krankheitsfälle und des Heilverfahrens aus dem Tagebuche meiner Erfahrung*, 2 vols. (Vienna, 1831), II, 18-19.

20. Robert Peirce (sometimes spelled Pierce), *The History and Memoirs of the Bath* (London, 1713), cases from pp. 12-13, 109-110; see also the cases of Mrs. Jane Chase of Yartee, pp. 8-10, and Mrs. Greene of Stratford-on-Avon, pp. 10-11.

21. Pierre Pomme, *Traité des affections vaporeuses des deux sexes* (1763), 3rd ed. (Lyon, 1767), pp. 83-93.

22. *Ibid.*, pp. 506-516.

23. The literature is summarized in Glafira Abricossoff, *L'Hystérie aux XVIIe et XVIIIe siècles* (Paris: med. thesis, 1897), pp. 144-145.

24. Jane Sharp, *The Midwives Book* (London, 1671), pp. 125-130, 317-322.

25. Richard Blackmore, *A Treatise of the Spleen and Vapours. . .* (London, 1725), pp. 102-113; there is a passing reference to a "rheumatism" in the limbs and lumbago, p. 111.

26. An example to edify the neurologists was offered by Georges Gilles de la Tourette, "Le Miracle opéré sur Marie-Anne Couronneau le 13 juin 1731," *Nouvelle iconographie de la Salpêtrière* 2 (1889): 241-250.

27. For example, when Eugène Bouchut was at the Hotêl-Dieu in Paris in 1848, he remembered that a young girl from the countryside who had been raped was brought in with a sudden paralysis of the tongue and the limbs. "Tout le monde s'intéressa à cette victime, et les soins de la médecine locale ayant échoué, chacun pensa qu'il n'y avait qu'à Paris et à l'Hôtel-Dieu où l'on pourrait trouver le grand médecin qui pourrait guérir cette paralysie. Une collecte fut faite avec peine, parmi les dames charitables du voisinage, afin de pourvoir aux frais du voyage du père et de l'enfant." Bouchut, "De l'influence des impressions morales sur la production et sur la guérison de certaines paralysies," *Gazette des hôpitaux* i (1877): 323.

28. Hector Landouzy, *Traité complet de l'hystérie* (Paris, 1846), pp. 112-114; the case continued for many years, the patient sinking into a chronic neurosis.

29. John Wilson, "Nervous Affections Peculiar to Young Women, Causing Contraction of the Musckes of the Extremities," *Royal Medico-Chirurgical Transactions* 21 (1838): 107-112 for these three cases; he presents several others.

30. Henry J.M. Bond, "Tetanus and Hysteria," *London Medical Gazette*, (24 March 1832): case from pp. 931-933.

31. Maruice Macario, "De la paralysie hystérique," *Annales médico-psychologiques* 3 (1844): 62.

32. George W. Lefevre, *An Apology for the Nerves* (London, 1844), pp. 166-167; he thought he was dealing with strokes.

33. John Abernethy, *Constitutional Origin and Treatment of Local Diseases* (1809), reprinted in Abernethy, ed., *The Surgical and Physiological Works*, 2 vols. (London, 1825), I, 61-62. Her course was uneven over the next few years, sometimes "muscular and fat," sometimes "so ill . . . that she wished to have issues made in the back." Abernethy felt these vicissitudes coincided with the state of her bowels.

34. Edward Sutleffe, *Medical and Surgical Cases* (London, 1824), pp. 226-227, 292-293.

35. Thomas Brown, "On Irritation of the Spinal Nerves," *Glasgow Medical Journal* 1 (1828): 131-160, esp. pp. 154-156 on the uterus. He first read the essay in 1823 to the Glasgow Medical Society. Helping to broadcast the doctrine of spinal irritation was also Thomas P. Teale's *A Treatise on Neuralgic Diseases, Dependent upon Irritation of the Spinal Marrow and Ganglia of the Sympathetic Nerve* (London, 1829); pp. 4-6 review the previous literature.

36. Thomas Watson, *Lectures on the Principles and Practice of Physic* (1843), 5th rev. ed., 2 vols. (Philadelphia, 1872), I, 650.

37. Frederic Skey, *Hysteria* (New York [and London], 1867), pp. 42-43.

38. *Ibid.*, p. 49. He noted that "a moderate sprinkling of young gentlemen was added" to the ladies.

39. Augustus Bozzi Granville, *The Spas of Germany*, 2 vols. (Brussels, 1838), II, 149.

40. *Ibid.*, I, 45.

41. Paul Richer, one of Charcot's assistants at the Salpêtrière, considered them the most common symptom. *Paralysies et contractures hystériques* (Paris, 1892), pp. 155-157; the work had been drafted a decade earlier. Deutermann, however, says they "belong to the rarities," especially in Germany, *op. cit.*, p. 425.

42. Jean-Albert Pitres, *Leçons cliniques sur l'hystérie et l'hypnotisme*, 2 vols. (Paris, 1891), I, 52. The largest category was 34 seizures.

43. Cornelius W. Suckling, "Exhaustion Paralysis," *Lancet* 23 March 1889: 573. Here again, an embolus might provide an alternative explanation for her symptoms.

44. Margaret A. Cleaves, *The Autobiography of a Neurasthene* (Boston, 1910), quotes from pp. 99, 108, 115. The account is thinly veiled in the fiction that one of her physician-patients is telling the story to Dr. Cleaves.

46. According to Pitres, Charcot and Richer first paid attention to abasia in 1883, in a publication which I have not seen, "Su di una forma speciale di impotenza motrice degli arti inferiori per diffetto di coordinazione," *Medecina contemporanea* no. 1 (1883): 6 (Pitres, *op. cit.*, I, 457).

47. Paul Blocq, "Sur une affection caractérisée par de l'astasie et de l'abasie," *Archives de neurologie* 15 (1888): 24-51, 187-211.

48. Frank R. Smith, "A Case Presenting the Group of Symptoms Termed Astasia-Abasia," *Johns Hopkins Hospital Bulletin* 5 (1894); 13-16.

49. Josef Breuer and Sigmund Freud, *Studies on Hysteria* (1895), trans. James and Alix Strachey (Harmondsworth, 1974), quotes from pp. 210, 218-219.

50. For an overview see Richer, *op. cit.*, pp. 74-82. Diabetes and other organic diseases can, to be sure, cause contractures in the young, but of a much milder variety than those reported in the literature on hysteria. A brief review may be found in Arlan L. Rosenbloom, "Joint Contracture Preceding Insulin-Dependent Diabetes Mellitus," *Arthritis and Rheumatism* 26 (1983): 931.

51. Examples in James N. Brawner, *The Mind and Its Disorders* (Atlanta, 1942), p. 197; Ap Morgan Vance, "Hysteria as the Surgeon Sees It," *American Journal of Obstetrics* 58 (1908); 763. As Vance cut off the plaster cast from a 14-year-old girl whose leg had "drawn up" a year previously, she cried, "It is going to draw up; it is going to draw up," at which Vance said severely, "If it does draw up, I will break your d___d little neck."

52. Skey, *op. cit.*, pp. 96-98.

53. Johannes K.A. Wertheim-Salomonson, "Hysterische Hüfthaltung mit Skoliose," *Deutsche Zeitschrift für Nervenheilkunde* 19 (1901): 87-91.

54. Armand Hückel, "Über psychische Lähmungen und ihre Behandlung," *Münchener medizinische Wochenschrift*, (19 March 1889): 195.

55. Pitres, *op. cit.*, I, 450-451.

56. Benjamin C. Brodie, *Lectures Illustrative of Certain Local Nervous Affections* (London, 1837), pp. 50, 52. The copy I consulted was bound in with some larger work, and pagination began at "p. 33."

57. Benjamin Travers, *A Further Inquiry Concerning Constitutional Irritation and the Pathology of the Nervous System* (London, 1835), p. 273; he implied it was lower-class women who requested amputation to be able to earn a living as beggars.

58. Skey, *op. cit.*, pp. 83-84.

59. Silas Weir Mitchell, *Lectures on Diseases of the Nervous System, Especially in Women* (London, 1881), p. 48.

60. Oswald Bumke, *Lehrbuch der Geisteskrankheiten* (1919), 2nd ed. (Munich, 1924), p. 452.

61. Robert T. Edes, "The New England Invalid," *Boston Medical and Surgical Journal* (18 July 1895): 54.

62. Rudolph Burkart, "Zur Behandlung schwerer Formen von Hysterie und Neurasthenie," *[Volkmann] Sammlung klinischer Vorträge*, no. 245 (n.d. [1884]), pp. 1801-08. At the time he wrote this Burkart was a doctor in Bonn.

63. Mitchell, *op. cit.*, p. 221.

64. *Ibid.*, p. 218.

65. Charles F. Taylor, "Effect on Women of Imperfect Hygiene of the Sexual Function," *American Journal of Obstetrics* 15 (1882): 170.

66. In a discussion of the "Biologische Abteilung des ärtztlichen Vereins Hamburg," of 18 June 1907, reported in the *Münchener medizinische Wochenschrift* (12 Nov. 1907): 2305.

67. William Allen Pusey, *A Doctor of the 1870s and '80s* (Springfield, 1932), p. 87.

68. Arthur E. Hertzler, *The Horse and Buggy Doctor* (New York, 1938), p. 241.

69. Theodor Fontane, *Effi Briest* (1895), Eng. trans. Douglas Parmée (Harmondsworth, 1967).

70. Boston, 1883.

71. [U.S. National Library of Medicine], *Index-Catalogue of the Library of the Surgeon-General's Office, United States Army,* 2nd series, vol. 7 (1902), entries on "Hysteria (Manifestations of) by disorders of motion," pp. 783-786; 3d series, vol. 6 (1926), "Hysteria (Manifestations of)," including "laryngeal," "motor," and "spastic and paralytic," pp. 943, 946; 4th series, vol. 7 (1942), "Hysteria, manifestations," including "motor" and "motor: paralysis," pp. 968-969.

72. Paul Chodoff, "A re-examination of Some Aspects of Conversion Hysteria," *Psychiatry* 17 (1954): 75. In his view, "To some extent, the disappearance of conversion hysteria is probably a fiction; it may be that there has been less change in people with neuroses than there has been in fashions of labelling and describing them." Yet he did concede that "hysterical conversion phenomena undoubtedly do occur less frequently than formerly. . ." (p. 76).

73. Henry P. Laughlin, *The Neuroses in Clinical Practice* (Philadelphia, 1956), pp. 252-253.

74. Merskey, *op. cit.*, p. 102. He added, "The only places in which I have personally observed or obtained evidence of frequent classical manifestations have been during military service or. . . [in] indigenous North American populations or in work associated with a neurological hospital or department" (p. 103).

75. Israel S. Wechsler, *The Neuroses* (Philadelphia, 1929), p. 185.

76. Patria Asher, "A Case of Rapidly Cured Hysterical Paralysis," *British Medical Journal* (9 March 1946): p. 355.

77. Alec Roy, "Hysteria: A Case Note Study," *Canadian Journal of Psychiatry* 24 (1979): 157-160.

78. J.G. Stefansson, et al., "Hysterical Neurosis, Conversion Type: Clinical and Epidemiological Considerations," *Acta Psychiatrica Scandinavica* 53 (1976): 122, 126, for data. An apparent decline in the incidence of conversion disorders in 1965-69 was mainly the result of including only new cases in those later years, p. 130.

79. Jerome K. Myers, et. al. "Six-Month Prevalence of Psychiatric Disorders in Three Communities, 1980 to 1982," *Archives of General Psychiatry* 41 (1984): 966, tab. 14. Somatization occurred 0.1 times per 100 population in each of the three cities surveyed, New Haven, Baltimore, and St. Louis.

80. Arnold Lévy, *Über Astasie und Abasie: Ein Beitrag zur Hysterie* (Berlin: med. diss., 1889), pp. 17-19.

81. Frederick Smith, "Hysterical Paraplegia in the Male," *British Medical Journal*, (16 Jan. 1904): 125-126.

82. The major contemporary study was Joseph Babinski and Jules Froment, *Hystérie-Pithiatisme et troubles nerveux d'ordre réflexe en neurologie de guerre* (Paris, 1917).

83. Walter G. Spencer, "Neuromimesis: Two Cases in Which the Hip-Joint Had Been Held Fixed For Nine Months," *Lancet* (28 April 1894): 1065.

84. W.C. Weber, "Astasia-Abasia," *Medical Record* (23 Dec. 1893): 808.

85. Michael R. Trimble, *Post-Traumatic Neurosis: From Railway Spine to the Whiplash* (New York, 1981); Esther Fischer-Homberger, *Die traumatische Neurose: Vom somatischen zum sozialen Leiden* (Berne, 1975).

86. James L. Halliday, *Psychosocial Medicine: A Study of the Sick Society* (New York, 1948), p. 61. He believed that the "incidence of gross physical manifestations of hysteria in women" had declined, and that in males, at least wartime hysteria was down between the two World Wars.

87. Edwin A. Weinstein, et al., "Conversion Hysteria in Appalachia," *Psychiatry* 32 (1969): 334-341.

88. Hart Randsdell and Tressa Roche, "Psychosocial Treatment of Psychoneurosis," in Joseph C. Finney, ed., *Culture Change, Mental Health, and Poverty* (Lexington, 1969), anecdote from p. 105.

89. Charles G. Watson and Cheryl Buranen, "The Frequencies of Conversion Reaction Symptoms," *Journal of Abnormal Psychology* 88 (1979): 210, tab. 1.

90. Norval Watson, "An Outbreak of Hysterical Paraplegia," *Paraplegia* 20 (1982): case from 154-155.

91. Macario, *op. cit.*, pp. 71-72.

92. Armand Hückel, "Über psychische Lähmungen and ihre Behandlung," *Münchener medizinische Wochenschrift* (26 March 1889): 216.

93. Ernst von Leyden, "Ein Fall von Schrecklähmung," *Berliner klinische Wochenschrift* (20 Feb. 1905): 193-196.

94. William A. Hammond, *Spinal Irritation* (Detroit, 1886), pp. 26-27. One notes, by the way, what a backwater American medicine was that even in the 1880s such a prominent figure as Hammond could still be writing books on this subject.

95. James C. Wilson, "On Astasia-Abasia, with a Case," *American Journal of the Medical Sciences* 118 (1899): 45-47.

96. H. Sutter, "Weiterer Beitrag zur Kasuistik der nervösen Erkrankungen im Wochenbett," *Zentralblatt für Gynäkologie* 30 (1906): 946-948.

97. Maurice Krishaber, *De la Névropathie cérébro-cardiaque* (Paris, 1873), pp. 6-9. He finally recovered his equilibrium, after however losing all his hair (which grew back in again).

98. Dr. Douglas communicated his case to a Dr. Fraser, who published it as a note, "A Case of Recovery from Reflex Paralysis," *Medical Times and Gazette* (19 May 1866): 518. The diagnostic possibilities in the case are even more complex: perhaps Dr. Douglas suffered an initial stroke,

and then developed some "functional overlay," as current clinical jargon puts it, to wit, psychogenic symptoms atop somatogenic symptoms.

99. Pitres, *op. cit.*, I, 184-188. Her doctors were able to satisfy themselves that no organic problem existed in the knee joint.

100. Hippolyte Bernheim, *Suggestive Therapeutics: A Treatise on the Nature and Uses of Hypnotism*, Eng. trans. Christian A. Herter from 2nd rev. Fr. ed. (1886) (New York, 1889), pp. 285-287.

101. Robert Sommer, *Diagnostik der Geisteskrankheiten* (Vienna, 1894), p. 141. Mary Vetsera was involved in the 1889 death of Crown Prince Rudolph at Mayerling.

102. Macario, *op. cit.*, p. 74.

103. Silas Weir Mitchell first explained his diet philosophies in "Rest in Nervous Disease: Its Use and Abuse," in Edward C. Seguin, *A Series of American Clinical Lectures*, vol. I (Jan.-Dec., 1875) (New York, 1876), 83-102; see, for example, the case of Mrs. B, brought to him on a couch. In two months of Rest Cure she gained 30 pounds (pp. 95-96).

104. Sommer, *op. cit.*, p. 141.

105. Breuer and Freud, *op. cit.*, p. 150.

106. Barbara Ehrenreich and Deirdre English, *For Her Own Good: 150 Years of the Experts' Advice to Women* (New York, 1978), p. 103. Ann Douglas Wood writes, "Ill health in women had become positively fashionable and was exploited by its victims and practitioners as an advertisement of genteel sensibility and an escape from the too pressing demands of bedroom and kitchen." "The Fashionable Diseases: Women's Complaints and Their Treatment in Nineteenth-Century America," *Journal of Interdisciplinary History* 4 (1973): 27.

107. Thomas Dixon Savill, *Lectures on Hysteria and Allied Vaso-Motor Conditions* (London, 1909), pp. 176-177.

108. This account is taken from Jean Strouse, *Alice James: A Biography* (Boston, 1980), pp. 97-122, 177-199, 221-236, 239 and *passim*.

109. Frank E. Peckham, "A Case of Hysterical Hip-Joint Successfully Treated by Hypnotism," *Boston Medical and Surgical Journal* (26 Oct. 1893): 419-420.

110. Jean-Auguste Crouzet, *Topographie médicale... de Lodève* (Montpellier, 1912), p. 211. It was originally written in 1898 and published by E. Hamelin after the author's death.

111. A. Fallik and M. Sigal, "Hysteria – The Choice of Symptom Site: A Review of 40 Cases of Conversion Hysteria," *Psychotherapy and Psychosomatics* 19 (1971): 312.

112. H.B. Hafeiz, "Hysterical Conversion: A Prognostic Study," *British Journal of Psychiatry* 136 (1980): 548-551.

113. Bumke, *op. cit.* p. 258.

114. Hans Strotzka, *Kleinburg: eine sozialpsychiatrische Feldstudie* (Vienna, 1969), p. 81.

115. Quote from Dewitt L. Crandell and Bruce P. Dohrenwend, "Some Relations Among Psychiatric Symptoms, Organic Illness, and Social Class," *American Journal of Psychiatry* 123 (1967): 1536. See also Frederick J. Ziegler, et al., "Contemporary Conversion Reactions: A Clinical Study," *ibid.* 116 (1960): 901-910. In Alec Roy's view, "Hysteria patients often lack verbal

and social skills and the confidence to express and communicate their emotional distress and personal unhappiness to [friends, etc.] as well as to their doctors. Thus they resort to a non-verbal method of communicating their distress and depression – the hysterical symptom." "Hysterical Neurosis," in Roy, ed., *op. cit.*, p. 91.

IV.
SYNTHESIS AND POLITICS IN SOCIAL HISTORY

13.

SOCIAL CHANGE AND THE
MEANING OF THE
AMERICAN REVOLUTION

Kenneth A. Lockridge

Several of us, students of colonial society rather than of the Revolution, think we see various changes occurring within that society prior to the Revolution. These changes were in fact extremely varied. They began as early as the 1720s, were most intense between then and the 1760s and were not reversed until well into the 1780s if at all.

We wonder whether these changes might help explain why certain Americans embraced the struggle which led to independence. Above all we wonder whether the difficulties of agreeing upon a frame for this changing society might help explain the long search for political definition which followed independence. It is the impact of social change on this definitive phase of the Revolution which concerns us most.

There is no obvious interpretative framework within which to discuss the issue. Conventional explanations of the search for political definition do not refer to a changing society. One school speaks of established American characteristics which became a national ideology in the course of the Revolution and were embodied in the Constitution. Another school looks more closely at the debates which intervened between independence and the Constitution, but sees there only an exacerbation of an enduring conflict between the haves and have-nots of American society. In neither case is there a systematic consideration of the effects of social change.

These speculations were prepared as the basis for a panel discussion at the meeting of the Organization of American Historians, New Orleans, April 1971. The "we" in the opening sentence refers to the members of the panel: Richard Bushman, Richard Brown, Daniel Scott Smith.

Decendants of the latter school are moving toward such a consideration. They are beginning to speak of a growing and complex polarization of society in the revolutionary era, a polarization which had strong if varying effects on the political debates of the 1770s and 1780s. As will be seen, my own views overlap considerably with those evolved by Jackson Turner Main, Van Beck Hall and especially Lee Benson.[1] But there remains about these interpreters of the internal Revolution a sense of limitation in the chronological depth and variety of effects of social change they are willing to consider. There is a feeling that they still focus too much on an immediate dualization of society with fairly direct political consequences. This is chiefly the fault of bibliographers who would label these men into the simplicities of their intellectual progenitors. But it is a real handicap, sufficient to lead us to want to consider the full workings of social change outside the framework being established by Benson, Hall and Main. To the extent that our independent studies of a changing colonial society lead us toward their conclusions about the internal divisions of the revolutionary era, we shall all be stronger.

The framework which comes closest to meeting our needs is the theory of modernization. This was evolved by social scientists to describe the transformation undergone by developing nations. It links certain economic and social changes to changes in attitudes, political behavior and political structure. The end product is presumably a modernized nation. We find the language of modernization useful because it speaks in terms of the varied political effects of dynamic social situations. We find that detailed studies of the attitudinal effects of social change in developing nations can help to confirm effects we think we detect stemming from similar changes in colonial America. We also find it valuable to note the ways in which theories of the modernization process do and do not fit the American case. But this is the limit of the usefulness of modernization theory. We cannot use any theory of modernization to explain the internal American Revolution because these theories all assume a much more convulsive and unidirectional process of change than can be found in pre-industrial America. The most we can say is that modernization helps us more than any other frame to think freely about the political effects of social change in colonial America. Ultimately this theory, too, is restrictive.

So we have decided to take a deliberately innocent approach. We have some indications that colonial society was changing during the half-century preceding the American Revolution. How might men have reacted to these changes? How might their various reactions have entered into the debates of those who sought to give political definition to the new nation? What effect could these reactions have had on the course and outcome of the debates? What might we learn thereby about the meaning of the Revolution?

My job is to provide a target. I was assigned to list the kinds of change which apparently were occurring and then to speculate on the effects of these changes on political attitudes. Then I was to ask whether in fact such attitudes appear to have entered into the political debates set off by independence. But here I find that Gordon Wood has anticipated me. His account of these debates reveals many of the political attitudes which several of us had anticipated would result from the changes taking place in colonial society. He even states that some of these attitudes seem to have been reactions to a changing society. My story therefore merges largely into his as we reach the time of the American Revolution. We agree that social change was in several ways a major energizer of the intricate exchanges which ultimately and half-inadvertently gave us the Constitution. We seem to agree that the entire process partook of polarization and modernization without fitting into any neat interpretative framework. Whether we agree on the meaning of the process I do not know, but certainly I shall give my opinions on its meanings.

II

As I see it, we begin around 1720 with a colonial society which in the aggregate is low in population density, has immediate access to land and is geographically immobile; a society in which wealth is widely distributed, which is socially undifferentiated and which is removed from dependency on the market economy, relative to the England of the eighteenth century or the America of fifty years later. In the aggregate this is a comparatively isolated, static, homogeneous society. On the other hand during the previous several generations upward intergenerational property mobility may have been unusually high, in relation to England or later America.[2]

Over the next fifty years this society was altered in a number of ways. Some changes already taking place within it simply continued, but as this occurred certain thresholds were crossed. Other characteristics increased their rate of change, while some that had previously been static began to change for the first time. Some of the more basic changes continued into the nineteenth century, but others leveled off toward a high plateau between 1750 and 1780. Certain trends even began to reverse in the 1780s as part of a second wave of social change which was not, however, fully evident until after 1790.

The mechanisms involved bear further elucidation, but let me list the central changes of the period between 1720 and the 1780s.

Population growth continued at a slightly higher rate after 1730 than before 1720. But basically the white population continued to double every twenty or thirty years, as before.

Population density continued to increase as the settlement of new areas lagged behind the explosive growth of the population. The average density of the smallest number of counties which would include a majority of the colonial population increased by a factor of three between 1720 and 1770. The rate of increase in density leveled off gradually with time, but the fact remains that the absolute density of the areas in which most colonists lived had multiplied severalfold from a very low base. By the time of the Revolution there were counties in America whose population density surpassed that of some of the less dense counties in England. The same could hardly have been said in 1720. The argument is that several socioeconomic thresholds were crossed in the process of this increase in absolute population density.

One of these thresholds was the exhaustion of undivided cultivable lands in many of the areas of increasing density, as indigenous population pressed against the local land supply. Between 1720 and 1750 an increasing proportion of counties experienced declining farm acreages. For these counties the aggregate rate of decline in average acreage increased sharply. Partly because of rising out-migration and partly because of the mathematics of the situation these trends began to level off after 1750. But by then the initially negligible proportion of colonial families subsisting from farms at or near the minimum necessary size had increased severalfold. It was some time before this proportion ceased growing altogether within the counties in question.

The overall rate of *migration* increased after 1720. This took the form of migration *to* newly settled areas more than ten miles from the migrant's point of origin, *out of* the most dense rural areas containing a majority of the population. Part of the migration also took the form of itinerant labor and of migration to suburban and urban areas.

The *concentration of wealth* rose to an increased rate, primarily because of the mounting pressure on the land supply. I have explained this mechanism elsewhere. I might add that the concentration of wealth *may* also have been accelerated by scattered local increases in per capita income which selectively benefited certain individuals. The trend to more rapid concentration was of course limited to the more dense areas; out-migration from some of these areas may have slowed the trend; and the new rural areas settled by many of the migrants did not at first show this trend. Nonetheless, the increased rate of concentration of wealth was intensive enough in areas containing sufficient population that it probably prevailed for the aggregate of colonial society. While the rate of concentration may have slowed temporarily after 1760, the process never ceased. It continued to add to the sudden increase in the concentration of wealth which had taken place toward the middle of the eighteenth century. A degree of *social polarization* accompanied the concentration of wealth. For a time the proportion of men labeled "gentlemen" increased faster than ever before, as did the proportion of men accepting poor relief, both proportions continuing to grow until the Revolution.

The overall level and rate of *social differentiation* also increased, largely as population density rose across various thresholds in areas containing a large portion of the population. Migration to new areas was not sufficient to do more than slow the rise in density and concomitant rise in differentiation in older areas. Nor is it likely that such new areas represented a sufficiently massive return to an undifferentiated society to counterbalance the effects of ever denser populations elsewhere. Richard Bushman has already outlined the process of differentiation in his book. In ever more localities the population became sufficient to support two churches instead of one, two schools in place of one and a full-time instead of a part-time storekeeper. Within larger areas, interest groups could more easily form as the absolute number of men sharing special interests—Baptists, for example, or storekeepers and inland merchants, or men seeking proprietorships in western lands—grew large enough to facilitate communication and organization. The Great Awakening did its share to accelerate the increase of choices men might make and the interests around which they might organize.

The level of *commercialization* also increased somewhat, perhaps at a slightly higher rate. Commercialization in one sense might be defined as the percentage of the total income of the population which would fluctuate significantly in response to fluctuations in the market economy of the region, the province or the larger world of international commerce. It is a measure of *dependency* on the market economy. Opposed to this is the proportion of income subject only to weather and to local contingencies. Increasing commercialization in this sense would probably have required a rise in per capita colonial agricultural exports and entailed a rise in per capita income. I think this was happening only within limited areas. I would add that within these areas the rise in per capita income need not have been evenly distributed. Some men may have been uniquely equipped to take advantage of increasing export demand, while others may have been forced to turn to these men for employ. One can imagine a locality in which everyone was increasingly dependent on the market economy: some men profited immensely while others barely improved their standard of living. And of course a parallel maldistribution was occurring on a regional level throughout America as well as on an individual level within those areas which had significant rises in per capita income. That is, certain regions were in fact enjoying substantial increases in per capita income, and in some of these everyone may have improved his standard of living at least a bit, whereas regions containing the bulk of the population experienced an insignificant if not a negative change in per capita income. This regionally selective commercialization amounted to a *geographic concentration of wealth*. A few counties increased their share of the national wealth faster than their share of the total population.

Other types of commercial dependency, which did not require the classic sort of rise in per capita output for market mentioned above, appear to have been increasing at a higher rate. As population density rose across a certain threshold, local farmer-artisans found sufficient nearby custom to become specialized artisans. Some may have been forced to such specialization by small inheritances of land. They relied for their incomes on the increasing number of semi-subsistence farmers within range of their shops. But on those continual occasions when local farmers either did not harvest their usual little surplus or could not get it to market or, once there, could not sell it, the newly specialized artisan would lose much of his income. Still another form of dependency rested on mechanisms too intricate for me to delineate, but seems to have gone like this: The concentration of landed wealth stemming from population pressure put some men in a position to offer, and others to need, loans—whether loans of cash or of land in the form of rented land. In the short run, while there were men who could pay interest or rent either by working harder or by lowering their standards of living, the landholder-creditors would prosper. They might even give employ to increasing numbers of laborers and artisans. Dependency relationships would proliferate. But it is difficult to imagine such a system stabilizing in the long run.

Implicit in all of this, then, is the assumption that one central change was *not* taking place: there was *little or no increase in aggregate per capita production and/or income between 1720 and 1770.* At most these measures increased by 10 percent, and the increase was concentrated in a few localities and there it most benefited those who were already relatively well off.

Increasing population density, land shortage, migration, interpersonal and interregional concentration of wealth, social differentiation and commercial dependency are abstractions which do not speak forcefully enough of the changing quality of life in colonial America. The impact of these trends can better be expressed by describing the modal life experience encountered by young Americans. Men coming of age in 1720 could typically expect to acquire sufficient land within their home counties to live out the lives of semi-subsistence farmers, as had their fathers. But the men coming of age in 1770 faced instead the typical choices of migrating and/or trying to enter more deeply into the market economy and/or accepting a lower standard of living than their fathers had. Furthermore these typical men of 1770 were far more likely to have experienced overt religious and political disputes within their communities as they came of age. Variations aside, such was the essential change in the American social experience.

Instead of speaking broadly of a new modal life experience, we might speak of the increased net frequency of a series of specific experiences. The concept of increased net frequency of a series of experiences still translates our sweeping social changes into human terms, but it is statistically more cautious than the idea of a new modal life experience, and it gives us a set of easily tested hypotheses.

Thus, I would venture that *there was a greater net likelihood in 1770 than in 1720 that any given American male would:* [3]

1. Live in a county whose population density was greater than 25 persons [4] to the square mile and still increasing. Also, live in a town or county, whichever was the basic unit of local jurisdiction, whose absolute population surpassed 1,750 white inhabitants and was not decreasing. Also, live in a basic unit of local jurisdiction founded more than 90 years previously. (All these probabilities increased substantially in Massachusetts between 1720 and 1770; for example, the percentage of the population living in towns more than 90 years old rose from less than 10 percent to over 50 percent.)

2. Not hold sufficient land to be able to bequeath more than one son enough land to maintain the father's standard of living considering the anticipated productivity of land at the time. (Or at least not have sufficient such land in or contiguous to the locality of present residence.) Not hold sufficient other resources to guarantee other sons their fathers' standard of living. Pass on his land by primogeniture, or at any rate pass on more than 75 percent of his land to one son.

3. Obtain the major portion of his land (in value) by purchase rather than by inheritance or grant.

4. Hold less than 100 acres of land. Hold less than 40 acres of land. Hold less than 1 acre of land.

5. Till land described by assessors or in an inventory as "worn" or once labeled "waste" or "poor" or "rocky" and since brought into production.

6. Rent land from an American whose own possession of the land did not stem directly from a proprietary charter granted prior to 1700.

7. Work as a farm laborer, migrant or otherwise.

8. Owe a debt larger than 1 percent of total estate, incurred to maintain rather than to improve standard of living, and owed to a man with at least five such loans out and whose income was more than triple that of his average debtor.

9. Marry after, and probably because, the bride was pregnant.

10. Never marry.

11. Produce goods and services and/or earn a real income of no greater value than that produced or earned by his father. Or, have a standard of living no higher than that of his father. Or, hold property whose real value was no greater than that of his father. (These are various ways of getting at the same point. I should make it clear here that we are not necessarily speaking of average per capita production or income or standard of living or property, all of which may have risen a little. We are speaking of the net frequency with which individuals failed to surpass their progenitors.)

12. Receive poor relief.

13. Live in local jurisdictions in which the wealthiest 10 percent of men own more than 35 percent of the total wealth and the poorest 10 percent own less than 5 percent.

14. Earn an income of which more than 25 percent depended upon employment by another person and/or upon ultimate participation in a market other than the internal exchanges of the immediate locality and/or upon the availability of loans or rented land.

15. Engage in a non-agricultural occupation. (Again, I recognize that a significant shift to commercial dependency and to non-farm occupations without substantial increases in per capita production and income is a phenomenon uncongenial to economists. But a mild increase in production and income selectively distributed, and/or population pressures which forced a lower standard of living on a substantial minority of the population while relatively and absolutely enriching a smaller minority, could have opened the way to such a shift. In Russian and Pakistani villages similar pressures appear to have led at least temporarily to changes very like those listed here. Unfortunately, for all the talk of Malthus, few economists have left their developmental models to work out the economics of Malthusian or semi-Malthusian situations.)

16. Petition his county court or legislative assembly at all. Petition in the name of an interest not common to more than 75 percent of the members of his local jurisdiction. Petition in the name of an interest not held by more than 5 percent of his local jurisdiction. (Both pressure on resources and social differentiation would lead to this and to the following changes.)

17. Live in a community which during the first 30 years of his lifetime experienced more than one internal conflict severe enough to provoke recourse to or require settlement by higher authority. Live in a community which during the first 30 years of his life had spent at least five years involved in one or more such conflicts. Live in a community in which dissenting votes were recorded on at least 5 percent of possible issues. Live in a community in which a challenge to a man's eligibility to vote had been recorded within the past 30 years.

18. Participate in a religious revival, a religious movement or group conviction based on the assumption that existing religion was in some sense corrupt and that a more pure conformity to the authority of God was required of individuals and of the community.

19. Participate in an effort to split a new congregation from an old one and/or a new community from an old one.

20. Consciously select from among several a congregation and/or a community in which respectively to worship and live.

I might also list several social experiences which had undergone a net increase, but were still the experiences of very small minorities. It became more likely that a man would:

21. Possess more than four times the median wealth of his local jurisdiction.

22. Call himself a gentleman and be called a gentleman by others, with all concerned meaning by that term something more profound than is meant today.

23. Possess more than four times the median wealth of his county without ever having held office above the county level.

I have saved migration because it led to an experience which increased without representing a net increase for the aggregate of society. Thus:

24. There was a net increase in the likelihood that a man would obtain land outside the county in which he resided at age 21.

25. There was net increase in the likelihood that a man would move his residence from the county in which he resided at age 21. Some of this migration took the form of itinerancy or movement to "urban" areas, but most was to new agricultural areas.

26. The net increase in migration thus led to some increase in the likelihood that a man would live in a county whose population density was less than 15 persons per square mile and in a locality whose white population was below 500 and which had been founded less than 30 years previously. (In Massachusetts the proportion of the population living in towns less than thirty years old rose from perhaps 20 percent circa 1720 to around 30 percent in 1760.) *But* this reversion to a "frontier" environment was overwhelmed by the massive increase in the proportion of the population living in localities two or three times as dense, large and old, as also occurred in Massachusetts. So we have as a result of migration an increase in an experience which nonetheless did not undergo a net increase. While much depends on how the opposing sub-environments are defined, the trend to a population living in areas significantly more dense and in communities significantly more populous and old than was the norm in 1720 appears to have overbalanced the trend back toward a population living in areas less dense and in communities smaller and newer than the norm of 1720.

(The asymmetry of these emerging social sub-environments raises questions about the claim that increasing geographic mobility led to increasing anxiety and individualization because it stripped an ever higher proportion of men of the context of their nearby kin. Perhaps it did, but on the other hand there was an even greater increase in the proportion of the population living in areas of significantly greater density than in time 'x' in the past. One definition of "significantly greater density" might be a density sufficient to increase significantly the numbers of kin living close enough to a man for him to have daily contact with them. It is possible that increasing density took more of the population across this threshold of familiarity than migration took away from their kin. If so, we would have to conclude that for most of the eighteenth century the *net* trend was toward rather than away from extended kinship contact.)

Aside from its asymmetry, this growing differentiation of social experiences is itself worth noting. Another submerged counter-trend created further such differentiation:

27. The geographic selectivity of such increases in per capita output and income as occurred, meant that beneath the general inertia of these characteristics, some regions experienced substantial increases in output and income. Within some of these regions we might expect that sons surpassed their fathers' output, income, standard of living, property, etc., with an increasing net frequency. These regions were often among those older areas which experienced substantial increases in population density and local population size, but they were unique in their prosperity, which was not the prevailing experiential trend.

These, then are some of the specific human experiences which increasing population density, pressure on the land supply, migration, concentration of wealth, social differentiation and commercial dependency, in the absence of a substantial rise in per capita income, might have brought with increasing frequency to the Americans of the eighteenth century. I do not maintain that the frequency of the experiences consequent on social change increased to such a level that American society was utterly transformed. But I do wonder what such a counterpoint of more frequent experiences, even if none of these surpassed a moderate absolute frequency, could have done to attitudes conditioned by the social environment of the early eighteenth century.

The issue is posed most dramatically if one looks beneath net experiential changes to examine the social sub-environments emerging within colonial America. That "typical" social environment of 1720 still existed, and increased migration had extended its most extreme simplicities to a larger proportion of the population (20 percent to 30 percent?). On the other hand the proportion living in distinctly more dense, large and old communities had increased faster and farther (15 percent to 50 percent?). Many (2/5?) of these communities had begun to experience pressure on the land supply and increasing out-migration, concentration of wealth, social polarization, commercial dependency and social differentiation, along with a reversal of a tradition of net intergenerational upward mobility in property, all without a significant increase in per capita income. Others (2/5?) had, however, benefited from substantial increases in per capita income. These also experienced pressure on the land and increasing concentration of wealth, social polarization, social differentiation and commercial dependency—indeed they often experienced all to an especially intense degree—but here it was much more unusual for anyone's standard of living to fall, somewhat more unusual for a man at a given age to fail to equal his father's property at the same age. In such areas, too, there may have occasionally been in- rather than out-migration. These communities were the heirs of (and often included) the commercialized urban, suburban and cash crop areas of fifty years before. They now encompassed somewhat more of the population and still more of the wealth of America. It would be absurd to equate these growing divergencies in the social environment with divergencies in social attitudes. But one wonders at the potential effects of such a divergence of experiences.

We might dismiss the idea that such social changes had political implications by pointing out that many of them had slowed down by 1750 or 1760 while by 1780 Americans were accustomed to them all. In fact we might ask whether the reversal of some of these trends very late in the eighteenth century did not have some effect on the politics of the 1780s. I am open to both possibilities.

But for now I wish to proceed on the assumption that the changes I have listed did affect attitudes of many men who in turn played a role in the search for political definition which culminated in the Constitution. Certainly most such men came to maturity while these changes were in full swing or still fresh.

III

The object now is to guess at the impact of these social changes on political attitudes, political behavior and the political system.[5] Then we shall see whether the politics of the internal Revolution bear out any of my suppositions.

The fundamental point is that we would expect a general increase in demands per capita on the political system. A shortage of land, commercialization and social differentiation all *lead* in fairly obvious ways—through contracts, petitions, instructions, complaints and court cases—to increasing per capita contact with the sources of political power. These contacts either took the form of direct demands or became political demands once disputes arose. Such an increase in demands must have activated and perhaps strained the political system, an overall effect with which I shall deal later.

Yet on this level the hypothesis as to the political impact of social change is too general. To be more specific, the social changes hypothesized should have given rise to two major and overlapping modes of political demand, each with its own effect on politics. There should also have been two more or less secondary effects arising from the general process by which social change increased political demands. Each of these four political consequences of social change deserves a separate discussion:

1. First, we might expect a number of political demands and concerns to arise from the sudden increase in the concentration of wealth in this still not overwhelmingly prosperous society.

More was involved than just having a wealthy group rise above the rest of society by acquiring even more of that society's resources. It was a matter of dependence, too, as an ever larger proportion of men actually depended upon their more wealthy fellows for the land, loans and employment which would maintain their standard of living. And thus it was a matter of deeply differing interests, for some offered while others asked for the essential land, money or employment. Surely someone reflected on the implications of this growing dependence which before was rare? Surely those with little came ever more into conflict with those with plenty?

These are real issues we ought to see manifested in the political writings of pre-revolutionary America. I think we will, once we get beneath the surface in our analysis of the writings of the day. Jack Greene has seen in the contemporary rhetoric of social declension chiefly a reaction to prosperity. When we look more closely we see that what is involved is not personal guilt over the accumulation of wealth. Men are objecting to the effects of the *disproportionate* prosperity of one segment of society. The corruption of which they speak is above all the corruption of an already wealthy group enhancing its wealth by pursuing its own interests and by abusing its control of the political machinery intended to serve all men.

True, these complaints about the economic and political engrossments of the wealthy could nonetheless be consistent with a general trend toward prosperity. In the rush for wealth some men would do better than others and might attempt to hold others back; many men would become more dependent; and some would fall by the wayside. But most sooner or later would benefit. In this perspective all complaints about the engrossment of wealth or power are merely signs of a painful adjustment to new economic structures which were leading to new economic heights. Yet I maintain that what was in fact occurring was a process which involved all the inequities of a headlong race for prosperity without the concomitant benefits of a general increase in prosperity.

We need to look very closely for evidence that men were aware of and concerned about just such a development. There are hints of it in statements that one class was becoming disproportionately wealthy at the expense of the whole society. Jefferson's desire to avoid a densely settled, land-short, seacoast society may have involved more than a wish to avoid the concomitant dependencies and corruptions; he may also have concluded from his experience of pre-revolutionary America that such a society would actually lower the standard of living of the mass of its inhabitants. On a more mundane level, might we not take more seriously the repeated statements in petitions for relief of debt and taxes (and later in objections to property suffrage requirements) that large and increasing proportions of men were simply too poor to meet their obligations? From such evidence we might at least conclude that, if America was going through an economic change which actually involved a long-range increase in per capita income, any such increase was at the time less than overwhelming and was temporarily maldistributed.

I do not believe that the sharpened concern over the concentration of wealth and the decline in social equality, over the concentration of political power, over increasing dependence, over the division of society by interests and over apparently declining material opportunity, was spread evenly through the society. Certain regions had more reason to be sensitive to these trends, while others may have been oblivious to many or all of their effects. Thus, on the one hand there were some older, more dense areas which were experiencing pressure on the land supply without benefiting from increases in per capita income. With these were the less dense inland regions settled increasingly by men who had to move there because of inadequate inheritances at home, and who had had to obtain land from private entrepreneurs rather than by grant or inheritance. Out of necessity or by choice, these latter areas were removed from the market economy. Their wealth was limited and, though it was at first relatively widely distributed, they would eventually evolve into the dense, land-short condition of the older rural areas whence they were settled, in what was a continuing process in early American history. In both areas, men's interests were chiefly that the government not strain by its levies their limited wealth, and that new land be continuously and readily available as needed. At the other extreme was the small but growing minority of the population living in densely settled areas which were ever more deeply and profitably involved in the market economy. The society's wealthiest and most powerful men tended increasingly to concentrate in these areas.

This is in essence the polarization described in Jackson Turner Main's *Social Structure of Revolutionary America*. It had always existed in embryo; the argument is simply that in degree of market involvement, per capita income and overt economic need, these social poles were farther apart in 1780 than in 1720. The extremes also embraced a larger proportion of the total population. Such a polarization must have had its political effects, and Main may describe these in his recent work on state political "parties" in the 1780s. One finds that representatives from inland, less commercialized areas tended to vote together against higher taxes, (or for higher taxes on commercial property), in favor of soft currency and, at times, in favor of a more ready availability of land. Representatives from older, more commercialized areas preferred giving the state a higher income with which to accomplish its tasks, especially when that income came from taxes on real property, feared and opposed a soft currency and tended to be more concerned than their opponents about the regular collection of debts. In short, there was in this period an unprecedentedly intense geographic division over specific economic and political interests which may have arisen from the fact that different geographic areas had increasingly different incomes, power, interests and material opportunities.

I must admit that I have not drawn in precisely the links between my suggested social changes and the more intense social and geographic conflicts which I claim followed from these changes. I am only suggesting that we *do* have on the one hand evidence of increasing concentration of wealth, social inequality, concentration of power, dependence, separation of interests, actual and prospective deprivation and perhaps differentiation of socioeconomic sub-environments along these lines, *and* on the other hand actual complaints about an emerging American aristocracy, about poverty and, in addition, a discernible geographic division of politics along lines of differing regional interests. I merely want to observe that there may actually have been real reason to believe that an American aristocracy was emerging and to believe that its emergence was not part of a process that benefited the great majority of Americans. This so-called aristocracy may also with reason have been increasingly associated with areas whose market involvement and per capita income were greater than that which prevailed in the rest of the society, and whose interests were accordingly different.

In searching for evidence that in some form such economic and social polarizations affected the politics of the day, certain crucial distinctions must be kept in mind. On the national level, effects would take the form primarily of concerned observers reflecting on the consequences of interpersonal and/or interregional polarization. A prime example is the concern over "Europeanization" or "feudalism" manifested by leaders of the revolutionary generation even before independence was mentioned. Why was Adams worried about feudal and canon law, or Jefferson about primogeniture and entail? As I have implied in an article, and as Rowland Berthoff and John Murrin now suggest with considerable evidence from the 1760s and 1770s, the social changes of the eighteenth century may have caused these leaders and others to fear that American society was in fact evolving away from the relative equality and opportunity of its past, toward a more European or "feudal" future. On the colony level, on the other hand, we will have to sort through a complex interplay of conflicting political demands to see whether and in what forms the hypothesized polarizations of the era were manifesting themselves in politics. Professor Main has given us a start here, but the analysis of the social sources of political rhetoric on this level is very difficult and has a long way to go. On either level, references to the problems of the society must be cast in the rhetoric of process if we are to assume they arise from social change. I find it significant that men on all levels were in fact speaking of trends, of growing threats, of impending or developing dangers, in their political rhetoric. Future inquiry will have to bear this out if we are to validate the hypothesis that in some form increasing social polarization was a force in the politics of the later eighteenth century.

Shortly I will mention what I see in Gordon Wood's study of the internal Revolution that seems to confirm my suppositions here. Meanwhile, I wish to consider a second mode of political demand arising from the social changes chronicled. I am convinced that these changes had results more profound than the mere intensification of concern over social opportunity and led to differences deeper than differences of interest.

2. Let us return to the America of 1720. I have said that vis-à-vis the England of the eighteenth century this was a society unusually low in population density, hence one in which each settlement was unusually isolated from exposure to outsiders. Geographic mobility, especially in the form of migratory labor or urban-rural exchanges, was relatively low. So was involvement in the market economy. The power of higher authorities over the locality was also less than prevailed in England. Within each locality social differentiation was limited to the usual minor variations common in semi-subsistence agriculture. Both land and the suffrage were widely available, so few men were distinguished from their fellows by the lack of either. The distribution of wealth was wide. In short, this society was unusually isolated, independent and homogeneous. This is not to deny that the rural America of 1720 was also in certain senses mobile, new or unstable. It was all of these, but it was nonetheless unusually isolated, independent and homogeneous relative to England or to the America of 1770. By 1720, for that matter, much of the aggregate novelty and instability of colonial society had diminished, as Professors Bailyn and Ver Steeg have pointed out, leaving isolation, independence and homogeneity as the most notable characteristics.

What were the values of this society? Quite simply that it was good to be isolated, independent and homogeneous. New England was the world of Michael Zuckerman's *Peaceable Kingdoms*. Men desired nothing so much as to be left alone to run their own affairs. Strangers were treated with suspicion, the same suspicion accorded the actions of higher authority, because either might impair local freedom of action. Within the town, formal votes were seldom taken as most issues were talked over so that a vote became superfluous because it would have been unanimous. The emphasis on unanimity had several functions. It prevented the emergence of conflicts severe enough to lead to the interference of higher authorities; hence unanimity helped preserve independence. It also maintained that homogeneity of opinion which was thought essential to a truly peaceful society. Finally, the stress on unanimity prevented individuals from furthering their particular interests by clever use of political power. The treatment of leaders was consistent with this: While respected as leaders of the consensus, they were sharply limited in their presumptions to superiority. There seemed to be a fear of letting anyone get too far ahead of anyone else.

This was also most often a radically Protestant society whose religion echoed the values of the community. Congregations only reluctantly accepted even a weak structure of higher church authority. Ministers fulminated against selfish interests. Sermons repeatedly assured men that the simple, sturdy life which their emigrant forefathers had bequeathed them was the very life the Protestant God had had in mind when he prepared this chosen land. The attitude toward change found in these sermons is particularly interesting because rarely does one find men so openly contemplating the meaning of change. Change was equated with evil except in the case of a closer adherence to the actual or imagined simplicities of the fathers.

In some ways, admittedly, this was two worlds: One was a world of intense little communities clustered around their meetinghouses; the other, a world of feckless dirt farmers living like their hogs amid the pine trees. But in two senses these worlds converged. They literally converged in the sense that New England towns tended to scatter into hamlets and farms, while elsewhere hamlets and little towns coalesced among the farmers. They converged in attitude in that Byrd's Lubberland, like Zuckerman's Peaceable Kingdom, was isolated, suspicious, certain of its rectitude and skeptical of social presumption.

This, then, was the major social experience of colonial America. It has already been sketched by Lee Benson in his social reinterpretation of Beard. It is rather like the life striven for by the men of Eric Wolf's closed, corporate, peasant communities. His peasants, likewise removed from the mainstreams of commerce and living in self-regulating groups on the land, likewise sought to minimize interference from the outside. They looked upon higher authority and upon commercial involvement as necessary evils, to be handled gingerly. They saw in homogeneity a way to preserve themselves from outside interference, from internal strife and from dangerous imbalances in the internal distribution of wealth or power. Religion reinforced these attitudes at every turn. The chief difference is that by 1720 many colonial Americans had more or less succeeded in realizing these ancient desires. The American environment virtually gave them what generations of peasants had desired and later would desire: isolation, independence, homogeneity. Why many colonists wanted this or why having it they did not eventually lose the fear on which the ethos is based is beyond my scope. They had it and, from all evidence, they wanted it to continue.

If the word *peasant* is offensive, let me suggest instead that the colonist raised in this environment was like Alex Inkeles' "pre-modern man." Pre-modern man as Inkeles has encountered him in several developing nations has little experience of such socializing institutions as consolidated schools, advanced commercial exchanges or factory employment. He is the man of the under-commercialized countryside. He wants above all to be left alone in order to lead his life as he has in the past. He respects any local authority which will insulate him from change. He is therefore skeptical of new ideas and only dimly aware of higher authority, whose basis he may not understand. Political activism seems to him at best fruitless and at worst morally wrong.

(Neither Wolf's model nor Inkeles' is a perfect description of even one of the variants of rural America circa 1720. Yet the broad similarities in circumstance and in attitudes are striking enough to warrant the suggestion that we may learn something about that American of 1720 by studying Wolf's peasant and Inkeles' pre-modern man. Certainly I find these men more appropriate models than the mobilized, activated, entrepreneurial, individualistic man read back into colonial history by Whigs nurtured on their own image of the age of Jackson.)

The point I want to make is this: What happens when we take such men—who in fact or in myth have and want isolation, independence and homogeneity—and confront them with the prospect of a shortage of land, with the need to move to and purchase new land elsewhere, with an increasing concentration of wealth, especially of landed wealth, with the pressure (and/or temptation) to enter into relations of economic dependence characteristic of the market economy, with growing social and religious diversity, with attendant strife and with attendant interference from higher authorities? The point is clear. Virtually every social change I have hypothesized involved a threat to the isolation, independence, homogeneity and continuity of American rural society, a threat not simply to its economic interests but perhaps to an integral world view. When one considers that religion usually permeates the rural world view, it is easy to imagine that many Americans of the eighteenth century could have become convinced that their world was coming to an end by action of the devil himself.

Or so I would suggest. But prediction is difficult because at this point our parallels from the social science literature disintegrate. Inkeles says little about his subjects' reactions to change, short of the total modernization of the attitudinal structure brought about by the advent of radical forms of socialization. Wolf at least suggests that it is the very threats posed by scarcity, by the commercial sector in a context of scarcity, by change and by diversity which created the corporate ethos in his subjects in the first place. This would imply that an acceleration of such threats, short of a total structural change in the society, would serve chiefly to intensify the drive for isolation, independence and homogeneity. And Wolf observes that in its more irrational forms such a drive does often invoke the forces of religion against witches and devils.

But we need not go beyond Michael Zuckerman's work to get some idea of how rural America reacted to the social changes of the eighteenth century. There we can see man desperately insisting on peace and unity, resisting appeals to higher authority, accusing one another of infidelity to the simple virtues of the past, all in the face of changes which they cannot control and which are destroying first local homogeneity then local independence. And here, as later at the time of the Revolution, we can see a sort of psychologically snowballing effect at work: While life in rural America circa 1760 was not radically more complex than in 1720, that earlier life had become so idealized in the minds of later generations that the mild-to-moderate social changes which actually occurred appeared in men's minds as catastrophic alterations of an idyllic and holy past.

I would suggest, then, that we should expect to find that much of rural America was made ripe for a very special kind of political mobilization by the social changes of the eighteenth century. Men were of course mobilized over specific interests—an adequacy of land, paper money, lower taxes, etc. And these men were suspicious of those more skilled than themselves in the intricacies of economic politics. But beyond this I would expect an agitated conviction that a good, simple, unified world was giving way to an evil, complex, selfish world under the impact of incomprehensible forces. And I expect exhortations to moral reform would have found a wide following. In the face of such deterioration, mere petitions and the organization of political groups would seem inadequate, indeed inappropriate responses. Only a crusade would suffice.

Michael Walzer has already suggested that Puritanism filled such a function in seventeenth-century England. And then in the eighteenth century there was the Great Awakening throughout much of America precisely when most of the social changes of the century were in full swing. The mind also fastens on the need a Revolution might fulfill in reassuring men whose world seemed to be falling apart and on the vehicle a Revolution might offer to men determined to restore the isolation, independence and homogeneity of the real and imagined past.

By this I do not necessarily mean that disturbed rural America eagerly embraced the crisis over the Imperial constitution and turned it into a violent revolution out of their need to purge their world of social sin. Yet it seems possible that the crisis leading to independence further mobilized rural Americans through its exhortations to political action, its libertarian rhetoric and its nationalistic optimism. Their best and wisest leaders urged all Americans to seize control of their own destinies, to free themselves of the oppression of corrupt outside forces and, in so doing, to take their country back on the path of virtue. What those best and wisest men meant by these incitements may have been quite another thing from the spirit in which rural America took them. Ready for a purgative crusade and invited to what appeared to be such an event, traditional Americans may have shaped the event to their inmost needs. The important question is: What happened when those needs were not satisfied by independence?

So much for the two primary modes of political demand generated by social change, which had an obvious tendency respectively to polarize and to evangelize politics. Two less evident effects of the general increase in political demands generated by change must be considered, before we look into the internal Revolution for confirmation of these speculations.

3. Lee Benson, in his social reinterpretation of Beard, spoke of a social experience other than the insular experience of inland America. He spoke of an urbane, cosmopolitan experience, an eastern, largely urban world of wealth and high education. Presumably, the leaders of this world were as close to politically modernized men as could be found. Alexander Hamilton might be their quintessential product, although his vision of a commercialized, industrialized society led by an almost demonically manipulative elite went rather beyond the cosmopolitanism of this culture. Still, these were the men who had experienced diverse interests, the ups and downs of the market place, the power of the British State and, through reading history, experienced still greater vagaries of human experience. They were not isolated, they knew that men are interdependent as much as independent and, if most of them clung to an ideal of unity, most also knew that the ideal of a spontaneous homogeneity of values was unrealizable. They tended to see unity as a fragile product of wise leadership such as they might themselves supply. Quite evidently, they had their constituents, however these were held—by awe, lease, employ or common interests—for these men were elected to power even after the Revolution.

Very well, the point is that I am *not* about to speak directly of this culture or primarily of its constituents. What I wish to propose now is the increase, under the impact of the social and political changes listed, of the proportion of society which was modernized in a further sense; namely, in that they were prepared to accept a vision of society and politics identical to that presented in James Madison's *Federalist* No. 10. To be specific, I propose that an ever greater minority of men were prepared to agree that:

1. The first fact of human existence is that individuals are different in their abilities and in their perceptions.

2. This leads to the fact that society will tend to be a mixture of

differing interests and beliefs. The able will become rich and strive against the poor, and vice versa. Those with a talent for trade will at times conflict with those engaged in manufactures. Further, differing personal ambitions or religious convictions or visions of society or mere frivolities and fads will create still other clashes.

3. Because individual differences are ineradicable, it is not possible to eliminate this diversity by creating in all men the same opinions, the same passions, the same beliefs.

4. It is in any event wrong to suppress the differences in interest or belief which arise from the differences between unique individuals because a man does not truly exist if he cannot express himself through his own chosen pattern of avocations and convictions.

5. Enlightened statesmen will not always be available to adjust the resulting clash of interests for the good of the whole society.

6. Therefore, society and politics will and should be a world where individuals select from among many interests and convictions, and in which a multitude of groups united on particular interests or convictions strive for power.

7. The structure of government must be such as to balance these strivings so as to create order.

It is not by accident that I refer to these beliefs as "modern." They are similar to the attitudinal syndrome which Alex Inkeles found in his "modern" men as he interviewed them in a number of developing nations. The acceptance of diversity, the commitment to individual action in pursuit of individual goals, the conception of politics as an arena where these goals contest and the awareness of a national government which is at once the source of political power and the framework for an orderly clash of interest are all characteristic of "modern man."

Where do I imagine such men came from? From the cosmopolitan areas described by Benson but also from the increasingly dense, diverse, out-mobile areas which did not share the wealth of cosmopolitan America. A better question would be, why do I think there was an increasing proportion of men prepared to subscribe to such a view? Because our evidence indicates that an increasing proportion of Americans lived in an ever more diverse social environment in which ever more interests were ever more openly contending. While this merely disturbed some men and/or set them into action for or against specific interests, it seems plausible that an increasing minority would have experienced enough diversity to cross an attitudinal threshold. They would have been involved in enough conflicts over land, religion, taxes, local politics, etc., would have participated in enough commercial transactions, would have moved about enough and encountered enough men with views different from their own and would have read enough of the still more multifarious outside world to realize that the world was of far too great a diversity to be reduced to unity. It would be evident that neither sermons nor wise leaders could bring homogeneity out of that polyectic of interests which these men had come to realize was normal. Nor would they want either to happen, for in that polyectic they now found their indentities. They now defined themselves in terms of their choices.

Richard Bushman has described this sort of process in his *Puritan to Yankee*. It is broadly the process by which Inkeles' "modern" men were modernized, though their change of attitude seems to depend a great deal on very specific socializing contexts which may or may not have existed in equivalent form in eighteenth-century America. (This needs some looking into. Lawrence Cremin's new book on colonial education argues suggestively that increasingly in the eighteenth-century colonial schools provided contexts of socialization quite like those provided by schools in Inkeles' developing countries. A close examination of the political culture of Van Beck Hall's moderately commercialized towns may tell us whether these provided the contexts in which a "modern" attitudinal syndrome was emerging.) For now, however, there seem to be general grounds for hypothesizing the growth of a latently modernized group, possessing the manipulative individualism of Inkeles' modern man and prepared for the ideology of the tenth *Federalist*. For such men the Revolution would have come as an additionally liberating force, exposing them further to the diversities of human society and bringing all old ideologies into question. They were ripe for the time when someone would describe society as they saw it and endorse their freedom to act.

So far, I am suggesting that the social changes of the eighteenth century did more than polarize society along lines of wealth, interest and opportunity. I think it possible that on the one hand social changes latently mobilized a large segment of the rural population in defense of a world view which might be called pre-modern. The Revolution completed this mobilization by offering a crusading ideology under which this segment of society could undertake political action, which otherwise their own world view condemned. In many respects this movement coincided with the men and areas most hurt by the polarization of society, but its motives went far beyond an immediate concern over lessening opportunity into realms of fear, reaction and revivalism which no amount of deprivation real or imagined can explain. This was an ethos which did not stop at the rational in its response to the changes of the day. Yet I also believe that out of the total experience of diversity and of political mobilization there emerged ever more men with an acceptance of the clash of interests and beliefs, men who literally found themselves in the choices they had to or wanted to make. These "modernized" men were still few, but as they were too many to be merely the leaders and mediators of society, they formed a constituency.

4. Finally, we must ask what happened to the old colonial elite in the midst of all this change.[6]

Charles Sydnor, Robert Wier and most recently Robert Zemsky have shown that for the larger part of the eighteenth century a rather wealthy elite was allowed to run colonial politics, only occasionally challenged by lesser leaders or by the voters. Wier and Zemsky seem to feel that the deference shown this elite arose from the conviction that it served real functions. Wier implies that the members of the elite were seen as the mediators of society. Men had come to accept that there would be contending interests, and even to value somewhat each individual's freedom to advance his interests, yet they still craved homogeneity. They still felt that somewhere beneath all interests lay a common good which should be brought to the fore and which should prevail over any individual interest. They looked to the elite for the wisdom which would perceive the common good and for the skill which would unite society behind that good, without unduly repressing any individual. Presumably the experience and education which accompanied wealth would equip the elite for this difficult task, while wealth itself would insulate the elite from the biases of self-interest. Zemsky puts it more cautiously, observing that the

Figure I

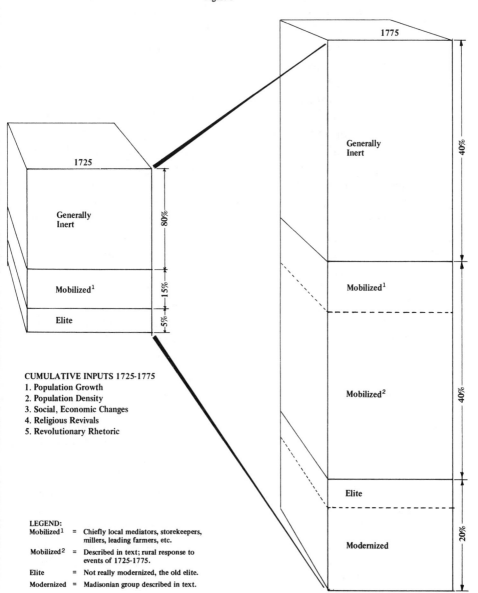

1775

Generally
Inert

40%

1725

Generally
Inert

80%

Mobilized[1]

15%

Elite

5%

Mobilized[1]

Mobilized[2]

40%

CUMULATIVE INPUTS 1725-1775
1. Population Growth
2. Population Density
3. Social, Economic Changes
4. Religious Revivals
5. Revolutionary Rhetoric

Elite

Modernized

20%

LEGEND:
Mobilized[1] = Chiefly local mediators, storekeepers, millers, leading farmers, etc.

Mobilized[2] = Described in text; rural response to events of 1725-1775.

Elite = Not really modernized, the old elite.

Modernized = Madisonian group described in text.

leisure and education which went with wealth at least made the elite the logical men to clarify policy choices. One might add that the adornments of wealth also made the elite the logical spokesmen for constituents whom a haughty Imperial bureaucracy was inclined to regard as hayseeds.

From this perspective the social changes of the eighteenth century would appear to have fortified the position of the elite. A society whose members longed for homogeneity might well have reacted to ever increasing diversity by relying ever more on the aristocratic mediators whom current ideology recommended. Likewise interested minorities would carry their cases to the existing leadership for an adjudication which if not favorable would at least not be repressive. As issues multiplied, the need for a leadership skilled in clarifying choices would increase apace. And the more socially distinct the local elite, the more impressive would be its credentials for dealing with English politicians in the interest of its constituents.

But this must have had limits. Both Wier and Zemsky made it clear that the deference shown the elite was never slavish dependence. To the contrary, the elite was watched closely, and its decisions might be ignored as often as followed. Confidence in the elite might easily have dissipated if it failed to perform as expected under the increasing demands of the day.

And if my description of the social changes of the eighteenth century is correct, demands on the political system must have been increasing at a tremendous rate. In America the growth of the population constantly outpaced the extension of political institutions so that each officer of state served an ever larger constituency. More important, the increasing pace of social differentiation in the eighteenth century led to an increase in per capita demands on the political system. Men pressed for this or that land scheme, this or that decision on the support of a pauper, this or that policy on currency, this or that exemption for a sect. The opportunities for the elite to fail multiplied proportionately. They were expected to resolve the conflicts of society without regard to their singular interests, their performance was watched and they were presented with ever more chances to dissatisfy someone with their decisions. I do not see how any idealized mediating group can survive such a situation.

It was more than a matter of unprecedented demands exhausting the limited credibility of a mediating group. I would argue that the credibility of the mediating elite was declining for more specific reasons. Their wealth and their personal and regional interests diverged ever more from those of the majorities in their respective colonies. Hence they could have become increasingly suspect in the eyes at least of certain regions, regions ever more conscious of their own ever more crucial interests. Further, if I am correct, the American populace was politically activated in two other senses, each of which served to undermine trust in the elite. On the one hand the traditional desire for homogeneity was sharpened by increasing diversity. Many men may have demanded a return to a simplicity far more extreme than anything the elite was prepared to impose. On the other hand an increasing proportion of men were reaching that stage of political sophistication at which they rejected the idea of a mediating elite because they knew that there were no men intelligent and impartial enough to impose any kind of valid unity on the diversities of society. Both groups, incidentally, may have been abetted by men with more conventional attitudes who, because of the ever smaller supply of high offices in proportion to demand, had been unable to find what they considered the proper political recognition of their relative status in their communities. Lastly we should not rule out the possibility that, whether out of temporary straits or developing greed, the elite actually gave in to the growing temptations of interest politics with greater frequency, thereby diminishing their own credit.

If half of these developments are borne out by evidence, the colonial elite was in a precarious situation by the eve of the Revolution. This suggests several things. In the first place, whether consciously or otherwise the members of the elite may have welcomed the constitutional crisis with Britain as an opportunity to restore their credibility by leading all Americans to the high ground of common principle. That was what elites were for—to discern the common interest, to sound the alarm when it was threatened and to unite society in its defense. By leading the early agitation against British impositions, the elite was not only fighting to preserve the constitutional basis for its own power, which is obvious, but also perhaps striving to recapture a dwindling popular deference by acting out the classic role which ideology prescribed for it.

This would, however, be a most difficult proposition to test. For by the very act of bypassing the colonial governments, Britain forced colonial leaders to strengthen their ties with their colonial constituency and ultimately to find in this constituency a new source of authority. So of course we will find the elite using the crisis to mobilize their constituents behind them, and such evidence will not prove that the elite was using the crisis to redeem itself from internal mistrust. The proof of this proposition will have to come from the period before the revenue acts. We would want to look for evidence that consciously or otherwise colonial leaders of the 1740s and 50s used conflicts with British authority in order to maintain their leadership over increasingly mistrustful constituents. By keeping tensions at a high point, the elite could have demonstrated the necessity for its continued existence. Having such evidence, we might then presume that this syndrome carried over into the early stages of the revolutionary crisis.

Yet this evidence still does not prove that the principle at stake in the crisis was not real or that it was not worth a war. Nor does it contradict the belief that a genuine sense of nationality evolved which further justified the war. In the case of our increasingly discredited elite searching for a way to reassert its value in its traditional role, as in the case of our fearful agrarians in search of a purgative crusade, I am only pointing out that certain groups may have responded to the revolutionary crisis in part because it appeared to offer a resolution to the problems presented by a changing society. I think the same thing occurred, to a much lesser extent, among men concerned about and/or affected by declining opportunity, the concentration of wealth and the polarization of society and of interests. They, too, may have seen in the coming crisis an opportunity to set things right within America. But in all cases I must admit that I regard these only as interesting overtones of an Imperial crisis which might have arisen and probably have run its course to war, had American society been fully as static as it is usually conceived as being.

Accordingly, what seems more significant is the possibility that we entered the period of intense political debate which followed independence, led by an elite whose competence and ideological justification were increasingly under fire as a result of changes in the society. It appears likely that this did happen. If my assumptions are correct, the elite's role in the movement for independence would not suffice to protect an individual leader or to renew for long the validity of the elitist principle of leadership. For one thing, by no means all of the elite were able to follow the alarm they had raised, all the way through to independence; that point gave many pause, and their pause eroded much of the credit they as a group had acquired early in the crisis. Moreover the social changes which were undermining the elite were not undone by the Revolution. These continued, while revolutionary rhetoric added a further source of political mobilization. If it were true that the elite emerged from the crisis of independence still pressed to justify the existence of a class of wealthy and disinterested social mediators, worthy of deference, we should expect to see their effort at self-justification as a major theme in the internal political debates which led to the Constitution.

In sum, if the changes in American society during the eighteenth century affected politics, I would expect the effects to take four major forms:[7] primarily (1) unprecedentedly acute interpersonal and interregional differences in wealth, in social status, in political power, in economic interest and in material prospects and (2) the latent mobilization of a profoundly reactionary rural world view; (3) a growing if still small constituency for an ideology of pluralistic individualism and (4) a political elite pushed as never before to justify its existence. I would also suggest that while rural reactionaries and a frightened elite probably intensified the movement toward independence, it is more important to study the impact of all four themes on the internal political debates which followed upon independence.

(None of these themes is entirely original. Professor Main is refining the first to a high degree; Richard Morris, Lee Benson and Alan Heimert have offered brief versions of the second; the third is rather close to other conclusions of Alan Heimert [and to current research by Richard Brown]; while a variant of the last has been hinted at by Gordon Wood and by Jack Greene. But in this case the themes gain credence because they emerge from the work of students of colonial society, who have no interpretive axe to grind when it comes to the Revolution. Further, the fact that all four themes derive from social change gives them an organic unity which enhances the power as part of an explanatory model. Finally, the emphasis on social change as the source of each theme facilitates the refinement and the validation of each theme.)

IV

There is no question that the four themes, although derived from a study of colonial America alone, emerge clearly in Gordon Wood's analysis of the political debates of the Revolution itself. The growing political contention of organized and differing interests, the reactionary desire to end such contention and such differences, the efforts of an elite to retrieve lost respect and the evolution of James Madison toward a newly skeptical political ideology suffuse this tale of the creation of the American Republic. And in several cases Professor Wood explicitly suggests that these themes arose from long-term changes in the society, basing this on his reading of the statements of the time. For the moment this would seem to me sufficient indication that social change, abetted by the Revolution, did give rise to the political themes anticipated and that these themes did enter into the dynamics of the internal Revolution.

While all four responses to social change were essential to the inimitably complex process which led to the Federal Constitution, Wood emphasizes that two of these responses fueled that debate and gave it its structure. On the one hand was a reactionary republicanism which sought to restore virtue and unity to American society, and which saw in the will of the local community the means of accomplishing this reform. As Wood points out, this ideology represented an almost quixotic attempt to vanquish the inevitable differentiation of society together with all its consequences. Or it would have been quixotic, had it not been so Puritanical. On the other hand was a shocked political elite, whose revolutionary credentials had not been sufficient to persuade an increasingly mobilized public to elect representatives for their wisdom. In their search for a sufficiently republican political frame which would nonetheless restore wise leadership, they inadvertently came up with a frame which would require neither popular virtue nor wise leadership—the Federal Constitution.

Yet at the same time another battle was raging at the level of political interests, a struggle whose contestants were partly identi-

cal to the contestants in the struggle between localistic republicanism and elite leadership. Men and regions who felt their unique
interests had been shunted aside by selfish establishments reached
out for power and came into organized contention with the
defenders of established interests. Regardless of the victor, this
increasingly overt struggle over more different interests guaranteed
that any new political framework would recognize men's right to
participate freely in the clash, as indeed the Constitution did.

Madison, a participant in the former battle and spectator of the
latter, moved the ideas embodied in the tenth *Federalist*, to wit
that neither the popular will nor wise leaders could be relied upon,
and that the state should be a just and stable arena for the clash of
interests. While his startlingly modern ideas did not entirely prevail,
he was a persuasive man whose ideas drew enough response to help
win ratification of the Constitution and who in fact described the
result in terms of a new ideology.[8]

Thus, as Wood's book seems to confirm, the four anticipated
responses to social change were involved in providing the framework of the new nation. It becomes impossible to imagine the
Revolution as anything but an event which took place in a
changing society or the Constitution as anything but the product
of such a society.

V

Was the process a "modernization"? It was a thing unto itself,
as any reader of Gordon Wood knows. Moderate social changes
away from a somewhat simple past whose simplicity was exaggerated by myth led to a complex but largely latent political
mobilization. The onset of a colonial war for independence
encouraged the political expression of the resulting social concerns
while adding a few concerns of its own. Several concerns arising
from social change then appear to have dominated the resulting
political debate. There was of course a generalized pressure for
more responsive government. Beneath this lay a rather tense
dialogue among polarizing interests and, more prominently, a
debate between a reactionary rural world view and an increasingly
outmoded elite. There was also an expansion of a constituency for
an individualistic ideology which accepted social diversity. Yet,
while the political outcome lent itself to such an ideology, there
was never any large-scale modernization of political attitudes and

the modernization was chiefly in the result. Largely inadvertently, the Constitution was what Madison said it was—a framework suitable for a mobilized society, with full leeway for the activities through which modernized individuals could realize themselves.

While it may not have fit a classic pattern, there was a great advantage implicit in this premature process. The varied impulses arising from the conjuncture of moderate social change with a colonial war for independence had produced quite unexpectedly an ideology and a political framework which would help America survive the strains of eventual modernization. We entered the age of industrialization, urbanization and immigration with a Constitution designed to accommodate contending interests. Ready at hand was an ideology which accepted such contention and endorsed the manipulative individual it would produce. Had the process been otherwise, the results might have been more constraining, and our vaunted Anglo-Saxon heritage might have proved less than enough to bring us intact through the crises of social modernization. Historians of the American Revolution may be surprised to hear an interpreter begin with social change and social polarization, and end with the conclusion that it was all for the best, yet that is the conclusion to be drawn from the evidence. It has been suggested before; Gordon Wood implies exactly this. Wood from his starting point and I from mine have come to view the Revolution as a unique and complex process whose result in the form of the Constitution was ultimately beneficial to America. The old attachments to any particular group or ideology become irrelevant when the Revolution is viewed as process.

Yet in the end the results of the whole process probably should not be described so optimistically. The Constitution only accommodated the present and future tensions of American society; it did not resolve them, and the social trends which created those tensions went on unchecked. Indeed, such philosophy as was implicit in the Constitution required that no move be taken to alter the development of the society. This philosophy was all very well when placed against the alternatives of a constantly interfering elite or a constantly interfering majority, but in the long run it did nothing to protect men raised on a heritage of rural isolation, independence and homogeneity. Furthermore, Madison's unrestrained individual might express himself in free competition by acquiring slaves or amassing immense industrial wealth. Eventually, certain of the free society's diversities and above all its accumulating inequalities would seem quite unbearable to many Americans. By that time it would be necessary to ask whether rural reactionism had not contained a grain of organic truth.

Postscript: The Devil's Advocate

The difficulties of this interpretation are too numerous to mention, but to list just a few:

1. Were any or all of the social changes listed really taking place, especially outside New England? How can we put these changes into testable form?

2. How do we know that any or all of the hypothesized responses to these changes actually took place? Gordon Wood musters considerable evidence that people were reacting to change, but the qualities of their reactions need to be further assessed. Even if their reactions take the predicted forms, it will remain possible that the turmoil of the Revolution itself, juxtaposed on an idealized portrait of the American past, created an impression of long-term change where in fact there was none. People were merely reacting to an impression, and the whole process was contained within the Revolution itself. Accordingly we must pay particular attention to the period immediately preceding the Revolution and look there for the types of political reactions hypothesized.

3. It is true that the themes stressed in this essay by no means exhaust the ways in which Americans may have perceived and reacted to the social changes of the eighteenth century. In this realm of evolving social perception lies the greatest opportunity for the historian of the American consciousness.

In sum, the limitations of this paper are obvious. The only reply is that we have evidence both of many real changes in eighteenth-century society and of the role of complex responses to social change in the Revolution. Given this evidence, we can hardly continue to treat the American Revolution as an event which took place in a society preserved in amber.

FOOTNOTES

1. The Bibliography lists publications referred to in the text.

2. Net upward intergenerational property mobility is here defined as the net proportion of sons surpassing their fathers in property at a given age.

3. This can also be stated as, "in 1770 as opposed to 1720 a greater (net) proportion of American males would be expected to":

4. These parameters are hypothetical.

5. As far as I know, only Daniel Scott Smith, and Rhys Isaac of La Trobe University in Australia, have attempted to trace such social changes through human perceptions to ultimate political behavior; their work is not yet complete.

6. Here defined as colonials serving in even minor positions of leadership in lower houses of assembly, or in higher colonial positions up to and including Royal offices and patronage positions, prior to 1775. When used for the post-1776 era, "elite" also includes men who believed in a mediating elite as described here and saw themselves as members of that elite. The elite as here defined overlaps extensively with Benson's cosmopolitan elite.

7. Not mutually exclusive.

8. This theme is being investigated with great sophistication by Rhys Isaac, who is giving particular attention to the effects of social change on political perception within Madison's native Virginia.

BIBLIOGRAPHY

Bailyn, Bernard, "Politics and Social Structure in Virginia," James M. Smith, ed., *Seventeenth-Century America* (Chapel Hill, 1959).

Benson, Lee, *Turner and Beard* (Glencoe, Illinois, 1960).

Berthoff, Rowland and Murrin, John, "Feudalism, Communalism, and the Yeoman Freeholder: The American Revolution Considered as a Social Accident," presented at the Williamsburg Conference on the American Revolution, March 1971.

Brown, Richard D., "Modernization and the Modern Personality in America, 1600-1865: A Sketch of a Synthesis," delivered at the session on Social Change and the Revolution, O.A.H. Meeting, New Orleans, 1971, and published in the *Journal of Interdisciplinary History*, II (Winter, 1972).

Bushman, Richard L., *From Puritan to Yankee; Character and the Social Order in Connecticut 1690-1765*, (Cambridge, 1967).

Cremin, Lawrence A., *American Education: The Colonial Experience* (N.Y., 1970).

Greene, Jack P., "Search for Identity: An Interpretation of the Meaning of Selected Patterns of Social Response in Eighteenth-Century America," *Journal of Social History*, III (Spring, 1970).

Hall, Van Beck, paper on commercialization and political behavior in Massachusetts' towns in the 1780s, given at the Brandeis Conference on New England Towns, 1970, from an unpublished Ph.D. dissertation at the University of Wisconsin, 1969.

Heimert, Alan, *Religion and the American Mind from the Revolution to the Great Awakening* (Cambridge, 1966).

Inkeles, Alex, see a forthcoming book to be titled *Making Men Modern;* also "The Modernization of Man" in *Modernization*, Myron Weiner, ed., (N.Y., 1966); and

"Making Men Modern; on the Causes and Consequences of Individual Change in Six Developing Countries," *American Journal of Sociology*, 1969. These articles refer back to other publications describing the Inkeles project.

Main, Jackson Turner, *The Social Structure of Revolutionary America* (Princeton, 1966); "Political Parties in Maryland, 1780-1787," *Maryland Historical Magazine*, 1967; and see his forthcoming book on state political parties in the 1780s.

Morris, Richard, "The Confederation Period and the American Historian," *William and Mary Quarterly*, XIII (1956).

Syndor, Charles, *Gentlemen Freeholders: Political Practices in Washington's Virginia* (Chapel Hill, 1952).

Ver Steeg, Clarence, *The Formative Years, 1607-1763* (N.Y., 1964).

Walzer, Michael, *Revolution of the Saints* (Cambridge, 1965).

Wier, Robert, "The Harmony We Were Famous For: An Interpretation of Pre-Revolutionary South Carolina Politics," *William and Mary Quarterly*, XXVI (1969).

Wolf, Eric, "Closed Corporate Peasant Communities in Mesoamerica and Central Java," *Southwestern Journal of Anthropology*, XIII (Spring, 1957); *Peasants* (Englewood Cliffs, New Jersey, 1966).

Wood, Gordon, *The Creation of the American Republic, 1776-1789* (Chapel Hill, 1969).

Zemsky, Robert, "Power, Influence, and Status: Leadership Patterns in the Massachusetts Assembly, 1740-1765," *William and Mary Quarterly*, XXVI (1969).

Zuckerman, Michael, *Peaceable Kingdoms: Massachusetts Towns in the Eighteenth Century* (N.Y., 1970).

14.

WORKING-CLASS CULTURE AND POLITICS IN THE INDUSTRIAL REVOLUTION: SOURCES OF LOYALISM AND REBELLION[1]

Alan Dawley and Paul Faler

I

It is the goal of revolution to change human nature. All the major political revolutions of modern times have tried to create a new kind of person liberated from the corruption of the old order: the Citizen of the French Revolution, the Proletarian Hero of the Bolsheviks, the New Man and New Woman of Cuba and China. The same is true of the Industrial Revolution. It gave birth to a new person among the laboring classes of Europe and America, one who put his/her own needs ahead of the demands of kin and community, who acknowledged no master but the self, and who located the virtues of self-control, self-denial, and self-improvement at the center of the moral universe. To working people, long accustomed to servitude and other forms of personal subordination, this new individualism fomented a fundamental challenge to customary ways of living. It divided people along cultural lines between the traditionally minded, who clung to old values and beliefs, and the modern-minded, who adopted the new personality. Further, the modern-minded worker, coming of age in the industrial era and faced with brutal attacks on his/her new-found sense of personal dignity, wrestled with the question of whether to be loyal to the system of industrial capitalism or to rebel against it. The central task of this essay is to sort out the origins of loyalism from the origins of rebellion, and to assess the relative historical impact of both.

We will proceed to that task in a moment, after setting out the boundaries of the subject. Although the ideas herein have a broad relevance to industrialization wherever it has occurred, we focus on the political and cultural experience of workers in the United States. We worked out the basic analysis in exhaustive studies of the shoe industry and the shoemaking community of Lynn, Massachusetts.[2] The shoe industry was of considerable importance to the American economy in the nineteenth century, second only to textiles at mid-century in numbers employed and product value. Its capital, its technology, and the bulk of its labor were all home-grown, and so its roots reach deep into the American economic subsoil. Lynn, for its part, was the largest center in the industry and was more fully dominated by shoe manufacturing than its close rival, Philadelphia. Together, then, Lynn and the shoe industry were a microcosm of the Industrial Revolution.

We have attempted to bridge the microcosm of Lynn and the macrocosm of the Industrial Revolution. Recognizing that the Lynn experience was not the only route to industrialization, we have attempted to take from Lynn only those ideas about the whole process that have some verification in the specific circumstances of other communities. Thus it may be that Lynn had more than its share of rebel workers while Boston abounded in bread-and-butter loyalists and Pittsburgh was filled with traditionally minded peasants, but this tripartite division between rebels, loyalists, and traditionalists appeared everywhere as the basic cultural cleavage among American working people through most of the nineteenth century. The time boundaries of the essay run from the rise of industrial capitalism in the Era of Good Feeling to its supremacy in the Gilded Age.

Lynn embarked on the path of industrialism in the 1820s and 1830s when a reorganization in the production of shoes underminded the old artisan/mercantile way of life and created a new social structure based on capitalist manufacturers and wage earners, the two core groups of the industrial class system. In the same two decades, the community saw the beginnings of industrial class conflict (strike organizations), the formation of working-class institutions (journeymen's societies and workingmen's parties), and the emergence of a new industrial culture – all before the advent of the factory system. The importance of this period is underlined by the fact that the main ideas, forms of organization, and social cleavages that developed before the factories would persist for a full generation under the factory system.[3]

None of these early innovations was more far-reaching than a new industrial morality. This moral code was characterized by a panoply of individualist values: self-discipline, self-control, and self-reliance. "Trust thyself," Emerson intoned, "every heart vibrates to that iron string." The code promised self-fulfillment through the faithful devotion to regular habits of toil. It stressed the virtue of work for its own sake, not as an expression of some higher calling. It demanded industry (labor aimed at self-improvement), frugality (economic self-sacrifice), and temperance (sensual self-denial). In the new code of morality, the self was at once supreme and suppressed, deified and denied, liberated and enchained.

Industrial morality bore a certain resemblance to an earlier set of virtues. It is clear that industry, frugality, and temperance had preindustrial (though not precapitalist) origins, and that an ethic of competitive individualism had put in an appearance among eighteenth-century laboring classes (among mechanics, at any rate, if not slaves, servants, or common laborers). But it is equally clear that the moral universe in which these values appeared remained bounded by traditional forms, and that those forms were broken only by the rise of industrial capitalism in the nineteenth century. In preindustrial times, individualism had been incorporated into a pattern of deference to social superiors, but in the new setting individualism was alloyed with a belief in equality of opportunity.[4] At one time industry had meant hard work; now it was redefined as devotion to a methodical work routine. Frugality was once consistent with charity; now it became associated with a definition of poverty as crime and a new stringency in poor relief. Temperance once meant moderation in drinking habits and prudent sexuality; now it was redefined as total abstinence and prudish sexuality. Thus, the new values were the result of the reassertion of traditional attitudes in new surroundings and represent both the effort of preindustrial America to keep itself going along traditional lines and the failure of that effort. This paradox of change emerging from an effort to conserve the past pervades American history in the 1820s and 1830s. To take another example, the Jacksonian movement sought to restore the foundations of the old Republic, but instead fostered the new democratic styles in politics and the very expansion in industry that undermined it.[5] The dialectical process of breakdown and repair thus resulted in the creation of something quite different than was intended.

We emphasize that industrial morality was a general feature of the industrial class system as a whole, not the particular values of one class within the system. It was neither bourgeois nor proletarian. It caused businessmen to organize the Society for the Promotion of Industry, Frugality, and Temperance, and prompted wage earners to join the Washingtonian Total Abstinence Society. It inspired businessmen to promote their new Institution for Savings with appeals to popular thriftiness, and it encouraged many working families to practice thrift at the expense of current living standards.[6]

Because industrial morality defined what industrial workers and industrial capitalists had in common with one another, it also defined how their values differed from the libertine culture of preindustrial class systems. The contrast is most striking when we compare industrial morality with the culture of slavery: individualism versus paternalism; the work ethic versus an ethic of leisure; free labor versus bond labor. Just as the industrial classes drew upon a common cultural reservoir, so, too, the classes of slavery drew their values from common preindustrial sources. Despite vast inequalities between slaves and masters, they shared certain cultural outlooks that set them farther apart from the industrial classes than from each other.[7] (This point will take on added importance later when we consider the political impact of the Civil War.)

Industrial morality was a source of cleavage within the working class between "traditional" and "modern" values. As each generation of preindustrial laborers came into contact with industrialism, some adopted the new code, while others rejected it and clung to preindustrial values. We term the latter "traditionalists" because they refused to give up their casual attitudes toward work, their pursuit of happiness in gaming and drinking, and the raucous revelry that accompanied fire and militia musters. Traditionalists still deferred to the silk vest, the gold watch, and the ivory-handled cane, still expected a rum ration from their employers, and still claimed Saturday afternoon and Monday morning as their own time. In 1820 virtually all the shoemakers in Lynn were traditionalists, and continual infusions of people with preindustrial backgrounds from the hills of New Hampshire and the rills of County Cork insured that a variety of traditional customs would persist well into the industrial period.

A second group adopted the new morality, and we term them "modernists." In terms of moral character, modernist workers resembled their employers (most of whom were also modernists) more than they did their traditionalist co-workers. They joined their employers in shunning the very things traditionalists cherished — the warm sociability of the drinking club, the "wasteful" amusement of the circus and the Jim Crow show, the easygoing work rhythm.[8]

If morality were the only determinant of behavior, then neither group of workers would have mounted an organized challenge to their employers — the traditionalists because they believed their employers were their betters and the modernists because they believed their employers were no different than themselves. But other factors threw wage earners into conflict with their employers and tapped industrial morality as both a motivation for struggle and as a means

to wage that struggle. The economic changes of the industrial revolution intensified competition among wage earners, cheapened their skills, undercut their
security, attacked their standard of living, increased their dependency, and
lowered their social position. In each case these changes conflicted head-on with
the values of industrial morality: self-reliance, self-discipline, and self-improvement. Given the situation in which scores of people were dependent upon a
single individual for their livelihood, what other recourse was there for those
who believed in equal rights and self-improvement but to take collective action?
Social and economic changes impelled the individualism of the modernists in
collective directions toward the mutualism of the benefit society, the fraternity
of the lodge, the common front of collective bargaining, and the solidarity of the
strike.

All the modernists were caught up in this process, but not all in the same
way. Some hastened its work; they devoted all their spare time to the moral
elevation of the laboring classes, sold subscriptions to labor newspapers, canvassed the town to promote support for a strike, and, after attending a temperance rally on Friday, spoke at a meeting of the journeymen's society on
Saturday. Others, however, slowed the process; they subscribed to a community
newspaper but not a labor journal, told the canvasser a strike was ill-advised, and
spoke at the temperance rally, but probably did not attend the journeymen's
meeting. In other words, the modernists subdivided into two different groups;
the first we term "rebels," the second, "loyalists." The rebels laid the foundations of the labor movement, saw sobriety and literacy as matters of self-pride
and as means to proclaim their independence from the external commands of
employer and liquor, and did not shrink from the prospect of a strike. On the
other hand, loyalists held aloof from the labor movement (or joined only in a
crisis), wore their sobriety and literacy as badges of middle-class respectability,
and tried to evade the issue of class conflict altogether. It is this division between
rebels and loyalists that commands our attention for the remainder of the essay.

Since rebels and loyalists shared the same underlying moral character, they
did not part company with each other (or with their bosses) over this cultural
issue. Rather, they divided over the question of political economy. Where the
loyalists saw an overriding mutuality of interests between labor and capital,
offset only by minor differences, the rebels saw an overriding antagonism, offset
only by minor points of agreement. To the loyalist, capital and labor were
mutually dependent, and each was entitled to a just reward – the entrepreneur a
fair profit, the laborer a fair wage. To the rebel, however, capital and labor stood
in direct opposition, since the interest of the former was to get as much work
from the latter for the lowest possible wage.

The explanation for this difference in outlook – a difference with vital
bearing on the question of class consciousness – lies in part outside the realm of
culture. A long period of economic prosperity reinforced the loyalist position,
while depression reinforced the rebels; by the same token, the loyalist argument
made more sense to well-paid, secure, skilled workers than to people who were
poorly paid and insecure (indeed, the true labor aristocrats in the shoe industry
– the cutters – were unquestionably the most loyal). But below the level of the
cutters, alignments were only tendencies, not hard and fast lines of demarcation.
In fact, the two outlooks cut across skill and wage differentials and must be
understood first on their own ground as cultural phenomena.

The breach in outlook was caused by the rebels' application of artisan radicalism to their own situation. They updated the egalitarian ideas of the American Revolution, the French Revolution, and English Jacobinism,[9] and combined them with the labor theory of value to produce an incisive critique of industrial capitalism. Believing that only labor could create value, they concluded that capital was nothing but the congealed labor of the producing classes. By itself, capital was inert and lifeless, not the living "head" of production, as the loyalists believed. Rebels argued that the large manufacturer who no longer performed labor in the shop and whose control over production rested exclusively on his ownership of capital was both a parasite and a thief. A Lynn cordwainer explained the labor theory of value to the readers of *The Awl* in 1844: "Is it not clear that the businessman stands debtor to the world for all which he receives over and above the amount of labor given? And is it not equally clear that the mechanic, I mean particularly the mechanics of Lynn, receives *less* than a compensation for the amount of labor given? It appears, therefore, that the world stands debtor to the mechanic for this surplus labor."[10] Pursuing this logic, rebels further contended that because the rise of capitalist manufacturing had divided labor from capital, and because labor suffered the consequences, the only road to reunion of labor and capital and the only ultimate remedy for the plight of the laborer was cooperative ownership.

This is as far as the early rebels took the labor theory. They were not Marxian socialists. While their views showed an affinity for socialism, largely because socialism rested on the same theory, they did not propose to seize existing private property rights. Nor were they middle-class reformers. While they often stood shoulder to shoulder with petty bourgeois democrats listening to some agrarian or currency reformer hawk his particular panacea, they maintained a distinct identity of their own. Some historians with ideological commitments to pure and simple trade unionism have mistaken the rebels as utopian middle-class meddlers, but these writers have missed their mark. The rebels were bona fide wage earners, not some offshoot of middle-class reformers.[11] Nor were they muddle-headed reactionaries who opposed the whole advance of industrialism; unlike the traditionalists, they did not seek cures for present ills in a return to the world of the past.

The accomplishments of the rebels were considerable and were far out of proportion to their numbers. A distinct minority, the rebels were, nonetheless, the catalytic element in Lynn and in the American working class as a whole. Their penchant for autodidacticism, their self-discipline, and their high level of literacy gave them the personal skills necessary to be effective organizers, and they took the lead in establishing unions, cooperatives, newspapers, workingmen's parties, and central labor councils. They authored the most incisive criticisms of industrial capitalism one can find in the annals of nineteenth-century social protest, and their ideas dominated the mainstream of the labor movement from the journeymen's societies and workingmen's parties of the 1830s through the National Labor Union, the Eight-Hour Movement, and the Knight of Labor after the Civil War. Thus the most vigorous opponents and the most trenchant critics of industrial capitalism were those workers who had accepted cultural values which they shared with their employers but used in their own class interest.

The foregoing discussion has shown that industrial morality was both a source of accord and a source of discord between labor and capital. Neither the stability of the industrial class system nor a revolutionary threat from below could be predicted on the basis of cultural influences alone. Thus before we make any final judgments on the fundamental cleavages of nineteenth-century American history, we must assess the weight of other factors. We will look further at the impact of economic changes before turning later to a consideration of political influences.

II

Surely the record of American industrial relations between the Civil War and World War II was a story of constant turbulence interrupted only intermittently by periods of relative peace. In this respect Lynn in 1860 represented what the United States would become, because in that year its shoemakers staged a massive walkout that soon became the largest strike the country had ever seen.[12]

In the five years before the strike, the chronic deterioration of the old artisan/mercantile order entered an acute phase in which the breakdown was especially severe. First, machine methods replaced hand methods in binding, the branch of the trade that had historically belonged to women. For more than a generation women had constituted about half the total workforce, but the establishment of several sewing-machine shops run as proto-factories compelled many married women with children to leave the trade completely. These changes also undermined the wages and security of women who could afford to buy a sewing machine and work at home, because household producers could only compete by accepting less pay for more work. Second, factory methods were introduced into certain branches of the trade, notably heeling, where machines had not yet been invented. Third, shoe bosses were sending an increasing part of their orders to domestic workers in the countryside, giving preference to outsiders at the expense of Lynn citizens. Lastly, the panic of 1857 lengthened into three years of hard times with resultant wage reductions and layoffs.

Virtually everyone was affected by the crisis at hand, but only the rebels had developed the methods to meet it. Only their analysis of the division between capital and labor made sense out of the recent economic changes and justified a strike as the means to combat them. Only their recognition of the need for the organization of labor and their organizing talents were adequate to the situation. In 1859 they formed the Lynn Mechanics Association and began publishing the *New England Mechanic.* In the winter of 1859-60 they called mass meetings and canvassed the city for strike support. They took the lead in a movement that gathered widespread support from loyalists and traditionalists alike, and on Washington's birthday in 1860 they led virtually the entire city out on strike.

The strike was a lesson in class conflict that strengthened the rebel outlook within the working class, even as it left the shoemakers in a weaker position vis-a-vis the manufacturers. Indeed, the very fact that the bosses had resolutely defeated the strike by sending work outside of town and importing out-of-town police to keep order verified the rebel analysis. Taken by surprise, many loyalists grew bitter over the manufacturers' resolve to defeat and disgrace them and swung over to the rebel position.

Economic changes over the next several years powerfully reinforced this trend. Although the economic squeeze was eased a bit by the return of prosperity during the war, the breakdown of the old order and the construction of the new was completed when the shoe industry converted to a full-fledged factory system by 1868, with all the accompaniments of a widening gap between capital and labor, a greater subordination of the wage earner to the owner's will, and an increasing share of wealth going to the owners. Traditionalists found it harder to hold on to the preindustrial ways, and loyalists found it harder to evade the issue of inequality. Consequently, the rebels were able to organize shoeworkers of all three types into the Knights of St. Crispin, a militant union of modern industrial workers that began its meteoric rise in Lynn in 1868.

Within two years the Knights of St. Crispin signed up more than half the male shoeworkers in the city as dues-paying members, mobilized hundreds more in a city-wide strike in 1870 that rivaled the magnitude of the Great Strike of 1860, and joined forces with the Daughters of St. Crispin, a sister organization that represented several hundred women shoeworkers. On a national scale the union's growth was equally impressive, making it the country's largest trade union. Labor historians have long recognized the importance of this remarkable group of unionists, but until very recently they have been just as mistaken in assessing who the Crispins were as they were correct in assessing their importance. Following John Commons, the original student of the order, they identified Crispins as old-time, skilled craftsmen fending off the influx of green hands.[13] Based on new evidence obtained from census information on 1000 names in the dues book of a Lynn Lodge, it is now possible to show conclusively that Commons was wrong. Crispins were not the most stable or the most highly skilled artisans, the groups who were assigned first rank in the order by the Commons interpretation. Instead, most Crispins were modern industrial workers: in terms of skill, income, property ownership, birthplace, and geographical mobility they represented a cross-section of the work force.[14]

Further insight into Crispin strength and militancy is provided by looking at three groups in the union whose background suggests traditionalism but whose behavior implies rebellion. First, Irish immigrants, who were less than a fifth of the work force, filled nearly a quarter of the Crispin membership rolls. The special Irish affinity for the union, a pattern repeated in the Knights of Labor a decade later, indicates that the factory system was fast undermining the peasant's traditional deference toward his employer and devotion to casual work rhythms. However, the size of the Irish contingent indicates the union contained men from both sides of the cultural divide — modernists who denounced the evils of demon rum for the Father Matthew Total Abstinence Society and traditionalists who found the convivial atmosphere of the drinking circle more to their liking. The union's adaptation to this hold-over from traditionalism broadened its base and put a larger army in the field under rebel leaders at strike time.

Second, Yankees from rural areas filled another quarter or more of the rolls. The small-town cobblers and farmer shoemakers who migrated to Lynn had been schooled in the values of rugged individualism, a fact which hastened their conversion to industrial morality and sharpened their reaction to the factory system. They were not used to being bossed, and their fierce independence clashed with the authoritarian rule of the factory, which not only drove them into the union but made many of them union militants.

Third, the prominence of women in Lynn's labor movement reveals the decline of patriarchy, a fundamental pillar of the traditional order. Women had benefited least from the great popular emancipations of the nineteenth-century laboring classes − the disappearance of servitude, the abolition of slavery, the opening of career opportunities, the granting of suffrage and other rights of citizenship − so that in the 1870s women retained their status as personal subordinates of their fathers and husbands. Yet the Daughters of St. Crispin, like the women strikers of 1860, held mass meetings, conducted work stoppages, and talked the rebel language of "equal rights." Clearly, the modern temper had invaded the "women's sphere" and weakened traditional beliefs. Once again, the base of the union was broadened, its position strengthened, and its militancy intensified.

As traditionalism waned, loyalism shifted ground. The inescapable inequality between employer and worker in the factory system caused the loyalists to reassess their position further, and they finally conceded the necessity for organization among the toilers. They no longer held aloof from the labor movement and even the most loyal of the loyalists, the cutters, eventually joined the Knights of Labor.

The rebels reassessed their outlook, too. In the 1870s and 1880s they showed an increasing affinity for a class analysis of the conflict between labor and capital. Crispin conventions discussed the concept of wage slavery and emphasized the abolition of the wage system through cooperation as the only true solution to the labor problem. Some of the letters in local newspapers and some of the testimony reported by the Massachusetts Bureau of the Statistics of Labor protested that the country was ruled by the industrial and financial monopolists. Some adherents of the Eight-Hour Movement located the source of social and political inequality in the exploitative process by which the worker was compelled to work a portion of each day solely for the profit of the owner. The Lynn Labor Reform party called for the nationalization of the means of communication and transportation.[15]

The overall impact of the economic changes in the shoe industry after 1860 was to reduce the cultural divisions within the working class. The factory system inducted traditionalists into the modernist viewpoint faster than any pre-factory experience. It persuaded loyalists to join the labor movement. And it produced tons of grist for the rebels' mill.

III

Taking stock of the argument so far, we have seen the development of a new type of person − one who believed that he could improve his lot in life by following a strict regimen of regular labor and by avoiding the pitfalls of excessive drink and excessive spending. In contrast to the traditionalist, who clung to the libertine morality and customs of an earlier era, the modernist lived by a tighter code of personal and social conduct that he shared with his employer. This cultural bond became the basis for political loyalty for some workers, but we have also seen an opposing development: the emergence of a rebel outlook from the clash between the worker's individualist beliefs and his actual economic situation, in which he was dependent on a money wage and subordinated to his employer's command. Further, we have seen the growing strength of the rebel outlook within the working class, the intensification of class conflict, rising organization and militancy, and the increasing affinity of the rebel outlook for a class explanation of labor's predicament.

Surely this is sufficient to demonstrate the potential for the development of a pervasive, class-conscious, radical outlook among American workers. By the 1870s workers in Lynn, as in other sections of the country, appeared ready to believe that the unequal distribution of wealth and power was caused by an interlocking economic, social, political, and cultural mechanism that brought about the oppression of all who labored with their hands.

But this potential was never fully realized. By the end of the century most workers probably linked their desire for collective self-help to a conception of labor as an interest group rather than a class. What, then, had contained the spread of radicalism? What historical alchemy had transformed rebellion into reconciliation?

The question is no less interesting for not being new. In one variation or another, it has been posed in a dozen ways ranging from the ridiculous (Daniel Bell) to the sublime (Selig Perlman).[16] The most recent answers have frequently taken one of two forms: (a) the diverse ethnic and religious origins of the American working class have divided it internally against itself, thus blocking the development of a common group identity; or (b) the high incidence of social mobility — in particular, movement up the ladder — gave workers a satisfying taste of success within the existing system and thwarted class identity.[17] While both perspectives shed considerable light on the question, and the second has opened a treasure chest of new evidence, neither constitutes a decisive solution to the problem. Diversity did not prevent the formation of the collectivist notion of labor as an interest group, and the incidence of rapid social mobility was consistent with a high level of class consciousness in several European countries.

Our own answer focuses on the intersection of working-class culture and American politics and is divided into three parts: (a) the ritual of democracy, (b) the impact of the Civil War, and (c) the interclass character of the party system.

During the 1820s and 1830s American politics became a mass ritual for the expression of popular culture. For the first time anywhere in the world, ordinary folk (at least the white males among them) regularly expressed their values and beliefs in the ongoing political process through the hoopla of conventions, the pageantry of parades, the camp-meeting style of rallies, the frenetic electioneering of voting day, and the final victory celebrations. All the bunting, brass bands, banners, and flags that festooned election campaigns merely demonstrated that politics had become a popular form of mass entertainment.

Industrial morality had a key role to play in the new ritual of democracy. Working people who believed in their own self-worth, and no longer deferred to the silk vest, the gold watch, or the ivory-handled cane, insisted that their own voices be heard and their own votes counted. Sooner or later most politicians learned to court them with phrases about the bone and sinew of society that flattered even their own high self-esteem. Democrats were the first to adopt the new style, but Whigs were not far behind, as they proved in the Log Cabin and Hard Cider campaign of 1840. The new style, with its banners, floats, and parades, thus incorporated into the election campaign itself many of the tamer features of old 'Lection day, a preindustrial festival of popular culture abolished by the Massachusetts General Court in 1831.[18] In other words, the ritual of democracy reinforced the individualist code of ethics adopted by modernist workingmen, but also provided popular entertainment for the traditionalists.

Further, the ritual emphasized the common political culture workers and employers shared. In contrast to several European countries, political democracy did not arise in the United States from the class demands of dispossessed workers against the propertied interests that controlled the state. Instead, it arose from an interclass movement that included both propertyless workers and small entrepreneurs, and was dominated by property-owning artisans and farmers. Thus the first generation of industrial workers often cooperated with industrial employers in joint political ventures. Lynn shoemakers who saw the wealth and power of some manufacturers increasing daily at their expense could turn to politics and make common cause with other manufacturers against an enemy — real or imagined — of the democratic political culture. In this fashion, antimasonry swept Lynn with a call to alarm against a secret, conspiratorial aristocracy. Nativism arose out of the fear of an internal threat to American republicanism posed by an authoritarian foreign power that used ignorant Irish Catholics as its pawns for gaining control. The powerful Free Soil movement attacked the Southern slaveocracy on the grounds that it was the epitome of aristocratic power, a death threat leveled at the producing classes, and the antithesis of industrial morality. Finally, the conflict between workers and employers was frequently softened by their joint cooperation as producers against the parasitic money power.[19] Just as inequality waxed in economics, it seemed to wane in politics.

Thus for the first generations of industrial workers, politics was a continual re-enactment of a ritual embodying the social relations of an earlier era of unity among the "producing classes." Industrial culture interacted with the political system in just the opposite way that it interacted with the economic system. The consequence was to retard the spread of rebellion and to advance the politics of loyalism.

The Civil War gave an enormous impetus to the politics of loyalism. At the outset of the War, Lynn was bitterly divided along class lines drawn during the strike of 1860. Strike passions boiled over into electoral politics as strike leaders organized a Workingmen's party to vent their outrage against the use of out-of-town police and their frustration over losing on all their formal strike demands. As the economic struggle resolved into a political struggle, economic defeat was offset by an overwhelming political victory. The Workingmen's party captured nearly every position in the Lynn city government. But then, just at this decisive moment, Fort Sumter fell. Rebel workingmen got back in step with their employers, strikers and bosses submerged their differences in the Yankee cause, and together they marched off to fight confederate traitors. The effect of the War on class consciousness was written in the next election returns: the Republican party, dominated by local shoe manufacturers, won its first city election, and soon worker opposition withered away to nothing. Literally *nothing*. Not a single vote was cast against the incumbent Republican mayor in 1863.[20]

The suffocating embrace of wartime unity persisted through the next decade as the issues created by the War continued to dominate the nation's political affairs, again despite massive economic dispute and division. Questions of reconstructing the Union overshadowed the social and economic issues of industrialization, so that when labor discontent re-emerged after the War, it did not define the main lines of political debate. Thus during the most critical years of industrialization, the United States was more keenly divided politically between industrialism and slavery than between industrial workers and industrial capitalists.

The War gave workers and manufacturers a common historical legacy. Both groups agreed that the history of their country after 1850 was, in effect, the history of class struggle. They regarded bleeding Kansas, the John Brown raid, the Civil War itself, and the military occupation of the South afterwards as incidents in a mortal battle for state power waged by antagonistic social and economic interests. Workers and manufacturers regarded their joint victory as a judgment on the superiority of the northern, industrial way of life. Both groups rejoiced in the defeat of the common enemy, the vindication of industrial morality, and the preservation of democratic values against their subversion by a would-be aristocracy. Both believed that the Federal government and the Union armies had served their basic interests well.

Class consciousness, like all forms of collective thought, is based on actual historical experience transformed into myth. The mythology that arose from the Civil War tended to persuade workers that their power and destiny were inextricably linked to the military heroes, civilian leaders, and the existing frame of government that had won the war. It was not necessary for bourgeois ideologists to go about preaching a "false" consciousness to working people who had risked their lives to bring down the slave power; workers needed only to compare their death toll at the hands of the slaveocracy with their death toll at the hands of company guards, police, and militia. Although the violent suppression of the Mollie Maguires and railroad workers in 1877 began to add up, the result was still dozens against thousands.[21] Had the war ended differently, with the Union in disgrace, or had slavery not been rooted so deeply in American history that it required the greatest military effort of the nineteenth century to extirpate it, the experience and the myths would have been different. Perhaps the conflict between the industrial and preindustrial systems would have been less severe and the conflict between the industrial classes more severe, but as it turned out, things ran the other way. The War took grist from the rebels' mill and gave it to the loyalists.

Working-class political culture emerged from conflicting cross-pressures, some encouraging and others discouraging a class view. As the effect of the Civil War waned, perhaps the most crucial pressure against class consciousness and the major outlet for working-class discontent was electoral politics. Its effect derived from the interclass character of the political parties, and it was crucial because it bore directly on the rebel worker, without whom no widespread radical movement was possible. Whether a rebel became a Democrat, Republican, Labor Reformer, or Greenbacker, he invariably came into close contact with middle-class politicians (a point David Montgomery has emphasized in his perceptive analysis of postwar politics), and this itself demonstrated the openness of the political process. No one has captured the essential relation between social discontent and electoral politics better than Wendell Phillips, firebrand of social reform, Labor Reform candidate for governor of Massachusetts, and hero to rebel workers. "We rush into politics," Phillips explained, "because politics is the safety-valve."[22]

The most powerful political organization in Lynn between 1878 and 1890 was a Workingmen's party that emerged under exactly the same circumstances as its predecessor in 1860: outrage and frustration in a strike launched a political movement for revenge against city officials that carried a Workingmen's candidate to overwhelming victory. The candidate, George P. Sanderson, was a man of clear rebel credentials. The son of a small-town, New Hampshire preacher, he had been a partner in a shoemakers' cooperative. His campaign was infused with rebel rhetoric about the conflict between labor and capital, a conflict personified by Sanderson himself, who had been a shoeworker most of his life, and his opponent, who was the owner of the largest shoe factory and the largest fortune in the city.

But soon after taking office, the rebellion petered out. Although Sanderson acted on his promise to fire the hated police chief, he brought forth nothing else in the way of a distinctive labor program. Having turned the rascals out of office and satisfied the popular taste for revenge, he had nothing further to do except reward the party faithful. Once in office, he became a loyalist by default.

The pattern set by Sanderson persisted throughout the Workingmen's reign. The party was effective in winning elections, manipulating city contracts and patronage jobs, and in controlling the local police force. Each of these accomplishments was important to the city's labor movement, and it is not necessary to belittle the bread-and-butter benefits provided by the Workingmen's party to make the point that it did nothing to pursue the broader interests of the class or to take the rebel outlook into such areas as municipal ownership, health and safety regulations in the factories, or expanded assistance to the poor. The Workingmen's party avoided areas of potential friction between wage earners and middle-class supporters and, instead, sought out the areas of agreement between them.[23] The Workingmen's party was not a party of the proletariat.

IV

We have seen that the Industrial Revolution twice divided American society: first, along industrial and preindustrial lines, and second, along class lines within the industrial order itself. The first division pitted a modern code of morality against a traditional code, industrialism against slavery, the Union against the Confederacy, and it proved to be the deeper division. The second pitted labor against capital, strikers against employers, rebels against owners, and in the time span we are considering from 1820-1890, this division was not as deep. Indeed, industrial class conflicts were often resolved in common struggles against preindustrial influences: the movements for moral reform, the ritual of democracy, and the war against the slave power united wage earners with their employers in battles against common preindustrial enemies.

Recognition of this double division — one between classes, the other between class systems as a whole — clarifies the conflicting cross-pressures that bore down on the nineteenth-century industrial worker. The pressures generated in class conflict tended to make the worker rebellious in his attitudes toward capital and conscious of his own class interests, whereas those generated by conflicts between the preindustrial and the industrial systems tended to make him loyal to the existing order, despite its gross inequalities. American historians, who have ignored such complexities too often, would do well to pose questions that recognize these divergent potentials. Historians who ask only, "Why isn't the

American worker class conscious?" get flat, one-dimensional answers. Better to ask "What conditions promoted class consciousness and what promoted the interest group mentality?" Why, for example, did vigorous strike activity, on any comparative basis, arise amid relatively docile politics? Likewise, historians who wonder, "Why is there no socialism in the United States?" get caught flat-footed when confronted with actual workers who had socialist ideas. Better to ask "Why is socialism weak among certain groups of workers, but strong among others?"

The experience of the first generations of industrial workers influenced the cultural and political development of later generations as America's industrial society matured in the twentieth century. First, the "traditionalist" was reborn whenever a displaced ex-peasant immigrated to America and set about to find work. While some of the children of the immigrants found steady employment and adopted modern ways, others became trapped in an economic maelstrom of low wages and high unemployment that made a mockery of the modern virtues of thrift, temperance, and self-improvement. Before the mid-twentieth century, the descendants of European immigrants would be joined by southern Blacks, Appalachian whites, and Puerto Ricans in this economic underworld. The tragedy of these hard-living, street-corner, marginal workers was that, having lost the anchor of traditional values, they became demoralized when they were unable to find a replacement. Neither traditional nor modern, their aimless, hopeless, disorganized life style was as much the cause as the consequence of their entrapment in a vicious cycle of poverty.

Second, the loyalists not only made peace with the labor movement, but took over large segments of it. Ironically, they often operated under the leadership of conservative ex-rebels like Samuel Gompers in the AFL and James Tobin in the Boot and Shoe Workers' Union. They came to see the trade union as a vital ally in their drive for economic security within the system, and, concurrently, they became bulwarks of the two-party system as an expression of their overall loyalty to the existing order. Their loyalty was severely tested by the Great Depression, but they jumped at the chance to reaffirm it by voting in droves for Franklin Roosevelt and enlisting to fight the fascist armies of Hitler and Tojo. Much like the Civil War, the Second World War strengthened loyalism in the American working class; so much, in fact, that it could be perverted to support the totalitarian, antiradical impulse in the country after the War.

Finally, the rebels cut a channel in American soil that enabled the egalitarianism of the late eighteenth-century revolutions to flow into the twentieth-century labor movement and join up with the streams of immigrant socialism. Rebels established a pattern of labor support for third parties that influenced the formation of socialist and labor parties in the first half of the twentieth century. Although frequent setbacks to industrial unionism and the post-World War II purges of radicals weakened the rebels' influence in the labor movement, the contemporary relevance of their ideas becomes apparent whenever hardship and frustration expose the cruelties of modern industrial capitalism and drive its victims to revolt.

FOOTNOTES

1. An earlier version of this article was presented at the 1974 meeting of the American Historical Association.

2. The ideas herein are a synthesis of the views of both authors; however, we have approached the subject from different perspectives. Paul Faler has specialized on the cultural life of pre-factory artisans, and he originated the cultural typology and terminology used here ("traditionalists," "rebels," "loyalists," industrial v. libertine morality). He introduced this material in "Cultural Aspects of the Industrial Revolution, Lynn, Massachusetts, Shoemakers and Industrial Morality, 1826-1860," *Labor History,* vol. 15, no. 3 (1974): 367-94. Alan Dawley has specialized on the economic and political life of factory workers and has written on these subjects in *Class and Community: The Industrial Revolution in Lynn* (forthcoming, Harvard University Press). In addition, see the following works: Dawley, "The Artisan Response to the Factory System: Lynn, Massachusetts, in the Nineteenth Century" (Ph.D. diss., Harvard University, 1971); Faler, "Workingmen, Mechanics, and Social Change: Lynn, Massachusetts, 1800-1860" (Ph.D. diss., University of Wisconsin, 1971); and Faler, "Working Class Historiography," *Radical America,* vol. 3, no. 2 (1969): 56-68. These studies revise an earlier body of literature on the shoe industry, of which the leading work is John Commons, "American Shoemakers 1648-1895: A Sketch of Industrial Evolution," *Quarterly Journal of Economics* 74 (1909): 39-84. Two other important works are Blanche Hazard, *The Organization of the Boot and Shoe Industry in Massachusetts Before 1875* (Cambridge, Mass., 1921), and Don Lescohier, "The Knights of St. Crispin," *Bulletin of the U. of Wisconsin,* no. 355 (Madison, 1910): 19-24.

3. Between 1830 and 1837 the first strike meeting occurred, the first journeymen cordwainers' society was formed, and the first workingmen's party appeared.

4. The co-existence of individualism and deference in preindustrial New England is described by Charles Grant, *Democracy in the Connecticut Frontier Town of Kent* (New York, 1961); an interesting recent perspective on the decline of deference can be found in James S. Young, *The Washington Community, 1800-1828* (New York, 1966).

5. The paradox has been explored by Richard Hofstadter, *The American Political Tradition* (New York, 1948); Marvin Meyers, *The Jacksonian Persuasion* (New York, 1957); and Oscar Handlin, *Commonwealth* (New York, 1947).

6. There was an "interlocking directorate" between the Society for the Promotion of Industry, Frugality, and Temperance and the Lynn Institution for Savings, both founded in the late 1820s; the full impact of the temperance movement on working people came in the early 1840s with the rise of the Washingtonian Total Abstinence Society.

7. Eugene Genovese has explored the culture of the slave system in *Roll, Jordan, Roll: The World the Slaves Made* (New York, 1974).

8. See Faler, "Cultural Aspects."

9. For a good introduction to eighteenth-century artisan radicalism, see the handy summary of E.P. Thompson's work on England and Albert Soboul's on France by Gwynn Williams, *Artisans and Sans-culottes: Popular Movements in France and Britain during the French Revolution* (New York, 1969).

10. *The Awl,* Aug. 7, 1844.

11. For a case of mistaking the origin and identity of the rebels see Norman Ware, *The Industrial Worker, 1840-1860* (Chicago, 1964).

12. Amazingly, Commons and his followers ignored the strike. The best treatment is in Philip Foner, *History of the Labor Movement in the United States* (New York, 1947), 1: 240.

13. The "green hands" theory can be found in Commons et al., *History of Labour* (New York, 1966), 2: 78; Lescohier, "Knights of St. Crispin," pp. 19-24; and Norman Ware, *The Labor Movement in the United States, 1860-1895* (New York, 1929), p. 20.

14. David Montgomery was the first to see through the "green hands" theory in *Beyond Equality* (New York, 1967), p. 154; full documentation for the Lynn Crispins is in Dawley, "Artisan Response," pp. 212-20.

15. Cooperation was endorsed in the *Proceedings* of the Third Annual Crispin convention, pp. 23-24; consecutive issues of the *Lynn Transcript* in January 1880, contained letters from "Scrib," who demanded an end to the political stranglehold of the rich; a Lynn respondent in the *Fourth Annual Report* of the Massachusetts Bureau of the Statistics of Labor (1873, p. 306), warned that the results of the factory system "have been altogether in favor of capital and against labor"; a letter (July 25, 1885), in the *Knight of Labor* said failure to enact an eight-hour law was like taxing labor for the benefit of capital, and the result would be the same as the outcome of unjust taxation in 1776.

16. For an example of the former see Daniel Bell's brilliantly written but foolishly conceived *Marxian Socialism in the United States* (Princeton, 1952); for an example of the latter see the best single work of the Wisconsin school, Selig Perlman, *Theory of the Labor Movement* (New York, 1928).

17. The first argument can be found in David Brody, *Steelworkers: the Non-Union Era* (Cambridge, Mass., 1960), and Marc Karson, *American Labor Unions and Politics* (Carbondale, Ill., 1958). The second argument has been set forth in recent quantitative studies; the study of working-class social mobility is virtually synonymous with Stephan Thernstrom's pathbreaking *Poverty and Progress* (Cambridge, Mass., 1964), and his more recent *The Other Bostonians* (Cambridge, Mass., 1973).

18. The abolition of 'Lection Day is discussed in Faler, "Cultural Aspects," pp. 381-82.

19. The political movements are treated in Dawley, *Class and Community*, chs. 2, 8.

20. Dawley, "Artisan Response," pp. 252-56.

21. Other relevant body counts include the death toll in the June Days of 1848, and the slaughter of the Paris communards.

22. Montgomery, *Beyond Equality*, passim; Wendell Phillips, quoted in Richard Hofstadter, *The American Political Tradition* (New York, 1948), p. 160.

23. The city government elected at the height of the Workingmen's strength was composed of almost equal numbers of working-class and middle-class council members.

15.

HOUSEHOLD ECONOMY, MARKET EXCHANGE AND THE RISE OF CAPITALISM IN THE CONNECTICUT VALLEY, 1800-1860

Christopher Clark

The rise of capitalism in the rural North involved two distinct but interrelated economic and social transformations. There was, on the one hand, a shift from local self-sufficiency in food and clothing toward increased dependence on outside markets for the sale and purchase of produce. On the other, control of manufacturing activity was removed from independent household producers into the hands of entrepreneurs, and the process begun of concentrating industry in workshops and factories. Each of these changes took a long time to complete, but, at least in the settled regions of the Northeast, the six decades from 1800 to the start of the Civil War witnessed the crucial phase of the process. It was then that the magnitude of the transformation became apparent, and then that contemporaries began to speculate on its effects — to talk, as Horace Bushnell did in 1851, of the "complete revolution of domestic life and manners" that was under way.[1]

When we seek the explanation for these changes, however, we are faced with a curious problem in the historical literature. While the economic history of ante-bellum New England has been adequately described, and while we now know a great deal about colonial society, there has up to now been relatively little written on the complex social processes involved in the development of early 19th century capitalism, particularly insofar as these affected the countryside. This is not to say that there is lack of explanations as to how the transformation came about. The most common of these integrates interpretations both of late colonial history and of early national economic development. It posits the existence of a predominantly profit-oriented rural culture in the 18th century, rooted in independent landholding and a significant degree of production for market, and based on individualistic values engendered particularly by the Great Awakening. While the level of economic development and available technology remained low, the entrepreneurial character of the rural population was not fully realized, but with the upheavals of the Revolutionary period, the growth of international and domestic trade in the ensuing fifty years, and in particular with the transportation revolution of the first half of the 19th century, the potential for capitalist enterprise was at last released, and the changes that we have noted given full force.[2] Recently, however, there has been an upsurge of work that in various ways criticizes this view. Two recent articles in particular, viewing rural society in its own terms rather than in those of the capitalist society that later grew out of it, and drawing on the agricultural histories of Bidwell, Shumacher and Danhof, have highlighted the need for a reinterpretation of early 19th century social history. Michael Merrill, describing the household mode of production in the late colonial period, has argued that most rural output was for family or local consumption, that involvement in the market was usually limited, but that a complex network of exchange relations existed within each rural community. Production was geared not to profit but to needs. This in turn generated a rural culture as much concerned with co-operation as with individual advancement and therefore less ripe for entre-preneurial development than the earlier interpretation had suggested. James Henretta, expanding the critique of the significance of the profit motive, has further argued that the single most important feature of rural culture was the strength of family values — the desire to transmit accumulated property and beliefs from one generation to another and the conservation of family interests. Moreover, this set of values remained significant far into the 19th century.[3]

The merit of Merrill's and Henretta's arguments lies in part in their ability to explain many of the features of rural life and culture in the 18th and early 19th centuries, but also in the fact that they accord due weight to the role of forces *within* local society in bringing about economic and social change. Theirs is a more convincing picture than that of latent entrepreneurship simply waiting for the "rise of the national market" and the "transportation revolution" to link it up with the outside world. They have not assumed the inevitability of the changes which were brought about, but have presented them as a product of conscious action, of struggle and uncertainty. But a major problem remains — if local society was not profit-oriented at first, and if the household and family interests were at the core of economic existence, then how did the rise of capitalist production come about? What processes *did* produce the result? This essays seeks to suggest an answer to this problem by examining the role of household production and family interests in the transformation of a particular region — the Connecticut Valley section of Hampshire County in Massachus-etts, an area containing Northampton, the county seat, and the towns surround-ing it.[4]

I

The extension of market relations was already under way in the Connecticut Valley by 1800, but it was more rapid after that date than at any time before. The improvement of existing roads, the building of turnpikes and the introduc-tion of stage routes had begun in the last decade of the 18th century, together with the improvement of the Connecticut River by the building of canals at South Hadley and at Turner's Falls. During the 19th century the construction of the New Haven - Northampton canal and the building of the first railroads in the 1840s and 1850s would complete a revolution in the region's communica-tions with outside markets. But changes were occurring within the region also. From the 1780s onwards a small number of local individuals began to peddle surplus produce and other goods to neighboring communities and as time went on there were an increasing number of references to itinerant traders in the area.[5] But beyond this, long-term changes were beginning which would set both agriculture and manufacturing in the region on a market-oriented basis to an extent that they had never been before.

Although it had long been known as an exporter of wheat, beef and timber products, by 1800 the proportion of the Valley's total agricultural output that was shipped elsewhere was still small. Indeed, Clarence Danhof has suggested that as late as 1820 perhaps as little as 25 per cent of local output was available for export.[6] Similarly, except for such items as salt and sugar the bulk of the Valley's food supply was locally grown. With increasing rapidity as the 19th century went on, this pattern changed, and the region's inhabitants became involved in the marketplace both as exporters and as consumers of agricultural goods. The number of farmers involved in fattening cattle for the Boston market grew significantly, for example, as did the size of their herds. In Hatfield and Hadley in the 1790s it was unusual for one farmer to sell as many as eight or ten animals in a year. By the 1850s some farmers were fattening 100 head each season, and herds of 40 to 50 animals were common.[7] On the other hand, an increasing proportion of the region's food came to be supplied from elsewhere. Imported wheat flour was being advertised for sale in Hadley as early as 1809. By the late 1820s Rochester-milled flour was widely available and in the subsequent decades not only townspeople but many local farmers were buying flour rather than growing grain themselves.[8] As we shall see, the Valley's dependence on outside markets was not complete by 1860, but it was established to an unprecedented degree. From being a region concerned largely with general farming for the supply of local needs, it had become increasingly subject to competition from other parts of the country and increasingly engaged in the production of cash crops which the south or west could not yet supply sufficiently. Beef-cattle, dairy produce and fodder crops became particularly important, together with broom-corn and — after the mid-1850s — tobacco.[9]

The shift toward market production in manufacturing was even more rapid and more visible. In the first decade of the century and at an increasing pace after 1820, progress was made in building up workshop and factory production, based largely on the water-power of Connecticut River tributaries. Distinct factory villages grew up in Amherst, Northampton and Williamsburg. This process involved the replacement of the old household manufactures. Early developments, in the adaptation of existing grist- and sawmills to use as fulling or carding mills, were intended at first to provide a service to the home producers of textiles.[10] But from the early 1800s millowners began to take in work on their own account or on shares, and thus began the process of centralizing production. Some, like the Bodmans of Williamsburg began to extend their fulling operations to embrace spinning and weaving.[11] However, despite this, and despite the appearance of such larger industrial concerns as the Northampton Woolen Manufacturing Company (about 1808), there was little direct challenge to household production until after the disruptions of the Embargo, the War of 1812 and the subsequent flow of British manufactures had passed away. Once these shields were removed the collapse of the household industry was rapid. For part of her marriage portion in 1824, Elizabeth Huntington of Hadley was given as much linen and woolens as she could spin the yarn for in a season, and her sisters still spun wool until around 1830. But references to such work in family papers disappear after this. Sylvester Smith's family in Hadley stopped making its own woolen cloth in 1822, and references to home-made cloth, quite common in Amherst account books up to that time, are few after the late 1820s.[12] Independent textile production did continue in a few places but it was rare — most people had begun to buy their cloth, or even their clothes, ready-made.

Much of the supply of manufactured goods of course came from large industrial centers elsewhere in New England and beyond, but industrial production within the region also grew rapidly. Between 1820 and 1840 alone, the area's manufacturing population doubled, growing in proportion from about one-fifth to just under one-third of the labor force.[13] The new industries fell into three broad categories: textiles and related products, organized in workshops and factories, and relying to some extent on extensive putting-out networks; products based on or related to agriculture, organized mainly in workshops; and finally — again mainly in workshops — the production of tools, machinery and other metal goods.[14]

Underlying all these changes in farming and manufacturing was a rapid growth in the commercial activity of the Valley. Merchant families already established in trade in the late 18th century began to emerge as major local figures, while some country traders began to turn themselves into substantial merchants. This was the foundation of the commercial elite which was to dominate local society for much of the antebellum period. Northampton's first bank was founded in 1803 and its second ten years later. Long before 1860 the town center was filled with workshops, stores and offices. Besides banking, the town provided insurance services, printing shops and several newspapers. Between 1831 and 1860 its total stock in trade quadrupled, from $73,450 to $281,800, representing a substantial per capita increase, from $20.33 to $44.89 per head.[15] By the middle of the century Amherst was also acquiring the trappings of a small commercial center — it had its own newspaper, as well as substantial stores and workshops. Nor was this commercial activity merely local in compass. Of the 350 tradespeople listed in the Northampton business directory for 1860, I estimate that about 70 percent also had credit listings with R.G. Dun and Company in New York, and the company listed several dozen Amherst businesses too. This suggests that at least part of their trade lay outside the local area.[16]

II

These, very briefly, were the dimensions of the shift to market exchange and capitalist production in the Valley. With local variations, it is a familiar pattern, and in recounting it we have not really learned much that we did not know already. The more interesting question is, *how* did these changes come about? In order to answer this we shall have to examine the household system of the late 18th and early 19th centuries more closely, and then analyze the role of this system in the dynamic of future change.

The Valley's economy at the turn of the century still exhibited many of the features that Merrill has described in his article on the household mode of production. It was not predominantly profit-oriented. The outside market was resorted to mainly to acquire necessities that were not available inside the region — such as iron, sugar, salt and rum — or, in certain instances, to purchase luxury items that similarly could not be produced locally. Except perhaps in Northampton, the amount of trade generated in this way was small until quite far into the 19th century. Between 1815 and 1820, for example, the inventory of the one store in Westhampton included about 150 types of goods, but their total value ranged only between $400 and $500 — or roughly between 45¢ and 65¢ for each inhabitant of the town.[17] Similarly, crops or goods which were sent from the region for sale in outside markets were rarely raised or produced specifically for this purpose. They were taken from the surplus that was left over after household and community needs had been met.

Rather than relying on the market, rural families supplied their wants both by producing their own goods for consumption and by entering into complex networks of exchange relationships with their neighbors and relatives in order to provide for needs that they could not, or chose not to, provide for themselves. Although a majority of the population were engaged in farming, and although there were few who had no connection to the land, there was still a fairly complex division of labor, along with the wide range of skills necessary for local self-sufficiency. On the one hand was the division between male and female tasks within the household — in which farming and trading were largely conducted by men, and the preparation of food and the production of clothes and other necessaries were largely in the hands of women. On the other hand was a certain division between households, and the products of craft skills, in blacksmithing, tanning, cooperage and so forth, were exchanged within the community for the food, manufactured products or labor of other households. In this way, for example, farmers could procure the services of itinerant weavers or tailors in return for food, and men like Elijah Norton, who farmed in Westhampton from 1785 until his death in 1828, could "carry on his farm, in part at least, by making shoes for his neighbors in return for which they could work on his farm."[18] Cash played little part in these exchanges. On the local level they tended to be made directly with goods or labor. A Frenchman, after a visit to the U.S. around 1790 described the system as he had found it:

> Instead of money going incessantly backwards and forwards into the same hands, . . . they supply their needs in the countryside by direct reciprocal exchanges. The tailor and the bootmaker go and do the work of their calling at the home of the farmer who requires it and who, most frequently, provides the raw material for it and pays for the work in goods . . . [T]hey write down what they give and receive on both sides and at the end of the year they settle a large variety of exchanges with a very small quantity of coin.[19]

When cash was used, it tended to be for specific purposes — to make settlement, to purchase imported goods or to pay taxes. Transactions were entered in account books and assigned a money value, but this was regarded primarily as a convenient method of calculation. It did not mean that money was widely regarded as having value in itself, beyond its uses for these specific needs. The lists of debits and credits in account books were often allowed to accumulate for long periods of time. This was due partly to habit, but also in part to needs — a farmer might obtain a bushel of rye from his neighbor at the end of the winter when his supply had run low, but he would not be expected to repay until either he had goods enough to make the return, or the lender had work that he needed doing at plowing, hoeing or harvesting. Work was commonly performed with the understanding that it would be paid for at some future date in a specific form. We find Dan Huntington of Hadley writing to his son in 1825: "I have been constantly hurried . . . [h]aving a good deal of wood to get this winter, to pay off men hired the last summer about the barn."[20]

Settlements were often irregular, and when they were made, payment was not always in cash. A note might be written, thus extending the debt further, an order made out to a third person to provide owed goods or services to balance, or goods accepted in payment. When Joseph Eastman of Amherst reckoned with Eliphalet Spear in 1810, he found "due to him in Produce three Dollers Eighty Nine Cents," and he made these payments over the following months.[21] Judging by the amount of work that was often put in by the adminstrators of estates, it is clear that death commonly intervened before peoples' accounts could be straightened out.

Some examples, drawn mainly from surviving Amherst account books, will illustrate how these local exchange networks operated. William Boltwood left more or less complete records of dealings with thirteen of his neighbors between 1794 and 1817. In six accounts no cash at all was used, and in only two of the remaining seven did it figure as a significant proportion of the total. In most instances, he traded produce from his farm: rye, wheat, corn, pork, veal, hay, timber, flax and potatoes, or performed day-work, plowing or similar services. In 1799 he lent Widow Mary Billings his horse so that she could ride to Brattleborough, Vermont, and the next spring he gave her 200 pounds of hay. She balanced the account eventually, making a "harnis" for him in 1801 and giving him six loads of stone in 1813. Joseph Douglas worked for Boltwood, made barrels and hogsheads for him, slaughtered his cows and pigs and gave him tea, sugar and salt. Boltwood reciprocated with produce, wool, cloth, his son's work ["Lucius one day . . .1/6"] and the use of his oxen and tools.[22] As these examples show, exchanges were made to provide food and to accomplish the various tasks of a rural existence. Money was seen not as an end to itself, but as a means to perform these tasks. In only four of the twenty-two accounts that Eleazer Cowles of Amherst recorded after 1816 does cash appear at all except at settlement times and even then it was in small amounts. Even Asa Dickinson, who sold rum, sugar and other imported goods in North Amherst early in the 19th century — items which more commonly demanded cash payment — did the majority of his business in produce and services. Of thirty-three people he served between 1804 and 1806, only twelve paid him entirely in cash, fifteen supplemented their cash payments with grain, flax or wool and six settled without cash at all.[23] The more formal instruments of exchange also reflected the frequency of non-cash payment. Samuel Smith, for example, gave a note to Asa Dickinson in June 1806 in which he promised to pay "for value received . . . the sum of five cords of pitch pine wood cut and split[,] d[e]l[ivere]d at his dore . . . by the first of October." Such practices were still common over twenty years later, when in 1827 Eliphalet Spear sent a third party to Chester E. Marshall with a note asking Marshall "Plese to let the Barer hav Six Bushels of rye and charge the same to me."[24]

This evidence illustrates the extent to which the people of the Valley were accustomed to rely on their neighbors and relatives for part of their livelihood. Whether they traded regularly for the goods and labor of other households, or whether they used the exchange networks more sporadically to tide them over seasonal or periodic shortages of particular goods, their economic planning was geared to the needs of their households within the context of the local community, rather than to the demands of production for profit in the marketplace.

It can be argued that this system was simply the product of necessity — the shortage of cash, perhaps — but the fact that these practices continued in use far into the 19th century, and that they were still not uncommon (as we shall see later) in the Civil War period, suggests that there was a deeper cultural attachment to kinship and neighborhood ties and to a spirit of mutual co-operation. Certainly, the system was "functional." It was flexible and to a considerable extent met the needs of producers. But it was more than that — it was at the center of a distinct culture. It generated its own values, of co-operation, of work-swapping, of household integrity and family advancement, that were to be influential throughout the early period of capitalist development. This is not to say that rural life was idyllic. Individual landholding and the activities of families to protect their interests produced friction and competition enough, as the proliferation of lawsuits attests. The young Hannah Dickinson wrote of Amherst in 1813, while she was a student at Westfield Academy, "the people are generally avaricious; they want to get as much property as they can; they are generally honest, but tight in their dealings."[25] However, although they contained seeds of change, the aspirations engendered by these values were different from those which were to grow up as the 19th century progressed. As James Henretta has pointed out, "success" was measured by the ability of families to conserve and expand their resources so as to be able to pass on sufficient property to "succeeding" generations. Not riches, but a comfortable living was the greatest attainment in life:

> Reason's whole pleasure, all the joys of sense
> Lie in three words, health, peace and competence.[26]

However, the early 19th century found this system already under pressure to change. A number of forces acting in the period following the Revolution came to effect a crisis in the household economy which would lead rural society to embark on the course of market development that we have already outlined. Some of these forces came from "outside" rural society, but it is clear that the crucial influences that led to the transformation stemmed from factors intrinsic to the household system itself. Together, they helped change the circumstances in which rural families were seeking to achieve their aims, and forced them to find new ways to reach old ends.[27]

The first disruption, whose impact was intermittent at least until the second decade of the 19th century, was the increasing flow of foreign manufactures into the Valley towns. From the 1760s on, the availability of cheap British clothing, textile products and other goods began to undermine the household manufacturing system. The process was interrupted, especially by the Embargo and the War of 1812, but its long-term effect was as a leavening process, gradually broadening the channels of local trade and increasing the opportunities for profit of local merchants and shopkeepers. When the rush of American manufactures into the region finally demolished household textile production in the 1820s, their path had already been carved by the successive influxes of British goods in the preceding 40 to 60 years.

A more dramatic disruption lay in the crisis of the 1780s which culminated in Shays' Rebellion. This crisis seriously affected the operation of the rural exchange system in Western Massachusetts. Credit was stopped, debts called in and hundreds of farmers sued and imprisoned. Trading in goods for imported necessities became difficult. These conditions were temporary, but in the context of a general growth of market exchange in the wider economy, they signalled a systemic weakness. Rural people had to intensify their efforts to supply their needs.[28]

Unfortunately, the chief way in which they had been accustomed to do this, by the acquisition of land, was being closed off to them by the end of the 18th century. This is not to say that there was a general land shortage or the makings of a crisis of subsistence, but that the completion of settlement in the region, linked with the inequalities that existed in property distribution, effectively limited the further expansion of landholding. Access was made more difficult for families which did not already own land, and new problems of inheritance were posed for those which did. There was a gradual increase in the numbers of landless or land-poor inhabitants, who attempted to make their livings either by selling their labor or by engaging in trade. At the same time, landholders began to cultivate their properties more intensively. From the 1790s onward there was a progressive cutting-back of unimproved acreage and extension of tillage, mowings and pasture.[29] Both these developments encouraged the growth of market relationships, by increasing the potential surplus of goods available for trade. Some families, still in pursuit of their long-standing goals of passing on the means of subsistence to their offspring, began to adopt the strategy of using market exchange to obtain them. The growing market economy expanded the possibility of using a trade, some education or some other skill as an "inheritance," and permitted the household system to adapt to the crisis.

For reasons of family, economy, rather than competitive profit-seeking, farmers and others began to seek new outlets for their produce, and to grow new crops for market sale. Their motives were often simple enough. Hannah Dickinson observed of Amherst, that "most of the farmers fat cattle and send them to Boston, or some other market, which helps to supply them with money to educate their children."[30] Some farmers took up business as a sideline for similar reasons. Dan Huntington of Hadley had a substantial farm, but also seven sons and four daughters to provide for. As one means of doing this he entered into partnership with a succession of small merchants, and by the late 1820s was owner of the store in North Hadley in conjunction with his son Edward. Edward's share of the profits, however, were not for his own use — they were put towards the expenses of one of his brothers, who was preparing for the ministry at Harvard.[31] As time went on, more families sought outlets for surplus produce, doing so often in small and risky ways. Seth Nims left his home in Conway around 1822 to find work in the South, carrying with him a bolt of cloth with which his parents hoped to raise some ready cash. Their letter to him in Georgia, written in the spring of 1823, bespeaks the continuing modesty of many families' aspirations where involvement with the market was concerned:

> We sent a pice of Cloth by you and we expected to receiv'd the money for it this spring, for we are in great want of it[.] If you have sold the cloth and got the money for it[,] if you have any chance to convey the money with safety I should be very glad[.] if you could send forty or fifty dollars more you would ablige me very much and I would endever to make it out to you when you come home.

After warning him to take care of his health and not to "let money carry your mind from things of more importance," they returned to the subject of the cloth: "if you can have the opportunity to send us the money for we are drove."[32] This is evidence not of a family's entrepreneurial spirit, but of its attempts to survive. Gradually, however, this involvement with the market was to undermine the old culture and the old economy.

III

When country merchants, who long had served as the channel by which local surpluses had been transmitted to outside markets, began to seek greater quantities of produce to trade with, they found, in the first place, that there were rural families willing to participate, and secondly, that a system for collection already existed in the local exchange networks. Similarly, as the availability of imported goods speeded the decline of household manufactures, especially in the 1820s, local families relied on these merchants increasingly for the industrial goods that they needed. The names of merchants and storekeepers began to appear in the account books more often alongside those of farmers and artisans, and farmers and sons grew accustomed to performing labor and other services for merchants and even factory agents, just as they had done, and continued to do, for their neighbors.[33]

To an increasing extent during the first few decades of the 19th century storekeepers advertised their willingness to sell their dry goods, groceries, shoes or crockery in exchange for "farmers' produce" or for specified farm goods. In the late 1820s the practice was almost universal. Fields and Dickinson of Amherst offered their range of goods for wood, rye, corn, oats and butter, while Luke Sweetser — one of the town's leading traders — announced that he wanted "Cider Brandy . . . in exchange for goods," and offered "a liberal exchange . . . in salt" for flaxseed. When the Huntingtons were collecting their daughter's marriage portion in 1824, they acquired furnishings from a store in Northampton, and sent two young sons into town with a fattened ox to make the first payment.[34] After about 1830 there was a tendency, especially among the leading Northampton merchants, to set business on a cash-only basis. From what can be deduced, for example, from the surviving account books of the firm of Wright and Rust, it seems that most of their transactions were conducted in cash in the mid-1830s; while early in the 1840s Dun and Company reported that Stoddard and Lathrop, Northampton's largest dry goods store, was doing "mostly a cash business."[35] But although by that time the practice of quoting lower prices for cash purchasers than for others was widely established, few merchants were able to deal entirely in cash. The North Hadley store, for example, sold goods worth a total of over $3,350 in 1839-1840, but only 18.5 per cent of this value was redeemed directly in cash.[36] Into the 1840s and beyond, trading with goods remained common — indeed for many shopkeepers and farmers, it was probably still the only way of doing business at all. In Northampton, Lewis McIntire advertised groceries for sale in 1845 for "Wood, Butter, Cheese, Eggs, Poultry and Farmers' Produce generally," while the blacksmith, Edwin Kingsley, still wrote notes to his creditors "for work at my shop." In Amherst and elsewhere, payments were still being made to storekeepers in goods in the mid 1860s.[37]

These practices, rooted not simply in expediency, but in deeply-felt habits and values, enabled the growth of markets to complement rather than destroy at once the old household system. Many rural families went along with the change, but a farmer's participation in this kind of exchange did not necessarily signal an immediate alteration in his attitudes toward profit-seeking. Certainly he might be sharp in his dealings — as the *Hampshire Gazette* once commented of farmers in Hatfield, they "commonly have their dish the right side up when it rains" — but he was not automatically transformed into an entrepreneur. Indeed, insofar as the early market sytem perpetuated many of the old forms of household exchange, it probably tended to shelter him from confronting this option. The merchant who acquired his goods would certainly perceive them as an opportunity for gain, but for the farmer the transaction still retained much of its old aspect of fulfilling a specific need. He was trading with the merchant rather than with his neighbors merely because he had to use his surplus to obtain goods that increasingly had to be found from outside markets.

If there was a continuity between old and new in farming, there was also one in manufacturing, although changes came about more quickly here. Under the household system, farming and manufacturing had been mutually supporting, as this proposal from a song collected in Miller's Falls suggests:
[She sings:]

> If you will find me ten acres of land
> Between the salt water and the sea sand
> And plow it all up with an old ram's horn
> And seed it all down with one kernel of corn
> Then come unto me and you shall have your shirt
> And then you can be a true lover of mine.[38]

The decline of household manufacturing threatened this relationship from the 1820s onward, as control of production was shifted from family to entrepreneur. Rural families, seeking new ways to provide for their own support, contributed to the change by sending workers to the new factories or by participating in the outwork system. Thus in many instances the labor which had previously been devoted to manufacturing tasks for the benefit of the household was turned to good account by workshop and factory owners. For the people — especially the young women — who entered factory employment, the change was often a liberating one, because it permitted them to escape from patriarchal authority and the confines of the household. But this freedom was gained only by submission to the authority of new masters. Outwork similarly held contradictions for the families involved in it. It enabled industrial production to remain in the home, but, as we shall see, "domestic industry" became an agent, first of mercantile, then of industrial capitalism.[39]

There were a few instances in which farm women were able to continue manufacturing on their own account for other members of the community.

Carpet and rug making was one such activity which, in the 1840s at least, continued partly in the hands of independent weavers, who owned their own tools and materials. Mary Nutting of South Amherst wrote to her brother in 1841 that "mother will take in all the weaving she can get hold of . . .," and apparently this was the woman's major occupation for the next several years. In 1845 she apparently wove a piece for the house of the president of Amherst College, and in July 1847 she was reported to be resting after having woven 124 yards of rag carpeting.[40] But this kind of work was increasingly rare — even the tailoring and sewing work that had long been a corollary of household textile manufacture was in decline. To a growing extent it was done either in the household for the family's own use, or it was done commercially by tailors' businesses at centralized shops.

Most women engaged in production had to find work with outside employers. Some, especially younger women, travelled to work in Eastern Massachusetts, or to the factories closer by in Springfield and Chicopee. Belchertown women were working in these latter towns from the mid-1820s onwards.[41] Until foreign immigration reduced the supply of such jobs from the later 1840s onwards, and speedups and wage cuts reduced their attractiveness, factory work continued to be regarded by families as an option open to their daughters along with the other emerging forms of female employment. Harriet Nutting wrote to her brother in 1847:

> Eli, what do you think John wants me to do[?] — He told Mother, that if I could keep school he thought I was able to *work in a Factory* — then I could be earning something. Had I better send on to Lowell and engage a place?[42]

Often these factory women returned home, perhaps to marry, and then found employment in the outwork system, so that their participation in the two types of labor was sometimes less a function of choice than of their place in the life cycle. It is probable that from the 1810s onward some Connecticut Valley families took work from distant eastern Massachusetts or Rhode Island factories, but this source of employment dried up in the 1820s as factories found more stable local labor supplies or came to rely on direct employment of workers.[43] However, new sources of outwork were growing up in the Valley itself, at first in small textile mills along the Mill River in Northampton and Williamsburg, subsequently in the button trade of Williamsburg and Easthampton, and finally in the palm-leaf hat industry, which was centered largely in Amherst.

These sources of outwork gave a new shape to the local economy and played an important part in the lives of the families who engaged in them. In 1840, when the average per capita value of domestic production in Massachusetts as a whole was 31¢, in Hampshire County the average was $1.28. Even in 1860, when the county figure had fallen to 86¢ per capita, this was over four times the state average and the highest in the state.[44] Outwork gave women, both married and unmarried, a chance to accommodate their work to the needs of other household tasks, in the way that had been possible under the household system. As Hannah Nutting reported to her brother in 1845 on her own and her sisters' activities:

I sewed for Doria Cook, the girls braided [hats]. [T]his week we have took up the carpets and cleaned house and made soap and cut five dresses and made two or three sun bonnets[.] Amelia has been to the Academy one day . . . all this besides braiding (we won't say anything about).[45]

In this part of New England outwork was an important factor in permitting rural families to survive economically during a period of fluctuating farm prices and extended market relations. It helped households remain independent, and this in turn helped preserve something of the old household exchange system into the Civil War era. But there was a price to be paid for this, because the very outwork system that helped preserve the independent rural household was also a source of the capitalist development that would ultimately undermine that independence altogther. The Amherst hat industry provides us with a classic illustration of this contradiction. It reflected a common pattern, both in the development of small capitalist industry and in the evolving relationship between capitalism and the rural household.

The first palm-leaf hat entrepreneurs were storekeepers, like Leonard M. Hills, who started his "boutique" for hats in Amherst in 1829. Over the next decade hat making became an important channel for investment of local merchant capital. By the mid-1840s at least ten merchants in Amherst, including all the leading general dealers, were involved in the business, while there were others in Hadley and in such outlying towns as Shutesbury, Leverett and New Salem.[46] Some of these merchants' outwork networks were quite extensive. Sweetser, Cutler and Co. of Amherst had over 280 people on their "braiding account" in the late 1840s and early 1850s.[47] They put out leaf to local families, who split, braided, bound and shaped it. The families then returned it to the merchants, who paid them largely in goods from their stores. In the winter of 1843 and 1844, for example, Charlotte Dickinson of North Amherst made a total of fifty-nine hats   for Sweetser and Cutler, for which she received salt, a whip, ribbons, cord and a length of calico. Four years later she made thirty three hats for another trader, in this case exchanging them for ribbon, candy, tea and ten yards of gingham.[48] From the start several of the merchants had kept small workshops in which the finishing processes were carried out. During the 1840s and 1850s these shops were enlarged, and various stages in the production process concentrated in them. Women workers were now hired to work in the shops — Oliver Clapp of East Amherst, for example, had 25 females employed at sewing in the shop behind his store by about 1844, most of them paid in goods. Finally in the late 1850s the Hills company consolidated most of its production on two factory sites, leaving only the actual braiding of leaf in the hands of outworkers. By 1862 the firm was employing up to 200 men and women in its various departments during the height of the season.[49]

Here we can see the interaction that occurred between the market, capitalist production and the life of the rural household. Local storekeepers increased their businesses by trading for the surpluses of farmers, which they acquired by entering the local exchange networks. As they accumulated profits many merchants expanded their interests into manufacturing and so created a further link with the family, this time by giving farm women employment in the outwork system. Finally, they recruited women out of the home to work in their shops and factories. The families involved had participated in this process initially in an attempt to preserve their old way of life. As it turned out they were helping to bring about a radical social change. The old household system had a profound impact on early industrial capitalism, but soon found its impact turned against itself. "Store pay," after all, was a ready adaptation from the exchange customs that had long been acceptable to rural families — they had traded labor for goods for generations, and here was now an opportunity to use it to gain access to wider markets. But in the hands of entrepreneurs, and in the context of an expanding cash market, the system rapidly became the tool of exploitation and a burden to outworkers and factory employees that was to make it a target of the labor movement for the ensuing seventy years. As Mary Nutting Bridgeman wrote in 1843 of her sister Maria, who had just started work in Clapp's East Amherst hat shop, "she gets along real well and if she could have her pay in cash she might make it more profitable."[50] In this and in other ways family independence and authority found itself in conflict with the dictates of organizations whose concerns were alien to it. As early as 1827, Elizabeth Goodell was writing home to Belchertown from her Springfield factory with unexpected news: "I want Noble to come down after me the 21 of October. . . . [T]hey have low[ere]d the wages 1 cent and a quarter and if any they are not going to give after the 20 of October."[51] Even in the smaller workshops similar clashes could develop. Mary Nutting planned a trip to relatives in Ohio in the spring of 1848, but before going had to make up her mind to break with her employer:

> Mr Clapp says I *must* not go until the custom work is over. That will probably be the first of July. But I am not obliged to do *exactly* as he says. I know he wants my help very much this summer for several of his old sewers he cannot have.[52]

But the women who worked for the Hills company in 1862 had no such choice to make. As Henry F. Hills indicated in a letter, it was made for them by their employer:

> We are thinking to give the girls a vacation of two weeks commencing about July 4th but 'twill depend on the orders we may receive.[53]

The copartnership of capitalism with its household forebear was breaking down, to the permanent exclusion of the old system.

IV

For the time being the change was more apparent in manufacturing than it was in rural life generally. In certain respects life remained much as it had been, and substantial remnants of the household exchange system survived into the era of industrial capitalism. Among farmers in particular, old habits ran deep. Men like Horace Belding of Amherst continued to trade crops and labor with their neighbors in the 1850s very much as their fathers had done forty years before. The old practices persisted because they continued to make sense in their cultural and economic context. The household system had welcomed and complemented market development and not resisted it, and so it was able to continue. However, this very situation, and the ease with which hosuehold values were adaptable to the needs of market production and capitalist accumulation, were to produce an increasing tension and conflict as the 19th century progressed.

Independence, frugality and industry had long governed rural families in their strivings for a "competence," but as Austin Loomis recognized when he wrote to this future wife in 1820, there was nothing to stop them fastening on a further goal. His ambition seemed modest enough:

> As to [my] worldly prospects, they are not as flattering as I could wish, but [I] am in hopes they will be more so shortly. Though riches are not the chief good, it is desireable to have the comforts of life, and be in some respects independent.

But, as he concluded, "the love of wealth seems natural to all mankind, and but very few have sufficient of this world to content them."[54] The urge to accumulate wealth became stronger as time went on, and old values came to be used for new purposes. A short biographical sketch written in the early 1850s could have been the model for a later 18th or early 19th century farmer: "He was moral, industrious and frugal, and took a wife possessing the same qualities . . .", but it happens that the subject was Samuel Williston, an Easthampton manufacturer who had turned these attributes into a fortune of a quarter of a million dollars.[55] Such men had already discovered a theological formula that would justify their attention to worldly allurements, while at the same time reassuring them about their prospects in the hereafter: "Whilst we seek for the treasures of this world may we also seek to be rich in faith and heirs of Christ's kingdom."[56] These attitudes had a corrosive effect on the household system. The local economy was forced to move more closely to the rhythms of national trade. Farmers and artisans whose concerns had centered around the reciprocal exchange relationships of their neighborhoods died, and gave place to new generations who were ready to use their inheritances as means for acquiring wealth. Old attitudes towards debt and restraints on speculative enterprise became weaker — an increasing number of people were willing to sell their property for gain or to mortgage it to raise capital for investment in new enterprises.

To many, the growth of markets and of large-scale manufacturing appeared to provide unprecedented opportunities for agricultural profits. But as the 19th century unfolded an increasing bifurcation developed within rural society, between those who continued willingly to extend their connections with the market and those who began to draw back from the system growing up in their midsts because they feared its consequences. These people had never accepted the notion of a "drive for profits," and if they accepted the market at all, it was simply as a means for securing a competence to be passed on to their successors. When Moses Goodell of Belchertown died in 1854, one of his sons wrote of him,

> He always was too honest to get along in the world and get to be very rich. But he managed somehow to just about hold his own, but I suppose it has been tight work for the past few years.

A document from 1852 shows us that up to the end of his life, Goodell continued to grow the crops that had long been the staples of household production in the Valley — corn, rye and potatoes — and that he grew them in quantities that can have allowed little margin for cash sales.[57] As a writer in the

New England Farmer had advised the same year,

> As a general rule . . . it is better that the farmer should produce what he needs for home consumption. He may obtain more money from tobacco, hops or broom corn, than from breadstuffs, but taking all things into consideration will he be better off?[58]

Many Valley farmers would have answered this question in the negative. They continued to use the household system to protect themselves from the vagaries of the marketplace. Despite the ready availability of cheap flour from the west, for example, local cultivation of wheat in small quantities for home use or local exchange remained common. There was no permanent decline in wheat production in Hadley or Hatfield until after the Civil War, while a New Hampshire farmer still felt able to suggest in 1862 that New England would do well to "raise more wheat and purchase less western flour."[59]

So although by 1860 the household system had long been in decline, we can see that elements of its structure, values and practices remained intact. The rise of capitalism in rural areas had taken the course that it did precisely because it had grown out of the household economy, and because the old system long continued to exert its influence on the new. But there was no simple correspondence between the two. The contradictions we have noted in the process of change served to promote considerable conflict. As I would like to suggest by way of conclusion, the values of the household economy, while doing much to ease the transition to capitalist institutions, also provided a basis for objection to them. In places there remained the old disapproval of debt and speculation. This was linked to criticisms of the divisions in society, which led in turn to disapproval of the accumulation of excessive wealth. At times in the Valley region this was to gather into a critique of capitalism itself.

As more and more people became dependent on the market for their existence, wealth inequalities grew wider. The late 18th century pattern of wealth distribution, in which differentials were related partly to age, as sons waited to inherit their fathers' property, was replaced by a new one, in which differences emerged permanently on class lines. This situation and the devastating effect of successive business crises were common targets for criticism. Sylvester Judd, the Northampton editor and historian wondered during the 1837 slump "whether this gambling, speculating age for money making will receive any permanent check," and continued to entertain the hope that a more modest way of running the economy might prevail. When George Trask wrote his condemnation of tobacco production in the Valley in the 1860s, he did not confine himself to criticism of the "loathesome crop" itself, but attacked the market system in general, the tragedy of the honest farmer made a dupe by the "paying crop," and the ruination caused when prices fell. He had the farmer in his story sum up:

> I am a poorer man today than when I began. I have nearly three years' crops on hand. My notes are in the bank . . . I have injured all my choice lands: and I should have been better off had I stuck to my old crops.[60]

Such opposition to the changes that were taking place was sporadic and often confused, but there is no doubt that many people were concerned at what they found happening around them. The most concerted criticism came in the early

1830s, from the Workingmen's Party, which for several years was active in Northampton. The party's discontent took a form that looked both forwards and backwards — toward a critique of capitalist society, but based on many of the values and practices of the household economy. Indeed its very existence was predicated on the existence of an alliance between farmers, artisans and laborers — an alliance which was rapidly becoming impossible in a world of market relations, but which made a great deal of sense in the older reciprocal economy of household production and exchange, in which these groups were dependent on each other and the distinctions between them were blurred in any case. At the base of the Workingmen's program was the claim to "Equal Rights," both to the fruits of labor and to participation in the political system. The courts in particular, "operate with peculiar oppressiveness on the poor and unfortunate class of the community," and they should be avoided in time-honored manner, by settling disputes through the arbitration of neighbors. The party attacked the "perversion of government" which kept ordinary people from a share of political authority, and explained economic and political inequalities in terms which implied a direct criticism of capitalist accumulation and market exchange. Grave dangers arose from the "monopoly of wealth and income in the hands of the few," and from "the union of Political Power with the monopoly of wealth." And as George Bancroft wrote in a nomination letter in 1834, "where the people possess no authority their rights obtain no respect and the gulf between the rich man and Lazarus grows wider and deeper." Moreover, this danger was inherent in the very operation of a market economy:

> When the merchant demands that his interest should prevail over those of liberty, . . . when the usurer invokes the aid of society to enforce the contracts which he has wrung without mercy from the feverish hopes of pressing necessity, it is the clamor of capital, which, like the grave, never says, It is enough.[61]

This represented the high-point of critical activity in the Valley. But the ideas of the Workingmen's party, its claims to political equality and the fruits of labor were diffused into various channels and had their effect in shaping the temperance and abolition movements, the early labor movement and, to a degree, the policies of the Whig and Democractic parties. In this way values originally engendered by the household economy continued to be put to new uses even after capitalist dominance had been established, and they became merged with newer ideas thrown up by the problems of a changing society. As Judd wrote in his diary in 1843, after he had heard in a sermon the common assertion that "all the distinctions in society [are] from God,"

> Many of the distinctions and inequalities among men come from the selfishness, the avarice and ambition of those who call themselves upper classes, who have governed the world for their own benefit, and not for the advantage of the many.[62]

It was becoming increasingly clear as the century passed its mid-point that the world of the market and of capitalist production was tying up "the many" in lines of exploitation and of class division that created new barriers in rural society. Their misfortune was that the values of household integrity, and of neighborhood co-operation and reciprocity, the only refuge from this condition that they knew of, had lost their effectiveness as a cohesive political force.

These values had drawn them into a new system, but had no longer the power to get them back out.

Acknowledgements

I am deeply indebted to Christopher Jedrey for his comments on various versions of this paper. I have also benefitted greatly from the remarks of John Bukowczyk, Nancy Folbre, Bob Gross, David Jaffee, Steve Nissenbaum and Patricia Wilson. Responsibility for errors remains entirely mine.

FOOTNOTES

1. Horace Bushnell, "The Age of Homespun," in *Work and Play* (New York, 1864).

2. Douglass C. North, in "Location Theory and Regional Economic Growth," *Journal of Political Economy* 63, no. 3 (June 1955): 243-258, suggests that North American settlement was a capitalist venture from its inception and that the development and economic growth of new regions "were shaped by the search for and exploitation of goods in demand on world markets," (pp. 244-245). Charles S. Grant, *Democracy in the Connecticut Frontier Town of Kent* (New York, 1961) and Richard L. Bushman, *From Puritan to Yankee: Character and the Social Order in Connecticut* (Cambridge, Mass., 1967) both emphasize the entrepreneurial spirit of northern rural society in the late colonial period. On the economic growth of the early 19th century and the role of transportation, see in particular George R. Taylor, *The Transportation Revolution* (New York, 1951).

3. The articles I refer to are Michael Merrill, "Cash is Good to Eat: Self-Sufficiency and Exchange in the Rural Economy of the United States," *Radical History Review* (Winter 1977): 42-71, and James A. Henretta, "Families and Farms: *Mentalité* in Pre-Industrial America," *William and Mary Quarterly*, 3rd series, 35, no. 1 (January 1978): 3-32. My debt to both these authors is very great. See also Percy W. Bidwell, "Rural Economy in New England at the Beginning of the 19th Century," *Transactions of the Connecticut Academy of Arts and Sciences* 20 (1916): 241-399; Bidwell, "The Agricultural Revolution in New England," *American Historical Review* 26, no. 4 (July, 1921): 683-702: Bidwell and John I. Falconer, *History of Agriculture in the Northern United States, 1620-1860* (Washington, 1925); Max Schumacher, *The Northern Farmer and His Markets during the Late Colonial Period* (1948; reprinted New York, 1975); and Clarence Danhof, *Change in Agriculture: The Northern United States, 1820-1870* (Cambridge, Mass., 1969). These comment in various ways on the importance of local self-sufficiency well into the 19th century. I disagree with D.C. North's remark in "Location Theory and Regional Economic Growth," (p. 246) that while "many homesteaders maintained a subsistence existence," this "was not significant in shaping the economic development" of regions. As I hope to show, the household economy of rural New England, and the local self-sufficiency on which it rested, *did* help to shape future change, however much that change was ultimately to outmode it. For some comments on a comparable problem in the history of the British industrial revolution — the importance of small industry and hand technology — see the editorial "British Economic History and the question of work," in *History Workshop Journal* 3 (Spring 1977): 1-4.

4. This study concentrates in five towns in particular, apart from Northampton — Amherst, Hadley, Hatfield, Westhampton and Williamsburg.

5. On transportation and trade in the region, see Gilbert Cestre, *Northampton, Massachusetts: Evolution Urbaine* (Paris, 1963), pp. 35-38: Margaret E. Martin, "Merchants and Trade of the Connecticut River Valley, 1750-1820," *Smith College Studies in History* 24 (1938-1939); and Thelma Kistler, "The Rise of Railroads in the Connecticut River Valley," *ibid.*, 23 1937-1938). On peddlers and small traders, see Judd Manuscript, "Northampton with Westfield," vol. II, p. 194 (Manuscript Collection, Forbes Library, Northampton): Judd MS., "Hadley" vol. III, p. 19: Sylvester Judd, *History of Hadley* (Northampton, 1863), pp. 381-383, 388.

6. Danhof, *Change in Agriculture*, pp. 10, 13.

7. See Judd, *History of Hadley*, p. 377; Judd MS., "Hadley" vol. III, p. 50. For figures on the expansion of pasture land, compare entries in Massachusetts General Court (Committees), Aggregates of Valuations, 1791 with those in Valuation of Massachusetts, 1831 (manuscript returns on microfilm, State Library, Boston. Hereafter cited as "Mass., Valuations, 1791," etc.).

8. Judd, *History of Hadley*, p. 48; Rochester flour was advertised by such traders as Fields and Dickinson of Amherst in *New England Inquirer*, April 3, 1828.

9. For crop outputs, see Mass., Valuations, 1831, 1850. See also Margaret R. Pabst, "Agricultural Trends in the Connecticut Valley Region of Massachusetts, 1800-1900," *Smith College Studies in History* 26 (1940-1941) and Elizabeth Ramsey, "The History of Tobacco Production in the Connecticut Valley," *ibid.*, 15 (1930).

10. Judd MS., "Hadley" vol. III, p. 15; Judd, *History of Hadley*, p. 380n.; Elizabeth Porter Phelps, Diaries 1763-1812 (MSS., Porter-Phelps-Huntington House, Hadley), entries for November 4, 1804 and September 8, 1805.

11. Agnes Hannay, "A Chronicle of Industry on the Mill River," *Smith College Studies in History* 21 (1935-1936): chapters 1-3; Catherine C. Roach, "A Study of Classes and Social Mobility in a Massachusetts Mill Town: Williamsburg, 1850-1900" (unpublished honors thesis, University of Massachusetts, Amherst, 1976), pp. 13-14.

12. Rolla Milton Tryon, *Household Manufactures in the United States, 1640-1860* (Chicago, 1917); the reference to Elizabeth Huntington is in Theodore G. Huntington, "Sketches . . . of the Family and Life in Hadley, written in letters to H.F. Quincy," (bound, undated typescript, Porter-Phelps-Huntington House), pp. 45-46, 50; and that to Sylvester Smith in Judd MS., "Hadley" vol. III, p. 15. For Amherst see, for example, Joseph Eastman and Chester Marshall, Account Book, 1801-1835 (Boltwood Collection, Jones Library, Amherst). I am grateful to The Jones Library, Inc., for permission to quote from manuscripts in the Boltwood Collection, hereafter cited as "BCJL."

13. U.S., *Census for 1820* (Washington, 1821), book 1; *Sixth Census or Enumeration of the Inhabitants of the United States . . . in 1840* (Washington, 1841).

14. See the Massachusetts Censuses of Manufacturing for 1837, 1845 and 1855. A survey of manufacturing in Northampton and Williamsburg is available in Hannay, "Chronicle of Industry on the Mill River," *passim.* For other towns, the best compilations are in town histories, but for an analysis of Amherst industry, see George R. Taylor, "The Rise and Decline of Manufactures and other matters," in *Essays in Amherst's History* (Amherst, 1978), pp. 43-77.

15. There is an account of Northampton during the 1840s in Henry S. Gere, *Reminiscences of Old Northampton* ([Northampton], 1902); for statistics, see Mass., Valuations, 1831, 1841, 1850, 1860.

16. *Northampton Business Directory* (Northampton, 1860); R.G. Dun and Co., Credit Reports, Massachusetts, vol. 46 (Dun and Bradstreet Collection, Baker Library, Harvard Business School, used with permission).

17. Sylvester Judd, "Book of Fragments," (MS. Collection, Forbes Library), entries for April 1815 and July 1820.

18. Samuel Wright, *Westhampton Local History* (3 vols., unpublished typescript, n.d., Forbes Library): I, 68.

19. Etienne Clavière and Jacques Pierre Brissot, quoted in Fernand Braudel, *Capitalism and Material Life, 1400-1800*, translated by Miriam Kochan (New York, 1974), p. 335. The following discussion of this question owes much to Merrill's article cited in note 3, above.

20. Dan Huntington to Edward Huntington, Hadley, January 14, 1825 (Porter-Phelps-Huntington House).

21. Joseph Eastman and Chester Marshall, Account Book cited in note 12, above.

22. William Boltwood, Account Book, 1789-1830 (BCJL).

23. Eleazer Cowles, Account Book, 1784-1849; Asa Dickinson, Account Books, vol. II, 1804-1811 (both in BCJL).

24. Asa Dickinson, Account Books, vol. II, entry for June 6, 1806; Eastman and Marshall, Account Book, fragment dated January 30, 1827.

25. Hannah Dickinson, "Geography of the Town of Amherst," (MS. composition, Westfield Academy, 1813, BCJL).

26. See Henretta, "Families and Farms," p. 30; the couplet was printed on the cover of a bound notebook belonging to Sylvester Judd, now Judd MS., "Sunderland" (Forbes Library).

27. The notion of a crisis in household production is suggested in Merrill, "Cash is Good to Eat." The social history of Shays' Rebellion and other aspects of this crisis in western New England remain to be treated thoroughly. I have been helped in drawing the brief summary that follows by conversations and correspondence with Nancy Folbre and Patricia Wilson.

28. See Martin, "Merchants and Trade," esp. p. 145, for comments on trading difficulties in this period.

29. Acreage figures are in Mass., Valuations, 1791 and 1831. A check on the pattern in Amherst in the first two decades of the 19th century, using town valuation lists for 1802 and 1822 (Town Clerk's Office, Amherst Town Hall), suggests that while the total acreage of settled land had stopped growing and while population was rising at an average rate of over 20 per cent per decade, there was only a slight fall in the average landholdings within the town of its resident taxpayers — from 56.7 acres to 52.6 acres. There was, however, a substantial increase in the proportion of improved acreage to the total, from 20.6 per cent in 1802 to 47.2 per cent in 1822. This suggests that families which owned land in the late 18th century were often able to provide for themselves by expanding onto their reserves of unimproved land. Families with little or no land at the turn of the century, or with large numbers of heirs, would presumably have been forced to start moving out of the area, to accept wage labor or to enter a non-farming business on their own account. This leads me to the tentative suggestion that it was inequalities in access to land, rather than a general problem of "overcrowding," that helped produce the crisis in the household system. (See Kenneth Lockridge, "Land, Population and the Evolution of New England Society, 1630-1790; and an Afterthought," in Stanley N. Katz, ed., *Colonial America: Essays in Politics and Social Development* (1st edition, Boston, 1971): 467-491.) Almost certainly, average family size reached a peak in this region at the end of the 18th century; in nearby Deerfield, the maximum mean completed family size found by H. Temkin-Greener and A.C. Swedlund was 7.8 children, for women of childbearing age between 1756 and 1809 ("Fertility Transition in the Connecticut Valley, 1740-1850," forthcoming in *Population Studies*, table 2.) Overall population density was also increasing quite rapidly: in Amherst it rose from 24.4 people per square mile in 1765 to 46.7 in 1790 and 69.2 in 1820, and the figures for Hadley were 23.5, 36.1 and 64.2 respectively. (Taylor, "The Rise and Decline of Manufacturing," p. 48, table 1.) But these densities were low by European standards. Much more research is needed on the land question.

30. Hannah Dickinson, "The Farmer's Annual Employment," (MS. composition, Westfield Academy, 1813, BCJL).

31. Theodore Huntington, "Sketches," p. 57.

32. Israel to Seth Nims, Conway, May 3, 1823 (BCJL).

33. For supplies by farmers to factories, see Taylor, "Rise and Decline," pp. 65-66, which discusses data in the *McLane Report* (1832) relating to produce delivered to the Amherst Cotton Manufacturing Co.; see also Joseph F. Warner, Account Book, 1851-1858 (MS. Coll., Forbes Library), which records supplies made — in return for goods — to Josiah Hayden's company store in Williamsburg.

34. *New England Inquirer*, November 22, 1827 and January 24, 1828. For the Huntingtons, see Theodore Huntington, "Sketches" p. 45.

35. One ledger, dated 1827-1839, from the store of Ansel Wright and Theodore Rust, survives in the Forbes Library's MS. Coll.. For Stoddard and Lathrop, see Dun and Co., Reports, Mass., vol. 46, p. 102 (Dun and Bradstreet Coll., Baker Library).
36. Ledger for the store at North Hadley, 1839-1840 (Porter-Phelps-Huntington House). Even if we add the amount given in notes, the total reaches only 42.5 per cent of repayments.

37. The advertisement is in *Hampshire Herald*, November 4, 1845. Kingsley's notes are in the collection of loose papers enclosed in the supplement to his account book, in the MS. Coll., Forbes Library. For later references to Amherst, see the account books of Noble Dickinson and Horace Belding and the papers of Asahel Goodell in BCJL.

38. Helen H. Flanders, comp., *Ancient Ballads Traditionally Sung in New England* (4 vols., Philadelphia, 1960-1965): I, 77.

39. For the argument that it was not the "Protestant Ethic," but the "tenacious resistance . . . of pre-capitalist labour," that lay behind the development of industrial capitalism in Europe, see Hans Medick, "The Proto-industrial Family Economy: The Structural Function of Household and Family during the Transition from Peasant Society to Industrial Capitalism," *Social History* 3 (October 1976): 291-315. On outwork in Europe see also Rudolf Braun, "The Impact of Cottage Industry on an Agricultural Population," in David S. Landes, ed., *The Rise of Capitalism* (New York, 1966) and Franklin Mendels, "Proto-Industrialization: The First Stage of the Industrialization Process," *Journal of Economic History* 32 (1972): 241-261.

40. Mary to Eli Nutting, Amherst, September 29, 1841; Hannah to Eli, June 6, 1845; Harriet to Eli, July 3, 1847 (Nutting Correspondence, BCJL).

41. Elizabeth to Susanna Goodell, Springfield, August 25, 1827; Susanna to Moses and Susanna Goodell, Cabotville [Chicopee], April 8, 1837 and February 7, 1838. (M.W. Goodell Papers, BCJL).

42. Harriet to Eli Nutting, Amherst, October 23, 1847 (Nutting Correspondence, BCJL).

43. See Johnathan Prude, "The Coming of Industrial Order: A Study of Town and Factory Life in Rural Massachusetts, 1813-1860," (unpublished Ph.D. dissertation, Harvard, 1976), pp. 85, 88 table III.

44. Tryon, *Household Manufactures*, pp. 314-315, table XVIII.

45. Hannah to Eli Nutting, June 6, 1845 (Nutting Corresp., BCJL). On the importance of outwork, see Prude, "The Coming of Industrial Order," p. 93.

46. See advertisements in *Hampshire and Franklin Express*, 1845-1848. For Leonard M. Hills, see Edward Carpenter and Charles Morehouse, *History of the Town of Amherst, Massachusetts*, (Amherst, 1896), p. 195 and Dun and Co., Reports, Mass., vol. 46, pp. 1, 47 (Dun and Bradstreet Coll., Baker Library).

47. Sweetser, Cutler and Co., Ledgers (BCJL).

48. Charlotte Dickinson, Account Books, 1812-1848 (BCJL).

49. Carpenter and Morehouse, *History of Amherst*, p. 306; Taylor, "Rise and Decline," pp. 60-61; see also *Amherst Record* May 3, 1871.

50. Mary Nutting Bridgeman to Eli Nutting, Amherst, April 24, 1843 (Nutting Corresp., BCJL).

51. Elizabeth to Susanna Goodell, Springfield, August 25, 1827 (Goodell Papers, BCJL).

52. Maria to Eli Nutting, Amherst, March 12, 1848 (Nutting Corresp.).

53. Henry F. Hills to Adelaide Spencer, Amherst, June 19, 1862, in Isabelle Carlhian, "The Hills Houses in Amherst," (unpublished paper, Hampshire College, 1973, copy in BCJL), appendix.

54. Austin Loomis to Mary Dickinson, Bolton, Ct., April 7, 1820 (Austin Loomin Papers, BCJL).

55. A. Forbes and J.W. Green, *The Rich Men of Massachusetts* (Boston, 1851), pp. 143-144.

56. Loomis to Dickinson, cited in note 54, above.

57. Nathaniel D. to Asahel Goodell, Sacramento, December 26, 1854 (Goodell Papers); Moses Goodell, Rental Agreement with John Thayer, Belchertown, February 13, 1852 (Goodell Papers).

58. Quoted in Danhof, *Change in Agriculture*, p. 23.

59. Pabst, "Agricultural Trends," p. 54; Levi Bartlett, "Wheat Growing in New Hampshire," in *Report of the Commissioner for Agriculture for the Year 1862* (Washington, 1863), pp. 96-104.

60. In Northampton by 1860 the richest decile of the population controlled 72 per cent of the town's real and personal estate, while the poorest six deciles held no recorded property at all [Robert Doherty, *Society and Power: Five New England Towns, 1800-1860* (Amherst, 1977), p. 47, table 5.1]; the distinction in Amherst was not as sharp, but still clear — the richest decile owned nearly half the town's wealth (Amherst Valuation List, 1860, Town Clerk's Office, Amherst Town Hall). On the 18th century see John J. Waters, "Patrimony, Succession and Social Stability: Guilford, Connecticut, in the Eighteenth Century," *Perspectives in American History* 10 (1976): 131-160. Judd's comments are in Judd MS., "Miscellaneous" vol XIV, pp. 286-287 and in his "Notebook" vol. I, entry for October 1, 1839 (MSS. in Forbes Library).

61. On the Workingmen's Party, see *Hampshire Gazette*, September 8 and 15, 1830; October 22 and 29, 1834. This brief summary of the party's ideas is taken from resolutions or addresses printed here. Bancroft's letter was published in the *Gazette*, October 8, 1834.

62. Judd, "Notebook," vol. II, January 31, 1843.

16.

POLITICS, CLASS STRUCTURE, AND THE ENDURING WEAKNESS OF BRITISH SOCIAL DEMOCRACY

James E. Cronin

I.

The notion that what social history lacks and desperately needs is politics, is curious indeed. For social history has always been among the most political of all the varieties of historical research and writing, and its practitioners have generally had a clearer understanding of the linkages between social history and politics than have those who have written and, continue to write, the history of politics and of political ideas with little or no appreciation of the social context in which these are normally embedded. Even the least sophisticated social historian, I would suggest, exhibits a better sense of the interrelatedness of politics, ideas and material life than do some of the most eminent writers of narrative political history. Take the worst of cases, for example, such as the late G.M. Trevelyan, author of the infamous definition of social history as "the history of a people with the politics left out." If one checks the origins of that statement, one finds that his actual point was not that one could legitimately "leave out the politics from the history of any people, particularly the English people," but that, because "so many history books have consisted of political annals with little reference to their social environment, a reversal of that method may have its uses to redress the balance." The aim, then, was not to degrade politics but to root its analysis: "Without social history, . . . political history is unintelligible," Trevelyan argued, but he never claimed it was unimportant.[1]

Any reasonable review of the evolution of social history would show, moreover, that political issues broadly conceived have lurked behind — or in some cases, quite explicitly determined — the agenda for research in social history.[2] What, after all, is the purpose of the enormous labour expended upon reconstructing the daily lives of ordinary people if not to assert their importance as historical actors or, at least, as the key objects of other historical actors? Can anyone explain the intensity of interest in the history of the family — outwardly the least political variety of social history — without taking account of feminism, and without recognizing that its aim is to reveal the changing forms of domination and cooperation within the domestic sphere? Is not the major question underlying the study of social mobility its relationship to process of class closure, formation and mobilization? Still more directly to the point, how can the critique of social history as apolitical be reconciled with the recurring interest shown by social historians in the development of the state?[3] It may well be, of course, that the products of social historical research are inadequate, and it definitely is the case that its political implications or inspirations are seldom made explicit; nonetheless, it is difficult to think of a major area within social history where political considerations are not important in the conception and execution of research.

Nor is the reluctance of social historians either to draw out explicitly the political consequences of their findings, or to confess their political assumptions, entirely to be deplored. For a certain separation between social and political history might well be a necessary precondition for the advance of research.

Successful research strategies do not always or necessarily replicate in their methodology the complexities of the real world, but often require some simplification and some delimiting of the objects of analysis. Indeed, it is generally necessary to narrow the focus of research in order to see the complex and contradictory nature of phenomena that are normally embedded in a dense context. More specifically, a proper recognition of the complexity of social historical development may only be possible when the equally complex interactions between politics and society are temporarily removed from the picture. Trevelyan again, not generally noted for his methodological expertise, nonetheless seems to have grasped this point when he wrote that "social history does not merely provide the required link between economic and political history. It has also its own positive value and peculiar concern." A generation or two of practising social historians have found Trevelyan's insights confirmed in their work. Inspired frequently by a vision of social "totality" and of the social basis of political and cultural events, they have focussed their attention on the evolution of one or another aspect of social life, only to find that its course was so contradictory and complex that any simple attempt to link it with politics would not do justice to the topic itself, or to the linkages between society and politics. They have found instead that the spheres of human activity studied by social historians each have their own logic and history which require study in and of themselves and which cannot simply be subsumed by extant models of social change or simply appropriated to political analysis as "influences" or "background." To put the matter historiographically, initial progress in social history required a temporary disengagement of social history from politics. Its increasing sophisticaton, however, has made the subsequent reconstruction of the linkages a still more difficult, and hence more distant, prospect. In this context, ritual incantation about the importance of political events and exhortation to infuse political content into social history are worse than useless — they do positive harm by seeming to suggest that the connection can be made quickly and easily if only there is a will to do so.

The burden of this essay is to argue for a different approach, one which recognizes the "relative autonomy" of social historical research and which defines the connection between social history and political history as in and of itself problematical. More specifically, I propose to review the problem of the historical development of the British working class in the twentieth century and, in that context, to argue (1) that that history has political and social-structural dimensions whose evolutions do not run parallel and which should be analyzed separately; (2) that the present scholarly consensus on this issue is deficient precisely for its failure to disentangle the social and economic from the political history of the class; and (3) that, when one does analyze these spheres separately, what appears to have mattered most is neither the development of social structure nor of politics within the working class, but the shifting linkage between the two types of change. We begin with a brief excursion into the beliefs and attitudes of working people at the end of the Great War and the ensuing political trajectory to 1945, then discuss the pervasive sense that something has radically changed in the postwar era. We analyze this perception and the arguments which it has produced in some detail, and suggest that they elide crucial distinctions between social and political history. We then try, in a brief and tentative way, to review several bodies of research which tend to show that the evolution of various aspects of social structure and politics has been more complicated than previously thought or allowed in the simpler attempts to link social and political history. We argue further that these distinct evolutions have combined to produce a growing disjuncture betweeen class relations and political alignments. The marshalling of evidence for these arguments is, of course, a far more difficult task which would transcend the limits of this largely methodological essay. This particular piece is offered as a preliminary to that effort. Writing it has helped to focus my research in this broader area; I hope others will find it useful as well.[4]

II.

The British working class thrust itself into the center of political and social life during a protracted period of militancy lasting from 1910 to 1926. This bursting upon the scene quickly produced a series of efforts aimed at making sense of the phenomenon. In particular, the broad-based "labour unrest" that preceded the Great War stimulated several attempts to diagnose the malady that was agitating the minds of British workers. Virtually everybody had something to say —Ramsay MacDonald, Tom Mann, George Askwith, and even H.G. Wells showing no shyness in pronouncing upon the hopes and complaints of ordinary people.[5] It seemed quite unnecessary, with such talent available, to ask working men and women directly.

This quaintly Victorian faith in the ability of labor leaders and middle-class commentators to discern the consciousness and feelings of the lower orders remained strong right up to 1914. One of the many effects of the war, however, was to shatter such simple notions about the ability of men of different classes to understand one another. The war also served to demonstrate the enormous, if normally latent, economic power which an organized working class could possess, and this revelation led directly to a recognition of the autonomy, complexity, and independence of working-class attitudes. The war made "public opinion" genuinely popular and, for that reason, less accessible to those whose views prevailed in established public discourse.[6] And the core of the new public in Britain was the working class, who were transformed from a mere physical presence — and, given the snobbery of urban ecology, often a barely visible one — into a political and cultural force.

The change was registered in many arenas, but most notably in attempts to capture the shifting mood of the populace during the war. The famous Commission of Enquiry into Industrial Unrest of 1917 was perhaps the first public acknowledgement of the fact that the interests of workers were not being adequately expressed through existing forums, and of the need to recast existing methods of inquiry and opinion-taking. The response was to send Commissioners into the industrial areas to hold hearings there rather than to invite spokesmen to London to speak on behalf of their various constituencies. The ensuing reports, though not quite the collection of *cahiers de doléances* that they could easily have been, nonetheless have a ring of authenticity lacking in previous inquiries or even in the tradition of social investigation begun by Booth, Rowntree and the rest.[7]

But official surveys were surely the least interesting and subtle of the products of that new awareness of the distinctive quality of working-class life and opinion, and the very best is probably the least well-known. It appeared, seemingly without an author, in 1919 with the unalluring title, *The Equipment of the Workers*, and was produced by a voluntary society in Sheffield.[8] The actual author was Arnold Freeman, head of the St. Philip's Settlement and architect of the study. Its aim was an "interrogation of the future" involving an assessment of "what the workers are capable of doing" and of, "what, later on, they are likely to do."

This unique inquiry went on to determine that, among the manual workers, about one-quarter were "well-equipped," nearly three-quarters "inadequately-equipped," and a small portion, about one in fifteen, positively "mal-equipped." The former were "men and women who have been awakened . . . to the seriousness and splendour of existence." The great bulk in the middle were described as "*asleep*" — "They muddle through life, . . . they desire to rest and be left alone . . . ," — while the remaining minority were judged "incapable of discharging reasonably the duties of man in society." The terms of this classification are as quaint as they are objectionable, but what is important here is how the totals add up. The overwhelming majority were in one of the two top groups. Thus, more than 95% of the workers were judged either intensely aware of thier environment and its potential, or at least capable, when once awakened, of achieving such a level of personal competence. Only a tiny fraction were considered beyond hope. Despite its tone, therefore, the *Equipment of the Workers* is far more sensitive to the intelligence running through working-class attitudes than almost any earlier studies of poverty and social life.

The core of the survey involved extensive interviews with 816 members of the Sheffield working class, half men and half women, and divided by age and occupation in much the same way as the underlying working population. From these were derived a summary of workers' political attitudes and a detailed picture of their daily lives, and the published volume of analysis reproduces sufficient data to bring these together and to suggest just what kind of person held various sorts of political opinions. The main political facts were stunning in their unanimity:

> It is our conclusion that the Well-equipped men and women workers (about one-fourth of the whole) will be intelligently determined, beyond all possibility of statesmanlike denial, to achieve extremely far-reaching changes in the existing civilization; and that the Inadequately-equipped workers (comprising the bulk of the remainder), without knowing definitely what they want, and without much willingness for self-discipline and patient endeavour, will violently react against a continuance of the pre-War industrial and social order or of any approximation to it.

Such a result contradicted the most cherished belief of the middle and upper classes that discontent found its breeding ground among the poor and those least capable of resisting. Those labelled "well-equipped" by the rigorous standards of the St. Philip's Settlement would certainly have been among the most intelligent, active and often the most influential members of their class, and yet their politics were the most obviously insurgent. Take Mrs. Leaning, a 24-year-old machine tender in a shell factory with a husband at the front. Fond of her family, "because of the ties attached to home," she felt that "nine women out of ten work against their feelings, chiefly because the work is too hard and coarse." In her own job she "experience a dreadful feeling of monotony" and has decided that "there are lots of things preferable to work of slavery." As for politics, she sometimes "feels almost too tired to take interest in anything," but when asked about her view of Socialism responded that it was "the greatest and best movement in the whole world. The only hope of the working-classes." Or Mrs. Quarles, age 28 and a housewife. Knowledgeable about history and local affairs, a member of the Women's Liberal Association, she was no radical, Socialists being in her view "rather wild and unbalanced people but harmless." Nevertheless she was convinced that "there is likely to be in the near future *Control of Industry by the Democracy*; the workers will never consent to return to pre-War conditions; the wage-system is doomed."

The "well-equipped men" exhibited much the same attitudes but were, on the whole, even more active in and integrated into unions, WEA classes and co-ops. Mr. Dalson, an engine tester of 27, exemplified all these characteristics. "He believes his home is the finest place in the world; he is very fond indeed of his wife and child." "In no sense a 'craftsman,'" he is nonetheless an adequate worker. "He works on the 'shift system' and this prevents him from systematic attendance at chapel or institute, etc.," but he has been a member of the National Union of General Workers for five years, and "booms the [Co-operative] Movement at every opportunity." As for Socialism, he professes to believe that it is "The only means of establishing the 'Kingdom of God' on earth." As for his city, "He thinks Sheffield is 'A Dirty Picture' with 'A Beautiful Frame.'"

Mr. Youngson, a 35-year-old fitter with a bad heart, was less of an activist than Dalson, but not any less militant or self-confident. He had recently moved to Sheffield from Middlesbrough, where "I was actively engaged in the trade union movement," and found his new surroundings "ugly and dirty." His rent was recently increased but he had refused to pay, and so was now given notice to quit. Nevertheless, he was proud of his home and relatively happy at his work. In politics, he was committedly left-wing: "I disagree entirely with the present constitution, and would abolish the House of Lords" and much else. Socialism was "The only way for us," and he very much hoped that the present "trials" would "awaken" the workers "to the power they possess."

Not all of even the "well-equipped" were so clear about their preferences as these, and the views of the not so well equipped were more confused still. And, of course, labour in Sheffield may have been more advanced in 1917 than it was in Wales or Wigan or, for that matter, London. Nonetheless, the compilers of the Sheffield report were much impressed by the fact that large numbers of the most articulate, stable and active workers were possessed of a very definite and radical vision of present ills and future solutions, and that this group was strategically located to move the whole class towards that vision. They assumed, too, that roughly similar processes were having comparable effects throughout Britain. The result could only be a body of "well-equipped" men and women intent upon social transformation. The report concluded on a lofty note:

> Eight millions of workers, each of them effective in trade union, co-operative society, local and national politics; all of them . . . increasingly homogeneous in their political and industrial purposes; these men and women will be the makers of English history from 1920 to 1950; upon a bridge made of their stalwart backs our children will cross from the shame and wretchedness of today to the Land in which the dreams of humanity are coming true.

III.

The confident prediction of 1919 seems to have been confirmed by the events of 1920-45. Despite the setbacks of 1924, 1926 and 1931, and the toll of pain and defeat inflicted by the slump, the "forward march of labour" was sustained from 1920 through the elections of 1935 and even of 1950 and 1951. By the end of the Labour government of 1945-51, over 8 millions were in trade unions, and close to 14 millions were voting Labour. Even in its hour of electoral defeat in 1951, Labour outpolled the Conservatives. Despite the distribution of seats, the "huge vote of 1951, still in conditions of postwar austerity and planning, was," as Raymond Williams has argued, "the most conscious working class determination ever recorded in Britain, to reject the conditions of pre-war society and go on with the new system."[9]

The sequence of events leading from the emergence of labour as a major industrial *and* political force after 1910 to its electoral triumphs of 1945-51 helped to confirm the rhetoric of the movement itself about the inevitable "forward march of labour." The notion has come to inform the historiography of both the class and the party for the period, despite the fact that the record of the 1930s was anything but encouraging. Neither the unions nor the Labour Party made steady progress during the interwar years, and any account formulated in 1939 would most likely have had readier recourse to metaphors from pathology than to those suggesting growth. Whatever the course of events making for the postwar victories, however, the image of a strong and united working class movement marching solidly behind the socialist banners of the party has stuck in the popular and historical memory, and constitutes the "base line" from which subsequent changes are measured.

It is obvious to all that the expressions of solidarity registered during 1945-51, however ambiguous their origins, did not provide entry into that "Land in which the dreams of humanity are coming true." Rather, since the first post-war Conservative victory there has been a mounting sense that Labour has lost its political momentum and entered into a prolonged and deepening crisis. At first, it appeared to be a simple product of exhaustion and the petering out of imaginative new ideas as the welfare state, hurriedly put in place during 1945-48, began to generate those goods it was supposed to deliver. But by 1960 the "visible moral decline of the labour movement" and its electoral impasse were beginning to be interpreted as merely surface manifestations of deeper processes leading to the decomposition of the working class itself.[10] The disappointments of the Wilson-Callaghan years, culminating in the catastrophe of 1979, only reinforced the sense of decline and have tended to confirm the most pessimistic of diagnoses about the implications of social change for labor politics.

Gloom over the fate of labor is now pervasive, and it is no longer the critics of labor who are most prominent in announcing its demise. Such a sympathetic and subtle analyst as Eric Hobsbawn, for example, was moved in his Marx Memorial Lecture for 1978, to ask why "the forward march of labour and the labour movement . . . appears to have come to a halt in this country about twenty-five or thirty years ago."[11] The crisis of labour, as he and others have described it, has been first and foremost a matter of weakening "support for the Labour party;" and certainly the pattern of elections and polls since 1978 have told in the same direction. The crisis of labor has been manifest also, it is alleged, in the changed tone and demeanor of other aspects of the movement. The conduct of strikes, for example, has altered so that it now appears that "the strength of a group lies not in the amount of loss they can cause to the employer, but in the inconvenience they can cause to the public, i.e., to other workers . . . " The very demands of strikes seem also to be somewhat lacking in nobility. Inflation and full employment have eroded the old sense of "a fair day's pay for a fair day's work," and have taught workers the amoral values of the market. Wage demands have escalated, and the combination of seemingly limitless claims and sectional styles of protest has been seen as straining the ties of class loyalty among workers while also alienating the broader, middle-class public.

The sense of malaise grasped by Hobsbawm is echoed by countless, particularly older, workers. One working-class woman, from among the many interviewed recently by Jeremy Seabrook, expressed poignantly the "dislocation in working-class tradition" when she explained: "What we've got now, it's nothing to do with socialism. It's a mocking of all the things we fought for . . . I don't know what's happened to folk. They've all got greedy-grabbing, that's the trouble." A worker from Nottingham put it more concisely: "When we had nowt, we threatened the rich. Now we act like they did." And another expressed bitter disappointment at the futility of chasing after wages when he commented, "You can't ruin the capitalist system simply by taking money off it, and that's what the working class is doing. You can't beat them economically. There's got to be an awakening of the working class, a spiritual awakening. I don't know whether it will come." A middle-aged worker from the East Midlands, keenly aware of the obsolesence of his own skills and the degradation of work in the most modern plants, conveyed a near-total disillusion: "In my lifetime I've seen working-class people become more cynical. People actually get through their lives without believing in anything. Now when I was young, the labour movement had a meaning; it had a moral content. It could challenge the morality of capitalism, and appeal to something in us that was generous and magnanimous . . . What the working-class had to oppose to capitalism is running pretty thin now."[12]

The malaise and the disintegration to which Hobsbawm alludes and which Seabrook seeks to describe may be real or imagined, but the perception that it is real pervades political discourse and social analysis alike in contemporary Britain. Debate, in fact, centers not upon whether it is so, but upon how this state of affairs came to be. Neither Hobsbawm, nor Seabrook nor numerous social scientists who have worked in and around the problem, can at this stage confidently assert a clear answer. Throughout the discussion, however, certain common themes surface again and again, suggesting both the assumptions that govern the discourse and the main contours of the answer that is likely to emerge. To begin, Hobsbawm, Seabrook and others are critical of the narrow minds that have dominated the Labour party and the unions in the postwar years, and would locate some of the problem in their activity or, in most cases, planned in activity. They would hesitate to attribute major significance to failures of leadership, though, and would tend rather to seek the basic roots of the difficulty in the various social processes that appear to have broken up and fragmented the traditional working class. To Hobsbawm, for example, the starting point for analysis is the simple failure of the manual workers to continue their numerical growth and the consequent rise within the work-force of white-collar and service sector employees. Even among manual workers, there have been sectoral shifts away from the old centers of trade union strength and working-class culture, like textiles, mining and shipbuilding, and a tendency for adult male workers in old and new industries to be replace by women who, he seems to feel, are less committed to the "common style of proletarian life" or to the values of trade unionism.

It is also argued that the dispersal of old working-class neighborhoods and their replacement by blocks of flats or council estates somehow have lessened solidarity as well. Years ago, as Hobsbawm explains, the working class was "a collection of localized communites locally rooted to a much greater extent than the middle classes." But this comfortable, older pattern has been replaced by a new, more planned, but more sterile social ecology, that has produced, in J. Seabrook's words, "the desolation of ruined communities and broken associations" that characterizes contemporary urban Britain. The destruction of community, so the argument runs, has reinforced the transformation of the economy so as to marginalize, isolate and "privatize" the working class.

While these factors have been undermining the solidity of the workers as a class, rising living standards have removed the edge from their material grievances. Thus to the extent that workers still pursue wage gains, as the record of strikes indicates they do, this very expression of militancy is taken as evidence not of class consciousness or even of resentment at inequality but of a growing acceptance by working people of the culture of consumption that previously was thought to affect mostly the middle classes. Hence wage militancy becomes the symbol of the absence of proletarian values and so loses its former meaning as a battle between rich and poor.

The argument, fleshed out in these terms, has a familiar ring, and many will hear in it echoes of the theories worked out in the 1960s about "the affluent worker" or the process of *embourgeoisement*. That theory has indeed made a curious and surprising rebound in the last few years. When first proffered in the wake of Labour's 1959 electoral defeat, it was linked to an explicit political program. The idea was that because Labour's traditional working-class base was being eroded by the social trends of an increasingly "affluent society," the party should be wary of relying upon old-fashioned appeals to class consciousness and to socialism. The theory became indentified in the context with the attempt to push Labour "to the right," which received its clearest expression in the movement to excise Clause 4 from the party constitution. When social scientists attempted to test the argument in the 1960s, therefore, they did so with a bit of an axe to grind. Not surprisingly, they found the theory wanting. Moreover, as the 1960s progressed and workers began in ever larger numbers to defy the government and union leaders first in "unofficial" and, finally, in the 1970s, in a series of "official" confrontations, the attention of researchers shifted away from debates on class structure in general. By 1981, Howard Newby could argue that research into state of Britain's class structure was at an impasse, stalled by the failure of the *embourgeoisement* hypothesis and yet unable to generate internally an alternative.

Just as sociologists have decided to bury the argument, it has been taken up again by the general public, by journalistic writers like Seabrook and by Britain's most eminent labor historian. To be sure, there are differences. Hobsbawm, for one, refuses to use the term embourgeoisement, or the phrase "the affluent worker," and even criticizes the former for what it implies about white-collar workers. And certainly there is lacking the celebratory tone which marked at least some of the early advocates of the theory, especially Ferdynand Zweig. But the similarities are in the end more striking than the differences. The "affluent worker thesis," in short, is alive and well and will remain so until the sociologists come up with something that is not only more methodologically and conceptually rigorous but that also satisfies as well as the *embourgeoisement* argument the need to explain British labor's evident crisis. In the meantime, the notion that what lies behind the political trends of the postwar years is the very decomposition of the working class will dominate the analysis of labor's history and current status.[13]

IV.

These most recent arguments about the fate of the working-class and the labor movement thus remain very much in that tradition of sociological analysis which derives its strength from its attempt to link up the evident decrease in the *elan* of the labor movement with the equally visible post-war changes in class structure. Though the labels attached to the analysis have shifted, it has a continuity and a continuing allure. The reasons for this are not hard to find: the facts about shifting political allegiances are well-documented and more or less incontrovertible, and the reshaping of society is so obvious as to be beyond debate, and it seems quite logical to assume that the twin transformations have been closely related.[14]

Looked at historiographically, moreover, the *embourgeoisement* argument is one which fits very nicely with the desire expressed by critics of social history to see social and political analysis closely combined. It infuses the study of shifting social structures with ready political import, and definitely avoids the tendency to treat the detailed description of material life as an end in itself. And it has great political relevance, for not only does such an analysis explain politics but in subtle hands can be used to proscribe political strategy. If there were an ideal towards which the advocates of a "politicized social history" should strive, it would seem to be an analysis akin in method and logic to that used by those who have framed and argued for the "affluent worker" hypothesis.

But is it really logical to move so quickly and easily between the analysis of social structure and of political behavior? It would certainly be foolish to suggest that there is no connection between the shape of Britain's class structure and its political life, and it would be equally absurd to reject the massive accumulation of empirical findings that demonstrate the changes that have occurred in both spheres. The past failures of the early versions of the argument ought, however, to warn us of any too facile connection between these sets of changes. The rejection of the "affluent worker" argument by social scientists was based, after all, not merely upon changing fashions in social research but also on findings that did not fit well with the model. More important, we have suggested above that a proper appreciation of the complexities of political and social development alike might well require a temporary severing of the links that connect them in order to understand each on its own terms. This would seem especially prudent in this particular case because, as we shall see, the link has been built for the most part upon an assumption which is in fact historically untenable. Rejecting that assumption and dissolving, at least for analytical purposes, that linkage, it will be further shown, opens up major new analytical possibilities.

The assumption in question, of course, is that "the political expression of class consciousness . . . means in practice . . . support for the Labour party." There is, in fact, much in the historical record to justify such an identification of the class with its class-based party.[15] The parallel growth of the working-class itself, of working-class organizations like Friendly Societies and trade unions, and of the Labour Party from the late nineteenth through the first half of the twentieth century, demonstrates a firm linkage. However, the connections were never so close and automatic as the happy coincidence of outcomes might seem to suggest, and it was never obvious to contemporaries that class membership was easily translated into political ideologies or allegiances or that social structural change had inevitable political consequences. A closer look at the timing of the growth of unions and of Labour party support, rather than a review of its sociology, would show further that the main spurs to class expression in politics were the two World Wars, which apparently had the effect of creating more space within the political arena for class-based alternatives.[16] Add to this the uneasy alliance between the Labour Party and its working-class base since 1950, and the enduring weakness of the connection, rather than its strength, becomes the more interesting fact to be explained.[17]

Perhaps it is time, then, to reject the temptation for premature synthesis based on such an assumption and, instead, to begin to pry apart the analysis of political allegiance from that of economic and social change. Such a separation opens up several new possibilities for research and argument and affords a much more complex and rounded view of the sturctural evolution of the working-class and of its behavior. By allowing separate foci, directed in the first instance at class structure and in the next at political alignments, it is possible to develop a much subtler view of the ambiguities and unevenness that characterize both. And by positing an initial separation, such an approach forces us to take more seriously the question of how the connections are actually forged and maintained at different points in time. In the remainder of this essay, I shall try to suggest very briefly what kind of views of social structure, of working-class culture, and of Labour politics are likely to emerge from an analysis conducted on the lines proposed here. No claim is made here to original research, although in fact such efforts have helped to generate this argument, but rather to the value of a new approach. Here I shall confine my empirical references to summary judgments of extant research. Needless to say, if the argument makes better sense of existing material, it clearly deserves further efforts to produce confirming evidence.

We have seen that as soon as the identification of the Labour party as the one and only vehicle for the political articulation of working-class interest is questioned, one begins to ask about relations between the party and the class and to realize that they have always been problematical, forever troubled and uneasy. Similarly, immediately one decides to study the evolution of social structure in its own right, the more ambivalent do its trends appear. Those structural processes which have supposedly been eroding class solidarity — the shifting sectoral distribution of workers, the increase in women's employment, the expansion of non-manual occupations, and the new patterns of recruitment into these white-collar or, for men, black-coated, categories — turn out upon examination to have been highly uneven and to have had contradictory effects. For example, the decisions of so many married women to return to, or to continue, working may well have removed so many "Mums" from the snug home that is so treasured an element of the traditional image of English working-class culture. But this trend has also generated needed income for workers' families, achieved greater, if still limited, personal independence for women, and usually has resulted in new recruits to the trade unions. More important, the phenomenon may, and occasionally has, added the leaven of women's unique sense of grievance and their interest in social provision to the rhetorical complex of working-class concerns.[18] The evolution of white-collar work has been similarly contradictory. Though it cannot be claimed that white-collar workers, especially if they are men, have been "proletarianized" in terms of lifestyle or education, their incomes and certain aspects of their working conditions probably have been. Moreover, they have themselves begun to act more "proletarian" and "class-conscious" by starting up and joining trade unions and by beginning to entertain, and occasionally put into practice, notions of workplace action.[19] That this is a genuine development rooted in the structural changes of these jobs, and not simply a temporary copying of tactics from industrial workers, is attested to by the resiliency of white-collar opposition to the Thatcher regime. The most protracted battles against Thatcher's policies have come from civil servants and health service workers and, though they have not been notably successful on pay issues, the conflicts have shown the unions of white collar workers in the public sector to be much stronger than had previously been thought.

Other sorts of social structural changes — e.g., in technology and industrial organization, in the degree of concentration in the economy, in the sectoral distribution of industry, and so on — could be shown to have equally contradictory effects upon the solidarities of the workplace and the community and, at one remove, upon electoral alignments. Thus, the initial result of dissociating social and political analysis is, and would seem inevitably to be, to enhance the appreciation of the contradictoriness of structural change and of political allegiances. The second effect of such a methodological distinction is to reveal the gaps and elisions which other kinds of analysis ignore or paper over. There is an enormous space, both in theory and in real life, between the mere assembling of the workforce in the factory or the office and the expression of workers' feelings and desires in party membership or electoral preference. The space is filled, of course, with all those various and complementary processes that contribute to "class formation" and that constitute the structures of everyday life for workingmen and women: personal relations with family, neighbors and friends; patterns of courtship, marriage and childrearing; leisure habits, cultural symbols and rituals; social life within the production process, workers' membership in unions and other formal organizations, their participation in strikes and other relatively non-political forms of resistance. These aspects of workers' lives have each been accorded their share of study — mostly under the separate rubrics of "working-class culture" and "industrial behavior" — but most of the results are fragmentary and poorly conceptualized.

Still, there is material enough to suggest the major outlines and the predominant trends and to show how poorly they fit with notions of class decomposition and *embourgeoisement*. Accepting, for the moment, the rather artificial distinction between "industrial behavior," and "working-class culture" one can discern the most important findings in each area and their implications for the present argument. Students of the former have been struck by two sets of facts. First, despite all the structural inequalities that work in an essentially capitalist society implies, British workers have exercised an amazing amount of on-the-job control.[20] This control has been greater for craftsmen than for the less skilled, and, in particular, for men as opposed to women, but overall the power of management to control the details of the labor process has been a largely unsuccessful battle. Only during the long slump of the interwar years did the balance tilt sharply in the employers' favor, and even then only in the most depressed industries or in those very new sectors where workers' organization had not been implanted, and only, it must be noted, for a time.[21] Intimately linked to this workers' power at the workplace has been the extensive character of organization on the shop floor. The network of shop stewards that has spread throughout British manufacturing since the late 1950s is a most impressive achievement. So, too, is the crystallization of this local strength in formal trade union organization, which since 1935 has continued to grow absolutely and proportionally, in spite of the rundown of the older centers of unionism in textiles, coal and shipbuilding.[22]

The second, interconnected phenomenon revealed by the study of labor's "industrial behavior" is the ubiquitousness and persistence of conflict. If there were a serious decline in the saliency of class interest and allegiance in twentieth-century Britain, one index would surely have to be a declining trend in strike activity. Yet the actual tendency has been quite otherwise. Since 1918, there have been three major outbursts of strikes — the first extending from the Great War through 1926, the second from about 1957 to 1962, and the third during 1968-72. There has also been recorded since 1956 a vastly increased propensity to strike throughout the economy, in recent years including even workers in the public sector. By a truly perverse logic, the greatest and longest lull in overt industrial conflict lasted from 1927 to 1955, more or less the precise period noted for its class-based politics.[23] The evidence from the purely industrial side, it would seem, gives scant support for those who see mainly decline resulting from the social structural changes of the postwar years.

Studies of working-class culture reveal other levels of reality that do not seem to fit the model. This is, in a sense, rather curious, for the tradition of cultural studies was a very important component in shaping the paradigm upon which arguments of decay and decomposition have been built. The first serious texts in the field, by Hoggart and Williams, enshrined an image of the working-class as inherently collectivist, introverted, localized and culturally distinct. They were seen to live in closely-knit communities based upon the overlap of stable, self-contained neighborhoods and extended families centered upon the mother, defensive by nature and by preference and put further on the defensive by the onslaught of mass media and their corrosive consumerist message.[24] The first fruits of the prolific Institute of Community Studies told the same story, featuring the cozy world of London's East End against the stark loneliness of the new council estates.[25]

With the subsequent development and refinement of cultural studies and analysis of the family and community patterns, and with the added perspectives provided by the growth of women's history and the use of oral interviewing in the rewriting of history, these over-simplified contrasts have been replaced by more sophisticated understandings of all these processes. The old, working-class family, for example, has come to be seen with a bit more critical distance. A source of strength in times past it may have been, but, as the testimony of men, women and children reveals, it was also the focus of the arbitrary exercise of authority and of much physical and mental pain. If "mum" was at the center of the networks of neighbors and relatives, she was also usually either worn-out by frequent pregnancies and the incessant demands of children or stuck with the double duties of home-maker and wage-earner. The demise of what might be called the Victorian proletarian family cannot, in this light, be regarded as an unambiguous loss to the working-class. Rather, the smaller families, the better medical care for women and children, the more rational practice of family planning, the greater ease of divorce and the increase in paid women's employment, while perhaps undermining the rationale for certain traditions of sharing tragedy, must be seen overall as a net gain in the quality of working-class life.[26]

It seems clear now, too, that the stability and sociability of communities does not rigidly depend upon having the woman chained to the hearth by patriarchal authority, nor can they flourish only in the poorest areas, like Salford or the Gorbals or the East End. This was more or less assumed to be the case in an entire genre of studies of working-class culture and families. A recurring theme in such works was the alleged tendency for networks to atrophy as workers achieved the material resources, mainly better housing and higher wages, and adopted the family structure with which to live a privatized, home-centered existence. These new, privatized workers were said to be found most readily in the newer, mass-production industries like motor cars or electronics and living in the council estates or tracts of homes that have come over the years to house the majority of British workers. Research, in consequence, focused on the contrast between the received idyllic portrait of warm and tight working-class communities of the prewar era and the present behavior and ethos of people living and working in such sites.[27]

It has failed to convince, however, at both ends. Historically, working people in Britain have for years valued their homes above all else and cherished absurdly sentimental notions of family life, whatever the underlying reality. Respectable, mid-Victorian artisans restricted family use of their parlours and were as proud of their homes as were the workers of Lancashire in the heyday of the textile industry before 1914, when the women scrubbed stoops and ironed curtains all day Saturday in preparation for the family rituals of Sunday.[28] Even in the Sheffield of 1917, as we have seen, working people battled an extremely ugly environment to make their homes livable. Accounts of the interwar years show no sign that these traditions were broken by the depression, and in 1957 Hoggart begins his description of working-class culture, derived from memories and studies of the 1930s and 1940s, by insisting on the centrality of the home.[29]

On the other end of the comparison those many sociological studies seeking to discover isolation and alienation on a council estate or in a new town have generally been unconvincing. Perhaps the classic case concerns Dagenham, that mammoth settlement of working people built during the 1920s just across the border in Essex and filled up by Londoners from older neighborhoods, especially the East End. Apparently repelled by the exterior of the estate, commentators began, even before it was completed, to speculate upon the dearth of social life that they felt must be going on inside it. The series of reports in the 1950s by the Institute of Community Studies on the traumas experienced by the elderly when they moved from old to new neighborhoods, from places like Bethnal Green to council estates like Dagenham, seemed to confirm this picture. However, when Peter Willmott set out in 1958-59 to analyze community life in Dagenham directly, he came to a surprising conclusion:[30]

> "Throughout this book," he explained, "Dagenham has been compared with the 'traditional' working-class community. At the end one is impressed with how similar, not how different, they are. Local extended families, which hold such a central place in the older districts, have grown up in almost identical form on the estate, and so have local networks of neighbors — people living in the same street who help each other, mix together and are on easy-going terms. In people's attitudes to their fellows, their feelings about social status and class, their political loyalties, again, there are close parallels between the two districts. In part, Dagenham is the East End reborn."

Although there is little doubt that planners have shown a marked insensitivity to the social life their housing schemes have disrupted, it seems equally true that the networks of working people have been extremely resilient. They are not so visible as the formal, voluntary associations that link up the rate-payers of middle-class suburbs, they are not as often sponsored by churches as churchmen would hope, and not ordinarily part of national political formations, but they serve working people well enough. They cannot and do not provide a mechanism for overcoming all the pains of working-class life, for making pensioners happy to leave their old neighborhoods, or for easing the hardships of unemployment. But they do suffice to knit together in an informal fashion the people of a street, a block of flats or an entire estate so that they can cope with the normal needs of a community. It may be that, because the state has come to provide so many social services, such informal networks have lost part of their *raison d'être* and begun to atrophy in a few places, but it is more likely that their focus has simply been shifted away from coping with crisis toward helping out in more fortunate circumstances. It may be, too, as some have suggested, that the rise of youth gangs and such unpleasant phenomena as football hooliganism and "Paki-bashing" betokens a frustrated attempt to recreate among youth the sense of community that has been lost by the postwar changes in the working class, but, again, it is more likely a reflecton of the strength of locally-rooted peer groups which, for a variety of reasons, take on temporarily deviant forms.[31]

The persistence of local loyalties, and the plain fact that most people like their homes and neighborhoods, together suggest that the picture of the traditional defensive working-class community being eroded by the anomie of privatized dwellings and the lure of consumerist mass media, is more than a litle overdrawn. Indeed, posing the analysis in terms of such a contrast between old and new lifestyles would seem to obscure the changes that have occurred by ruling out implicitly the possibility that established values and patterns of association can take on qualitatively new dimensions and significances when the context changes. Yet on purely *a priori* grounds that is a more likely prospect than the alternative. Though it is obviously not possible to demonstrate it here, I would argue that this is precisely what has happened in postwar Britain, where long-term prosperity transformed the defensive posture of the working class into an aggressive assertion of working-class interest. Workers' expectations and demands have escalated as their sense of the limits of their needs has expanded, and there is an apparently novel mood of self-assertion. To some, of course, this chasing after goods represents an abandonment of the ideals of the labor movement, a degradation of workers. But it is hard to see how, in a society where a man's worth is judged by his ability to consume and where women have been trained in the arts of consumption from the nursery on, an increase in working people's sense of personal worth could be registered in any other manner. Moreover, to lament the passing of the defensive and diffident aspect of working-class culture would be to sanctify, by implication, those terrible deprivations experienced by workers in the past, especially during the interwar years, which forced their aspirations to stay within the limits that poverty, recurring unemployment and political impotence set for them.[32]

Neither the study of working-class culture nor that of industrial behavior, then, lends credence to the image of decline which the rhetoric of politics and political analysis has created. It seems that the different levels at which class operates — those of production, of cultural reproduction, of workplace action and of politics — do not mesh, and this brings us to the final, and surely most important consequence, of separating political and social analysis. That is the impetus it gives to refocusing study more directly upon the historical processes that link social structure, industrial behavior, cultural patterns and political allegiance, and upon the varying extent to which these levels of the social totality fit together or pull in opposite directions at any given moment. Not only are such processes complicated and important, but they are also constantly changing. Just as the social bases of political behavior alter, so, too, does the way in which the two are related and the strength of the connection. A synthetic picture of working-class life and politics can therefore only be successfully approached when one understands that in reality there may not be synthesis at all, but rather confusion, contradiction and tension.

V.

This would seem to be especially the case for the historical evolution of labor, for there is nothing about the structure of politics in industrial society to compel the translation of solidarities based upon economic status and social location into political loyalties. Much about political life militates against it, so much, in fact, that the most useful analytical procedure might well be to turn around the normal question asked about working-class politics in Britain — what social processes have caused and are causing the decline in working-class political consciousness? — and to ask instead what special circumstances in the history of 20th-century Britain allowed for such a close, if temporary, identification between membership in the working class and political support for the Labour Party as obtained in 1945-51?

This form of asking the question may be much more fruitful than the usual way of posing the problem and its very framing suggests a different perspective on it. For what seems to have happened is that, for the first half of the century, events and processes combined to create a growing bond between the workers and the

Labour party, while events since 1950 have had the effect, not of decomposing the class or turning it selfish or "affluent" or into poor copy of its betters, but of loosening the tie with Labour as a political instrument. More precisely, the working class grew in numbers, in organization and in political competence consistently from late in the 19th century to about 1950, and during that time neither of the two established parties — the Liberals or Conservatives — could wrench itself from its class moorings to become the party of the workers. Labour became the vehicle for workers' entry into the polity, and the hostility of the Conservatives and the incoherence of the Liberals meant that there was little genuine competition for the working-class vote. Labour also had the political good fortune not to be identified with the horrors of the Great War, the agony of the slump (after 1931, at least), the foreign policy blunders of the late 1930s or the ineffective prosecution of the Second World War in 1939-40. By 1935, they were the party of the working-class — demobilized and demoralized though the class was at that time. In the next decade they became the party of an increasingly organized and vital working class and, of great importance, of those numerous members of the middle classes determined to discard the old ways of the Tories.

The rise of Labour was based, therefore, in part upon the formation and self-activity of the working class. But it also derived great strength from the failure of the established parties and their lack of any serious program for the national leadership. Having established itself by the Second World War as the carriers of workers' interest, the Labour party proceeded to become as well the party of national progress behind which all sorts of non-working-class voters could unite.[33] For a brief moment, the class interest of workers in social reform and the national interest in reconstruction were united by an implicitly Keynesian program serving as both economic and political theory. But even in the best of times, Labour fudged critical issues of policy and was never truly united on a detailed and shared vision of the future. In consequence, for most of its history the Labour Party has received only grudging support from the majority of the workers. Working-class cynicism was strong even in 1945, and Labour's penchant since 1945 for calling upon its firmest supporters for the greatest sacrifices toward the goals of price stability and export-led growth has constantly justified at least that degree of detachment.

By 1948, or at the latest 1951, the "Social Democratic synthesis" thus began to falter. Much of Labour's program had been enacted in its first four years of office and the basis of reconstruction laid. By the 1950s Labour ceased to offer a compelling reformist vision or even, as time went on, a clear alternative to the Tories. In consequence, its middle-class supporters began to swing back and forth between Labour and the Conservatives depending on the fickle perceptions of the moment, and its working-class base began to alternate between political abstention and reluctant support. But this was not due to the disintegrating effect of social change upon class loyalty. Rather, from 1950 until the mid-1970s, Britain exhibited a pattern of structural change whose undiluted political effect could well have been to maintain, or possibly to increase, Labour support. For example, the maintenance of full employment and the slow pace of growth cushioned the impact of industrial shifts upon the economy, the occupational structure and working-class communities. This allowed trade unions — the main determinant of Labour Party voting — to adapt to the changing composition of the working class and to maintain and even slightly increase their membership. The economic climate also helped to stimulate the growth of shop stewards' organization in manufacturing, especially after 1956, and hence to provide a means to sustain workers' demands for higher wages and the strikes that inevitably ensued.

Two other major structural changes effected by postwar economic development were, as we have seen, the increase in women's paid employment and the proliferation of white-collar jobs, and these, too, resulted in trade union growth. The introduction of women into industry did not in most cases lead to a decrease in union density, and although the substitution of female for male clerical labor has been associated with a decline in average clerical earnings, it has not prevented the spread of organization into these types of employment. Rather, white-collar unionization grew in close relation to the increase in white-collar workers generally from 1948 to approximately 1965 and then, during the late 1960s and early 1970s, took a giant leap forward to encompass over 39% of non-manual employees by 1974, an increase of a third from the level of 1964.[34]

This deepening of organization throughout society, coupled with the resiliency of working-class values but mixed, too, with a measure of increased expectations, led to substantial increases in trade union militancy that came in the waves of strikes of 1957-62 and 1968-72 and that has yet to truly subside even in the depressed years that have followed. The Labour Party, however, has had little to offer in the way of a political program for the realization of workers' enhanced sense of collective and personal worth. They have been lukewarm at best to the spread of shopfloor organization and antipathetic towards what they see as irresponsible wage demands. Toward the numerical strengthening of the unions they have been more favorably disposed, for obvious reasons, but towards the necessary accoutrements of union power — the independent power of shop stewards, the increase of industrial democracy, the politicization and democratization of corporate decisions — they have by and large not been sympathetic. In place of encouragement have come a flawed income's policy, a restrictive industrial relations bill, and, finally, deflation dictated by the International Monetary Fund and administered by the most recent Labour government.

In retrospect, what is surprising about this contradiction between the trends of social change, opinion and action among working people, and the inert (or worse) response of the Labour Party is not that it has led to a weakening of the ties between Labour and the working-class and, thus, between the direction of class formation and the evolution of politics. Much more surprising is the residual strength of the relationship, and the fact that so many working people still hope and work for a party that has so often since 1951 failed to live up to the hopes and needs of its supporters.

The sources of this growing lack of correspondence between social structure and political allegiance or, more precisely, between the possibilities inherent in the shifting social structure and their actual crystallization or mobilization in politics, are many and varied. A share of the responsibility must surely be borne by individuals, by those whose personal careers have spanned the decades of stagnation in Labour's style and strategy. Yet another share can be allotted to the paralytic effects of the intellectual legacy of "labourism," that amalgam of Fabian faith in the collectivist state, of the quintessentially "English" belief in the primacy of Parliamentary solutions to the problems of class conflict, of contempt for any systematic plan or program that could be labelled utopian or dogmatic by Labour's opponents. But the most important factor, it would seem, is the sheer difficulty involved in achieving a political consummation of social structural relations.

Modern democratic politics creates this difficulty in several ways. First, there is the gross asymmetry between the resources working people can bring to bear in political struggle and what is needed for victory in that struggle. Working-class strength is overwhelmingly local in character, centered in the workplace or the community and best tapped by such forms of collective action as strikes or local elections. Projecting such loyalties into the arena of national politics does not come easily. The national power of unions helps, but in general the result is a very troubled relationship between the political party oriented to the capital and its local bases of support. This is a problem that has plagued the Labour Party since before the First World War, and it has never been solved.

The drift of power from the locality to the center and the increasing involvement of the state in all aspects of economy and society further accentuate this imbalance between the strengths of working people and the requirements of politics. Economic management in particular places great strains on any potential aspirant or insurgent, and dictates a level of expertise and commitment that is not highly compatible with the inefficiencies and confusions of democratic process within a vital social movement. It also taxes the theoretical apparatus of social movements, for it forces Labour not simply to identify enemies and injustices or to propose simple, once-and-for-all reforms, but to develop a plan for economic and social development and a set of devices for overcoming bureaucratic inertia and vested interests.[35]

Finally, to do all this necessitates the elaboration, by a political movement that is largely class-based, of a program and a set of leaders that can appeal to a broader spectrum of electors than those encompassed by the local solidarities of unambiguous working-class membership. The great electoral victories of 1945-51, it is becoming increasingly clear, were not won by the mobilization of pure working-class support, but by the conjuncture of working-class loyalty and substantial, if scattered, instances of middle-class disloyalty to their traditional class party. The ambiguities of structural evolution since 1945-51 make it even more necessary for Labour, if it is to tap the potential latent in that change, to attract the support of those whose class locations have become less clear or more contradictory.

The sum of these difficulties means that politics is likely to be the most problematic index of class formation. Taken together with the inhospitable findings lurking in the separate literatures on the distinct spheres of working-class life, this suggests that the study of the evolution of labor should henceforth depart from previous approaches, based upon the assumed identity of class and politics, and begin by emphasizing the lack of articulation or correspondence between the various levels of working-class existence. Work and occupation, social life and culture, family patterns, industrial organization, and politics each have to be studied on their own terms and as processes subject to their own inner logic. Yet, because in the end they do join together and produce those manifestations of class allegiance and conflict that so dominate the historical landscape, it will also be necessary in the final analysis to see how these different aspects of class formation increasingly fit together in the years up to 1950, and how they have pulled in different directions since then. And only by adopting a style of research that allows for such separate evolutions of social and political phenomena will it be possible ultimately to construct a synthetic history that does equal justice to the complexities of social and political history.

FOOTNOTES

1. G.M. Trevelyan, *English Social History* (London, 1942), pp. vii.

2. The most notable feature of the current criticism of social history is the absence of any such credible review and analysis of the field. Particularly lacking in this regard is Tony Judt's "A Clown in Regal Purple: Social History and the Historians," *History Workshop* ff7 (Spring, 1979): pp. 66-94.

3. One area in which this is evident is in the social-historical study of crime and policing. The state plays an even more direct role in the analysis of collective action undertaken by Charles Tilly. See, for example, Charles, Richard and Louise Tilly, *The Rebellious Century* (Cambridge, Ma., 1975); Edward Shorter and Charles Tilly, *Strikes in France, 1830-1968* (Cambridge, 1974); and Charles Tilly, ed., *The Formation of National States in Europe* (Princeton, 1975). The advance which such work represents over extant theory and research within political history and political science can be readily seen by comparing it with Eric Nordingler's limp defense of nonsocial analysis, *On the Autonomy of the Democratic State* (Cambridge, Ma., 1981).

4. This more extended research project will appear as *Labour and Society in Twentieth-Century Britain* (London, forthcoming).

5. The documentary literature on the working class is reviewed and well worked over by Standish Meacham, *A Life Apart* (Cambridge, Ma., 1977); but see also Ross McKibbin, "Social Class and Social Observation in Edwardian England," *Transactions of the Royal Historical Society*, 5th Series, Vol. XXVIII (London, 1978), pp. 175-199.

6. See A.L. Lowell, *Public Opinion in War and Peace* (Cambridge, Ma., 1923).

7. Report of the Commission of Enquiry into Industrial Unrest, Cmd. 8696, *Parliamentary Papers*, (1917-18), Vol. X.

8. St. Philip's Education and Economics Research Society, *The Equipment of the Workers* (London, 1919). References organized by category and individual respondent.

9. Raymond Williams, *The Long Revolution* (New York, 1961), p. 329.

10. Williams, *Long Revolution*, 329-335; Mark Abrams and Richard Rose, *Must Labour Lose?* (Harmondsworth, 1960); Ferdynand Zweig, *The Worker in an Affluent Society. Family Life and Industry* (New York, 1961).

11. Eric Hobsbawm, "The Forward March of Labour Halted?" *Marxism Today* (September, 1978). The article touched off a considerable debate in the journal's pages, much of which —and more — has been republished in book form under the same title (London, 1981) and edited by Martin Jacques and Francis Mulhern.

12. Jeremy Seabrook, *What Went Wrong?* (London, 1978), pp. 31, 131, 133, 254-7.

13. See J.H. Goldthorpe, D. Lockwood, F. Bechhofer and J. Platt, *The Affluent Worker: Industrial Attitudes and Behaviour* (Cambridge, 1968); *Affluent Worker: Political Attitudes and Behaviour* (Cambridge, 1968); *The Affluent Worker in the Class Structure* (Cambridge, 1969). A review of this literature and of the current state of the debate is Howard Newby's proposal to the SSRC, "Economic Stagflation and Social Change," 1981. Presumably the results of Newby's study will go some way toward advancing the debate, but its completion is still some distance away.

14. D. Butler and D. Stokes, *Political Change in Britain. The Evolution of Electoral Choice*, 3rd Edition edition (London, 1974); Dennis Kavanagh, ed. *The Politics of the Labour Party* (London, 1982).

15. Hobsbawm, *Forward March of Labour Halted?*, p. 16; see also Anthony Heath, *Social Mobility* (Harmondsworth, 1981), pp. 224-246, for a classic identification of this sort.

16. See Ross McKibbin, *The Evolution of the Labour Party* (Oxford, 1974) on the First World War era; and on the Second, Angus Calder, *The People's War* (London, 1971); and Paul Addison, *The Road to 1945* (London, 1975).

17. See Barry Hindess, *The Decline of Working Class Politics* (London, 1971), and Tom Forrester, *The Labour Party and the Working Class* (London, 1976).

18. Sheila Lewenhak, *Women and Trade Unions* (London, 1977).

19. G.S. Gain, *The Growth of White Collar Unionism* (Oxford, 1970);l A. Steward, K. Prandy and R.M. Blackburn, *Social Stratification and Occupation* (London, 1980), esp. pp. 91-113; J.H. Goldthorpe, *Social Mobility and Class Structure in Modern Britain* (Oxford, 1980).

20. Richard Price, "Rethinking Labour History: the Importance of Work," in J. Cronin and J. Schneer, eds., *Social Conflict and the Political Order in Modern Britain* (New Brunswick, 1982), pp. 179-214; Andrew Friedman, *Industry and Labour. Class Struggle at Work and Monopoly Capitalism* (London, 1977) and Stephen Wood, ed., *The Degradation of Work? Skill, Deskilling and the Labour Process* (London, 1982).

21. Alfred Barrett Brown, *The Machine and the Worker* (London, 1934), is an important early statement.

22. G.S. Bain and R. Price, *Profiles of Union Growth* (Oxford, 1981).

23. J. Cronin, *Industrial Conflict in Modern Britain* (London, 1979).

24. Chas Critcher, "Sociology, Cultural Studies and the Post-war Working Class," in J. Clarke, Critcher and R. Johnson, eds., *Working Class Culture* (London, 1979), pp. 13-40 is a thorough review of this development.

25. Ronald Frankenberg, *Communities in Britain* (Harmondsworth, 1969).

26. Women's Cooperative Guild, *Maternity Letters from Working Women* (London, 1917); Margery Spring Rice, *Working Class Wives* (London, 1981, reprint of 1939 edition); E. Slater and M. Woodside, *Patterns of Marriage. A Study of Marriage Relationships among the Urban Working Classes* (London, 1951); M. Young and P. Willmott, *The Symmetrical Family* (London, 1973).

27. The most subtle version of the position was that put forward by Brian Jackson in *Working Class Community* (London, 1968); perhaps the least was Josephine Klein's *Samples from English Cultures*, 2 vols., (London, 1963).

28. R. Gray, *The Labour Aristocracy in Victorian Edinburgh* (Oxford, 1976); G. Crossick, *An Artisan Elite in Victorian London* (London, 1978).

29. Richard Hoggart, *The Uses of Literacy* (London, 1957).

30. P. Willmott, *The Evolution of a Community* (London, 1963), pp. 109ff.

31. For review of the issues and major studies, see Chris Waters, "Badges of Half-Formed, Inarticulate Radicalism: A Critique of Recent Trends in the Study of Working Class Youth Culture," *International Labor and Working Class History* ff19 (Spring, 1981); pp. 23-37.

32. The evidence on changes in working-class expectations is highly inconclusive, primarily because it has been so closely bound up with the notion of broad versus narrow reference groups developed by W.G. Runciman in *Relative Deprivation and Social Justice* (London, 1966). A PEP Survey of 1975 claimed to have found little change in the breadth of workers' comparisons and hence, it would seem, little alteration of expectations. See W.W. Daniel, *Wage Determination in Industry* (London, 1976), esp. pp. 19-24.

On the other hand, Martin Harrop's research seems to show a significant lessening of working-class tolerance for inequality. See Martin Harrop, "Democracy and Inequality: Mass Conceptions of Stratification in Britain," Ph.D. thesis, Yale University, 1979. Obviously, one needs a more refined approach to the issue based upon a broader sense of social change and cultural values. For a beginning, see Bernice Martin, *A Sociology of Contemporary Cultural Change* (Oxford, 1981); and for a brief summary of at least some of the research to date, see Ian Maitland, "Disorder in the British Workplace: the Limits of Consensus," *British Journal of Industrial Relations* XVIII (1980): 353-364.

33. See Gareth Stedman Jones, "Marching into History." *New Socialist* ff3 (Jan.-Feb., 1982): 10-15, on the cross-class alliance behind the victory of 1945.

34. R. Price and G.S. Bain, "Union Growth Revisited: 1948-1984 in Perspective," *British Journal of Industrial Relations* XIV (1976): 339-355.

35. On the structural difficulties surrounding working-class political movements in industrial societies, see Adam Przeworksi, "Social Democracy as a Historical Phenomenon," *New Left Review* ff122 (1980): 27-58; Przeworski and Michael Wallerstein, "The Structure of Class Conflict in Democratic Capitalist Societies," *American Political Science Review* LXXVI (1982); 215-238; and, for a less deterministic and dismal view, Charles Tilly, "Social Movements and National Politics," Center for Research on Social Organization, University of Michigan, Working Paper ff197, May, 1979.

17.

FROM COP HISTORY TO SOCIAL HISTORY: THE SIGNIFICANCE OF THE POLICE IN AMERICAN HISTORY

Eric H. Monkkonen

Americans have been writing about their urban police for over one hundred years. Much of the writing has been neither critical nor very deep, but the original fascination with the police runs through it all. In the past fifteen years historians have examined police with greater care and detail than ever before. Yet, though they have moved closer to a really striking analysis of the police, there remains much work of synthesis and generalization to be done. Some of the best work on the police fails to locate them within the context of urban institutions. Reconceptualizing their organizational shape, development, and role within their urban environment assists us in better understanding both the police and the policed. This article sketches some suggestions toward forming such a synthesis and makes some empirical generalizations which are intended to stimulate and help define a provocative set of research problems. The intention is to keep the research lively and to steer the topic away from becoming a narrow specialization unrelated to broader problems in U.S. history.[1]

Section I: Recent Historiography

The historiography of U.S. urban government languished between the progressive era and the 1970s — a hiatus best symbolized by the gap between the publication of the second and third volumes of Ernest Griffith's history of U.S. city government — volume two appeared in 1928 and volume three in 1974.[2] In the interim, most exciting substantive work had been done on municipal reformers, with an emphasis on reformers rather than on municipal.[3] Literature on police often reflects the general historiographical interest in reformers and their impact by focusing on attempts to change police. This focus may best be seen in Fogelson's *Big City Police,* which is essentially an analysis of police reform, rather than of the police themselves.[4] Of course, had historians working with urban police wanted to place them more in the context of urban governmental organization, as opposed to urban reform, they would have been hard-pressed, simply because Griffith's muck-raking work did not offer much description or analysis within which to place police as an organization. But recent research in the history of the city as a municipality has begun to change the historiographic landscape, providing those interested in police organization and behavior with a perspective and the beginnings of a substantive analysis. This research starts with Frisch's work on Springfield, Massachusetts, continues through the work of Fox on urban accounting, Teaford on the legal status of cities within the various state governments, and into newer, quantiative work on urban fiscal behavior and political economy, especially that of the Hollingsworths and McDonald.[5]

This recent research in what might be called municipal history has both a perspective and substantive material to offer the historian working with police. Teaford, for instance, dramatically rejects the notion, found in writings of progressives like Griffith and perpetuated by many others, that city governments were powerless legal orphans whose prospects fluctuated at the whim of ignorant state legislators. Instead, Teaford shows that until at least the 1920s the very ignorance of the legislators worked to give the cities effective *carte blanche* in deciding those questions affected by legislation. With only a handful of exceptions, Teaford found that the legislative committees dealing with urban affairs simply followed the expert advice of urban representatives or of city officials themselves. His point makes intuitive sense: much of what cities had to request was of a detailed and technical nature, and to be actively anti-city a rural legislator would have to become an expert in each specific problem. Resistance to and limitation of city power in the legislatures came in the 1920s with the rise of suburban municipalities which no longer depended on central city government. Even with these competing municipalities, the major restriction on city-related legislation was of annexation and expansion powers which threatened adjacent municipalities. Such legislation can be read simply as mediation of inter-urban disputes.

Teaford has shown us the need to be alert to the strength and importance of city government as an actor, rather than as a prostrate victim of whim, ignorance, and prejudice. By implication, this is the way we should try to conceive the police — an organization of fiscal importance within a municipal government with rather independent power. This perspective represents a shift from that usually taken, which envisions the police as an organization active in its behavior, but passive and unimaginative in its role as an organization within city government. For in many respects, and particularly in scale, city government was an innovative actor in the changing organizational world of the nineteenth and early twentieth century. Rather than thinking only of police corruption, incompetence, participation in factional politics, brutality, and the like, we must stand at a different location and also see the police as a part of the inchoate but creative actions of city dwellers, inventing a formal and bureaucratic world of municipal services and controls hitherto unforeseen. This angle of vision will help remind us that uniformed urban police were nineteenth-century innovations, that New York City, not to mention London, had functioned without a uniformed police when it had a population of nearly a million people, apparently with no enormous crises of order.

The research of Fox on municipal accounting shows how the very way in which fiscal accounts were kept by cities and, in the twentieth century, by the federal government, mirrored the confusion of categories created by the new municipal organizations. It took a major effort of national reformers to separate fiscal accounts into capital and operating expenditures. This change is important to historians of police for two reasons. First, it demonstrated a conscious recognition that the very urban organizational forms were of a new order, one which could no longer be accounted for as had the cities of early nineteenth century. And the police were very much a part of this new form, a part, incidentally, which used mainly operating as opposed to capital expenditures. The second reason this rethinking of urban accounting is important to the historian of the police is that in creating the new system of accounting, city fiscal reformers laid the basis for the destruction of a wonderful system of police record publication, usually found in the annual reports of the chief to the mayor or city council.[6] For over a half century, police departments dutifully noted everything, or nearly everything, which they officially did, endlessly chronicling the behavior of their part of the emerging municipal government. In a literal sense, the discovery of the fiscal significance of city government took the formal record keeping out of the hands of the actors and laid the basis for the eventual nationalization of reporting on municipal topics. Thus, in the second decade of the twentieth century, the time-honored form of police reports began to disappear from city to city, often to be replaced with slickly printed brochures designed to serve the same purpose as corporate annual reports and about as useful.

The annual reporting of municipal governments as fiscal entities has begun to attract the attention of historians who utilize the time series of fiscal data as an indicator of urban behavior. McDonald, for instance, uses fiscal data to ask just what the city government of San Francisco did and to compare different political regimes. The Hollingsworths use the data to develop behavioral models of middle-sized cities, trying to classify cities as different types of actors. Work of this kind should also have a substantive and methodological impact on the study of urban police. First, as more cities are analyzed, we may see expenditure patterns and typologies which will account for policing differences and developments. Second, methodologically, the analysis of fiscal time series suggests that the same kind of data can be used to analyze police, their behavior, their relative position in city government, and their variation in position between regions and over time.

Because the history of the police is so much a part of the history of the city, it is essential that the history of the city provide the first and most dominant framework within which to analyze the police. Unfortunately, until recently, much of the social history of the city did not illuminate even the basic shape of the urban container within which the police acted. However, the recent work on urban government, of which just a sample has been cited here, has begun to give us a picture of an independent, active, emerging form of organization. This picture urges us to take a broad and rather basic approach, asking how the police spent their time, comparing their fiscal status to other segments of government, and establishing simple, baseline statistics.

We must describe the broad quantitative dimension of police location, dates of emergence, the size and shape of police behavioral activities, and answer the classic and basic historical questions of where, when, how many and how much change. It may come as a surprise to some that these simple questions had not been very thoroughly answered long ago, but the general focus of prior researchers on case studies or on problems which did not lend themselves to such basic issues, such as reform, have left these questions to languish.

The case studies have established the fundamental scenarios of the creation of uniformed police in enough cities so that we may detect the modal characteristics in this urban innovation process, and these similar characteristics can be used to compare cities. Both Lane and Richardson show how the rather lengthy process which occurred before the police of Boston and New York had been transformed varied between the two cities, making it imperative to focus a national comparison on one consistent and regular part of the transformation process.[7] There are several reasons to choose the uniform as the decisive moment. The uniform finalized the unique position of the police as a semi-military presence in the city; the uniform declared the constant availability of the police; the uniform almost always came at the same time which the command hierarchy of the organization was completed; the uniform symbolized and was often coterminous with a unified police (as opposed to separate day and night police, for instance); the police themselves saw the uniform as an important, if controversial statement of their purpose; the police uniforms led to the introduction of uniforms in other civil occupations in the United States, indicating their innovative nature even outside of the police changes; finally, the switch to uniforms can be consistently, if not easily, dated.

New York City uniformed its police first, in 1853, after an earlier short-lived attempt in the 1840s. The cities of Savannah, perhaps Albany, Charleston, Jersey

City, Philadelphia, Baltimore, San Francisco, Chicago, Washington, Boston, Cincinnati, Manchester, New Hampshire, and Utica, New York, in that order, complete the list of those cities which followed in the 1850s. The 1860s and 1870s saw a deluge of smaller and smaller cities uniforming their police. Denver, for instance, uniformed its police in 1874, when its population was less than 17,000. The timing and patterns in this sequence will be pursued further below, but several preliminary observations should be made here.

Clearly the major metropolises took the initiative in the creation of the uniformed police, New York and Boston explicitly imitating London. The early innovators not in the group of leading metropolises had two or three characteristics which account for what may be termed their premature change to the uniformed police. First, some of the early innovators were virtual suburbs of New York City — Jersey City, for instance. Other cities were regional centers with many of the chracteristics of primate cities — Charleston or San Francisco, for instance. Finally, many of the early innovators were southern, slave cities, where the police were very much in the military mode of slave control. Richard Wade, for instance, has asserted that southern cities had virtual standing armies in the form of police to control slaves.[8] This thesis deserves more research, for the early uniforming of non-slaveholding San Francisco's police suggests that southern cities may have innovated more because of their roles as regional centers rather than for slave control alone. Nevertheless, this sequential list of cities suggests that the timing of innovation in urban police followed an important basic pattern in the urban network, determined primarily by size, but also heavily influenced by region. Moreover, the pattern shows the importance of a nested set of urban hierarchies, with London the central example for the largest cities, radiating from this a national American network, and within this several regional networks.[9] Thus, even in the matter of locating and dating the emergence of the uniformed police, the history of cities and their systematic relationships maintains an underlying importance.

Once we have located police in time and space, we need to describe their size and how it changed as the organizations became entrenched in city government and matured. One measure of this dimension is simply the total number of police personnel per 1,000 city population. This measure very nearly approximates an expenditure index, for salaries took up most of the police budget. Also, it has the advantage of offering comparability with modern data. Did the police get created at a modern strength, or did they grow? If they grew, when did they grow, and why?

In 1977, the mean number of police personnel per 1,000 population for all U.S. cities over 10,000 persons was 2.67.[10] This figure varied with city size in nearly linear fashion, as might be expected, with values ranging from 4.12 for central cities over a million down to 2.08 for places between 25,000 and 10,000. For comparative purposes, a better sense of police per capita distribution can be gained by controlling for metropolitan status: central cities had a mean figure of 3.02 personnel per 1,000 — as contrasted to the substantially less 2.02 for suburban cities. Over a century before, for a sample of twenty cities with populations over 50,000, the mean figure for the decade of 1860-1870 for fledgling police departments varied between a low of 1.4 and a high of 1.65. If we take the mean of these means as about 1.5, we can conclude that police personnel per capita increased somewhere between 35 to 100 percent over the past century. The amount of drama one wishes to accord this change is up to the analyst: while real, I find the difference to be rather small. The 1860s value is, for instance, virtually the same as the figure for the group of cities with the lowest per capita police personnel figure for 1976, cities in the west north-central U.S. with a population between 25,000 and 50,000.[11] Moreover, the advent of these forty hour work week significantly reduced person hours on patrol, for nineteenth and early twentieth century police typically worked sixty hours or more per week.[12]

When graphed over the period 1860-1920, the shape of the mean police personnel per 1,000 in the same twenty cities shows a decline until 1882, followed by a steady rise to a 1909 peak of 2.1, and a slight decline to 1920. In other words, the graph shows a basic rise with two slight downturns. The rising trend is consistent with the somewhat larger mean size of police personnel in the 1970s compared to a century earlier. It is also consistent with and largely caused by the growth in city size over the period 1860-1920, because larger cities tend to have more officers per capita.

The mechanism of the causal sequence has not yet been explored and should prove important. Because departmental size is legislatively mandated in absolute numbers, not in per capita rates, simple maintenance of the status quo required legislative action. Were police department requests for more officers automatically granted, or was this a subject of continual political struggle? How did the great density of central cities turn into greater police per capita? Did large places have more legislative influence or was there a shared perception of the "need" for more police per capita in major cities?

When the annual change in police per 1,000,000 population is regressed against the annual change in urban population for the 1860-1920 period, the R^2 is .86, with a b coefficient of .000091.[13] This indicates that while a very high population of the police growth in strength can be accounted for by the denser policing of large cities, the actual multiple was quite low — a change of 10,000 persons yielding one more officer per million persons. The modern coefficient, which can only be roughly estimated from cross-sectional rather than change data, appears to be similar but to be distorted upward by the much more intensive policing of the five central cities over a million.[14] (Note the implication for our era as central cities lose population and independent municipalities multiply — personnel should decrease per capita, simply from the decrease in the mean size of municipalities. Or, perhaps the ages of cities offset this tendency, with older places maintaining their higher ratios.) The only other data to compare with this sample are for both urban and rural places, over the period 1910 to 1970: these data show a continuous increase in the ratio, with the exception of the depression decade of the 1930s.[15] For the whole United States, the percent increase in police officers per 1,000 population was: 19%, 1910-1920; 34%, 1920-1930; no increase, 1930-1940; 10%, 1940-1950; 10%, 1950-1960, 28%, 1960-1970. These data inflate the actual city based component of the increase, because they mask both the rapidly increasing proportion of the population in cities and the more dense policing in large central cities. Presumably, if the twentieth century increase could be adjusted to account for the growth of city size and percent of the population in the cities, we would find a much more modest increase, one even less than that of the modest increase of the twenty sample cities followed from 1860 to 1920.

Several conclusions may be drawn from these various quantitative hints. First, the major change occurred at the moment of the creation of the modern police. The transformation symbolized by the uniform was indeed a transformation, one which set an enduring precedent. Second, although police size relative to the population has increased, a large if unknown proportion of this increase can be accounted for simply because of the increased size and age of cities. Third, maintenance of the departmental status quo required constant augmentation of police departments as cities grew. Fourth, the formulation of urban police occurred within a national and even international context of change in municipal government.

The significance of the basic transformation signalled by the creation of the uniformed police leads to an examination of demands made on them. Demands on police came from elected city officials or politically powerful persons, from within the police themselves, and from the various groups and classes of the public, either acting through political representatives or autonomously. The context of demands is much more difficult to describe than the contexts of urban development or measurable components of policing, for its manifestations include public statements, private actions of political persons, that almost hidden job culture of rank and file police officers, and most nebulous, the demands of the public. Here, case studies provide clues. Miller's work comparing the London and New York police comes the closest to analyzing demands on police, for he has explored the public and private records in as much depth as possible.[16] He shows the origins of the feeling of personal responsibility for punishment, or justice, within the organization and structure of the police. Only the research of Watts on St. Louis promises to have a greater range and depth of records.[17] Watts' work should also provide insight to the job culture of early twentieth-century police, an area which has been mainly explored by Levine and Wilentz.[18] Levine's work shows that by the 1890s New York City rank and file police had a clearly defined job-consciousness which had the important consequence, even then, of creating a resistance to change and an organizational inertia, a phenomenon which has persisted for almost one hundred years. Other work, that of Johnson, Haller, Haring, and Schneider, has helped describe the impact of changing crime patterns and of governmental demands. All of this analysis suggests that from the last third of the nineteenth century on the police had strongly internalized and informally implemented demands which gave them a feeling of sole responsibility for containing crime and disorder, a feeling which structured their self-perceptions and often set them in conflict with public demands.

As the decade of the 1970s has shown, public demands on police have been difficult to voice and even more difficult to implement when they run contrary to intertia and job cultures of police departments. Not all public demands on police are so controversial as those which have motivated efforts to create civilian review boards, but even less controversial demands have run into resistance as the reference to lost children, below, will show. The major point to be made concerning public demands on police is that, whether the demands are for disarming, for civilian control, for less corruption, or for a "law and order" type of justice, no one asks for dis-establishment. The demands are for more and more fair service, for different kinds and qualities of basically the same service. This reminds us of the unqualified success of the police in establishing themselves as a fundamental municipal service.

Three more conceptual frameworks for examining the police have been developed in the recent literature. They are the social control thesis, the notions of order and disorder, and the idea that criminal behavior itself influences the development of the police. Although the social control interpretation of much social history has been misused and too often substituted for a more careful analysis, it remains exciting and an important element to consider in any history of social organizations.[20] First used to analyze varioius benevolent groups and reformers, the social control theorists discovered that underlying religious benevolence, or social welfare programs, was a conscious or semi-conscious intent to control rather than to aid the afflicted. That is, the impulse to aid and assist those in need masked a deeper attempt to force them to act in ways determined by the benevolent. This discovery could account for the motives of the benevolent, explain apparent contradictions in aid programs, and show how hegemony could be subtly established and discreetly preserved.

Of course, the control goals of police are hardly discreet or subtle, and this might be why only a few historians concerned with social control have investigated the establishment and behavior of nineteenth-century police.[21] These exceptions have argued that police were established to control immigrants or workers and that they worked directly for the labor management needs of local capitalists. Although these arguments have found few direct rebuttals, many other historians have established that the police-labor-capital relationship exhibited considerable variation from place to place.[22] In certain ways, the uniformed police have proved less amenable to social control strategies in favor of one class or special group than other social organizations, for police visibility makes them somewhat open to observation and vulnerable to complaints of bias. Because their role is known, demands of fairness can be made upon them. This does not mean the police have in fact been fair, but it shows why less visible arms of city police — secret police, plain clothes operatives, or other special groups — must function as social control agents where there is conflict. Today most police activity involves consensual social control — traffic law enforcement, apprehension of felony suspects and the like — and the conflicts occur over relatively limited substantive areas — drug enforcement — or over overtly biased and wrongful activities — the Chicago convention in 1968.

In the nineteenth century the police provided a broad range of welfare services, including the provision of overnight shelter to the homeless and indigent. This range of services gave the police considerable scope for class-oriented social control activities. It is this class-oriented, if consensual, social control which is of historical interest. Although the police in every city did not necessarily act at the whims of local capitalists, they did take care of the "wandering armies" of workers. They formed an integral part of a system which saw industrial workers leave the cities in the summer for farm work and return in the winter for day labor and industrial work. The social control was often a positive rather than a negative or repressive effort on the police's part. In addition to this form of social control, Schneider's work has reinforced our understanding of how police cooperated and made emerging shopping and commercial areas attractive, as they sometimes ignored requests of neighborhoods for similar kinds of order maintenance and vice control.[24] Both of these forms of police behavior preserved the status quo and spatial separation, but in neither case was there the continuous repressive stature implied by the social control perspective. Thus, the social control perspective helps us gain an analytic tool to understand some of police activities, but it does not provide as powerful an explanatory device as one might expect.

Another conceptual framework which has some promise for examining the police and their role is that of social order and disorder. Unlike anthropologists, who mainly consider order and disorder to be perceptual categories, historians accept the concept of order as reflective of reality. Even though we use the term with often wildly different definitions, there seems to be a loosely acceptable set of observable characteristics around which these definitions hover. These include objective predictability, consensus or structured conflict, consistency in rules and behaviors, and consensually defined decorum. Subjective order includes perceptions of rationality, predictability, a modicum of fairness, and safety. These definitions are not value free and can be seen as layered — that is, a society can have deep disorder and surface order. In spite of the complexities of the notion of order, we can see that police in nineteenth-century cities, among other things, used their power to preserve or create order, particularly in public places. The actual public orderliness of cities provides the daily working context for the uniformed police.

If we have a "willing suspension of disbelief" for a moment, some arrest data for drunk and disorderly conduct can give us a powerfully suggestive insight into the order context of policing. The rate of arrests per 1,000 population by urban police between 1860 and the present decreased from over 45 to around 15.[25] With the one major exception of the brief period immediately following World War II, there has been a steady and unmistakable trend downward for the past 120 years. For whatever reason or reasons that caused this shift in arrest behavior — the rise of private drinking space, changed perceptions, use of the automobile, urban regimentation or cooling of the earth — its decline demonstrates a clearly changed context of urban policing, a decrease in urban disorder. This decrease has affected the day-to-day life of the police officer. A century ago over half of the officer's arrests were for order related offenses. Today only one arrest in five is for an order related offense. The first uniformed police officers entered a city that was a good deal less orderly than that of today. They had predictable physical contact with drunks, disorderly persons and public disorder. In other words, the daily public context for uniformed police was decidely rougher than that of today.

The causes of the increase in order are too complicated to account for here, but the increase does show that the daily priorities of policing have changed dramatically. With this change, criminal behavior has gradually assumed much greater importance. Perhaps it is because of this slowly increased public order that today we automatically associate the police with crime, a perception which obscures our basic understanding of the police. One of the explicit functions of the newly uniformed police in the 1850s was to be the prevention of crime as well as disorderliness. James W. Gerard, who studied the London police before making his well-known recommendations for creating the New York police, had a touching belief that the sight of a uniform would strike a deterrent fear into the hearts of would be criminals.[26] Thus, the uniformed police would prevent crime rather than trying to catch criminals after their offenses. Perhaps some of the contemporary resistance to the modernized police may have come from the absurdity of this argument, and the ultimate pervasiveness of the innovation may have come fron a realization of the many other benefits of a modern police organization. In any case, the concept of crime control was definitely in the heads of early police innovators: it was also behind the forming of departmental detective bureaus, and prompted the late nineteenth and early twentieth-century creation of a national identification bureau.[27] But the assessment of criminal behavior as an adequate interpretive framework within which to place the police remains elusive and difficult. Johnson has made the only major attempt to do so, and while interesting for other reasons, the actual or even implied impact of criminal behavior and its development on the police is the least successful part of his work.[28]

Implicitly, crucial aspects of criminal behavior are quantitative, yet measurement of the phenomenon presents a classic difficulty of positive social science, and the data referred to here should only be seen as suggestive. During the period 1860-1920, for the twenty largest U.S. cities, arrest rates for felony crimes declined or stayed relatively stable until the turn of the century, then begin to rise.[29] Homicide arrest rates exhibited a similar pattern, though the upturn came in the mid-1880s. Lane, in his study of violent death in Philadelphia, found the homicide rate upturn to be at a later date, in the early decades of the twentieth century.[30] Gurr's work on western Europe found a similar upturn in felony crimes in the late nineteenth century.[31] Although there is a disagreement on dates among these three studies which may come from the varying methodologies, the identified pattern is similar enough to suggest that the underlying trend has some basis in fact. Whatever the causal matrix, the amount of criminal behavior with which the police were ostensibly to deal has changed since their mid-nineteenth-century introduction. In the nineteenth century the rate seems to have been steady or declining steadily, even though urban disorder was high by modern standards. Cities were more disorderly than dangerous. In the twentieth century, on the other hand, the cities have become more orderly but also more dangerous. It is mainly this changed twentieth-century aspect of criminal behavior which has given the charge of police to deal with crime its public importance.

Section II: A Developmental Overview

By 1920 four major transformations of urban police in America had occurred. Two of these involved the spread of the innovation of the police and the unintended consequences of this innovation, and the other two involved the focus and function of police behavior. The introduction and spread of the uniformed police has been usually handled by historians in a particularistic manner, only partly because of the case study nature of their research. Most have accepted one of three arguments for the innovation: (1) the police were created in response to rising crime; (2) the police were created in response to urban disorder and riots; (3) the police were created to control the growing immigrant and industrial working classes. The first two arguments are empirical but unverifiable — did crime or disorder increase prior to the introduction of the police? No one has tried to show this was a general situation across many cities immediately prior to their creation of the police. Instead, most case studies show that prior crimes or disorders made up a part of the arguments of the police innovators. Only Levett has approached the problem systematically, using data on changing proportions of immigrants to support his argument that cities created police to control a new immigrant population.[32] His argument, however interesting, founders on the cities which did not have even large populations yet still created uniformed police — Denver, for instance, which was hardly a city when it created its police.

An approach suggested by the basic urban perspective on policing holds more promise and is simpler. In the United States, uniformed police were simply the first of other urban services to be formalized along organizational models provided by London, the seed city for innovation in early nineteenth-century urban governance. The underlying communications pattern which determined the diffusion of other kinds of information and innovation through the urban nework determined the speed and direction of the diffusion of the police. The literature on diffusion of innovations in geography and sociology emphasizes one of two basic diffusion models, one with a constant or point source and the other where each new innovator in turn becomes a new source of information, the contagious diffusion model.[33] Had London continued to be the only model for policing, U.S. cities would have been following a point source process, but in fact each new city became a model for imitation by other cities, so the spread of uniformed police in the United States followed the contagion model.[34] In fact, the diffusion of police paralleled the mid-nineteenth century paths for the diffusion of cholera epidemics, an ironic verification of the contagion process.[35] This pattern does not mean that the diffusion of the uniformed police innovation came about automatically or that other causal factors did not enter in. It reminds us that the police were a part of changing municipal governments and avoids an explanatory account for their spread which needlessly emphasizes vague forces or localistic explanations. As pointed out above, not all cities conformed to either model's predictions: the south got its police too early, as did some suburban cities. But the burden of analyzing these variations should be on explaining deviations from the diffusion model's predictions, those places which truly deviated meriting intense local study.

The second transformation of U.S. police came as an unintended consequence of their introduction. Never before had an urban service provided easy public access and centralized communication. Urbanites for the first time could have direct contact with easily visible, regularly available, and authoritative city workers. They immediately began to place on the police demands unrelated to crime control, but more reflective of other urban problems. As a result, police busily reported health hazards and open sewers, took censuses, gave advice to travellers, and returned lost children to their parents. This last activity gives a reasonable indicator of the quickly growing demands on police, for shortly after each city reorganized and uniformed its police, the rates of lost children returned to parents began to soar as urban people found a new ear for their demands for service and public order.[36] Whether these demands resulted in the continuing increase in public order is untestable, but it is clear that the problem of lost children found a solution unmatched by previous methods.

The third transformation was of police behavior relating to social control and crime. The new police, in providing urban services, were either formally charged with or quickly assumed the burden of temporary care for the destitute. Not only did police distribute food and coal in the winter, but they regularly took in lodgers, who sometimes slept on crude bunks, other times in cells or simply on hard hallway floors.[37] While an unintended consequence of their introduction, the police did end up actively engaged in a kind of social control, focused on the care and management of what was then called the "dangerous class." This class control did not involve indoctrination — lodgers gave police their names, ages, occupations and homes, but only so the police could identify them and keep repeaters from staying over three to five days. Lodgers slept on crude beds and the police rousted them out at daybreak, thus minimizing the time and effort they spent on lodgers. The lack of indoctrination and the lack of discrimination against "unworthy" aid recipients ended up becoming one of the main complaints against police lodging from social reformers who were more interested in social control.

The transformation of the class management of police came towards the end of the nineteenth century when the police function began to shift from class control to crime control. A multiple regression analysis of arrest rates and lodger rates as determined by police strength shows a shift in emphasis occurring in the period 1890-1920, when variation in policing no longer produced a variation in lodgers or in crimes of public order, but did begin to affect the arrest rates for felony crimes.[38] Not too surprisingly the degree of the statistical relationship declined significantly, for while police could easily control the production of public order, which included the more devious public behavior of the "dangerous class" but also an apparent upturn in felony crime, this transformation in the focus and function of the police makes sense and also helps account for the fourth transformation of policing.

The formal national communication networks established by police chiefs in the 1890s and the decline of the local management of the "dangerous class" signaled the fourth transformation of police, which came in the context of the new police focus on crime control.[39] Symbolized by the permanent formation of the organization which eventually became the International Association of Chiefs of Police (the Police Chiefs Union) in 1893, this fourth transformation responded to the need for systematic information transfer from one city to another. For several years the IACP floundered with various schemes to create a national identification program which would help one police department communicate the positive identification of one person with another department. Catching offenders outside the boundaries of one department without information coordination was difficult, and prior to the National Bureau of Identification's efforts, such publications as the *Police Gazette* had been the major source of inter-city information. The growth of the IACP, its identification system, and its continued efforts to get congressional funding created the precedent for nationally coordinated police with a focus almost completely limited to crime. The fourth transformation, like the urban network within which it was embedded, has never really been completed in a tidy fashion. Instead its complexity parallels that of the federal/municipal government relationship. One can predict that future changes in the structure of municipal government will contain or be preceded by changes in the police organization. As the previous model of urban government proved durable and flexible enough to last into the mid-nineteenth century, it may well be that the present mode of uniformed police and the municipal government within which they exist may be around a long time.

Section III: Further Research Problems

The picture sketched above is probably controversial in some aspects and is certainly incomplete. In this concluding section of the article I wish to indicate avenues in need of further exploration. The nineteenth-century decline and the twentieth-century rise of felony crime needs to be tested as an hypothesis, using more rigorous and systematic measurements than any so far.[40] Lane's use of coroner's records for Philadelphia, for instance, suggests the potential for a cross-city study of death by violence. Did it really decline in the nineteenth century? If such a curve can be established more precisely and surely, then its causal origins will also need a rigorous exploration. Several appealing but ad hoc explanations have been advanced, but none has been systematically tested. Thus, if the curve is real, the problem cries for an approach which tests the several competing hypothesis. Does the curve really chart the advent of industrialism and subsequent post-industrialism, as claimed by Lane? Or is the curve more an artifact of some other deeper (or shallower) urban change?

Or, perhaps, is a crime rate itself too dependent a variable to even try to analyze in a rigorously defined time-series? A reasonable argument can be made that there are so many independent variables whose relationships may be non-linear and inter-related in unspecified ways, variables which affect different offense rates differently, that the analysis of offense rates is bound to be speculative and untestable. When considering demographic variables, cultural variables, economic variables, opportunity variables, deterrence variables, and random perturbances with unknown effects — wars and depressions, both of which moved millions across the country, affecting both the denominators of rates and the actual number of offenses — the measurement and modeling problems may be overwhelming. Of course, if historic crime rates are not open to causal analysis, and if the criminal justice system is to a certain extent driven by the real crime rate, then the system is doubly dependent, both on crime and the multiplicity of factors that drive crime.

Even with this uncertainty, there are several problems in the history of the police in need of feasible and potentially interesting research. First and foremost, we need more series of data. While tedious to collect, the data must be developed to begin to fill in the basic context of police development and change. This is not a call for mindless data collection, but we have no reason to prolong our state of ignorance. There is no collected arrest or offense data for the period between 1920 and 1931, and the FBI considers the data it has published since 1931 to be unreliable for cross-city comparison prior to 1957. These data inconsistencies between the 1920s and the 1957 period, although not easily bridged, should yield an interesting series when it is sketched in. For example, the post-World War II burst in drunk and disorderly arrests discussed above is an hitherto unknown event discovered only by the creation of the arrest series. The major flaw of earlier data will be the absence of "offenses known to the police," long considered the most important data, but continued care and experience in dealing with these data should narrow the range of uncertainty.

We need to use more carefully articulated models with this data, and the use of advanced non-least squares based time-series statistics should be considered. The research of Blumstein and his associates provides a challenge in this regard, although it may be that advanced statistical techniques will only be useful for the more robust imprisonment data.[41] For instance, we now have the methods, historiography, and sources for detailed studies of homicide, suicide, and accidental death which should be able to confirm one of the three current impressions of crime: that "things" are falling apart, that mid-twentieth century homicide is a blip on the long decline of the crime or that the post-industrial urban crisis has made the *Clockwork Orange* come true.[42]

We must not confuse police/policy derived questions and concepts with historical/scientific ones, that the two might better and more carefully inform each other. Much work on the police answers policy related questions as asides, but the precise separation of the two should help clear up confusion and make the analysis of data more sensible. Historical data often can make significant contributions to policy and planning, but it does so best when unconfused with historical concerns. This is best exemplified by the work of Blumstein and his associates, who analyze series of imprisonment data which move through political and economic change in order to sharpen understanding of the dynamics of imprisonment, not of social change. They do not ignore historical social change, but when it seems to intrude on their material, they simply note that the unexplained variation probably came from social change, and move to other questions.[43] These footnoted variations are those of most interest to historians. For instance, by carefully separating the origins of change, Blumstein and his associates have helped identify two major eras of historical imprisonment levels, one period of relative stability from 1880 to around 1920, the other from 1920 to at least 1979. Their work shows that by proceeding with explicit policy questions, they could very carefully distinguish the kind of change which is of interest to historians from the change which attracts the attention of policy analysis. These distinctions are, finally, more than methodological. The historian wants to understand society, the policy maker to control it. But we argue that understanding is a prerequisite for control, and most of us are in favor of crime control. So as federal money works on the aim of police officers, we work on understanding their long term relationship to crime.

We also need more comparative work on the police: not simply work of regional and international comparison, of which Miller's remains the major example, but work comparing organizations. The obvious beginning is to compare fire and police organizations, which have similar periods of emergence and similar transitions from volunteer or volunteer-based models to uniformed and hierarchically organized city services. But other organizations will also provide useful comparisons — public schools, hospitals, and perhaps various businesses or federal bureaucracies. Only Rothman has tried such an approach, and his book, *Discovery of the Asylum,* is the stronger for it.[44] Since one of the emerging interpretations of nineteenth and early twentieth century history is known as the "organizational synthesis," the comparative analysis of the police and other organizations should improve both our understanding of the police and of organizations in history.[45]

In addition to the organizational basis of comparison, the comparison of police to other specifically governmental bureaucracies should also be illuminating. Economic historians have just begun to study the behavior of government bureaucracies as economic actors.[46] Although the main concern of the econometricians seems to be in discovering the causes of growth and estimating the overall economic impact of the growth, their work will provide financial data and economic frameworks within which to place police, or any other branch of the criminal justice system for that matter.

In a similar vein, but from a somewhat different perspective, the work in progress of political scientists Herbert Jacob and Robert Lineberry on governmental responses to crime contains two implicit challenges for historians.[47] First, as their research takes it beginning point as 1945, they have given historians a convenient end date for directly comparable work. Second, the political science perspective of the researchers invites quantitative political historians, who in large part focus on electoral politics and ignore other facets of political behavior, to shift toward thinking about the political history of public policy and crime.

We also need more straightforward descriptive legal histories of policing and crime control. Until recently, most legal history has focused on the analysis of Supreme Court decisions, and relatively little work has been done on the day-to-day operations of the lower courts, where most police originated business entered and left the judiciary.[48] The records of these lower courts do not seem to be systematically preserved, and much work on this topic will depend on luck, the aggressiveness of archives and a researcher's pluck.[49] Wunder's research on the lower courts of the northwest territory shows what can be done with the sensitive combing of statues and sporadically preserved materials. One can only hope that the Mayor's and Police Justices courts will find similar historians.

Conclusion

Police history continues to attract historians new to the field even when other forms of social and urban history are on the ascendant. It is of critical importance that the historians and other social scientists who pursue the subject stay alert to historiographic and social scientific trends in order to avoid repetition and to ask penetrating questions. The generalizations in this article should be seen as hypotheses to be tested, and the suggestions for further research should be taken as coherently related research topics, not just minor information gaps. If the field builds on previous work, becomes self-critical, and consciously works at being a part of a much larger social and political history, it promises to contribute a major component of U.S. history.

FOOTNOTES

1. The research reported in this paper has been supported by grants from the Academic Senate of the University of California, Los Angeles; the Social Science Research Council, and the American Philosophical Society. Portions of the substantive analysis in Section II have been drawn from my book, *Police in Urban America, 1860-1920* (New York, 1981). An earlier version of this paper was presented at the First Conference on the History of Crime and Criminal Justice, College Park, Maryland (September 1980), sponsored by the International Association for the History of Crime and Criminal Justice. I wish to thank David Waterhouse for his research assistance. Jon Butler, Eugene Watts and Terrence J. McDonald made invaluable comments on the manuscript.

2. Ernest S. Griffith, *History of American City Government: The Colonial Period*, v. 1 (New York, 1938); *The Modern Development of City Government in the United Kingdom and the United States* (London, 1927); *A History of American City Government: The Conspicious Failure, 1870-1900* (New York, 1974); *A History of American City Government: The Progressive Years and Their Aftermath, 1900-1920* (New York, 1974).

3. Samuel P. Hays' work has stimulated much of this research. See his, *American Political History as Social Analysis: Essays by Samuel P. Hays* (Knoxville, 1980).

4. Robert M. Fogelson, *Big City Police* (Cambridge, 1977).

5. Michael H. Frisch, *Town into City: Springfield, Massachusetts, and the Meaning of Community, 1840-1880* (Cambridge, 1972); Kenneth Fox, *Better City Government: Innovation in American Urban Politics, 1850-1937* (Philadelphia, 1977); J. Rogers and Ellen Jane Hollingsworth, *Dimensions in Urban History: Historical and Social Science Perspectives on Middle-Size American Cities* (Madison, 1979); Terrence J. McDonald, "Urban Development, Political Power and Municipal Expenditure in San Francisco, 1860-1910: A Quantitative Investigation of Historical Theory,'" (Ph.D. dissertation, Stanford University, 1979).

6. For a discussion of annual reports, see Monkkonen, "Municipal Reports as an Indicator Source: The Nineteenth Century Police," *Historical Methods* (Spring, 1979), 57-75.

7. See Monkkonen, *Police in Urban America*, App. I, for complete details.

8. Richard Wade, *Slavery in the Cities: The South, 1820-1860* (New York, 1964).

9. For two examples of historical geography using a network perspective, see, Allan R. Pred, *Urban Growth and the Circulation of Information: The United States System of Cities, 1790-1840* (Cambridge, 1973), and Michael P. Conzen, "Maturing Urban Systems of the U.S., 1840-1910," *The Annals of the Association of American Geographers* (March 1977): 88-108.

10. U.S. Department of Justice, LEAA, *Sourcebook of Criminal Justice Statistics, 1978* (Washington: G.P.O., 1978), 86.

City Size	Mean Police Personnel Per 1,000 Population
1,000,000 +	4.12
500,000-999,999	2.63
250,000-499,999	2.40
100,000-249,999	2.44
50,000- 99,999	2.14
25,000- 49,999	2.06
10,000- 24,999	2.08

11. *Sourcebook*, p. 87.

12. Eugene Watts, "Police Priorities in Twentieth Century St. Louis," *Journal of Social History* (June, 1981): 649-674.

13. The specific first difference regression results are:
Total Police = 127.6 + .91 (d - 10) Population^2
r^2 = .865; D-W = 2.5254; DF = 58.

14. *Sourcebook*, p. 86.

15. Data from U.S. Department of Commerce, Bureau of the Census, *Historical Statistics of the United States: Colonial Times to 1970* (Washington, 1976), Series D 590, 591, p. 144.

16. Wilbur R. Miller, *Cops and Bobbies: Police Authority in New York and London, 1820-1870* (Chicago, 1977).

17. Watts, "Police Priorities."

18. Jerold E. Levine, "Police, Parties and Polity: The Bureaucratization, Unionization, and Professionalization of the New York City Police, 1870-1917" (Ph.D. dissertation, University of Wisconsin, 1971); Sean Wilentz, "Crime, Poverty and the Streets of New York City: The Diary of William H. Bell, 1850-1851," *History Workshop* (Spring 1979): 126-155.

19. David R. Johnson, *Policing The Urban Underworld: The Impact of Crime on the Development of The American Police, 1800-1887* (Philadelphia, 1979); Mark H. Haller, "Illegal Enterprise: Historical Perspectives and Public Policy," in James A. Inciardi and Charles E. Faupel, eds., *History and Crime: Implications for Criminal Justice Policy* (Beverly Hills, 1980), 77-90; Sidney Harring and Lorrain McMullin, "The Buffalo Police, 1872-1900: Labor Unrest, Political Power and the Creation of The Police Institution," *Crime and Social Justice* (Fall-Winter, 1975): 5-14; John C. Schneider, *Detroit and The Problem of Order, 1830-1880: A Geography of Crime, Riot and Policing* (Lincoln, Neb., 1980).

20. For the most recent critique of the social control thesis, see David J. Rothman, "Social Control: The Uses and Abuses of the Concept in the History of Incarceration," paper presented at the First Conference on the History of Crime and Criminal Justice, College Park, Maryland (September 1980).

21. Allan E. Levett, "Centralization of City Police in the Nineteenth-Century United States" (Ph.D. dissertation, University of Michigan, 1975).

22. Bruce C. Johnson, "Taking Care of Labor: The Police in American Politics," *Theory and Society* (Spring 1976): 89-117; Samuel Walker, "The Police and the Community: Scranton, Pennsylvania, 1866-1884: A Test Case," *American Studies* (1978): 79-90; Daniel Walkowitz, *Worker City, Company Town: Iron and Cotton-Worker Protest in Troy and Cohoes, New York, 1855-1884* (Urbana, 1979), 135, 192-218, 233-239.

23. Walkowitz, *Worker City, Company Town*, 197-217, 219-238.

24. Schneider, *Detroit and The Problem of Order*.

25. Data from Monkkonen, "A Disorderly People? Urban Order in the Nineteenth and Twentieth Centuries," *Journal of American History* (Dec., 1981): 539-559.

26. James W. Gerard, *London and New York: Their Crime and Police* (New York, 1853).

27. Donald C. Dilworth, ed., *Identification Wanted: Development of the American Criminal Identification System, 1893-1943* (Gaithersburg, Md., 1977).

28. Johnson, *Policing the Urban Underworld;* see also the review by Joseph G. Woods, *Journal of American History* (June 1980): 141-142.

29. Monkkonen, *Police in Urban America,* chap. 2.

30. Lane, *Violent Death.*

31. Ted R. Gurr and Hugh D. Graham, *Violence in America: Historical and Comparative Perspectives* (Beverly Hills, 1979); see especially Gurr, "On the History of Violent Crime in Europe and America," 353-374. See also Lane, "Urban Police and Crime in Nineteenth-Century America," *Crime and Justice: An Annual Review of Research,* 2 (1980): 1-44.

32. Levett, "Centralization of City Police."

33. Gudmund Hernes, "Structural Change in Social Processes," *American Journal of Sociology* (Nov. 1976): 513-547.·

34. Monkkonen, *Police in Urban America,* chap. 1, figures 1 and 2.

35. G.F. Pyle, "The Diffusion of Cholera in the U.S. in the Nineteenth Century," *Geographical Analysis* (Jan. 1969): 59-75.

36. Monkkonen, "The Consequences of Police Reform: Lost Children and Public Perceptions," Paper presented at the International Economic History Congress (Aug. 15, 1979), Edinburgh.

37. Sidney L. Harring, "Class Conflict and the Suppression of Tramps in Buffalo, 1892-1894," *Law and Society Review* (Summer 1977): 873-911.

38. See Monkkonen, *Police in Urban America,* chap. 4 and Appendix III.

39. Donald C. Dilworth, ed., *The Blue and the Brass: American Policing, 1890-1910* (Gaithersburg, Md., 1976).

40. See Ted R. Gurr, "Historical Trends in Violent Crimes: A Critical Review of Evidence," in *Crime and Justice: An Annual Review of Research,* 3 (1981): 295-353, for an example of a test of the hypothesis of the felony crime rate reversal.

41. Alfred Blumstein and Jacqueline Cohen, "A Theory of the Stability of Punishment," *Journal of Criminal Law and Criminology* (June 1973): 198-207. Also Blumstein and Soumyo Moitra, "An Analysis of the Time Series of the Imprisonment Rate in the United States: A Further Test of the Stability of Punishment Hypothesis," *Journal of Criminal Law and Criminology* (Fall 1979): 376-390.

42. Roger Lane, *Violent Death in the City: Suicide, Accident, and Murder in 19th Century Philadelphia* (Cambridge, 1979).

43. Alfred Blumstein and Soumyo Moitra, "Growing or Stable Incarceration Rates: A Comment Cahalan's 'Trends in Incarceration in the United States Since 1880'," *Crime and Delinquency* (Jan. 1980): 91-94.

44. David J. Rothman, *The Discovery of the Asylum: Social Order and Disorder in the New Republic* (Boston, 1971).

45. Robert F. Berkhofer, Jr., "The Organizational Interpretation of American History: A New Synthesis," *Prospects* (1979): 611-630.

46. Thomas E. Borcherding, ed., *Budgets and Bureaucrats: The Sources of Government Growth* (Durham, N.C., 1977); Roger L. Ransom, "In Search of Security: The Growth of Government in the United States," Department of Economics, Working Paper Number 40 (Jan. 1980), University of California, Riverside.

47. Herbert Jacob and Robert L. Lineberry, Governmental Responses to Crime Project, Evanston, Ill. See Jacob and Lineberry, "Governmental Responses to Cime, 1948-1978," Paper presented at Social Science History Association Annual Meeting (Nov. 1980), Rochester, New York; see also, Jacob and Michael L. Rich, "The Effects of Police on Crime: A Social Look," *Law and Society Review* (1980-81): 109-122.

48. Michael S. Hindus deals with court behavior in *Prison and Plantation: Crime, Justice and Authority in Massachusetts and South Carolina, 1767-1878* (Chapel Hill, 1980). John Wunder, *Inferior Courts, Superior Justice: A History of the Justices of the Peace on the Northwest Frontier, 1853-1889* (Westport, Conn., 1979), carefully details lower court operations and quantifies some court behavior. The important book by Lawrence M. Friedman and Robert V. Percival, *The Roots of Justice: Crime and Punishment in Alameda County, California, 1870-1910* (Chapel Hill, N.C., 1981) appeared too late to incorporate in this essay.

49. Monkkonen, "Systematic Criminal Justice History: Some Suggestions," *Journal of Interdisciplinary History* (Winter 1978): 451-464. Hindus, et al., *The Files of the Massachusetts Superior Court, 1859-1959: An Analysis and Plan for Action* (Boston, 1980), detail a systematic survey and sampling of a century of criminal court records. These data are available through the Criminal Justice Archive and Information Network, University of Michigan.

18.

THE CIVILIZING OFFENSIVE: MENTALITIES, HIGH CULTURE AND INDIVIDUAL PSYCHES

Arthur Mitzman

"Que de choses, effacées à demi dans nos moeurs populaires, semblaient inexplicables, dépourvues de raison et de sens, et qui reparaissant pour moi dans leur accord avec l'inspiration primitive se sont trouvées n'être autre chose que la sagesse d'un monde oublié."

Jules Michelet

Preface

To describe the proper relationship between ego and id, Sigmund Freud once used the metaphor of rider and horse; the rational ego must master and direct the instinctual id-drives in the same way that the rider masters and directs his horse.

Comparable prescriptions for wellbeing can be found centuries before Freud, among the ideologists of absolutism. In 1621, Père Maldonnat, in a dictum charged with implications for the social relations and mentalities of the past three and a half centuries, argued that the will should command the desires "like the father his son, the pedagogue his disciple, the lord his servant, and the king his subjects." To understand the historical connection between psychology and society implicit in this ancient wisdom, we shall have to invoke the shade of Max Weber as well as that of the creator of psychoanalysis, and consider what can be said on Père Maldonnat's subject from the triple standpoints of the history of mentalities, cultural history and psychohistory.

The analysis based on these standpoints, then, examines the relation between, on the one hand, the normative psychology of secular and religious authorities in the period since the renaissance and, on the other, traditional popular mentalities, a relation I shall call the "civilizing offensive." As such, it scouts out a scholarly no-man's land, adjacent to the historical imperium, that has been earlier subject to the wondering gaze of Norbert Elias, Michel Foucault, Jacques Donzelot and Robert Muchembled. The present exploration attempts to extend and correct the maps they have drawn.

Introduction

This essay addresses a problem that appears to be endemic in psychoanalytically oriented history writing: the missing link to large social-historical concerns.[1] To search out this connection, I shall examine a stratum of broadly interpretive social-historical literature — the literature that deals from the standpoint of changing mentalities with what Norbert Elias has called the "civilizing process." I believe that a close look at the fields of mentalities, culture, and psychohistory will, in demonstrating their interrelation, lead to an important modification and integration of the two theoretical corpuses which are implicit in these branches of inquiry: a Weber-based historical sociology, whose principle of increasing rationalization underlies the more interesting developmental theories of individuation, centralization of power and corresponding value change in culture and mentalities;[2] and Freudian theory, which is indispensable for the understanding of individual personality but whose notorious ahistoricity has been a major stumbling-block for the psychohistorical enterprise. In short, I wish to show that a hermeneutical alliance between the fields I have mentioned can lead to a more responsible and more integrated use of both psychoanalytic and sociological categories by historians.

Essential to the connection between mentalities, cultures and individual psyches are the socializing agencies which transmit social values: the family, the youth peer group, and other traditional and modern networks of sociability: confraternities, corporations, educational institutions, churches, armies, trade unions, etc. In the analysis both of the structure of these socializing agencies and of their evolution, the work of the psychohistorian and the historian of mentalities is complementary rather than mutually exclusive.[3] For the mental baggage of norms and values that individuals unthinkingly absorb from the religious, social and political structures of their societies — the terrain of collective mentalities — is an indispensable Greek chorus of support or rebuke for the parental sources of conscience and ambivalence that the psychohistorian studies. Indeed, Freud recognized this Greek chorus effect when he coined the term "cultural superego." Nonetheless, there are two central shortcomings of Freudian theory which are thrown sharply into relief when looked at from the perspective of the history of mentalities: a general neglect of the extra-parental sources of superego formation and an underestimation of the pre-oedipal influences on culture and personality. For it is arguable that the historical process of rationalization, by drastically eliminating pre-oedipal characteristics from the mediating agencies between the individual and the dominant mentality, as well as by pre-empting, containing and institutionalizing the social frameworks for oedipal revolt,[5] has fundamentally altered the prevailing "cultural superegos" and thereby the shape of individual personality.

This last is crucial for the connections we are exploring. The rationalization of public and private life postulated by Weber has had as its social-psychological corollary a process of individuation and of steadily increasing control by centralizing political and ideological authorities over traditional cultures and mentalities which has modified the shape, the values and the significance for the individual of the family as well as of non-familial agencies of socialization. Indeed, it is arguable that this process is the major historical tendency of the past 500 years.

Forming a continuity with it, but primarily of relevance for the European social and cultural history of the past two and a half centuries, are three other, inter-related processes, which have similarly influenced the individual, the familial and the supra-familial sources of superego formation: 1) the evolution of a disenchanted and goal-oriented modern consciousness, connected with the rationalization and centralization of economic and political life, with the spread of scientific thinking and the decline of religion; 2) as a paradoxical response to the first: the development and intensification of national consciousness, partly as a surrogate for traditional religious beliefs, partly to fill the gap left by vanishing corporate and local solidarities; and 3) – both as a means of levelling the opposition to 1) and 2) and as a reconciliation of their contradictory elements – the attack on behavior presumed by those in authority to be immoral or uncivilized. This had been a prevailing justification for the suppression of popular culture between 1500 and 1800, motivating condemnations of witchcraft, of the festive violence of the young and of irregular sexuality in the 16th, 17th, and 18th centuries. In the 19th century, it took the characteristic form of medical-ethical attacks on masturbation, prostitution and concubinage; in the 20th century, of condemnations of drug use and homosexuality; and, throughout the modern era, of efforts to reform what was viewed as the incurable licentiousness, vulgarity and lack of a work ethic of the lower classes.

This attack, which I call the "civilizing offensive",[6] will be the main focus of this essay. Using this perspective, I shall examine the conflict of popular and elite cultures in France during the 14th to 19th centuries, as evidenced in studies by Muchembled, Le Roy Ladurie and Darnton. Because Robert Muchembled's *Culture populaire et culture des élites* places this conflict within a framework that takes account both of the sociological processes of centralization and rationalization and of social-psychological collisions of mentalities and values, I shall direct my remarks in the first place to his work.[7]

I

Muchembled Weberianized: criticism; predecessors; repression of popular culture; peasant culture and nature; *Montaillou* as confirmation – porosity of man and nature.

Muchembled's book, useful though it is, is far from flawless. Some of the key concepts he used, such as "culture populaire," "religion populaire," and "culture des élites," as well as his overly simple conflict model, have been the subject of extensive criticism and debate by his colleagues.[8] In general, this criticism of Muchembled suggests that he constructed the oppositions popular culture-elite culture and popular religion-church doctrine in a manner that overlooked the innumerable accommodations, shifts and compromises within these pairs. One example among many, of the unstable interpenetrations of popular and elite cultures, was the religious organization of the laity. In the countryside and the towns, the devotional societies – "confréries" – functioned since the late middle ages to give the church a grip on popular society and culture. In some cases, Natalie Zemon Davis has pointed out, they seem to have been established to co-opt the older anarchic and morally unreliable organizations of young adults, such as the *abbayes de jeunesse*.[9] Yet in southern France, the *confréries* became in the 18th century partly secularized into associations of Freemasons, and in the 19th century, many of the remaining Catholic *confréries* became the seed-beds of local republican and anti-clerical organizations.[10]

Perhaps what is missing in Muchembled is the equivalent, at the level of an historical sociology of village and city culture, of an intermediary stage between "archaic" and "modern," comparable to what Max Weber demonstrated for political sociology in his descriptions of "patriarchal and patrimonial rule," as part of the evolution from feudal (or despotic) to bureaucratic control.[11] Carlo Ginzburg (in *The Cheese and the Worms*) and Emmanuel Le Roy Ladurie (in *Montaillou*) have both revealed irrefutably, at the level of individual experience, this large intermediate zone where modernizing and archaic mental structures partly combine and partly conflict. Inasmuch, however, as this paper is concerned not with the correction of Muchembled's lack of nuance, but with the utility of the broad line of development he has sketched from archaic to modern mental structures, his book will remain its central focus.

My positive arguments about Muchembled are three-fold: First, that looking at Freudian theory in the light of the value conflicts Muchembled has shown between popular and elite cultures suggests the normative and anachronistic character of certain aspects of this theory when applied to periods before the nineteenth century.[12] Secondly, that reversing this procedure – i.e., looking at Muchembled's portrayal of value conflict in a Freudian perspective – could give his work a more systematic character. Thirdly, that by extending Muchembled's perspective into the nineteenth century, one can also see the relativity of an important aspect of the Weberian theory of rationalization that underlies his work: the notion that this rationalization is an inexorable one-way street, a permanent iron cage.

Muchembled is of course not the first scholar to write a broad, synthetic work that uses the process of centralization and rationalization as a sociological framework for dissecting value change. Norbert Elias did this in 1939 in *Über den Prozess der Zivilisation*, and Weinstein and Platt did it in 1969 in *The Wish To Be Free*.[13] In both works, systematic use was made of psychoanalytic categories, which are rather incidentally applied by Muchembled. But their efforts, situated in the decades before historians of mentalities were fully engaged in questions of value change, were restricted to portraying conflicts within the elites themselves, and thus by-passed both the mentalities of the large majority of the population and the conflict between these popular mentalities and those of the upper orders of society. Concomitant with this neglect of the popular classes, their work also tends to emphasize and to value the more rational and moralizing aspects of personality – ego and superego in Freudian terms – and neglect or devalue the non-rational and largely unconscious force of instinctual drives – what Freud called the Id.

Muchembled differs in both these respects from his predecessors. His focus is not on the aristocratic and bourgeois elites as the object of the civilizing offensive and the process of individuation – both of which are implicitly recounted in his work – but on the common people and their *culture populaire*. And his view of the processes of change, does not contain the implicit judgment that moral progress is attained by them.[14] To the contrary, his work shows primarily what has been lost by the destruction of the pre-absolutist popular culture.

This last, though it no doubt reflects Muchembled's own values, is his strong point, particularly for the psychoanalytically informed historian. For although Muchembled does not refer to personality systematically in depth-psychological terms, his argument about the impact of absolutism on traditional popular culture can be of great value in the historical relativizing of Freudian categories. In fact, through references to Erikson and Roland Jaccard, and through the use of the notions of sexual repression and the return of the repressed, Muchembled does involve psychoanalytic discourse in his work.

In the first place, he implies that there is a similarity between the ongoing repression of popular culture *by* the elite culture and repression of the body *within* it. That is, from the standpoint of the elite culture, there was a crucial parallel between the separation, control and repression of the lower social stratum and that of the lower bodily stratum. Indeed, despite the folk culture's intricate systems of controlling and channeling drives and impulses, its social organization and mentalities were generally viewed with the same aversion and repressive tendencies as the court authorities maintained against the "irrational" or "uncivilized" aspects of the behavior of the elite.

Secondly, Muchembled describes the process by which this aversion became internalized by those members of the popular culture who were open to the discipline and education emanating from the dominant elite culture. On the whole, he views literacy as well as a modest degree of wealth and local power as the most important criteria for establishing such colonization by the elite culture, and he views the more "modern" mentality of this layer of rural culture as exerting the same sort of "civilizing" pressure on the rest as Elias views being exercised in the royal courts against the warrior aristocracy. This pressure from within the peasant community explains much of the persecution of witches as well as the suppression of other aspects of the older culture which one labored to repress in one's own personality as well as in the community as a whole.

Thirdly and most importantly, he describes in both material and psychological terms the object of these repressions, the traditional rural mentality. In general, Muchembled posits a dependence on and proximity to nature that shaped every aspect of personality and mentality in the folk culture. Cut off by inadequate transportation from larger economic units and by inadequate technology from surpluses above immediate needs, traditional societies were usually remote from any notion of material, social and scientific "progress." Yoked as they were to the recurrent cycles of nature, the concept of time in them was in general not linear but circular. The character of religious thought that arose under such conditions lacked most of the presuppositions of Christianity: the teleological movement toward the kingdom of God, the monotheistic notion of a single all-powerful deity, and the unique relation of every individual soul to this deity. To the contrary, natural forces and objects everywhere merged with supernatural ones, individuals were profoundly embedded in collective kin, age-group and professional networks; one feared the spirits of the dead but nonetheless invoked their intercession to overcome the anxiety caused by capricious nature. One did so in the first place to insure a proper return of the sun, warm weather and fertility during the short winter days, when the abundance of nature had disappeared; in the second to protect the crops and the local community from the caprices of drought, flood and pestilence, and from the dangers of human cupidity and aggression. Most of the beliefs, festivities and ritual practices of folk culture were based on the need to allay these anxieties and to insure the recurrence of what they viewed as the eternal life-giving cycle.

In opposition, then, to the religious and philosophical tendencies that increasingly identified the purely spiritual, the non-natural, non-material aide of man with his proximity to God, and the natural, with his evil and corruptibility, many elements of the traditional popular culture maintained an integration of man into the world of nature. Le Roy Ladurie shows how the Cathar heresy adopted by so many in the medieval mountain village of Montaillou established spiritual links with the animal kingdom which Catholicism shunned: the souls of humans migrated after death into the bodily apertures of cows, horses and donkeys, to lodge there until their ultimate return to human form.[15] The choice of religion in this Pyrenean village showed in other ways the sharply differing attitudes of the local people and the Catholic Church to the animal world. Most of the Cathari missionaries (the *parfaits*) were, like their converts, shepherds, involved in the daily care of their flocks, animal as well as human, whereas the only interest of the local bishops in either one was in their literal potential for "fleecing" – i.e., the collection of the tithe. This interest was so repugnant to the shepherds that their preference for Catharism was sometimes barely distinguishable from tax evasion.

The local attitude toward the cult of Mary is especially noteworthy in connection with nature religion, since this cult was, the author of *Montaillou* argues, thrown out the door by the heretical doctrine (bitterly misogynist as well as purist), only to be smuggled back through the window by the shepherds and peasants because of the identification in regional folklore of Mary with an archaic earth goddess:

> This chthonic aspect of the marian presence appears to me highly essential. Incontestably, the Virgin Mother...generally in the high Ariège, is in the earth. Just as God the Father, at the opposite end, is in the sky. The two form a couple at the two ends of the vertical dimension. Mary of Montaillou and of Sabarthes is tied to the very old cult of stone emplacements that surround the herds of cows and the pairs of plow oxen. Towards her and towards these stones, fall the gifts of sheared wool. She receives, under her altar and in the cemetery which adjoins her chapel, the cadavers that return to the nourishing maternal soil. The Mother Goddess is an Earth Goddess...Vessel of flesh, she accepts the urine and the manure, the cadavers and the bovine tramping. She incarnates in fact the cults of uterine and agricultural fertility.[16]

Montaillou deals, of course, with a remote mountain village in the early fourteenth century. By the time the civilizing offensive really got underway, in the sixteenth century, the archaic elements of local peasant culture were more Christianized, with the result that many of the prohibitions imposed by the Church on popular festivities such as the charivari and on dancing in houses of worship and cemeteries were invoked against practices that western Christianity had earlier tolerated or even sanctioned. At a certain point, a compromise which generations earlier the Church had been glad to accept, since it gave it control over popular customs, was perceived as incompatible, because of its violence or its mixture of the profanely material and the sacred, with a more purely spiritual morality.[17] The repression of dancing by both Calvinist and post-Tridentine Catholic authorities is a particularly interesting case, as I will demonstrate.[18]

In general, the early modern period saw the rapid growth of a movement toward purity which was at once religious, ethical, logical and political. This movement toward purity was the psychological corollary, indeed the epistemological basis, for the process of rationalization and desacralization described by Weber. Although most of its manifestations still appeared in the moral garb of Christian doctrine, there were distinct signs of secularization. Descartes laid the basis for a strict separation of mental and physical faculties; Hobbes, for a naked state power that could do without religious pretences; Locke, for a theory of property that would render obsolete and illogical the overlapping forms of ownership that underlay the corporate system of the old regime. Contrariwise, the inexactitude of the boundaries between mine and thine, between secular and religious, had gone together both in the archaic folk culture and in the Christianized universe imposed on it, with a parallel, if diminishing, vagueness about the boundaries between man, nature and the supernatural, and between one human body and another. This was particularly so for the popular culture which Le Roy Ladurie glimpses behind the inquisitorial transcripts on Montaillou's citizenry, and which Muchembled discusses in archetypal terms in *Culture populaire et culture des élites*. Now this porosity of social relations and concepts at all levels of the old regime resonates interestingly with certain Freudian and post-Freudian theories that deal with the earliest and most fundamental stages of mental development.

II

From Weber to Freud: Freud and Lacan on ego boundaries and pathology; traditional culture and lower bodily functions; nature, sex and the devil; socialization, oedipal revolt, paternal power.

In contrast to the appearance of clearly defined ego-identity ("autonomous and unitary, marked off deceptively from everything else") which corresponds roughly to the personality ideal propagated by the civilizing offensive, Freud posited that "the ego is continued inward, without any sharp delimitation, into an unconscious mental entity which we designate as the id and for which it serves as a kind of facade."[19] Furthermore, maintained the Freud of *Civilization and Its Discontents*, the deceptive sharpness of ego-delimitation originates ontologically in its opposite, the fusional relationship between child and mother:

> An infant at the breast does not yet distinguish his ego from the external world as the source of the sensations flowing in on him. He gradually learns to do so[20]. . . . Originally the ego includes everything, later it separates off an external world from itself. Our present ego-feeling is, therefore, only a shrunken residue of a much more inclusive – indeed an all-embracing – feeling which corresponded to a more intimate bond between the ego and the world about it.[21]

It is arguable that in pre-modern cultures, whether feudal, corporative or popular, residues of this "more intimate bond" were expressed precisely by that porosity of social relations and concepts which I have noted.

Freud himself viewed any recurrence in adulthood of "states in which the boundary lines between ego and the external world become uncertain" – with the exception of the state of being in love – as "pathological.[22] Moreover, he inclined to minimize the significance for later development of this early fusional relationship to the mother.[23] But what Freud stigmatized and depreciated in the early mother-child relation has been viewed as normal, essential, and of permanent influence in the post-Freudian work of Lacan, Klein and Schachtel.

To discuss only the first of these: Lacan, like Freud, sees the mother-child relationship, in Sherry Turkle's words, as "fusional, dual and immediate, dominated by the desire to lose self in the other."[24] But its order of importance is much greater than with Freud. Based on this fusional relationship with the mother, Lacan postulates an initial, pre-Oedipal mode of experiencing the world, which he calls the imaginary order, in which the self seeks fusion with the other. This phase – the "mirror phase" – is for Lacan the basis of aesthetic creativity and sensibility. The increasing intrusion of the father into the dual relationship of mother and child creates a symbolic, rational way of experiencing the world, which leads the child away from the narcissism and symbiosis of the first phase and prepares it for social interaction.

Nonetheless, Turkle indicates, Lacan's symbolic order does not actually replace the imaginary one, since identification with people and images is a normal feature of adult life, and this capacity is based on the model of infantile fantasy life – the "imaginary identifications" of the mirror phase, "a direct, fusional mode in which self is lost in other."[25] I would argue that it is precisely the aim of the modernizing missionary morality, whether at the level of theology, political ideology, epistemology or ethics, to obliterate the expressions of the "fusional mode" which constituted the porosity of the older style of social relations and concepts.

Because the cosmos of the traditional popular culture was in general characterized by recurrence, and the divisions between man, nature and the supernatural were perceived as relative and porous rather than absolute, it is plausible that normal personality development within it was less unidirectional than Freudian and other therapeutic civilizers now deem proper, that there was a less rigorous repression of oral and anal stages of sexual evolution operative before the genital phase, and that the institutions of the traditional culture allowed more open expression of id-impulses and anxieties associated with all stages of development than the centralizing missionary moralities of the modern era found acceptable. Urine and excrement, for example,

> are not the objects of profound disgust as in our day. They constitute, for the peasants as for Rabelais, the "joyous matter" which Bakhtin has described in an admirable book. For, as this author emphasizes, urine and excrement are connected, by their place in the lower part of the body, with eminently sacred phenomena such as fecundity and birth and, by this fact, with "renewal and well-being."[26]

Peasant sexuality also lacked the sense of shame and guilt that the missionary morality of the Church began propagating in the sixteenth century. Muchembled writes of "a solid licentiousness, even among women, who are frightened neither by the sight nor by the evocation of the virile organ."[27]

Some of the fairy folk tales recounted at the *veillées* similarly give evidence for a rather different attitude toward bodily functions, though these, even in the oldest versions to which we have access, often seem to reveal the conflict between the old and the new moralities. Here I shall shift to examples provided by Robert Darnton in his lively essay "Peasants Tell Tales."[28]

One of the stock ingredients of these tales, for instance, is the conflict between stepmother and stepchild. Darnton is of course correct in pointing to the large number of such conflicts in a culture where so many women died young, leaving children behind to be brought up by second wives who gave preference to their own children. This is not merely indicative of a different demographic and economic structure from ours, however: it suggests, just as does the work of Muchembled, a different mental structure as well. For the prevalence of stepmothers meant that the way of consciously conceptualizing motherhood which became dominant in the 19th century family ideology — consistently loving, dependable, and symbolized by the nurturant goodness of the mother of God — was improbable in the earlier period. Too many people had the experience of stepmothers, apart from the fact that biological mothers, pressured by poverty and the Church's inflexible demands for reproductive efficiency, rarely had the emotional energy to play the all-loving role bourgeois ideology later came to expect of them. To the contrary, the good mother-bad mother antithesis that post-Freudian theory has discovered in the fantasy life of infants receives more direct expression in traditional folk culture than we can find anywhere in modern society (except perhaps in 20th century folklore about mothers-in-law).[29] Salvation from the viciousness of the wicked stepmother usually came through the intervention of a fairy godmother, who seemed to conflate elements of pagan nature goddesses with those of the Virgin Mary.

Take for example the tale of the "three gifts," translated in full by Darnton.[30] We begin with the usual second wife who detests and mistreats her little stepson. The latter is exploited as shepherd, dressed in rags and given no more than a piece of bread and butter each day to stay alive. A fairy disguised as a beggar woman appears on the scene, and tests the boy's goodness by asking three days in a row for a piece of his meager ration. When he has passed inspection, she identifies herself as a fairy, suddenly appears beautifully dressed, young and fresh, and offers him three wishes. His desires are simple: He wants to be able to hit any small birds he aims at with his crossbow, to force everyone in the vicinity to dance whenever he plays his flute, and to have the power to compel his stepmother to fart loudly whenever he sneezed.

The next day, the shepherd boy tries out his new-found sneezing powers in church: "His stepmother, despite all her efforts to contain them, immediately let out a salvo of farts and turned so red in the face that everyone stared at her and she wished she were a hundred feet under the ground."[31] After being turned out of the church for disrespect, the stepmother complains to the priest that it was her stepson's sneezes that precipitated her ignominy. The priest, sensing foul play, scolds the shepherd youth, but the latter, instead of confessing. leads the priest into the fields, where he shoots a bird with his crossbow and asks the priest to fetch it. The place where the bird had fallen is full of thorn bushes and, as soon as the priest is in them, the boy plays his flute, which, as promised, induces in the priest uncontrollable and, because of the thorns, painful dancing. When the boy stops, the priest brings him to the justice of the peace and demands he be punished as a witch.

The shepherd boy, sure of his powers, again starts fluting: "The priest, who was standing, began to dance; the clerk began to whirl on his chair; the justice of the peace bounded up and down on his seat; and everyone present shook their legs so wildly that the courtroom looked like a dance hall."[32] To stop this undesired exercise, the lad was allowed to go in peace if he would cease playing.

Like so many folk tales, the story of the shepherd boy's revenge has the character of a world turned upside down, both in the social sense of his coming out (temporarily) on top in a society that destined him for the bottom, and, to use the same terminology, of doing so by a fantasized victory of the bodily bottom over the top — a little boy's magic revolt against the civilizing offensive, a revolt clearly endorsed by the popular mentality that transmitted these tales to the young. Interestingly, it is the cruel stepmother who is associated with Christian missionary morality and the fairy godmother who arms the lad with the weapons of nature. In fact, the first two gifts she gives him — the ability to hit any bird with his crossbow and the capacity to force people to dance by playing his flute — are respectively the traits of Diana and Pan, the two principal Greek nature deities.[33]

Two things are evident from this tale: the conflict of old and new cultures is in full swing and the tale's peasant narrators are clearly out to ridicule the civilizing offensive and its priestly and step-motherly agents. Wild dancing to a shepherd's flute and a scatological practical joke — the provinces of Dionysus and Rabelais — are used to turn the tables on the missionary morality of sitting still in church and controlling and repressing the body. The general effort to discipline and repress the lower parts is implicit in the use of these parts as weapons against the oppressive alliance of priest and stepmother.[34]

Apart from the greater accessibility of archaic fantasies and the profound connection to the natural world, the peasant cultures of early modern Europe also displayed a radically different pattern of socialization than the one that gave rise to Freud's theories. From the age of about twelve, adolescent and unmarried young males were organized in the various *bachelleries* and *abbayes de jeunesse*, and these were probably as important a conduit for the cultural superego of the community as a boy's biological parents.[35]

Though some of the customs prevalent in these associations reveal a barbarism the world is well rid of — such as the group rape of village girls as a means of sexual initiation[36] — they functioned on the whole as an essential element of the local social structure, organizing festivities and rituals and guarding morality through the humiliating and noisy practice of the charivari. Muchembled and others have argued that the attack on these youth groups by church and state that began around the time of the Reformation aimed not simply at ending barbaric customs but at the suppression of the anarchic popular culture as a whole and at the imposition on peasant society of the patriarchal Christian values of the new absolutism.[37] In terms of this pattern, we might see in the organized youth groups of the older society — despite their conservative function as the transmitters of communal values — an embodiment of what later came to be called oedipal revolt, directed not against the biological fathers, but, implicitly, against the paternal power epitomized by king and bishop and by the upper classes in general.[38] The bloody class warfare in the carnival at Romans in 1580 was in any case replete with symbolic fantasies of oedipal revolt: fears on the part of the communal notables that the plebeians planned literally to eat them and rape their women.[39]

A brief glance at the family values propagated by the civilizing offensive in the early modern period suggests the reality of this "oedipal" aspect of the conflict between elite and popular cultures. To support the authority of the king's and of God's agents, the ideologists of Absolutism proclaimed a sweeping reinforcement of paternal power, that aimed to undermine all horizontal bonds capable of generating resistance to the constituted secular and religious system, whether at the level of insubordinate offspring, contumacious aristocrats, the urban commune, the village community or the local youth group. Bishop Bossuet argued that kings were made on the model of fathers. Malebranche saw parents as the "lieutenants" of God. In 1705, the catchism of Montpellier stated:

> All superiors are comprehended under the name of fathers and mothers, because they ought to love their inferiors like their children and because the inferiors, from their side ought to love, fear, respect their superiors like their fathers.[40]

Georges Snyders, Muchembled's principal source on this question, emphasizes the mutual support and mutual justification of the various kinds of hierarchical relations — of fathers over children, the king over his subjects, and God and His church over his creatures — and reveals the profound significance of this structure of domination for the evolution of personality:

> Here we find a characteristic element, which we have located repeatedly in the authors of the period: this domination has in each of us an interior model which is nothing but the subordination of the different faculties of the soul: "Nature has wanted our appetites to be obedient to our reason." — And in the same sense, Père Maldonnat... affirms that the will commands the desires "like the father his son, the pedagogue his disciple, the lord his servant, and the king his subjects."[41]

In this passage, interdependence between, on the one hand, political and religious authority, and, on the other, what is called individual reason and will, is transparent, as is the equation between the "appetites" and the subservient orders of society. To translate these terms into Freudian ones: the domination of ego and superego over id is clearly seen as the desired psychological equivalent and support of the domination of the reinforced patriarchal authority over its subjects.

Muchembled closes his essay on a bleak note. Much like Tocqueville, he sees the French Revolution's aim of "improving the lot of the human race" as largely a mask for continuing under more effective leadership "the centralising and unifying struggle which had characterized the two preceding centuries."[42] All the regimes since 1789, he argues, implemented "the same universalist, patriotic, centralizing aspirations." Despite the shift in proclaimed ideals, the legacy of the absolute monarchy — the condemnation of local and regional diversity, the repression of popular culture — was retained.

III

The Nineteenth Century: revolution and romanticism as return of the repressed; conclusion.

There is no doubt a grain of truth in Muchembled's somber analysis, but the diagnosis is too absolute. Whatever its long-term implications, the French Revolution, like the sorcerer's apprentice, released social forces over which it had little control. William Sewell has demonstrated the persistence of the corporate impulses of the artisanry in the midst of a revolution which was based in theory on the anti-corporate individualist values of the Enlightenment.[43] This was probably inevitable, considering the dependence of the lawyers and bureaucrats of the third estate on the popular muscle of artisans and peasants in overthrowing and demolishing the old regime. Sewell also demonstrates the recurrence of the corporate spirit in the compagonnages and mutual aid societies of the first half of the nineteenth century. In fact, what was being resurrected in the nineteenth century was not the corporate system as a whole – the upper orders of bourgeois society fully embraced the new individualism – but that part of it which had been co-opted and, for purposes of control and repression, integrated into it, from the pre-revolutionary urban popular culture.[44] (This popular culture aspect of the traditional artisanry and its recalcitrant hostility to the upper orders are strikingly illustrated in Darnton's "The Great Cat Massacre.")[45]

The persistence of the traditional values of the artisanry was in turn aided by the revaluation, in the eyes of a part of the elite culture, of the pre-industrial "people" and its popular culture. Just as the armed people had been indispensable to the success and momentum of the Revolution between 1789 and 1794, the two recurrences of the revolution – 1830 and 1848 – had equally depended on the resurrection of the link between the common people and the revolutionary segment of the bourgeoisie. For this segment and its intellectual representatives, who included the bulk of the social-romantic writers of the July Monarchy, a positive orientation toward the common people conveyed an inclination to view its culture with an interest and openness which had been obliterated among French elites since the rise of absolutism in the late 16th century.[46]

The popular culture was not, of course, cultivated by the revolutionary leadership of 1789. To the contrary, their roots in the Enlightenment led them to disdain it as superstitious and – by 1789 – priest-ridden; their mission to complete the job of national integration that the monarchy had botched led them to attempt to replace local patois, rituals, customs and beliefs with a national language, school system and scientific reason.[47] Nonetheless, the cause of popular culture, particularly in the cities, was enormously advanced by the indispensable role of the pre-industrial populace in the revolution and, as early as 1801, the police were noting that carnival processions in Paris were greater than they had ever been under the Ancien Regime.

Indeed, Alain Faure interprets the whole period of Louis Philippe's rule as an epoch of carnivalesque rebellion and political charivaris.[48] It is hardly accidental that the sharpest satirical paper of the July Monarchy, in which Daumier published his series of lithograhs on that epitome of bourgeois knavery,

Robert Macaire, was called *Le Charivari*. The resurrected popular theater in Paris, the melodrama of the Boulevard du Temple, decisively influenced the most advanced playwrights of the '20's and '30's, Hugo and Dumas, in restoring blood and emotional reality to a theatrical tradition that had been drained of both by classicism.[49] Hugo began his *Notre Dame de Paris* with a late medieval festival of fools, and George Sand, borrowing from Agricol Perdiguier, wrote extensively on the *compagnonnages* and their *tour de France*.

Popular carnivals, characterized by scatological humor and wild dancing, thus brought back to the Parisian heart of elite culture, as part of a general return of the repressed folk culture, just those aspects of the pre-modern popular personality against whose prohibition the embattled shepherd boy of "The Three Gifts" aimed his flute and his sneezes.[50] Darnton has suggested another subversive conduit from the peasant culture to the French elites in the wetnurses and nannies who transmitted folk tales and popular traditions to the offspring of the wealthy.[51] We know that Flaubert, who integrated carnivalesque and scatological elements in his private crusade against bourgeois hypocrisy, was one of the children so introduced to popular culture by a nanny.

In terms of the social composition of elite culture, the most crucial element that ensured a certain receptivity to the popular culture was one which was as inherent and necessary a part of the personality development of bourgeois youth as the *compagnonnage* and the mutual aid societies were for the artisans: the informal peer group, equivalent in elite culture to the youth groups of traditional society.[51] The new individualism of bourgeois society dictated a dissolution of all the formal and many of the informal extra-familial networks of socialization that had existed under the Old Regime. But in fact the isolated nuclear family, which was allocated sole responsibility by this individualism for shaping the character of the young, was generally inadequate. Oldest sons in a cohesive nuclear family might be in the position hypothesized by Freudian theory for a healthy relation of conflict and identification with the father, but most children were not. Hence the crucial significance of household personnel, neighbors and friends for early socialization, evident in the case of the younger son Flaubert and of countless others where a tight father-son relation was lacking.[53] During adolescence, character was frequently formed by identifying with father substitutes (teachers and culture heros) and intimate peers. Thus Michelet's personality was shaped by his teachers Villemain and Cousin and by his friend Poinsot; Hugo's by Chateaubriand and Lamennais and also by his peers in the *cénacles* of the 1820's; and Flaubert's by Hugo himself as well as by his friends Le Poittevin and Chevalier.

In many cases during the first half of the nineteenth century, the peer group tie was reinforced by an ideological current that via the French Revolution transmitted values of the older communal culture both to the micro-level of the romantic movement and the macro-level of the informal youth group: the ideals of fraternity and social harmony. Given the incapacity of the nuclear family to take on the exclusive burden of socializing the young, the alternatives to it, particularly the adolescent friendship ties and the ideological value on fraternity and social harmony, aided the proliferation, throughout broad circles of middle class adolescents, of profound and sometimes permanently influential horizontal bonds to friends and siblings.[54] The sociologist Jesse Pitts has called these friendships, which he believes have had a lasting influence on faction-forming in French politics and culture, the "delinquent peer group."[55] Indeed, with the breakdown of the salon system of aristocratic patronage in the arts, they became the basis in literary and artistic circles of the characteristic organizational form of the romantic rebellion, the *cénacle*.

Flaubert is one of the literary artists whose personality was most clearly shaped by these peer-relations, though he was too young to participate in the *cénacles*. We know more, because of the life-long character of Flaubert's friendships and his remarkable correspondence, about him than about, for example, Hugo, central figure in all the romatic *cénacles* of the twenties, but it is clear from other cases I have examined that these friendships were a structural feature of the socialization and personality development of a major part of elite culture.[56]

At the level of the high cultural tradition, manifestly in the work of Hugo and Michelet, these elements merged with ideas of historical recurrence found in Vico and Ballanche[57] and with the revival of what Bakhtin called the "grotesque realism" of Rabelais and Shakespeare,[58] to introduce into the romantic world-view something of the cyclical notion of time, the cosmological perspectives and the frank acceptance of the lower bodily parts that the civilizing offensive had attempted to root out of the older peasant culture.

Thus despite the evident mutilation and decline of this folk culture, it reemerged in 19th century France: the ideological circumstances of the first half of the nineteenth century, together with the socialization problems I have indicated, opened up many personalities of this period to what the elite culture had for two centuries disdained and suppressed in the name of the civilizing offensive.

We must of course be careful about the significance we attach to the apparent defense of aspects of the traditional culture by the social romantics. At one level, men like Hugo and Michelet aided the revival of interest in Rabelais and in the Rabelaisian aspects of popular culture. Hugo hailed the doomed Cambronne's reply to a summons to surrender at Waterloo — "Merde!" — as a carnivalesque victory that redeemed a crushing national defeat, and he explicitly invoked the spirit of Rabelais. Michelet explored the connections between the cause of progress and the popular culture in several books of his middle period. The Church maintained a particular abhorrence for the lower body, for Rabelais, for the undisciplined and still somewhat heathen rural popular culture, and especially for Hugo and Michelet. Yet, in many respects these two were closer to the bourgeois and Christian ideals of their epoch than they were to its surviving pre-modern mentalities. At one point or another in their careers, they shared a belief in the mission of the transcendent free spirit to overcome the barriers of material and natural "fatality," and though rather free in their personal lives, they tended to look down prudishly on overt sensuality. Indeed, Flaubert was not motivated merely by professional jealousy when he described Les Misérables as "fait pour la crapule catholico-socialiste."[59]

Nonetheless, the romantic openness to popular culture was symptomatic of an enfeeblement of the civilizing offensive which, by fits and starts, has continued to the present. It was not only the lengthy assimilation, via the French Revolution, of the populace and its culture to the radical bourgeoisie which weakened the stranglehold on the civilizers on the elite culture. In fact, for comprehensible social psychological reasons, both they and the resistance to them have become common features of life in the second half of the twentieth century. That the European and American middle classes have taken over much of the repressive morality that began with Christianity's ascetic rejection of this world was evident to Weber himself at the turn of the century. But what Weber failed to take into account, was the stubborn challenge to this morality that the rapid expansion of the bourgeois world itself would bring to bear.

For one thing, what Pareto called the circulation of elites, the upward and downward mobility of a large part of the European and American population of the past two centuries, has guaranteed a continual stream of businessmen, managers, bureaucrats, and members of the professions from social backgrounds that gave them direct knowledge of the popular culture, and made them frequently ambivalent about the civilizing offensive they felt compelled to conform to. Furthermore, the clear limits to any nation's capacity, after a century of rampant imperialism and two world wars, to even control, much less to rule the world outside its borders has led to a decline in mass belief in the combined demi-gods of nationalism and science, which together were supposed to replace or at least supplement the moribund missionary morality of Christianity. Among scholars, there has been a sharp drop in the nineteenth century positivist faith in progress through science: a decline that is understandable in an age in which the destructive potentialities of unfettered scientific development – exhaustion of resources, pollution and thermonuclear war – appear to outweigh its possibilities for alleviating human misery. Historians in particular seem less inclined to chronicle the traditionally positivist sub-disciplines of politics and economic advance and more open to study the large groups of people that the triumphs of civilization have left estranged, uprooted and disoriented. The extension of the western hegemony to ever larger areas of Africa and Asia, and the constant migration of labor from the less advantaged corners of the world to do the dirty work in the more advantaged parts has also put the missionary morality in question, heightening defensiveness and xenophobia in some and increasing the sense of cultural relativity and pluralism in others.[60]

This essay has explored the historical dimensions of such an ongoing relativization of the civilizing offensive. Using the scholarly literature of recent decades, I have sought to summarize some of the shapes and contents of the popular mentalities that were partly repressed and partly reshaped in the course of the centuries-long dominance of the missionary morality. By doing so, I have suggested the convergence of the Weberian model of rationalization with the Freudian one of ego development, as well as the partly anachronistic and normative character of both these models.

The implications are, I believe, particularly clear for the application of Freudian theory to historical problems. Freud's ideas can be useful to historians dealing with individual personalities or group mentalities, insofar as he postulates a method for analyzing personality based on a distinction between inborn drives, socially given norms and the development of ego capacities to cope with the tensions between the first two as well as with the threats of the external environment. Systematization of these ego capacities in terms of mechanisms of defense — repression, projection, transference etc. — is also valuable as is the notion of oral, anal and genital stages of early development and their significance for subsequent character formation as worked out by Freud, Fromm and Erikson. In the light of the history of pre-modern mentalities, however, I would suggest that there are normative and anachronistic elements in the assumption of the universality of the oedipus complex and the related notions of the parents as the decisive influence on the early shaping of personality, as well as in the postulate that ego can only be healthy if it breaks totally with the earliest phase of mother-child symbiosis. In these areas, one has the impression that orthodox Freudians are simply reflecting certain norms and ways of thinking of their own western society rather than reacting critically to them.

Interestingly, Marxism displays a dichotomization and distortion of social reality analogous to that of Freud. As the latter minimizes the influence of the mother on the child, and generally ignores the peer influence and the broader social environment, leaving only the Oedipal hostility between father and son as the motor of personal development, Marx ignores the influence on the industrial proletariat of the pre-industrial popular strata out of which it was born in the 19th century, and focuses exclusively on the class hostility of factory proletarian and capitalist as the motor of historical develpment. For Marx, social development, as for Freud, personal development, has an end-goal: replacement of the dominating paternal figure (the capitalist) by his progeny (the proletarian) through the internalization of the former's cultural perspective and social role. In both areas of inquiry, the exclusion of the "maternal" origin has been a source of embarassment to later, independent-minded researchers. Since E.P. Thomspon, Marxist historical inquiry has attempted to account for the pre-industrial artisanal influences on working class consciousness, just as Klein, Mahler and Lacan have attempted to integrate maternal influence into the Freudian scheme of personality development.

Relating both Marx and Freud to the civilizing offensive of the 19th century offers some interesting possibilities for explaining their common myopia about "maternal" origins. We have seen how so much of the "bourgeois" vision of the world was taken over from its Christian predecessors of the reformed and post-Tridentine moralities: purely individual connections to God and the State, based on sharp, unitary categories of thought and social relations, as opposed to the porous concepts and collective relations of the pre-modern traditional cultures; linear concepts of time, leading teleologically to the kingdom of heaven or to the indefinite accumulation of material and spiritual well-being, as opposed to cyclical time concepts based on eternal recurrence and the assumption of ecological equilibrium; transcendence of the natural world as ethical mandate, as opposed to the acceptance of an immanent rootedness in it. I would argue that the denials of social and conceptual porosity, of cyclical time and of an immanent rootedness in the natural world are aspects of a broad repression of the maternal and of nurturance in the bourgeois-Christian mentality, and that this repression forms the general condition that shapes the specific neglect of the "maternal" in the theories of Marx and Freud. Both Freud and Marx shared the underlying values of this bourgeois-Christian ethic; with all their brilliance, their struggles to analyze and overcome it were as ambivalent as their points of origin as Jews in an overwhelmingly Christian environment. Their contradictory desires to subvert, convert and be integrated into their world were paradigmatic for the plight of the 19th century bourgeois youth as a whole, and it is no wonder that the movements they originated reproduced these incompatible desires. In other words, their powerful analytic capacities and emancipatory inclinations were probably bent in a particular direction by the bourgeois cultural superego that shaped their own rather isolated and antagonistic relations to their fathers: rational, masculine, individualistic and authoritarian in a linear top-down direction.

Without the Jewish background — and without the eschatological impulse that may be related to it — Max Weber shared this general characteristic with Freud and Marx. I do not think it is accidental that these three were raised and educated in a similar cultural milieu, the 19th century German variant on the cultural superego of the European bourgeoisie. The starkness of the antagonisms pervading their theories, a certain exclusion of the maternal element, and a tendency to minimize the mediating role of horizontal social elements outside the vertical power dichotomy of high and low (somewhat less evident in Weber), reflected the lack of alternatives to the topographic model of the bourgeois cultural superego: dominance above, and below only the alternatives of submission or subversive analysis. This central European situation was in crucial respects *sui generis*. The absence of a successful popular revolution, such as that which prevailed in France at the end of the 18th century and whose tradition influenced subsequent French history as well as the French bourgeois mentality, together with the continuities between the rational asceticism and principles of domination inherent in the traditional state (especially the Prussian), in the German idealist tradition and in German bourgeois society, help to explain the sharpness of the vertical oppositions in the theories of all three men.

If historians in the late twentieth century show increasing restiveness with these models, it is for good reason. As I have suggested, there are a multitude of justifications for our present skepticism about the vertical social relations, linear, irreversible processes and watertight conceptualizations that Marx, Freud and Weber derived from their central European reality. Contemporary French historical thought, in which this skepticism is evident, received a powerful impulse to question its positivist heritage in 1968, from the most recent ritual enactment of the French revolutionary tradition. I have stressed the importance of this popular revolutionary current in the evolution of the civilizing offensive. It is therefore noteworthy that the historiographical point of departure for much of the present interest in popular mentalities is that artisan's son, Jules Michelet, who viewed himself as a child of the French people and their revolution, whose best-known books were impassioned examinations of both of these, and whose work on the popular culture and beliefs of the pre-industrial strata was symptomatic not only of the radical bourgeois mentality in the social-romantic epoch but also of the pattern of cyclical recurrence which is discernible in aspects of French culture as well as in contemporary historical thinking.

That Michelet himself incarnated – alongside of a number of values taken over from the missionary morality – the humanist leaven of the revolutionary tradition as well as the narrow chauvinism of modern nationalism, poses another of those paradoxical entanglements, illustrative of a still present cultural reality, whose analysis demands the combined energies of the historian of mentalities, the cultural historian and the psychohistorian.

FOOTNOTES

This paper was prepared for the round table on psychohistory of the 16th International Congress of Historical Sciences, held at Stuttgart in August 1985. The questions it deals with have arisen in the course of two and a half decades of study in the areas of modern French and German cultural and intellectual history. These questions became more sharply defined, thanks to the probing of my students, in the course of a year-long seminar on mentalities and psychohistory that I gave at the university of Amsterdam in 1984-85. Special thanks are due to the stimulus and criticism of Willem Frijhoff, Anton Blok, Fritz Ringer, Rod Aya, Bernard Kruithof, John Gillis and Michael Seidman, of my assistants Jan Aarts and Peter de Back, and of my wife, Marleen Mitzman-Wessel.

1. The problem was recognized some time ago by Fred Weinstein in "The Coming Crisis of Psychohistory" (*Journal of Modern History*, 47[2], 1975, pp. 202-28). But Weinstein and Platt's contribution to a solution (in *The Wish to Be Free, Society, Psyche and Value Change* [Berkeley, 1969]) suffers from internal inconsistencies (the incompatibility of their twin categories of autonomy and inclusion) and a culture-bound commitment to ideals of individuation and ego development that obscures understanding of the pre-modern culture. John Demos (in *The Little Commonwealth: Family Life in Plymouth Colony* [1970]; and *Entertaining Satan: Witchcraft and the Culture of Early New England* [1982]) and Peter Loewenberg (in "The Psychohistorical Origins of the Nazi Youth Cohort," *American Historical Review* [1971] pp. 1457-1502) did link a psychohistorical approach to social-historical concerns, but did not do so in a way that showed a general theoretical connection and their methods have found little resonance among social and cultural historians or among psychohistorians. The recent tours de force of Peter Gay (*The Bourgeois Experience, Victoria to Freud. Vol. 1, Education of the Senses* [New York & Oxford, 1984]) and Carl Schorske (*Fin-de-Siècle Vienna. Politics and Culture* [New York 1980]), despite their brilliance and new insights are keyed into cultural history and, except for the implications of Gay's work for the history of family life, are remote from the ongoing concerns of social historians. In fact, most psychohistory that is not cultural history veers toward a perverse resurrection of the great-man variety of history, and psychohistorians too often are ignorant of and indifferent to what historians of mentalities are doing. The exception – apart from Demos – is David Hunt (*Parents and Children in History. The Psychology of Family Life in Early Modern France*, [Boston 1970]). Patrick Hutton, an historian of the Blanquist movement, has also offered an interesting effort to reconcile psychohistory and the history of mentalities, but he too largely restricted himself to the history of the family: "The Psychohistory of Erik Erikson from the Standpoint of Collective Mentalities" (*Psychohistory Review*, 12 (1) [1983]: 18-25).

2. Weber presented his notion of an inexorable rationalization of public and private life primarily in terms of "goal-rationality" – the ever more rational adjustment of means to ends and thereby the attainment of increasing efficiency, which he saw as manifested in increasing division of labor and specialization. He perceived this process in all institutionalized areas of human activity: political, economic, military, scientific, religious and educational. Weber's ideas on rationalization as historical process appear in *Wirtschaft und Gesellschaft* (Tübingen, 1956), passim, in the last part of *The Protestant Ethic and the Spirit of Capitalism (New York, 1930)* (original German edition 1904), in "Religious Rejections of the World and Their Directions" (in Gerth & Mills, eds., *From Max Weber* [London 1948], pp. 323-359 – originally in Weber's *Religionssoziologie* Band I [Tübingen, 1922]) and in "Science As A Vocation," Gerth & Mills, *op.cit.*, pp. 129-156. For the scholarly discussion, see Wolfgang Mommsen, "Universalgeschichtliches und politisches Denken bei Max Weber," *Historische Zeitschrift* (1965): pp. 557-612; Karl Löwith, "Max Weber und Karl Marx" in his *Gesammelte Abhandlungen* (Stuttgart, 1963), pp. 1-67; Arthur Mitzman, *The Iron Cage, An Historical Interpretation of Max Weber* (New York, 1970). For a brief, clear presentation, the parts on "Bureaucracy" and "Rationalization and Disenchantment" of Lewis A. Coser's treatment of Weber in his *Masters of Sociological Thought* (New York, 1977), pp. 230-234. The developmental theories referred to in the text are those by Elias, Weinstein and Platt, and Muchembled (see below). For an interesting approach to the Weberian paradigm which supplements it with Habermas's theory of communicative action, see Detley Peukert, "Neuere Alltagsgeschichte und Historische Anthropologie," in Hans Süssmuth (ed.) *Historische Anthropologie* (Göttingen, 1984). According to Peukert, Habermas "describes the constitution of modern society as a dialectical tension between systemic and everyday logics. The modern regulatory systems of the capitalist market economy and the bureaucratic state apparatus develop, accoding to Habermas, within a systemic logic that is independent of experience. Contrariwise, the realms of culture, socialization and social integration are subject to a this-worldly communicative logic that is based on experience" (p. 63-64). With certain modifications, this theory fits well with my concluding argument (see below).

3. Although Demos, Hutton and Hunt recognize this (see note 1) they do so only in a limited framework (primarily applied to family history). At the level of youth sociability and its 20th century interrelation with nationalism, there are fine works by John Gillis (*Youth and History, Tradition and Change in European Age Relations, 1770-Present* [New York 1974]) and George Mosse (*Nationalism and Sexuality, Respectability and Abnormal Sexuality in Modern Europe* [New York, 1985]) but neither one brings in a psychoanalytic perspective.

4. An explanation of "cultural superego" limited to the influence of "the personalities of great leaders," appeared in *Civilization and Its Discontents* (New York 1961, p. 88f – original ed. 1931). Later Freud expanded the concept as follows: "The parent's influence naturally includes not merely the personalities of the parents but also the racial, national and family traditions handed on through them as well as the demands of the immediate social milieu which they represent. In the same way an individual's superego in the course of his development takes over contributions from later successors and substitutes of his parents, such as teachers, admired figures in public life or high social ideas. (*An Outline of Psychoanalysis*, [New York, 1963], p. 17 – original German ed. 1940)

5. By this last I mean to signify the replacement of spontaneously organized, or anthropologically based, youth groups, such as those discussed by Natalie Zemon Davis and Jacques Rossiaud, by the disciplining of adolescents and young adults from above through schools, the boy scouts, trade unions and armies. The organization of apprentice artisans in the guild systems of the Ancien Regime was clearly a step in this direction, though, as Darnton's "Cat Massacre" reveals, much of the older, anarchic style of oedipal revolt persisted within the guild framework. See below and notes 35 and 36.

6. I have translated here the term currently in use in Dutch historical discourse by Bernard Krutihof and others, "het beschavingsoffensief." See B. Kruithof, "De deugdzame natie. Het burgerlijk beschavingsoffensief van de Maatschappij tot Nut van 't Algemeen tussen 1784

en 1860," *Symposion, Tijdschrift voor maatschappijwetenschap* jrg.2, nr.1, (1980): 22-37. The concept is, of course, derived from Norbert Elias (see note 13). Frijhoff, without using my nomenclature, refers to it as follows: "Cultural historians have by now generally adopted a basic model of cultural change, probably under the (usually unconscious) influence of widely diffused sociological theories stressing the crucial importance of politically dominant groups for the modernization of society. This model consists of the acculturating (and partly destructive) influence of cultural politics of elite groups upon the life of common people, whatever may be meant by this term. The language of that model leans heavily on military imagery: cultural strategies of advanced groups trying to score a victory over their adversaries or opponents. Thus Burckhardt's or Huizinga's morphological or typological description of the cultural *forms* and their transformations has been replaced by the analysis of the cultural *process*, of its influence on the social groups involved and of its functions in the wider society." (W. Frijhoff, "Elite and popular cultures in the Dutch Republic: Notes on the Specific Forms of their Relationship," in *Images of the World, Dutch Genre Painting in its Historical Context* [London 1986]) Frijhoff discusses this model critically but his list of "only a few outstanding investigators" who use it reads like an honor role of modern historical scholarship: "Michael Bakhtin, Yves Marie Bercé, Marc Bloch, Peter Burke, Julio Caro Baroja, Natalie Zemon Davis, Jean Delumeau, Carlo Ginzburg, Emmanuel Le Roy Ladurie, Alan Macfarlane, Robert Mandrou, Robert Muchembled, Keith Thomas, Michel Vovelle."

7. Robert Muchembled, *Culture populaire et culture des élites (XVe-XVIIIe siècles)*, (Paris 1978). (Will be referred to as Muchembled.)

8. Frijhoff, for example, points out six different connotations of "popular culture" in the paper cited in note 6. On the connotations of popular religion, see Jean-Claude Schmitt, "Religion populaire et culture folklorique," *AESC* (1976): 941-53. Cf. also Peter Burke, "Popular Culture between History and Ethnology," *Ethnologia Europeaea* XIV, 1 (1984): 5-13.

9. Natalie Zemon Davis, "Some Tasks and Themes in the Study of Popular Religion" in C. Trinkaus and H.A. Oberman, eds, *The Pursuit of Holiness in Late Medieval and Renaissance Religion* (Leiden, 1974), pp. 207-336.

10. Maurice Agulhon, *Pénitents et Francs-Maçons de l'ancienne Provence* (Paris 1968), and idem., *La République au village* (Paris, 1970).

11. Max Weber, *Wirtschaft und Gesellschaft* pp. 739-794.

12. By this normative and anachronistic character I mean the emphasis on the relation to parents as the only socializing agency and on the emergence of an autonomous rational ego as the only way of combining social order with individual freedom, and the notion that the reappearance in adulthood of fantasms and behavior associated with pre-oedipal stages of development constitutes an undesirable neurotic regression.

13. Norbert Elias, *Über den Prozess der Zivilisation; Soziogenetische und psychogenetische Untersuchungen*, 2 vols. (Basel, 1939); and Weinstein and Platt, *op.cit.*

14. Stuart Clark's critique of Muchembled in his "French Historians and Early Modern Popular Culture" (*Past and Present*, no. 100 [August 1983]: 62-94) misconstrues Muchembled's intent on this point. He uses Muchembled's emphasis on the pervasive poverty and anxiety of the traditional rural society and his nomenclature for popular beliefs, such as "superstitions," as a means of placing Muchembled in the line of positivist detractors of popular culture, whereas it is clear from the second half of Muchembled's book that he by no means endorses the statist and Christian attack on popular culture, and does not at all fit into the procrustean bed in which Clark would place him.

15. Emmanuel Le Roy Ladurie, *Montaillou, Village occitan de 1294 à 1324* (Paris, 1976), pp. 454, 537.

16. Ibid, pp. 493 ff.

17. See for example André Burguière, "The Charivari and Religious Repression in France during the Ancien Regime," in R. Wheaton and T.K. Haraven, eds, *Family and Sexuality in French History*, (Philadelphia 1980), pp. 84-110. Burguière distinguishes two phases in the church repression of charivaris. In the first (late 15th and 16th centuries) "the religious authorities generally endeavored to oversee them more than combat them" (p. 87); condemnations were limited to cases where local customs, interpreted as heretical, forbade marital practices permitted by the church. In the second phase (17th century) it was the form of the charivari – violent, disorderly – which the church condemned, and with it, implicitly, the youth sociability that underlay the charivari.

18. Infra, p. ff., on the repression of dancing by the protestant and the post-tridentine Catholic Church, see Peter Burke, *Popular Culture in Early Modern Europe* (New York, 1978), pp. 209, 225, 236, 237; and Schmitt, *op.cit.* pp. 948, 949, 950.

19. Sigmund Freud, *Civilization and its Discontents*, p. 13.

20. Ibid., p. 13f.

21. Ibid., p. 15.

22. Ibid., p. 13.

23. In *Civilization and Its Discontents*, he even denied its significance in the development of religious consciousness, which he rather saw as originating in the child's need "for a *father's* protection." (p. 19 – my emphasis, A.M.)

24. Sherry Turkle, *Psychoanalytic Politics, Freud's French Revolution* (New York, 1978), p. 56.

25. Ibid., p. 58.

26. Muchembled, p. 95.

27. Ibid.

28. In *The Great Cat Massacre and other Episodes in French Cultural History* (London, 1984), pp. 9-72, Darnton makes a different argument from mine, seeing in his material on the one hand an expression of a peasant mentality shaped by acute scarcity, brutality and danger, and on the other a means of distinguishing German from French popular culture. Some of his examples, however, show other things.

29. In a number of folk tales, the cannibalistic propensities of wicked mothers and their surrogates (as in "Little Red Riding Hood") reveal the most primitive fear of the *mère terrible*. As does the practice found by Van Gennep in certain areas of France of *scier la vieille* – cutting the old lady in two – during Lent. Practiced of course on papier maché models, it probably reflected the unconscious identification of the lean, late-winter period of nature's harshness, in which the perishables preserved from the autumn harvest were no longer available, with the angry, non-nurturing mother. Most interestingly, this custom followed shortly after the feast-day of Saint Agatha (February 5), whose martyrdom consisted in the amputation of her breasts. (On "scier la vieille": A. Van Gennep, *Manuel du folklore français*, tome III [Paris, 1947], p. 942ff., and N. Belmont, *Mythes et croyances dans l'ancienne France* [Paris, 1973], pp. 72f.) The Italian custom of burning "La vecchia" as the symbol of Lent is reported in Peter Burke, *Popular Culture in Early Modern Europe*, p. 222. (On Saint Agatha,see Jacques de Voragine, *La Legende dorée*, [Paris 1942], tome I, p. 81.) The reverse of these fantasies of oral deprivation that surfaced during the Lenten period of fasting were the fantasies of an oral paradise of abundance during carnival itself, the "Land of Cockaigne... where houses

were thatched with pancakes, brooks ran with milk, there were roast pigs running about with knives conveniently stuck in their backs..." (Burke *op.cit.*, p. 190). See also Jean Delumeau, ed., *La Mort des pays de Cockaigne, comportements collectifs de la Renaissance à l'âge classique*, (Paris, 1976).

30. Darnton, *op.cit*, p. 69-72.

31. Ibid, p. 72.

32. Ibid, p. 72.

33. Muchembled, p. 88. For a recent treatment of the connection between archaic fertility rituals and Maria-worship: Haralds Biezais, "Religion des Volks und Religion der Gelehrten," in H.P. Duerr, *Der Wissenschaftler und das Irrationale* I (Frankfurt, 1981), p. 565-600. See also R. Briffault, *The Mothers*, vol. III (London, 1927) p. 184: "The Holy Virgin is universally identified with the moon"; and Van Gennep, *op. cit.* t.VI pp. 2393f. for harvest festivals associated with the Assumption on August 15. The combination of hunting goddess with Marian cult was also said, in an ideologically tinted work, to underlie the now forgotten Hertjesdag, celebrated around Amsterdam on the Monday after the feast of the Assumption of Mary until the early 20th century. Cf. Jan Ter Gouw, *De Volksvermaken*, n.d. & no place of publication (1885?), pp. 150-154.

34. In "Comment Kiot-Jean épousa Jacqueline," it is the witch that gives the young man the power to make others fart, and he applies his gifts to the wealthy and hostile family of his would-be bride (thus also to his future mother-in-law) and to their priest. This happens through some magic goat dung, which the youth hides in the ashes of the hearth of the haughty family that refuses his candidacy. When they blow on the ashes, they fart uncontrollably, thus demonstrating – just as in "The Three Gifts" – the power of the forbidden combination of oral and anal wind to overturn the social barriers and bring down the mighty. (Darnton, p. 58) The witch was of course an ambivalent figure in the popular imagination, since, from the standpoint of the civilizing offensive, she could represent the dangerous wicked mother, who dines on naughty children, and, from the standpoint of the older folk culture, the protective "good mother" of the world of nature. The fairy godmother also expressed this ambivalence. In a version of Cinderella discussed by Darnton, the place of the fairy godmother was taken not by a witch but by the Virgin Mary, who in a later stage of the story seems to be metamorphosed into a tall fruit tree that, to nourish the underfed heroine, "bends its branches down to her whenever she approaches" – like all good mothers. (Darnton, p. 32)

35. See Natalie Zemon Davis, "The Reasons of Misrule," in her *Society and Culture in Early Modern France* (London, 1975); Yves-Marie Bercé, *Fête et révolte*, (Paris, 1976); Jacques le Goff and Jean-Claude Schmitt, eds, *Le Charivari (actes de la table ronde organisée à Paris, 1977)* (Paris, 1981).

36. Jacques Rossiaud, "Fraternités de jeunesse et niveaux de culture dans les villes du Sud-Est à la fin du Moyen Age," *Cahiers d'histoire* 31 (1974): 67-102) and "Prostitution, jeunesse et société dans les villes du Sud-Est au XVe siècle," *Annales E.S.C.* 31, 2 (1976): 289-325.

37. Muchembled and Bercé, *op.cit.* More cautiously, Burke (*op.cit.* p. 234f) sees "reform" of the popular culture in the century before 1650 as the work primarily of "Catholic and Protestant clergy," and in the subsequent period, increasingly, of "lay reformers."

38. Bercé, *op.cit.*, pp. 82f ("Les attributs du Carnaval devenus emblêmes de révolte"). Here too, Burke is more cautious, seeing in the festival explosions primarily a "safety valve", tolerated by the powers that be. He nonetheless acknowledges that the "rituals of revolt did coexist with serious questioning of the social, political and religious order and the one sometimes turned into the other" (pp. 202f).

39. E. Le Roy Ladurie, *Carnival in Romans* (New York, 1980); idem, *The Peasants of Langue-doc* (Urbana, Ill, 1980), pp. 196-197.

40. Muchembled, p. 277f.

41. Georges Snyders, *La Pédagogie en France aux XViie et XVIIIe siècles* (Paris, 1965), p. 264.

41. Muchembled, p. 389,

43. William H. Sewell, Jr., *Work and Revolution in France, The Language of Labor from the Old Regime to 1849* (Cambridge, 1980), pp. 92-142.

44. The precise relationship of the sans-culottes to the corporate mentality is not clear from Sewell's book. On the one hand, he implies that they continued, in an anti-corporate climate, much of the corporate way of thinking, a point on which he is criticized by Michael Sonenscher in "The Sans-Culottes of the Year II: rethinking the language of labour in Revolutionary France," (*Social History* [October, 1984]; 301-328). On the other hand, Sewell himself argues in an article just published that the sans-culottes expressed a "variant of revolutionary ideology" that "was constructed out of the same terminology with the same essential set of concepts: popular sovereignty, natural law, the general will, representation, virtue, property, aristocracy, the people." ("Ideologies and Social Revolutions: Reflections on the French Case," *The Journal of Modern History* [March, 1985]: pp. 75,77.) Theda Skocpol, in a thoughtful reply to Sewell, associates the sans-culottes neither with the revolutionary enlightenment idiom he now sees them using nor with the corporate mentality, but with "traditional norms of social solidarity and 'just prices,'" ("Cultural Idioms and Political Ideologies," ibid, p. 93) Sonenscher's material on artisan values in the 18th century supports my view (which is implied by Skocpol) that the sans-culottes represented that part of the corporate structure – the artisanry – which had been forcibly integrated into it from the pre-existing popular culture. Sewell's book shows how this culture survived the demise of both corporatism and the French Revolution until the second half of the 19th century, though his emphasis on organizational forms and language used in worker's literature somewhat misleadingly exaggerates its corporate side. On the popular culture of the French urban artisanry in the 19th century, see Georges Duveau, *La vie ouvrière en France sous la Second Empire* (Paris, 1946), especially chapter IV, "les moeurs", pp. 419-537; Michelle Perrot, "La femme populaire rebelle" in *L'historie sans qualités* (Paris, 1979); Gerard Jacquemet, "Belleville ouvrier a la Belle Epoque" in *Mouvement Social* no. 118 (janv-mars, 1982): 61-77; J. Kaplow, "La fin de Saint-Lundi. Le Paris populaire au XIXe siècle," *Temps Libre* (1981).

45. In Darnton, *op.cit.*, pp. 75-106.

46. James Smith Allen makes a similar point in his *Popular French Romanticism, Authors, Readers, and Books in the 19th Century* (Syracuse, 1981): "Essentially, the [romantic] movement in its broad appeal and emphasis on free creation marked the end of the bifurcation of literature high and low in the eighteenth century." (p. 210) "Part of the intellectual world of elites filtered downward and encouraged a brief cultural interaction of a very particular sort between social classes high and low in early nineteenth century Paris. This marked a decidedly urban version of an important development noted by recent historians of rural France. Maurice Agulhon and his students, for instance, have documented a similar interaction between local notables and their peasants in which republican values were expressed in the guise of traditional fêtes...For perhaps the first time in French cultural history since the seventeenth century, the middle classes and respectable artisans and shopkeepers shared a common literary activity – the new popular literature, much of it romantic in the period." (p. 220) Allen's emphasis on top-down influence is a bit one-sided, as my examples (*infra*) indicate. Louis Chevalier's excellent *Labouring Classes and Dangerous Classes in Paris During the First Half of the Nineteenth Century* (London, 1973), does seem to show an anxious identification by the bourgeois of working with criminal classes, but in fact Chevalier's main sources for this are the socially conservative (if politically liberal) surveys of Villermé, Buret and Fregier – men whose hostility

to any further recurrence of the revolution made them unwitting bearers of the July Monarchy's version of the civilizing offensive. Moreover, the focus of Chevalier – and his sources – is not on the pre-industrial "people" of artisans and shopkeepers, but on the new industrial proletariat and, above all, the floating lumpenproletariat. Michelet, who had an early orientation toward the liberal political economists but later – after 1840 – adopted social romantic views, illustrates the distinction I am trying to make. In *Le Peuple* (1846) he showed serious concern for the moral condition of the new factory workers but idealized the traditional artisanry. And he refused to believe that the French urban working force would ever lose its predominantly artisan character. Allen, of course, would emphasize the extent to which even the traditional artisan-shopkeeper group was being absorbed into a mass culture that bore the imprint of the civilizing offensive rather than the traditional popular culture. I am convinced, however, that as long as a major section of the middle class remained in radical opposition to the political status quo – which was the case during the July monarchy – there was appreciation and support for many aspects of the recalcitrant pre-industrial culture. This political, social and cultural search for an alliance with the people was the basis, I would contend, of social romanticism. Only in the second half of the 19th century did the bourgeoisie, frightened by June 1848, abandon its dreams of revolutionary alliance, join ranks, and *uniformly* try to impose the missionary morality on the common people. Together with the rapid evolution of mass media and of social-economic modernization, this precipitated the dissolution of the traditional culture and, in the generations before 1914, the absorption of large masses into the culture preferred by the civilizing offensive. (That for the popular strata subject to this cultural hegemony many areas of rebellion and creativity have persisted, has been plausibly argued by historians of 20th century culture such as Michael Seidman.)

47. Michel de Certeau, Dominique Julia, Jacuqes Revel, *Une Politique de la langue, la Révolution Française et les patois* (Paris, 1975).

48. Alain Faure, *Paris Carème-Prenant, Du Carnaval à Paris au XIXe siècle* (Paris, 1978).

49. Robert Baldick, *The Life and Times of Frederick Lemaître,* (London, 1959); Frederick Brown, *Theater and Revolution, The Culture of the French Stage* (New York, 1980), pp. 83-131. For a comparable analysis of the relation of popular to elite theater in Munich around 1900, see Peter Jelavich, "Popular Dimensions of Modern Elitist Culture: The Case of Theater in Fin-de-Siècle Munich," in La Capra and Kaplan eds, *Modern European Intellectual History, Reappraisals and New Perspectives* (Ithaca and London, 1982), pp. 220-251.

50. According to Burke (*op.cit.*, p. 190), carnival represented "Nature, or in Freudian terms, the Id." That the popular culture was, if diminished, still alive in the 19th century is attested not only by the vitality of carnival in July Monarchy Paris, but by the use of folkloric elements in rural riots and uprisings: the "demoiselles of the Ariége" discussed by John Merriman (in his anthology *1830 In France* [New York, 1975] pp.87-118), the political charivaris discussed by Robert Bezucha (in "Masks of Revolution: A Study of Popular Culture During the Second French Republic," in R. Price, ed., *Revolution and Reaction, 1848 and the Second French Republic* [London, 1975], pp. 236-253), the archaic symbolism of the "new mass rural radicalism", again during the second republic, presented by Peter McPhee (in "Popular Culture, Symbolism and Rural Radicalism in Nineteenth-Century France", *The Journal of Peasant Studies* 5 [1978]: 238-253), and the equally archaic elements in the southern French armed resistance to Louis Napoleon's coup d'état (in Maurice Agulhon, *La République au village* [Paris, 1970]). That rural dancing continued to be attacked by the civilizing offensive is evident by Paul Louis Courier's defense of it in 1820. (P.L. Courier, "Petition à la chambre des députés pour les villageois que l'on empêche de danser," *Oeuvres* [1874], tome 2, pp. 24-43.)

51. Darnton, *op.cit.*, p. 63.

52. See John R. Gillis, *op.cit.*, which gives examples for Germany around 1800 (pp. 73, 76, 79). I have identified the same phenomenon in France in the adolescences of numerous romantic writers (Hugo, Musset, Gautier etc.) as well as of Flaubert, Du Camp, Vallès and

Alfred Dumesnil, Michelet's son-in-law. (With Michelet himself, it was limited to one very close friend, Paul Poinsot.)

53. See A. Mitzman, "The Unstrung Orpheus, Flaubert's Youth and the Psycho-Social Origins of Art for Art's Sake," *The Psychohistory Review* (Summer, 1977): 27-42.

54. Of the cases mentioned in note 52, Flaubert, Gautier, Vallès and Dumesnil are good examples of writers who revealed a life-long influence of their adolescent attachments. In the unpublished correspondence of Dumesnil and Eugène Noel (Bibliothèque Historique de la Ville de Paris) these bonds with the ideology of fraternity are explicit.

55. Jesse Pitts, "Continuity and Change in Bourgeois France" in Stanley Hoffman et al, *In Search of France* (New York, 1965).

56. The friendship of Dumesnil and Noel, for example (note 54) was embedded in a larger group of about half a dozen youths with a common secondary school experience in Rouen. Because Dumesnil became an author in his own right as well as Michelet's son-in-law, his correspondence has been preserved. Judging by his letters with the other friends of his youth, I would judge that such bonds were the norm rather than the exception.

57. Michelet was the translator of Vico's *Nuova Scienza* into French and his work showed the life-long influence of the Neapolitan philosopher. Anne-Maria Amiot has noted the similarity between certain historical ideas of Hugo and the notion of *"accouchement"* used by the Lyonnais mystic Ballanche to designate the character of change as both death and new birth — a notion cognate with the idea of time as cyclical found in popular culture. See her "Les fondements théologiques de la Révolution française dans *La fin de Satan* de Victor Hugo" in *Philosophies de la Révolution française*, (Paris, 1984), p. 162. Michelet, at a decisive moment in his life — the death of Madame Dumesnil — also made use of the concept of *accouchement*. On Ballanche see Paul Bénichou, *Le Temps des prophètes* (Paris, 1978), pp. 74-104.

58. Mikahil Bakhtin, *Rabelais and His World* (Cambridge, Mass., 1968). On the anticipation of Bakhtin in Hugo's work, especially the carnivalesque, grotesque and scatological aspects of it, see Victor Brombert, *Victor Hugo and the Visimary Novel* (Cambridge, Mass., 1986). Hugo wrote on Rabelais in *William Shakespeare* (Paris, 1973), pp. 80-83; Michelet, in his *Histoire de France*, where he freely acknowledged his debt to the work of the young Eugène Noel (see notes 51, 53, 55 supra). Noel emphasizes, as does Bakhtin (who starts his book with quotes from Michelet) the rootedness of Rabelais in the popular culture of his time (Eugène Noel, *Rabelais* [Paris, 1850], and *Le Rabelais de poche* [Paris, 1860].

59. Gustave Flaubert, *Correspondance* (Conard) (Paris, 1929), tome 5, p. 35. On the church's abhorrence for the traditional boisterousness of peasant Christianity see Edward Berenson, *Populist Religion and Left-Wing Politics in France, 1830-1852* (Princeton, 1984) pp. 58f.

60. In an essay of 1967 that is sharply critical of certain leftist intellectuals' infatuation with third world primitivism, François Furet has examined similar themes: "Les intellectuels français et le structuralisme" in his *L'atelier de l'histoire* (Paris, 1982). I disagree with Furet's conclusions but he raises the right questions.

INDEX